PRINCIPLES-FOCUSED EVALUATION

Also from Michael Quinn Patton

Developmental Evaluation: Applying Complexity Concepts
to Enhance Innovation and Use
Michael Quinn Patton

Developmental Evaluation Exemplars:
Principles in Practice
*Edited by Michael Quinn Patton,
Kate McKegg, and Nan Wehipeihana*

Principles-Focused Evaluation

The GUIDE

Michael Quinn Patton

THE GUILFORD PRESS
New York   London

Library of Congress Cataloging-in-Publication Data

Names: Patton, Michael Quinn, author.
Title: Principles-focused evaluation : the guide / Michael Quinn Patton.
Description: New York : Guilford Press, [2018] | Includes bibliographical
    references and index.
Identifiers: LCCN 2017003135| ISBN 9781462531820 (pbk.) | ISBN 9781462531905
    (hardcover)
Subjects: LCSH: Evaluation research (Social action programs) | Social
    service—Research.
Classification: LCC H62 .P32174 2017 | DDC 001.4—dc23
LC record available at *https://lccn.loc.gov/2017003135*

Part opener graphic: "Inukshuk" by IYAK (Fred Iyak Trimble);
photographed by Lynsey Tjaden

To Charmagne Elise Campbell-Patton—
my daughter, partner in Utilization-Focused Evaluation,
and inspiration for principles-focused evaluation—
who exemplifies the new generation of evaluators
and the future of the evaluation profession

Preface

Authors generally write the preface after completing the book. Thus, while writing this preface marks a stopping point, at least for now, in my journey through principles-focused evaluation, you, the reader, are at the beginning of this book. To help you get oriented, I thought it would be useful to provide a brief overview of the journey: how principles-focused evaluation emerged and its development so far. In so doing, I should note that this book assumes some familiarity with program evaluation basics, like traditionally defining evaluation as rendering judgments of merit, worth, and significance; the distinction between formative and summative evaluation; logic models and theories of change; and standards for evaluation (Yarbrough, Shulha, Hopson, & Caruthers, 2010). Understanding those basics will help in making sense of the specific niche, purpose, and contributions of principles-focused evaluation.

Developmental evaluation first emerged as an option within utilization-focused evaluation (Patton, 2008, 2012). Principles-focused evaluation then emerged as an option within developmental evaluation. This book elevates it to a full-fledged, distinct evaluation approach with its own niche, framework, and focus. Chapter 5 explains the relationship between utilization-focused, developmental evaluation, and principles-focused evaluation in more detail. Here's an overview.

Developmental Evaluation as Context

Developmental evaluation focuses on evaluating innovations in complex dynamic environments. Innovation is a broad umbrella that includes creating new approaches to intractable problems, adapting programs to changing conditions, applying effective principles to new contexts (scaling innovation), catalyzing systems change, and improvising rapid responses in crisis conditions. Developmental evaluators track, document, and help interpret the nature and implications of innovations and adaptations as they unfold. They gather data about the processes, outcomes, and contexts of innovation, and help extract lessons and insights to inform the ongoing adaptive innovation process. How do innovative programs and initiatives adapt within and navigate the turbulence and uncertainties of complex systems change? *They adhere to principles.*

Principles-Based Initiatives Led by Principles-Driven People

Principles inform and guide decisions and choices. They do so by telling us how to act. Principles-focused evaluation examines (1) whether principles are clear, meaningful, and actionable, and, if so, (2) whether they are actually being followed, and, if so, (3) whether they are leading to desired results. Principles are derived from experience, expertise, values, and research. Principles-based initiatives are led by principles-driven people. This book will examine, explain, and elaborate these themes. But first a note on language.

I refer to principles-based initiatives, principles-driven people, and principles-focused evaluation as a way of distinguishing the primary role of principles in each case. The meanings are straightforward. Principles-based initiatives, including programs, projects, collaborations, and change efforts of all kinds, base what they do and why they do it on guiding principles. *Initiatives* is a generic term encompassing the full variety of change endeavors but most often takes the form of programs for evaluation purposes. Principles-driven people are motivated by deeply help values expressed through principles that translate values into behaviors. Principles-focused evaluation makes principles the focus of evaluation. But *these language designations are arbitrary,* a matter of preference, not operational significance. One could just as easily refer to principles-focused initiatives, principles-based people, and principles-driven evaluation; or principles-driven initiatives, principles-focused people, and

principles-based evaluation. Or one could refer to them all in the same way: principles-focused initiatives, principles-focused people, and principles-focused evaluation. I have chosen to distinguish the role of principles for people, initiatives, and evaluation by referring to principles-based initiatives (programs), principles-driven people, and principles-focused evaluation. Bottom line: These are stylistic preferences, not substantive distinctions.

So then, returning to substance, principles-based initiatives are led by principles-driven people. That's what Frances Westley, Brenda Zimmerman, and I found in studying major social movements that successfully solved problems and changed systems. In *Getting to Maybe: How the World Is Changed* (2006) we reported what we found, that social innovators are motivated by a strong sense of calling, based on deeply held values. They see some social or ecological problem and act. These are people who look at the way things are, find the status quo intolerable, and want to make a difference. They engage based on their principles.

Principles-focused evaluation has emerged as a major inquiry framework and focus for developmental evaluation. For example, in their insightful volume *Evaluating Complexity*, Preskill and Gopal (2014) advise, "Look for effective principles of practice in action, rather than assessing adherence to a predetermined set of activities" (p. 16). Studying the implementation and outcomes of effective, *evidence-based principles* is a major new direction in developmental evaluation relevant to addressing complex problems in a rapidly changing and turbulent world.

Principles-Focused Evaluation

Principles-focused evaluation has now evolved from a type of developmental evaluation to an evaluation approach unto itself. That's because principles constitute a distinct *evaluand*, a specific and unique focus for evaluation. Evaluation, we say, "grew up in the projects." The profession's origins were in evaluating projects, and, from my perspective, we remain in the grip of a self-limiting project mentality. Such tools as logic models and SMART goals work well for project evaluation. They do not work well, in my judgment, for different kinds of evaluands like evaluating mission, strategy, advocacy, policy change, social and ecological systems change, complex dynamic interventions, and principles. The new challenges for evaluation as a transdisciplinary profession have to do with new units of analysis and broader areas of focus for evaluation, what we call the *evaluand*, that is, the thing evaluated. Chapter 4 discusses the challenge of new evaluands and the corresponding need for matching evaluation approaches.

Principles-focused evaluation informs choices about which principles are appropriate for what purposes in which contexts, helping to navigate the treacherous terrain of conflicting guidance and competing advice. What principles work for what situations with what results is an evaluation question. Thus, from an evaluation perspective, principles are hypotheses, not truths. They may or may not work. They may or may not be followed. They may or may not lead to desired outcomes. Whether they work, whether they are followed, and whether they yield desired outcomes are subject to evaluation. Learning to evaluate principles, and applying what is learned from doing so, takes on increasing importance in an ever more complex world where effectiveness depends on adapting to context. Principles guide adaptation.

New Directions in Evaluation

In doing workshops and webinars on both developmental evaluation and principles-focused evaluation I get asked how (and why) I identify these alternative types of evaluation. Well, I don't just sit around dreaming up new approaches. Quite the opposite, these alternative approaches are responses to my evaluation clients' needs and interests. I am a full-time independent evaluation consultant. I aim to design evaluations that meet my clients' evaluation and decision-making needs, which is the heart of utilization-focused evaluation. My professional standing and livelihood depend on doing so effectively, ethically, credibly, and responsively. Developmental evaluation emerged as a response to innovators, and funders and supporters of innovation, who needed and wanted an evaluation approach specifically attuned to the processes and challenges of social innovation in complex dynamic systems. Principles-focused evaluation has emerged from consulting and working with principles-driven people implementing principles-based initiatives who wanted and needed an evaluation approach that focused on principles. This book is the result. It's a response to the evaluation needs of a specific group of primary intended users, those for whom adhering to principles is the core of how they engage in their attempts to make the world a better place for people in need and to ensure the sustainability of ecological systems.

The distinguishing characteristic of principles-focused evaluation is the focus on principles as the object of evaluation, as the evaluand. Three core questions bring the utilization focus to principles-focused evaluation: To what extent have meaningful and evaluable principles been articulated? If principles have been articulated, to what extent and in what ways are they being adhered to in practice? If adhered to, to what extent and in what ways are principles leading to desired results?

Overview of the Book

Part I of this book introduces principles: what they are, why they matter, and their niche in program development and evaluation. Part II presents the GUIDE framework for effectiveness principles. Effective principles provide meaningful *guidance* (G) and are *useful* (U), *inspiring* (I), adaptive *developmentally* (D), and *evaluable* (E). The chapters in Part II explain, illustrate, and illuminate each criterion (represented by each letter) in the GUIDE framework. Part III presents six case exemplars of principles-driven initiatives evaluated by principles-focused evaluations. Three of the exemplars are completed evaluations and three are still under way. Part IV turns to principles for evaluations and evaluators, including reflections and insights from three experienced principles-focused evaluators. Part V aims to be practical and practice oriented, offering tools and checklists to use in conducting principles-focused evaluation.

Contributors to the Book

While the book is inevitably dominated by my experiences and perspectives, I learned from editing *Developmental Evaluation Exemplars* how important and informative it is to include the experiences and insights of others, including the occasional skeptic and nay-sayer. Thus, I want to express special thanks to the colleagues who contributed directly and insightfully to this book with their reflections. I introduce each of these contributors at greater length where their perspectives are shared. Here I want to acknowledge and thank them for their contributions, and alert readers to these delectable embellishments.

▶ Chapter 9 includes a dialogue about principles with a longtime colleague and friend, and distinguished adult education scholar, Stephen Brookfield.

▶ Chapter 13 describes the varied and important contributions of principles in every aspect of the work of a youth-serving organization in Minneapolis. Heather Huseby, Executive Director of YouthLink, and Nora Murphy, the principles-focused evaluation consultant to YouthLink, highlight the utility of principles.

▶ In Chapter 16, John Wilson, a community organizer based in southern Africa, has contributed examples of grassroots principles-focused organizational development and evaluation from his work. I met John at a meeting of the Global Alliance for the Future of Food, where we found we had shared interests in principles as a source of inspiration and evaluation in community-based organizations and programs.

▶ Charmagne Campbell-Patton, to whom this book is dedicated, and about whom I will say more shortly, contributed Chapter 17, "Inspiring Principles: Distinguishing Overarching Principles from Operational Principles."

▶ Chapter 19 provides an extended case example of the developmental, contextual, and adaptive nature of principles through a citizen journalism initiative that involved adapting both facilitation and evaluation principles in an open-space event. Yve Susskind and Peggy Holman teamed up to write the chapter in a creative, interactive, and dialogic format. Yve was the developmental evaluator for the initiative described. Peggy Holman led the development of the initiative and is an experienced facilitator as well as author of *Engaging Emergence: Turning Upheaval into Opportunity* (Holman, 2010).

▶ Chapter 20, on simple rules and minimum specifications, spotlights complexity concepts with developmental implications for principles-focused evaluation. Glenda Eoyang and Royce Holladay, leaders of the Human Systems Dynamics Institute and longtime colleagues in Minnesota, contributed their expert perspectives. Mark Cabaj, an experienced developmental evaluator based in Canada, added his own connoisseurship reflections to the conclusion of the chapter.

▶ The Epilogue includes reflections and insights by the pioneering developmental evaluator and author Jamie Gamble (2008) on the relationship between developmental evaluation and principles-focused evaluation.

Part III also draws on the experience of editing *Developmental Evaluation Exemplars,* which affirmed the importance of providing in-depth case exemplars. Thus Part III presents examples of principles-focused initiatives with principles-focused evaluations. Each chapter illustrates a different approach to and purpose for principles. These examples show what focusing on principles looks like in practice for both change initiatives and evaluation of those initiatives. Three of the exemplars report on evaluations that have been completed: evaluation of the implementation of the Paris Declaration Principles for International Development Aid; program-level principles for working with homeless youth; and community-level principles for a community-based anti-poverty initiative in Canada, Vibrant Communities. The case presentations are derived from their final reports and interviews with those involved, as well as my own involvement. I conducted the meta-evaluation (evaluation of the evaluation) of the Paris Declaration principles evaluation featured in Chapter 25. I consulted on the design and interpretation of the youth homelessness program evaluation highlighted in Chapter 26. Mark Cabaj and Jamie Gamble helped me adapt the Vibrant Communities case example, Chapter 27, to fit the purpose of this book. *My experiences with these three exemplars of principles-focused evaluation are the bedrock of this book.* Indulge me in reiterating and emphasizing this point: without the Paris Declaration Principles evaluation and the youth homelessness program evaluation, there would be no principles-focused evaluation book. The relationships that formed with the people involved in the Paris Declaration and youth homelessness evaluations have sustained this writing effort over several years. Moreover, my interactions with Mark

Cabaj and Jamie Gamble about their experiences evaluating Vibrant Communities as a principles-driven initiative enlarged my understanding significantly and took me beyond my own limited experiences and perspectives.

The other three exemplars present ongoing and still-developing principles-based work: the Global Alliance for the Future of Food, a collaboration of major philanthropic foundations (Chapter 28); The McKnight Foundation's Collaborative Crop Research Program, an international agricultural research program working in Africa and South America (Chapter 29); and the emergence of agroecology as a new interdisciplinary field of scholarship and practice (Chapter 30). The chapters are based on their progress reports, interactions with key leaders, and developmental evaluation experiences with principles-focused evaluation, and my consultations with them. My thanks to the Global Alliance for the Future of Food and The McKnight Foundation for giving me permission to share their experiences with principles-focused programming and evaluation. Ruth Richardson and Jane Maland Cady have been especially visionary in articulating principles as the foundation of the collaborations they help lead and in using evaluation to further develop and strengthen the effectiveness of those collaborations. I have had the privilege of consulting with both the Global Alliance and The McKnight Foundation on their initiatives, and in doing so, have deepened my understanding of principles-focused evaluation through work with these ongoing, global collaborations. All of the people I've worked with in those collaborations have contributed to the ideas and practices presented in this book. Marah Moore, the evaluator for The McKnight Foundation collaboration, has been an important fellow traveler on this journey for several years now. Ernesto Méndez, whom I met through The McKnight Foundation work, is at the forefront of agroecology; he provided the research, his own and others, that is the basis for Chapter 30.

Part IV, "Principles for Evaluations and Evaluators," includes three chapters that take readers inside the practice of principles-focused evaluation. Ricardo Wilson-Grau, the creator of Outcomes Harvesting, presents Outcome Harvesting principles in Chapter 32. Donna Podems, an independent evaluator based in South Africa, shares her experiences and reflections as a principles-focused evaluator in Chapter 33. Nora Murphy, the principles-focused evaluator of the youth homelessness programs featured in Chapters 13 and 26, reflects on how her personal principles for living intersect with her principles as a principles-focused evaluator. An independent reviewer of the book, one not given to hyperbolic praise, who provided critical feedback with a discerning eye and a commitment to speak truth to the author, wrote of this sequence of chapters, "I was BLOWN AWAY by this section and particularly the three voices introduced at the end. All three are like a symphony coming to a crescendo!"

Acknowledgments

Acknowledging the many people who have influenced my thinking and practice beyond the direct contributors to this book just noted is daunting. You'd have to look at all the prefaces to all my books to begin to get a sense of the many people who have contributed in some way to this latest manifestation of my evaluation journey. I've been at this work for nearly five decades. Colleagues, clients, students, friends, family, supporters, and antagonists have all contributed. Acknowledging that long lineage of influence, I'll just highlight a few of the people who have contributed most directly to this book while I was writing it.

Randi Roth, Executive Director of Interfaith Action of Greater Saint Paul, and former Executive Director of the Otto Bremer Trust, has been engaging with me around the ideas that have finally taken shape in this book for a decade now, from the perspective of her deep engagement with the youth homelessness evaluation and, more recently, Project SPIRIT, an African American after-school program. Shanene Herbert, director of Project SPIRIT, both broadened and deepened principles-focused evaluation with her leadership in directing a principles-driven program (see Chapter 22). Over a 2-year period, the senior staff of the Blandin Foundation engaged with me in reflective practice focused on principles embedded in the foundation's strategic framework and theory of philanthropy (Annette, Fauth, & Ahcan, 2015; Patton, Foote, & Radner, 2015). Working with Steve Rothschild (2012) on his book about principles for nonprofits provided momentum for this book on evaluating those principles.

Among evaluation colleagues, Kate McKegg and Nan Wehipeihana, my co-editors of *Developmental Evaluation Exemplars,* have long been on the leading edge in practicing principles-focused evaluation in New Zealand. The insights from working with Kate and Nan are embedded deeply throughout this book. Stewart Donaldson provided the first opportunity for me to do a workshop and webinar on principles-focused evaluation through the Claremont Evaluation Center professional workshop series. After only a brief discussion with Stewart, he immediately grasped its niche and purpose, and urged me to create and offer the first principles-focused evaluation workshop. I did so in 2013, and have returned annually ever since. Several other evaluation colleagues have been encouraging and have provided feedback as the book developed: Tanya Beer, Julia Coffman, Miriam Fultz, Meg Hargreaves, Jennifer Jewiss, Jean King, Leah Moses, Patti Patrizi, Hallie Preskill, Patricia Rogers, Jamie Radner, and Kay Sherwood.

I owe special thanks to Publisher and Senior Editor C. Deborah Laughton at The Guilford Press. When I first told her about the focus of this book, she immediately understood its niche and potential contribution. What I've said about working with her on previous books merits repeating: She is a consummate, hands-on, meaning-focused, clarity-of-message-oriented *editor*. Yes, an actual *editor*, someone who improves chapter titles, quality and clarity of writing, and helps separate the wheat from the chaff *in service of readers*. Editing is becoming a lost art in academic publishing. I'm not talking about copyediting (ensuring consistency of style and correct grammar). I'm talking about editing that makes a book better, that supports book authors in deciding what to keep, what to discard, and how best to present what is kept. Deborah has a keen editorial eye, an astute editorial mind, and a willingness to spend time applying both. She also has a diplomatic editorial tone in offering suggestions and an irrefutable rationale for those suggestions she offers: to improve the experience for readers.

Serendipity also visited and contributed while I was writing. Out of the blue I received an e-mail inquiry from Glenn Page, who had been in a few of my training workshops and serves as both Developmental Evaluator in Residence at the Centre for Environmental Change and Human Resilience (CECHR), University of Dundee, Scotland, and Principal at SustainaMetrix, his consulting organization. Glenn had noted my comment in *Developmental Evaluation Exemplars* about principles-focused evaluation emerging as a major inquiry framework and focus for developmental evaluation. He wanted to know more. I was about two-thirds of the way through writing this book and offered to share the draft manuscript. What came back to me 4 days later was a detailed review both substantively and editorially. Glenn offered insightful comments about gaps, identified confusing sentences, asked for more detail about certain examples, suggested ways of enhancing the flow, critiqued incomplete exhibits, and affirmed the overall contribution of the book from his perspective as a developmental evaluation practitioner interested in principles-focused evaluation. And, oh, he did superb copyediting with a keen eye for missing commas, among other errors of omission and commission. Glenn personified my target audience, in the abstract, when I began the book. He became my target audience in flesh and blood as I finished the book. He subsequently reviewed the revised draft and the remaining chapters as I wrote them. I am deeply grateful to Glenn as should you, the reader, be, for he greatly improved the book throughout.

The only other person to have read every word of the book, and multiple versions as the book evolved, was my daughter, Charmagne Campbell-Patton. Two years ago she announced that she wanted to become an independent evaluator. She had been doing evaluation part-time as one of her responsibilities in an education nonprofit. She had decided she wanted to do more on a greater variety of projects and initiatives. I welcomed her to join me as a consulting and business partner, which she did. We've been doing projects together, teaching together, and writing together. She agreed to review the manuscript as I wrote and, as we discussed what was missing, to contribute Chapter 17, in which she had a better example than I had on my own. While Glenn Page reviewed the manuscript as an experienced evaluator, Charmagne brought the fresh eyes and inquisitive mind of a relative newcomer to the profession. She represented readers who would come to this book without a lot of prior evaluation knowledge and experience. She identified areas that needed clarification, assumptions that needed to be made explicit and explained, language that was overly jargonish, and sections and chapter sequences that lacked coherence and flow. Her comments led to a major reorganization of the book and strengthened the whole as well as the parts. She is one of a handful of second-generation evaluators (children of evaluators who helped establish the profession), a number I hope grows substantially in future years, which I would treat as one indicator of the vitality and allure of the profession. More generally, Charmagne represents the future of evaluation and, in dedicating the book to her, I dedicate it to the new and next generation of evaluators.

The solitude and intensity of writing can be tough on relationships. My partner, Jean Gornick, and I have built a place in the Minnesota woods, along the Snake River near the Wisconsin border, where we can have a life together. Here we host family gatherings and play with our grandchildren. We kayak in summer, and snowshoe and cross-country ski in winter. We plant indigenous flowers, grasses, and bushes, plant and nurture native trees, garden, keep bees, maintain a monarch butterfly habitat, and sustain a small fruit tree orchard. She brings important balance to my life, both supporting my writing and making sure it doesn't consume me—and us. My writing and, more importantly, my quality of life and our relationship benefit from that effort at balance. I am deeply grateful for her support, understanding, and commitment to a rounded life.

Note on Chapter Epigraphs

I use quotations to introduce chapters, like The Grateful Dead quote that opens this preface. Let me repeat here what I have said previously about employing quotations in this way:

> I think of such quotations as garnishes, seasoning, and a bit of *amuse-bouche* (a French gourmet tradition of serving an appetizer that is not on the menu but, when served, is done so without charge and entirely at the chef's discretion and preference). For the most part, these are not scholarly quotations, nor are they usually referenced. In the spirit of the gastronomic metaphors offered here, they are *palate cleansers* as you move from one topic to another.
>
> Some people, I am told, find such quotations annoying. . . . Well, you know, you don't have to eat the garnish. You don't like it, skip it. Like spam or unwelcome e-mails that you instantly delete, move past them quickly. (Patton, 2015a, p. xiii)

For my part, I'm a quotations addict. As a writer, one not given to brevity, I'm impressed when someone expresses a pithy insight succinctly. A well-articulated principle has that same quality.

A Note on the Cover Art

The cover features a stone sculpture of an inukshuk I was given in Banff, Alberta, when I keynoted a Canadian Evaluation Society meeting there in 1986. It was sculpted by an indigenous artist named IYAK (Fred Iyak Trimble). An inukshuk (pronounced in-ook-shook) is a stone landmark, like a cairn, created by indigenous communities to guide their people through desolate landscapes, like the great expanses of tundra in the Arctic region of North America. For the Inuit, Inupiat, Kalaallit, Yupik, and other aboriginal people of the Arctic Circle, inukshuks, often shaped like the human form, were used for navigation and guidance, especially to locate good hunting and fishing locations, food caches, and places of veneration and special cultural significance. Principles are inukshuks composed of words.

Contents

List of Exhibits

Principles

What They Are, Why They Matter, and Their Niche in Program Development and Evaluation

Three ancient and enduring questions to contemplate:

1. What are your principles?
2. To what extent do you adhere to them in your behaviors?
3. If you do adhere to them, what are the consequences and results of that adherence? And if you do not, what are the consequences and results of not adhering?

You can ask and answer them as an individual, in the privacy of your own thoughts. You can ask and answer them as a couple, in your significant relationship. You can ask and answer them as a family, or as a group of people who work and engage together.

You can also ask and answer these questions as a program, organization, community, change initiative, or social innovation endeavor. You can ask and answer them informally or formally, casually or systematically, and as a brief distraction or a concentrated commitment. When you do so formally, systematically, and as a concentrated commitment, you have moved into the territory of seriously evaluating principles: evaluating their meaningfulness; evaluating adherence to them; and evaluating their effectiveness. That is what it means to become engaged in *principles-focused evaluation*.

To facilitate others in undertaking a principles-focused evaluation is to become a principles-focused evaluator. That means adhering to the principles of principles-focused evaluation. Part I of this book introduces, explains, contextualizes, and illustrates those principles.

1

First Principles

There are three constants in life . . . change, choice and principles.
—Stephen R. Covey, author of *The 7 Habits
of Highly Effective People*

Change confronts us on all sides, envelops us from all directions, is omnipresent. We have choices about how we face, engage, and deal with change. Principles inform and guide those choices. They do so by telling us how to act. Principles-focused evaluation examines (1) whether principles are clear, meaningful, and actionable, and if so, (2) whether they are actually being followed and, if so, (3) whether they are leading to desired results.

Principles are derived from experience, expertise, values, and research. They operate at different levels. They can guide individual, program, policy, organizational, and community choices and actions. There are design principles, relationship principles, principles of professional practice, philanthropic principles, accountability principles, policymaking principles, sustainability principles, research principles, and so forth. You may recall introductory high school textbooks on principles of algebra, biology, and physics. Every arena of human inquiry and endeavor has generated guiding principles, often conflicting. For example:

"The early bird gets the worm" but "The second mouse gets the cheese."

"Fail often, fail fast, learn much" versus "Failure is not an option."

"Think strategically, understanding the big picture" though "The devil is in the details."

What conflicting guidance do you experience? How do you decide which to follow when two principles guide you in opposite directions? "Haste makes waste," but "Fools rush in where angels fear to tread."

Principles-focused evaluation informs choices about which principles are appropriate for what purposes in which contexts, helping to navigate the treacherous terrain of conflicting guidance and competing advice. What principles work for what situations with what results is an evaluation question. Thus, from an evaluation perspective, principles are hypotheses, not truths. They may or may not work. They may or may not be followed. They may or may not lead to desired outcomes. Whether they work, whether they are followed, and whether they yield desired outcomes are subject to evaluation. Learning to evaluate principles, and applying what you learn from doing so, takes on increasing importance in an ever more complex world where our effectiveness depends on adapting to context. Principles guide that adaptation.

First Principles First

As this book progresses, I'll distinguish a number of different kinds of principles, for example, program principles in contrast to evaluation principles, or principles to guide individual behavior as distinct from principles of organizational effectiveness. But we begin at the beginning, by distinguishing *first principles:* propositions so basic and foundational that they cannot be deduced from any other proposition or assumption. In mathematics, first principles are referred to as axioms or postulates. Sir Isaac Newton, in his *Mathematical Principles of Natural Philosophy* (1687), derived the laws of planetary motion from his mathematical explanation of gravity. He then used the same principles to account for the trajectories of comets, the tides, and other natural phenomena, thereby forever undermining the belief that the Earth was the center of the solar system. He also demonstrated that the motion of objects on Earth and of celestial bodies followed the same principles. In fact, his principles are really *laws:* universal observations about how the world works. His first law of motion posits that an object either remains at rest or continues to move at a constant velocity, unless acted upon by an external force. Newton's laws state insights about how the world works. They are so basic and foundational that they constitute first principles.

Blaise Pascal (1623–1662) was a French mathematician and scientist who formulated *Pascal's principle,* which states that a pressure change occurring anywhere in a confined incompressible fluid is transmitted throughout the fluid such that the same

change occurs everywhere. Pascal ruminated at length on first principles, concluding they were so basic that they couldn't be deduced by reason alone but had to be intuited by experience and feeling. He wrote, "Principles are intuited, propositions are inferred, all with certainty, though in different ways" (Pascal, 1910, p. 99). Propositions about the details of how the world works are inferred from first principles about the nature of nature.

Natural Principles versus Human Guidance Principles

Philosophy is the science by which the natural light of reason studies the first causes or highest principles of all things—is, in other words, the science of things in their first causes, in so far as these belong to the natural order.
    —JACQUES MARITAIN, An *Introduction to Philosophy*

Natural principles explain how the world operates. Darwin's principle of natural selection posits that within any environment, those most advantaged in that environment will survive (survival of the fittest). The natural sciences formulate, validate, and study natural principles. They can be and are evaluated using scientific principles of inquiry, but that is not our primary focus here, though there is a chapter on evaluating natural principles.

We'll be focusing on human guidance principles. These are principles that advise us how to live and what to do in the face of certain conditions—for example, "When in Rome do as the Romans do" (a sentiment first expressed by Saint Augustine in 390 C.E.). Such oft-repeated, widely applicable, time-honored, and well-established principles are a kind of first principle in the social realm. They are socially constructed and verified through shared human experience. Other principles are influenced by and can be derived from such axiomatic first principles, even as they may depart in important ways from the first principle. "When in Rome" directs us to pay attention to and respect other cultures. The American Evaluation Association (AEA) has adopted a statement on cultural competence based on the principle that "to ensure recognition, accurate interpretation, and respect for diversity, evaluators should ensure that the members of the evaluation team collectively demonstrate cultural competence."

> Cultural competence is a stance taken toward culture, not a discrete status or simple mastery of particular knowledge and skills. A culturally competent evaluator is prepared to engage with diverse segments of communities to include cultural and contextual dimensions important to the evaluation. Culturally competent evaluators respect the cultures represented in the evaluation. (American Evaluation Association, 2011)

In this book, I examine how general, overarching principles ("When in Rome . . .") lead to more specific, highly contextual operating principles, like the statement above on cultural competence.

Two Kinds of Human Guidance Principles: Moral Principles versus Effectiveness Principles

Philosopher Immanuel Kant (1724–1804), in his essay *Fundamental Principles of the Metaphysics of Morals* (1785), famously distinguished "hypothetical imperatives" from "categorical imperatives." An action deemed good in and of itself, and not done as a means to achieve something else, was categorically good and constituted a moral imperative. In contrast, an action done in the hopes of achieving some desired result was hypothetically imperative, meaning that its value depended on determining that the desired result was attained by the hypothesized action. Kant's hypothetical imperatives constitute effectiveness principles. His categorical imperatives are moral principles.

Moral principles tell us what is right. Effectiveness principles tells us what works. "Do unto others as you would have them do unto you" provides moral guidance. "Think globally, act locally" offers guidance about how to be effective. Both can be evaluated. Moral principles are evaluated on whether they are being followed, that is, whether you are behaving rightly. Effectiveness principles are evaluated on whether they are being followed *and* whether, in following them, you achieve what you want to achieve. In that regard, effectiveness principles can be evaluated for their meaningfulness, feasibility, adherence, utility, and results. This book is concerned with evaluating effectiveness principles, and I will offer a framework for doing so. Identifying and evaluating moral principles requires a framework for determining what is moral (Julnes, 2012; Minnich, 2017; Schwandt, 2002).

I hasten to add that whether something is a moral or effectiveness principle can be a matter of perspective. "Do unto others as you would have them do unto you" provides moral guidance but can also be viewed as offering effective advice or how to enrich relationships, or win friends and influence people. "An eye for an eye" can be viewed as a moral principle (let the punishment fit the crime) or as an effectiveness principle (deter future crime). Or both. "Think globally, act locally" offers guidance about how to be effective but can be viewed as a moral imperative. The value of making the distinction is to learn the perspective of those who adhere to and advocate a particular principle because the evaluation implications are different.

Consider the principle of racial integration (versus the principle of "separate but equal"). If it is viewed as a moral principle, the primary evaluation question is whether it is being done and the nature and quality of the integration. But if it is considered an effectiveness principle, that is, a means to higher school achievement or a more harmonious society, then it is evaluated both on the extent to which it is occurring and whether it is leading to the desired outcomes. Likewise keeping kosher or following a vegan diet can be viewed as either a moral principle (eating the right diet) or an effective one (eating a healthy diet). The evaluation criteria are different. Actions may be a combination of moral and effectiveness principles, but, in my experience, the two are rarely equally weighted. So I find it useful to distinguish moral principles (intrinsically right and good guidance) from effectiveness principles (instrumental toward some desired result). This involves distinguishing between doing things right (effectively) versus doing the right things (what is moral). Both are important, and both kinds of principles *can and should be evaluated.*

Principles Can and Should Be Evaluated

Principles are many-splendored and marvelously diverse things. They encapsulate ancient wisdom, call on us to be thoughtful and act nobly, and inspire us to be purposeful and effective. On the other hand, often being general and ambiguous and requiring interpretation, they can frustrate, foment uncertainty, and generate intense arguments about how to apply a principle in a given situation, which is why evaluating them is so important. Thus, the fundamental message and guidance of principles-focused evaluation: *Principles can and should be evaluated.* To illustrate the possibility, necessity, and challenge of undertaking principles-focused evaluation, Exhibit 1.1 presents 14 classic principles, divided into moral, natural, and effectiveness categories, with corresponding evaluation questions.

The evaluation column in Exhibit 1.1 illustrates evaluative thinking and inquiry applied to natural, moral, and effectiveness principles. Each principle provides guidance, and that guidance can be evaluated. Effectiveness principles provide guidance about how a certain kind of action, in principle, will produce a certain result or consequence. The eight effectiveness principles

in Exhibit 1.1 are so well established, universally applicable, and oft repeated that they might be considered *first principles.* What do you think?

Principles-focused evaluation inquires into the real-world efficacy of an effectiveness principle within some context. The evaluator asks: Based on the evidence, how does the principle work, and with what results, if any? Take, for example, Thomas's theorem, which posits that *what is perceived as real is real in its consequences.* Eminent Columbia University sociologist and president of the American Sociological Association, Robert K. Merton, proclaimed Thomas's theorem, by sociologist William Isaac Thomas (1863–1947), "probably the single most consequential sentence ever put in print by an American sociologist" (Merton, 1976, p. 174). As a theorem (aka principle), "it refers to an idea that is being proposed or accepted as sound, consequential, and empirically relevant." Following Thomas's theorem as a principle means that if you are trying to bring about change, you will pay particular attention to what people perceive about their current situation and the proposed change. The evaluation would examine how, and how well, you did this, and how it informed your intervention approach and results. Correspondingly, you may also follow sociologist George H. Mead's theorem, a derivative principle: "If a thing is not recognized as true, then it does not function as true in the community" (1936, p. 29).

Practice Exercise: Your Baseline

Identify a principle that informs and guides your life choices and decisions. Any kind of choice. Work. Family. Money. Relationships. Faith. Any principle. Write it down and date it. Put it someplace where you can find it, refer to it, and use it in the practice exercises I'll offer in this book. That's your baseline, your starting point, *your first principle.* See if it changes, or your approach to following it changes, as you read this book.

EXHIBIT 1.1. Fourteen Classic Principles and Corresponding Evaluation Questions

Principle	Premise of the principle	Sample evaluation questions
Moral principles	**Do what is right:** **Guidance to live morally**	**Is the principle being followed?**
1. *Golden Rule relationship principle*	Do unto others as you would have them do unto you.	How do those you interact with perceive that they are treated by you?
2. *Unconditional love principle*	Love the sinner, hate the sin.	Can you actually do it? And can you act in a way that expresses and communicates the distinction? Can the person you love tell the difference and appreciate its significance?
Natural principles	**How the world works**	**Is the principle accurate, true, and predictive in the real world?**
3. *Darwin's principle of natural selection*	Within any environment, those most advantaged in that environment will survive (survival of the fittest).	What explains the difference between those species that survive and thrive compared to those that languish and perish?
4. *Newton's principle of motion*	For every action, there is an equal and opposite reaction.	What explains motion? Measure actions (e.g., inputs) against reactions (e.g., outputs).
5. *Michels's iron law of oligarchy*	All forms of organization, regardless of how democratic they may be at the start, will eventually and inevitably develop oligarchic tendencies.	What happens to democratic organizations over time? What explains the emergence of oligarchic patterns?
6. *Campbell's law of corrupt indicators*	The more any single quantitative social indicator is used for high-stakes decision making, the more subject it will be to corruption pressures and the more apt it will be to distort and corrupt the social processes it is intended to monitor.	How are high-stakes indicators used over time under varying conditions? How does measurement validity change over time, if at all?

(continued)

Principle	Premise of the principle	Sample evaluation questions
Effectiveness principles	**Do what works to achieve desired results.**	**Is the principle being followed and does following it produce the desired results?**
7. *Occam's principle of parsimony*	That explanation requiring the fewest assumptions is most likely to be correct.	What are the merits of alternative and competing explanations? Compare and contrast.
8. *Pareto's 80/20 distribution principle*	80% of results are caused by 20% of the action or actors.	What is the actual percentage of actions or actors responsible for 80% of results? What's the consistency of this finding?
9. *Thomas's social construction theorem*	What is perceived as real is real in its consequences.	What do people perceive as real and what are the consequences of those beliefs?
10. *Parkinson's productivity principle*	Work expands to fill the time available for its completion.	What is the relationship between time available to complete a task and the time actually taken for completion?
11. *Murphy's low-expectations principle of pessimism*	Whatever can go wrong will go wrong.	What are the reasons that things go wrong? What are reasons why something might have gone wrong but didn't?
12. *The Confucian principle of the mean*	Moderation in all things; never act in excess.	What constitutes moderation for a given activity or situation? Compare experiences and results for those who exercise moderations versus those who engage in excess.
13. *Principle of least effort*	Less is more; do only as much as necessary to achieve the desired result.	What are variations in effort exerted to achieve a desired outcome? What explains the variations in effort and corresponding results?
14. *Grassroots engagement principle*	Think globally, act locally.	What does it mean to think globally? What actions follow from such thinking?

CHAPTER 2

Effectiveness Principles
What? Why? When? How? Who? Where?

I keep six honest serving-men
(They taught me all I knew);
Their names are What and Why and When
And How and Where and Who.
—RUDYARD KIPLING, "The Elephant's Child"

What?

An effectiveness principle is a statement that provides guidance about how to think or behave toward some desired result (either explicit or implicit), based on norms, values, beliefs, experience, and knowledge. The statement is a *hypothesis* until evaluated within some context to determine its relative meaningfulness, truth, feasibility, and utility for those attempting to follow it.

Consider the *abundance principle:* Give what you want to receive.

▶ If money feels tight, make a small contribution someone else's well-being.

▶ If you are feeling pressed for time, consider letting a single car go ahead of you in traffic, rather than impatiently tailgating the car in front of you.

▶ At a time when you are feeling low on energy, challenge yourself to give some positive attention to someone else (Whitman, 2016).

Program effectiveness principle: Plan your work and work your plan.

▶ Set and focus on priorities.

▶ Avoid mission drift.

Why?

A good principle provides guidance for making choices and decisions, is useful in setting priorities, inspires, and supports ongoing development and adaptation.

Twenty-one philanthropic foundations focused on improving food systems for the poor decided to collaborate in order to have greater collective impact. To do so, they concluded that they needed to identify and commit to shared principles. So they did. They are now the Global Alliance for the Future of Food. Chapter 7 presents their principles and the process they used to develop them. Chapter 3 offers a number of other examples of principles-driven programs and initiatives, and their rationales for making principles central to their work.

When?

Here's my response to the question "When?"

When ready. When needed. When able. When motivated. When committed.

The members of the Global Alliance for the Future of Food identified principles at the beginning of their collaboration. In contrast, the McKnight Foundation's Collaborative Crop Research Program, featured in Chapter 29, operated for more than 20 years before the leadership team decided to make explicit the principles that brought coherence to their work on 65 research projects with small farmers and agricultural researchers in 12 countries in four regions of the world on 24 different crops across the agricultural development spectrum, from seed development and breeding to agronomy to markets to food preparation to storage to postharvest processing. The Paris Declaration on Aid Effectiveness, whose evaluation is discussed in Chapter 25, were adopted by more than 100 countries and international agencies in 2005. This breakthrough agreement represented the culmination of 60 years of international negotiations, high-level forums, meetings, commissions, and treaty conventions.

Time is always of the essence, but timing varies.

How?

How are principles used? How do principles make a difference? Let me count the *hows*. Here are 10 ways principles operate that will be illustrated throughout this book.

How principles guide. They . . .

1. inform choices at forks in the road;
2. are grounded in values about what

matters to those who develop, adopt, and attempt to follow them;

3. provide direction, but not detailed prescription, so they offer opportunities to adapt to different contexts, changing understandings, and varied challenges;

4. must be interpreted and applied contextually and situationally to ensure their relevance; and

5. are the rudder for navigating complex dynamic systems.

How principles make a difference. They . . .

6. can enhance effectiveness when based on experience, knowledge, and evidence about how to be effective;

7. require judgment in application, so their effectiveness is somewhat dependent on the quality of decision making and judgment in applying and evaluating them;

8. have opposites that point in a contrary direction, so they force consideration of alternative courses of action based on comparing competing principles;

9. point to consequences, outcomes, and impacts; and

10. can be evaluated for both process (implementation) *and* results so that their hypothetical effectiveness and relevance can be tested.

Who?

Who employs effectiveness principles to guide change initiatives? Who needs principles-focused evaluation and evaluators?

Principles-driven change makers and innovators include idealists and pragmatists. Idealists embrace the admonition of Thomas Jefferson: "In matters of principle, stand like a rock; in matters of taste, swim with the current." Pragmatists are more likely to resonate with an approach attributed to

Abraham Lincoln: "I never had a policy; I have just tried to do my best each and every day," or perhaps the even more adaptable position of World War II general George S. Patton, whose position was "A leader is someone who can adapt principles to circumstances."

The point is that principles-driven people encompass the full diversity of humankind. Whatever brings them to principles, and whatever principles they express, the role of evaluators is to invite them to examine the extent to which they are adhering to principles, and if so, the implications and results of doing so—and if not adhering, the reasons for and implications of whatever lapses may be found and documented. Principles-focused evaluators, like all evaluators, bring a healthy skepticism to whatever claims are made, of whatever kind. That skepticism is nicely captured by the observation of highly respected Supreme Court justice Oliver Wendell Holmes Jr. in an 1897 Boston speech: "A man is usually more careful of his money than of his principles."

However, skepticism can be problematic if that's all an evaluator brings to an inquiry. Principles-focused evaluators share an interest in determining the effectiveness of principles. As an evaluator I am intrigued and stimulated by those with whom I work who are open to principles-focused evaluation. These are people willing, and sometimes even eager, to undertake reality testing and find out whether they are walking the talk of their principles and whether their work, initiatives, interventions, programs, and projects are adhering to espoused principles, and if so, whether that adherence is leading to the changes they envision for a better world. Those who fund principles-focused initiatives as well as the intended beneficiaries of principles-driven change, and the general public, also have a stake in testing the hypothesis that principles are effective. The next chapter provides examples of principles-driven initiatives and interventions.

Where?

In complex dynamic situations. This answer deserves elaboration because it provides important insight into the niche of principles-focused evaluation.

As noted above, principles are especially powerful rudders for navigating complex dynamic systems. To appreciate this niche for principles-driven initiatives and interventions, and therefore principles-driven evaluation, it is useful to differentiate between simple, complicated, and complex challenges.

▶ *Simple challenges.* The problem to be addressed is well defined and a great deal is already known about it. Clear, direct, linear, predictable, and controllable cause–effect patterns of success with strong evidence have been documented from evaluation research. Examples include immunizations to fight disease, well-tested new plant varieties in agriculture, and a rigorously evaluated math curriculum.

▶ *Complicated challenges.* Things become complicated when disagreements exist about how to define the problem and what to offer as a solution. In such situations diverse types of stakeholders with competing perspectives are affected and/or involved. Conflicting or confusing evidence from past research and/or evaluations foment controversy and tension. The problem of interest manifests multiple dimensions that interact, thereby increasing uncertainty and reducing predictability. Cause–effect linkages are context-contingent; they are discoverable with careful analysis, but neither obvious nor certain. Some contingencies are discernible, that is, there are known unknowns. Examples include bringing together diverse stakeholders in a diverse community to work together on environmental issues, or working on problems that extend across different sectors, such as health, nutrition, and safety issues in schools.

▶ *Complex challenges.* Complex dynamic situations are characterized by high uncertainty about how to even define the nature of the problem. There is typically great disagreement among diverse perspectives about what the issue is and strongly opposed opinions about what to do. The situation is turbulent, dynamic, ever changing, and variable from one place to another; nonlinear interactions exacerbate the problem and solutions are sought within a dynamic system. Key variables and their interactions are unknown in advance. Each situation is unique and in flux. Causal explanations are elusive. Examples include persistent problems like family and community violence, deeply entrenched poverty, the influx of new drug problems like opiate addictions, and complex issues like obesity in Western societies and chronic hunger in food-insecure areas. Climate change is a global example of a complex dynamic system where definitions of the problem are contentious and solutions elusive and controversial.

Interventions are usefully conceptualized as having complex aspects where they are inherently dynamic and emergent, rather than following a path that has been tightly defined in advance to achieve tightly specified objectives. Planning is done with an overall vision in mind, but it acknowledges that plans will develop as different people become engaged and as the program unfolds. Community capacity-building programs have many emergent aspects, as they work by identifying needs and strengths and then iteratively planning and implementing specific actions as priorities and opportunities change (Rogers, 2011, p. 35). Complex interventions are "nonstandardized and changing, adaptive, and emergent in response to changing needs, opportunities and understandings of what is working" (Rogers, 2011, p. 37). Complex interventions articulate a vision but not specific objectives and have no integrated approach or formal governance structure but self-organize as the work emerges. Both

processes and results are nonstandardized, contextually variable, changing, adaptive, and emergent.

How do those working to bring about change function under such complex conditions? Principles provide rudders for navigating complex dynamic systems.

What is the appropriate approach to use in evaluating complex interventions addressing complex challenges? *Principles-focused evaluation.*

Establishing causal attribution between interventions and results is especially problematic under conditions of complexity. Complexity theory posits that causality is not knowable in advance and can only be made somewhat coherent in retrospect. Once identified, causal chains and iterations will be inherently unique to the complex interactions that produced change within a particular time and context. Complexity theory rules out prediction-oriented, explanation-focused theories as irrelevant because complexity is its own explanation and prediction is not possible under conditions of complexity. These are clearly radical, paradigm-shifting premises, which may be why it is so tempting and easy to reframe complex challenges as merely complicated or even assert that the appropriate principle to follow is to simplify the complex.

Forss, Marra, and Schwartz (2011) have observed that "doing an evaluation is more of a mess than it used to be" (p. 7). They go on to assert that "evaluation tends to be more complex today than it was a decade ago" (p. 12). However, these challenges are not due to the nature of evaluation. Rather, they are due to the more complex policies and interventions evaluators are called on to evaluate in the face of a more densely populated, highly interconnected, and rapidly changing world. An evaluation of complex policies is more difficult than an evaluation of simple policies, strategies, programs, and projects, but the complexity resides in the evaluated object. How the evaluation handles that process is a step toward understanding, recognizing, and making sense out of the complexity "out there" (p. 13). What, then, are the characteristics of a complex intervention or policy? Four are highlighted: (1) it is nonlinear; (2) there is an asymmetric relation between policy and management on the one hand, and impact and results on the other hand; (3) change may be fast or slow, and both at the same time; and (4) the degree of uncertainty and risk is very high (p. 12). This is the "where" of principles-focused evaluation. Where these conditions characterize the situation and intervention, principles-focused evaluation has the agility, adaptability, and responsiveness to match the agility, adaptability, and responsiveness of principles-driven change makers and social innovators.

When distinguishing between simple, complicated, and complex situations and interventions it is worth emphasizing that these are not absolute categories. These distinctions do not constitute a taxonomy of operationally distinct, mutually exclusive, and exhaustive categories. Rather, the distinctions constitute a typological continuum. Situations are *relatively* simple, *relatively* complicated, and *relatively* complex. Moreover, identifying simple, complicated, and complex elements within a situation, intervention, and, correspondingly, an evaluation, may be most accurate and useful.

> Interventions can have some simple aspects, some complicated aspects and some complex aspects, and it is more useful to identify these than to classify a whole intervention as complex. An intervention without any complicated or complex aspects would have a clearly defined and agreed intended outcome, standardized and stable implementation processes that work through a single causal path to achieve the intended outcome, and would be implemented by a single organization, without significant contributions from other organizations. It is reasonable to report on

these types of interventions in terms of "what works."

> Many interventions have complicated aspects such as different components which all need to work effectively and together, or processes that work differently in different contexts, or which only work in combination with other programs or favorable environments. It is essential to report on these in terms of "what works for whom in what contexts."

> Some interventions have aspects that are intrinsically dynamic and emergent. While there is an overall goal in mind, the details of the program will unfold and change over time as different people become engaged and as it responds to new challenges and opportunities. Effective evaluation will not involve building a detailed model of how the intervention works and calculating the optimal mix of implementation activities because what is needed, what is possible, and what will be optimal will be always changing. (Rogers, 2013, p. 1)

When what is needed, what is possible, and what will be optimal will be always changing, principles provide guidance and direction for those working for change, and principles-focused evaluation offers an appropriate evaluation match. It is precisely because the challenge in any evaluation design is to match the inquiry framework to the nature of the problem being studied, the situation one faces, and the questions being asked that it can be helpful to distinguish between the simple, the complicated, and the complex. (For more on these distinctions and their evaluation implications, see Patton, 2011, 2012a, 2015a, 2016a, 2016b.)

Principles in Simple, Complicated, and Complex Situations and Interventions

Finally, simple situations and simple interventions may be in part guided by principles. For example, the World Health Organization follows the principle that immunizations should be voluntary, not forced on people. Complicated situations and interventions may also be in part principles-driven. *Seek consensus in collaboration* is a principle relevant to complicated interventions based on multiple actors working together. But complex situations and interventions are especially appropriate for principles-driven initiatives and principles-focused evaluation. *Adapt to context* is a complexity-sensitive principle. *Principles are particularly useful and appropriate for navigating complexity.*

Practice Exercise

At the end of Chapter 1, I asked you to identify a principle that guides your choices and decision making. How, if at all, has that principle helped you adapt to a new or different context? How, if at all, has that principle been useful in helping you navigate complexity? Be specific. What choice or decision? What context? What complexity? How was the principle meaningful and useful? And if it was not meaningful and useful, why not?

CHAPTER 3

Examples of Principles-Driven Change Initiatives and Programs

Policies are many, principles are few.
Policies will change, principles never do.
—JOHN C. MAXWELL, American author,
speaker, and pastor

Individual choices are informed and guided by principles. So are group choices and actions. The niche of principles-focused evaluation is principles-driven change initiatives and programs. Below are examples of principles-driven collective action. These will be elaborated and discussed in more depth as we go along, but these brief synopses will give you a sense of the nature and variety of principles-driven programs, collaborations, and reform efforts.

▶ In April 2002, 15 communities and the three national sponsors met for a 3-day forum in Guelph, Ontario, to create Vibrant Communities Canada. They jointly developed an experiment designed to test a "new" way to tackle poverty that acknowledged the complex nature of poverty and the challenge of achieving scale in poverty reduction efforts. The new way was not a model, but rather a set of five core principles that local communities agreed to follow in mounting locally unique campaigns.

▶ Over 100 countries and international development agencies signed an agreement to transform the international development assistance system. The agreement, signed in Paris in 2005, consists of five principles that, if and when implemented, would fundamentally alter how development assistance is given, received, administered, and implemented to achieve greater impact. A principles-focused evaluation examined both implementation and impacts of the Paris Declaration on International Aid.

▶ He Oranga Poutama is a sports and recreation health initiative among the Māori people of New Zealand. The initiative has involved developing a practical, grounded understanding of what engaging in health and recreation *as Māori* looks like in diverse activities. Core principles were developed and adapted in various local settings along with a system of national coordination and support to facilitate local effort. The principles-focused developmental evaluation received the 2013 Australasian

Evaluation Society's Best Evaluation Policy and Systems Award.

▶ In 2012, a group of community colleges began collaborating to scale up innovation in the form of guided pathways, programs of study, and evidence-based strategies to improve student outcomes and programs, organization, and system performance. Studying patterns across successful but greatly diverse innovations among the participating community colleges, the Transformative Change Initiative (TCI) discovered that the core of transformation was best expressed as seven overarching guiding principles.

▶ In late 2003, several legal petitions on behalf of juvenile offenders facing the death penalty were filed with the Supreme Court. On January 26, 2004, the Court granted certiorari in *Roper v. Simmons,* and the case was argued on October 13, 2004. In the brief window of time between when cert was granted and the case was argued, roughly nine months, a coordinated "final-push" campaign aimed at overturning the juvenile death penalty was organized and funded. The campaign was led by a small group of advocates without any formal organizational structure. Instead they based campaign coordination on a set of principles to which they all committed, beginning with decision making by consensus. On March 1, 2005, the Supreme Court ruled 5–4 that capital punishment for juveniles was unconstitutional.

▶ The McKnight Foundation began supporting the Collaborative Crop Research program in 1983. Over the subsequent 30 years the program evolved, expanded, and adapted. The program funded over 200 projects, developed research protocols, a theory of change, a development framework, and strategic plans. But the parts did not seem to cohere into a meaningful whole until a core set of principles emerged that captured and communicated both how and why they engage in development as they do.

▶ A community journalism initiative convened a gathering of journalists, community leaders, young aspiring journalists, and policymakers to discuss and deliberate on a new approach to community-engaged journalism. The interactions were facilitated through an open-space, world café, unstructured, self-organizing, and emergent process over three days. The dynamic and adaptive interactions were documented through developmental evaluation. Open-space facilitation principles, supported by developmental evaluation principles (presented in Chapter 5), provided the anchoring foundation for the fluid and adaptive process.

▶ In 2014, the Thrive Foundation, acting on its new mission to "guide disadvantaged youth to reach their full potential by strengthening the presence and impact of caring adults in their lives," searched across the nation for organizations providing services to disadvantaged youth with a caring adult at the center of their program delivery model. The search turned up eight exemplary organizations. Thrive then embarked on an evaluation of these organizations to see what they were doing with youth that made them effective. The inquiry identified and validated nine common principles that guided the work and explained the effectiveness of these diverse national organizations (Samuelson, 2016).

Principles-Driven Programs

Change efforts typically are organized and implemented as carefully planned, standardized models aimed at achieving specified program goals. Principles-driven initiatives, in contrast, typically operate in dynamic environments striving to meet and serve the diverse needs of diverse participants. A common mantra of such programs is that "one size doesn't fit all." Services are matched to participants' situations. Processes vary by participant. Outcomes vary for different people. Diversity demands responsiveness. Responsiveness generates variability based on determining what's appropriate, possible, and relevant. What is the anchor in the midst of such dynamic adaptation? Principles.

Six agencies serving homeless youth in Minneapolis and Saint Paul had long worked independently as autonomous organizations. They had developed their own distinct mission statements, strategic frameworks, value statements, program models, and staff operating manuals. When they came together to exchange ideas and learn from each other, they found, unexpectedly, that they shared fundamental principles about how to work with homeless youth. Those principles, taken together, constitute a coherent approach to overcoming youth homelessness. Here is the introduction to their report *Nine Evidence-Based Guiding Principles to Help Youth Overcome Homelessness:*

All homeless young people have experienced serious adversity and trauma. The experience of homelessness is traumatic enough, but most also have faced poverty, abuse, neglect or rejection. They have been forced to grow up way too early. Most have serious physical or mental health issues. Some are barely teenagers; others may be in their late teens or early twenties.

Some homeless youth have family connections, some do not; all crave connection and value family. They come from the big city, small towns and rural areas. Most are youth of color and have been failed by systems with institutionalized racism and programs that best serve the white majority. Homeless youth are straight, gay, lesbian, bisexual, transgender or questioning. Some use alcohol or drugs heavily. Some have been in and out of homelessness. Others are new to the streets.

The main point here is that, while all homeless youth have faced trauma, each homeless young person is unique. Each homeless youth has particular needs, experiences, abilities and aspirations. Each is on a personal journey through homelessness and, hopefully, to a bright future.

Because of their uniqueness, how we approach and support each homeless young person also must be unique. No recipe exists for how to engage with and support homeless youth. As homeless youth workers and advocates, we cannot apply rigid rules or standard procedures. To do so would result in failure, at best, and reinforce trauma in the young person, at worst. Rules don't work. We can't dictate to any young person what is best. The young people know what is best for their future and need the opportunity to engage in self-determination.

This is where principles come in. Organizations and individuals that successfully support homeless youth take a principles-based approach to their work, rather than a rules-based approach. Principles provide guidance and direction to those working with homeless youth. They provide a framework for how we approach and view the youth, engage and interact with them, build relationship with them and support them. The challenge for youth workers is to meet and connect with each young person where they are and build a supportive relationship from there. Principles provide the anchor for this relationship-building process. (Homeless Youth Collaborative on Developmental Evaluation, 2014, p. 2)

Exhibit 3.1 presents their nine evidence-based guiding principles to help youth overcome homelessness. Later, in Chapter 26, I'll describe how the principles were generated, evaluated, and are now being used for staff training and development, strategic planning, and ongoing engagement with homeless youth. For now, this is a real-world example of principles that serve as the compass (navigational system) for a dynamic collaboration.

Practice Exercise

Identify a principles-driven program in your arena of interest and expertise. Try an Internet search for the tag "principles" and your program area of interest. To what extent and in what ways is the program principles driven? What does this seem to mean? Keep this program in mind as we further define and refine what it means to be principles driven.

EXHIBIT 3.1. Nine Evidence-Based Guiding Principles
to Help Youth Overcome Homelessness

The principles begin with the perspective that youth are on a journey; all of our interactions with youth are filtered through that **journey** perspective. This means we must be **trauma-informed, nonjudgmental**, and work to **reduce harm**. By holding to these principles, we can build a **trusting relationship** that allows us to focus on **youths' strengths** and opportunities **for positive development**. Through all of this, we approach youth as **whole beings** through a youth-focused **collaborative** system of support.

Journey-oriented: Interact with youth to help them understand the interconnectedness of past, present, and future as they decide where they want to go and how to get there.

Trauma-informed: Recognize that most homeless youth have experienced trauma; build relationships, responses, and services on that knowledge.

Nonjudgmental: Interact with youth without labeling or judging them on the basis of background, experiences, choices, or behaviors.

Harm reduction: Contain the effects of risky behavior in the short term and seek to reduce its effects in the long term.

Trusting youth–adult relationships: Build relationships by interacting with youth in an honest, dependable, authentic, caring, and supportive way.

Strengths-based: Start with and build upon the skills, strengths, and positive characteristics of each youth.

Positive youth development: Provide opportunities for youth to build a sense of competency, usefulness, belonging, and power.

Holistic: Engage youth in a manner that recognizes that mental, physical, spiritual, and social health are interconnected and interrelated.

Collaboration: Establish a principles-based, youth-focused system of support that integrates practices, procedures, and services within and across agencies, systems, and policies.

Note. Principles developed by the Homeless Youth Collaborative on Developmental Evaluation and adopted on December 5, 2013, by collaboration participants: Avenues for Homeless Youth; Catholic Charities (Hope Street); Face to Face (Safe Zone); Lutheran Social Services (StreetWorks Collaborative); the Salvation Army (Booth Brown House); and YouthLink (Youth Opportunity Center).

CHAPTER 4

Evaluating Principles

Historical Context and Forward-Looking Challenge

A rose is not an orange is not a cat is not a rock.
—HALCOLM,[1] "How Things Are"

I date the beginning of the evaluation profession to 1975 and publication of the first *Handbook of Evaluation Research* (Guttentag & Struening, 1975)—in an impressive two volumes. That was also the era when the first professional evaluation associations were formed: the Evaluation Research Society and the Evaluation Network, which merged in 1984 to become the American Evaluation Association; the Australasian Evaluation Association; and the Canadian Evaluation Society. Now we have a number of evaluation journals, handbooks, textbooks, training institutes, annual conferences, webinar series, and online libraries. We now have more than 200 national and regional organizations for professional evaluators around the world, with more than 75,000 evaluators, and the year 2015 was designated as the International Year of Evaluation by the United Nations.

So what have we learned in more than 40 years? What are we still figuring out? And what are the emergent challenges for evaluation that we're just beginning to confront? Having been involved full-time as an evaluator over that entire span of four-plus decades, in this chapter I offer my perspective on these questions. Others would no doubt answer differently. My purpose in undertaking this assessment of the state of evaluation knowledge and practice is to identify the niche and contribution of principles-focused evaluation. *Spoiler alert:* Evaluating principles is one of evaluation's emergent challenges, an approach to evaluation that we're just beginning to learn how to do. This book aims to deepen our theory, knowledge, skill, and practice in evaluating principles, particularly principles-driven programs and change initiatives.

What Evaluators Do Well

We've learned to evaluate projects and programs. We know how to specify SMART goals (specific, measurable, achievable, relevant, and time-bound) and develop

---

[1]Halcolm (pronounced "how come?") is my sage philosophical alter ego and muse, who pipes in every so often to remind us that evaluation is grounded in fundamental philosophical underpinnings about how and why the world works as it does.

performance indicators. We have become skilled at developing logic models and theories of change. We know the importance of distinguishing monitoring from evaluation and how to do so, different types of evaluation (utilization-focused, impact, theory-driven, cost–benefit, empowerment, participatory, social justice, etc.), diverse uses of evaluation (accountability, learning, decision making, enlightenment, etc.), and how to work with diverse stakeholders (program staff, policymakers, funders, participants, etc.). We know how to enhance evaluative thinking among those engaged in evaluations. We have standards for what constitutes evaluation quality and checklists for what should be included in an evaluation. We know the importance of specifying intended use by intended users. We have a variety of ways of reporting findings and facilitating evaluation use. This is by no means a comprehensive or exhaustive list, but, hopefully, it provides a sense that we've learned a lot, know how to do a lot, and merit the designation of being a knowledge-based profession and transdiscipline, an umbrella discipline like philosophy and statistics that is essential and foundational for all other disciplines (Scriven, 2008).

What We Aim to Do, and Know We Should Do, but Are Still Learning to Do Well

My assessments of evaluation's accomplishments and future challenges are based on nearly a half century of full-time evaluation practice across a broad range of evaluation purposes, diverse programs, and levels of engagement from local to national and international. In my view, we've largely moved beyond the qualitative–quantitative paradigm debate and have come to value mixed methods. But evaluation reports remain largely siloed, with separate qualitative and quantitative sections, rather than integrating methods to provide triangulated data on common core questions. This is

analogous to what is called "parallel play" among toddlers in a sandbox, each aware of the other and both enjoying being in the same space, but lacking the skills to actually engage and play with each other.

The evaluation profession has recognized the importance of being competent at more than methods though that remains the focus of most training. We're still figuring out how to train for other professional competencies like interpersonal skills, reflective practice, project management, adherence to standards and guiding principles, and building capacity for cultural competence and responsiveness. Likewise, substantial attention is being devoted to incorporating systems thinking, complexity concepts, visualization, diverse and conflicting values, rapid feedback and real-time data, and the ability to treat failure as an opportunity for learning. The last decade has brought prominence to process use (learning and capacity building that occurs among those involved in an evaluation as distinct from using findings). We know that evaluations should search for unanticipated consequences and side effects, but too few designs include adequate resources and open-ended fieldwork to actually do so. Evaluators are getting better at incorporating explicit ethical frameworks and making underlying values explicit, but these directions need improvement and further development. Again, this is by no means a comprehensive or exhaustive list, but my message is that we're continuing to develop, innovate, and adapt to deepen and expand our relevance, utility, and excellence as a profession.

Emergent Challenges for Evaluation

The emergent challenges for evaluation, from my perspective, primarily have to do with new units of analysis and broader areas of focus for evaluation, what we call the evaluand, that is, the thing evaluated (Scriven, 1995, p. 68). Evaluation, we say, "grew up in the projects." As evidenced by what we do well, the profession's origins were in evaluating projects, and, from my perspective, we remain in the grip of a self-limiting project mentality. Such tools as logic models and SMART goals work well for project evaluation. They do not work well, in my judgment, for different kinds of evaluands like mission fulfillment, strategy, advocacy campaigns, policy change, systems change, and complex dynamic interventions. Projects are closed systems, or at least treated as such in most evaluations, in which boundaries can be established and control can presumably be exercised within those boundaries by both program staff and evaluators. In contrast, complex dynamic interventions, advocacy campaigns, and strategic initiatives are open systems characterized by volatility, uncertainty, and unpredictability, all of which make control problematic. Evaluating community impacts, regional and sector-wide initiatives, cross-sector initiatives, networks and collaborations, leadership, innovation, and collective impact poses new conceptual and methodological challenges. Treating these complicated and complex evaluations like more simple projects is inappropriate, ineffective, and insufficient. Indeed, it can do harm by misunderstanding, misconceptualizing, and misrepresenting the very nature of complex change and thereby generating results that are inaccurate and irrelevant. In addition, and along parallel tracks, evaluators are being challenged to develop new approaches to scaling innovations, assessing the effects of social media, and using "big data" to examine large and open systems. We are evaluating both theories of change and theories of philanthropy (Patton, Foote, & Radner, 2015). Evaluating global systems dynamics poses a particularly daunting challenge as we learn to view the Earth and the Earth's inhabitants as a holistic, interconnected, and interdependent global system. Viewed from outer space the Earth looks like a blue marble,

so I have referred to global systems change evaluations as Blue Marble Evaluations (Patton, 2016b).

This brings us to principles. Evaluating principles is also different from evaluating projects. Principles-driven programs are different from goals-driven programs. Principles constitute a different kind of evaluand. Principles take on added importance among the new challenges for evaluation because, as discussed in the last chapter, *principles are the primary way of navigating complex dynamic systems and engaging in strategic initiatives.* Principles undergird efforts at community change and collective impact. Understanding how to evaluate principles and adapting evaluation concepts, approaches, methods, and processes through principles-focused evaluation will, I believe, provide valuable direction for how to evaluate other new evaluands as we grapple with other and related emergent challenges. This book addresses those challenges and positions principles-focused evaluation on the cutting edge of evaluation.

Exhibit 4.1 summarizes this discussion.

Practice Exercise

If you are an evaluator, use Exhibit 4.1 to do an assessment of your expertise:

What do you do well as an evaluator?

What are you still figuring out?

What are the emergent challenges you face as an evaluator?

If you are **not** *an evaluator,* assess your experience of and knowledge about evaluation:

What activities and purposes do you associate with the word and activity *evaluation*?

What, if anything, have you wondered about how to evaluate because evaluation seemed difficult in some way?

What was the difficulty or challenge?

EXHIBIT 4.1. What Evaluators Do Well and Are Still Figuring Out,
and the Emergent Challenges for Evaluation
A Partial Inventory from One Veteran's Perspective

What evaluators generally do well, or at least know how to do	What we aim to do and know we should do but are still learning to do well	Emergent challenges for evaluation
Evaluating . . . • projects and programs • models • policies • philanthropic grants • clusters of projects or grants • goal attainment • outcomes • implementation *Generating . . .* • logic models • theories of change • performance indicators • lessons • recommendations • standards for evaluation • rubrics • evaluation checklists *Distinguishing . . .* • purposes of evaluation (formative, summative, accountability, monitoring, knowledge generating, developmental) • types of evaluation (utilization focused, impact, theory driven, cost–benefit, empowerment, participatory, social justice, etc.) • uses of evaluation (accountability, learning, decision making, enlightenment, etc.) • diverse stakeholders (program staff, policymakers, funders, participants, etc.)	*Conducting evaluations that attend to and integrate . . .* • mixed methods • cultural responsiveness and cultural competence • systems thinking • complexity concepts • visualization • diverse and conflicting values • rapid feedback and real-time data • learning from failures • process use (capacity-building effects of being involved in the evaluation as opposed to using findings) • unanticipated consequences and side effects • explicit ethical frameworks • making values explicit	*Evaluating . . .* • principles • global systems change dynamics (Blue Marble Evaluations) • mission fulfillment • strategies • advocacy campaigns • systems change • complex dynamic interventions • contextual factors and influences • community impacts • regional and sector-wide initiatives • cross-sector initiatives • environmental ecosystem sustainability • networks • collaborations • leadership • innovations • collective impact • scaling • social media • big data • rights-focused evaluation

CHAPTER 5

The Niche and Nature
of Principles-Focused Evaluation
Serving Diverse Purposes

Expedients are for the hour, but principles are for the ages.
—HENRY WARD BEECHER, American preacher,
orator, and writer

In the chapter on evaluation focus options in *Utilization-Focused Evaluation* (Patton, 2008), I identified and discussed 80 different evaluation options. Summative evaluation. Formative evaluation. Developmental evaluation. Theory-driven evaluation. Empowerment evaluation. Outcomes evaluation. Process evaluation. Cost–benefit evaluation. Internal evaluation. External evaluation. Realist evaluation. Quality assurance. Responsive evaluation. Independent evaluation. Real-world evaluation. Accountability. Monitoring. Utilization-focused evaluation. Where does principles-focused evaluation fit in the landscape of evaluation options? More particularly, what is the relationship between developmental evaluation, utilization-focused evaluation, and principles-focused evaluation? Let me take up the second question first.

Utilization-Focused Evaluation

Utilization-focused evaluation is a comprehensive decision framework for designing and implementing an evaluation to fit a particular situation and, in that situation, meeting the information needs of primary intended users to enhance their intended use of the evaluation. Utilization-focused evaluation is done for and with specific primary intended users for specific, intended uses. It begins with the premise that evaluations should be judged by their utility and actual use; therefore, evaluators should facilitate the evaluation process and design any evaluation with careful consideration for how everything that is done, from beginning to end, will affect use. Use concerns how real people in the real world apply evaluation findings and experience the evaluation process. Therefore, utilization-focused evaluation provides systematic, research-based guidance and a set of steps for deciding what approach to evaluation is most appropriate for a particular situation and specific primary intended users. This means that utilization-focused evaluation encompasses every evaluation option methodologically, conceptually, theoretically, analytically, and process-wise. Any of the

80 options mentioned above, or the many other options that have been articulated to meet particular evaluation needs and demands, can be used in a utilization-focused evaluation. In essence, utilization-focused evaluation doesn't prescribe what to focus on but rather prescribes a process for determining what to focus on based on unwavering attention to intended uses by intended users. Exhibit 5.1 summarizes some common utilization-focused evaluation options. Within those options, you will see that developmental evaluation is a purpose option while principles-focused evaluation is both a focus (evaluand) option and a type of evaluation. Each of these is discussed below.

Developmental Evaluation

Developmental evaluation serves the purpose of innovation development. Developmental evaluation provides *evaluative* information and feedback to social innovators, and their funders and supporters, to inform adaptive *development* of change

EXHIBIT 5.1. Options for Focusing an Evaluation		
Ways of distinguishing evaluations	**Sample options**	**How to choose among options in utilization-focused evaluation**
1. Purpose distinctions	a. *Summative evaluation:* Make overall judgments of merit, worth, and significance to inform a major decision like continuing, ending, expanding, or contacting a model program. b. *Formative evaluation:* Identify strengths and weaknesses and provide feedback to improve a model and get it ready for summative evaluation. c. *Accountability:* Determine if resources are being applied as prescribed by funders and if specific mandated ways of operating are being followed. d. *Developmental evaluation:* Support innovation and adaptation in complex dynamic environments. e. *Knowledge generation:* Extrapolate lessons to inform initiatives and evaluations in the future.	• Purpose determines and drives use. • Negotiate with primary intended users and be clear about the priority intended purpose of an evaluation. • Watch for and manage conflicts and tensions between different purposes. • Purpose determines evaluation questions, design, methods, analysis, reporting, and use.
2. Focus of evaluation (evaluand)	a. Program b. Project c. Product d. Personnel e. Strategy f. Policy g. Principles (as the intervention)	• Be utilization-focused regardless of the evaluand; the same processes and steps apply to enhance use.

(continued at the top of the next page)

Ways of distinguishing evaluations	Sample options	How to choose among options in utilization-focused evaluation
3. Types of evaluation	a. Outcomes b. Process c. Implementation d. Impact e. Cost-effectiveness f. Cost–benefit g. Strategy focused h. Principles focused i. Combinations of the above	• Focus on the most important concerns, issues, and questions of the intended users. • Ensure adequate resources and time to do a high-quality evaluation of whatever type is being conducted.
4. Evaluation approaches	a. Theory driven b. Participatory c. Empowerment d. Randomized controlled trials (experimental designs) e. Quasi-experimental designs f. Realist systems g. Feminist h. Culturally responsive	• Be sure primary intended users understand the assumptions, values, requirements, evaluator skills, and kinds of results associated with different evaluation approaches.
5. Evaluator roles	a. Independent, external b. Independent, internal c. Team with internal and external d. Collaborative e. Evaluator as coach/facilitator f. Interactive g. Embedded	• Ensure that primary intended users understand the implications of role options for evaluation costs, findings credibility, evaluator skill requirements, and expectations of stakeholder engagement.

initiatives in complex dynamic environments. Developmental evaluation brings to innovation and adaptation the processes of asking evaluative questions, applying evaluation logic, and gathering and reporting evaluative data to inform and support the development of innovative projects, programs, initiatives, products, organizations, and/or systems change efforts with timely feedback. Social innovators, funders of social innovation, advocates and supporters of social innovation, and change agents are the primary intended users of developmental evaluation—and clearly identified as such in any specific developmental evaluation. The intended use (purpose) of developmental evaluation is to support

adaptation and development of the innovation. This is done through ongoing and timely evaluation. The developmental evaluation feedback and findings are used by social innovators and change agents to illuminate and adapt innovative strategies and decisions. That's intended use by intended users. That's utilization-focused evaluation with a developmental purpose. Funders of social innovation use developmental evaluation findings to inform funding decisions and meet accountability expectations and demands. That's also intended use by intended users. That's also utilization-focused evaluation. In short, developmental evaluation is a particular kind of utilization-focused evaluation. All that has been learned about enhancing use over 40 years of utilization-focused evaluation practice and research undergirds developmental evaluation (Patton, 2008, 2012a, 2015a, 2016a, 2016b).

The developmental evaluation niche focuses on evaluating innovations in complex dynamic environments because that's the arena in which *innovators* are working. Social-ecological innovators, for example, integrate understandings of and actions on the human and natural worlds as interdependent and interactive complex dynamic systems. Social-ecological innovators deal with people and places, and interventions within contexts. Innovation is a broad framing that includes creating new approaches to intractable problems, adapting programs to changing conditions, applying effective principles to new contexts (scaling innovation), catalyzing systems change, and improvising rapid responses in crisis conditions. Social-ecological innovation unfolds in social systems that are inherently dynamic and complex, and often turbulent. The implication for social innovators is that they typically find themselves having to adapt their interventions in the face of complexity. Funders of social-ecological innovation also need to be flexible and adaptive in alignment with the dynamic and uncertain nature of social innovation in complex systems. Developmental evaluators track, document, and help interpret the nature and implications of innovations and adaptations as they unfold, both the processes and outcomes of innovation, and help extract lessons and insights to inform the ongoing adaptive innovation process. At the same time, this provides accountability for funders and supporters of social innovations and helps them understand and refine their contributions to solutions as they evolve. Social-ecological innovators often find themselves dealing with problems, trying out strategies, and striving to achieve goals that emerge from their engagement in the change process, but which they could not have identified before that

engagement, and that continue to evolve as a result of what they learn. The developmental evaluator helps identify and make sense of these emergent problems, strategies, and goals as the social innovation *develops.* The emergent/creative/adaptive interventions generated by social innovators for complex problems are significant enough to constitute *developments,* not just improvements, thus the need for *developmental* evaluation.

Traditional evaluation approaches advocate clear, specific, and measureable outcomes that are to be achieved through processes detailed in a linear logic model. Such traditional evaluation's demand for upfront, preordained specificity doesn't work under conditions of high innovation, exploration, uncertainty, turbulence, and emergence. Indeed, premature specificity can do harm and generate resistance from social innovators, as, indeed, it has, by constraining exploration, limiting adaptation, reducing experimental options, and forcing premature adoption of a rigid model not because such a model is appropriate, but because evaluators, funders, or other stakeholders demand it in order to comply with what they understand to be good evaluation. Developmental evaluation emerged as a response to criticism of traditional evaluation by social innovators and their expressed need for an alternative way to engage in evaluation of their work.

Developmental evaluation involves evaluative thinking throughout. Judgments of merit, worth, significance, meaningfulness, innovativeness, and effectiveness (or such other criteria as are negotiated) inform ongoing adaptive innovation. Such evaluative judgments don't just come at the end of some fixed period (e.g., a 3-year grant); rather, they are ongoing and timely. Neither empirical conclusions and interpretations nor evaluative judgments are reached and rendered by the evaluator independently. Developmental evaluation is a collaborative, interactive, utilization-focused process. It unfolds in complex dynamic systems where the particular meaning and significance of information may be difficult to predetermine, so developmental evaluators need to interpret patterns in the data *collaboratively* with social-ecological innovators, funders, advocates, change agents, and systems change supporters to make sense together of emergent findings. Through this empirically focused interaction, developmental evaluation becomes an integral part of the innovative process.

Principles-Focused Evaluation

Here are the distinctions so far. Utilization-focused evaluation is a comprehensive decision-making framework for determining what kind of evaluation is appropriate for a particular situation and to serve the intended uses of specific primary intended users. Developmental evaluation is one particular purpose of evaluation: supporting development of social innovations introduced by social innovators into complex dynamic situations. Principles-focused evaluation calls attention to and focuses on one particular object of evaluation, on principles as the *evaluand*. Outcomes are the evaluand of outcomes-focused evaluation. A project is the evaluand of project-focused evaluation. A theory of change is the evaluand of theory-of-change-focused evaluation. Program processes are the evaluand of process-focused evaluation. And, follow me closely here, principles are the evaluand of principles-focused evaluation.

Principles-Focused Developmental Evaluation

A principles-focused developmental evaluation would evaluate how principles are informing innovative developments in a complex dynamic situation. Because developmental evaluation often unfolds without predetermined or fixed processes and outcomes, the innovative process may be guided by adherence to principles. Adapting

those principles to particular challenges and changing contexts is often a primary focus of developmental evaluation. For example, an innovative, community-based anti-poverty initiative may be committed to the principle of inclusion. A principles-focused developmental evaluation focused on inclusion would be appropriate for such an initiative because it combines the purpose of supporting and evaluating innovation development with a focus on principles as the rudder for navigating complexity in the process of developmental adaptation.

But not all developmental evaluations are principles focused, and not all principles-focused evaluations are developmental in purpose. So let's consider some other purposes and applications of principles-focused evaluation beyond developmental evaluation. Exhibit 5.2 presents examples of how principles-focused evaluation can serve diverse purposes and/or involve varied types of evaluation.

Evaluating Principles

As this book illustrates, principles-focused evaluation can evaluate processes of implementing principles, outcomes associated with principles, longer-term and broader impacts that result from principles-driven programming, and innovative approaches to principles adaptation. Principles-focused evaluation can serve a variety of purposes: accountability, formative, summative, developmental, and knowledge generating. In all these applications, principles-focused evaluation should be utilization-focused. Across all these applications, diverse purposes, and varying uses *the distinguishing characteristic of principles-focused evaluation is the focus on principles as the object of evaluation,* as the evaluand. Three core questions bring the focus to principles-focused evaluation: To what extent have meaningful and evaluable principles been articulated? If principles have been articulated, to what extent and in what ways are they being adhered to in practice? If adhered to, to what

EXHIBIT 5.2. Principles-Focused Evaluation Serving Diverse Purposes		
Evaluation purpose	Principles-focused evaluation questions	Concrete examples
1. Formative evaluation	How can the program's adherence to principles be improved?	The evaluation shows that staff in a program for homeless youth are interpreting the principle of "trauma-informed care" in different ways. Staff training to improve shared adherence to the principle is recommended.
2. Accountability evaluation	Is the program following principles as specified in funding and policy mandates?	A major housing renovation project in a low-income community mandates community consultation on playground and green space design. The evaluation documents the nature, extent, and types of community consultation and reports the findings in a public accountability report.
3. Knowledge-generating evaluation	What can be learned about the effectiveness of principles?	An online course following principles of online student engagement conducts an evaluation to gather and analyze feedback from faculty and students to generate lessons about the effectiveness of the online course principles that can be used in future online courses.
4. Summative evaluation	Are the principles currently being followed relevant and effective? Should they be maintained, changed, or dropped altogether (and replaced with "best practices")?	An innovative higher-education program follows learner-centered principles that give students major control over the curriculum. The evaluation gathers data from graduates and their employers about whether students learned what they needed to succeed, with the findings used to judge if the learner-centered approach is working in the employment marketplace, or if a more employer-focused program should be designed and implemented.
5. Developmental evaluation	How are principles being applied in adaptation of an innovation to new locations?	A microfinance program based on women's empowerment principles is evaluated to document how the principles of empowerment are being adapted in different cultures and among women with different characteristics: younger, older; married/unmarried; with and without children; with varying degrees of education.

extent and in what ways are principles leading to desired results?

Comparing Principles of Utilization-Focused Evaluation, Developmental Evaluation, and Principles-Focused Evaluation

To illustrate how principles can differentiate approaches and further illuminate the distinctions and interconnections between utilization-focused evaluation, developmental evaluation, and principles-focused evaluation, I am concluding this chapter by presenting the essential principles of each. Exhibit 5.3 presents utilization-focused evaluation principles. Exhibit 5.4 presents developmental evaluation principles. Exhibit 5.5 presents principles for principles-focused evaluation. Exhibit 5.6 shows the relationships among the three approaches,

namely, that utilization-focused evaluation is the overarching framework within which developmental evaluation and principles-focused evaluation are distinct options, sometimes overlapping, as in *principles-focused developmental evaluation,* but each sometimes constituting a distinct approach. (Part IV will discuss in greater detail the role of principles in differentiating alternative evaluation approaches and share reflections from principles-focused evaluators about their experiences.)

> **Practice Exercise**
>
> Compare and contrast the sets of principles for utilization-focused evaluation (Exhibit 5.3), developmental evaluation (Exhibit 5.4), and principles-focused evaluation (Exhibit 5.5). What is common across the three sets? What is distinctive about each set? How do principles serve to define an approach?

EXHIBIT 5.3. Principles of Utilization-Focused Evaluation

1. *Situational analysis.* Analyze the situation in which the evaluation will occur.

2. *Intended users.* Identify and engage with the primary intended users of the evaluation.

3. *Intended uses.* Engage with primary intended users to determine the evaluation's priority uses.

4. *Intended use by intended users.* Focus all aspects of the evaluation (questions, methods, design, measurement, analysis, timing, reporting) on intended uses by intended users.

5. *Ongoing focus on use.* Make attention to use the driving force of the evaluation from beginning to end.

6. *Engagement.* Be active-reactive-interactive-adaptive in working with intended users.

7. *Process use.* Be aware of and strategic about how being involved in the evaluation affects those involved.

8. *Adaptation.* Adapt to changed priorities, turnover among intended users, reallocation of resources, changed timelines, and other factors that emerge over time; avoid rigidity.

9. *Follow-up.* Work with intended users to interpret and act on the evaluation's findings.

10. *Learning.* Reflect on the strengths and weaknesses of the utilization–focused evaluation process and results to learn and improve.

Source: Patton (2008, 2012a).

EXHIBIT 5.4. Developmental Evaluation Principles

1. *Developmental purpose.* Illuminate, inform, and support what is being developed, identifying the nature and patterns of development (innovation, adaptation, systems change), and the implications and consequences of those patterns.

2. *Evaluation rigor.* Ask probing evaluation questions, think and engage evaluatively, question assumptions, apply evaluation logic, use appropriate methods, and stay empirically grounded, that is, rigorously gather, interpret, and report data.

3. *Utilization focus.* Focus on intended use by intended users from beginning to end, facilitating the evaluation process to ensure utility and actual use.

4. *Innovation niche.* Elucidate how the change processes and results being evaluated involve innovation and adaptation, the niche of developmental evaluation.

5. *Complexity perspective.* Understand and interpret development through the lens of complexity and conduct the evaluation accordingly. This means using complexity premises and dynamics to make sense of the problems being addressed, guide innovation, adaptation, and systems change strategies, interpret what is developed, adapt the evaluation design as needed, and analyze emergent findings.

6. *Systems thinking.* Think systemically throughout, being attentive to interrelationships, perspectives, boundaries, and other key aspects of the social system and context within which the innovation is being developed and the evaluation is being conducted.

7. *Co-creation.* The innovation and evaluation develop together—interwoven, interdependent, iterative, and co-created—such that the developmental evaluation becomes part of the change process.

8. *Timely feedback.* Time feedback to inform ongoing adaptation as needs, findings, and insights emerge, rather than only at predetermined times (like quarterly, or midterm and end-of project).

Source: Patton (2016a).

EXHIBIT 5.5. Principles Guiding Principles-Focused Evaluation

1. *Matching.* Conduct principles-focused evaluations on principles-driven initiatives with principles-committed people. Principles are the evaluand (focus of evaluation).

2. *Distinctions matter.* Distinguish types of principles: natural, moral, and effectiveness; distinguish principles from values, beliefs, lessons, rules, and proverbs.

3. *Quality.* Support development of principles that meet the GUIDE criteria: They *Guide*; are *Useful*; *Inspire*; support *Developmental* adaptations; and are *Evaluable*.

4. *Evaluation rigor.* Systematically inquire into and evaluate effectiveness principles for both implementation (Are they followed?) and results (What difference do they make?).

5. *Utilization focus.* Focus on intended use by intended users from beginning to end, facilitating the evaluation process to ensure utility and actual use.

6. *Beyond rhetoric.* Support using principles comprehensively; use them or lose them; don't let them become just a list; apply them across functions (staff development, working with clients, strategic planning, monitoring, and evaluation).

7. *Interconnections.* Interconnect principles. The eight principles of principles-focused evaluation are an interdependent, interconnected whole (not a pick-and-choose list). For any set of principles being evaluated, examine how individual principles are aligned (or not) and interconnected (or not).

8. *Learning.* Reflect on the strengths and weaknesses of the principles-focused evaluation process and results to learn and improve; engage in principles-focused reflective practice. Deepen learning about principles-driven programming and principles-focused evaluation; extract and apply lessons.

EXHIBIT 5.6. Relationships among Utilization-Focused Evaluation, Developmental Evaluation, and Principles-Focused Evaluation

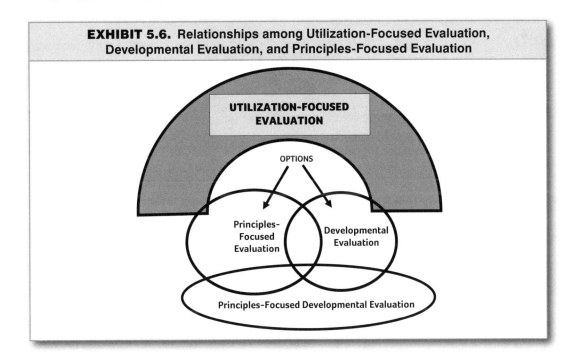

GUIDE
Criteria for Effectiveness Principles

People are different. People choose different criteria. But if there
is a better way among many alternatives, I want to encourage
that way by making it comfortable. So that's what I've tried to do.
—YUKIHIRO MATSUMOTO, Japanese computer scientist
and software programmer

Criteria are central to evaluation. Judging quality requires criteria. Evaluative reasoning is built around criteria. Determining how good something is begins with criteria. Think about the criteria you apply to the things that matter to you. What are your criteria for music you prefer? What criteria have you used in buying car? A computer? Furniture? Clothes? What are your criteria for a fine dinner? For your favorite movies? For political candidates worthy of your vote?

Part II of this book presents and discusses *criteria for effectiveness principles*. Principles-focused evaluation evaluates the meaningfulness of principles, degree of adherence to avowed principles, and the results that follow from adherence. But first we have to address what constitutes a high-quality principle, which is the focus of Chapter 6. *No principles, no principles-focused evaluation.* Principles-focused evaluators often have to help develop, fine-tune, reframe, or better articulate principles to enhance their guidance, utility, inspirational nature, developmental adaptability, and evaluability.

Here is an overview of Part II.

GUIDE for Effectiveness Principles
The Characteristics
of High-Quality Effectiveness Principles

We learn by practice. Whether it means to learn to dance by practicing dancing
or to learn to live by practicing living, the principles are the same.
—MARTHA GRAHAM, American choreographer

The Up-Front Clarifying Role of Evaluators

Traditionally, evaluation has been synonymous with measuring goal attainment. The classic evaluation question was: To what extent is the program attaining its goals? In order to answer this question, clear, specific, and measureable goals were needed. And that's where the trouble began. As I noted in discussing goals in *Essentials of Utilization-Focused Evaluation* (Patton, 2012a):

> The evaluation literature is replete with complaints about goals that are fuzzy, vague, abstract, too general, impossible to find indicators for, and generally inadequate. An example: Improved quality of life. What are the dimensions of "quality of life"? What constitutes improvement? Thomas Jefferson's "pursuit of happiness" would not pass muster. (p. 204)

In addition to vague goals, programs often have multiple and conflicting goals, and different stakeholders may emphasize different goals for the same program. This has meant that evaluators are called on not only to evaluate goal attainment, but to facilitate goals clarification in order to evaluate whether intended goals are being achieved. Enter *evaluability assessment*.

Evaluability assessment involves determining if a program is ready for evaluation, which usually includes clarifying goals. Evaluators have become heavily involved in goals clarification because, when we are invited in, we seldom find a statement of clear, specific, prioritized, and measurable goals. This can take novice evaluators by surprise if they think that their primary task will be formulating an evaluation design for already established goals. Even where goals exist, they are frequently unrealistic, having been exaggerated to secure funding—what are called BHAGs (big hairy audacious goals). One reason evaluability assessment has become an important pre-evaluation process is that, by helping programs get ready for evaluation, it acknowledges the frequent need for a period of time to work with program staff, administrators, funders, and participants on clarifying goals—making them realistic, focused, agreed on, and measureable. Evaluability assessment can include interviews to determine how much consensus there is among various stakeholders about goals and to identify where differences lie.

As evaluators became involved in working with program people to more clearly specify the program's model (or theory), it became increasingly clear to those engaged in clarifying program models that evaluation was an *up-front activity*, not just a back-end activity. That is, traditional planning models laid out some series of steps in which planning comes first, then implementation of the program, and then evaluation, making evaluation a back-end, last-thing-done task. But to get a program plan or design that could actually be evaluated has meant evaluators taking on the up-front role of clarifying goals, logic models, and program theories of change. This has had huge implications for evaluators. It has meant that evaluators have to be astute and skilled at working with program people, policymakers, and funders to facilitate their articulation of goals in a way that can be evaluated. *The same up-front process of clarification is often needed in principles-focused evaluation to develop and clarify principles.*

SMART goals (specific, measurable, achievable, relevant/realistic, time-bound/timely) emerged as a framework for goals clarification.

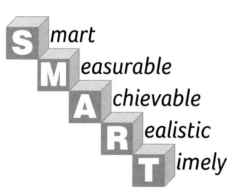

In this chapter I offer the GUIDE framework as a set of criteria for clarifying effectiveness principles, that is, a tool to help a principles-based program ensure readiness for principles-focused evaluation. GUIDE is an acronym and a mnemonic specifying the criteria for a high-quality principle statement. A high-quality principle (1) provides guidance, (2) is useful, (3) inspires, (4) supports ongoing development and adaptation, and (5) is evaluable.

Essentially, GUIDE criteria provide an evaluability assessment framework applied to principles. After presenting the GUIDE framework in detail, I'll return to further discussion of the difference between goals-based evaluation and principles-focused evaluation, and to the integration of the two.

Elucidating the GUIDE Criteria and an Example Applying the Criteria

To illuminate the GUIDE criteria, let me present the fundamental principle that undergirds utilization-focused evaluation. Then we'll examine this principle using the five GUIDE criteria.

> **Utilization-focused evaluation principle:** Focus on intended use, by and with intended users, in every aspect of, and at every stage of, an evaluation.

Now let's examine that principle against the five GUIDE criteria.

G Guiding

A principle is prescriptive. It provides advice and guidance on what to do, how to think, what to value, and how to act to be effective. It offers direction. The wording is imperative: *Do this.* The guidance is sufficiently distinct that it can be distinguished from contrary or alternative guidance.

The utilization-focused evaluation principle prescribes identifying intended users from the beginning and involving them in determining how an evaluation will be used, then designing the evaluation accordingly. Alternative and contrary principles are: Design an evaluation to be credible to scholars. Attend to use when you have findings to be used. Worry about accuracy, not use. Identifying and articulating alternative possible principles clarifies a particular principle's guidance.

U Useful

A high-quality principle is useful in informing choices and decisions. Its utility resides in being actionable, interpretable, feasible, and pointing the way toward desired results for any relevant situation. The principle provides guidance for translating knowledge into action.

The purpose of the utilization-focused evaluation principle is to enhance actual use of an evaluation by those for whom and with whom it is being done. It can be applied to any evaluation situation. The principle advises focusing on use throughout the evaluation from the beginning, not just at the end when findings are ready. That's useful advice; not easy, but doable, interpretable, and actionable.

I Inspiring

Principles are values based, incorporating and expressing ethical premises, which is what makes them meaningful. They articulate what matters, both in how to proceed and the desired result. They articulate how to do things right (effectively) and the right thing to do (express the values basis for action). That should be inspirational.

The utilization-focused evaluation principle values use. Valuing use is both an ethical and pragmatic stance. It implies that evaluations should not be done as a matter of compliance or window dressing but should be conducted so as to be useful—and actually used. This, the principle asserts, is the evaluator's calling. This is what makes evaluation worthwhile, meaningful, and a contribution to solving societal problems and improving lives. To behave otherwise is wasteful and unethical. The desired result is enhanced use of the evaluation by those for whom it is intended for social betterment. For evaluators who care about a better world, use is the vehicle for realizing that noble vision, so the principle is hopefully inspiring, both in the vision it offers and the implication that the desired result (greater evaluation use) is possible by following the principle.

D Developmental

The developmental nature of a high-quality principle refers to its adaptability and applicability to diverse contexts and over time. A principle is thus both context sensitive and adaptable to real-world dynamics, providing a way to navigate the turbulence of complexity and uncertainty. In being applicable over time, it is enduring (not time-bound) in support of ongoing development and adaptation in an ever-changing world.

The utilization-focused evaluation principle applies to any context in which an evaluation is being conducted. It applies across levels from local, to regional, to state, national, and international. It applies as an intervention, change initiative, policy, or program develops and on through its implementation. It provides guidance for any number of intended uses and applies to different purposes for evaluation (accountability, program improvement, strategy analysis, overall summative judgments of merit and worth, monitoring, or knowledge generation).

E Evaluable

A high-quality principle must be evaluable. This means it is possible to document and judge whether it is actually being followed, and document and judge what results from following the principle. In essence, it is possible to determine if following the principle takes you where you want to go.

The utilization-focused evaluation principle can be evaluated by following up with intended users to find out if the evaluation was used in intended ways and to get their feedback on the extent to which their involvement affected how they used the evaluation. There is a substantial literature reporting on evaluation of the utilization-focused evaluation principle (Patton, 2008, 2012a).

Exhibit 6.1 summarizes the GUIDE framework.

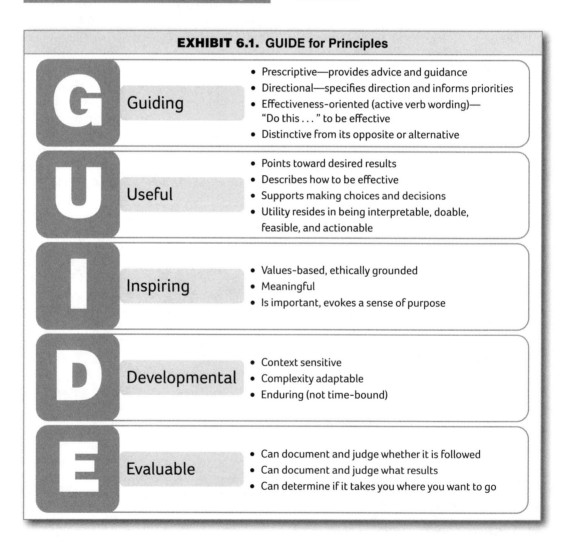

EXHIBIT 6.1. GUIDE for Principles

G — Guiding
- Prescriptive—provides advice and guidance
- Directional—specifies direction and informs priorities
- Effectiveness-oriented (active verb wording)— "Do this . . . " to be effective
- Distinctive from its opposite or alternative

U — Useful
- Points toward desired results
- Describes how to be effective
- Supports making choices and decisions
- Utility resides in being interpretable, doable, feasible, and actionable

I — Inspiring
- Values-based, ethically grounded
- Meaningful
- Is important, evokes a sense of purpose

D — Developmental
- Context sensitive
- Complexity adaptable
- Enduring (not time-bound)

E — Evaluable
- Can document and judge whether it is followed
- Can document and judge what results
- Can determine if it takes you where you want to go

SMART Goals Compared to GUIDE Principles

Because SMART goals and objectives are so extensively advocated, it is instructive to compare them with GUIDE principles. Exhibits 6.2 and 6.3 make this comparison. Exhibit 6.2 presents SMART goals for the worldwide campaign to eradicate polio. Exhibit 6.3 provides GUIDE effectiveness principles for the same campaign. Whereas SMART goals are specific and precise, GUIDE principles provide general guidance. Whereas SMART goals mandate quantitative indicators and statistical measures, GUIDE principles can be evaluated with multiple methods, both quantitative and qualitative. For example, adherence to the utilization-focused evaluation principle that advises focusing on intended use by intended users could be evaluated by intended users' ratings of the utility of findings as well as case studies of how findings were used. Whereas SMART goals are calculated and articulated to state outcomes that are achievable, GUIDE principles aim to be inspiring by making explicit and articulating values that guide both how something is

---

EXHIBIT 6.2. Example of a SMART Goals Framework
Polio Eradication

SMART goal criteria	SMART goal examples
Specific—precise outcome	Eradicate polio worldwide.
Measurable—quantitative, statistical precision	By 2017, no children will be paralyzed by the wild poliovirus. The World Health Organization (WHO) reports at least 3 years of zero confirmed cases due to indigenous circulation of wild poliovirus anyplace in the world.
Achievable—a logic model or theory of change can be created to show how the goal will be achieved	**The four key strategies for eradicating poliomyelitis are:** 1. Routine immunization of infants with oral polio vaccine (OPV) in the first year of life 2. Supplementary immunization activities, national immunization days, and subnational immunization days (NIDs and SNIDs), during which all children under 5 years of age are vaccinated, regardless of whether they have been vaccinated before 3. Mop-up campaigns to ensure that every child is vaccinated and to break the final chains of transmission 4. Effective disease surveillance for acute flaccid paralysis (AFP) to find and investigate every newly paralyzed child and determine if poliomyelitis is the cause of the paralysis (*www.unicef.org/newsline/poliopkabout-printer.htm*)
Relevant/realistic—achievement of results can reasonably be expected with the inputs and activities specified in the logic model	Detailed WHO plan supported with WHO and philanthropic funding (e.g., The Bill and Melinda Gates Foundation, Rotary International, the US Centers for Disease Control and Prevention [CDC], and the United Nations Children's Fund [UNICEF]).
Time-bound/timely—target date for when outcome will be achieved	No new cases of polio by the end of 2017 onward. (*http://apps.who.int/gb/ebwha/pdf_files/WHA69/A69_25-en.pdf*)

EXHIBIT 6.3. Example of a GUIDE Framework Application
Polio Eradication Principles

GUIDE principles criteria	GUIDE principles example
Guiding—provides direction and informs priority setting	Take a holistic approach to the polio eradication campaign. (Educate, support appropriate policy changes, and build health system capacity.)
Useful—informs decision making; is interpretable, feasible, and actionable	Conduct the campaign so that communities value what has been provided in the immunization initiative and the lessons of effective immunization are captured and adapted for other health and development initiatives.
Inspiring—values are explicit, motivational, and meaningful for ongoing, long-term engagement	Ensure the quality of the immunization campaign. Quality is as important as quantity (number vaccinated) for long-term effectiveness; therefore, emphasize the quality of interactions with children and families in the eradication campaign to deepen their understanding and cooperation.
Developmental—context and complexity sensitive; enduring, not time-bound	Adapt the campaign to local contexts by being aware of and sensitive to religious, cultural, economic, political, and social issues that can affect cooperation in the eradication campaign.
Evaluable—uses mixed methods, understanding that both qualitative and quantitative data will require interpretation and judgment	Focus on the countries where paralytic poliomyelitis due to wild poliovirus type 1 is endemic (e.g., Afghanistan and Pakistan); evaluate to determine that the vaccinations are voluntary (not imposed) and that the campaign is holistic.

done and what the desired result is. Principles are not achievable in the sense that the task is completed and the outcome accomplished; rather principles guide ongoing engagement across many discrete projects and multiple change initiatives. Whereas SMART goals are written to express the outcomes of a specific project or program, GUIDE principles emphasize broader values-based, ethically grounded utility. Being useful incorporates and subsumes being relevant, because following principles must be meaningful. However, SMART goals focus only on outcomes and not on the process for attaining outcomes; in contrast, as just noted but worth reiterating, GUIDE principles apply to both process and outcomes, to both what is to be achieved and how it is to be achieved.

Finally, whereas SMART goals are time-bound, GUIDE principles provide enduring and ongoing guidance. This is the difference between the project mind-set of SMART goals and the more general strategic thinking and action mind-set of GUIDE principles. Exhibits 6.2 and 6.3 summarize and illustrate these distinctions using the example of polio eradication globally.

Principles and Goals

This chapter has contrasted principles with goals, more specifically GUIDE principles with SMART goals. The two sets of criteria are not directly comparable; "specific" is not contrary to "guiding"; "measurable" is not in conflict with "evaluable"; "achievable" may be an element of "inspiring";

"relevant" and "useful" can be mutually re-inforcing; and "time-bound" versus "devel-opmental" is a matter of appropriate time perspective, and each has value. Thus, prin-ciples and goals can, and typically do, coex-ist. Principles provide general guidance for how to understand and take action in the world. Goals frame the intended outcomes of specific actions (projects, programs, and policies) within some limited time frame. *Principles and goals can be complementary, but the extent to which they are aligned and mu-tually reinforcing is an evaluation question.* Thus, both principles and goals can and should be evaluated, and the alignments (or conflicts) between them may be part of the effectiveness evaluation inquiry. That said, the key point in this chapter is that principles and goals constitute different evaluands, and the ways in which they are evaluated will be different. Given their na-ture as clear, specific, measurable, relevant, achievable, and time-bound, SMART goals are evaluated by whether or not targeted indicators are met. In contrast, evaluating principles requires examining both pro-cesses and results and may rely more heavi-ly on qualitative data (interviews, fieldwork, observations, and documents). Evaluating principles as if they are goals or projects is inappropriate and distorting. The chapters that follow go into detail about how to de-velop and evaluate principles, and I return to how principles and goals go together by examining specific examples from real programs and change initiatives. Part III of this book provides concrete examples of principles-driven interventions and the cor-responding principles-based evaluations. With those examples to draw from, I re-turn to the GUIDE criteria for principles-focused evaluation.

Beyond Evaluation as a Measure of Goal Attainment

One final comment about goals versus principles. Evaluation is still often defined as measuring goal attainment, which is a quite narrow perspective both methodolog-ically and conceptually. Because principles explicitly incorporate and express values, and evaluating principles involves attention to both processes of following principles and the outcomes that result from doing so, principles-focused evaluation is more comprehensive than mere goal attainment evaluation. Pioneering evaluator and phi-losopher of science Michael Scriven has emphasized eloquently the limitations and distortions of equating and defining evalu-ation only or primarily as an assessment of goal attainment. He attacks the American Psychological Association (APA) *Dictionary of Statistics and Research Methods* (2014) for incorrectly defining summative evaluation as "an attempt to assess the overall effec-tiveness of a program in meeting its objec-tives and goals after it is in operation":

> [That] definition . . . means the Nazi prison camps would score very well (at least for sev-eral years), or that stoning a woman to death for infidelity is good work (when locally sanctioned), or that the U.S. Food and Drug Administration is wasting our time and tax money in checking drug side-effects when they are not included in a drug designer's goals. The basic idea that evaluation is de-termining the degree of goal achievement persists partly, one suspects, because of one of its flaws—it avoids the necessity for evaluat-ing the goals and their supporting values, a process that was of course a capital offense in positivist philosophy of science. . . . But it also omits the rest of what evaluation does that cannot be omitted without disaster, for ex-ample, finding side effects and side impacts, doing cost analysis and risk analysis, identifi-cation of and comparison with alternatives, and evaluating the intervention's process—including the ethics of its procedures, its self-description, and its self-assessment. (Scriven, 2016, p. 28)

Measuring goal attainment helps deter-mine if a program is doing things right (effectively), but principles also invite us to ask whether the program is doing the right things. The values on which principles are based, and the inspiration provided by articulating and acting on those values, invite questioning assumptions and engaging in double-loop learning.

> For example, single-loop learning might help a practitioner improve a particular way of working with a particular client; double-loop learning would require a rethinking of whether this way was appropriate, or even whether the entire concept of service was appropriate. Sometimes this is described as "doing things right" as compared to "doing the right thing." . . .
>
> Much evaluation focuses on single-loop learning—that is, identifying errors and correcting them, but staying largely within the existing framework of worldviews, stated goals, and intended processes. While this can be useful, it can also be important to engage in double-loop learning that questions the assumptions about how the program works, how the environment works, and how the organization works. Not just "Did the program meet the stated goals?" but also "Do the goals of the project really suit the needs of the target group?" (Rogers & Williams, 2006, p. 78)

Double-loop learning requires skilled facilitation, as does questioning assumptions (Patton, 2017a). Evaluation involves assessing the merit, worth, and significance of whatever is the focus of evaluation, be it goals or principles. The point of this chapter has been that evaluating principles involves quite different criteria from evaluating goals. Evaluating principles, we shall see, is as much an ethical enterprise as a methodological one. Exhibit 6.4 summarizes the GUIDE framework for effectiveness principles and adds a rubric for assessing each criterion.

The remaining chapters in Part II explore in greater depth the implications of the GUIDE criteria. See the preceding overview of Part II for an outline of the GUIDE-based chapters that follow. Examples of principles-driven change initiatives and programs in Part III illuminate the GUIDE criteria in practice.

Practice Exercise

At the end of Chapter 1, I invited you to identify a principle that informs and guides your choices. Any kind of choice. Any principle. I suggested that you write it down and date it. Put it someplace where you could find it and use it in a later practice exercise. This is that time. That principle was your baseline, your starting point, *your first principle*. How does it stack up against the GUIDE criteria in this chapter? Based on what you've read so far, revise your principle, or if you find it doesn't need revision, reflect on how you can evaluate your adherence to it.

EXHIBIT 6.4. GUIDE Framework and Rubric for Effectiveness Principles		
GUIDE	**Each criterion defined**	**Sample quality assessment rubric**
G = **Guiding**	A principle is prescriptive. It provides advice and guidance on what to do, how to think, what to value, and how to act to be effective. It offers direction. The wording is imperative: *Do this . . . to be effective.* The guidance is sufficiently distinct that it can be distinguished from contrary or alternative guidance.	*Rating of guidance provided by a particular principle:* • Excellent • Good • Fair • Poor • Worthless
U = **Useful**	A high-quality principle is useful in making choices and decisions. Its utility resides in being actionable, interpretable, feasible, and pointing the way toward desired results for any relevant situation.	*Rating of utility of a particular principle:* • Very useful • Fairly useful • Somewhat useful • Slightly useful • Useless
I = **Inspirational**	Principles are values based, incorporating and expressing ethical premises, which is what makes them meaningful. They articulate what matters, both in how to proceed and the desired result. That should be inspirational.	*Inspiration rating:* • Very inspiring • Fairly inspiring • Somewhat inspiring • Slightly inspiring • Uninspiring
D = **Developmental**	The developmental nature of a high-quality principle refers to its adaptability and applicability to diverse contexts and over time. A principle is thus both context sensitive and adaptable to real-world dynamics, providing a way to navigate the turbulence of complexity and uncertainty. In being applicable over time, it is enduring (not time-bound), in support of ongoing development and adaptation in an ever-changing world.	*Rating for developmental potential:* • Highly adaptable and applicable to diverse contexts and complex situations • Fairly adaptable and applicable to diverse contexts and complex situations • Somewhat adaptable and applicable to diverse contexts and complex situations • Slightly adaptable and applicable to diverse contexts and complex situations • Not adaptable and applicable to diverse contexts and complex situations
E = **Evaluable**	A high-quality principle must be evaluable. This means it is possible to document and judge whether it is actually being followed, and document and judge what results from following the principle. In essence, it is possible to determine if following the principle takes you where you want to go.	*Evaluability assessment:* • Highly evaluable • Fairly evaluable • Somewhat evaluable • Slightly evaluable • Can't be evaluated

A principle is prescriptive. It provides advice and guidance on what to do, how to think, what to value, and how to act to be effective. It offers direction. The wording is imperative: *Do this.* The guidance is sufficiently distinct that it can be distinguished from contrary or alternative guidance.

"Somehow, some way, we have to guide these people back to reality!"

Source: The Cartoon Bank; © Condé Nast.

Chapters 7–11 elucidate the ways in which principles provide GUIDANCE.		
GUIDE framework for effectiveness principles	Chapter 6	GUIDE for Effectiveness Principles: The Characteristics of High-Quality Effectiveness Principles
G = GUIDING	Chapter 7	Guidance for Developing and Distinguishing Principles: Principles versus Rules, and the Alternative Principles Test
	Chapter 8	Referring to Something as a Principle Doesn't Make It One: Further Guidance on Distinguishing Effectiveness Principles
	Chapter 9	Still More Guidance on Developing and Distinguishing Principles: Principles Derived from and Contrasted with Assumptions, Truths, and Lessons
	Chapter 10	Conceptual Triangulation: Evaluating the Similarities of Parallel Principles
	Chapter 11	Holistic, Sequential, and Pole Star Approaches to Principles

CHAPTER 7

Guidance for Developing and Distinguishing Principles
Principles versus Rules, and the Alternative Principles Test

The function of reason is to distinguish things which in reality are united and to unite together, after a fashion, things that are distinct by comparing one with another.

—THOMAS AQUINAS, Italian philosopher and theologian

Quick Review

Chapter 1 distinguished three kinds of principles: natural principles, moral principles, and effectiveness principles. This book focuses on evaluating principles for effectiveness. Chapter 2 described the niche of principles used to help social innovators and change makers navigate change in complex dynamic situations. Chapter 3 provided examples of principles-driven programs and initiatives. Chapter 4 made the case that evaluating principles is new territory for evaluation, which has been and still is dominated by project and program evaluation. Principles as the evaluand, the thing evaluated, is different from projects and models as the unit of analysis for evaluation. Chapter 5 discussed the relationships between utilization-focused evaluation, developmental evaluation, and principles-focused evaluation. Chapter 6 provided

the GUIDE framework for generating and evaluating principles.

This chapter begins a sequence of five chapters that elucidate and illustrate how principles provide guidance: the *G* in the GUIDE framework. This series of chapters goes much deeper into the process of distinguishing and locating the niche and nature of principles-focused evaluation by providing advice on developing and distinguishing effectiveness principles. Remember the admonition: *No principles, no principles-focused evaluation.* As explained in the opening of Chapter 6, the role of principles-focused evaluators often includes evaluability assessment for principles-based programs: Do the principles meet the GUIDE criteria? To help support development of principles ready for adherence and evaluation, I'll begin by distinguishing principles from rules and recipes and discuss the evaluation implications of this distinction. That will lead to *the rules test for high-quality principles.* Then I'll show how identifying an opposite or alternative principle can help clarify an effectiveness principle, which will lead in a straightforward manner to *the alternative principles test for high-quality principles.*

Principles versus Rules and Recipes

Rules are not necessarily sacred, principles are.
—FRANKLIN D. ROOSEVELT, U.S. President

Rules prescribe precisely: You must do this specifically and precisely. Principles provide guidance: Do this in such a way that your actions fit the situation. Principles, unlike rules, must be interpreted and adapted to context. "Stop at a stop sign or red light" is a rule. "Proceed with caution along a winding mountainous road" is a principle, and though providing guidance, it must be interpreted and adapted based on driver experience and skill, knowledge of the road, and conditions at the time (weather, time of day or night, other vehicles, pedestrians, or obstacles on the road). What factors to take into account, and how to do so, is also a matter for evaluative inquiry and judgment. Thus, guiding principles provide direction but must be interpreted and adapted to context and situation, like the following advice on how to be a good student: *Make your studies your priority.* What that means in practice will depend on what you're studying and what else is going on in your life. The alternative principle is: *Have fun, hang out, hook up, and study just enough to get your degree.* Different principles. Different guidance. Pick your poison. Exhibit 7.1 shows the rules for a girls' residence at the Minnesota State Public School for Dependent and Neglected Children (an orphanage) in the 1940s. Those are rules! Exhibit 7.2 compares rules with principles.

A recipe, like a rule, tells you exactly what to do: *Add one-quarter teaspoon of salt.* A cooking principle, in contrast, provides guidance: *Season to taste.* A time management "best practice" prescribes setting aside the last hour of the workday to respond to non-urgent e-mails. The principled approach guides you to *distinguish urgent from nonurgent e-mails* and manage e-mail time accordingly. Best-selling management books like *In Search of Excellence* (Peters & Waterman, 1982), *Good to Great* (Collins, 2001), *The Seven Habits of Highly Effective People* (Covey, 2004), and Peter Drucker's many works offer effective principles, not rules.

Principles should to be succinct, pointed, and specific enough to provide direction but open enough to be adapted to context. Principles are grounded in values about what matters, must be interpreted and applied contextually and situationally, require judgment in application, and can be evaluated for both process (was the principle followed?) and results (did the desired outcome get accomplished?).

The cooking principle *season to taste* meets these criteria. The principle doesn't tell you what seasonings to consider, or even what a seasoning is. It doesn't tell you how to taste, exercise taste, judge taste, or who is doing the tasting. Novices learning to cook may be better off initially following the recipe that says add a quarter teaspoon of salt, then experiencing how that tastes as they develop the confidence to season to taste. Acting on a principle requires enough knowledge and experience to be able to interpret and apply that principle at a particular time in a specific context. Some knowledge of cooking is necessary to season to taste. Exhibit 7.3 compares principles versus rules using the example of season to taste versus add a quarter-teaspoon of salt.

The Rules Test for Clarifying Principles

Distinguishing principles from rules provides a good way of testing to see if a principle has been stated as a principle and not

EXHIBIT 7.1. Rules for Girls at the Minnesota State Residence School

BEDTIME RULES FOR GIRLS' COTTAGE 4
1940s
As described by Vivian (Swan) Manthe

Morning Wake-Up Rules

- The girls that worked in the Main Kitchen had a 5:30 a.m. wake-up call - all others girls were up at 6:00 a.m.
- We IMMEDIATELY made our bed PERFECTLY (or re-made it until it was perfect).
- We then folded our blankets and returned them to the cupboard.
- We proceeded downstairs to the first floor to dress by our chair.
- Those awakened at 5:30 went to their jobs. The rest of us had to sit in our chair until it was time to go to breakfast in the Main Building.
- NO TALKING was allowed while waiting to go to breakfast.

Evening Bed Time Rules

First Floor:

- Our nightgown was kept in a cloth bag hung on the back of our chair.
- We all undressed by our chair in the Main Room (no privacy).

Second Floor:

- We got our blankets out of the cupboard.
- We were in bed - with lights out - at 7:30, 8:00, or 8:30 p.m. depending on our age. The only exception was Christmas Eve when everyone could stay up until 9:00 p.m.
- Absolutely NO TALKING was allowed after lights out.

Source: The Minnesota State Public School Orphanage Museum (*www.orphanagemuseum.com*).

lapsed into formulation as a rule. As noted, Exhibit 7.2 provides examples for distinguishing a principle from a rule. Exhibit 7.1 provides examples of rules. *Stating a rule version of a principle is a good test for determining that the principle is, indeed, a principle and not a rule.*

From Rule to Principle

When a rule proves too rigid, it may be revised to become a principle. An excellent example is the rule "No screens under 2." The American Academy of Pediatrics first issued this guideline in 1999, unambiguously directing parents and other caregivers to avoid letting young children watch television, computers, smartphones—indeed, any devices with screens. The new guideline, issued in October 2016, is a principle rather than a rule: *Interact with young children when watching screens.* The nature of the interaction will depend on the age of the child, who is with the child, and what's on the screen. For example, screen time is especially appropriate when a family member or friend is interacting from a distance. Thus, the revised guidance shifts the focus from the screen itself to how the screen is used. In so doing, a rule was transformed into a principle.

EXHIBIT 7.2. Rules versus Principles
Select Examples

Focus of guidance	Rule	Principle
Cooking recipe	Add ¼ teaspoon of salt.	Season to taste.
Time management	Set aside the last hour of the workday to respond to non-urgent e-mails.	Distinguish urgent from non-urgent e-mails and manage e-mail time accordingly.
Investing	For individual small investors, own only three diversified mutual funds and no more than 10 individual stocks, which is all a small investor needs and can manage.	For individual small investors, own as few or as many mutual funds and stocks as you can understand, regularly monitor, and reasonably manage.
Staff meetings	Start each week with a staff meeting of no more than 1 hour.	Hold staff meetings at regular intervals and as needed based on the nature of the staff and the purpose of the meetings.
Education	Every primary-school-age child should read at least 15 minutes a day.	Children should read regularly and consistently based on their interest and ability.
Children watching television	Limit TV to 1 hour daily.	Monitor and set limits on TV watching so that children are involved in a range of development activities.
Exercise	Engage in 30 minutes of aerobic exercise every day.	Create a regular exercise regimen that is sustainable to meet your fitness and health goals given your age and lifestyle.
Evaluation	Deliver the final report by the date specified in the contract or terms of reference.	Target delivery of the findings to be useful for informing important decisions and actions. Monitor emergent issues that may influence and change the time when findings will be most useful to primary intended users.

Source: From Patton (2011, p. 168). Copyright 2011 by The Guilford Press. Reprinted by permission.

	EXHIBIT 7.3. Principles versus Rules			
	Guiding principles	**Example, illustration**	**Rules (recipes, best practices)**	**Example, illustration**
Nature of knowledge	Principles provide guidance, not detailed prescription.	Season to taste.	Rules tell you exactly what to do.	Add ¼ teaspoon salt.
Approach to context	Principles must be interpreted and applied contextually and situationally.	Determine whose tastes to satisfy and the context within which taste preferences will be expressed (e.g., holiday occasion, celebration, normal meal).	Rules are meant to transcend context, to provide the same result regardless of context.	Always add ¼ teaspoon of salt.
Judgment	Principles require judgment in application.	What seasoning options should be offered?	Rules remove the need for judgment; just follow the rule.	Always add salt. Always add ¼ teaspoon.
Approach to choice	Principles inform choices at forks in the road.	When circumstances and people change, seasoning can change.	Rules remove the need to choose.	Always follow the rule.
Approach to complexity	Principles are a rudder for navigating complex dynamic systems to support adaptation.	As more factors come into play, more situation analysis, interpretation, and judgment are needed.	Rules simplify.	Maintain fidelity to the rule to achieve consistency and stability.
Evaluation emphasis	How has the principle been implemented, with what variations, and with what range of outcomes?	What variety of seasonings were used? How do taste preferences vary? Have different taste preferences been satisfied?	Has the rule been followed precisely, with high fidelity, to achieve the desired standard result?	The recipe always has the same salty taste, a high-fidelity, highly predictable outcome each time.

Making It a Principle to Follow a Rule

Principles and rules sometimes intersect in bizarre ways. It can be a principle to follow a rule. Here's the story that followed the headline "New CEO Stands on Principle in Midst of Mental Health System in Chaos." Rules govern how mental health patients on a waiting list for residential care are admitted. A county judge ordered a mental health facility to admit a patient with dementia. The director of the mental health facility responded that she was following rules for admission from the waiting list, and she refused to let the dementia patient "jump the line" and enter ahead of those assessed with greater needs. She insisted that it was a matter of principle to follow the waiting list rule, and despite a threat of contempt of court and possible jail time, she stood on the principle that she would adhere to the rule (McCambridge, 2016).

In the real world the distinction between principles and rules can become muddled, complex, dynamic, and interconnected. This is especially the case in complex systems theory where the term *simple rules* is used to describe observed and emergent patterns of behavior. Chapter 20 discusses this complexity notion of *simple rules* in relation to principles.

The Alternative Principles Test to Enhance Clarity

One cannot say of something that it is and that it is not in the same respect and at the same time. . . . It is impossible, then, that "being a man" should mean precisely not being a man. . . . And it will not be possible to be and not to be the same thing.
—ARISTOTLE, *Metaphysics*, Book IV, Part 4

Nothing can both be and not be. Two or more contradictory statements cannot both be true in the same sense at the same time.
—The logical principle of noncontradiction

Another test of whether a principle provides distinct and meaningful guidance is that you can conceptualize its opposite or a specific alternative. In 2002, representatives from 15 Canadian communities and their national sponsors met in Guelph, Ontario, to create an anti-poverty initiative called Vibrant Communities. Each community was represented by someone from the private, public, and nonprofit sectors, as well as someone with experience living in poverty. Over the course of 3 days of deliberations they committed to tackle poverty based on five core principles that local communities would follow to mount their own unique campaigns. The format of the principles statement articulated both what they would do and, contrariwise, what they would not do.

1. *Poverty reduction*—a focus on reducing poverty as opposed to alleviating the hardships of living in poverty.

2. *Comprehensive thinking and action*—addressing the interrelated causes of poverty rather than its individual symptoms.

3. *Multisectoral collaboration*—engaging individuals and organizations from at least four key sectors—business, government, nonprofits, and persons who've experienced poverty—rather than just one sector in a joint effort.

4. *Community asset building*—building on the community's strengths rather than focusing on its deficits.

5. *Learning and change*—embracing a long-term process of learning and change rather than simply undertaking a series of specific interventions.

The Clarity of Opposites

The developmental evaluation collaborative that developed and evaluated effective principles to help youth overcome homelessness (see Chapter 26) explicitly drew contrasts between their approach and programs based on contrary principles. That exercise accentuated the distinct nature of their principles. For the sake of brevity and focus, they did not include the opposites in their statement of each principle as Vibrant Communities did, but they drew the contrasts in supporting discussions. Exhibit 7.4 presents these alternatives.

Principles as Thesis and Antithesis

To expand on the point of this chapter about the value of conceptualizing opposites and alternatives so as to increase the meaningfulness and distinctiveness of any given principle, Exhibit 7.5 suggests alternatives for the 14 classic principles presented in Chapter 1. These are presented in dialectical terms as thesis and antithesis: an original principled premise (thesis) and its opposite proposition (antithesis).

Evaluating Opposites in Principles-Focused Evaluation

Hegelian dialectics provide a powerful conceptual framework for clarifying alternatives. This is the analytical logic of contrasting the thesis with the antithesis, an original premise with its counterfactual, and a principle with its opposite or alternative. Principles-focused evaluation can include contrasting, comparing, and gathering evidence about the relative effectiveness of alternative principles. Instead of counterfactuals, we examine *counterprinciples*.

Chapter Summary

This chapter has offered two ways to develop and distinguish effectiveness principles: (1) distinguishing them from one or more corresponding rules and (2) identifying an opposite or alternative principle.

▶ *The rules test:* State a rule that pertains to but contrasts with your principle (see Exhibits 7.2 and 7.3 for examples).

▶ *The alternative principles test:* Conceptualize an opposite, contrary, or alternative principle (see Exhibits 7.4 and 7.5 for examples).

By way of illustration, Exhibit 7.6 applies the *rules test* and the *alternative principles test* to the utilization-focused evaluation principle used in Chapter 6 to illustrate the five GUIDE criteria.

Practice Exercise

At the end of Chapter 1, I invited you to identify a principle that informs and guides your choices in life. Then, at the end of Chapter 6, I asked you to assess how well your principle meets the GUIDE criteria and to revise your principle accordingly, if needed. Now, to further conceptualize your principle, do two things: (1) state a rule that pertains to but contrasts with your principle, and (2) conceptualize an opposite, contrary, or alternative principle. Basically, subject your principle to both the *rules test* and the *alternative principles test*.

EXHIBIT 7.4. Opposing Principles for Serving Homeless Youth

Effective principles to help youth overcome homelessness*	Alternative and opposite principles for serving homeless youth
1. *Be journey oriented:* Interact with youth to help them understand the interconnectedness of past, present, and future as they decide where they want to go and how to get there.	1. *Solve the immediate problem:* Get kids off the streets.
2. *Trauma-informed care:* Recognize that all homeless youth have experienced trauma; build relationships, responses, and services on that knowledge.	2. *No excuses:* Follow the rules, behave appropriately, or no shelter and no services.
3. *Be nonjudgmental:* Interact with youth without labeling or judging them on the basis of background, experiences, choices, or behaviors.	3. *Tell it like it is:* "You're screwing up your life."
4. *Harm reduction:* Contain the effects of risky behavior in the short term and seek to reduce its effects in the long term.	4. *Zero tolerance:* No risky behavior allowed, ever. Drunk, high on drugs, disorderly, disrespectful behavior—no bed, no meals, no services.
5. *Build trusting youth–adult relationships:* Build relationships by interacting with youth in an honest, dependable, authentic, caring, and supportive way.	5. *Maintain boundaries:* The program is about getting kids into housing, not building relationships. There's no time or money for relationships. Stay focused on the housing outcome.
6. *Strengths-based:* Start with and build upon the skills, strengths, and positive characteristics of each youth.	6. *Deficits-based:* Focus on meeting needs, filling gaps, supplying what is missing.
7. *Positive youth development:* Provide opportunities for youth to build a sense of competency, usefulness, belonging, and power.	7. *Narrowly outcomes focused:* Get youth in housing for 6 months, the indicator of success.
8. *Holistic:* Engage youth in a manner that recognizes that mental, physical, spiritual, and social health are interconnected and interrelated.	8. *Focused:* It's about housing, housing, housing.
9. *Collaborative:* Establish a principles-based, youth-focused system of support that integrates practices, procedures, and services within and across agencies, systems, and policies.	9. *Competitive:* Resources are limited; every program is competing for a small pot; shine your own light bright.

*See Chapter 26 for the background on these principles.

EXHIBIT 7.5. Twelve Classic Principles
Thesis and Antithesis

Original principle (thesis)	Opposite or alternative principle (antithesis)
A. Universal moral principles: Do what is right.	**Relativism:** What is right depends.
1. *Golden Rule relationship principle:* Do unto others as you would have them do unto you.	1. *Platinum Rule:* Treat others the way they want to be treated (which may not be how you'd like to be treated).
2. *Unconditional love principle:* Love the sinner, hate the sin.	2. *Conditional love principle:* Love engenders and nurtures love, but love must be earned and deserved.
B. Universal natural principles: How the world works can be known.	**Popper's impossibility of proof principle:** Things can be disproved but never definitively proved; we never know for sure, for there are always other possibilities.
3. *Darwin's principle of natural selection:* Within any given environment, those most advantaged will survive (survival of the fittest).	3. *Intelligent design:* God created diverse environments and corresponding species.
4. *Newton's principle of motion:* For every action, there is an equal and opposite reaction.	4. *Nonlinearity* (complexity theory): Small actions can generate large reactions.
C. Effectiveness principles: Do what works to achieve desired results.	**Skepticism about effectiveness:** What works is a matter of chance and cannot be controlled or predicted.
5. *Occam's principle of parsimony:* That explanation requiring the fewest assumptions is most likely to be correct.	5. *Complicated world principle:* Things are always more complicated than we think; we deceive ourselves with simple explanations.
6. *Pareto's 80/20 distribution principle:* 80% of results are caused by 20% of the action or actors.	6. *50–50 distribution principle:* Results are a matter of chance, like a coin toss; causality cannot be apportioned.
7. *Thomas's social construction theorem:* What is perceived as real is real in its consequences.	7. *Positivist reality theorem:* Only what can be measured and verified with the senses is real; the world is what it is and perceptions cannot change reality.
8. *Parkinson's productivity principle:* Work expands to fill the time available for its completion.	8. *Shakespeare's productivity principle:* Toil and trouble, work is never done.

(continued)

Original principle (thesis)	Opposite or alternative principle (antithesis)
9. *Murphy's low-expectations principle of pessimism:* Whatever can go wrong will go wrong.	9. *Boy Scouts principle of planning ahead:* Be prepared. Preparation expects, foresees, and overcomes adversity.
10. *The Confucian principle of the mean:* Moderation in all things; never act in excess.	10. *The hippie principle of live for today:* Life is short, live to the maximum in the moment. Carpe diem.
11. *Principle of least effort:* Less is more; do only as much as necessary to achieve the desired result.	11. *Principle of maximum effort:* A job worth doing is worth doing well, so always give 110%.
12. *Grassroots engagement principle:* Think globally, act locally.	12. *Einstein's systems change principle:* Problems cannot be solved at the same level they were created. Think globally, act globally.

EXHIBIT 7.6. Contrasting a Principle with a Rule and an Alternative Principle		
Principle	Contrasting rule formulations	Opposite or alternative principle
Utilization-focused evaluation principle: Focus on intended use, by and with intended users, in every aspect of, and at every stage of, an evaluation.	**User evaluation rules:** 1. For formative evaluations, only involve program staff. 2. For summative evaluations, make funding decisions the priority.	**Evaluator independence principle** Authorize and empower an external evaluator to make all major decisions about an evaluation to ensure the evaluation's independence and credibility.

CHAPTER 8

Referring to Something as a Principle Doesn't Make It One

Further Guidance on Distinguishing Effectiveness Principles

> The authenticity principle is a marketing strategy that goes for truth in marketing. It's based on the idea that genuine messages are more effective because they ring true with customers. . . .
>
> Marketing messages that align with the realities of your business, brand, corporate culture and customer experience are more effective.
>
> —ANNA MAR (2013)

Street vendors offer Gucci luggage and Rolex watches at substantial discounts from retail store prices. But are they genuine or imitations? And do you know how to tell the difference?

Gertrude Stein famously postulated that "a rose is a rose is a rose." Are artificial roses still roses? Does the rose postulate apply to principles? A principle is a principle is a principle. This chapter asserts that referring to something as a principle doesn't make it one. Thus, principles-focused evaluation must begin by determining if a statement purported to be a principle actually constitutes one. This turns out to be a tricky business. Determining the authenticity of antiques—and principles—requires some careful examination and expertise.

There is no shortage of principles to assess. Lists of principles abound. Books promising illuminating principles proliferate. Many appear to follow the Hype Principle: *exaggeration sells.*

▶ *20 Principles of Success Not Taught in School* (Groover, 2012)

▶ *The Success Principles: How to Get from Where You Are to Where You Want to Be* and, from the book's website, Discover 67 of the World's Most POWERFUL Principles Guaranteed to Give You Everything You Want out of Life! (Canfield, 2015)

▶ *8 Key Principles to Succeed: Dominate Your Life* (Farber, 2013)

▶ *21 Success Principles: 21 Powerful Ways to Help You Immediately Become More Productive, Happy and Successful, for Life!* (Ledger, 2014)

Some principles are originals. Some are knockoffs. Some are not principles at all. Indeed, to enter into the territory of principles is to enter into a landscape riddled with hype, quick fixes, silver bullets, mirages, quicksand, swamps, dead ends, morasses, tempests, and even toxins.

Well-articulated, clear, meaningful, inspirational, and evaluable principles are powerful, beautiful, and rare. More common, I'm afraid, are muddled ruminations, biases and personal preferences posing as universal wisdom, and self-congratulatory exhortations about being principled, following principles, leading the principled life, and being a principled organization, much of it drivel. To become a principles-focused evaluator is to take on the challenge of separating the classical wheat from the chaff, to tell the fakes from the real things, and to distinguish the well-intentioned but mistaken and untestable from the well formulated and evaluable—and worthy of being evaluated. This chapter provides further elucidation of the *G* in the GUIDE framework by looking at and distinguishing examples that meet the GUIDE criteria for effectiveness from statements that purport to be principles but don't meet the criteria offered here. In so doing, this chapter aims to provide support and direction for developing meaningful and evaluable principles.

Good Examples of Bad Examples

Consider as a precursor to the challenge of identifying meaningful and evaluable principles these four relatively commonplace examples to be found in the principles terrain.

▶ *Fortune* business magazine featured "6 Principles That Made Nelson Mandela a Renowned Leader": He anticipated. He challenged. He interpreted. He decided. He aligned. He learned (Schoemaker & Krupp, 2014). These are behaviors, not principles. They describe his exemplary character and leadership traits, which are important and inspirational. But the point here is that to undertake principles-focused evaluation for principles-driven people and initiatives, we need to distinguish principles from other ways of engaging in change. Caleb Storkey (2014) has written a book presenting

and discussing Mandela's principles. They include "Lead with conviction," "Forgive those who oppress you," "Be authentic," and "Know when to step down." But note: Not all of what Storkey calls Mandela's principles meet the GUIDE criteria either, for example, "Make the Impossible Possible." Knowing the difference is one of the requisite skills for facilitating principles-focused evaluation.

▶ *Time* magazine political columnist Joe Klein wrote about the 2016 presidential election in the United States and opined: "America was founded on the principle that the things we have in common are more important than the things that divide us. The fundamental principle of marketing is the opposite: you sell to the things that make us different" (Klein, 2016, p. 29). These are his political opinions wrapped in a gilded allusion to principles. People routinely gold-plate as principles their beliefs, speculations, feelings, notions, impressions, judgments, and opinions. Politicians debate whether American foreign policy is based on advancing "universal principles" rather than "national interests" without saying what those supposedly universal principles actually are (Roth, 2016, p. 4).

▶ *Principles and Practice of Structural Equation Modeling* (Kline, 2016) is in its fourth edition, the leading textbook in the field. It is rich with axioms, concepts, definitions, postulates, fundamental assumptions, premises, operating prescriptions, models, statistical rules, equations, common errors to be avoided, advice, exemplars, guidelines, standards, and tools—and *devoid of principles*. There is a section on "principles over computer tools" that promises principles but never states any (p. 3). The summary of Chapter 1 promises that "fundamental principles" will be featured in Chapter 2, but none are presented. There is the blunt admonition: "Death to stepwise regression, think for yourself" (p. 38), which constitutes a strong recommendation and clear advice but isn't a principle, in my judgment. The book's index has no entry for principles. There is a concluding chapter on best practices, but these are quite different from principles (see Chapter 24 in this book for the distinction). I should add that this is but one example I've come across in many books, articles, reports, organizational statements, and blog posts that have "principles" in the title but no identifiable principles within. The widely used *Facilitator's Guide to Participatory Decision-Making* (Kaner, 2014) promises "design principles" for establishing agendas but offers six steps to be followed, not principles. An example from my own discipline of sociology: "Teaching Sociological Principles in an Evaluation Research Course" (Eckberg, 2015) implies, but never says explicitly, what those principles are.

▶ Under the pen name "Miss Manners," author Judith Martin has published bestselling guidebooks on excruciatingly correct behavior (2005), rearing perfect children (2002), a dignified wedding (2010), eating (1997), communication (1996), civility (1999), business manners (2013), the right things to say (1998), and domestic tranquility (1999). She equates manners with principles. I make a distinction between manners and etiquette—manners as the principles, which are eternal and universal, etiquette as the particular rules, which are arbitrary and different in different times, different situations, different cultures. Her expertise on manners may well be second to none. Her expertise on principles, dubious. Manners are socially constructed and approved ways of behaving. They prescribe outward bearing, correct behavior, and the appropriate stance to take toward others behaviorally. Principles state fundamental truths, actionable values, and/or philosophical premises that guide behavior, including manners. *Know and display appropriate manners for the situation* is a principle. What those manners are is a matter of context, culture, and circumstance. Whether displaying appropriate behaviors

is effective is an evaluation question. Miss Manners can assert that manners are principles, but that does not make them so.

Exemplary Principles

Lest my review of certain common shortcomings in identifying principles appear to be mere lulz (look it up, it's recent Internet slang that has become a useful term and can be found in the *Oxford English Dictionary*), or snarkiness, my experience is that we learn from both good examples and bad ones. Having offered some poor ones, let me offer some exemplars, and do so in the three categories of principles introduced in Chapter 1. These are all from Robert Heinlein (1973), science fiction author and astute observer of the human condition.

1. *Natural principle* (how the world works): "Everybody lies about sex."

2. *Moral principle* (how to live life): "Everything in excess! To enjoy the flavor of life take big bites. Moderation is for monks."

3. *Effectiveness principles* (what works):
   a. *Fair witness principle:* "Speak precisely." When asked the color of a building, answer, "It's white on this side."
   b. *Effective parenting principle:* "Do not handicap your children by making their lives easy."
   c. *Lifelong learning principle:* "Unlearn old falsehoods."

Semantic Principles

Words are loaded pistols.
　　　　　—JEAN-PAUL SARTRE, French philosopher

As the *Miss Manners* example portends, this chapter is partly about semantics. Some people detest semantic arguments. If you are among them, you may want to skip the rest of this chapter. What would you be skipping? Sorting out various meanings of what gets called a principle, especially the subcategory *effectiveness principles*. Why does this matter? Because to evaluate principles, one has to have a sense of what they are. And in many instances, as the case exemplars later in Part II demonstrate, principles-focused evaluators are called on to facilitate a group that is developing their principles. Just as evaluators have become involved in helping programs clarify their goals, develop program logic models, and generate theories of change, principles-focused evaluators help programs identify and articulate their principles clearly. It helps in such situations to know what needs to be developed: clear, specific, and measureable goals; a logical logic model; a testable theory of change; or effectiveness principles. This chapter, then, delves more deeply into the definitional and semantic question of what is, and is not, an effectiveness principle.

Semantics is the branch of linguistics and logic concerned with the meanings of a word, phrase, sentence, or text. "That's just a matter of semantics" can be a dismissive way of minimizing different interpretations of something said. Words matter. Definitions matter. Lives and fortunes hinge on definitions of what constitutes *abuse, torture, war, genocide, violence, wealth, justice, love,* and *being alive*. Principles-focused evaluation depends on what constitutes a principle. To further our inquiry in that regard, let's examine a few general principles of semantics outlined by Milton Dawes (2013), some of which, I shall argue, are not principles at all. But then, what are they if a semanticist, who specializes in the meaning of words, says a statement is a principle? First up, the *principle of non-allness*.

> We cannot imagine, think, say, understand, know all about anything or anyone—including ourselves. Where applicable, modifying our thinking with words including "some," "sometimes," "usually," "probably," and others, can help us avoid "allnessing." (Dawes, 2013, #2)

Researchers will recognize this statement as a caution against overgeneralizing. Evaluators will recognize this as a warning against making grandiose claims that can't be fully substantiated. More generally, this semantic statement is a version of admonitions to be modest and balanced in what we say. The label "non-allness" states what not to do rather than what to do and requires explanation rather than standing on its own as meaningful. The first sentence of the explanation states a premise or observation, namely, that we can't know everything about anything. That leads to a recommendation for language modifiers (e.g., *sometimes* rather than *always*). Turning the principle of non-allness, as stated and explained, into an effectiveness principle takes some work; that principle might read something like one of the options below.

▶ *"Speaking precisely" principle:* State precisely what you know and the degree of certainty with which you know it, not more and not less.

▶ *"Avoiding overgeneralizations" principle:* Carefully state both what and where your knowledge applies and where it doesn't or is uncertain.

▶ *"Known knowns" principle:* Distinguish known knowns from known unknowns, and be watchful for unknown unknowns.

Divergence, Then Convergence

In working with groups to articulate principles, I've found that we begin with several statements that contain elements of what the people involved want to commit to. The three optional principles just listed are an example of what might emerge from an initial discussion. We list the options and get reactions and eventually find common ground around shared meanings. As some options are discarded and others are subjected to revising toward consensus, I invite them to apply the GUIDE criteria:

1. Does the principle provide meaningful guidance for action? (Construct a scenario where guidance is needed and test the principle's value.)

2. Is it likely to be useful in decision making and priority setting?

3. Is it inspiring, that is, do people care about the principle?

4. Is it developmental, that is, relevant to various challenges and situations?

5. Is it evaluable? Can adherence to results be assessed? What would be accomplished by adhering to the principle?

Let's try another semantic principle: the *principle of non-identity* (the word is not the thing):

> A label, or name, is not the thing labeled and named. "Things" are not what we think, say, imagine, believe them to be. Words, things, situations, etc. do not in themselves have meanings: We give meanings. Many words can be thought of as names of "sets." Each one of us decides (mainly non-consciously) what belongs to our "set": What characteristics would you put in your set "friend"? (Dawes, 2013, #5)

This semantic principle brings to mind U.S. president Bill Clinton's answer when asked in sworn testimony whether his statement that he had not had sex with Monica Lewinsky was false. "It depends on what the meaning of the word *is* is," he famously replied. But I digress.

The *semantic principle of non-identity* begins, again, with a premise and an observation. It is not stated in the form of an effectiveness principle, so some conversion would be needed to make it one. The parallel research and evaluation principle alerts us to distinguish a measure from the thing measured. A reading score is not the same as reading.

Dawes (2013) offers 10 semantic principles, none of which are stated as effectiveness principles. They represent one approach to principles that I encounter quite often, which is to state a premise, express a belief, or make an observation, and call the statement a principle. Consider the semantic *etc. principle:*

> A way to *remind* ourselves that there is always *more* to what we think, believe, define, know, understand, imagine, see, hear, etc. When we ignore or forget the factor of "more," we set ourselves up for shocks, disappointments, distress—among other factors. (Dawes, 2013, #9)

I'd call this a musing or rumination rather than a principle.

The principle that's hopefully emerging for you in this chapter is a version of the "word is not the thing" semantic principle. Let's call it the *name delusion principle:* **Referring to something as a principle doesn't make it one.**

The final semantic principle is the scientific orientation principle, and it nicely illustrates the name delusion principle. See what sense you can make of this.

> The scientific approach can be thought of as "A heuristic cumulative enterprise evolving from wonder, curiosity, and imagination: Through careful observations, hypotheses, experiments, theories, predictions, and a time-binding self-correcting process of learning involving revisions, and refinements of theories, 'Scientists seek to create "maps" (theories, explanations, patterns of relationships, etc.) that most accurately represent territories mapped.'" In developing a scientific orientation, we can anticipate significant improvements in our ventures. We can be creative and artistic without becoming "artists." We do not have to become "scientists" to develop a scientific orientation. (Dawes, 2013, #10)

So let's cut to the chase on this one.
Scientific orientation principle: Think scientifically. You don't have to have an advanced degree in science to think like a scientist.

Clarifying Principles

The preceding examples of semantic principles illustrate the kind of muddle I find in a great many exhortations under the moniker *principles*. To evaluate principles, evaluators will often have to clarify the principles and help articulate them in a way that is clear and evaluable. The language used matters. Philosopher, social scientist, and novelist Aldous Huxley (1949, p. 3) spent a lot of time contemplating and writing about language. I conclude this section on semantic principles with his extended reflection on words and meanings:

> A great deal of attention has been paid . . . to the technical languages in which scientists do their specialized thinking. . . . But the colloquial usages of everyday speech, the literary and philosophical dialects in which people do their thinking about the problems of morals, politics, religion and psychology—these have been strangely neglected. We talk about "mere matters of words" in a tone which implies that we regard words as things beneath the notice of a serious-minded person.
>
> This is a most unfortunate attitude. For the fact is that words play an enormous part in our lives and are therefore deserving of the closest study. The old idea that words possess *magical* powers is false; but its falsity is the distortion of a very important truth. Words do have a magical effect—but not in the way that magicians supposed, and not on the objects they were trying to influence. Words are magical in the way they affect the minds of those who use them. "A mere matter of words," we say contemptuously, forgetting that words have power to mold people's thinking, to canalize their feeling, to direct their willing and acting. Conduct and character are largely determined by the nature of the words we currently use to discuss ourselves and the world around us.

Alleged Principles That on Closer Examination Aren't

The Pollyanna Principles by Hildy Gottlieb (2009) aim to "reinvent nonprofit organizations to create the future of our world." The six "principles" state beliefs about how the world works that Gottlieb calls "undeniable truths" (p. 39). In that regard, they aspire to be natural principles like Sir Isaac Newton's *Principia Mathematica* (see Chapter 1). But Newton's principles were empirically verified, validated, and generalizable. Beliefs about how the world works are just that: beliefs, neither truths nor principles. Consider Pollyanna Principle #1: "We accomplish what we hold ourselves accountable for" (p. 42). This is stated as a prediction and established truth of nature, but is basically a belief. No evidence in support of this proposition is offered, perhaps because it is "undeniable." But we evaluators know a bit about accountability (Bemelmans-Videc, Lonsdale, & Perrin, 2007). We promote accountability. We worry about accountability. We measure processes and outcomes for accountability. We also know that there is seldom a direct causal link between holding ourselves accountable and achieving results, in contrast to these assertions:

> It is hard to imagine how limitless our potential is simply as a result of what we choose to hold ourselves accountable for!
>
> If we hold ourselves accountable for fiscal prudence, we will be fiscally strong. . . . Imagine the potential, then, if we held ourselves accountable for making our communities healthy, vibrant, resilient, humane, places to live? If we accomplish what we hold ourselves accountable for, our potential is limited only by use! (Gottlieb, 2009, p. 42)

Keep in mind that these are called the Pollyanna Principles. To be Pollyannaish is to be excessively cheerful and optimistic. These principles fit the bill. "They are about inspiring and encouraging our human potential to achieve what we want" (p. 39). Now suppose, as a thought experiment, we were asked to convert the Pollyanna Principles into effectiveness principles that meet GUIDE criteria and design a principles-focused evaluation approach for each effectiveness principle. Exhibit 8.1 suggests what that might look like. I've taken the six Pollyanna Principles and revised them to make them effectiveness principles that manifest the GUIDE criteria. An evaluation framework and questions for each principle are then identified. Pay particular attention to the evaluation questions because they illustrate how principles-focused evaluation can support and enhance a principles-driven organization.

Referring to Something as a Principle Doesn't Make It One

From the beginning of this book I've been emphasizing two primary questions that are fundamental to principles-focused evaluation: To what extent are expressed principles actually being adhered to (the implementation question)? If adhered to, to what extent and in what ways is following the principles leading to desired results (the outcomes question)? But those two questions assume

EXHIBIT 8.1. Gottlieb's (2009) Six Pollyanna Principles Converted to Effectiveness Principles and Corresponding Evaluation Questions

Pollyanna Principles stated as "undeniable truths"	Conversion to effectiveness principles	Principles-focused evaluation questions and implications for the converted effectiveness principles
1. Holding ourselves accountable: We accomplish what we hold ourselves accountable for. (p. 42)	1. Be accountable.	What are the organization's messages, processes, procedures, incentives, and uses for accountability? a. Who is accountable to whom for what? b. What are criteria for meeting accountability expectations? c. Evaluate adherence to accountability framework including enabling factors, barriers, areas for improvement, and lessons.
2. Creating the future: Each and every one of us is creating the future every day, whether we do so consciously or not. (p. 54)	2. Be future oriented: Examine planned actions and activities through the lens of future likely consequences.	What are the organization's messages, processes, procedures, incentives, and interactions in considering the future? a. Who is involved in futuring scenarios and contemplations? b. What results from such sessions?
3. Interconnected and interdependent: Everyone and everything is interconnected and interdependent, whether we acknowledge that or not. (p. 69)	3. See the world through interconnections and interdependencies: Examine how planned actions and activities, and unplanned events and interactions, affect interconnections and interdependencies.	Map the organization's interconnections and interdependencies. How did these develop? What are the implications for effectiveness? What interconnections warrant further strengthening? Track interconnections and interdependencies over time; reflect on their implications for effectiveness.

(continued)

Pollyanna Principles stated as "undeniable truths"	Conversion to effectiveness principles	Principles-focused evaluation questions and implications for the converted effectiveness principles
4. Being the change we want to see: This means walking the talk of our values. (p. 78)	4. Live your organizational values in what you do.	What are the organization's priority values? How do people inside and outside the organization experience and perceive these values? How, to what extent, and in what ways are these manifest in actions, processes, interactions, interconnections, and future planning?
5. Strength builds upon strength, not our weaknesses. (p. 90)	5. Know, use, and build on strengths.	What are the organization's perceived strengths and weaknesses? How are these determined? How do people inside and outside the organization experience and perceive the organization's strengths and weaknesses? How, to what extent, and in what ways are strengths used and nurtured in actions, processes, interactions, interconnections, and future planning?
6. Systems: Individuals will go where systems lead them. (p. 99)	6. Engage in systems and systemic thinking. (This means, at a minimum, examining interrelationships, perspectives, and boundaries when analyzing something.)	What is the organization's capacity for systems thinking? What is evidence of systems and systemic thinking? How, to what extent, and in what ways does systems thinking inform the organization's work? How can systems thinking be deepened and enhanced?

principles expressed in a sufficiently clear and meaningful way that they can be evaluated. What this chapter has emphasized is that what is called a principle is often not, on closer examination, a principle, especially not an effectiveness principle. Thus, returning to first principles (Chapter 1), the first principles-focused evaluation questions to ask are: What are the principles to be evaluated? Do they constitute effectiveness principles? Are they stated in a way that can be evaluated for adherence and results? These are essential baseline, starting-point questions. The message of this chapter is that referring to something as a principle rhetorically doesn't make it one. That's the essence of what the *G* criterion in the GUIDE framework calls for:

A principle is prescriptive. It provides advice and guidance on what to do, how to think, what to value, and how to act to be effective. It offers direction. The wording is imperative: *Do this.* The guidance is sufficiently distinct that it can be distinguished from contrary or alternative guidance.

Practice Exercise:

Do an Internet search for principles on a topic of interest to you. Assess whether the alleged principles meet the *G* criterion in the GUIDE framework.

CHAPTER 9

Still More Guidance on Developing and Distinguishing Principles

Principles Derived from and Contrasted with Assumptions, Truths, and Lessons

> The ability to think critically about one's assumptions, beliefs, and actions is a survival necessity.
> —STEPHEN D. BROOKFIELD, *Teaching for Critical Thinking* (2011, p. 2)

Quick Review

Chapter 6 presented the GUIDE framework for effectiveness principles: A high-quality principle provides guidance (G), is useful (U), inspires (I), supports ongoing development and adaptation (D), and is evaluable (E). Chapter 7 provided guidance for developing and distinguishing effectiveness principles using the rules test (Can you distinguish each principle from a corresponding rule?) and the alternative principles test (Can you identify an opposite or alternative principle?). Chapter 8 made the case that referring to something as a principle doesn't make it one and provided more guidance on distinguishing effectiveness principles by offering examples of bad and good principles statements. This chapter offers still more advice on developing and distinguishing principles by discussing how principles are derived from assumptions, truths, and lessons. All of this has been aimed at identifying, generating, developing, and articulating high-quality principles that meet the

GUIDE criteria generally and, as a starting point, the *G* criterion specifically. In effect, evaluators have to assess the quality and meaningfulness of principles before evaluating adherence to them and the results of adherence.

Identifying, Generating, Developing, and Articulating Principles

Let me reiterate what should by now be obvious: *Principles-focused evaluation begins with principles.* No principles, no principles-focused evaluation. But principles don't just happen. They don't suddenly appear. They aren't always obvious. Indeed, they may be well disguised. Or there may be resistance to them or reasons for not calling principles by that name. Thus, the work of facilitating and undertaking principles-focused evaluations can include identifying, generating, developing, and articulating principles, or alternatives to principles. The result of developing a statement of principles may, or may not, resonate with and be useful to those whose presumed principles have been identified, generated, and articulated. But until they've been made explicit, their meaningfulness and utility, let alone their evaluability, cannot be judged. This chapter presents a case example of the challenge and possibilities of articulating principles courtesy of a longtime colleague whose whole career manifests a commitment to critical reflection. In that spirit, the light of principles-focused critical reflection is turned on his framework for nurturing skillful college teachers.

Stephen Brookfield is Distinguished University Professor and the John Ireland Endowed Chair at the University of Saint Thomas in Minneapolis–Saint Paul, Minnesota. Six times he has received the Cyril O. Houle Award for Literature in Adult Education. He has written, cowritten, or edited 18 books on adult learning, teaching, critical thinking, discussion methods, and critical theory. He has also received the Imogene Okes Award for Outstanding Research in Adult Education and the Philip E. Frandson Award for Literature in Continuing Higher Education (2013), awarded by the University Professional Continuing Education Association. His work has been translated into German, Korean, Finnish, Chinese, Japanese, Polish, Farsi, and Albanian. He is a distinguished scholar, brilliant thinker, and a superb writer, and reticent about calling his knowledge principles. Such has not always been the case, as we shall see. Because he is also a longtime colleague and friend, he was open to sharing his journey away from principles while indulging my insistence that, whether he acknowledges them as such, his cumulative work deserves to be formulated as effective principles and evaluated as such. He has kindly and thoughtfully reacted to my reformulations of his work at the end of this chapter. What follows provides an opportunity to compare and contrast truths, assumptions, and lessons with principles based on Stephen Brookfield's writings. Let's start with assumptions.

Assumptions about Skillful Teaching

In the third edition of his widely used book *The Skillful Teacher: On Techniques, Trust, and Responsiveness in the Classroom* (Brookfield, 2015), the second chapter is devoted to "the core assumptions of skillful teaching." The first edition of this book appeared 25 years earlier. Since that time these core assumptions have been extensively tested, studied, reviewed, examined, debated, affirmed, and widely disseminated. What might have been modestly appropriate to posit as assumptions in a first book, I suggested to him, would seem reasonably to have evolved into more definitive statements 25 years later in a third edition. Might such statements take the form of principles? Exhibit 9.1 offers the contrast. I invited him, and you, to consider this. How do the two types of statements differ? Do the differences, if there are any of significance, matter?

Testing Assumptions Generates Principles

The perspective I am offering here is that principles provide strong guidance on how to achieve a desired result, in this case, becoming a skillful teacher. Assumptions are hypotheses and foundational premises. They are a reasonable beginning point for supporting action and learning, but the purpose of making them explicit is to examine their implications and test their validity. When that is done systematically over a period of years, as Brookfield has done, the evidence accumulated supports the transition from assumptions to principles. Principles, *integrating values and evidence of effectiveness,* provide guidance, utility, inspiration, developmental opportunities, and evaluation direction (GUIDE) to support meaningful and effective action.

Brookfield's response offers an important perspective that has implications beyond his own reticence. Knowing how the notion of "principles" is perceived is crucial for working with people to evaluate the effectiveness of principles. Here is his response:

EXHIBIT 9.1. Skillful Teaching *Assumptions versus Principles*	
Brookfield's assumptions about skillful teaching*	**Conversion to effectiveness principles for skillful teaching addressed to teachers**
1. Skillful teaching is whatever helps students learn.	1. Teach what helps students learn.
2. Skillful teachers adopt a critically reflective stance toward their practice.	2. Be critically reflective about your teaching practice.
3. The most important knowledge the teachers need to do good work is a constant awareness of how students are experiencing their learning and perceiving teachers' actions.	3. Monitor constantly how students are experiencing their learning and perceiving your actions.
4. College students of any age should be treated as adults.	4. Treat college students as adults.
*Brookfield (2015, pp. 8–9).	

In general, "guiding assumptions" and "principles" are very close. I think I avoid the term "principles" because of the self-importance I sense emanating from it—as in a principle being an axiomatic statement of truth. The word has a sense of axiomatic finality about it—the revealed truth aspect.

The word "assumption" has more openness to me. An assumption is something that might be revised at a later date as experience, as reflection, or research dictates. I'm sure that's how you think about principles too—as being open to subsequent revision. (Brookfield, personal correspondence; this chapter closes with a more extensive response from Brookfield)

Indeed, the purpose of evaluating principles is to determine their meaningfulness, the degree of adherence to them, and, if adhered to, their effectiveness. Those results can support revisions and adaptations of the principles in that, as emphasized throughout this book, they are different from rules and laws, which are more rigid and static. Brookfield makes his use of the word *assumptions* closer to principles by calling them "guiding assumptions." But assumptions aren't typically viewed as "guiding." They are foundational premises that may or may not be tested—or even testable. Googling for a definition of "assumptions,"

the first result that came up was "a thing that is accepted as true or as certain to happen, without proof."

Truths

Brookfield is concerned that principles imply an "axiomatic statement of truth." An "assumption" is more open, less definitive and rigid than truth, he says. Of course, the whole focus of principles-focused evaluation is to evaluate the effectiveness of principles, which treats them not as truth but as guidance subject to ongoing review, contextual evidence, critical reflection, learning, and revision. What strikes me as especially ironic about Brookfield's concern is that in the opening chapter of *The Skillful Teacher*, the chapter before the one on his four core assumptions, he offers his "personal truths" in a section entitled *Growing into the Truth of Teaching*.

Each of us comes to certain understandings and insights that just seem so right, so analytically consistent, and so confirmed by our experiences, that describing them as truthful seems entirely justified. The truth I'm talking about here is not universal truth. . . . It is a more personal truth, one smelted and shaped in the fire of our practice so that it fits the situations we deal with every day. . . .

Over a period of time each of us develops this personal truth to the point where we depend on it and sometimes declare it. I've been teaching since 1970 and it's only in the last few years that I felt confident enough to do some truth telling to myself about the frustrations and fears that are always there in my work. I feel I've grown into the truth of my own teaching.

By growing into the truth of teaching I mean developing a trust, a sense of intuitive confidence, in the accuracy and validity of our judgments and insights. Much of my career has been spent growing into truth. Here are some of the most important truths I've established for myself about teaching:

▶ I will always feel like an imposter and will never lose the sense of amazement I feel when people treat me as if I have something valuable to offer.

▶ I will never be able to initiate activities that keep all students engaged all the time.

▶ Attending to my credibility at the outset of a new course is critical so I need to watch out for my tendency to engage in too much self-deprecation.

▶ The regular use of examples, anecdotes, and autobiographical illustrations in explaining difficult concepts is strongly appreciated by students.

▶ Making full disclosure of my expectations and agendas is necessary if I am to establish an authentic presence in a classroom.

▶ I always have power in the classroom and I can never be a fly on the wall withering away to the point that students don't notice I'm in the room.

▶ Modeling critical thinking is crucial to helping students learn, but students will probably resist critical thinking whatever I do.

▶ Resistance to learning is a highly predictable presence in my classrooms; its presence does not mean I'm a failure.

▶ I've learned racist impulses and instincts and I will never lose these, though I could become more aware and struggle against them.

▶ I cannot motivate anyone to learn if at a very basic level they don't wish to. What I can do is try to remove whatever organizational, psychological, cultural, interpersonal, or pedagogic barriers are getting in the way of their learning, provide whatever modeling I can, build the best possible case for learning, and then cross my fingers and hope for the best.

These truths are experiential truths, confirmed repeatedly by my own analyses, colleagues' perceptions, and students' anonymous feedback. They have not been revealed to me in a series of Road to Damascus epiphanies, there has been no instantaneous conversions. Instead there has been an incremental building of recognition and confidence, a growing readiness to accept that these things are true for me, Stephen Brookfield, even when they are contradicted by conventional wisdom, omitted from manuals of best practices, or denounced by authoritative experts. . . . I have grown confident enough to speak these truths publicly. (Brookfield, 2015, pp. 8–9)

Personal Truths as Operating Principles

In what follows I am not in any way arguing with how Brookfield characterizes his personal truths. They are powerfully stated, evocative, and carefully contextualized as personal. That said, they also offer an opportunity to illustrate how an evaluator working with a principles-centered person, which I know Stephen Brookfield to be, could offer a layered framework of overarching and operational principles to provide comprehensive and coherent guidance. Overarching principles provide general guidance for effectiveness. Operating principles provide more specific guidance for effectiveness. Chapters 17, 27, and 31 provide more detailed examples and explanations of overarching effectiveness principles as an umbrella for more specific operating principles to guide effectiveness. Treating Brookfield's core assumptions as overarching principles and his personal truths as operating principles, we get the principles framework for the skillful teacher presented in Exhibit 9.2.

EXHIBIT 9.2. Assumptions and Personal Truths Reframed as Overarching and Operating Principles for the Skillful Teacher

Overarching principles (derived from core assumptions)	Operating principles (derived from personal truths)	Brookfield's reflections illustrating operating principles
1. Teach what helps students learn.	a. Use examples, anecdotes, and autobiographical illustrations in explaining difficult concepts. b. Model critical thinking to help students learn.	a. "The regular use of examples, anecdotes, and autobiographical illustrations in explaining difficult concepts is strongly appreciated by students." b. "Making full disclosure of my expectations and agendas is necessary if I am to establish an authentic presence in a classroom."
2. Be critically reflective about your teaching practice.	a. Reflect on how you feel about yourself as a teacher. b. Reflect on the feedback you receive from others. c. Expect students will probably resist critical thinking. d. Be aware of and struggle against racist impulses.	a. "I feel like an imposter." b. "I feel amazed when my expertise is valued." c. "Resistance to learning is a highly predictable presence in my classrooms and its presence does not mean I'm a failure." d. "I've learned racist impulses and instincts, and I will never lose these, though I could become more aware and struggle against them."
3. Monitor constantly how students are experiencing their learning and perceiving teachers' actions.	a. Attend to your credibility at the outset of a new course. b. Pay attention to how your power as teacher affects what is occurring in the classroom.	a. "I need to watch out for my tendency to engage in too much self-deprecation." b. "I always have power in the classroom and I can never be a fly on the wall withering away to the point that students don't notice I'm in the room."
4. Treat college students as adults.	a. Remove whatever organizational, psychological, cultural, interpersonal, or pedagogic barriers are getting in the way of students' learning. b. Provide whatever modeling you can.	a. "I will never be able to initiate activities that keep all students engaged all the time." b. "I cannot motivate anyone to learn if at a very basic level they don't wish to."

Once-upon-a-Time Principles

It turns out that Stephen Brookfield was not always reticent about principles. His classic book *Understanding and Facilitating Adult Learning* (Brookfield, 1986), the first book to receive both the Imogene Okes Award and the Cyril O. Houle World Award for Literature in Adult Education, was sub-titled: *A Comprehensive Analysis of Principles and Effective Practices*. In that book he identified and discussed six "principles of effective practice" for adult educators. Exhibit 9.3 presents these principles with my commentary. My comments are aimed at illustrating how an evaluator might work with a principles-centered person or program to clarify draft principles and make them more evaluable to test their effectiveness.

From Lessons to Principles

Brookfield's work offers yet another opportunity to examine the development of principles, this time converting lessons to principles. Lessons are a form of evidence of effectiveness. Lessons constitute knowledge. One way to make lessons actionable is to convert them to effectiveness principles to guide behavior and support further learning through evaluation.

Stephen Preskill and Stephen Brookfield (2008) published a book titled *Learning as a Way of Leading: Lessons from the Struggle for Social Justice*. The book examines nine leaders they believe "were among the greatest activists of the twentieth century and who, by virtue of their thirst for knowledge, empowered millions of others to continue their own learning for the cause of social justice" (p. x). Here's what they found.

> More than anything else, the leaders we are interested in are learners. They revere learning, they learn from their experience and from their co-workers, and they are constantly sharing with others the fruits of what they have learned. They also regard as paramount responsibility to encourage the learning of others.

What are some of the ways learning leaders demonstrate their commitment? Well, they listen with close attention, observe with a discerning eye, and read texts of all kinds—including the text of people's experiences—with critical acumen. They are constantly on the alert for new information, novel insights, deepened understanding. For these learning leaders, everything learned is potentially grist for the leadership mill. They try constantly to make connections between what they have learned, the issues that matter to them most, and the goals they are trying to achieve as leaders. Nothing is too trivial or insignificant, at least at first, to be taken into account and used in some way to lead more effectively or to bring about change more proactively. Such leaders do not hide their enthusiasm for what they are learning, either. They eagerly and overtly share their reflections on experience, what they are reading, what new ideas they are coming up with, what interesting connections they are making, and how they are revising earlier ideas and practice because of new learning. They do this in part because they are unabashed lovers of learning. But they also do so for strategic effect, to stir up their co-workers' excitement about their own learning and its potential for stimulating creativity and further change.

The raison d'être for modeling a public commitment to learning is to induce co-workers to launch their own learning projects. Everything that learning leaders do should be linked in some way to supporting other people's learning. . . . Most significant of all outcomes, perhaps, are the long-term relationships that occur as a result of working together on learning projects. Such relationships not only increase one's willingness to learn and lessen one's vulnerability about admitting ignorance, but also fuel future projects in public works. (pp. 5–6)

They found that learning leaders:

▶ Learn to be open to the contributions of others.

▶ Learn critical reflection.

▶ Learn to support the growth of others.

EXHIBIT 9.3. Six Principles of Effective Practice for Adult Educators, with Commentary	
Principles for effective practice (Brookfield, 1986)	**M. Q. P. commentary**
1. Participation in learning is voluntary; adults engage in learning as a result of their own volition.	This strikes me as a precondition for effective adult learning, not a principle. However, given evidence that only voluntary learning is effective, an adult educator might assert the following professional principle: *I teach only with learners who choose to learn; avoid mandated and involuntary teaching situations.* An institutional principle would be: *Make adult learning voluntary.*
2. Effective practice is characterized by a respect among participants for each other's self-worth. Foreign to facilitation are behaviors, practices, or statements that belittle others or that involve emotional or physical abuse.	This is stated as a finding: "Effective practice is characterized by. . . ." The principle that can be extrapolated from this finding is something like the following: *Create and maintain a climate of mutual respect based on valuing each other's self-worth.*
3. Facilitation is collaborative. Facilitators and learners are engaged in a cooperative enterprise in which, at different times and for different purposes, leadership and facilitation roles will be assumed by different group members.	Though a declarative statement, almost definitional in form, this can be interpreted as a value preference (facilitation *should be* collaborative). Combining that value preference with evidence of effectiveness, the adult learning principle becomes something like this: *Make facilitation collaborative.*
4. Praxis is placed at the heart of effective facilitation. Learners and facilitators are involved in a continual process of activity, reflection upon activity, collaborative analysis of activity, new activity, further reflection and collaborative analysis, and so on.	This describes the facilitation process. The principle would appear to be: *Put praxis at the center of facilitation as part of an ongoing cycle of action and reflection.*
5. Facilitation aims to foster in adults a spirit of critical reflection. Through educational encounters, learners come to appreciate that values, beliefs, behaviors, and ideologies are culturally transmitted and that they are provisional and relative.	This states the goal and outcomes of facilitation. The principle appears to be: *Foster critical reflection.*
6. The aim of facilitation is the nurturing of self-directed, empowered adults. Such adults will see themselves as proactive, initiating individuals engaged in a continuous re-creation of their personal relationships, work worlds, and social circumstances rather than as reactive individuals, buffeted by uncontrollable forces of circumstance.	This statement elaborates the purpose of facilitation and further describes expected outcomes. The principle embedded in this statement is: *Nurture and empower self-direction.*

▶ Learn collective leadership.

▶ Learn to sustain hope in the face of struggle.

▶ Learn to create community.

Exhibit 9.4 converts these lessons into principles with accompanying evaluation questions for reflective practice.

Illustrations of Conceptual Options

I trust that readers will appreciate the learning opportunity afforded by Stephen Brookfield's openness to having his work examined and reframed through the lens of principles-focused evaluation. The importance of his contributions to adult education is validated by the many awards he has received. His writings manifest high-quality scholarship, reflective practice, critical thinking, and practical advice. It is precisely the high quality and importance of Brookfield's works that lend significance to the opportunity to consider the potential value of conceptualizing his contributions through the lens of principles and principles-focused evaluation. He has kindly and thoughtfully provided the following response to my suggested reframing of his work, after which I conclude this chapter with lessons for principles-focused evaluators.

Stephen D. Brookfield Responds

I love disagreeing with friends. Indeed, when I team teach with my longtime friend and collaborator Steve Preskill the best moments for me are when we start disagreeing

in front of students. According to students this is also a highlight. Steve and I are having fun, but we're also striving to do the important work of showing what constructive and searching disagreement looks like. Such disagreement doesn't stop at "here's my view and here's yours"; instead, it moves into inquiry and curiosity. We want to know why each of us disagrees with the other, so we ask question after question—Why do you think that? What's the evidence or experience you take most seriously? How would you respond to this point? How does what you're saying now connect to what you said 5 minutes ago? So I want to state and reiterate some specific disagreements with Michael and to make some general comments on his argument.

First off, the "principles as axiomatic" thing. Michael says I wasn't always reticent about using the term *principles* and quotes a book I wrote 30 years ago as evidence. My first response is that 30 years ago I was a callow untenured professor trying to keep a job at Columbia University and coming up for tenure. I can't possibly recall my state of mind when writing that book, but I think it's reasonable to assume that in my effort to make an impression I had less hesitancy about using the word *principles*. *Principles* sounds important, portentous, definitive. If I have principles, then I'm a morally good person who does things in a principled way. If I have principles, then I've discovered some universal truths that are enduring and axiomatic guides to good practice.

I do remember that after the *Understanding and Facilitating Adult Learning* (Brookfield, 1986) book came out someone asked me where my principles came from, and I remember immediately answering, "I just made them up." I don't think that was far from the truth. I probably thought "this chapter needs an introductory statement of principles so let's get them down." Now I admit that they didn't come totally out of the air and that, however spontaneous it might have seemed, whatever I claimed as

EXHIBIT 9.4. From Lessons to Principles and Evaluation (Reflective Practice) Questions			
Findings about learning leaders*	Leadership lessons	Principles derived from the lessons	Reflective practice questions for learning leaders
1. Learning leaders listen with close attention, observe with a discerning eye, and read texts of all kinds. They are constantly on the alert for new information, novel insights, and deepened understanding.	1. Learning is a way of leading.	1. Lead by learning.	a. What are your primary sources for ongoing learning? b. What have you learned from these sources recently? c. How has what you've learned informed what you do, that is, informed your leadership behaviors and actions?
2. Learning leaders try constantly to make connections between what they have learned, the issues that matter to them most, and the goals they are trying to achieve as leaders. Nothing is too trivial or insignificant, at least at first, to be taken into account and used in some way to lead more effectively or to bring about change more proactively.	2. Everything learned is used to increase effectiveness.	2. Use learning to increase effectiveness.	a. How do you connect what you've learned to the issues you care about and the goals you are aiming to achieve? What are examples of those connections? b. In what ways have you become more effective? How has what you've learned led to that increased effectiveness?
3. Learning leaders eagerly and overtly share their reflections on experience, what they are reading, what new ideas they are coming up with, what interesting connections they are making, and how they are revising earlier ideas and practice because of new learning.	3. Learning leaders share their learnings openly and enthusiastically.	3. Share your learnings openly and enthusiastically.	a. What learnings have you shared with others? b. How do you share what you've learned? c. How is what you've learned received by others? How do you know?

(continued)

Findings about learning leaders*	Leadership lessons	Principles derived from the lessons	Reflective practice questions for learning leaders
4. Learning leaders regard as paramount the responsibility to encourage the learning of others. They stir up their co-workers' excitement about their own learning and its potential for stimulating creativity and further change. The raison d'être for modeling a public commitment to learning is to induce co-workers to launch their own learning projects. Everything that learning leaders do should be linked in some way to supporting other people's learning.	4. Learning leaders model learning to support learning and growth by others.	4. Support learning by others.	a. How are you supporting learning by others? b. How do you know that others feel their learning is supported? c. How does supporting the learning of others contribute to the goals you're aiming to achieve as a leader?
5. For learning leaders, the most significant of all outcomes, perhaps, are the long-term relationships that occur as a result of working together on learning projects. Such relationships not only increase one's willingness to learn and lessen one's vulnerability about admitting ignorance but also fuel future projects in public works.	5. Learning leaders create community through deepened relationships that flow from shared learning and shared leadership.	5. Strengthen relationships and create community through shared learning and shared leadership.	a. How do you experience relationships with those with whom you share learning? b. To what extent and in what ways are you nurturing a community of learning and learners? c. How do you share leadership through learning?
6. Learning leaders demonstrate critical acumen. Everything learned is potentially grist for the leadership mill.	6. Learning leaders engage in critical reflection.	6. Engage in critical reflection.	a. How do you engage in critical reflection? b. What does "critical reflection" mean to you? How is it a leadership function? c. What's an example of a change you've made based on critical reflection?

*Source: Preskill and Brookfield (2008).

principles were things I'd thought about a lot and things I'd experienced. But I do believe I threw the word around too lightly in a way that was designed to give the book an aura of significance.

I'm reminded of two quotes as I make this point: Bob Dylan's line in "My Back Pages"—"I was so much older then I'm younger than that now"—and W. B. Yeats's line in his poem "The Second Coming"—"the best lack all conviction, while the worst are full of passionate intensity." I read both these quotes as illuminating why I moved away from using the term *principles*. The longer I try to understand teaching, learning, and leadership, the more I become skeptical of anything smacking of universal prescriptions. One thing I've learned—is this a principle, Michael?—is that nothing stays the same. So a belief I hold about teaching and leadership—that transparency is the best policy—is something I'll willingly contradict depending on the situation. There've been times when I've been very comfortable playing my cards close to my chest, not making full disclosure and manipulating the flow of information.

I'm also disturbed by the language of attempting to translate principles into effective practices. This is a neat contrivance that foundations and institutions love because it simplifies the world's complexity. But anyone who's awake and alert knows that in classrooms, staffrooms, communities, and organizations everything is contextual. Practices and actions that are highly effective for some *always* get in the way for others. We live our lives as change agents, evaluators, teachers, and leaders constantly taking actions that, on the whole, have more advantages attached to them than disadvantages. Nothing I do as a teacher or leader is effective for everyone affected by it. Everything has drawbacks. It's just that at that time, in that place, with those learners, clients, or colleagues, a certain choice, decision, or judgment makes the best overall sense.

Lessons about Developing and Evaluating Principles Based on Working with Stephen Brookfield's Adult Education Writings

Again, my thanks to Stephen Brookfield for indulging me in reframing some of his writings and in offering a collegial response. Here are some lessons I extrapolate from our exchange.

1. *Negative connotations associated with "principles" can be a barrier to both principles-based programming and principles-focused evaluation.* For Brookfield, principles connote "axiomatic truths," a form of knowledge about which he is appropriately skeptical. My advice is to avoid rhetorical discussions about such connotations and turn, instead, to developing actual statements of principles, as illustrated by the examples in this chapter. That moves the discussion from the abstract to the concrete, focusing on real potential principles and their meaningfulness and utility.

2. *No principles, no principles-focused evaluation.* This chapter opened by noting that principles don't just happen. They aren't always obvious. Indeed, they may be well disguised. Or there may resistance to or reasons for not calling principles by that name (lesson 1 above). Thus, part of the work of facilitating and undertaking principles-focused evaluations can include identifying, generating, developing, and articulating principles or alternatives to principles, like rules, assumptions, operating truths, values, and lessons. Which kinds of statements are most useful, appropriate, and meaningful within the context of and for the people involved in the principles development and clarification exercise? The point is to find out if a principles-driven approach is meaningful, appropriate, and useful to those who are trying to bring about change in the world. There are other ways of conceptualizing change. But to find out if a principles-based approach resonates

with and inspires the change makers, the evaluator may have to generate examples for discussion and consideration.

3. *Principles may lurk in and have to be extracted from other kinds of conceptual statements like assumptions, beliefs, values, findings, lessons, and premises.* Much of the work of identifying, generating, developing, and articulating principles involves taking statements that are conceptualized as something else and mining them for potential principles. Principles, like gold, may have to be extracted and refined from other raw material. They don't just show up already polished and radiant. Extracting and polishing principles from other kinds of statements is part of the work involved in principles-focused evaluation.

4. *Generate evaluation questions to illuminate the connection between principles-driven change processes and principles-focused evaluation.* Just as it is helpful to move discussion about principles from the abstract to the concrete, so it is important and useful to move discussion of principles-focused evaluation from the abstract to the concrete. As principles (or potential principles) are identified and developed, pose evaluation questions about the principles to illustrate what principles-focused evaluation offers for principles-driven people and principles-based programming.

5. *Principles aren't for everyone, nor is principles-focused evaluation.* I fully appreciate and respect Stephen Brookfield's reservations about principles and do not believe that pushing principles would have any value for his work. He has taken a different road. Following his example of drawing on song lyrics (Stephen is a musician and leads a band), I'm happy to "Let it be."

Practice Exercises

1. I have chosen not to respond to Stephen Brookfield's reaction to my review of his work (see pp. 72–75). What is your reaction to his rejoinder to me? What do you imagine my response would be? Indeed, go ahead and formulate my response as a practice exercise.

2. In your area of interest and expertise, identify an expert, prominent scholar, or other personage held in high esteem who espouses lessons, premises, assumptions, values, recommendations, principles, or some other such statement of advice.
If principles are advocated, to what extent do they meet the GUIDE criteria? If the advice takes some other form (for example, recommendations or lessons), try your hand at converting them to principles. Assess the results you generate against the GUIDE criteria.

CHAPTER 10

Conceptual Triangulation
Evaluating the Similarities of Parallel Principles

> The grass is not always greener on the other side of the fence. Sometimes,
> if you look carefully, in the right light, it's the same color, or at least pretty
> close, even though a different variety. But you have to look carefully.
> —HALCOLM, "Principle of Color Coordination"

Chapter 7 discussed testing the distinctness and meaningfulness of a principle by conceptualizing its opposite or another specific alternative. This chapter goes in the opposite direction and looks at the value of finding similarities among sets of principles. This is a form of conceptual or theoretical triangulation. Finding that a new set of principles generated for a new situation bears similarities to well-established principles in a different field of endeavor can be part of the validation and evaluation process for the new set of principles. In so doing, we're examining yet another way to meet the G criterion in the GUIDE framework that calls for principles to provide meaningful guidance for action.

Chapter 30 will present and discuss agroecological principles. Agroecology applies ecological principles to the design of sustainable farming systems. In formulating and validating agroecological principles, Méndez, Bacon, and Cohen (2016) took a transdisciplinary approach "to integrate different types of knowledge systems"

with special attention to farmer-generated knowledge (p. 5). Participatory action research (PAR), an approach that engages local people in using research to understand and solve local problems, is a parallel field that also emphasizes locally generated knowledge. Participatory approaches in agroecology and participatory approaches in action research adhere to similar principles. Exhibit 10.1 shows the comparison. By comparing the principles of a relatively new and still-emergent field like agroecology with a well-established and credible field like PAR, the agroecologists sought to enhance the legitimacy and relevance of their underlying principles.

Cooperative Extension and Evaluation: Parallel Principles

Extension and evaluation both center on getting useful information to people. Extension provides information aimed at such things as improving farm productivity,

EXHIBIT 10.1. Comparison of Selected PAR and Agroecological Principles

PAR principles	Agroecological principles
1. PAR prioritizes empowerment, as community-based partners contribute to the define the research agenda.	1. Agroecologists work with farmers, consumers, communities, agricultural ministries, food advocates, and others to support empowering people.
2. PAR processes are context dependent, as they bring together trans/interdisciplinary teams responding to stakeholder aspirations.	2. Agroecology establishes farming and food systems that adjust to local environments.
3. PAR research processes inform action at multiple scales for positive social change.	3. Agroecology offers principles and analysis toward the creation of more sustainable agriculture and food systems.
4. PAR processes deepen as long-term relationships are formed and multiple iterations of the cycle occur.	4. Agroecology seeks to develop strategies to maximize long-term benefits.
5. PAR processes listen to a diversity of voices and knowledge systems to democratize the research and social change processes.	5. Agroecology incorporates farmers' voices and knowledge into the research process and seeks to diversify biodata, landscapes, markets, and institutions.

Source: From Méndez, Bacon, and Cohen (2016, p. 5). Copyright 2016 by Taylor and Francis. Reprnted by permission of Taylor and Francis Group, LLC, a division of Informa PLC.

improving nutrition, and improving the quality of life in the home, community, or business. Evaluation provides information aimed at improving programs, improving the effectiveness of personnel, and assuring accountability. While working as an evaluator in the Minnesota Extension Service, I aimed to increase the acceptance and use of program evaluation by extension staff by demonstrating that effective extension education and useful evaluations involved nearly identical principles. Evaluation, I argued, could be viewed as a specialized application of more general extension principles because both extension and evaluation involve making research knowledge understandable, packaging information for decision making, educating information users, and encouraging people to act on the basis of knowledge (Patton, 1983). I was hoping to show that evaluation shouldn't be viewed by extension staff as something alien, threatening, or unknown but rather as a particular application of already-known,

well-established, validated, and accepted extension principles.

I began by comparing five parallel steps in effective extension and useful evaluation as shown in Exhibit 10.2. The basic processes of effective extension work are derived from the diffusion of innovations and change-agent literatures (Rogers, 1962; Rogers & Shoemaker, 1971). The processes of useful evaluation are derived from research on ways of increasing the effectiveness and use of evaluation (Patton, 2008, 2012a).

The first step in these parallel processes is identifying the people who are to benefit and be served by an extension program or an evaluation. Extension staff can't serve everyone. Some targeting is necessary. Likewise, evaluations must be targeted. No single evaluation can answer everyone's questions. Effective extension programs and effective evaluations are carefully targeted.

Step 2 emphasizes the importance of needs assessment in both extension program development and evaluation design. Needs assessment includes finding out from clients and decision makers what's worth doing. Many rigorously designed evaluations go unused because evaluators failed to find out what program staff and decision makers really needed and wanted to know. Both effective extension and effective evaluation include attention to the *real* information needs of targeted groups.

Step 3 emphasizes that the information disseminated by both extension staff and evaluators is based on research. Extension information comes from experiment station research, university faculty studies, and private sector research and development work. Evaluation information comes from studies of program processes, outcomes, and consequences. Regardless of the type of study conducted, the source of information, or the rigor of methods used, *both* extension and evaluation are research based. Both try to provide valid information for decision making and change for decision making.

Step 4 focuses on the information delivery process. It's not enough for researchers and evaluators to generate new knowledge. Research and evaluation information must

be *extended.* No idea is more fundamental to extension than the idea that research knowledge must be translated, packaged, made understandable, made practical, and adapted to local situations. Likewise, evaluation findings must be translated, simplified, and made understandable to targeted decision makers and information users.

Finally, Step 5 calls attention to the importance of follow-up. It's not enough to just deliver information to people. To bring about real change in behaviors and practices, it's usually necessary to work with people over time to help them apply and use information they've been given. An effective evaluation process isn't completed when the report is written and the findings officially delivered. The evaluation utilization process involves personal follow-up, clarification, discussion, and work with decision makers to help them use and apply evaluation findings.

Having laid the foundation of parallel processes, I turned to parallel principles using the Joint Committee Standards for Educational Evaluation as the basis for comparison. Exhibit 10.3 shows the parallel principles.

EXHIBIT 10.2. Parallel Processes in Extension and Evaluation

Basic extension processes	Basic evaluation processes
Step 1: Determine who's to be served by an extension program. Who are the clients or targets of a program?	*Step 1:* Determine whose information needs are to be met by an evaluation. Who are the decision makers and information users for the evaluation?
Step 2: Determine the information and program needs of the clients.	*Step 2:* Determine the evaluation information needs of decision makers and information users.
Step 3: Gather the needed information and develop the needed program.	*Step 3:* Gather the needed information.
Step 4: Deliver information and recommendations to clients.	*Step 4:* Present evaluation findings to decision makers and information users.
Step 5: Work with clients to apply and use what they've learned.	*Step 5:* Work with decision makers to apply and use evaluation findings.

EXHIBIT 10.3. Parallel Extension and Evaluation Principles

Extension principles	Evaluation principles
Extension utility principles	***Evaluation utility principles***
1. *Targeting extension programs:* Programs should be developed to meet the identified needs of specifically targeted audiences.	1. *Targeting evaluation:* Evaluations should be designed to meet the information needs of specifically targeted audiences.
2. *Extension staff credibility:* The people conducting programs should be both trustworthy and competent to achieve credibility and acceptance.	2. *Evaluator credibility:* The people conducting an evaluation should be both trustworthy and competent to achieve credibility and acceptance.
3. *Information scope:* Information provided should address pertinent questions and be responsive to the needs and interests of participants in programs.	3. *Information scope:* Information collected should address pertinent questions and be responsive to the needs and interests of specified audiences.
4. *Report clarity:* Extension materials should be readily understandable with clear recommendations, where appropriate.	4. *Report clarity:* Evaluation reports should be readily understandable with clear recommendations, where appropriate.
5. *Follow-through:* Extension programs should be planned and conducted in ways that encourage follow-through by participants.	5. *Follow-through:* Evaluation should be planned and conducted in ways that encourage follow-through by members of the audiences.
Extension feasibility principles	***Evaluation feasibility principles***
1. *Practical considerations:* Extension programs should be planned with attention to participants' availability and time constraints.	1. *Practical procedures:* Evaluation procedures should be selected with attention to known time constraints and participants' availability.
2. *Political viability:* Extension programs should be planned and conducted with anticipation of the different positions of various interest groups, so that their cooperation may be obtained, and so that controversies can be anticipated and misunderstandings averted.	2. *Political viability:* The evaluation should be planned and conducted with anticipation of different positions of various interest groups, so that their cooperation may be obtained, and so that possible attempts by any of these groups to curtail evaluation operations or to bias or misapply the results can be averted or counteracted.
3. *Cost-effectiveness:* Extension programs should be of sufficient value to justify the resources expended.	3. *Cost-effectiveness:* Evaluations should produce information of sufficient value to justify the resources expended.

(continued)

Extension principles	Evaluation principles
Extension propriety principles	*Evaluation propriety principles*
1. *Human interactions:* Extension staff should respect human dignity and worth in their interactions with clients and others involved in extension.	1. *Human interactions:* Evaluators should respect human dignity and worth in their interactions with other people associated with an evaluation.
2. *Balanced presentations:* Extension information and programs should be complete and fair in presenting both sides of issues and problems under discussion, and both strengths and weaknesses of proposed innovations or changed practices should be discussed.	2. *Balanced reporting:* The evaluation should be complete and fair in its presentation of strengths and weaknesses of the object under investigation, so that strengths can be built on and problem areas addressed.
3. *Fiscal responsibility:* The extension agent's allocation and expenditure of resources should reflect sound accountability procedures and otherwise be prudent and ethically responsible.	3. *Fiscal responsibility:* The evaluator's allocation and expenditure of resources should reflect sound accountability procedures and otherwise be prudent and ethically responsible.
Extension accuracy principles	*Evaluation accuracy principles*
1. *Defensible information sources:* The sources of information drawn on for extension presentations and programs should be described in enough detail that the adequacy of the information can be assessed.	1. *Defensible information sources:* The sources of information in an evaluation should be described in enough detail that the adequacy of the information can be assessed.
2. *Justified conclusions:* The recommendations made by extension staff should be explicitly justified, so that participants in extension programs can assess them.	2. *Justified conclusions:* The conclusions reached in an evaluation should be explicitly justified, so that the audiences can assess them.
3. *Objective presentations:* Extension services and staff should take steps to guard against distortions in extension materials and presentations due to personal feelings and biases.	3. *Objective reporting:* The evaluation procedures should provide safeguards to protect the evaluation findings and reports against distortion by the personal feelings and biases of any party to the evaluation.

Source for extension principles: Patton (1983); source for evaluation principles: Joint Committee on Standards for Educational Evaluation (1981).

The comparison of extension and evaluation principles concluded:

> As people who know the value of information-based decision making, extension educators are in an ideal position to provide leadership in evaluation processes, both in conducting evaluations and in using evaluation information for program improvement.
>
> By understanding the similarities between extension and evaluation, extension staff may become involved in evaluations with greater confidence, even instructing evaluators in the principles of extension, so as to improve the practice of evaluation. By applying the new standards of evaluation, extension personnel can improve both the usefulness and quality of evaluation. At stake is the quality of both evaluations and extension programs. (Patton, 1983)

Common Principles, One List

The examples of comparable principles presented thus far have taken the form of similar but not identical principles in two arenas of action, agroecological principles compared to those of participatory action research, and evaluation principles compared to extension's. The final example is of a single set of identical principles applicable to two fields: humanistic psychology and qualitative inquiry. Exhibit 10.4 presents the 10 shared principles. The purpose of this unified list was to demonstrate to humanistic psychologists that qualitative research was appropriate for and compatible with their therapeutic principles.

The Value of Comparisons

Comparisons enlighten. Understanding when principles in two arenas of endeavor are different, similar, or the same helps us appreciate and fine-tune those principles with which we are concerned. Examining and understanding participatory action research principles both validates and sheds light on agroecology principles. Comparing extension principles with evaluation principles when working with extension staff helps make the unfamiliar (evaluation principles) more familiar (extension principles). Identifying identical principles for humanistic psychology and qualitative inquiry establishes common ground and common evaluation criteria.

EXHIBIT 10.4. Common Principles Undergirding Qualitative Research Inquiries and Humanistic Psychology Therapies

1. Treat each person as unique.

2. Treat each person as deserving respect.

3. Negotiate what is to occur based on reciprocity rather than imposing, forcing, or mandating.

4. Be open, honest, and transparent about what will and does occur.

5. Listen to the perspective and learn about the experiences of those you encounter in the process of engagement.

6. Be person centered by authentically attending to the effects of your process on people.

7. Treat emotions and feelings as natural, healthy dimensions of human experience.

8. Be empathically nonjudgmental.

9. Be sensitive to context and its effects on what unfolds.

10. Communicate that the process (how things are done) is as important as the outcomes (what is achieved).

All the examples and comparisons in this chapter meet the *G* criterion in the GUIDE framework. There's more than one way to develop meaningful and evaluable principles. *Conceptual triangulation*—comparing and assessing the similarities of parallel principles as illustrated in this chapter—is one option.

Practice Exercise

Search for parallel sets of similar principles in your own fields of interest. Examine the similarities and differences between the two sets of principles.

CHAPTER 11

Holistic, Sequential, and Pole Star Approaches to Principles

My humanity is caught up and is inextricably bound up in yours. I'm human because I belong. The spirit of *ubuntu* means wholeness. It is knowledge that we belong to a greater whole and are diminished when others are humiliated or diminished, when others are tortured or oppressed, or treated as if they were less than who they are. Our purpose is social and communal harmony and well-being.

—Archbishop Desmond Tutu (1997, p. 7)

This is the final chapter focused on illuminating the *G* criterion in the GUIDE framework. Thus far I have been focusing on identifying and articulating specific, autonomous effectiveness principles. But any given program or initiative will typically have multiple principles. Chapter 22 reviews the seven Kwanzaa principles that guide an African American after-school program. Those principles are interconnected and together constitute a whole. Chapter 25 highlights evaluation of the five Paris Declaration principles for international development assistance. Each is important in its own right, but together they constitute a comprehensive shift in how international development assistance was meant to be done. Chapter 26 examines nine evidence-based principles for helping youth overcome homelessness. Those principles reinforce each other. Chapter 29 discusses the eight overarching principles of the McKnight Foundation Collaborative Crop Research Program. Here again, the principles together provide a depth of

coherence that supersedes the significance of each alone. Thus when, as is typical, a program or initiative has multiple principles, the question arises of how, if at all, they interconnect and interrelate. In many cases, each principle provides important and distinct guidance, and the evaluation assesses the meaningfulness, adherence to, and results of adhering to each principle on its own merits. But in other cases, the separate principles are viewed as intrinsically interconnected and interactive such that they are meant to be viewed holistically and evaluated for collective adherence and impact.

Holistic Set of Principles

Chapter 28 presents and discusses the principles of the Global Alliance for the Future of Food, a group of more than 20 philanthropic organizations from around the world collaborating on issues related to the sustainability of global agriculture and food systems. The Alliance members went through a process of identifying shared principles and ended up with six. (See Exhibit 28.1, p. 262.) As part of testing and verifying the relevance and utility of the principles to guide the work of the Alliance, small groups participated in a simulated diagnostic process in which the principles were used to describe and assess particular food systems. That diagnostic exercise gave rise to the question of whether all the principles had to be applied to an initiative of the Global Alliance or whether they should be treated as a menu of options. This question generated intense discussion. The end result was a shared commitment to treat the six principles as a whole, integrated framework, not a list of options. This also resolved a corresponding question of whether they were to be listed in some order of priority. All were determined to be equally important and essential to the work of the Global Alliance.

Chapter 3 ended with the nine evidence-based principles for helping youth overcome homelessness (see Exhibit 3.1, p. 18). Those principles are introduced as a holistic framework:

The principles begin with the perspective that youth are on a journey; all of our interactions with youth are filtered through that *journey* perspective. This means we must be trauma *informed, nonjudgmental,* and work to *reduce harm.* By holding these principles, we can build a *trusting relationship* that allows us to focus on *youths' strengths* and opportunities for *positive development.* Through all of this, we approach youth as *whole beings* through a youth-focused *collaborative* system of support.

Integrated Principles

Each time any program, initiative, or collaboration identifies and adopts a set of principles, the question arises as to whether they constitute a pick-and-choose list or an integrated, interrelated whole. The McKnight Foundation Collaborative Crop Research Program, discussed in Chapter 29, identified eight principles and determined that they constitute an interrelated, mutually reinforcing, dynamically interconnected whole. Exhibit 11.1 shows the visual depiction of the interdependent principles.

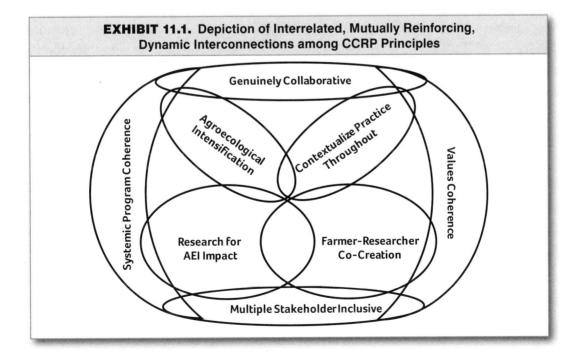

EXHIBIT 11.1. Depiction of Interrelated, Mutually Reinforcing, Dynamic Interconnections among CCRP Principles

Genuinely Collaborative

Agroecological Intensification

Contextualize Practice Throughout

Systemic Program Coherence

Values Coherence

Research for AEI Impact

Farmer-Researcher Co-Creation

Multiple Stakeholder Inclusive

Developmental Evaluation as an Example of Integrated Principles

The integrated framework diagram (Exhibit 11.1) has been used to depict other integrated sets of principles, including the eight developmental evaluation principles (see Chapter 5 and Exhibit 5.4; Patton, 2016a, Ch. 15). Each of the developmental evaluation principles is essential, and all of the principles are interrelated and mutually reinforcing. *Together,* the developmental evaluation principles constitute *an integrated whole.* Being utilization focused (principle #3) requires staying attuned to the priority purpose of the evaluation, namely, being developmental (principle #1) in support of innovation and adaptation (#4). Developmental evaluation occurs in a complex dynamic system (#5) that requires an evaluator to understand and apply complexity concepts and systems thinking (#6) with timely feedback (#8). Utilization-focused engagement is collaborative (#7) and evaluative (#2), making the developmental evaluation part of the intervention. (Each principle is defined in Exhibit 5.4, p. 30.) This means that for an evaluation to merit the label "Developmental Evaluation," all of the eight principles should be addressed to some extent and in some way. The eight principles are not a pick-and-choose list. All are essential.

In contrast, consider the 10 principles of empowerment evaluation:

1. Improvement
2. Community ownership
3. Inclusion
4. Democratic participation
5. Social justice
6. Community knowledge
7. Evidence-based strategies
8. Capacity building
9. Organizational learning
10. Accountability

Miller and Campbell (2006) systematically examined 47 evaluations labeled "empowerment evaluation" and found wide variation among practitioners in adherence to the principles. Cousins (2005), in another review, concluded that any particular empowerment evaluation approach will depend on "which combination of principles are most important, given the needs of the local context and the impetus for the empowerment evaluation in the first place" (p. 201).

When asked which of the 10 empowerment evaluation principles he had identified as essential, David Fetterman responded that there are "high, medium and low levels of each of these principles. . . . You don't always have to do the highest. It depends on your circumstances and situations, but [the principles] gives you a gauge and a guide of how to do these things" (Donaldson, Patton, Fetterman, & Scriven, 2010, p. 49). Moreover, empowerment evaluation theorists emphasize that it is "a systematic way of thinking" rather than adherence to specific principles (Fetterman, Wandersman, & Kaftarian, 2015). They argue that empowerment evaluation principles are like principles of democracy, such as free speech and freedom of religion; democratic countries vary in their adherence to these principles, but that doesn't mean they aren't still democracies. The latest book on empowerment evaluation (Fetterman, Shakeh, Kaftarian, & Wandersman, 2014) clarifies that there are can be *zero levels* of adherence to, implementation of, or attention to particular principles. It's a pick-and-choose menu. That said, Fetterman (2005) has stated that incorporation of more empowerment principles is better than fewer.

As a general rule, the quality [of an empowerment evaluation] increases as the number of principles are applied, because they are synergistic. Ideally each of the principles should be enforced at some level. However, specific principles will be more dominant than others in each empowerment evaluation. The principles that dominate will be related to the local context and purpose of evaluation. Not all principles will be adopted equally at any given time or for any given project. (p. 9)

What is true for sets of evaluation principles (developmental evaluation principles, empowerment evaluation principles, and other evaluation principles discussed in Chapter 31) is also true for sets of effectiveness principles more generally, whether for programs, initiatives, or policies. A core question is: To what extent do principles in a set (or on a list) constitute separate and autonomous principles versus an integrated whole? These contrasting ways of regarding principles involve different conceptual and evaluation criteria as shown in Exhibit 11.2.

Sequential Principles

A sequential principles framework specifies a set of steps and a sequential order for implementing a set of principles to achieve an overall desired result. An excellent example is the framework developed in South Africa and led by Bishop Tutu for the Truth and Reconciliation Commission in 1996 following apartheid.

1. Bring together the oppressor and the oppressed
2. Speak the truth
3. Confession
4. Forgiveness
5. Reconciliation

EXHIBIT 11.2. Autonomous Principles in a Framework Compared to Integrated and Interdependent Principles in a Framework		
Set of principles	List of separate, distinct, and autonomous principles	Set of integrated, interdependent, and interacting principles
1. Conceptualization of principles in a set	Each principle is distinct and independent of the other principles in the set.	The principles in a framework are viewed as interacting, interdependent, and interconnected.
2. Implications for judging meaningfulness	Each principle is judged on its individual meaningfulness.	Individual principles are judged both separately and as part of an integrated, coherent whole.
3. Implications for adherence	Those adhering to the principles decide which ones on the list to follow, and/or to what degree to follow any particular principle.	All principles in the set should be adhered to for any given implementation of the principles-based approach.
4. Implications for principles-based results	Each individual principle has its own expected results when adhered to.	Individual principles are expected to point to individually relevant results, but the integrated and cumulative impacts of the principles in combination is expected to be greater than the sum of the individual principles.
5. Implications for principles-focused evaluation	Evaluate individual principles for meaningfulness, adherence, and consequences of adherence.	Evaluate both individual principles and their collective meaningfulness, adherence, and impacts.

This sequence is both temporal and logical. The process calls for direct interaction between oppressors and oppressed, so they must be brought together in a safe place where speaking the truth is possible. The truth is the basis for confession, which must precede forgiveness, and then reconciliation.

Archbishop Desmond Tutu (1997) has explained the nature and importance of the sequence:

> True reconciliation is based on forgiveness, and forgiveness is based on true confession, and confession is based on penitence, on contrition, on sorrow for what you have done. . . . Equally, confession, forgiveness and reconciliation in the lives of nations are not just airy-very religious and spiritual things, nebulous and unrealistic. They are the stuff of practical politics. . . .
>
> Forgiveness gives us the capacity to make a new start. That is the power, the rationale, of confession and forgiveness. It is to say, "I have fallen but I am not going to remain there. Please forgive me." And forgiveness is the grace by which you enable the other person to get up, and get up with dignity, to begin anew. Not to forgive leads to bitterness and hatred which gnaw away at the vitals of one's being. (pp. 60–61)

Evaluating Truth and Reconciliation Processes

Truth and reconciliation commissions are convened to uncover and bring to light oppression by those in power in the hope of resolving conflicts and creating the conditions for a transition to power sharing in a new system of social justice. In the 1980s and 1990s human rights violations were the focus of public hearings in Bolivia, Argentina, Chile, El Salvador, Uganda, Zimbabwe, Nepal, and the Philippines. Rwanda held truth and reconciliation hearings following the genocide there in 1994. More recently there have been truth commissions in Canada and Australia concerning the treatment of aboriginal populations historically. Germany has held truth commissions on human rights violations in the former East Germany. These and other truth commissions around the world have been the object of evaluation (Bakiner, 2016; Hayner, 2010; Martin, 2009; Rotberg & Thompson, 2000). For my purpose here, Exhibit 11.3 provides generic evaluation questions for the sequence of truth and reconciliation principles.

Evaluating Sequential Principles

The general point in this section goes beyond truth and reconciliation processes. I have highlighted truth and reconciliation principles because they exemplify an important and influential sequential principles framework. The larger lesson is: when developing principles and a framework for evaluating principles, *inquire into whether there is an intended, hypothesized, or expected sequence.*

Pole Star Principles

Keep going north.
—Principle followed by escaping slaves seeking freedom in the United States before the Civil War

This chapter has been discussing sets of principles and how the individual principles in a set may relate to each other either interactively as a dynamic system or sequentially, one following the other. Most principles-based programs and initiatives have multiple principles. Occasionally, however, a single principle is so important that it dominates all others. Such a principle is called a "pole star principle."

A pole star is a prominent visible star that is closely aligned with the Earth's axis of rotation such that it lies approximately directly overhead when viewed from the North Pole or South Pole. The term *pole star* usually refers to Polaris, also known as the North Star.

The south celestial pole lacks a bright star like Polaris to mark its position, though it is possible to navigate and locate the South Pole using the Southern Cross

EXHIBIT 11.3. Generic Evaluation Questions for the Sequence of Truth and Reconciliation Principles

Sequence of principles	Principles-focused evaluation questions
1. Bring together the oppressor and the oppressed	Who participated in the truth and reconciliation process? Who represented oppressors? Who represented victims of oppression? Who from both groups did not participate and why? What was the scope of participation in the process compared to the numbers of people who were engaged in oppression and those who were victims of that oppression?
2. Speak the truth	What "truths" were spoken by whom? To what extent did participants (both oppressors and oppressed) feel safe and trusting to speak truth? What structures, agreements, understandings, assurances, and processes were put in place to facilitate speaking the truth?
3. Confession	What confessions were heard? What was the experience of confessing? How complete, honest, comprehensive, accurate, and truthful were the confessions perceived to be by those participating in the process, both confessing and hearing confessions?
4. Forgiveness	What forms and formats did forgiveness take? What was the experience of forgiveness among those forgiving? What was experience of being forgiven? What short-term actions followed forgiveness?
5. Reconciliation	What patterns of reconciliation emerged? What is evidence that reconciliation was meaningful, genuine, authentic, and enduring? What have been the impacts and consequences of the truth and reconciliation process for the people involved and for the country where the process occurred?

constellation. The single star most directly above the South Pole is Sigma Octantis, which despite being a faint star, is sometimes known as the South Star.

Prior to the Emancipation Proclamation issued by President Abraham Lincoln on January 1, 1863, escaping slaves journeyed north trying to reach Canada, where slavery was prohibited and runaway slaves could not be captured legally and returned to their owners in the American South. The principle they followed was to keep going north. They were taught that moss usually grew on the north side of trees and that migrating birds flew north in the summer. But the most consistent and trustworthy navigational sign was to follow the North Star. Unlike other stars, it never changes position and always indicates where true north can be found.

In *Hamlet,* Shakespeare has Polonius state a Pole Star Principle to his son, Laertes, who is leaving for Paris:

> This above all: to thine own self be true,
> And it must follow, as the night the day,
> Thou canst not then be false to any man.
> (Act 1, Scene 3)

The Principle of Nonviolence

Nonviolence is a Pole Star Principle. For Dr. Martin Luther King Jr., nonviolence was an overarching effectiveness principle. It has moral underpinnings, to be sure, but King's effectiveness premise was that "Nonviolence seeks to win friendship and understanding. The end result of nonviolence is redemption and reconciliation. The purpose of nonviolence is the creation of the

Beloved Community. Nonviolence seeks to defeat injustice" (n.d., p. 1).

Under the overarching umbrella principle of nonviolence, Dr. King articulated a sequence of principles for engaging in nonviolent social change.

▶ *Principle 1: Gather information.* Learn all you can about the problems you see in your community through the media, social and civic organizations, and by talking to the people involved.

▶ *Principle 2: Educate others.* Armed with your new knowledge, it is your duty to help those around you, such as your neighbors, relatives, friends and co-workers, better understand the problems facing society. Build a team of people devoted to finding solutions. Be sure to include those who will be directly affected by your work.

▶ *Principle 3: Remain committed.* Accept that you will face many obstacles and challenges as you and your team try to change society. Agree to encourage and inspire one another along the journey.

▶ *Principle 4: Peacefully negotiate.* Talk with both sides. Go to the people in your community who are in trouble and who are deeply hurt by society's ills. Also go to those people who are contributing to the breakdown of a peaceful society. Use humor, intelligence, and grace to lead to solutions that benefit the greater good.

▶ *Principle 5: Take action peacefully.* This step is often used when negotiation fails to produce results, or when people need to draw broader attention to a problem. It can include tactics such as peaceful demonstrations, letter-writing, and petition campaign.

▶ *Principle 6: Reconcile.* Keep all actions and negotiations peaceful and constructive. Agree to disagree with some people and with some groups as you work to improve society. Show all involved the benefits of changing, not what they will give up by changing. (n.d.)

While presented by Dr. King as sequential, it is clear that these six operational principles are not simply linear steps. They also interact and have recursive feedback effects as they are adhered to and take effect. *Gathering information* (#1) continues throughout a nonviolence intervention for social change, as does *educating others* (#2). *Remaining committed* (#3) is likewise ongoing. The first three principles set the stage for the remaining three in the sequence: *peacefully negotiate* (#4), *take action peacefully* (#5), and *reconcile* (#6). These operational and sequential principles provide detailed guidance for adhering to the overarching principle of nonviolence. Both the Pole Star Principle and the six sequential principles meet the GUIDE criteria: They provide guidance (G), are useful (U), inspire (I), are developmentally adaptable (D) to a variety of situations, and can be evaluated (E).

The importance and utility of having operational principles to provide more detailed and nuanced guidance for adhering to an overarching Pole Star Principle is insightfully illustrated in this dialogue spoken by the character President Abraham Lincoln in the 2012 movie *Lincoln*:

A compass, I learnt when I was surveying, it'll . . . it'll point you True North from where you're standing, but it's got no advice about the swamps and desert and chasm that you'll encounter along the way. If in pursuit of your destination, you plunge ahead, heedless of obstacles, and achieve nothing more than to sink in a swamp . . . What's the use of knowing True North?

Advanced Practice Exercise

Chapters 7, 8, and 9 were devoted to identifying and articulating high-quality effectiveness principles that meet the GUIDE criteria. The sequential principles illustrated by the Truth and Reconciliation Commission process led by Archbishop Desmond Tutu in South Africa provide an opportunity to evaluate the quality and nature of a set of principles that aim to reconcile truth commissions and criminal prosecutions. International legal scholar and human rights advocate Lyal S. Sunga (2009) has proposed "Ten Principles for Reconciling Truth Commissions and Criminal Prosecutions." See Exhibit 11.4 for six of those principles. To what extent do these "principles" constitute principles as defined and discussed in this book? Evaluate these principles as a practice exercise in distinguishing and judging high-quality effectiveness principles. My answers are in Exhibit 11.4a on page 92.

EXHIBIT 11.4. Select Principles for Reconciling Truth Commissions and Criminal Prosecutions	
Proposed principles (Sunga, 2009)	**Assess these as meeting the GUIDE criteria for high-quality effectiveness principles**
1. No government or international authority, such as the UN, or regional collective security arrangement should ever grant blanket or unconditional amnesties from criminal prosecution because they negate criminal justice and contribute little to truth or reconciliation.	
2. In the case that a government has granted a blanket amnesty, no international or foreign court or tribunal should respect it.	
3. Truth commissions should be vested with mandates to investigate violations and report on them in a way that does not cause prejudice to eventual criminal prosecutions, even where the criminal justice system does not yet function adequately.	
4. Criminal proceedings should accord much greater attention to the rights of victims to an effective remedy.	
8. The international community should never grant amnesties from criminal prosecution for aggression, genocide, war crimes, or crimes against humanity.	
10. The UN should make every effort within the parameters of international law to apprehend perpetrators of crimes under international law, including those who attempt to extort, by force or threat, amnesty from criminal prosecution in regard to such crimes.	

EXHIBIT 11.4a. My Answers to Exhibit 11.4	
Proposed principles (Sunga, 2009)	**M. Q. P. assessments of the "principles"**
1. No government or international authority, such as the UN, or regional collective security arrangement should ever grant blanket or unconditional amnesties from criminal prosecution because they negate criminal justice and contribute little to truth or reconciliation.	This is stated as an absolute rule, not a principle. See Chapter 7 for the difference and why it matters.
2. In the case that a government has granted a blanket amnesty, no international or foreign court or tribunal should respect it.	Same as number 1.
3. Truth commissions should be vested with mandates to investigate violations and report on them in a way that does not cause prejudice to eventual criminal prosecutions, even where the criminal justice system does not yet function adequately.	Stated as a policy recommendation, not a principle. Restated as a principle it could read: *Conduct truth commissions in a way that does not cause prejudice to eventual criminal prosecutions.*
4. Criminal proceedings should accord much greater attention to the rights of victims to an effective remedy.	Stated as an opinion and policy recommendation, not a principle. Restated as a principle, it could read: *Attend to the rights of victims to an effective remedy in criminal proceedings.*
8. The international community should never grant amnesties from criminal prosecution for aggression, genocide, war crimes, or crimes against humanity.	Same as number 1 above.
10. The UN should make every effort within the parameters of international law to apprehend perpetrators of crimes under international law, including those who attempt to extort, by force or threat, amnesty from criminal prosecution in regard to such crimes.	Stated as a policy recommendation to the UN, not a principle. Restated as principles, two emerge: a. Pursue perpetrators of crimes under international law. b. Resist attempts to extort, by force or threat, amnesty from criminal prosecution by those who commit international crimes.

Useful

A high-quality principle is useful in informing choices and decisions. Its utility resides in being actionable, interpretable, feasible, and pointing the way toward desired results for any relevant situation.

CHAPTER 12

Principles Point the Way
to Desired Results

Confirmation bias: A tendency to favor information that confirms pre-existing views and to ignore information that contradicts pre-existing views. The bias is strongest for beliefs in which there has been significant emotional investment.
—WILLIAM LIDWELL, KRITINA HOLDEN, and JILL BUTLER (2015, p. 26)

A senior executive in a philanthropic foundation told me that principles-driven programming and principles-focused evaluation sounded *too process-oriented*. "We're all about results here," she insisted. I regularly encounter this perception. When principles are associated with processes rather than results, confirmation bias can ensue, leading to undervaluing or even opposing focusing on principles for either programming or evaluation. At the end of this chapter, I'll ruminate on our societal outcomes mania and the downside of overly simplified distinctions between process and outcome, but the primary focus here is making the case that effectiveness principles point to results. By results I mean outcomes, impacts, consequences (both intended and unintended), and any other ways that changes are labeled. The language of results is inconsistent and can be confusing. I don't want to get into the terminological quagmire. I'm basically talking about what difference it makes, if any, to follow principles. The emphasis in this chapter is that principles-focused evaluation involves assessing both implementation and outcomes. To what extent are effectiveness principles being followed in practice (implementation question)? If followed, to what extent are effectiveness principles supporting attainment of desired results (outcome question)?

As the GUIDE framework utility criterion for a high-quality principle (Chapter 6) states: A high-quality principle is useful in informing choices and decisions. Its utility resides in being actionable, interpretable, feasible, and pointing the way toward desired results for any relevant situation. A well-conceptualized, well-articulated, and useful principle points to consequences, implications, and results. This chapter provides examples of how principles-focused evaluation clarifies and addresses the outcome implications of principles.

Establishing a Baseline for Assessing Change: The Paris Declaration Example

The Paris Declaration on Aid Effectiveness was endorsed in 2005 by over 100 countries and organizations including the more developed aid-donor countries like the United States, developing countries from around the world, and international development institutions like the World Bank, the United Nations Development Group, and the Organization for Economic Co-operation and Development (OECD). It was a landmark international agreement and the culmination of several decades of attempts to improve the quality of aid and its impact on development. The 2005 Paris Declaration on Aid Effectiveness remains the dominant international statement on the aid relationship. The Paris Declaration aimed to reform how aid was done by (1) placing priority for aid on national strategies developed by countries receiving aid, (2) aligning donor strategies with receiving country priorities, (3) harmonizing aid strategies among donors, (4) managing for results, and (5) mutual accountability.

One effective way of pointing to outcomes is to begin with baselines, namely, the status of the international aid system at the time the Paris Declaration was signed. Then changes in outcomes can be assessed against those baselines. Chapter 25 presents details of how implementation of the Paris Declaration Principles was evaluated, an exemplar of principles-focused evaluation. The five Paris Declaration Principles imply outcomes. This becomes especially clear when the baseline for each principle is made explicit. Exhibit 12.1 takes the five Paris Declaration Principles and makes explicit the baseline and outcome implications of each principle.

By conceptualizing baselines and outcomes embedded in principles, whether the outcomes are explicit or implied, a principles-focused evaluation framework is created that makes outcome evaluation

part of the design. In the case of the Evaluation of the Paris Declaration Principles (see Chapter 25), the three overarching evaluation questions were addressed—(1) compliance with the principles, (2) outcomes of adherence to the principles, and (3) larger impacts—and that's how the evaluation data collection and final report were organized.

1. What are the factors that have shaped and limited the implementation of the Paris Declaration reforms and their effects? (Compliance with principles)

2. What improvements have been made in aid effectiveness as targeted in the Paris Declaration? (Aid effectiveness outcomes)

3. What contributions have improvements in aid effectiveness made to sustainable development results? (Impact)

The evaluation of the Paris Declaration Principles provides a fairly straightforward way of seeing how principles-focused evaluation can be outcomes oriented. Chapter 25 details how adherence to the principles and the resulting outcomes were measured. The next example is more nuanced because the interim outcomes are implicit.

Youth Homelessness Programs

Chapter 26 presents and discusses principles for overcoming youth homelessness. These were also presented in Exhibit 3.1. These principles were developed by a collaboration among six distinct programs working with homeless youth. While the overall goal shared by these programs (and for which they were funded) was getting homeless youth into affordable and sustainable housing, the principles articulated and shared by the collaborating programs imply and point to interim outcomes that contribute to the overarching housing goal. Exhibit 12.2 takes four of the principles and suggests an interim outcome implied by each

EXHIBIT 12.1. Paris Declaration Principles of Aid Effectiveness *Baselines and Outcomes*		
Paris Declaration Principles	**Baseline situation at the time the Paris Declaration was signed**	**Desired outcomes and evaluation evidence needed to assess degree of outcome attainment**
1. **Ownership:** *Developing countries set their own strategies for poverty reduction, improve their institutions, and tackle corruption.*	Country development agendas are heavily influenced by international agencies and the national interests of donor countries.	Developing countries take control of their strategies for poverty reduction, improving their institutions and tackling corruption. *Evaluation evidence needed:* Independent analysis of developing country priorities and how they are determined.
2. **Alignment:** *Donor countries align behind these objectives and use local systems.*	Donor countries impose their own agendas on developing countries in providing development assistance.	Donor aid aligns with developing country priorities. *Evaluation evidence needed:* Independent analysis of donor programs in relation to developing country priorities.
3. **Harmonization:** *Donor countries coordinate, simplify procedures, and share information to avoid duplication.*	Donor countries operate autonomously in their development assistance and programming.	Donor countries coordinate their development assistance with each other. *Evaluation evidence needed:* Independent analysis of donor programs and how they are determined.
4. **Results:** *Developing countries and donors shift focus to development results and results get measured.*	Developing countries and donors focus on program activities, not results.	Developing countries and donors focus together on program activities and whether they lead to mutually agreed-on desired results. *Evaluation evidence needed:* Independent analysis of evaluation approach.
5. **Mutual accountability:** *Donors and partners are accountable for development results.*	Only donor countries are required to be accountable.	Mutual accountability becomes the norm. *Evaluation evidence needed:* Independent analysis of donor and developing country accountability approach and relationship.

Note. See Chapter 25 for background and details on the Paris Declaration Evaluation as an exemplar of principles-focused evaluation.

EXHIBIT 12.2. Youth Homelessness Principles
Examples of Interim Outcomes and Corresponding Evaluation Questions

Principles for helping youth overcome homelessness	Implied interim outcomes	Principle-focused evaluation questions	Connection to the overarching housing outcome
1. **Journey oriented:** Interact with youth to help them understand the interconnectedness of past, present, and future as they decide where they want to go and how to get there.	a. Youth understand and can articulate the interconnectedness of their past, present, and future. b. Youth have a plan for their future.	a. To what extent can youth articulate the interconnectedness of their past, present, and future? b. Do youth have a future plan? Do they express ownership of the plan? What is the nature and quality of the plan?	Youth are more likely to attain and maintain housing if they (a) understand what led to their homelessness and (b) have a future plan to which they are committed that includes having housing.
2. **Trauma informed:** Recognize that most homeless youth have experienced trauma; build relationships, responses, and services on that knowledge.	a. Youth understand the nature and effects of the trauma they have experienced. b. The trauma is being treated to make it manageable.	a. To what extent are youth aware of the trauma they have experienced and its effects on them? b. How is trauma being treated, and with what results?	Acknowledging and dealing with the trauma of homelessness is necessary to take the steps needed to reduce the effects of trauma, which makes having the capacity to maintain housing more likely.
3. **Harm reduction:** Contain the effects of risky behavior in the short term and seek to reduce its effects in the long term.	a. Youth reduce risky behaviors.	a. To what extent are risky behaviors addressed and reduced?	Risky behaviors increase the risks of homelessness. Reducing risky behaviors increases the chances of keeping a job, staying in school, and maintaining housing.
4. **Trusting youth–adult relationships:** Build relationships by interacting with youth in an honest, dependable, authentic, caring, and supportive way.	a. Youth learn how to create and manage healthier relationships. b. Youth experience trust and learn how to create and manage trusting relationships.	a. To what extent and in what ways do youth learn how to create and manage healthier relationships? b. What do youth learn about trusting relationships? How does this learning affect them?	Youth are often homeless because of bad relationships with parents, roommates, landlords, teachers, and others in positions of authority. Learning to manage these relationships in a healthier way increases the chances of having positive relationships that affect having housing.

one. Corresponding principles-focused evaluation questions are then made explicit. Finally, the connection between the interim outcome and the ultimate outcome (housing) is identified. This is offered as a way of showing how outcomes can be extracted from principles to make a principles-focused evaluation outcomes oriented. It also represents a framework for how interim outcomes embedded in principles can be connected to ultimate outcomes and desired impacts.

Principles Can Integrate Processes and Outcomes

The Blandin Foundation is a private, independent foundation in Grand Rapids, Minnesota. Endowed with assets of approximately $360 million, it is one of only a handful of foundations in the United States focused exclusively on rural communities and is the largest rural-based private foundation in Minnesota. The foundation's philanthropic model and strategic approach are informed by the principle "Nurture committed connections." Senior leadership undertook a yearlong reflective practice evaluation in which they examined (1) what that principle means, (2) the degree to which it was being adhered to in the foundation's work, and (3) the results of adhering to the principle. A major insight emerged: *committed connections constitute both a process (a way of engaging with communities) and an outcome (strong, healthy relationships and increased social capital).* How this insight emerged through the principle-focused evaluation and its implications for the foundation's philanthropic work reveal the significance of *integrating processes and outcomes through the lens of principles-driven programming and principles-focused evaluation.*

The Principles-Focused Evaluation Context

The Blandin Foundation supports and works with rural Minnesota communities

"as they design and claim vibrant, resilient futures" (Annette, Fauth, & Ahcan, 2015, p. 43). The foundation awards grants in rural Minnesota (about $12 million per year), operates a community leadership program (7,000 served over 29 years), engages in public policy and community engagement (broadband, student success, etc.), and invests in strategic communications. In 2012, the foundation's trustees and senior leadership team decided to take a new look at their annual review process, giving equal weight to "What are we learning?" and "In what ways are we delivering on our strategic plan?" They generated a menu of possibilities for systematic reflective practice.

> We went to where our energy took us, to dive deeply into an element of the foundation's strategic framework: *committed connections.* What patterns could we see in our work and experiences as we stood with communities, grantees, policy partners, peers and many other long-time partners in strengthening rural Minnesota communities? (Annette et al., 2015, p. 43)

Focus on Committed Connections

The leadership team's deep dive into committed connections

> brought us a flood of new understanding, and ways we could strengthen our role as a perpetual connector. It was exciting—for us, for our trustees. We reported the following insights in our annual assessment report to our trustees:

▶ Committed Connections are core to the Foundation's work.

▶ Committed Connections deepen over time.

▶ A Committed Connection is both process and outcome.

▶ Committed Connections can take many forms:

  ▷ Connecting people to each other (individually, small groups)

  ▷ Connecting people to networks

  ▷ Connecting people to knowledge

  ▷ Connecting people to issues

▷ Connecting issues to issues (breaking down silos between issues)

▷ Connecting people to resources

▷ Connecting people to opportunities

▷ Connecting people to action (from talk to action)

▷ Connecting people to organizations

▷ Connecting organizations to each other

▷ Connecting people to communities

▷ Connecting communities to each other

▷ Connecting communities to regions

▷ Disconnecting people from ineffective or dysfunctional connections

These insights formed the basis for recognizing and nurturing the full continuum of different connector roles played by the Foundation staff. Through cross-case thematic analysis as a staff team, we deepened our shared understanding of, commitment to, and actions focused on *committed connections*. We also strengthened how we engage in case-based reflective practice. (Annette et al., 2015, p. 43)

What I want to reiterate here is the breakthrough insight that the principle of nurturing committed connections integrated process dimensions (how staff engage with communities and do their work) and outcomes (strong, healthy relationships and increased social capital). The next section, with a different foundation and a different result, takes this point further.

Reframing Processes and Outcomes: Mapping Systemic Interrelationships

I opened this chapter with the comment from a senior executive in a self-identified "outcomes-driven" philanthropic foundation that principles-driven programming and principles-focused evaluation sounded *too process-oriented*. I then indicated that at the end of this chapter I'd ruminate on the downside of simplistic distinctions between processes and outcomes. That time has arrived.

The executive's foundation funded programs that promote human rights

internationally. The foundation was resistant to requests to fund capacity building, including evaluation capacity building. They understood that capacity needed to be developed, but in their strategic framework they distinguished between processes and outcomes, and capacity in their framework was identified as process, that is, about getting ready to achieve outcomes rather than actually achieving them. To open up the possibility of reframing how they were thinking about processes and outcomes, I took the staff through an exercise like the examples in this chapter, showing how principles point to outcomes. Increased capacity is an interim (immediate or short-term) outcome that organizations promoting human rights need to attain if they are to be effective in increasing human rights protections, the ultimate outcome. Identifying immediate, intermediate (interim), and longer-term outcomes and connecting them together as a hierarchy of outcomes presents a different way of thinking than dividing that hierarchy of outcomes into processes versus outcomes. Increased organizational capacity becomes an outcome needed to increase organizational effectiveness and attain desired societal changes (ultimate outcomes). Outcome mapping (International Development Research Centre, 2007) and outcome harvesting (see Chapter 32) are frameworks that employ this logic.

The foundation was implicitly operating on a principle of promoting human rights. I say "implicitly" because this statement was considered a strategy, not a principle, which was fine. The outcome embedded in that principle, or strategy, was an increase in human rights protections. The process to achieve that outcome was grant making to human rights organizations. This is standard, linear logic model thinking, which is widespread and can be helpful in clarifying the pathway to outcomes. But such thinking also can have a downside.

Making a hard-and-fast distinction between process and outcome is a manifestation of Cartesian dualism that leads to the compartmentalization and separation of phenomena, emphasizing their categorical distinctiveness rather than their interconnectedness. In the current outcomes mania, attention to processes (how one gets to outcomes) has somehow become of secondary importance, if attended to at all. Black box experimental designs epitomize this inattention to and neglect of process. But process, like context, matters. Outcomes depend on and flow from processes within some particular context. That is one way of seeing interconnections, the traditional and dominant linear framing.

But the influence of dualism runs deep and hinders seeing, framing, understanding, and acting on interconnectedness. In graduate school I participated in a sociology of development seminar in which a major focus was on whether democracy is a means or an end. Recently, I've encountered discussions (more like arguments) concerning whether human rights, or capacity building, or leadership development, or even evaluation are a means or an end, and correspondingly, whether principles-focused evaluation should be thought of primarily as process oriented or outcomes oriented. At stake in these arguments are intervention designs, program models, conceptual frameworks, evaluation questions, policy formulations, and funding for all of the preceding.

Systems thinking shifts the focus from categorical separations and siloed distinctions to interconnections and interrelationships. So in the human rights foundation we took on the question: How are human rights, democracy, evaluation, and evaluation capacity interconnected and interdependent? This took us in quite a different direction from asking which is process and which is outcome, and what processes lead to what outcomes.

So let's connect the dots to show how principles point to outcomes while also valuing process. A values commitment to human rights is a foundation of inclusive democracy. Informed, inclusive decision making is critical to democracy. Informed decision making requires credible, meaningful, and relevant information on which

to base democratic deliberations and decisions. Generating credible, meaningful, and relevant information is the function of evaluation. Without evaluation capacity, including the capacity to think evaluatively, informed decision making is not possible, which undercuts democracy and threatens the commitment to human rights. This web of interconnections cannot be reduced to distinct processes and outcomes. These are system, and systemic, interrelationships, each element of which must function for the whole to function.

These are also complex, nonlinear, and dynamic interconnections. Evaluation capacity is not some fixed state, some predetermined, operational outcome. Changes in technology, demographics, cultural context, politics, the global economy, public health, climate change, gender relationships, ideological conflicts, and civil unrest, to name but a few of the more obvious factors, pose new challenges to human rights, democratic structures, and decision-making processes, and meaningful, trustworthy, useful evaluation. Evaluation capacity must evolve to deal with changing conditions and emergent evaluands beyond traditional projects and programs. Principles are one such new evaluand (focus of evaluation). Evaluation must evolve to assess the effectiveness and system impacts of new evaluands like strategies, cross-sector interventions, integrated development initiatives, interconnected sustainability development goals, and global systems change.

Evaluation is more than a compliance activity, a bureaucratic accountability imperative, and a paperwork mandate. Capacity to comply, feed the bureaucratic monster, and get paperwork done—these do not inspire. These are the shadow forces that undermine evaluation capacity building by making evaluation itself a mere administrative or managerial task.

But the vision of evaluation capacity building as critical to healthy, inclusive, human-rights-affirming, and democratic dialogue, engagement, and decision making—that is a vision of evaluation capacity building as *both* process and outcome, as both means and ends, and as part of the integral web of our highest ideals.

From this perspective, evaluation capacity is not a destination. It is a journey without a fixed or even certain destination. And the fellow travelers on that journey, among many others, are human rights and democracy.

Conclusion: The Utility of Principles

This chapter has provided examples of how principles-focused evaluation clarifies and addresses the outcome implications of principles. Exhibit 12.3 presents the sequence of evaluation questions that constitute a comprehensive principles-focused evaluation, one that begins by evaluating the meaningfulness of the principles, then addresses adherence and concludes with attention to outcomes and impacts. A well-conceptualized, well-articulated, and useful principle points to consequences, implications, and results of adhering to the principle so that those hypothesized consequences, implications, and results can be evaluated. The next chapter takes an even broader look at the utility of principles, further elaborating the *U* in the GUIDE framework for effectiveness principles.

Practice Exercise

Exhibit 12.2 analyzed four principles for working with homeless youth by making explicit implied and embedded interim outcomes and their connections to the overarching outcome of getting homeless youth into affordable and sustainable housing. Below are four more principles for working with homeless youth. Using the outcomes framework in Exhibit 12.2, identify the interim outcomes for the principles below and articulate how those interim outcomes are connected to and supportive of achieving the overarching housing outcome.

Nonjudgmental: Interact with youth without labeling or judging them on the basis of background, experiences, choices, or behaviors.

Strengths based: Start with and build upon the skills, strengths, and positive characteristics of each youth.

Positive youth development: Provide opportunities for youth to build a sense of competency, usefulness, belonging, and power.

Holistic: Engage youth in a manner that recognizes that mental, physical, spiritual, and social health are interconnected and interrelated.

EXHIBIT 12.3. Full Sequence of Principles-Focused Evaluation Questions

Principles-focused evaluation questions	Evaluation criteria
1. To what extent are the principles meaningful?	Apply the GUIDE criteria to the principles.[*]
2. To what extent are the principles adhered to behaviorally?	Adherence means *walking the talk:* Are the principles being followed in practice?
3. What are the results of following the principles?	Identify and evaluate desired outcomes and impacts that flow from the principles.

[*]Chapter 35 provides tools and rubrics for applying the GUIDE criteria to principles.

CHAPTER 13

Diverse Uses of Principles across an Organization

NORA F. MURPHY

HEATHER HUSEBY

Previously, I have referred to and drawn on the principles-focused evaluation titled *Nine Guiding Principles to Help Youth Overcome Homelessness* (Murphy, 2016). Chapter 3 presents the nine principles that were evaluated (Exhibit 3.1). They are not repeated here, so do a quick review before reading this chapter (see p. 18). Chapter 26 presents details about the evaluation. Nora Murphy conducted the principles-focused youth homelessness study and has continued working with one of the six collaborating agencies, YouthLink in Minneapolis, on how the principles apply to all aspects of the organization. Her contribution in this chapter is to elaborate and elucidate the ripple effects of the principles-focused evaluation, thereby expanding and deepening what the *U* for *useful* means in the GUIDE framework. (In Chapter 34, Nora shares her perspective on and experiences with becoming and being a principles-focused evaluator.)

Heather Huseby, Executive Director of YouthLink for 10 years, reflects on what it has meant to become strategically principles based over the last 4 years. In 2004, YouthLink was undergoing leadership and organizational turmoil and fragmentation. The board terminated the executive director and hired Heather as a part-time consultant because of her expertise in strategic leadership development. She designed a plan for improvement and growth. Working part-time for a year, she brought unity and vision back into what had become a chaotic, fragmented organization. She reorganized programming, put finances on solid ground, terminated some staff, and established strategic priorities. After staying on for 1 more year as a consultant to monitor the implementation of the design, she was hired as the executive director of YouthLink. Over the course of her decade of leadership, she has continued to develop the organization, focusing most recently on making all aspects of the work principles-based.

My thanks to Nora and Heather for this multidimensional look at the utility of evidence-based effectiveness principles.

—M. Q. P.

Serving Homeless Youth

On any given night in Minnesota, 4,000 young people will experience homelessness. Many of these young people, ages 16–23, will visit YouthLink, located in downtown Minneapolis. Established more than 40 years ago, YouthLink connects young people with a community of resources and support including assistance meeting basic needs, meeting employment or educational goals, accessing mental and physical health resources, or finding supportive housing. YouthLink was named as the host site for the Youth Opportunity Center (YOC), a unique collaborative model bringing together a variety of organizations and agencies that provide resources young people experiencing homelessness may need—all in one location. This center was a key recommendation in the *Ten Year Plan to End Homelessness in Minneapolis and Hennepin County* (Commission to End Homelessness, 2006). YouthLink's mission is to "support and empower young people on their journey to self-reliance," and their vision is "a community in which all youth, without regard to their living situation, have an equal opportunity to pursue their goals and dreams, and an equal likelihood of achieving them."

Transitioning to a Principles-Driven Organization

Readiness

YouthLink's executive director, Heather Huseby, EdD, was and is committed to transitioning YouthLink to a principles-driven organization. She invited Nora to YouthLink to start the conversation about what that could look like and how evaluation could support the transition. We began by sitting down with the entire leadership team, a signal to me that, as executive director, she wanted this to be an integrated effort agency-wide. We had people representing community partnerships, programming,

operations, development, and communications around the table. All of the participants described how they saw the principles as relevant to their roles within the organization, their hopes for how principles might impact their work, and their vision for principles applied to the organization as a whole. As I listened, two readiness factors became apparent: (1) everyone in the group seemed genuinely supportive of this organizational shift, despite varying levels of understanding, and (2) they seemed to like and respect each other. While these things may seem trivial or extraneous, staff who don't work together well, or staff resistant to the impending change, make it hard to create a positive evaluation and change culture.

Testing the Principles

The first step in this partnership was to pull together groups of stakeholders from the YouthLink community and engage them in a mapping activity that would allow them to think deeply about the principles and platform for change concepts, provide feedback about what was missing or what didn't belong, and ask questions for clarification and understanding. Members of the Terra-Luna organizational development team held five sessions with different groups of stakeholders: directors and supervisors, housing staff, drop-in staff, and youth. The following six ideas are themes that emerged across the four groups.

1. The principles were accepted as essential. None of the principle statements was edited. However, it was noted in one session that they were "race-free" statements. The group felt this was problematic given that race is such an important factor in the lives of the youth.

2. People fundamentally saw the principles as connected and intertwined, not separate. Certain principles naturally clustered together for some people, and clustered in different ways for other

groups. But the bottom line is that they are interrelated and cannot be learned about and done in isolation from one another.

3. Staff generally expressed that they appreciated being able to spend time working on creating common understandings.

4. Articulating the principles allows staff to "place a stake in the ground" and to validate the things they do that are important—but not always valued—such as relationship building and collaboration.

5. Staff generally do not want to help youth within a broken and oppressive system but want to work in a way that creates systemic change. Race and oppression were mentioned in four of five sessions, and staff members pointed out on numerous occasions that equity and social justice are missing from principles. As one person observed, "We don't want to be a part of the problem. Social services are late to fight for social equity."

6. Building community and social connectedness is essential to the work. Staff felt that part of services is offering youth a community.

Developing a Shared Vision

TerraLuna was invited to participate in YouthLink's annual staff retreat to share the themes that emerged from staff interviews. The YouthLink leadership team felt it was crucial that all YouthLink staff hear the results of the report on TerraLuna's concept-mapping activities and provide a space for staff input on the developmental evaluation's next steps. But they also felt it was important to include the perspectives of board members and youth served by YouthLink. With the center closed for a day, staff, leadership, board members, and a small group of youth were convened to (1) develop a common understanding of the

principles and good practice; (2) share the themes that surfaced in the staff mapping exercise; (3) discuss how YouthLink can become a "principles-driven" agency; and (4) interact, inform, enjoy, and have fun. The following agenda was developed by the TerraLuna team; Marney Thomas, director of partnerships and community engagement at YouthLink; and Bob Nelson, director of operations at YouthLink.

TerraLuna compiled all of the data collected that day, and the main themes that emerged across all five stakeholder sessions were:

1. The *principles are essential* to the work.

2. People fundamentally saw the principles as *connected and intertwined,* not separate.

3. Staff generally noted that they appreciated being able to spend time *working on creating common understandings.*

4. Articulating the principles allows staff to "*place a stake in the ground*" and to *validate the things they do that are important*—but not always valued—such as relationship building and collaboration.

5. Staff generally do not want to help youth within a broken and oppressive system, but want to *work in a way that creates systemic change.*

6. *Building community and social connectedness* is essential to the work. Staff generally felt that part of their services is offering youth a community.

7. In addition to the themes identified, there were two emergent principles: *systems change/social justice* and *community/sense of belonging.*

This day was critically important. The energy was one of possibilities and trust. Principles-based work creates space for creativity and innovation and encourages people to think of new possibilities. It demonstrated the commitment to transparency in the process, ensured that everyone had the same information regarding the process and what was learned, and supported a shared vision for the next phase of the work. Staff and youth reported that they felt that administration trusted and respected their wisdom and ideas. Dr. Heather Huseby felt that the staff retreat with the youth and board was "the most impactful, unifying retreat YouthLink ever held—with the most positive results—as a result of the focused on the principles."

Organizational Change toward a Shared Vision Anchored in Reflective Practice

The retreat left the staff with a lot of possible next steps. TerraLuna shared in its report that "There's a lot here. We know that. But it all seems to be do-able. There is staff buy-in. There is trust that these are the *right* principles. There is excitement around the direction the organization is taking. There is goodwill and positive regard among staff members. But your vision, leadership and a consistent commitment to co-creating the shared vision for a principles-driven Youth-Link makes this feasible." Together we developed a reflective practice approach that

engaged organizational development, staff development, and innovative program development (see Exhibit 13.1). The following sections describe what these components look like.

Innovative Program Development

Youth Engagement and Youth Voice

The Youth–Adult Principles Advisory Committee (PAC) was convened over a 5-month period from October 2014 to February 2015. With positive energy, PAC was productive in bringing youth more fully into engagement with the principles.

YouthLink Connector Pilot Project

While this project is guided by the nine guiding principles, its overarching principle, community connectedness, emerged through an iterative process with the Youth-Link community. The overarching goal is to help young people develop a healthy network of support with other youth by nurturing and deepening existing relationships and creating new connections intentionally

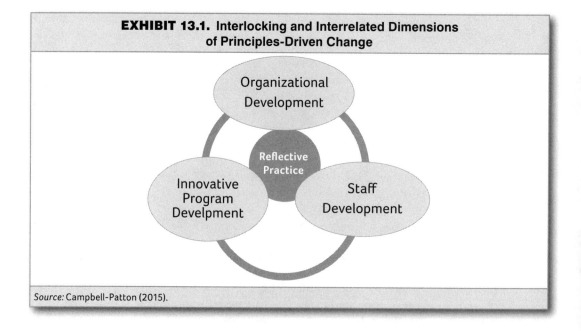

EXHIBIT 13.1. Interlocking and Interrelated Dimensions of Principles-Driven Change

Organizational Development

Reflective Practice

Innovative Program Develment

Staff Development

Source: Campbell-Patton (2015).

with community representatives. The project proposal outlined how the connector program was principles driven and articulated principles-based outcomes for youth and adults. The purpose of the principles-focused evaluation was threefold: (1) to tell the story of what happened, (2) to document processes and outcomes, and (3) to inform learning so adaptations could be made for future iterations of this program.

New Housing Site

A new 47-bed permanent supportive housing facility was being planned onsite at YouthLink at the time of this writing. Leadership saw this as an opportunity to consider how the principles could inform all aspects of the conceptualization of the new housing and programming. The architecture design included specific attention to the nine principles. The new housing model's platform for change as well as its overall operating handbook will be principles focused.

Staff Development

Performance Evaluations

We heard repeatedly from staff in different roles that annual performance evaluations should be revised to address the shift to principles-based work. The director of operations took the lead on this work, partnering with the office manager to revise the existing performance evaluation. Evaluators and staff worked together to review and make changes to the section of the performance review document that focused on principles. The most significant change was to ask how the principles were used in interacting with colleagues and youth. Something that staff voiced as important at the all-staff retreat was that they also work together in a principles-based way, so we wanted to reflect that in the performance evaluations. The document was finalized and ready to pilot for staff reviews in December 2014. Because they were piloting

the principles-based section of the performance evaluation, they didn't use scores in that section when assigning points to a person's overall score.

New Staff Orientation

The principles training for new staff ensures that everyone understands principles both conceptually and in their practical applications. Each person can connect through his or her strengths using this model. The longer-term plan is to produce a video for each principle, another video that talks about the development of the principles, and a video describing the set of principles as a whole. The videos will be supported by a training manual as well as other downloadable documents. It is possible that in the future, YouthLink could copyright the training manuals.

Organizational Development

Hiring

Integrating principles into hiring was not on the initial list of ways that the organization felt it needed to develop. However, at a supervisors' meeting focused on integrating the principles into their work, the supervisors noted that it would be helpful if they knew whether applicants were able to think and work in a principles-based way. As a result, the principles have been posted on the website and applicants are asked to address the principles in their cover letter.

Supervising

In October 2014, housing staff looked at how each individual principle is relevant to their work. Even with this support, staff at housing sites were struggling to put the principles into the programming itself. When this reaction was brought to a supervisors' meeting, the leadership group decided that they would spend 2 weeks focusing on one principle at a time. Every 2 weeks, they began discussing a principle in staff meetings. It has become an ongoing cycle to be repeated sequentially. During the week, they look at one specific principle and discuss how it plays out. They focus on the implications for practice and share what they learn through their observations and reflections. Once they have gone through all of the principles, they plan to circle back to the first one, allowing them to deepen their learning and understanding developmentally over time.

YOC Partners

As of October 2014, the YOC partners had been introduced to the principles and engaged in discussion around principles-based work. It was agreed that it would be helpful for them to have a handbook that described YouthLink's principles-based approach. Staff finished the handbook and has given it to YOC partners. The developmental evaluation team suggested an organizational self-assessment focused on the principles. This is under development as YouthLink has created a principles-based memorandum of understanding for the partnership.

Board of Directors Development

At a board meeting, staff introduced the stories of two young people and asked the directors to think about what the stories mean for their work as board members. The stories were used to help them understand how the principles work in practice and affect youth. This led to a shift from the nuts-and-bolts focus of a typical board meeting to reconnecting with why they became board members in the first place. The principles gave voice to inspiration.

Reflective Practice and Evaluation

Reflective Practice

Reflective practice is what it takes to make sure things are not getting separated and siloed. The tendency is to create projects and programs—and this is sometimes appropriate—but when projects happen separately from everything else and they don't feed into the larger conversation, things get siloed. The principles are the glue. The reflective practice keeps the glue fresh.

In reflective practice meetings, staff shared that:

▶ Principles-focused conversations between supervisors and staff have become deeper, more meaningful, and less defensive.

▶ Group dynamics have shifted. Instead of recognizing the same staff over and over, a focus on principles has intrinsically elevated a variety of staff members for their different strengths.

▶ Principles are showing up in unexpected places. Supervisors talked about asking themselves, for example, "How is my office space arranged as it relates to the principles?"

▶ The principle "strengths-based" has been powerful in helping supervisors reframe youth behaviors that staff would typically see as problematic by having a conversation about strengths.

▶ Some principles are harder to integrate than others. "Harm reduction" and "trauma informed" were identified as particularly challenging.

▶ "Positive youth development" is a big topic and one that supervisors feel Youth-Link hasn't yet tackled in a meaningful way.

Evaluation

The overarching hope is to develop an ongoing evaluation plan for the organization that is principles based, allows the organization to meet its reporting commitments, and supports the organization's ongoing learning and development.

Conclusion

The principles certainly provide meaningful direction and inspiration. They are supporting ongoing development, which includes evaluating adherence and effects. In all these ways, the principles are proving useful. Staff at YouthLink are far too busy to just go through the motions of complying with some model. If what they're asked to do isn't useful, it doesn't get done. The principles are being judged by staff for their utility and, at least so far, the judgment is highly positive.

Likewise, the youth served by YouthLink are astute about what matters and sensitive to and turned off by meaningless rhetoric. The principles resonate with youth. The principles are affirming and anchoring, and useful without creating the feeling that something is being forced on them.

For the developmental evaluation team, the principles are highly utilization focused. We are keenly alert to, aware of, and take into account who the intended users are, and what the intended uses are, for any particular principles-focused initiative and the corresponding principles-focused evaluation.

Overall

Overall, the focus on principles has transformed the organization from a more "crisis-response, basic needs organization" to an organization that has adapted its overall design to the journey orientation of the youth. As Dr. Huseby described it:

"We have become an organization that is rooted in an evidence-based foundation of design and operation. This shift has changed the trajectory of the agency from . . . focusing simply on crisis [and] basic needs . . . [to] also focusing attention, resources and collaborative efforts on transformative services, including education, employment and housing. This is reflect[ed] by the planning of a new 47-bed permanent supportive housing facility onsite, GED school onsite, career development center planning, career pathway planning and hiring of education and employment navigators."

This shift is not accidental, and the path hasn't been easy or straightforward. In the three years since the finalization of the principles, Dr. Heather Huseby has taken a stand on the principles, consistently placing them at the heart of the work, of decision making, and of envisioning the future of YouthLink. She describes what this was like.

"We, as an organization, benchmark everything against the principles. This does require strong, consistent leadership; it requires leadership with a consistent vision and focus, and it requires leadership that understands the significance of an informed leadership team."

During this time frame the organization has gained national attention, growing from a budget of $3 million to $5 million, and launched a $6 million comprehensive campaign. Dr. Huseby observed, "This doesn't happen without a base of quality and the evidence-based principles are the root of this quality."

If the executive director had not gone through the reflective practice process around effective evidence-based principles of practice, this transformation to an evidence-based principles-focused organization may have taken longer to achieve. And even though there has been a tremendous shift, the work is not over. The organization will continue to change, as will the world and the youth it serves. Thus, YouthLink will need to continuously engage, deepen, and adapt its principles-based strategy. Focusing simultaneously on organizational development, staff development, and innovative program development creates a multilayered approach to support this learning-focused commitment to the principles.

Concluding Reflection

YouthLink's executive director offered these final reflections as we completed this chapter:

"I don't know how you can find a service provider organization that has embraced, integrated and become more principles-focused and evidence-based than Youth-Link has since our first conversations about principles-focused evaluation with the homeless youth collaboration almost 4 years ago. YouthLink has transformed over these years. This has included the challenge of adapting to the transformation of the young people we serve from being just 16–21 years old to being 16–24. This was a big change for us, serving this population of 'opportunity youth.' They require more transformative services, more 'bundled services' and better alignment with adult system support services/pathways. We've found how important it is to talk with those 'receiving' our youth [for other services] about 'evidence-based principles' and inform them about our principles-based approach to all of what we do."

CHAPTER 14

Evaluating the Utility
of Research-Derived Principles
for Enhancing Online Learning

Back in 1987, Chickering and Gamson articulated seven principles of good teaching. Then came the web, online learning, MOOCs, and myriad directions in support of student success. With clarity and verve, Bonk and Khoo combine a memorable acronym with motivational principles that move us into meaningful action.
—ANN HILL DUIN, Professor of Writing Studies, University of Minnesota
(Back cover blurb for Bonk & Khoo, 2014)

TEC-VARIETY is an acronym for a set of "motivational principles" for "online educators to appropriately harness the many affordances of the Web" (Bonk & Khoo, 2014, p. 5). Curtis J. Bonk, professor of instructional systems technology at Indiana University, was awarded the Most Outstanding Achievement Award from the U.S. Distance Learning Association Outstanding Adult Educator Award for the TEC-VARIETY framework. The framework "synthesizes the varied ways for enhancing Web pedagogy into a few principles . . . that, when combined, can powerfully boost the chances for online learning success. . . . Each letter of TEC-VARIETY stands for one or more motivational principles" (p. 10). Exhibit 14.1 presents the framework.

How to Approach and Evaluate a Set of Principles for Utility

In this chapter I'm going to use the TEC-VARIETY framework to illustrate one approach to evaluating a set of principles focusing on the U (Useful) criterion in the GUIDE framework. However, the other GUIDE criteria will also inevitably and necessarily come into consideration. Remember, principles-focused evaluation begins by asking if a principle is meaningful, coherent, and understandable. A principle can neither be implemented nor attain desired results if it's not reasonably clear in its guidance. Clarity of guidance increases usefulness. For each of the 10 principles in the TEC-VARIETY framework, it's appropriate to ask, using the GUIDE criteria, whether its guidance (G) is clear; whether it is useful (U), meaning actionable; whether it inspires (I); whether it can be *developed* contextually (D), meaning adapted to situational variations; and whether it is evaluable (E). To do so, I'll generate specific evaluation questions for each TEC-VARIETY principle, but with a particular emphasis on utility. The focus on utility comes from the authors of the TEC-VARIETY set of principles, for they posit the purpose of the principles as

EXHIBIT 14.1. Principles of the TEC-VARIETY Framework

1. *Tone/climate:* Ensure psychological safety, comfort, sense of belonging
2. *Encouragement:* Provide feedback, responsiveness, praise, supports
3. *Curiosity:* Offer surprise, intrigue, unknowns
4. *Variety:* Incorporate novelty, fun, fantasy
5. *Autonomy:* Ensure choice, control, flexibility, opportunities
6. *Relevance:* Make learning meaningful, authentic, interesting
7. *Interactivity:* Create collaborative, team-based, community-oriented processes
8. *Engagement:* Support and reward effort, involvement, investment
9. *Tension:* Include challenges, dissonance, controversy
10. *Yielding products:* Be goal driven with purposeful vision and ownership

being useful for online teaching. To set the stage for this exercise, let me briefly review how the TEC-VARIETY principles were developed.

Research Origins of the TEC-VARIETY Principles

The TEC-VARIETY framework is based on research about learning adapted and interpreted to identify and elaborate factors affecting online learner success and generate strategies to mitigate online learner attrition. Here is an overview of some of the research from which the TEC-VARIETY principles were extracted.

Encouragement and Feedback Principle Based on Behaviorism: Learner Motivation through Carrots and Sticks

A central aspect of behaviorism is that students, like all humans, learn by associating a stimulus with a response. Human behavior, being malleable, can be reinforced or extinguished. The theory of behaviorism and supporting research emphasize the importance of positive and negative feedback (carrots and sticks) and corrective learning. Bonk and Khoo (2014, p. 33) extrapolate

the principle of encouragement and feedback from behaviorism and apply it to online learning.

Autonomy Principle Based on Cognitivism: Learner Motivation through Intentional Goals, Beliefs, and Expectations

Bonk and Khoo (2014) reviewed studies documenting how to facilitate learner intrinsic motivation by supporting student needs for autonomy, competence, and relatedness (p. 36). Attribution theory, self-efficacy theory, goal orientation theory, and self-determination theory and supporting research in each of these specializations within cognitive psychology provide the basis for extrapolating principles of online learner autonomy and curiosity (pp. 35–36).

Tension, Variety, and Tone-Setting Principles Based on Constructivism: Learner Motivation through Active and Social Construction of Meaning

Constructivist theory and research has focused on how knowledge is socially constructed through social interactions and the creation of shared meanings. Specific constructivist-advocated teaching strategies include many active learning principles such as "situating tasks in real-world contexts, goal-based learning attuned to learner interests, and guiding and coaching a novice toward expert performance as in a cognitive apprenticeship" (p. 37). The Interaction Principle is supported by constructivist theory and research.

Relevancy Principle Based on Sociocultural Views: Learner Motivation through Considerations of the Cultural Milieu

Bonk and Khoo (2014) observe that "Perhaps the most widely researched teaching strategy of this recent sociocultural learning era is that of making learning relevant, authentic, and meaningful to students" (p. 39). They later note that "the notion of relevancy is pivotal in many contemporary pedagogical frameworks that recognize learner-centered principles such as authenticity, collaboration, and active engagement" (p. 40).

From Research-Derived Principles to Principles-Focused Evaluation

This brief overview cannot do justice to the extensive review of theory-based research findings that are the source for and undergird the 10 TEC-VARIETY principles. What is noteworthy is that a great deal of synthesis, interpretation, and extrapolation is required to move from research findings to principles. It is by no means a straightforward process. Indeed, it is necessary and appropriate to evaluate the results of such synthesis, interpretation, and extrapolation. Therefore, based on and inspired by the TEC-VARIETY Framework, I offer a set of criteria for evaluating research-derived principles in Exhibit 14.2.

Evaluating the Principles

Once principles have been identified, from research in this case, the action moves to evaluating both their implementation (whether they are actually being followed in practice) and, if followed, the results and impacts of doing so. That is the essence of principles-focused evaluation. Exhibit 14.3 makes explicit the utilization-focused evaluation questions connected to each principle. Usefulness, in this case, is judged by how well the principles inform decision making about teaching processes and the extent to which adhering to the principles leads to high-quality student learning online as hypothesized and asserted by the authors.

Conclusion

Embedded in principles are evaluation questions, typically both process and outcome questions. Surfacing, articulating, and posing those questions involves *process use,* meaning that the very process of examining the principles and generating evaluation questions is likely to have an impact on how the principles are understood and used. Posing and gathering data on outcome questions will support whatever the overall purposes of the evaluation are, whether formative, summative, developmental, accountability, knowledge generating, or some combination thereof. Exhibit 14.3 shows how to convert principles into useful principles-focused evaluation questions.

Practice Exercise

Complete Exhibit 14.3, p. 115, for Principles 3, 4, 7, 8, and 9. (See Exhibit 14.1, p. 112, for those principles.)

EXHIBIT 14.2. Criteria for Evaluating Research-Derived Principles Applied to the TEC-VARIETY Framework

Criteria for evaluating research-derived principles	TEC-VARIETY framework example	Evaluation questions
1. **Clarity of the principle**	Principle 1. Tone/climate: psychological safety, comfort, sense of belonging	Each of the 10 principles has a name followed by three additional clarifiers, but taken together do these cohere into a clear principle? Are psychological safety, comfort, and sense of belonging all dimensions of the same overall principle: *tone/climate*?
2. **Validity of the interpretation, extrapolation, and synthesis of the research findings and theory**	Tension, variety, and tone-setting principles are based on constructivism.	Is the line of reasoning from research findings and theory to the resulting principle(s) credible and persuasive?
3. **Balance of evidence**	"In sum, active and social collaborative strategies emphasizing the use of relevant and meaningful tasks (sixth principle), interactivity (seventh principle), engagement (eighth principle), and yielding products (tenth principle) underpin the entire TEC-VARIETY framework." (p. 40)	In presentation of the research findings in support of a principle, is the evidence presented in a balanced way, taking into account both research that supports the principle and research that leads to an opposite or contrary conclusion?
4. **Strength of evidence**	"The evolution of motivational models (including our TEC-VARIETY framework) portrays a shift from individual cognitive and affective processes to current views of a more dynamic and embedded relationship between the individual and her social context." (p. 41)	How strong is the cumulative research evidence that undergirds a principle?

		EXHIBIT 14.3. Examples of Utilization-Focused Process and Outcome Evaluation Questions for the TEC-VARIETY Framework		

Principle	Process evaluation questions	Outcome evaluation questions
1. *Tone/climate principle:* Ensure psychological safety, comfort, sense of belonging	What processes and activities are implemented to create a safe and comfortable learning climate?	To what extent do students feel psychologically safe and comfortable and have a sense of belonging?
2. *Encouragement principle:* Provide feedback, responsiveness, praise, supports	What feedback do students report experiencing? What are the nature of, mechanisms of, and modalities for feedback?	What do students learn from feedback? What is the impact? To what extent and in what ways do students feel supported?
5. *Autonomy principle:* Ensure choice, control, flexibility, opportunities	What choices, flexibility, and opportunities do students report? What are their reactions to those choices?	How does having choices have an impact on student participation and learning?
6. *Relevance principle:* Make learning meaningful, authentic, interesting	To what extent and in what ways do students report the course and learning they experience as being relevant, meaningful, authentic, and interesting?	How does relevance enhance participation, course completion, and learning outcomes?
10. *Yielding products principle:* Be goal driven with purposeful vision and ownership	How do students understand and react to the course goals and vision? To what extent do they feel ownership of the goals and vision?	To what extent and in what ways are participation, completion, and intended learning outcomes attained?

Inspiring

Principles are values based, incorporating and expressing ethical premises, which is what makes them meaningful. They articulate what matters, both in how to proceed and the desired result. That should be inspirational.

"I'm making this decision on principle, just to see how it feels."

Source: The Cartoon Bank; © Condé Nast.

Chapters 15–18 elucidate some ways in which principles INSPIRE.		
GUIDE framework for effectiveness principles	Chapter 6	GUIDE for Effectiveness Principles: The Characteristics of High-Quality Effectiveness Principles
G = GUIDING	Chapters 7–11	
U = USEFUL	Chapters 12–14	
I = INSPIRING	Chapter 15	Inspirational Principles Are Infused with Values
	Chapter 16	Principles-Focused Evaluation at the Grassroots in Africa: Inspirational Examples and Reflections *John Wilson*
	Chapter 17	Inspiring Principles: Distinguishing Overarching Principles from Operational Principles *Charmagne Campbell-Patton*
	Chapter 18	Principles-Focused Pedagogy of Evaluation: Inspired by Freirean Pedagogy

Inspirational Principles
Are Infused with Values

I believe it is an established maxim in morals that he who makes an assertion without knowing whether it is true or false, is guilty of falsehood; and the accidental truth of the assertion, does not justify or excuse him.

—ABRAHAM LINCOLN, U.S. president

Lincoln valued truth. In this quote, he sets a high standard for speaking truth. Without evidence to back up our assertions, we ought to be clear that we are expressing opinions. To assert that something is true without supporting evidence is immoral by Lincoln's standard. Principles-focused evaluation invites people to bring evidence to bear on their beliefs and assertions, to test whether they are adhering to their principles and examine the results of such adherence.

Lincoln was viewed as *a man of principle*. One of the highest accolades we can bestow on someone is to honor them as a woman or man of principle. Presumably such an accolade would meet Lincoln's standard of being backed up by evidence. We are rightly skeptical of self-evaluations in this regard. In Charles Dickens's classic story *A Christmas Carol*, the miser and misanthrope Ebenezer Scrooge says of himself: "I am a man of the highest principles and a most generous spirit!" Dickens uses the device of ghosts of Christmases past, present, and future to confront Scrooge with evidence of his miserliness and misanthropy, whereupon he is transformed. It's an inspiring story of evaluation evidence used to bring about change. Or at least I find it so.

The Personal Factor: Principles-Driven People

I find, generally, that principles-based programs and initiatives have been developed and are led by principles-driven people. This is the *personal factor* in principles-focused evaluation. In the research on evaluation that formed the basis for utilization-focused evaluation, we found that what we called "the personal factor" was a primary determinant, indeed, most often *the* primary determinant, of whether evaluation findings were used (Patton, 2008, 2011). Essentially, we found that an evaluation is more likely to be used if intended users find the evaluation meaningful and the questions relevant, and *care about the findings*.

119

They have to care. Caring comes from valuing. Valuing is at the core of rendering evaluative judgments. I'll say more about that below. For the moment, let's stay with the personal factor and engaging with principles-driven people as the primary intended users of principles-focused evaluation. The opportunity to work with principles-driven people is what inspired me to develop principles-focused evaluation. One such person was Steve Rothschild, whom I featured in a chapter in my book *Developmental Evaluation* (Patton, 2011, Ch. 2).

Steve Rothschild had a vision. He wanted to reduce poverty by providing corporate employers with chronically underemployed or unemployed workers, especially men of color, helping them get and keep jobs paying a livable wage plus benefits. Rothschild would bring to this vision considerable success in the business world. He is a former executive vice president of General Mills, where he led the marketing campaign that made Yoplait the number one yogurt brand in United States. He wanted to apply his knowledge, experience, and success in the private sector to alleviating poverty. The result was a major anti-poverty training and employment program called Twin Cities RISE!

Rothschild brought to this effort a strong commitment to making a difference. In our first meeting, when I cautioned that he was moving into an arena where many had tried and few had succeeded, he was undaunted and emphasized that the challenge appealed to him, much as the challenges of marketing Yoplait had almost 20 years earlier. He saw this new enterprise as a good fit with his intense desire to give something of value and importance back to the community in return for his own good fortune. In planning sessions he interwove vision, inspiration, and creativity with hard-core analysis, critical thinking, and thoughtful planning. He had reviewed and was openly critical of existing nonprofit and government-supported employment training programs. He was prepared to invest his own resources in this effort, put his credibility on the line, and visibly demonstrate a new way to do things.

He was motivated first and foremost by his commitment to combat racism, social injustice, and inequality. Before articulating intended outcomes, which he could do and valued the importance of (e.g., living-wage jobs with benefits), he talked about the principles and values that would be the foundation of the program. And he wanted to be sure that any evaluator he worked with shared those values and respected those principles, otherwise how could they trust each other? So, the first exercise I facilitated with his program design team was clarifying the values and principles on which the innovative program would be based. That was the very first document produced in the design process. To this day it remains the program's fundamental guidance document and action framework, revisited periodically. The seven guiding principles are: (1) be purpose-driven; (2) measure what counts; (3) be market driven; (4) create mutual accountability; (5) support personal empowerment; (6) create economic value from social benefit; and (7) be learning driven (Rothschild, 2012). Listed in the abstract like this, they may not appear to provide much guidance or be particularly inspiring. But through ongoing discussion, reflective practice, and reaffirmation, these principles have vitality and specific meaning within the organization and have provided ongoing inspiration and important direction at major forks in the road. For example, the principle of mutual accountability led to a formal, legal contract between participants and the program specifying the responsibilities and obligations of each. The early years of principles-focused developmental evaluation focused on what they meant in practice. Rothschild was a principles-driven social entrepreneur who created a principles-based organization that adopted principles-focused evaluation. He explained:

Throughout my corporate and nonprofit experience, I had been identifying and practicing what makes organizations strong and successful. Founding RISE! forced me to articulate the principles I've learned. . . .

I based our initial principles on my observations regarding what I had seen work in both sectors as both an executive and a member of corporate and nonprofit boards. As RISE! grew I revised them based on our experience. We learned exciting and often humbling lessons about what works and what doesn't. I've talked with the economists, researchers, and government officials and interviewed social entrepreneurs and the clients we serve. The seven principles are the distillation of insight from a lot of good minds and lessons learned from the frontline. (2012, pp. 11–12)

Inspirational Principles Grounded in Deeply Held Values

It is not the content of a company's values that correlates with performance, but the strength of conviction with which it holds those values, whatever they might be.
—JIM COLLINS, management consultant and author of *Good to Great* and *Built to Last*

Another updated example from *Developmental Evaluation* (Patton, 2011) concerns a family foundation that faced the challenge of transitioning to the next generation when the founding parents both died within a short time interval. This led to a substantial infusion of new assets into the endowment, a much larger philanthropic operation, more formal processes, increased staff, and greatly expanded grant making. I was asked to facilitate a board retreat (adult children and grandchildren of the founders and a couple of trusted longtime family friends) to begin a strategic planning process that would focus the foundation's mission going forward. After interviewing board members individually and hearing over and over again about the values that the founders lived by, I suggested that we devote the retreat to articulation of those values. Over the course of

a 2-day retreat, they told stories about the founders that made explicit how they lived their values. Those values became the foundation's guiding strategic document, one that they returned to year after year in subsequent retreats, always asking the values-driven evaluation question: *Are we walking the talk?* Are we operating in a way that the founders would recognize as upholding their values? Are the things we're accomplishing with the endowment they created true to what they cared about? And one of the things the founders cared about was courageously taking risks and supporting innovation. So we evaluated the grants portfolio using criteria based on innovation and risk taking.

I've found that many social innovators are driven as much, or more, by values than specifiable outcomes. Given the uncertainties of complex interventions and interactions, where the ends (outcomes, impacts, results) are uncontrollable, unpredictable, and emergent—values can become the anchor, the *only* knowable in an otherwise uncertain, unpredictable, uncontrollable, and complex world.

In *Getting to Maybe,* a book on successful social movements (Westley, Zimmerman, & Patton, 2006), inquiry into the motivations of social innovators revealed that those involved expressed *a sense of calling.* They saw things through their own personal and community lenses of strong values, and when they looked they saw things that were unacceptable, problems that were outrageous, and they felt compelled to act. They were driven by a vision of how the world should be and could be a better place. These were not management-by-objectives folks. These were values-driven visionaries. Martin Luther King Jr. said: "I have a dream," not "I have a metric." He inspired by offering a vision, not a rubric. Metrics and rubrics are valuable and useful tools, but inspiration moves people to action. The two must work together. That's why the GUIDE criteria for high-quality principles include both inspiration (I) and evaluation (E).

Values matter to values-driven social innovators because a deep sense of values undergirds their initiatives as their vision gets implemented through day-to-day operations and interactions. And if they are to engage with evaluators, those evaluators will need to be able to engage with them around their values. Strategies and tactics must be values based. Outcomes are thought of as manifestations of values. Innovation is what you promote, but *values are who you are.* American novelist Jennifer Crusie captured this insight when she responded to a question about the role of values in her writing: "Values aren't buses. . . . They're not supposed to get you anywhere. They're supposed to define who you are."

Which is where effectiveness principles come in, because *effectiveness principles are supposed to get you somewhere.* The perspective offered throughout this book is that an effectiveness principle is a statement that provides guidance about how to think or behave toward some desired result (either explicit or implicit), based on norms, values, beliefs, experience, and knowledge. Principles are derived from experience, expertise, values, and research. Principles are grounded in values about what matters to those who develop, adopt, and attempt to follow them.

GUIDE principles aim to be inspiring by making explicit and articulating values that guide both how something is done and what the desired result is. Principles are not achievable in the sense that the task is completed and the outcome accomplished; rather principles guide ongoing engagement across many discrete projects and multiple change initiatives. Principles that meet the GUIDE criteria are broadly values based, ethically grounded, and useful in informing decisions. Being useful incorporates and subsumes being relevant, because principles must be both meaningful and actionable. Effectiveness principles apply to both processes and outcomes, to both what is to be achieved and how it is

to be achieved, to both means and ends. When considering the inspirational nature of principles, this point deserves a bit of elaboration courtesy of Mahatma Gandhi. One of Gandhi's principles, as summarized by a Gandhi scholar, was to keep means and ends interconnected and apply the same values to both.

> It was Gandhi's firm conviction that means are at least as important as, and often even more important than, ends. It is, of course, desirable that ends should be good and reasonable. But they merely give a direction to life while the means adopted constitute life itself. Therefore, if the means are right, that is, if they conform to the tests of truth and nonviolence, even mistakes, errors and failures aid the growth of the individual. On the other hand, wrong means corrupt the soul and no good can ever come out of them. Gandhi repudiated categorically the idea that ends justify the means. (Santhanam, 2015, p. 1)

Gandhi's admonition is to be mindful that both means and ends are based on values, and to examine whether those values are consistent, meaningful, "good," and "right." The inspirational nature of principles is that they are grounded in values about what matters, are actionable, can be interpreted and applied contextually and situationally, require judgment in application, and can be evaluated for both process (Was the principle followed?) and results (Is following the principle taking us where we want to go?).

Outcomes-Based versus Principles-Based Mission Statements

Nonprofit organizations, nongovernmental agencies, philanthropic foundations, and government units vary in whether they frame their mission statements in terms of problems to be solved or principles to be followed. Exhibit 15.1 contrasts these different approaches to mission statements

	EXHIBIT 15.1. Problem-Focused versus Principles-Focused Mission Statements	
	Problem-focused mission aimed at specific changes	Principles-focused mission that states how the work is to be done
Mission statements	A *problem-focused mission* aims at solving a problem, for example: • reduce poverty • increase educational attainment • enhance the development of youth	A *principles-driven mission* describes how the work will be done, for example: • help people help themselves • engage and empower • build sustainable capacity
Mission example	*Promote immigration reform and improve the quality of life of immigrants.*	*Work collaboratively with community partners to develop new approaches based on shared values.*
Theory of change	A problem-focused mission should be undergirded by a *theory of change* that states how the desired results will be accomplished (e.g., how the quality of life for immigrants will be improved; how poverty will be reduced; how educational attainment will be enhanced; how youth will be developed).	A principles-driven mission should be undergirded by a *theory of action* that articulates how the work will be done (e.g., helping people help themselves). Such a theory of action can then be applied to any problem—helping immigrants, poverty reduction, youth development, disease prevention—but the mission focus is on how the work will be done.
General evaluation implications	A problem-focused mission is evaluated by its impact on the problem of concern (e.g., whether poverty is reduced).	A principles-focused mission is evaluated by how the organization engages in its work. Does it adhere to its principles? Does it walk the talk of its values? Use the GUIDE criteria for evaluation.
Principles-focused evaluation implications	Track, monitor, and provide feedback on progress and developments related to problem reduction and attainment of desired outcomes.	Track, monitor, and provide feedback on how the work is carried out, how values inform developments, and on the connection between values and developments. Process (how the work is done) is as important as, if not more important than, the solution of the problem (because the means matter as much as the ends).

Source: From Patton (2011, p. 250). Copyright 2011 by the Guilford Press. Adapted with permission.

with a look at the implications for evaluation. An earlier version of this exhibit (Patton, 2011, p. 250) compared values-based mission statements with problem-focused statements. Principles incorporate values but are more action oriented, thus this updated comparison.

Pushback against Principles as the Basis for Change Efforts and as the Evaluand

Exhibit 15.1, contrasting problem-focused missions with principles-focused missions, reminds us that people see the world differently and conceptualize change in diverse ways, only two of which are being compared here. We cannot make sense of the world without paradigms, lenses, and frameworks of some kind. What framework we use matters, as eminent evaluation theorist Ernie House has explained:

> The wrong frame has evaluators looking for the wrong things. Cognitive scientists tell us that we need such frames to interpret events. We have no choice. We necessarily think about the world in terms of stories and causes. Frames enable us to interpret events coherently and meaningfully. That's how our minds are structured. At the same time, inappropriate framing is a major source of cognitive bias. That's true for evaluations as well. We have work to do to understand our own (often implicit) frameworks. (2014, p. 31)

Introducing and comparing alternative frameworks provides an opportunity for me to note that not everyone is inspired by principles, much less principles-focused evaluation. I encounter diverse kinds of resistance to principles-focused evaluation, some quite intense, the nature of which strikes me as quite appropriate, understandable, and sensible within the contexts in which the resistance occurs. Exhibit 35.1 in Chapter 35 (pp. 348–350) presents some common pushbacks against principles-focused evaluation and potential ways of responding.

Evaluators, Values, and Valuing

Evaluation trainers, among whom I include myself, like to point out that in the middle of the word *evaluation* is *valu[e]*. The standards adopted by the evaluation profession mandate values identification and articulation so that the basis for value judgments can be known and assessed (Joint Committee, 1994, standard U4). But I find that many evaluators, well trained in social science methods, are much more comfortable with technical discussions than values discussions. The primacy of outcomes-driven

programming and evaluation ensures that discussions will turn quickly to specifying clear, specific, and measurable outcomes and then on to laying out the logic model that will presumably accomplish those outcomes. Values are more often left implicit and assumed rather than made explicit and examined.

George Julnes (2012) edited a special issue of *New Directions for Evaluation* titled "Promoting Valuation in the Public Interest: Informing Policies for Judging Value in Evaluation." That volume placed particular emphasis on the importance of context when dealing with values and valuing. The volume also highlighted the need to make values explicit in evaluation, make the valuing process transparent, and enhance evaluators' skills at engaging in values clarification and making values-based judgments. Judging value is the major purpose of evaluation, but evaluators have long struggled with how to do so (Schwandt, 2015).

In the context of this chapter, looking at the inspirational nature of principles, I would offer two powerful sources of inspiration for evaluators—at least I find them so. They are from evaluation pioneers and thought leaders Bob Stake and Ernie House.

Values and Evaluators: Neutrality or Advocacy?

Distinguished evaluation theorist and methodologist Bob Stake has written eloquently about evaluators' values and advocacy in an article provocatively entitled "How Far Dare an Evaluator Go toward Saving the World?" He began by noting that evaluators often care about the thing being evaluated—*and should care*. Evaluators don't have to pretend neutrality about the problems that programs are attacking in order to do fair, balanced, and neutral evaluations of those programs. Stake (2004) identified six things evaluators do and should care about:

1. We often care about the thing being evaluated.

2. We, as evaluation professionals, care about evaluation.

3. We advocate rationality.

4. We care to be heard. We are troubled if our studies are not used.

5. We are distressed by underprivilege. We see gaps among privileged patrons and managers and staff and underprivileged participants and communities.

6. We are advocates of a democratic society.

So, evaluators do not have to pretend neutrality about the problems innovators are attacking in order to do fair, balanced, and neutral evaluations of their programs. Who wants an uncaring evaluator who professes neutrality about homelessness, hunger, child abuse, community violence, or HIV/AIDS? My younger brother died of AIDS early in the epidemic. My entire family has been involved actively in AIDS walks and other activities. When I am engaged with HIV/AIDS monitoring and evaluation systems, I do not pretend neutrality. I want to see prevention programs work. That means I am motivated to hold staff's feet to the fire of evaluation to ensure that the program works—because I know from personal experience that lives are at risk (Patton, 2011, p. 249).

Truth, Beauty, and Justice

Ernie House, drawing on his roots in philosophy, has offered an insightful, provocative, and inspirational values framework for judging the quality and validity of evaluations: *truth, beauty, and justice:*

> Put simply, my broadening of the concept of validity was based on the idea that if an evaluation is untrue, or incoherent, or unjust, it is invalid. In other words, an evaluation must be true, coherent, and just. All three criteria are necessary. By contrast, sound fiscal judgment

is not necessary to establish evaluation validity, that is, if an evaluation is expensive, that doesn't make its findings invalid. To add some flair, I talked about "truth, beauty, and justice" in evaluation. The underlying concepts were argument, coherence, and politics. Truth is the *attainment* of arguments soundly made, beauty is the *attainment* of coherence well wrought, and justice is the *attainment* of politics fairly done. (2014, p. 31)

Jane Davidson has added her own provocative and inspirational twist to House's criteria:

> True "beauty" in evaluation is a clearly reasoned, well-crafted, coherent evaluation story that weaves all three of these together to unlock both truth and justice with breathtaking clarity. . . . House, in his 1980 book *Evaluating with Validity*, argued that truth trumps beauty and justice trumps them both. In other words, get the social justice priorities right, deliver valid answers relative to those, and then convey it all beautifully and believably.
>
> I'd like to flip House's idea on its head. What if beauty wasn't merely about how well the evaluative story is told? What if the *process* of creating a clear, compelling, and coherent (beautiful) evaluative story was in fact the key to unlocking validity (truth) and fairness (justice)? (2014, p. 43)

Values are embedded in and expressed by principles. Principles express values in a way that makes them actionable. Valuing truth, beauty, and justice leads to corresponding principles:

Seek truth. *Experience* beauty. *Work* for justice. At least those are the imperative verbs I would offer. What are yours? _____ truth. _____ beauty. _____ justice.

The Heart of Inspiration

Chapters 16 and 17 provide examples from evaluation practitioners of the inspirational nature of principles. The principles-focused evaluation exemplars in Part III

(Chapters 25–30) also provide illustrations and evidence of inspiration and its importance. Those involved in implementing principles-based programs and initiatives regularly report how refreshing, uplifting, and, yes, inspirational it is to articulate principles and dig deeply into their meaning, adherence, and consequences. These are principles-driven change makers and social innovators creating and running principles-based organizations—and they resonate to principles-focused evaluation.

As I've reiterated throughout this book, the work of principles-focused evaluation includes facilitating the identification, articulation, and collective meaning making of principles. Such work can be, and often is, emotional. The work of social change is emotional. Examining evidence of effectiveness can evoke strong emotions because those involved care, and care deeply, about making a difference. Principles-focused evaluators need to not only be comfortable dealing with emotions, including their own, but embrace the inspirational and emotional side of our work. It's not all research designs, data collection, and critical thinking. Our work involves values, caring, and

relationships. So I close this chapter with an assertion that is anathema to evaluators, the provocative and inspirational wisdom of Antoine de Saint-Exupéry, as expressed in *The Little Prince:* "And now here is my secret, a very simple secret: It is only with the heart that one can see rightly; what is essential is invisible to the eye." Perhaps not *only*. But at least partly. Therein lies inspiration.

Practice Exercise

This chapter presents six things evaluators do and should care about according to Bob Stake (see pp. 124–125). First, consider what six (or however many) things you care about as an evaluator, or social innovator, or change agent, or whatever role you play in the world. Use Bob Stake's list as a source of inspiration, but come up with your own list. Then, as the second part of this practice exercise, convert Stake's six things to effectiveness principles that meet the GUIDE criteria. Are they more inspiring or less inspiring reframed as principles? Or do you find no difference? Why? What does your answer tell you about yourself?

CHAPTER 16

Principles-Focused Evaluation at the Grassroots in Africa

Inspirational Examples and Reflections

JOHN WILSON

The end results are people with changed lives.
—PETER DRUCKER, business and private-sector management consultant
(when asked about the bottom line for not-for-profit organizations)

John Wilson has spent his career working on food security issues in Africa. He is a Zimbabwean currently working as a free-range facilitator in East and Southern Africa with community-based organizations, national NGOs (nongovernmental organizations), small farmers, and also at times with regional or continental networks.

John modestly aims to play a small part in helping to facilitate a stronger food movement in Africa that also benefits small-scale farmers and their communities and enhances ecological vibrancy. He sees collaborative and strategic work as being particularly important in the coming years, linking together much of the good work being done. We met at a meeting of the Global Alliance for the Future of Food (see Chapter 28), which led him to incorporate principles-focused evaluation into his work. As he sent me examples of the principles that were emerging from his work, I shared draft chapters from this book, and he provided valuable feedback.

The examples of principles identification and initial development in this chapter illuminate the inspirational dimension of the GUIDE framework: inspiration. Adherence to and the effects of the principles John has been developing with grassroots organizations have not yet served as a basis for evaluation, but it is hoped they will do so in the future. Nevertheless, articulation of principles that meet the GUIDE criteria has been meaningful, and the process of principles identification, with an evaluation framework in mind, has had an impact on those involved as well as their organizations.

John sent me many more examples than I could include here. What is especially valuable are his descriptions of how he facilitates identification of principles with grassroots groups and his reflections on what he's learned about the value of principles as an organizing and mobilizing framework. My thanks to the organizations featured here for sharing their principles and to John for sharing his facilitation processes and reflections. *Note to reader:* Don't worry about keeping the various organizations and acronyms straight; it's the process, format, and content of the principles that matters.

—M. Q. P.

Principles in Support of "Walking the Talk"

Let me begin with work I had the opportunity to do with an organization in Kenya to develop a set of principles and to discuss how they could use them to evaluate themselves and for ongoing decision making. This assignment grew out of a presentation that I did to the biennial gathering of Tudor Trust[1] grantees in Africa. The organization in question, Resources Oriented Development Initiatives (RODI), came back to me later to say that they would be interested in taking it further.

Eliud Ngunjiri, the director, wrote to me about the difficulty of "walking our talk," and it made me think about how there's often much discussion about "walking our talk" in civil society organizations. Civil society organizations complain about themselves in this regard. They complain about others. And it is true that organizations often don't "walk their talk" as much as they should or could. At times this may be due to opportunism, but often I think it's because organizations don't rigorously come back to looking at what "walking our talk" means. Principles-focused evaluation can do just that. I see it as a practical way to help organizations walk their talk. "Our talk" is what we stand for, what we believe in, what we know from experience will work, what we know must happen, our inspiration—our principles. And we can only "walk our talk" consistently if we have a way of regularly assessing ourselves on this score! Otherwise it will tend to be empty talk. So we undertook to make RODI's principles explicit.

At the beginning of our session, attended by 25 staff and board members, Eliud gave an eloquent introduction to principles-focused evaluation before handing the session over to me. He really gets the need for evaluation at another level, for the organization as a whole as opposed to just "project evaluation."

I did a 20-minute introduction that built on what Eliud had brought up, looking at the history of evaluation as a profession and where it is succeeding and where it is not. This led into discussing complex situations and the rise of developmental evaluation to deal with such situations; and then principles-focused evaluation as a significant method within this developmental evaluation umbrella. I used Patton's GUIDE acronym to describe what a good principle is, having discussed different kinds of principles, and making the point that the emphasis in principles-focused evaluation is on principles for effectiveness.

We spent the rest of the morning coming up with a set of principles for RODI. There was lots of very interesting discussion around each one, as there always is. We revisited them the next morning and made a few amendments in the fresh light of the morning.

---

[1] The Tudor Trust (*http://tudortrust.org.uk*) is an independent grant-making trust that supports voluntary and community groups working in any part of the United Kingdom. It also has a small, closed grants program in East and Southern Africa.

Draft of RODI principles

1. *The inherent potential of each person.* Appreciate the potential in everyone to transform themselves to be useful and valued members of their community.

2. *Crime prevention focus.* Reach out to work in situations where we contribute to crime prevention in Kenya and East Africa.

3. *Resources oriented.* Emphasize potential resources and opportunities rather than problems in any given situation.

4. *Rolling out capacity building.* Strengthen the abilities of people so that they in turn strengthen others toward improved livelihoods.

5. *Learning and influencing with others.* Network and collaborate with like-minded state and nonstate actors in the interests of complementarity, for mutual learning, and toward influencing policy, including service delivery enhancement.

6. *Nature harmony.* Promote natural resource management practices that are in harmony with nature.

7. *Self-reliance.* Ensure that our work always enhances self-reliance.

8. *Gender equity.* Advocate for gender equity in all our work.

9. *Emerging crosscutting issues.* Constantly assess the context we work in for emerging crosscutting issues that are critical to our work and respond appropriately to these.

10. *RODI resilience.* Work toward RODI being a resilient organization that is increasingly less dependent on external donors and its founders.

Engaging with the Principles

On the second morning, after the review of the principles, participants worked in groups, with each group looking at one of the above principles. The aim was to have an evaluation discussion in relation to each principle so that everyone could begin to get the idea of this. I gave these questions to guide the discussion:

1. What questions might you use to evaluate RODI against this principle?

2. Think about where evidence might come from to support your assessment.

3. How is RODI doing (1 = not at all well; 2 = not well; 3 = average; 4 = well; 5 = very well); and why do you give that score?

4. What suggestions do you have so that RODI improves in relation to the principle you are looking at?

We only had time to share and discuss five of the principles in the light of these questions. We finished off by doing some next steps. The plan is that they will look at two to three principles each time they do their quarterly review and then they will scan the whole set of principles at their annual review and planning. They are also going to produce a small booklet on their principles.

My Reflections

I was happy with the way the two-morning session went. And I know participants were too. Many recognized the added value that this approach could bring to RODI. I emphasized the need to come into this approach gradually. It was clear that looking at all 10 principles in evaluation mode at one time is too much, hence the decision to look at two to three each time. The group struggled to some extent with the exercise on the second morning but this is not that surprising; in fact, I would go further to say that this struggle will be an important part of what using principles in evaluation mode is all about because there is much to learn, and that learning challenges us to examine thoughtfully and honestly the effectiveness of what we do.

The more I work with this approach, the more I recognize its potential. There's nothing to lose. Just going that step further and turning values into principles of effectiveness is already a very useful step. And any efforts to then return to the principles and assess one's organization against them can only be useful. If this goes on to become a systematic approach, then I can see it becoming extremely useful to organizations.

I do sometimes wonder how many organizations will go that extra mile to make this approach an inherent part of their M&E, knowing the resistance to M&E in general! But at the same time I am hopeful that its potential meaningfulness, because it links to what the organization is all about, may give the added interest that will bring the discipline.

The Alliance for Food Sovereignty in Africa

This next example is from the Alliance for Food Sovereignty in Africa (AFSA). At one AFSA meeting we spent some time looking at principles, and the members warmed to the idea of using principles-focused evaluation in AFSA. Of course there is also the need to evaluate according to funder requirements, linked to the different funded "projects," but hopefully there will be some funders who recognize the value of the principles-focused evaluation work too. AFSA recognizes that holding this continental network of networks together will depend on strong bonds that go much deeper than structures and procedures. One AFSA elder from Benin gave a beautiful short "speech" on how we must keep looking beyond our minds to our hearts and will. And how the AFSA principles express all three.

The principles we came up with give AFSA a way of tracking how the alliance is moving forward based on what really matters to the members. As always, much discussion went into the final few words for each statement. The principles also give AFSA a framework to creatively explore possibilities for the future. And they give AFSA a "tool" to guide decision making at the forks in the road, given the great complexity of what it is dealing with and relating to. AFSA's world is extremely fast changing, and it has to be dynamic and light on its toes while also being consultative and involving of all the members. My feeling is that the principles will help AFSA juggle those two dimensions. If assessment and planning ahead keep coming back to the principles, AFSA will develop an inner rigor—driven by minds, hearts, and wills.

These are AFSA's principles:

1. Champion small African family farming systems based on agro-ecological and indigenous approaches that sustain food sovereignty and the livelihoods of communities.

2. Resist industrialization and commodification of African agriculture and food systems; massive land grabs; destruction of biodiversity and ecosystems; displacement of indigenous peoples, especially pastoral communities and hunter-gatherers; and the destruction of their livelihoods and cultures.

3. Emphasize African-driven solutions to African problems, and a belief in the richness of our diversity.

4. Be a strong voice to shape policy on the continent in the areas of community rights, family farming, promotion of traditional knowledge, the environment, and natural resource management.

5. Emphasize women and youth as key players in food sovereignty.

6. Contribute to land ownership and control in the hands of communities.

7. Reject the genetic engineering and privatization of living organisms.

8. Ensure a clear understanding and

continual analysis of the political dimension of agro-ecology and food sovereignty, communicating this clearly and having this inform the development of AFSA's strategies.

9. Work in synergy with all actors who empower what we as AFSA are doing.

10. Bring farmers and other grassroots voices forward to speak about agroecology, food sovereignty, and the work of AFSA.

11. Ensure cross learning and collaboration between members of AFSA.

Permaculture Research Institute—Kenya Principles

I always launch into the exercise of developing a set of principles saying "let's develop a first draft set of principles" so that they don't get too hung up on the wording at first. However, in the end the wording is important and I try to help them get it "right."

But what should also happen over time is that organizations modify them in the light of further experience. I say "further" because they initially grow out of experience. By regularly evaluating their principles, the groups will actively engage with them, and in that engagement I'm sure they will notice, as their experience deepens, that some of them might need to be stated slightly differently. Here are principles from an organization called PRI-Kenya (Permaculture Research Institute—Kenya):

1. Always be an accountable, honest, and transparent organization to ourselves and to our stakeholders.

2. Facilitate local and appropriate solutions to local problems and local ownership of projects.

3. Strengthen communities toward resilience and self-determination.

4. Contribute to greater equity within the organization, in the communities we work with, and the wider world.

5. Be an organization that shares information openly and widely.

6. Recognize the value of cultural diversity and identity, and that there are many sources of knowledge.

7. Continuously search out synergies with others toward greater impact.

8. Strive toward financial and organizational sustainability and independence.

9. Continuously invest in the organization's growth through an iterative review process.

Context-Specific Principles: A Sense of Ownership

Here are a few reflections after working on principles with PORET, a community-based organization in a hot and dry part of eastern Zimbabwe. It's a very rich environment in its own way, but fragile and degraded, and continuing to degrade. As always I found the discussion incredibly rich for each principle. For example, there were very interesting points made that led to the addition of the phrase "as the modern way" in principle no. 7 on the next page. I've realized that to some extent principles can seem fairly generic when you look at lots of different ones. But in fact they are incredibly unique to each group, especially when viewed as a set of principles.

It's all about people talking openly and freely, often from their hearts as much as their minds, and slowly but surely teasing out the principle. Though there are times, I find, when it just pops straight out! Doing the principles like this is such a good foundation for a new board. We discussed all the time as we developed them whether they could be evaluated. So right from the beginning they are seeing these principles, not just as something to put up on a wall or in their flier, but very much as something they will assess themselves against regularly. And, of course, though new to the organization, they come out of all the experience of those who took part.

Principles

1. Always work toward initiatives and activities that are self-driven by community members.

2. Ensure useful and used documentation, relating to PORET's work, for community members and other interested parties.

3. Recognize the special knowledge, effort, and skills of individuals and groups that are in line with PORET's purpose.

4. Revitalize understanding of the role of culture in sustainable development.

5. Strengthen the community to value their natural resources and their ability to protect these.

6. Be a united, effective, and accountable organization.

7. Promote a natural and holistic understanding of and approach to health as the modern way.

8. Support self-reliant farming.

9. Strengthen community understanding of the broader context, including policies and laws.

The Challenge of Follow-Through

I've come to realize that I need to spend more time thinking through how I will follow up with those organizations with whom I have worked to develop principles. So far it has been more about taking the opportunity of working with various organizations to help them articulate their principles and talking through with them about how they could use them as a significant part of their monitoring and evaluation work. The reality is that there aren't the resources for me to go back and work with all of them on this. I would love to be able to design a process all the way through.

STIPA

A co-facilitator and I spent a week working with a Kenyan organization called STIPA, based in Kisumu. They work in this part of Kenya and also in Somalia, Somaliland, and Pundtland. We started off at the beginning of the workshop by developing principles with the group for how we would work as a group during the week. We came up with two and we came back to these a couple of times during the week to monitor ourselves in the process of the workshop.

On the second day the participants drew a tree to depict their practice (which they call Participatory Integrated Community Development [PICD]), with the trunk as their philosophy (Exhibit 16.1).

On the third day, I worked with them to spell out their "trunk" into principles. This is how they turned out, after rich and in-depth discussion to get them expressed according to what they mean. It took time but didn't drag. I could tell that they were very involved in this and happy to do the exercise. *They knew them in their hearts and heads but just hadn't spelled them out.*

1. *Conflict sensitive:* Enhance peaceful co-existence in communities, including enabling communities to resolve existing conflicts.

2. *Gender sensitive:* Ensure significant and meaningful participation of both men and women, young and old, in decision-making processes.

3. *People driven:* Enable communities to lead their own initiatives and processes, at their own pace.

4. *Dialogue:* Create time and space for reflection, open sharing, and negotiation.

5. *People's   participation:*   Strengthen

relationships for sustained commitment toward a collective vision.

6. *All inclusive:* Ensure involvement of all the different groupings and categories of people in a community, especially the marginalized. (This is something they are particularly good at, comparing them with other organizations I know, who struggle with this and often end up not reaching those who perhaps they most want to reach.)

Following this, my colleague facilitated a session to plan a visit to a community the following day. The aim of the visit was to help STIPA in their reflection process about how their way of working with communities has been going and to get a community's perspective on this. The STIPA team immediately suggested that they would like to use the principles as a basis to get feedback from the community, in effect, evaluative input.

This exercise formed the heart of the work with the community the next day and was rich! There were some difficulties translating the principles into the local language, Luo, with perhaps some of the subtleties of the principles lost. This meant that there were some overlaps in community responses, but this wasn't a big issue. On the day after, back at the STIPA office, we reflected on the exercise with the community, again through the lens of the principles. This helped us identify areas that still needed to be addressed in relation to each principle. Again it was a rich and valuable exercise.

Helping them spell out these principles has given them a useful way to assess themselves and I'm sure they will continue to use them as such. They are very much a value-driven organization and this has given them a tool to link to those values. We discussed how principles-focused evaluation will add another dimension to the

---

EXHIBIT 16.1. PICD Tree Depicting Principles as Branches with the Trunk as the Program's Philosophy

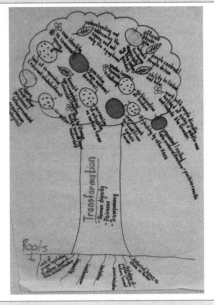

Reprinted with permission from Lucas Wadenya, Support for Tropical Initiatives in Poverty Alliance (STIPA), Kenya.

outcomes-oriented monitoring and evaluation they have to do for those funding their work.

Personal Reflections on Principles-Focused Evaluation

Principles-focused evaluation affirms and gives structure and direction to lots I have been trying to do over the years related to assessing progress against values. In complex and fast-changing situations, it's very difficult to predict outcomes. And being tied to predetermined and fixed outcomes often stifles creativity and the ability to respond to situations as they arise.

I understand principles-focused evaluation to be a particular kind of developmental evaluation. I particularly like this "be on your toes" approach; it is so important in situations of complexity where things are changing fast and you have to be ready to adapt and seize hold of opportunities. I think the private sector is better at this. The civil society sector, often because of donor requirements and accountability, tends to plan, plan, plan . . . and plod! Patton talks of "ready, fire, aim" rather than "ready, aim, fire"—a nice way of looking at it. Plunge in and keep learning.

The more I engage with principles-focused evaluation, the more I feel excited about moves in this direction. I'm realizing that up until now I have been rather tentatively moving in this direction, but being tentative often lacks clarity. I'm feeling much less tentative as I gain experience in this approach.

The Centrality of Values

For years I've known that what makes an organization really tick is its values, in the civil society sector anyway. I've understood that there is a need for reference points to measure progress and effectiveness. The focus on impacts and outcomes can serve a purpose, and one does need to get results, of course, but an effective organization keeps coming back to its values, *rigorously*. This is what creates integrity. To work in an ever-changing world and respond to opportunities and issues as they arise, you need a way of tracking yourself that keeps you light on your toes and dynamic, responsive, and creative, a way that keeps assisting decision making as you reach forks in the road. Going back to one's principles can do that— a principle in this sense is a value spelled out in a statement that captures exactly what that value means to you and your organization.

What Really Matters

Let me share an insight that suddenly came to me on a plane trip one day: effective organizations operate with principles, and this is what makes and keeps them effective. But these principles are usually subconscious. Of course organizations often list their values at some stage, but those values are not consciously used to guide and evaluate the organization, which is what principles-focused evaluation is about.

Think of a pioneer organization that operates with great passion and dedication. They are relentless in their pursuit of their work. They have rigor. They are thinking all the time about what they are doing. They keep learning. They may be a bit disorganized and don't document things well enough and don't have the proper systems. But they are effective. It suddenly came to me on the plane how these effective, pioneering organizations, operating on unarticulated principles, are then told they must now professionalize or words to that effect. They must put in systems. They must develop theories of change, do their logical frameworks, have all those indicators (very SMART) and so on. They get sucked into it all, and evaluation and monitoring revolves around the indicators, which are often a farce because you can't predetermine indicators in complex situations.

Now, we live in the real world and won't change the demand for logic models and results-based approaches. They are here to stay, in the short and medium term at least. *But,* if we can give organizations the option *also* of articulating their principles, which they have anyway, we can then give them a tool to evaluate themselves against what really matters to them and a tool to help make strategic decisions with.

This could mean that they still use the logic models without these taking them off course, because what will keep them effective is the principles-focused approach. I suspect it will also make them deal better with their logic models. They can approach these with more confidence rather than with trepidation, or loathing as is sometimes the case! It is a job to be done and managed, but not to be dominated by.[2]

I've observed repeatedly that the process of generating shared principles within an explicit evaluation framework, to be used for ongoing improvement and learning, not just done and forgotten, has the effect for those involved of stimulating creativity. I often watch how logframes stifle creativity. The usual compliance-focused and mandated evaluation exercises are deadly dull, just going through the motions of meeting funding requirements. In contrast, articulating principles evokes passion, caring, deeply held values, and engaged, creative interaction. Based on my observations and experiences, I think that discussion and identification of principles stimulate rather than stifle creativity.

In essence, principles evoke and state what people care deeply about.

Principles-focused evaluation challenges people to look at whether they are walking the talk of their principles. To do so means staying grounded in the realities and stories of the people who will, hopefully, be served by those principles.

Final Reflections

I've been thinking a lot about what draws me to principles-focused evaluation. It's more than just helping organizations be more effective. It's at a higher level. Those of us involved in the environment, in food issues, in holistic health, in trying to create more just societies, often get drawn away from our principles into a project delivery mode. We lose sight of what we are really about when this happens. Our resources are bound up in becoming good at delivering projects, and so some of us become good at that; often we are the ones who continue to get the money. Some of the big international NGOs are a prime example of this in my experience. But "we" may lose our raison d'être.

We must keep going back to our principles in order to be true to who we are and to be more effective (the two go hand in hand). And beyond that, I'm realizing, it's critical that we learn how to use our principles to guide us so that in turn we can help our wider society use principles to monitor and evaluate itself. If one looks around at many of the issues plaguing us today, there seem to be two underlying problems in particular that influence this:

1. We are not able to think holistically because we have a reductionist approach to things, based on our education.

2. We are not able to, and don't, bring our values to bear nearly enough and with enough rigor on what we are doing.

I think principles-focused evaluation can go some significant way in dealing with

---

[2]Inspired by John's ruminations here, see the Epilogue (pp. 390–392) for my own reflections on logic models and principles-focused evaluation—M. Q. P.

both these issues. By discussing principles (especially as a *set* of principles), one tends, in the process, to look at the bigger, more enigmatic picture, which neat, predetermined indicators and "project" approaches usually ignore. Principles are, to a large extent, the expression of core values, and so in principles-focused evaluation we are constantly bringing our values to bear on what we are doing. Perhaps the biggest problem for people is that it will be "messy"; there won't be neat answers. It means learning to accept and work with ambiguity. That, itself, may be a guiding principle.

Practice Exercise

My deepest thanks to John Wilson for the examples in this chapter and for his insightful and inspiring reflections. He ends by commenting that principles-focused evaluation "means learning to accept and work with ambiguity." Go more deeply into the challenges of accepting and working with ambiguity. Why is this so challenging? How can the capacity to deal with ambiguity be strengthened? How does the ambiguity of working with principles affect accountability demands? What issues arise for you in thinking about the ambiguities of being principles driven and engaging in principles-focused evaluation?

CHAPTER 17

Inspiring Principles
Distinguishing Overarching Principles from Operational Principles

CHARMAGNE CAMPBELL-PATTON

Charmagne Campbell-Patton comes to evaluation with a strong background in youth civic engagement, including capacity building around global citizenship. Youth are motivated by two things: peers and what they care about. If they don't care about what is going on, and their friends aren't with them, forget about it. Charmagne has found that youth resonate to and are inspired by global principles like the Universal Declaration of Human Rights and the Convention on the Rights of the Child. I am grateful to ChildFund International for sharing this example and to Charmagne for writing about and sharing her experiences. I am especially pleased that Charmagne, my daughter and the mother of my granddaughter, has been bitten by the evaluation bug and has become an evaluator. (For a more general treatment of conceptualizing and evaluating the complexities of youth civic engagement, see Campbell-Patton & Patton, 2010.)

—M. Q. P.

ChildFund International

The Convention on the Rights of the Child is the most rapidly and widely ratified international human rights treaty in history. The Convention changed the way children are viewed and treated—i.e., as human beings with a distinct set of rights instead of as passive objects of care and charity. The unprecedented acceptance of the Convention clearly shows a wide global commitment to advancing children's rights.
—UNICEF on the occasion of the 25th anniversary of the Convention on the Rights of the Child

ChildFund International is a children's charity that works in over 25 countries around the world to improve the lives of young people from birth to young adult-hood. Over the last few years, they have developed a new model for Youth Civic Engagement and Leadership (YCEL). This model was based on extensive research in the field as well as on ChildFund's experi-ence in child participation and youth civic engagement[1] throughout the Americas region and was intended to be adapted by local partners in the various countries where ChildFund operates.

Before beginning to implement pro-grams based on the model, however, Child-Fund was already thinking about evalua-tion. A dream client, right? It wanted to be sure that as it rolled out the model in differ-ent local environments, it was gathering the data to understand whether and how the model was working in these different situ-ations. ChildFund also wanted to be sure that lessons from each local community fed back into the model so that it continued to develop based on experiences in the field.

Beginning in early 2015, I began work-ing with the program development team at ChildFund to create a situation assess-ment guide that could walk local partners through a process of identifying assets and barriers to youth civic engagement and leadership in their communities. The pro-cess would provide a baseline for evaluation and inform program development. Since it was also participatory, involving a core group of stakeholders, including youth, it was also part of the initial intervention. This will become important later, but just hold on to that thought for now.

ChildFund decided to pilot the situation assessment process in the United States with one of its longest-standing partners—Operation Shoestring—which provides year-round academic, social, and emotional

support to elementary, middle, and high school children in Jackson, Mississippi. While the organization had not done youth civic engagement programming before, they had deep ties to the local community and the ability to engage a range of stake-holders in the process to develop a solid program model.

Inspiration

I spent some time with the staff of Opera-tion Shoestring training them in devel-opmental evaluation and walking them through the situation assessment process before they engaged the broader commu-nity. Over the next several months, they held three stakeholder sessions where they mapped the youth civic engagement and leadership landscape in Jackson. They also connected with another youth leadership program and were able to engage youth in workshops and activities that explored their perspectives on the community. Dur-ing these workshops, Operation Shoestring staff also introduced the youth to the Dec-laration of the Rights of the Child (UNI-CEF, 1959), which is a framing document for ChildFund's youth civic engagement model. Many of the youth had never heard of this document and were unaware that they had rights as children in the communi-ty. As they began to learn about their rights and assess the extent to which they were being upheld (or infringed upon) in their community, *many youth seemed inspired by the idea that they were rights holders.*

After nearly a year of engaging the com-munity in the situation assessment process, Operation Shoestring, ChildFund, and I came back together for an adaptive ac-tion session to ask three deceptively simple questions: What? So what? Now what? To-gether, we discussed the findings of the situation assessment, identified key themes and priority areas, discussed potential bar-riers, and made a plan for how to use the information gathered to inform program

---

[1]ChildFund defines civic engagement as an orga-nized action by a person or group that benefits the community and leads to the realization that young people exercising their rights and leadership have the skills to help a group of people reach a com-mon goal.

development and as a baseline for a developmental evaluation that would support the program as it developed and adapted during its first year.

Principles Emerge

Also, out of the adaptive action session emerged a set of 15 operating principles based on ChildFund's YCEL model. When we shared these principles with Michael Patton, he suggested grouping the operating principles into a few overarching principles in order to highlight those that are most inspirational, while making them easier to work with and evaluate. Exhibit 17.1 presents the working principles that emerged from the situation assessment in Jackson.[2]

So what's next for this project? These principles will inform program development and form the basis for developmental evaluation. We will gather real-time data with the youth involved in the program to identify the extent to which these principles are being upheld in the program and whether they need to be adapted based on emerging opportunities or challenges. In short, we will engage in a principles-focused developmental evaluation.

Practice Exercise

In the development of principles "many youth seemed inspired by the idea that they were rights holders." What does this mean? What does this observation suggest about "rights" as a source of inspiration in this case? What would be evidence that youth felt inspired?

---

[2] For other examples of distinguishing general overarching principles from more specific operating principles, see Chapters 29 and 31. One advantage of this distinction, when a group has generated lots of principles, is that all or most suggestions for principles can be included among operating principles to give voice and ownership to all who have participated, but only a small number are considered overarching principles to make the recall and use of principles manageable. Some groups prefer to treat operating principles as "practices" and call them that; doing so is also a viable solution to having too many overarching principles.—M. Q. P.

EXHIBIT 17.1. Working Principles from the Situation Assessment

Principles	Overarching principle defined	Operating principles to implement overarching principles
1. **Youth vision principle**	Support youth to dream of a better reality for themselves, their community, and the world.	• Provide young people with opportunities to reflect on and explore their own identity, situation, and community. • Support skills and competence in meaningful and inspirational vision statements. • Create an inclusive process that ensures broad representation of youth from different backgrounds and a feedback loop where a core group of youth takes back their ideas and plans to a larger group of youth.
2. **Youth voice principle**	Support youth to develop and express their own perspective and voice.	• Create spaces for young people to associate and develop their voice. • Build community openness to and valuing of youth perspectives. • Create interactive opportunities for the community to hear from young people. • Ensure that young people have the opportunity to express their unique needs and interests and speak as a group distinct from adults.
3. **Youth authentic inclusion principle**	Create opportunities for active and meaningful participation of young people in the daily life of the community.	• Create a community environment that includes and values the involvement and contributions of youth. • Promote authentic and ongoing inclusion of youth in any process or institution that affects their lives or those of their families. • Support youth to identify and take action to benefit themselves and their community.
4. **Community valuing youth principle**	Promote a view of youth as assets to the community who can make a positive contribution toward social change.	• Ensure that young people have access to information to enhance their civic knowledge and inform their participation. • Create opportunities for youth and adults to build relationships based on mutual understanding and respect.
5. **Youth development principle**	Provide opportunities for youth to develop knowledge and skills for effective civic participation and leadership that will benefit them throughout their lives.	• Reduce barriers for youth from different backgrounds to come together and work together.

CHAPTER 18

Principles-Focused Pedagogy of Evaluation

Inspired by Freirean Pedagogy

> Paulo Freire left us the legacy of ethical-political roots to support our practices—wings, that is, a theory to go beyond his work; and many dreams—the utopia of a society of equals; or, as he affirms at the end of *Pedagogia do Oprimido* (*Pedagogy of the Oppressed*): "the creation of a world in which it will be easier to love."
>
> —MOACIR GADOTTI, Director, Instituto Paulo Freire, São Paulo, Brazil

Paulo Freire has been an inspiration to millions. He epitomized what it means to be principles driven. I was inspired by Freire as a graduate student in the turbulent 1960s. In 2014, on a trip to Brazil, I had the opportunity to reconnect with his writings and found them inspirational in a new and unexpected way. He conceptualized and articulated a *pedagogy of the oppressed*. That is well known, as is the globally enduring influence of his pedagogical principles and practices. But what inspired me was the implications of his approach for *a principles-based pedagogy of evaluation*. This chapter, like the preceding chapter, aims to elaborate and elucidate the *I* in the GUIDE framework: inspiration. Principles inspire. Freire's writings have inspired a principles-focused pedagogy of evaluation (Patton, 2017b).

Pedagogy is the study of teaching. *Pedagogy of evaluation* entails examining how and what evaluation teaches. There is no singular or monolithic pedagogy of evaluation. Embedded in different evaluation approaches are varying assumptions, values, premises, priorities, and sense-making processes. Those who participate in an evaluation are experiencing sometimes explicit, more often implicit and tacit, pedagogical principles. Evaluation invites stakeholders involved to see the world in a certain way, to make sense of what is being evaluated through a particular lens, to make judgments based on certain kinds of evidence and values.

Pedagogy of evaluation is inspired by and builds on the works of Paulo Freire, especially his classic *Pedagogy of the Oppressed*. His other books include *Pedagogy of Indignation, Pedagogy of Hope, Pedagogy of Freedom, Ecopedagogy,* and *Critical Pedagogy.*

Those evaluation approaches that have been most influenced by Freirean pedagogy and share Freirean values, modes of engagement, and desired outcomes are social-justice-focused evaluations, democratic deliberative evaluation, empowerment evaluation, feminist, transformative evaluation, and critical systems evaluation. Evaluation's actual and potential role in examining the effects and implications of inequality is a core concern of the social justice perspective in evaluation (House, 1990, 2014; Rosenstein & Syna, 2015; Sirotnik, 1990). Other evaluation approaches value, teach, and strive for different results, that is, they are based on other pedagogical premises and principles.

The larger understanding that Freire's work reminds us of is that all evaluation approaches constitute a pedagogy of some kind. *All evaluation teaches something.* What is taught and how it is taught varies, but evaluation is inherently and predominantly a pedagogical interaction. Freire understood and taught us that all interactions between and among people are pedagogical; something is always being taught, conveyed, and proselytized. This chapter invites you to use Freire's works to reflect on your pedagogy of evaluation.

Freirean Principles

Paulo Freire developed a transformative method for teaching illiterates in Latin America many years ago, but his influence endures. He was born in Brazil in 1921 at a time of world economic crisis in which he experienced hunger and poverty at a young age. He became an activist working for a more democratic and universal approach to education in Brazil. In 1964, he was imprisoned for 70 days as a traitor and subsequently exiled. In 1968 he wrote his famous *Pedagogy of the Oppressed,* published in Spanish and English in 1970, but not in Brazil until 1974. In 1970, Freire was recruited to Geneva, where he worked for 10 years as a special educational adviser to the World Congress of Churches. In that capacity he traveled worldwide helping countries to implement popular education and literacy reforms.

Freirean principles, illuminated through his work and writings, remain relevant because inequality remains a global problem. In this chapter I'll summarize Freire's description of his method from *Pedagogy of the Oppressed* and then extract his principles and their relevance for evaluation today and looking forward. I will quote extensively from Freire to provide a sense of his language and perspective. The scenario and all quotations are from *Pedagogy of the Oppressed* (Freire, 2000) unless otherwise noted.

Freire's Engagement Process

Here's Freire's scenario: A plan is to be developed and implemented for adult education in a peasant area with high illiteracy. The process begins with a participatory situation analysis facilitated by "investigators." The investigators hold an informal meeting in the area where the literacy campaign is to take place. During this initial meeting with local people they explain what they propose to do and that "the investigation will be impossible without a relation of mutual understanding and trust" (p. 110). Volunteers are recruited at this meeting to serve as assistants in gathering data about the life of the area. Together the investigators and volunteers develop "a critical perception of the world, which implies a correct method of approaching reality in order to unveil it. And critical perception cannot be imposed. Thus, from the very beginning, thematic investigation is expressed as an educational pursuit, a cultural action" (p. 111).

> It is essential that the investigators observe the area under varying circumstances: labor in the fields, meetings of a local association (noting the behavior of the participants, the language used, and the relations between the officers and the members), the role played by women and by young people, leisure hours,

games and sports, conversations with people in their homes (noting examples of husband–wife and parent–child relationships). No activity must escape the attention of the investigators during the initial survey of the area. (pp. 111–112)

The process then moves from data to interpretation. During these "evaluation meetings" each person reports "how he perceived or felt a certain occurrence or situation. The initial investigation focuses on uncovering and understanding contradictions of consciousness among the people being studied. However, Freire cautions: "the fact that the investigators may in the first stage of the investigation approximately apprehend the complex of contradictions does not authorize them to begin to structure the program content of educational action. This perception of reality is still their own, not that of the people" (p. 114). Instead, a second stage of inquiry is initiated to further investigate these contradictions, with the investigators "always acting as a team."

Freire reports having learned with colleagues that the people in communities only become deeply interested and engaged when the inquiry is related "directly to their felt needs. Any deviation . . . produced silence and indifference" (p. 116). With further work, Freire and colleagues developed a pedagogy of critical consciousness that moved beyond mere needs identification to perceiving the *causes* of their needs. Therein lies the emergence of critical consciousness.

Extrapolation of Freirean Principles

There is no definitive list of Freirean principles. Different analysts drawing on and influenced by Freire's works emphasize different elements and articulate principles in varying ways. Thus, what follows is my interpretation of his principles with an eye toward particular influences on and relevance for evaluation (Patton, 2017b).

> **Principle 1:** Facilitate critical thinking to open up, develop, and nurture *critical consciousness.*

The conviction of the oppressed that they must fight for their liberation is not a gift bestowed by the revolutionary leadership, but the result of their own *conscientização*. (Freire, 1970, p. 67)

Critical consciousness, or *conscientização* (Portuguese), refers to attaining a deep, meaningful, realistic, and reality-based understanding of one's world. This includes becoming aware of how one has been indoctrinated and conditioned to think in particular ways by those with power and wealth who control traditional educational outlets including schools, governmental agencies, media outlets, and the business world. Freire (1970) introduced the idea of *conscientização* in his book *Pedagogy of the Oppressed* to emphasize that ordinary people, especially the poor, are oppressed by false consciousness, having internalized the message that they are inferior, without value, incapable, and useless. A pedagogy of the oppressed raises consciousness about the nature, sources, and implications of oppression, which include dominant and domineering myths, so as to help one escape control by those in power and come to act with freedom and consciousness as a self-determining and thoughtful human being. This realization empowers the oppressed to take action.

The best starting point for such reflections is the unfinishedness of our human condition. It is in this consciousness that the very possibility of learning, of being educated, resides. . . . Our capacity to learn, the source of our capacity to teach, suggests and implies that we also have a capacity to grasp the substantiveness/essence of the object of our knowing. (Freire, 2001, p. 66)

> **Principle 2:** Cultivate consciousness in communities of people, not just individuals.

When they [the oppressed] discover within themselves the yearning to be free, they perceive that this yearning can be transformed into reality only when the same yearning is aroused in their comrades. (p. 47)

The emergence and nurturing of critical consciousness is both a cultural and political activity and is therefore inherently a collective activity: *inquiry together*. Freire's pedagogy involves people together examining issues that are important to them and their situation, what he calls "thematics."

> The investigation of thematics involves the investigation of the people's thinking—thinking which occurs only in and among people together seeking out reality. I cannot think *for others* or *without others*, nor can others think *for me*. Even if the people's thinking is superstitious or naive, it is only as they rethink their assumptions in action that they can change. (Freire, 1970, p. 108)

Principle 3: Make critical consciousness pedagogy interactive and dialogical.

Freire provides an extensive critique of what he calls the "banking" concept of education in which teachers deposit information into students. In contrast, the pedagogy of the oppressed must be interactive and dialogical.

> Through dialogue, the teacher-of-the-students and the students-of-the-teacher cease to exist and a new term emerges: teacher-student with students-teachers. The teacher is no longer merely the-one-who-teaches, but one who is himself taught in dialogue with the students, who in turn while being taught also teach. They become jointly responsible for a process in which all grow. . . . Here, no one teaches another, nor is anyone self-taught. People teach each other, mediated by the world, by the cognizable objects which in banking education are "owned" by the teacher. (Freire, 1970, pp. 79–80)

Principle 4: Integrate reflection and action.

Freire was strongly and eloquently critical of the juxtaposition of reflection and action as separate and distinct arenas of human experience. For him, reflection is aimed at action and action is the content of reflection. *Critical dialogue presupposes action.*

> At all stages of their liberation, the oppressed must see themselves as women and men engaged in the ontological and historical vocation of becoming more fully human. Reflection and action become imperative when one does not erroneously attempt to dichotomize the content of humanity from its historical forms. . . .
>   The insistence that the oppressed engage in reflection on their concrete situation is not a call to armchair revolution. On the contrary, reflection—true reflection—leads to action. On the other hand, when the situation calls for action, that action will constitute an authentic praxis only if its consequences become the object of critical reflection. (Freire, 1970, pp. 65–66).

Principle 5: Value and integrate the objective and subjective.

Critical consciousness, reflection, and action must be grounded in objective reality that is subjectively experienced and understood.

> The radical is never a subjectivist. For this individual the subjective aspect exists only in relation to the objective aspect (the concrete reality, which is the object of analysis). Subjectivity and objectivity thus join in a dialectical unity producing knowledge in solidarity with action, and vice versa. (Freire, 1970, p. 38)

At the core of critical consciousness is the "capacity to apprehend reality" (Freire, 2000, p. 66). For Freire, poverty is a verifiable reality. Oppression is also a verifiable reality, not merely perception. Freire goes at length to distinguish both intellectual and academic objectivism and subjectivism from commonsense objectivity and subjectivity as understood and experienced by ordinary people. Moreover, Freire asserts that any hoped-for, alleged, or asserted transformation from oppression to liberation must be "objectively verified" (p. 50). He wrote: "One cannot conceive of objectivity without subjectivity. Neither can exist without the other, nor can they be dichotomized" (p. 50).

Principle 6: Integrate thinking and emotion.

Freire articulated a holistic and humanistic approach to dialogue that valued and integrated reason and emotions, especially in his last book, *Pedagogia da Autonomia* [*Pedagogy of Freedom*] (Freire, 1997). Freire insisted on connecting our emotions with our reason. He spoke of a "reason soaked with emotion."

Principle 7: Make critical consciousness pedagogy co-intentional education among those involved in whatever roles.

A revolutionary leadership must accordingly practice *co-intentional* education. Teachers and students (leadership and people), co-intent on reality, are both Subjects, not only in the task of unveiling that reality, and thereby coming to know it critically, but in the task of re-creating that knowledge. As they attain this knowledge of reality through common reflection and action, they discover themselves as its permanent re-creators. In this way, the presence of the oppressed in the struggle for their liberation will be what it should be: not pseudo-participation, but committed involvement. (p. 69)

Principle 8: Engage critical consciousness as both process and outcome, both method and result, both reflection and action, both analytical and change-oriented.

For Freire, the goal of critical consciousness as a pedagogy is "to be more fully human" (p. 55). He contrasts *being human* with the goal of having more wealth and possessions (p. 59). One doesn't attain critical

consciousness as a fixed and defined outcome; rather it is an ever-emerging result of ongoing engagement and inquiry. He viewed critical pedagogy as both a method for making sense of the world and a new way of seeing and experiencing the world that yielded significant outcomes of new knowledge, new attitudes, new behaviors, and, ultimately, social change (p. 69). This is achieved through a process of sense making that provides a new understanding of the world, which constitutes, as an outcome, a different kind of knowledge, which leads to social change.

> As a process of search, of knowledge, and thus of creation, it requires the investigators to discover the interpenetration of problems, in the linking of meaningful themes. The investigation will be most educational when it is most critical, and most critical when it avoids the narrow outlines of partial or "focalized" views of reality, and sticks to the comprehension of *total* reality. Thus, the process of searching for the meaningful thematics should include a concern for the links between themes, a concern to pose these themes as problems, and a concern for their historical-cultural context. (p. 108)

Principle 9: Acknowledge that all pedagogy is political.

Learning between teachers and students is what gives educational practice its gnostic character. It is a practice that involves the use of methods, techniques, materials; in its directive character, it implies objectives, dreams, utopias, ideas. Hence we have the political nature of education and the capacity that all educational practices have in being political and never neutral. In being specifically human, education is gnostic and directive and for this reason, political. It is artistic and moral as it uses techniques as a means to facilitate teaching; it involves frustrations, fears, and desires. It requires of a teacher a general competence that involves knowledge of the nature of knowledge itself as well as the specific knowledges linked to one's field of specialization (Freire, 2001, p. 67).

Principle 10: Engage critical pedagogy as fundamentally and continuously evaluative.

Critical consciousness involves ongoing evaluation. The development of a literacy campaign scenario presented earlier, which is the most extended example of Freire's approach in *Pedagogy of the Oppressed,* describes in depth and detail a participatory evaluation process. But critical pedagogy is not conceptualized as a project and the purpose is not to produce a report. Critical pedagogy is an ongoing process that aims to bring about long-term and lasting change.

A Holistic Freirean Evaluation Framework

Freire was philosophically grounded in Hegelian dialectics. What most strikes me about his pedagogy is his genius for synthesis. His capacity to transcend thesis and antithesis to generate integrated synthesis undergirds all 10 principles identified and discussed in this chapter. He emphasized throughout *Pedagogy of the Oppressed* that both the oppressors and the oppressed must achieve critical consciousness and do so for the advancement of each and both together (principle 1). He connected the individual to community (principle 2), and people to each other (principle 3). He integrated reflection and action (principle 4), objectivity and subjectivity (principle 5), thinking and emotion (principle 6), and evaluators and participants in evaluation (principle 7). He emphasized the interconnection and interrelationship between process and outcome, methods and results, analysis and engagement, and understanding and social change (principle 8). He portrayed cultural patterns, social interactions, community relationships, economic dynamics, socio-psychological manifestations, knowledge, education, and learning manifestations as fundamentally political; he made sense of everything through the lens of political economy and showed the oppressed how to understand their situations historically and currently through that lens. Thus, he connected the past to the present and future pedagogically and paradigmatically (principle 9). Finally, he brought what today we call evaluative thinking into his analysis, engagement process, and sense making, giving the oppressed, nonliterate, poor, and disadvantaged the facility to describe, compare, analyze, reflect, and render judgments as the basis for bringing about change (Patton, 2017b).

Principles-Focused Evaluation of Freirean Pedagogy

So, having extracted principles from Freire's writings and practice, how can we use them for evaluation? The first step would be to work with Freirean scholars and followers to review, refine, and validate the principles. For the sake of this example, let's presume that the principles are validated by those knowledgeable about Freirean pedagogy. They can then be used as a framework for evaluating initiatives based on Freirean pedagogy and principles. Here's a scenario in which that could occur.

The Paulo Freire Institute: Education to Transform

Dr. Moacir Gadotti, Professor of Education at the University of São Paulo and director of the Instituto Paulo Freire (IPF) in São Paulo, was a colleague of Paulo Freire (Gadotti, 1996a). He explains that the IPF was created in 1991 amid the political unrest that followed the events leading to the fall of the Berlin Wall and the end of the Soviet empire.

That was a defining moment for leftists worldwide. In a way, it was as if we had lost ground, lost our paradigm. Paulo Freire was asked at that time by the newspaper *Folha de S. Paulo* if he thought that was the "end of socialism." He replied that it was not the end of socialism but the end of a certain face of socialism. And added that, in this way, it would be easier to defend democratic socialism, socialism with freedom.

It was in this political context that the IPF was created, a context of paradigmatic crisis. It was the right moment to reassert and strengthen the paradigm of the oppressed that had nothing to do with the socialist authoritarian paradigm. (Gadotti, 2016)

When Paulo Freire left the Municipal Department of Education in São Paulo in 1991, Gadotti (2016) explains,

he was freer to devote himself to this new challenge he had always followed closely, even considering his busy schedule. Until 1997, he supervised all projects of the IPF. His last project was to organize with us the course he would begin in September that year in his celebrated return to Harvard University, where he had taught in 1969. We had already selected several texts that would be part of the readings we would recommend to his future students. Unfortunately, he died in May that year without fulfilling that dream. (p. 2)

To continue Freire's work does not mean to repeat it, but to reinvent it. As he once said, "the only way anyone has of applying in their situation any of the propositions I have made is precisely by redoing what I have done, that is, by not following me. In order to follow me it is essential not to follow me!" (Freire & Faundez, 1985, p. 41). This is what the IPF (*www.paulofreire.org*) attempts to do. The utopia that moves this institution is to educate, to transform, to create a planetary citizenship, a "planetarization" (Antunes, 2002), fighting social injustice caused by capitalist globalization, in the light of a new political culture, inspired by the Freirean legacy. A set of projects and programs contribute to the fulfillment of this institutional mission.

The Freirean Principles Extrapolated from His Writings and Practice Would Provide a Framework for Evaluating the IPF's Projects and Programs

Director Gadotti described the IPF approach to me in 2016. See if you infer how the Freirean pedagogical principles could be used to evaluate IPF programs by doing the two things I have emphasized throughout this book: (1) evaluate whether the principles are being followed, and (2) if the principles are being adhered to, identify and evaluate the outcomes of following principles. Here, then, are more details about the IPF approach and programs to be evaluated.

▶ Popular education and adult education have always been structuring programs of the IPF with numerous actions that have benefited thousands of people. We understand adult education as a fundamental human right, crucial in overcoming poverty and social exclusion. It is a human right since every human being seeks to become complete and, for that, they must read the world, build knowledge, and improve themselves. To recognize adult education as a human right implies considering all people able to produce knowledge, produce culture, and, through culture, transform nature and socially organize themselves.

▶ Another key IPF program is the citizenship school. The citizenship school opposes the theory of human capital, the movement of "total quality" and the "market-school" (Romão, 2000). Its main themes are school autonomy; integration between education, culture, and work; school and community; inter- and transdisciplinary vision; and critical education of teachers. This was one of the last dreams of Paulo Freire who, shortly before his death, in an interview at the IPF, defined the citizen school as "a school of community and camaraderie, which lives the tense experience of democracy."

▶ The IPF embraced the cause of ecopedagogy created by one of its founders, Francisco Gutiérrez (Gutiérrez & Prado, 1989), which was soon extremely well received. Ecopedagogy includes the study of planetarity, sustainability, global citizenship, and virtuality. It is broader than the pedagogy of environmental pedagogy and closer to a sustainable education, eco-education, than to environmental education, because it goes beyond the pursuit of a healthy relationship with the environment. It aims to discuss, based on everyday life, the deepest meaning of what we do with our existence. We understand ecopedagogy as a pedagogy of the earth, a new chapter of *Pedagogy of the Oppressed* since the Earth itself, a living and evolving thing, during the Anthropocene became very oppressed. The last text written by Paulo Freire was about ecology, published posthumously in *Pedagogia da Indignação* [*Pedagogy of Indignation*] (Freire, 2000).

▶ In 1998, one year after the death of Paulo Freire, the IPF created the Paulo Freire Forum, an international space for the study and actualization of his legacy, as well as for the strengthening of links between people and organizations developing work and research from the perspective of Freirean philosophy (*http://forum.unifreire. org*). The Paulo Freire Forum functions permanently on a virtual campus and organizes international attendance meetings every 2 years. In the Paulo Freire Forum of Bologna (Italy), in 2000, the UNIFREIRE (*Universitas* Paulo Freire) was founded. The UNIFREIRE was organized as a set of institutes and academic departments, with different independent programs linked by the same Freirean spirit, in more than 20 countries (*www.paulofreire.org/unifreire*).

▶ The IPF maintains the Centro de Referência Paulo Freire [Paulo Freire Reference Centre], dedicated to preserving the memory and legacy of the educator, providing videos of lessons, conferences, lectures, and interviews he gave in life, increasing the access of people interested in his life, work, and legacy. A digital collection (*www.acervo. paulofreire.org*) makes available a great part of his work for downloading free of charge.

▶ The IPF is a member of the World Social Forum International Council and the World Education Forum. These forums would not have been born in Brazil without the history of more than 50 years of struggle of the popular education movement which was so greatly inspired by Paulo Freire. By participating in and promoting, from the beginning, these forums, the IPF seeks to collectively construct the strategies required for the construction of "another possible world" (Gadotti, 2007). Educating for another possible world is to educate for the emergence of what is not yet, the not-yet, the utopia. Education for another possible world is also education for a break, for rebellion, for refusal, for saying "no," to shout, denouncing and announcing.

Gadotti explains that the IPF intends to be a broad, fruitful, and generous gathering of institutions, projects, dreams, and men and women who are subjects of our history, and therefore conditioned, but not determined beings, able to achieve social transformation. As Carlos Rodrigues Brandão affirmed,

> It is not about pettily thinking of specific practices of education based on Paulo Freire's ideas. This would be to radically reject Paulo Freire's ideas. Nothing is less Freirean than being a follower of ideas without knowing how to be a creator of spirits. It is a matter of creating conditions to fraternally put to the test our own capacity to create. To really dare. To open new horizons in the name of justice and equality. (as cited in Gadotti, 1996b, p. 706)

Gadotti notes that when Paulo Freire created the IPF, he wanted to bring together people and institutions which, driven by the same dreams of a humanizing education, could deepen their reflections, improve their practices and strengthen themselves in the struggle for the construction of another possible world. The IPF has been and still seeks to be a work of educators who deeply identify with the Freirean legacy and are driven by those dreams, seeking, in the daily work of the institution, to joyfully but also with seriousness, scientific-creative rigor, commitment, and solidarity, to build more just and sustainable realities.

Matching the Evaluation Approach to the Nature of the Initiatives Being Evaluated

The fundamental lesson of this chapter is the importance of matching the evaluation approach to the nature of the initiatives being evaluated. The initiatives of the IPF are presumably based on the principles of Freirean pedagogy. Therefore, a principles-focused evaluation would be the appropriate match for IPF projects and programs to assess fidelity to Freirean principles and attainment of outcomes consistent with Freirean values, ideology, philosophy, and practice.

Practice Exercise

Pick one of the 10 Freirean principles that you find particularly relevant to your interests and arena of engagement. What makes it meaningful and relevant to you? Now pick a Freirean principle that you find inappropriate or irrelevant for your work. Why? What's the difference between the more relevant and less relevant principle for your interest, values, and work?

Developmental

A leader is a man that can adapt principles to circumstances.
—GEORGE S. PATTON, World War II U.S. Army general

The developmental nature of a high-quality principle refers to its adaptability and applicability to diverse contexts and over time. A principle is thus both context sensitive and adaptable to real-world dynamics, providing a way to navigate the turbulence of complexity and uncertainty. In being applicable over time, it is enduring (not time-bound) in support of ongoing development and adaptation in an ever-changing world.

Chapters 19–20 elucidate the ways in which principles can support DEVELOPMENTAL ADAPTATION when navigating complex dynamic systems.		
GUIDE framework for effectiveness principles	Chapter 6	GUIDE for Effectiveness Principles: The Characteristics of High-Quality Effectiveness Principles
G = GUIDING	Chapters 7–11	
U = USEFUL	Chapters 12–14	
I = INSPIRING	Chapters 15–18	
D = DEVELOPMENTAL	Chapter 19	The Developmental Nature of Effectiveness Principles: A Case Example of Adapting Principles in Practice *Yve Susskind and Peggy Holman*
	Chapter 20	Simple Rules and Minimum Specifications: Spotlight on Complexity Concepts with Developmental Implications

The Developmental Nature of Effectiveness Principles

A Case Example of Adapting Principles in Practice

YVE SUSSKIND

PEGGY HOLMAN

This chapter presents the intersection of two sets of principles: principles for dialogic engagement with complex systems and developmental evaluation principles, each adapted to a particularly emergent situation, a challenging context, a high degree of uncertainly, and the dynamic interrelationship with the other set of principles. I know that's quite abstract, but what this meant in the real world of an innovative journalistic undertaking will all become clear, or at least clearer, shortly. To appreciate both the substance of this chapter and its positioning at this point in the book, a quick review will help.

Part I (Chapters 1–5) presented the purpose and niche of principles-focused evaluation. Part II opened with the GUIDE framework for effectiveness principles, presented in Chapter 6: A high-quality principle (1) provides guidance, (2) is useful, (3) inspires, (4) supports ongoing development and adaptation, and (5) is evaluable. Chapters 7–11 provided guidance for developing and distinguishing effectiveness principles, essentially elaborating the G (guiding) criterion in the GUIDE framework. Chapters 12–14

focused on the U (useful) standard for effectiveness principles. Chapters 15–18 provided examples of the inspiring (I) nature of meaningful effectiveness principles. That brings us to the developmental (D) characteristic of effectiveness principles.

> The developmental nature of a high-quality principle refers to its adaptability and applicability to diverse contexts and over time. A principle is thus both context sensitive and adaptable to real-world dynamics, providing a way to navigate the turbulence of complexity and uncertainty. In being applicable over time, it is enduring (not time-bound), in support of ongoing development and adaptation in an ever-changing world.

This chapter provides a case example that illuminates the developmental and contextually adaptable nature of principles. This principles-focused case has been prepared by two of the primary people involved, Peggy Holman, in the role of co-designing and facilitating the innovation process, and Yve Susskind, in the role of principles-focused developmental evaluator. I played a consultative role as the process and the evaluation unfolded. I asked Peggy and Yve to introduce themselves to you, after which they tell the story in a highly creative, emergent, and developmental way. I would only add that this example illustrates all of the GUIDE criteria, but I am placing it at this point in the book because it so engagingly portrays, highlights, and illuminates the developmental nature of effectiveness principles.

—M. Q. P.

The Intersection of Engagement and Developmental Evaluation Principles in the Experience Engagement Conference

Meet Peggy Holman

My work with dialogic practices took off in the early 1990s when I experienced Open Space Technology, a process that enables groups of any size to self-organize around complex, even conflicted, and important issues. I saw Open Space as a means to liberate spirits and make space for breakthroughs to emerge by engaging a diverse group that cared. It led me on a journey to learn about these strange system-oriented, high-participation practices in which the needs of individuals and needs of the whole could both be met.

To pursue my quest, I spearheaded the creation of two editions of *The Change Handbook* (Holman, Devane, & Cady, 2007), an anthology that showcases these practices. We moved from 18 to 61 methods between the two editions, in 1999 and 2007. That explosive growth led me to write *Engaging Emergence: Turning Upheaval into Opportunity* (2010), which articulates the underlying principles that inform my approach to design and hosting.

I began working with journalists in 1999 because of a racially motivated shooting that got me thinking about the role of stories in shaping our worldviews and actions. I wanted to take what I knew about engagement and storytelling and work with journalists—our cultural storytellers. Several journalism colleagues and I formed Journalism That Matters (JTM), a nonprofit that convenes conversations to foster collaboration, innovation, and action so that a diverse news and information ecosystem supports communities to thrive.

Meet Yve Susskind

In my consulting business, Praxis Associates LLC, I collaborate with nonprofits, community-based leaders, and activists to collect data and think critically about their work and the results they are achieving in order to continually build effective strategies and programs for organizational and social transformation. In my 53rd year on the planet, I now recognize that I am most comfortable living on the edges—socially, professionally, and personally. It has never seemed natural to me to separate evaluation from design and creation. It just makes sense to me that the processes of reflection, learning, questioning, trying, inventing, experimenting, and refining happen in an integrated way.

Imagine my delight when I discovered that there is a "legitimate" approach (books are written about it!) to evaluation that aligns with how I have been working all along but felt like I couldn't tell anyone about! What I love about developmental evaluation is that it uses the natural human tendency toward integrating doing and learning (action and reflection, a.k.a. praxis) to support social innovation and problem solving. I now work primarily with organizations that already understand that they are in the midst of change and are seeking to learn from and harness the feedback that comes from trying new things. I understand that cycle of evaluation/planning/reflection (i.e., praxis) to be a dialogic process, and so writing this chapter with Peggy has been profoundly liberating for me.

JTM and the Experience Engagement Conference: Principles in Practice

When issues are complex, answers unclear, and people hold passionate and conflicting perspectives, thinking you know the optimal course of action is at best foolish and at worst destructive. So what do you do when you don't know what to do?

JTM embraces disruption by creating a generative space in which people's differences become a source for innovation. The story of Experience Engagement (EE), a conference co-hosted by JTM that brought journalists and community members together, illustrates the approach. While JTM has designed and hosted highly participative conferences—often called "unconferences"—since 2001, this was the first time that developmental evaluation played a role in making innovations visible and extending the reach of a conference.

This chapter is about the intersections we discovered between the principles that guide JTM's conference design and the principles of developmental evaluation. (*Note:* The developmental evaluation principles are presented in Chapter 5, Exhibit 5.4, p. 30.) JTM's conference design includes *hosting practices*. We use the term *host* instead of *facilitator* because facilitator implies you are external to what is happening. In truth, there is no outside. Hosting acknowledges that you, too, are a participant, bringing your skills and consciousness, and can be changed by the experience. Our experience confirmed our hunch that these

two sets of principles are complementary and mutually supportive.

This chapter is presented as a dialogue between the authors, one of us being a systems change practitioner and the other an evaluator. The dialogue unfolded as we made sense of the experience we shared in designing, hosting, and developmentally evaluating the EE conference. Peggy brings her perspective from 20 years of working with and writing about dialogic practices suited to addressing complex, even conflicted situations. Yve is an evaluator specializing in understanding and strengthening the processes and results of social-change-oriented organizations. The perspective Yve brings to this chapter is informed by the rare (and joyous) collaboration with partners whose conscious, principled approach naturally reinforces the processes and principles appropriate for evaluating emergent, complex situations.

Peggy's sections provide background on JTM and the EE conference. They use dialogic principles from her book *Engaging Emergence: Turning Upheaval into Opportunity* (2010) as enacted in the EE conference. Yve's sections, which are presented in boxes, point out the intersections of the two sets of principles. Within the boxes, developmental evaluation principles are in **bold** and dialogic principles are in ***bold italics***.

Some Context

Since 2001, JTM has convened conversations that have enabled people across the "whole system" of journalism—journalists, media reformers, educators, students, technologists, and others who care about the role of news and information in civil society—to reimagine journalism that serves the needs of communities and democracy. We began convening these gatherings, with Open Space Technology at their heart, because, like many structures of civil society, journalism is in the midst of a death and rebirth, grappling with its role and relevance. As a process that invites people to self-organize by taking responsibility for what they love as a means to address complex, important issues (Owen, 2008), Open Space was ideally suited to reimagining journalism's future.

We've known from feedback from people who attended our conferences that we've made a difference. But we were searching for a way to (1) extend that reach from the fortunate few who could attend our face-to-face events and (2) make the impact of our work more visible. Because our approach to hosting is dialogic—based on a theory that change occurs through the conversations we have, the stories we tell, and the generative images that emerge—we sought an approach to evaluation that mirrored the emergent nature of our hosting practices. Developmental evaluation seemed promising.

We began our journey with a call to Michael Quinn Patton, who affirmed our suspicions that the underlying principles that guide our approach to process design married well with the principles of developmental evaluation. We were also fortunate to discover an evaluator, Yve Susskind, who brought an instinct for working with the uncertainty that is a given when designing a process intended to encourage breakthroughs in thinking and practice to emerge. With Michael as an adviser and Yve at our side, our work began.

Principles for Designing Dialogues

My quest to understand the principles of successful dialogues led me to study complexity science and to connect it to my experience with groups. I discovered a pattern that I could reliably work with, even though specific outcomes were unpredictable.

Warning: While the description that follows may sound neat, tidy, and linear, that's far from the case. That just makes it easier to read.

In brief, a disturbance (chaos) interrupts the status quo. In addition to natural responses, like grief or fear or anger, people differentiate—take on different tasks. For example, in an earthquake, while many are immobilized, some care for the injured, others look for food and water. Someone creates a "find your loved ones" site on the Internet. A few blaze the trails and others follow. They see what's needed and bring their unique gifts to the situation. A new order begins to arise. This pattern of change flows as follows:

▶ *Disruption* breaks apart the status quo.

▶ The system *differentiates* and, through random encounters, surfaces innovations and distinctions among its parts.

▶ As different parts interact, a new and more complex coherence arises. See Exhibit 19.1.

The following principles inform my approach to engaging with disruption, differentiation, and coherence. In essence, they support *pioneering*, better equipping people to enter into the mystery of not knowing outcomes in advance in hopes of achieving breakthroughs and creating innovations:

▶ Disrupt *compassionately* by creating a space for dialogue through:

  ▷ Asking meaningful, generative, bold questions.

  ▷ Inviting the diversity of the people and perspectives in the system.

  ▷ Welcoming who and what shows up.

▶ *Encourage random encounters* by crafting opportunities for individual expression and connection.

  ▷ *Reflect collectively to seek meaning* and emerging coherence, calling forth novel *simplicity* on the other side of complexity.

  ▷ And just when you think you're done, something or someone will disrupt what's happening. creating an opportunity to *iterate*—to do it all again (see Exhibit 19.2).

EXHIBIT 19.1. Patterns in Facilitated Groups

EXHIBIT 19.2. Actions for Dialogic Engagement

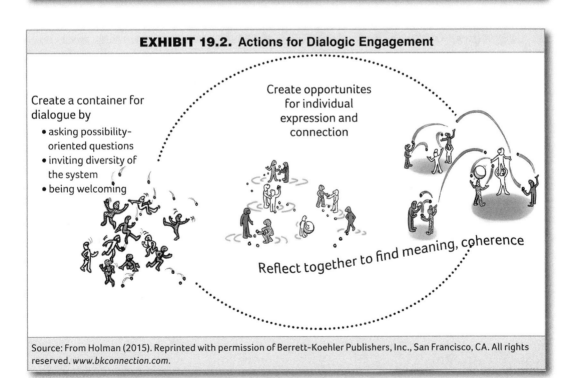

Yve reflects: An example of Peggy's description of *new coherence* emerging from disruption occurred in the design phase of the EE conference. The design team had already been working for a couple of months when Peggy and I met. So, at the next design team meeting, Peggy *introduced a disruption* into the planning that had been under way, in the form of a developmental evaluator (me) who was invited into the design process (**co-creation**). Prior to that disruption, the original coherence around the purpose of evaluation was that it would help measure the impact of JTM's dialogic practices on collective and individual understanding of engagement. With the disruptive idea that developmental evaluation would be something quite different and could be a powerful tool to foster a new understanding of the practice of journalism and community engagement, the purpose statement of the conference and the design itself were opened to renovation. Through the developmental evaluation processes of **defining the developmental purpose** and clarifying the specific **form that the innovation was taking**, the design team articulated the conference purpose as illuminating and supporting a new paradigm for community and journalism engagement. The next natural step was to confirm that the planned conference activities were congruent with that purpose. Thus the **co-creation** principle came into play. The developmental evaluation became part of the intervention when we aligned the conference activities and evaluation questions. By going through the conference design, we made sure that each activity was related to both the overall convening and development purposes and that there was a data source associated with each activity—a *new coherence*. Some of the specifics of conference activities, such as the end-of-the-day reflection questions, were left open to allow the design to respond (**co-creation**) to what was emerging from *disruption, randomness,* and *mystery.*

Designing EE

Often people fear emergent design because end goals are not articulated in advance. So how do you know where you're going? A distinction between aspirations and goals provides some guidance. Aspirations point in a direction without specifying details. It's an art to name an intention big and bold enough to hold a diversity of perspectives yet contained enough to not get lost. It's also an iterative process, holding the purpose lightly, knowing it will evolve as new players get involved and we learn more through working together.

Fear is also a common response to disruption. And disruption is a given in journalism. For years, journalism gatherings have been laden with "woe is me" commiseration. People told us that our JTM gatherings were different. That's because we met disruption by compassionately asking a bold, generative question. By being compassionate, we create a bubble in the dissonance to breathe and look around. Social science research tells us that we move toward what we can imagine (Cooperrider, 1990). An inviting question attracts those who care and implicitly says we'll figure it out together because no one has the answer.

The idea of dialogue has been entering into journalism for several years generally, as in the inclusion of the term *engagement* in the name of the EE conference. Yet few seemed to know the potential of engagement, using the term for activities like social media and business development. Given we had much to offer in this arena, it seemed time to host a gathering on journalism and community engagement. We reached out to the Agora Journalism Center at the University of Oregon, which, like JTM, focuses on the relationship between community and journalism.

Ask Generative, Bold Questions. The EE conference hosts included key players from the Agora Center and from JTM. We invited a diverse team of colleagues to form a design team, responsible for expressing conference aspirations, crafting an invitation, and inviting colleagues to attend. As the conference planning proceeded, an evaluation subteam of four plus Yve formed within the design team, aided by occasional advising calls with Michael Quinn Patton.

The team began with a preliminary conference design based on past JTM gatherings, tailored to the aspirations the hosts articulated for this gathering. Through the integration of developmental evaluation principles and practices into the conference design process, breakthroughs occurred in the convening question, the conference purpose, and the role of evaluation in investigating the question and supporting the purpose. Exhibit 19.3 shows this developmental journey from original aspirational statement for hosting to final, generative, and ambitious convening questions. Along this journey, the conference developmental purposes and the evaluation purposes became one and the same.

Yve reflects: Patton (2016b, p. 254) describes using the principles of developmental evaluation as *sensitizing concepts* that "remind us to engage with the concept throughout our fieldwork within a specific context." We used some of the developmental evaluation principles as sensitizing concepts to remind us what to include in both the design of the conference and its evaluation. The use of "**developmental purpose**" and "**innovation niche**" as sensitizing concepts focused the *iterative, collective reflection* that came so naturally to the design team. The result was a convening question aligned with the form of the innovation (open and generative) and a purpose statement that reflected the intent of the evaluation to midwife the emergence of an innovative engagement between journalists and communities that "contributes to thriving, inclusive communities." Thus, the conference purpose shifted from the original aspirational statement in column 1 of Exhibit 19.3 to the one in column 2. Because the whole conference was designed to deliberately create *random, unplanned encounters* to see what would emerge, and since

EXHIBIT 19.3. Example of Adaptation and Development of Principles	

Hosts' original aspirational statement: The conference focus is on:
 	
• Civic impact when journalists and communities engage.
• Media as a force for good.
 	
Our intent is to catalyze a network.
 	
• Work with the ecosystem and its power of connecting the players, increasing collaboration.
	Final generative, ambitious convening question: What is possible when the public and journalists engage to support communities to thrive?
	
	Developmental and evaluation purpose (they became one and the same):
	
	• Our intent is to *illuminate, inform, and support community information health* that contributes to *thriving, inclusive communities* by:
	  o learning about processes that grow it
	  o creating products that support it
	  o catalyzing a community of practice dedicated to it, and
	  o identifying actions to amplify it.
	• To begin to understand how engagement changes communities, the relationship between community members and journalists, and the field of journalism.

the group was experienced in using the feedback that comes from those kinds of "compassionate disruptions," there was an openness I have rarely experienced in other settings to the *iterative* refining of the **purpose of the conference in developmental** terms.

Our purpose also informed the evaluation.

Yve reflects: Before integrating developmental evaluation as the approach, the design team's language around evaluation included such phrases as "measuring participants' knowledge and perspectives on engagement before and after" and "identifying what people found valuable." By *embracing disruption* and **co-creating** the conference, evaluation, and the emerging innovation, the team's language around evaluation shifted away from terms such as *measuring, outcomes,* and *impact,* which imply a more developed model and a clearly defined set of expected outcomes. Early on, one of the hosting partners had suggested using their pre–post survey of impacts on conference participants' thinking as the centerpiece of the evaluation. The design team, focused on illuminating and supporting rather than measuring, prioritized a more ethnographic and qualitative approach, while the hosting partner carried out the pre–post survey in parallel. When the evaluation subteam was poring over the data that had naturally come out of the Open Space and the plenary sessions, we *welcomed what showed up* and incorporated the survey findings along with all the other naturally occurring data (such as Facebook posts, tweets, harvested sticky-note reflections). In so doing, we discovered additional support for listening as a key theme of engagement (the survey found that 20% of participants mentioned "listening" as part of the definition of engagement before the conference, and 30% did so at the end). The developmental evaluation

brought life to that data by identifying "Listening is our superpower" as one of three principles for engagement between journalists and community that emerged at EE. (To see the two other principles of engagement that emerged at the EE conference, see Exhibit 19.4 on p. 165. The three principles are listed in the curved line of text at the top.)

Additionally, our purpose gave us some sense of what we'd be listening for, while staying open to the unexpected. As we matched purpose with the products the conference would generate to aid our listening, we were astounded by the wealth of data that would be available to us: Open Space session notes, tweets and Facebook group posts, graphic recordings, photographs, audio and video recordings, Post-it notes used in clustering during group reflections. Yve kept a record so that we knew going in who was capturing what and how. It paid off down the road.

Yve reflects: Because of their experience using multiple dialogic practices to facilitate emergence, the design team easily embraced the developmental evaluation tenet to keep open to what is emerging and not prematurely force a meaning. There was an ease with knowing that the purpose of the endeavor was to illuminate and foster emergence of a new path (the **innovation niche principle**), that this was precisely the purpose of creating a setting where complex and unpredicted, *random encounters* would generate new order from chaos.

Engage the Diversity of the People and Perspectives in the System. If you want different results, then engage different people. Specifically, change the mix of people who are part of the system. It's another potential pain point, particularly with conflicted issues. After all, "those people," whoever the "other" is, can be disruptive. It can be messy. Typically, when a part of the system feels ignored, misheard, suppressed, misunderstood, it acts out. Yet people who are not the "usual suspects" bring an essential part of the puzzle precisely because the status quo ignores them. Their participation also contributes to the unpredictability of the situation. When you create a generative inquiry big enough to hold all who care and designing sufficient spaciousness for welcoming who and what shows up, new conversations focused on unexplored possibilities arise.

It's rare for journalists and community members to engage in extended dialogue with each other. It was part of what made EE unique. Without their interactions, the importance of listening might never have arisen. Yet it became an essential principle as voiced by a participant during the conference close: "Listening is our superpower."

Welcome Who and What Shows Up. Once the invitations have gone out, particularly when the gathering is open to the public, you never know who will show up. Or what external events might influence what's happening. Part of the art of dealing with disruption is to stay open and curious. It's where a personal practice that keeps one centered in a storm pays off. It's also helpful to work with a team when the situation is complex. So even if one host is emotionally triggered by something said or done, another can be present to ensure the space remains open for engaging with what's happening.

Yve reflects: Once the design team realized that the developmental (and evaluation) purposes were to illuminate and support, and not to measure outcomes, I understood the reason why Open Space Technology as the meeting process for EE made sense. OST is a *process based on principles* that purposely allows something new and unpredictable to emerge, where predetermined outcomes can be counterproductive, setting expectations in rigid terms that can blind us to the unexpected

emerging. Thus, OST exemplifies how the engagement principles of embracing *mystery* and *chance encounters* help generate **emergent meaning of the innovation.**

Encourage Random Encounters. What makes random encounters creative rather than a disruption that gets in the way? Our natural tendency when disrupted is to shut down, defend, or attack. For creative responses, we need room to work through triggers. By setting the stage with a meaningful, generative question, an invitation big enough to attract a variety of perspectives, and a commitment to being welcoming, the likelihood for generative encounters is increased.

Here's an example. At EE, an Oregon public figure who had been vilified by the Portland press signed up for the conference. Because we kept a public registration list, her presence at the conference was known to anyone who looked. We heard from several journalists warning us that she could be disruptive. So our ears were open as the convening began. Because our design provided the spaciousness for multiple perspectives to be authentically explored, she brought valuable contributions to numerous sessions. And if she was disruptive, it was with her creative gifts.

EE accomplished the task of using disruption creatively by spending almost two days in Open Space, inviting people to host sessions on what mattered most to them. In the process, they connected with others, often across divides.

People who have never experienced the process often fear chaos since no one knows what sessions people will call. What if it isn't relevant? Or if it's counterproductive? Or controversial? Welcoming disturbance prepares us to embrace mystery with curiosity and a sense of possibility.

In more than 20 years of opening space, sometimes in highly conflicted situations, I have never seen it fail. It's a seeming paradox: when we are invited to pursue what authentically matters to us, rather than selfishness, our actions become an act of service, contributing what we love on behalf of the whole. What in other circumstances might be disruptive differences become gifts to the whole.

Yve reflects: In looking back now at Peggy's and my first meeting, I clearly see that she was making good use of our **random encounter** by practicing the art of **welcoming who shows up.** She invited me to pursue what authentically matters to me (choosing the right evaluation approach for a given situation), which moved me to contribute what I love (using evaluation methods to support innovations that advance social change) on behalf of the whole (JTM's endeavor to reimagine journalism that serves the needs of communities and democracy). By doing so, she was able to create space for my authentic expression and drew out a connection to and commitment to the project that I didn't know I had. So, when she invited me to join the design process, with her characteristic openness to whatever might happen, I agreed to participate even though at that point there was not yet funding for evaluation. Our shared belief in the power of being open to what can happen when we trust the process gave me confidence it would be worth it.

At EE, the topics were rich and varied: *What does engagement mean? How do we really listen to communities? What is objectivity in journalism? Who determines what is newsworthy? Is there structural bias built into journalism that prevents rich engagement with communities of color?* These and other topics brought out authentic exchanges around deeply held beliefs. They led to both intimate and powerful exchanges on issues like journalism ethics when engaging communities and even discussions about the purpose and practice of journalism itself.

These sorts of exchanges are the norm at JTM gatherings. What was different this time was what the developmental

evaluation caused us to do: be mindful about gathering data, particularly from collective sense-making activities held at the beginning and end of each day, so that we could discern broader patterns across the conference.

Yve reflects: Through this process, toward the end of the conference the design team **welcomed and worked with a disturbance** that led to sharpened understanding of what was emerging. A **disruptive idea** was that journalism is not simply reporting, but that it is about change and making a difference for communities. Engaging with this idea then led to the even more disruptive idea that there may be a new role that is not journalism or the journalist, but the purpose of which is to support communities to tell their own stories. This disruption opened us to a breakthrough so that, as one participant said, "where we ended up at the conference was a completely different place, with community at the center rather than journalism at the center." Another observed, "If the focus is on the journalist, then it's often constrained by journalism training and the traditional role of journalism, where you're listening in order to write your story. You'll hear what fits your story, your frame, and you're not going to hear what the community has to say, which leads us to question who decides what's newsworthy. This is quite profound." In further reflection, the team began to see how that insight helps make sense of the "mistrust, lack of mutuality, suspicion of hidden agendas, separation, manipulation, and inauthentic voice" of the old paradigm. With that insight, a new framework of engagement began to take off (the **developmental purpose**). Through the practices of *embracing mystery* and allowing meaning to emerge from *random encounters,* the idea began to emerge that in a community engagement context, journalists' ideas and motivations should be removed from center stage. The journalists in the room were organically shifting their roles from having an idea of the story that they wanted to tell to being present and following leads, allowing the story to emerge—and then following the group's lead to tell its story, which became the story of the emerging role of the journalist.

Reflect Together to Discover Meaning and Emerging Coherence. We knew that we would gather a lot of data. And so we knew that the more we involved participants in making sense of their experience, the better off we'd be. We always design plenary sessions for reflection. They support us to step out of the flow of the intense conversations and look inward to ask what meaning is emerging for us.

By using our innate human capacity for pattern sensing, each time we gathered as a whole group, we did a different activity to surface the gems people had found. This was more than an intellectual activity. We invited them to draw from their whole self, to think critically, of course, but also to listen to their hearts, notice what touched their spirit, and what moved them to act. And then we'd involve them in discovering patterns across their individual yearnings so that collective insights, simply expressed, became visible.

Such activities are one of my favorite aspects of convening groups around complex issues. When people speak their authentic truths and find kindred spirits, something vital shifts in them. Many no longer feel so alone. They now know in their bones that others share deeper truths and aspirations that they may never have even consciously named before. And sometimes people with very different worldviews become unlikely partners to bring what matters to them to life. Often, an eloquent, deceptively simple generative image captures the essence of an emerging idea. We saw that in the closing reflections and tweets, which ultimately incorporated three widely expressed ideas into the journalism/engagement framework that emerged.

This collective sense making may be the greatest leap of faith for those who have not experienced the magic of emergence: that something useful can arise out of many seemingly disconnected interactions. Twenty-plus years of being present with groups meeting from a few hours to multiple days has left me with the unshakable confidence that when conditions are designed for creative engagement, something of value to the people attending always emerges. It may not be what they expected. In fact, it often isn't. [*Yve adds:* which is why an approach to evaluation that is not constrained by preconceived outcomes is so fitting.] But it can and does change lives and relationships. And it can inspire actions that have been frustratingly blocked for years.

Yve reflects: By generating data collected naturally through Open Space sessions and the harvesting and sorting of reflections, which integrate **meaning-making** directly into the conference activities, JTM has for years been exemplifying the developmental evaluation principles of **co-creation** and **timely feedback.** Opportunities for meaning making were certainly built into EE. Periodic activities allowed all attendees to reflect on a question, which the design team then incorporated into on-the-fly design change (**timely feedback principle**). At the end of each day, the team would do a quick review and summary of what had come out of the conference so far, what new ideas were emerging, and would then decide what the morning's generative reflection would be to draw out the fledgling new ideas and spur new suggestions for the next round of Open Space sessions. The *random encounters* of Open Space, the *shifting between opportunities for individual expression and connection* and reflective and generative focuses, led to disturbances that in turn led to real results for the **developmental goal** to illuminate the meaning of engagement.

At EE, the closing circle was predominated by gratitude. Many spoke movingly of falling back in love with journalism—practiced in the way they imagined it to be at the conference. Some students spoke of letting go of doubts about their chosen field, inspired anew by its potential to make a difference.

Because of the developmental evaluation, we were more mindful about capturing the insights garnered from these and other reflections. Our hope was that doing so would address one of the challenges that led to trying developmental evaluation: broadening our reach. Over the years, many people have told us how impactful their experience was. They changed their work, entered into partnerships, reframed the way they saw themselves or what they do, or were otherwise deeply affected by their experience. It's darn near impossible to share the impact of that, much less broaden its reach. We hoped the developmental evaluation might help us to do that.

Yve reflects: The use of **developmental purpose** as a sensitizing concept informed not only the design of the conference and the focus of the evaluation. That "illumination and support" were the stated developmental purposes was critical for driving the creation of a report that could be used by EE participants, funders, and others to envision new experiments and to make sense of what they were seeing in the changing media landscape. In past conferences, where *iterative* and *collective meaning making* took place, not having a purpose stated in **developmental** terms may have meant that, while the proceedings were collected and made available, there was, as a JTM board member expressed it, still sometimes a lingering frustration "that we didn't come away with a lasting document of record." The developmental goal to illuminate the new paradigm resulted in a tangible, groundbreaking, and actionable outcome (the framework, which is depicted below).

Ripples Beyond

Having gathered a great deal of data, including that derived from collective sense making across the days, we invited anyone who wished to do so to join us in diving into the material following the event. A team of five of us read through it all. Two of us drafted a report based on what we discovered. It wasn't easy! And it took the varied perspectives among us to tease out some elusive ideas.

Yve reflects: After the conference, as the developmental evaluation team worked with the proceedings, the copious data initially generated a feeling of overwhelm. "I have to admit that the moment of looking at the large data set and trying to turn it into a thesis was super overwhelming. That reduced my engagement," said one team member. The developmental evaluation principle of **utilization focus** helped the group realize that neither a "dissertation-level" analysis nor a traditional evaluation report was needed. In considering who would be using the product of the evaluation and what they would be using it for, the team identified JTM (to continue to develop the framework), community and journalist practitioners of engagement (who might want a set of guiding principles), funders and media organizations (who are looking for promising new directions for projects), and community-based organizations (that want to better understand how to work with journalists). None of these users needed a dissertation, or even a full conference or evaluation report. The reminder to focus on utility echoes the engagement principles of using *meaning making* as a doorway to *simplifying*.

Another breakthrough came when we made it visual (see Exhibit 19.4.)

We shared our synthesis of their words and ideas with the rest of the participants for comment and then made it widely available. It's a framework that provides a glimpse into how journalism and community are evolving together. It now guides our work and is being used by others. As a first step in putting language around what the collective wisdom of journalists, community members, educators, students, and others are sensing in the changing journalism ecosystem, it seems to resonate when we share it.

This framework has become JTM's calling card for describing our work. We produced a framework report that summarizes the emerging ideas about engagement that are reflected in the graphic. The full report can be found at the EE website (Journalism That Matters, 2016). We are also using it as part of a new developmental evaluation supporting a project by one of the conference attendees. It's influencing the way they think about their pioneering journey and causing them to dig deeper in learning how these principles apply to their real-world work. And it's raising the bar on the quality of their engagement.

Yve reflects: Indeed, it appears that results are already being seen. By taking a **utilization focus**, the team determined that

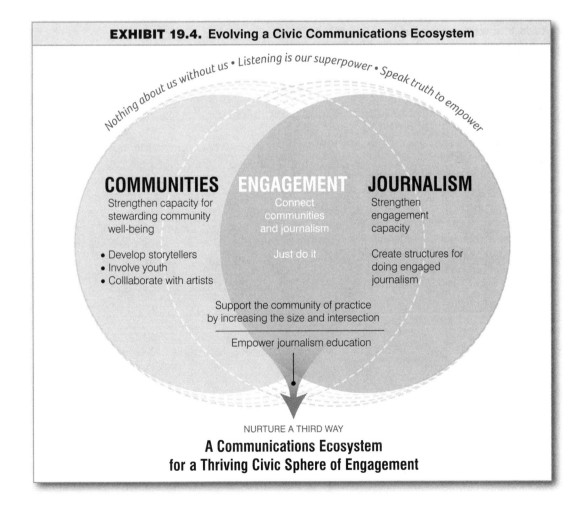

EXHIBIT 19.4. Evolving a Civic Communications Ecosystem

Nothing about us without us • Listening is our superpower • Speak truth to empower

COMMUNITIES
Strengthen capacity for stewarding community well-being

- Develop storytellers
- Involve youth
- Colllaborate with artists

ENGAGEMENT
Connect communities and journalism

Just do it

JOURNALISM
Strengthen engagement capacity

Create structures for doing engaged journalism

Support the community of practice by increasing the size and intersection

Empower journalism education

NURTURE A THIRD WAY
A Communications Ecosystem for a Thriving Civic Sphere of Engagement

among the key users of the framework report are funders and institutions that study and support journalism. A funder who attended the conference indicated it has impacted his thinking and work with local journalism. A potential project with a community developer became more likely because of our ability to express our philosophy. The developer has told us that what we are doing is what is missing in their community engagement process, and the head of the Agora Center used the framework to "think about where Agora fit in the model." By adding a **utilization focus** to emergence, we got results in the form of impact on institutions.

Following the developmental evaluation tenet that evaluation is part of the process of **supporting an innovation and then learning more about it through its adaptation to new contexts,** the design team identified two next steps that are currently in process. We are interacting with a handful of projects that were informed by EE by (1) supporting the projects' use of the framework as a guiding strategy and (2) by deepening our understanding of engagement by asking "What are we learning about the principles articulated in the framework from what is happening in the projects? What outcomes are we starting to see related to these ideas?" Essentially, the plan is to engage with the framework with a *pioneering* mindset—to jump in, try out the new ideas, and then through *collective reflection* work with the feedback that comes.

Ongoing Development

The framework that emerged from EE, complete with its generative visual, continues to be shared with journalists, community activists, funders, students, academics, and others. JTM is now using the framework in the next phase of learning about "what is possible when the public and journalists engage to support communities to thrive." Using developmental evaluation, we are working with several engagement projects around the country to support their use of the framework's emergent principles. Peggy, Yve, and other JTM members meet regularly to reflect on what we are learning about the framework and to deepen our understanding of what the principles mean and how they make a difference in these projects. And we stay open to what emerges as our journey continues.

Practice Exercise

As noted in the introduction to this chapter, the placement of this case example at this point was to portray, highlight, and illuminate the *D* (developmental) criterion in the GUIDE framework. Select at least one of the engagement principles presented by Peggy Holman and comment on the extent to which it meets the other four GUIDE criteria. Likewise, select at least one developmental evaluation principle portrayed by Yve Susskind and comment on the extent to which it meets the other four GUIDE criteria.

CHAPTER 20

Simple Rules
and Minimum Specifications
Spotlight on Complexity Concepts
with Developmental Implications

As long as you're dancing, you can break the rules.
Sometimes breaking the rules is just extending the rules.
Sometimes there are no rules.
—MARY OLIVER, "Three Things to Remember"

Principles are especially powerful rudders for navigating complex dynamic systems. Chapter 2 positioned complex dynamic situations as a particularly appropriate niche for principles-driven initiatives and interventions, and therefore principles-driven evaluation. This chapter returns to complexity with a focus on two prominent and widely used complexity concepts: simple rules and minimum specifications. In so doing, I hope to further illuminate the implications of the *D* (developmental) criterion in the GUIDE framework.

Simple Rules

In the complexity theory community, the phrase "simple rules" refers to emergent patterns that constitute rules of thumb that can be used to make quick decisions and act rapidly under conditions of complexity. "Simple rules tame complexity better than complex solutions" (Kinni, 2015, p. 1). Simple rules, to be effective, should be small in number, customized by and for those who need to follow them, and provide direction while giving enough latitude to exercise discretion (Sull & Eisenhardt, 2012). In fact, or at least in my opinion, based on the GUIDE criteria, simple rules are often not rules at all, but constitute principles.

In Chapter 7, I differentiated principles from rules. Rules are quite specific and meant to be followed. Rules do not provide latitude for exercising judgment and discretion. The purpose of a rule is to remove judgment and decision. Consider these rules on a public beach:

▶ No fishing
▶ No nudity
▶ No littering
▶ No unaccompanied children
▶ No boating

▶ No fires

▶ No cooking

▶ No alcohol

▶ No drugs

These are what most people would think of as simple rules. They provide absolutely concrete guidance. They demand complete compliance. No judgment or decision making is needed. Just follow the rules. What complexity theorists mean by simple rules is different in that they are patterns of behavior that have emerged to navigate in a complex dynamic system. So let's add principles to the mix.

Principles, in contrast to rules, provide guidance but must be interpreted in context and require judgment. Here is a set of principles for a public beach:

▶ Respect others using the beach.

▶ Help keep the beach clean and pleasant for all.

▶ Play safely.

▶ Supervise children.

▶ Have fun.

▶ Report suspicious activity.

Now here are some complexity-based *simple rules* for behavioral patterns at a public beach.

▶ Groups of people spread out over the available space rather than collect together.

▶ Areas of activity (volleyball) are separated from areas of just hanging out (sunbathing).

▶ People position themselves in the same direction in relation to water and sun.

As these examples show, complexity-derived simple rules are meant to refer to consistently observed and emergent patterns consistently followed, not rules imposed by authorities. Because the two

different meanings can be confused, I think the term "simple rules" is an unfortunate moniker in the complexity literature. Moreover, most lists of complexity-based simple rules are expressed more as principles than rules. In a widely cited article on simple rules in the *Harvard Business Review,* Sull and Eisenhardt (2012) tell the story of a company that faced and managed a crisis by developing and following four simple rules:

▶ Remove obstacles to growing revenues.

▶ Minimize up-front expenditure.

▶ Provide benefits immediately (rather than having them pay off in the long term).

▶ Reuse existing resources.

These are *not* rules in the usual sense. These are principles aimed at effectiveness derived from a combination of experience, situational analysis, and values. The distinction is not mere semantics, at least not from an evaluation perspective. Rules are evaluated by compliance. Principles are evaluated by effectiveness based on the GUIDE criteria. Exhibit 20.1 lists rules for a playroom in a coffee shop. These are rules in both content and visual imagery.

The most famous example of simple rules in complexity is the Boids simulation. In 1986, computer programmer Craig Reynolds simulated the flocking behavior of birds. It became famous as illustrating how complex adaptive systems can be based on a few simple rules. It came to be called Boids, mimicking someone with a stereotypical New York City accent saying "birds." The rules applied in the simplest flocks of Boids are as follows:

▶ Separation: steer to avoid crowding local flockmates.

▶ Alignment: steer toward the average heading of local flockmates.

▶ Cohesion: steer to move toward the average position of local flockmates.

EXHIBIT 20.1. All Rules All The Time

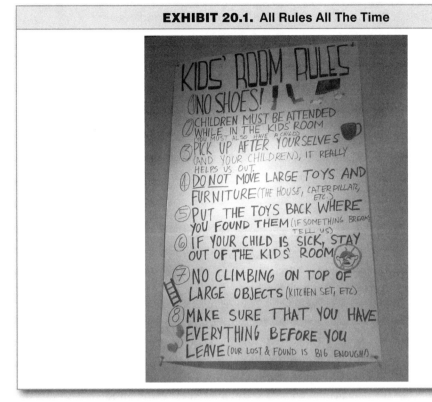

For an illustration of the Boids simulation and discussion of its implications, see Reynolds (2001).

I read these statements as closer to principles than rules, though in order to do the computer simulation, software rules had to be written. So the simulation is rules based. The difficulty with the Boids simulation is that it is an oversimplification and overgeneralization. It's not how all birds flock all the time. Go watch birds in the real world. You will not observe those three "simple rules" controlling their behavior. From my home in Northern Minnesota I spend a lot of time every fall and spring watching migrating flocks of Canada geese, ducks, and swans. The Boids simulation does not capture migratory flight behavior. It's a computer simulation, not a representation of real-world bird behavior. The semantic principle of non-identity reminds us: *The word is not the thing* (Dawes, 2013). Parallel insights: The map is not the territory. The computer simulation is not the real world.

That said, there are patterns in flocking behavior. But they are more accurately described as patterns than rules. Rules are absolute. Patterns are tendencies. Again, the distinction matters, especially for understanding the world (natural principles) and designing effective systems to meet the changes of complexity (effectiveness principles).

Sometimes an organization combines rules and principles. Exhibit 20.2 offers an example from an after-school program.

Simple Rules for Facilitation and Understanding of Human Systems Dynamics

Glenda Eoyang (2009), founder and director of the Human Systems Dynamics Institute, has specified the six "simple rules" that inform her facilitation work:

EXHIBIT 20.2. Combined List of Rules and Principles
Can You Tell Which Is Which?

---

1. Teach and learn in every interaction.

2. Reinforce strengths of self and other.

3. Search for the true and the useful.

4. Give and get value for value.

5. Attend to the part, the whole, and the greater whole.

6. Engage in joyful practice.

Again, in my view, these are principles, not rules. Each provides guidance but must be interpreted and applied contextually. Each requires judgment, not mere compliance.

An excellent example of Eoyang's skillful facilitation work is her consultation in redesigning a county's social service system, described in the important practitioner's toolkit *Systems Concepts in Action* by Williams and Hummelbrunner (2011). The results of her work took the form of a set of observed patterns expressed as "rules," all of which read to me like principles rather than rules. See what you think.

▶ Build success for yourself and others.

▶ Develop people and processes that improve outcomes.

▶ Stay connected.

▶ Learn your way into a shared future.

▶ Decide and trust others to decide. (pp. 148–149)

Royce Holladay, also a leader at the Human Systems Dynamics Institute, has written the online article "Four Principles of Change: Simple Rules," whose title makes principles and simple rules equivalent:

Human Systems Dynamics (HSD) helps you see, understand, and influence the patterns of interaction and decision making that shape your world. . . . We have been exploring a set of four principles that help you understand change in the complexity of human systems. These principles use the essence of HSD to offer options for understanding and taking action as you navigate change in complex systems. While HSD, as a field of study, presents many ways to think about change, these four principles establish a solid framework for affecting change in your organization:

1. Human systems change in response to system tension.

2. Change at a global level depends on change at the local level.

3. A short list of simple rules increases system-wide coherence.

4. Adaptive change happens through iterative cycles of Adaptive Action. (Holladay, 2015)

I asked Glenda Eoyang, a longtime friend and colleague, about calling these principles. She responded:

"I think that what you call principles, we would call simple rules.

"We used 'principles' in this piece in the sense of first principles: *a fundamental truth or proposition that serves as the foundation for a system of belief or behavior or for a chain of reasoning.*

"We don't get stuck on definitions usually. We have sometimes used principles rather than simple rules to talk about the MIN SPECS."

From my perspective, the four statements are neither principles (first or otherwise) nor simple rules. They are premises about how change happens. They are beliefs. They aspire to be natural principles (how the world works), but they are not sufficiently empirically validated or generalizable to be treated as natural principles. They can be considered natural principle hypotheses. But because the principles are directed at change and are meant to be used to facilitate change, it strikes me as potentially valuable to express them more directly as effectiveness principles. In Exhibit 20.3 I have done just that. I'm offering this rendering of how I think these premises could translate into evaluable effectiveness principles and corresponding principles-focused evaluation questions for illustration purposes. The evaluation questions invite rigorous

EXHIBIT 20.3. Translating Change Premises into Effectiveness Principles		
Original human systems dynamics premises	**Translation into effectiveness principles**	**Principles-focused evaluation questions**
1. Human systems change in response to system tension.	1. Identify and use system tensions to facilitate human systems change.	What tensions were identified? How were they identified? How were they used to facilitate systems change? What were the results?
2. Change at a global level depends on change at the local level.	2. Analyze and act on the interconnections between local and global change.	What global issue is the target of change? What is the local manifestation of that issue? How does change at the local level connect to global change?
3. A short list of simple rules increases systemwide coherence.	3. Build systemwide coherence through a short set of relevant and interrelated principles.	What is the baseline degree of coherence in the system of interest? How are relevant and interrelated principles identified? How are they used? How does their identification and use affect systemwide coherence?
4. Adaptive change happens through iterative cycles of Adaptive Action (Human System Dynamics, 2013).	4. Apply the Adaptive Action cycle interactively to achieve adaptive change.	How was the Adaptive Action cycle applied? What changes occurred? To what extent and in what ways were those changes "adaptive," if at all?

systematic inquiry into the implementation and effectiveness of principles.

Distinguishing Principles from Rules: Does It Matter?

One person says that my feeling is fancy, another that my fancy is feeling.
  We should have a rule. Reason offers itself; but it is pliable in every sense; and thus there is no rule.
    —BLAISE PASCAL, *French mathematician and philosopher*

The *I* in the GUIDE framework is for *Inspiring*. Principles inspire. Rules constrain. Principles are grounded in values. Rules are grounded in obeisance to the authority that sets the rule. Principles challenge us to walk the talk of our values. Rules evoke fear of the consequences of being caught breaking them. Principles move us toward a meaningful vision of what matters. Rules limit us to what is acceptable.

Clearly, I think it's worth distinguishing principles from rules, and that the distinction is important, as is clarity about the distinction. A core principle of evaluation practice is "Be clear." This means being as clear as you can be, and being clear about what you're not able to be clear about, and the implications for any particular evaluation of the degree of clarity that is possible in a given situation. Rules and principles are different, and the implications of those differences matter, often a great deal. Stopping at a stop sign is a rule (law) of driving. "Drive defensively" is a principle. In the United States, the "Three strikes, you're out" rule (three felony convictions means life in prison) removed judicial discretion, which is based on the principle that the punishment fit the crime and judges decide. The result contributed to the United States having the highest incarceration rate in the world, especially of young African American men. Immigration rules determine who can be in a country legally. Medicaid and health insurance reimbursement rules in the United States determine

what medical care people are eligible for in contrast to the principle that a doctor determines what is needed based on the best interest of the patient.

The Good, the Bad, and the Confusing

For there's nothing either good or bad, but thinking makes it so.
    —WILLIAM SHAKESPEARE, *Hamlet*, Act 2, Scene 2

Let me hasten to add that I'm not saying rules are bad and principles are good. I'm saying they are different—and evaluated differently. The "Three strikes, you're out" rule removed judicial discretion, but giving judges discretion to follow the principle that the punishment fit the crime can lead to (and historically has led to) racial, gender, age, and social class biases and injustices. Neither principles nor rules are inherently good or bad, just or unjust, fair or unfair. Much will depend on how they are interpreted and applied—and, when applied, what consequences result. That's where evaluation comes in for both rules and principles. Are they followed? If so, with what consequences?

The point here is that evaluating rules or principles will depend on clarifying the purpose of each and what criteria to apply in judging effectiveness. My judgment is that the complexity-based meaning of "simple rules" confuses rather than clarifies. Regardless, I don't expect complexity theorists to stop referring to observed and emergent patterns as *simple rules*. I'm merely hoping that principles-focused evaluators will be thoughtful about the different meanings of terms used in various contexts and take those differences into consideration when developing and evaluating principles (or rules).

Think about what rules you experience in your own world. Does it matter in your experience whether you are subject to rules, simple or otherwise, versus principles? In what area of your personal experience is this distinction clear, meaningful, and important?

Minimum Specifications

Let thy principles be brief and fundamental, which as soon as thou shalt recur to them, will be sufficient to cleanse the soul completely, and to send thee back from all discontent with the things to which thou returnest.

—MARCUS AURELIUS, Roman emperor, *Meditations of Marcus Aurelius*

Let's turn to another important and widely used complexity concept: MIN SPECS. (In the complexity literature, the shorthand for "minimum specifications" is MIN SPECS.) The basic idea of MIN SPECS is to "establish only those very few requirements necessary to define something, leaving everything else open to the creative evolution of the complex adaptive system" (Zimmerman, Lindberg, & Plsek, 2001, p. 161).

> We often over-specify things when designing or planning new activities in our organizations. This follows from the paradigm of "organization as a machine." If you are designing a machine, you had better think of everything, because the machine cannot think for itself. Of course, in some cases, organizations do act enough like machines to justify selected use of this metaphor. For example, if a person is having their gallbladder removed, they would prefer the surgical team operate like a precision machine; save that emerging, creative behavior for another time! Maximum specifications and the elimination of variation might be appropriate in such situations.
>
> Most of the time, however, organizations are not machines; they are complex adaptive systems [CAS]. The key learning from the simulations is that in the case of CAS, minimum specifications and purposeful variation are the way to go. (Zimmerman et al., 2001, pp. 161–162)

Guidance for developing MIN SPECS is principles focused rather than rules focused.

▶ Don't attempt to define the outcome or behavior of the system in detail.

▶ Generate principles that can be applied by those engaged in change.

▶ Specify a limited number of meaningful and relevant principles.

▶ "Allow complex behavior to emerge from the bottom-up in the system to interactions among agents, or between agents and the context" (Zimmerman et al., 2001, pp. 162).

In preparing to write their influential book *Edgeware*, which shares insights from complexity science, Zimmerman and colleagues (2001) generated minimum specifications for the book. They called these "rules," but they read more like agreements. Once again, for the sake of illustration, I have converted their agreements into principles with corresponding principles-focused evaluation questions. Exhibit 20.4 shows the results.

Brenda Zimmerman, the force behind and senior author of *Edgeware*, was a good friend and colleague, and coauthor with Frances Westley and me of the book *Getting to Maybe: How The World Is Changed* (Westley et al., 2006). We had many discussions about simple rules, minimum specifications, and principles. Brenda agreed that *principles* is a more fitting term for the kinds of simple rules and minimum specifications she helped groups generate; what terminology to use, she felt, was a matter of adapting to context. Because the terms "simple rules" and "MIN SPECS" are widely used among those engaged with complexity, trying to change the language to principles might be a distraction. Moreover, at that time, nothing had been written making the case for principles as the more appropriate term. This book hopefully fills that gap.

MIN SPECS Stated through Limitations

MIN SPECS are meant to be empowering in complex adaptive systems. Because of the

EXHIBIT 20.4. Converting MIN SPECS into Principles with Corresponding Principles-Focused Evaluation Questions

Does *Edgeware* offer MIN SPECS for writing?	Conversion of MIN SPECS to effectiveness principles	Principles-focused evaluation questions
1. Everyone has enough content to enable intelligent conversation.	1. Converse about complexity from a position of knowledge.	What knowledge base about and experiences with complexity did each author bring to the book? How did the authors' knowledge and experiences affect the conversations about complexity?
2. All agreed to be complementary learners, committed to continuous awareness and open, honest, safe reflection, both individually and collectively.	2. Commit to and stay aware of open, honest, and safe reflection.	How do the authors monitor their shared commitment to and awareness of open, honest, and safe reflection together? What are examples of such reflection? What threats to safe reflection emerged and how were they recognized and handled?
3. Good-enough diversity, ever-changing (as much as practical and possible to avoid inbreeding).	3. Bring diverse, dynamic understandings to the writing.	What was done to ensure diversity and dynamism? What is evidence of diversity and dynamism in the book?
4. Enough time together for rich information flow.	4. Ensure time for rich information flow.	How much time did authors spend together? What is the authors' assessment of how the quality and content of the book was affected by how much time they spent together? What are examples of rich information flow the authors experienced in the writing? How are those a function of time spent together?
5. A safe container for reflection.	5. Create a space and process for safe reflection together.	What are examples of "safe" reflection that occurred in the writing? What threats to safe reflection, if any, emerged and how were they handled? What processes and conditions were put in place to enable and enhance safe reflection? What results in the book are especially a result of safe reflection?

Source: Zimmerman et al. (2001, pp. 164–165).

turbulence, unpredictability, dynamism, uncertainties, and lack of control under conditions of complexity, MIN SPECS in the form of principles can provide a rudder for navigation through the tempests of complexity. Principles are typically stated in a positive tone with affirmative action verbs, as illustrated in Exhibits 20.3 and 20.4. Principles typically provide positive guidance: *Think globally, act locally.*

A contrary approach in support of empowerment is to state what cannot be done with the understanding that anything not restricted is allowed. John Carver created the Policy Governance model for boards of directors aimed at clearly distinguishing the board's policy-setting role from management's implementation role. This approach tries to keep boards focused on policy and help them avoid micromanagement. In Carver's Policy Governance model he has the board establish Executive Limitations, a list of things that the CEO cannot do in carrying out the organization's mission and specified policies. Anything not prohibited is allowed. Presumably, the list of prohibitions is much shorter and more concise than any effort to anticipate and specify all the things a CEO could do. Executive Limitations, then, are an alternative way of supporting leadership responsibility and creativity (Carver & Carver, 2001). They follow in the tradition of Hippocrates's principle (oath), which is now applied well beyond medicine: *First, do no harm.*

Weaving Together Principles and MIN SPEC Practices: The Case of Replicating Mentoring Models in Northern Alberta

MARK CABAJ

Mark Cabaj was the executive director of the Vibrant Communities anti-poverty initiative featured as a principles-focused evaluation exemplar in Chapter 27. He was also co-leader on its developmental evaluation. I have been collaborating with Mark for more than a decade. He is one of the pioneers in conceptualizing and conducting principles-focused evaluations. He wrote the reflections that follow especially for this chapter after a conversation we had about MIN SPECS. My thanks to Mark for sharing his experiences and insights.

—M. Q. P.

In 2012, the staff of Boys & Girls Clubs/Big Brothers Big Sisters of Edmonton (Alberta, Canada) was approached by nonprofit organizations from five rural communities in northern Alberta to replicate their "best practice" mentoring model, developed and codified in neatly organized manuals over decades of trial and error. (The Boys & Girls Clubs and Big Brothers Big Sisters completed the formal part of their merger—the first between organizations in their respective movements—the year before.)

While the Edmonton group was pleased to share its experience, and the local sites eager for the support of their well-regarded urban cousin, both sides quickly found out that the conventional approach to model replication—encouraging the would-be replicator to follow the best-practice recipe with high fidelity—was unworkable. The

Edmonton model, regardless of its obvious strengths, simply did not neatly fit into the smaller, rural, and diverse community contexts of its regional partners.

Undaunted, the Edmonton group returned to the drawing board and turned their strategy upside down through three simple (iterative) steps:

First, the group reconfirmed what they felt was the essence of effective mentoring. This they captured in the form of core principles such as "trustful relationship between child and adult based on mutual respect" and "ensuring the emotional and physical safety of the child."

Second, the group landed on a collection of "minimum specification" (aka MIN SPEC) practices (e.g., interview guides, safety checklists, training) by exploring two questions: (1) Which practices reflected these principles? and (2) Which practices should be in all mentoring models regardless of their unique contexts?

Third, and finally, the group reframed its orientation away from "assisting the five sites to replicate their practices with high fidelity" toward working with people in local sites to adapt the new mentoring framework to their local context. "We dropped the franchise approach and became a wholesaler to local retailers," explained one participant.

This approach resulted in an entirely different development process. Local groups were eager to participate in the process of adapting the framework, and the Edmonton group continually refined it based on the results of local testing.

The results were impressive. Over a period of several years, five similar but locally varied—and supported—mentoring models emerged, and all the partners were very satisfied with the local mentoring results. Unexpectedly, the Edmonton group found many of the local practices—such as group mentoring—worthy of embedding in their own best-practice model. "I think we ended up learning as much from them as they did

from us," noted an Edmonton team member.

Despite their success in finding a balance between rural and urban, and shared and locally varied practices, the partners continue to adapt their new mentoring framework:

"Our communities' needs and environments continue to evolve and therefore so should our mentoring principles and practices. So, for example, we are exploring whether, if, and how we can innovate our model to introduce young mentees to much-needed job experience—a powerful new idea in the mentoring field—while the uncertain funding environment is forcing us to explore the possibility of completely overhauling our regional partnerships. But we'll be OK because we know how we can manage the tension between standardization and local variation."

—LIZ O'NEIL, Executive Director,
Boys & Girls Clubs/Big Brothers
Big Sisters of Edmonton

The process of innovation and of adapting models to address tough social issues, even within a framework of principles and MIN SPEC practices, in increasingly complex, diverse, and dynamic environments will always be "unfinished business."

Practice Exercise

In the conclusion to the discussion of simple rules I suggested a clarifying exercise that I repeat here in case you skipped over it at the time. Think about what rules you experience in your own world. Does it matter in your experience whether you are subject to rules, simple or otherwise, versus principles? In what area of your personal experience is this distinction (subject to rules vs. principles) clear, meaningful, and important? How are evaluation criteria different for rules versus principles?

Evaluable

A high-quality principle must be evaluable. This means it is possible to document and judge whether it is actually being followed, and document and judge what results from following the principle. In essence, it is possible to determine if following the principle takes you where you want to go.

CHAPTER 21

Evaluable Principles

Methods and Measures for Evaluating the Effectiveness of Principles

To know how far you've come, you have to know where you started.
—HALCOLM, "Principalia et Alia"

The *E* (evaluable) in the GUIDE framework for effectiveness principles brings us to evaluation design, data collection, and analysis. *A high-quality principle must be evaluable.* While a great deal of the work in principles-focused evaluation may involve identifying, articulating, fine-tuning, and wording principles, ultimately, principles-focused evaluation is about evaluation.

Principles-focused evaluation involves assessing the meaningfulness of principles, degree of adherence to principles, and, if adhered to, the results and impacts of adherence. This chapter offers concrete data options and analysis approaches for these three types of assessment. I hasten to add that the options and approaches offered are examples of what is possible. Actual data collection and analysis will depend on the nature of the principles being evaluated, a particular evaluation's purpose, and the evaluation design generated to answer specific questions within an inquiry context. Moreover, principles-focused evaluations, like all evaluations, are subject to the Joint Committee on Standards (2010) criteria that call for evaluations to be useful, feasible, ethical, accurate, and accountable. That said, as a distinct and innovative focus of evaluation (i.e., a nontraditional evaluand as discussed in Chapter 4), principles pose particular methodological and measurement challenges that this chapter addresses.

Evaluating the Meaningfulness and Quality of Principles Using the GUIDE Criteria

A recurring theme of this book has been that principles-focused evaluation often involves facilitating development of principles. The GUIDE framework presented in Chapter 6 provides criteria for evaluating the meaningfulness and quality of principles. Let's look at how GUIDE criteria could be applied in practice with an example.

Evaluating Principles of Adult Education: An Illustrative Example

Chapter 9 presented principles for effective adult education based on the writings of and assumptions articulated by distinguished adult educator Stephen Brookfield. We can begin with three overarching evaluation questions:

1. To what extent are the principles meaningful to adult educators?
2. To what extent do adult educators follow the principles in classroom practice?
3. If the principles are followed, what are the results for students?

Exhibit 21.1 provides a framework for answering the first question. Exhibit 21.2 then offers an interview protocol for answering questions 2 and 3 by gathering data from adult educators.

Assessing Principles against the GUIDE Criteria

Exhibit 21.1 presents an inquiry matrix with adult education principles along the side and the GUIDE criteria across the top. Each cell in the matrix applies a GUIDE criterion to a principle.

Assessing the Extent to Which a Sample of Adult Educators Finds the Principles Meaningful to Their Own Teaching

Let us now suppose that we want to assess the extent to which a sample of adult educators finds the principles meaningful to their own teaching. A qualitative approach would be to interview them using the GUIDE criteria. A quantitative approach would be to rate each principle on the GUIDE criteria. I'll illustrate both approaches in a mixed-methods evaluation. Exhibit 21.2 provides an example of what such an evaluation interview protocol might entail for the first principle.

The qualitative interview protocol in Exhibit 21.2 illustrates open-ended questions for the first adult education facilitation principle. Similar questions could be asked for each of the principles.

Quantitative Ratings of GUIDE Criteria

A quantitative approach to evaluating the adult education principles would involve surveying adult educators by turning the GUIDE criteria into rating scales. Exhibit 21.3 presents such a survey. I have illustrated using a 5-point scale. Some prefer 4- or 6-point scales. The scale size is not an issue for this example.

Exhibit 21.3 provides examples for the first two GUIDE criteria, guidance (G) and utility (U). Similar ratings could be elicited for the other three GUIDE criteria: inspirational (I), developmental (D), and evaluable (E). (See Chapter 6 for all of the GUIDE criteria and Chapter 35 for additional tools and rubrics for evaluating principles.)

Evaluating Adherence to Principles

Thus far in this chapter I've illustrated how to evaluate the meaningfulness of principles using adult education principles. To evaluate adherence to those principles by adult educators we would need to observe their teaching, interview them about how they facilitate adult learning, and examine their syllabi, teaching plans, and course materials and student engagement exercises. To look in more depth at evaluating adherence to principles, let's turn to an example where this was actually done: the evaluation of the implementation of the Paris Declaration Principles, featured in Chapter 25.

An Exemplar of Evaluating Adherence to Principles

The Paris Declaration Principles committed donor and recipient countries to reforming the system of development aid. Change is evaluated by comparing a baseline situation with the situation after reform has been implemented. Assessing the progress of reform, then, meant making explicit the baseline situation that the Paris Declaration

EXHIBIT 21.1. Applying the GUIDE Criteria to the Revised and Focused Principles for Effective Facilitation by Adult Educators

Principles	G = Provides clear guidance to adult educators	U = Useful to adult education facilitators	I = Inspires adult educators	D = Developmental: can be adapted to variations in situation and context	E = Evaluable: can assess adherence to the principle and results of adherence
1. Create and maintain a climate of mutual respect based on valuing each other's self-worth.					
2. Make facilitation collaborative.					
3. Put praxis at the center of facilitation as part of an ongoing cycle of action and reflection.					
4. Foster critical reflection.					
5. Nurture and empower self-direction.					

Evaluation questions that could be asked of adult education facilitators for each cell:

G: Is the principle clear and actionable?
U: Is the principle useful for understanding, planning, and engaging in facilitation?
I: Do you find the principle inspiring?
D: To what extent can you adapt the principle to different learners and facilitation situations?
E: To what extent can you evaluate how well your facilitation is going and its effects on students' learning?

181

EXHIBIT 21.2. Sample Interview Protocol
GUIDE-Based Evaluation Questions for Adult Educators

Evaluating Principle 1. *Create and maintain a climate of mutual respect based on valuing each other's self-worth.*

G = Guiding. A principle is prescriptive. It gives advice and guidance. It provides direction. The guidance is distinct from contrary or alternative guidance.

Sample interview questions	M. Q. P. commentary
G1. To what extent, if at all, would you say that you currently follow this principle in your teaching? 1. Most of the time 2. Sometimes 3. Seldom 4. Never	This opening question is aimed at differentiating adult educators who say they are already following the principle from those who are not. The scale (1–4) is optional.
G2. How would you (or do you) create a climate of mutual respect in your classroom based on valuing each other's self-worth?	This question aims at finding out what specific behaviors the principle prescribes from the perspective of the adult educator being interviewed. (*Note:* Actual behavior is aimed at those who say they are already following the principle. Potential behavior is for those not currently following the principle but considering doing so.)
G3. To what extent and in what ways does this principle provide meaningful guidance to you as an adult educator? *Probe:* Please provide examples of how this principle applies to and informs your teaching.	This question asks about meaningfulness directly. The probes aim to find out what meaningfulness means in practice, in the classroom.
G4. Based on your knowledge and experience as an adult educator, what is the opposite of a "climate of mutual respect"?	This question tests whether the principle's guidance is distinct from alternative guidance. (See Chapter 7 on the value of identifying opposite principles as a test of meaningful guidance.)

(continued)

U = Useful. A principle should have a clear purpose. Its intended use is clear. Yet, it should be sufficiently general to be applicable to a range of situations and challenges. To be useful it must be doable.

Sample interview questions	M. Q. P. commentary
U1. How would you (or do you) use this principle in planning your teaching?	This question is aimed at finding out if the principle is actually used, or potentially useful. (*Note:* Actual use is aimed at those who say they are already following the principle. Potential use is for those not currently following the principle but considering doing so.)
U2. What do you do (or would you do) in following this principle? *Probe:* Please provide examples of how you use (or might use) this principle's guidance in facilitating adult learning.	This question asks directly about use. The probes aim to find out what use means in practice, in the classroom.
U3. In what ways, if any, is this principle not useful in your teaching situation? *Probe:* Ask about specific situations or challenges where the principle would not be useful.	This question tests whether the principle is viewed as applicable to a range of teaching situations and challenges.

I = Inspiring. Principles are values based, incorporating and expressing ethical premises, which is what makes them meaningful. They articulate what matters, both in how to proceed and the desired result. That should be inspirational.

Sample interview questions	M. Q. P. commentary
I1. What's your reaction to this principle?	This completely open-ended question is aimed at eliciting whatever reaction is salient to the adult educator being interviewed. It doesn't restrict or constrain reaction in any way, so those being interviewed can respond in whatever way is meaningful to them.
I2. From your perspective, what values about teaching, learning, and education are expressed in this principle? *Follow-up question:* To what extent, if at all, do you share those values?	This question asks about values directly. The follow-up inquires into a personal values connection.
I3. As a teacher, to what extent, if at all, do you find this principle inspiring? *Probe:* Why or why not?	This question asks directly about inspiration. The probe seeks to deepen and illuminate the response.

(continued)

D = Developmental. The developmental nature of a good principle refers to its adaptability and applicability to diverse contexts and over time. A principle is thus both context sensitive and adaptable to real-world dynamics, providing a way to navigate the turbulence of complexity and uncertainty. In being applicable over time, it is enduring (not time-bound), in support of ongoing development and adaptation in an ever-changing world.

Sample interview questions	M. Q. P. commentary
D1. Please describe ways in which the students you teach, the context in which you teach, or the situations you face in teaching have changed or varied over time.	This questions aims to find out what developmental challenges and variations the adult educator has experienced.
D2. Given the variations in teaching you've experienced, how applicable and relevant is this principle to those variations?	This question asks for an assessment of the adaptability of the principle to various teaching experiences and situations.
D3. In what teaching situations that you've encountered do you find this principle not meaningful and relevant, if any? Why?	This question asks about contextual applicability from the opposite point of view, that is, probing where it is not relevant as a counterpoint to where it is relevant. This invites a different point of view and analysis.

E = Evaluable. A good principle must be evaluable. This means it is possible to document and judge whether it is actually being followed, and document and judge what results from following the principle. In essence, it is possible to determine if following the principle takes you where you want to go.

Sample interview questions	M. Q. P. commentary
E1. How do you evaluate your classroom climate? What ways do you have of monitoring your classroom's climate?	This question introduces the idea of evaluating climate generally before inquiring more directly and deeply into the specific climate prescribed by the principle.
E2. Turning to this principle specifically, how do you know (or how might you find out) if your teaching creates and maintains a "climate of mutual respect based on valuing each other's self-worth"?	This question asks for evaluation practices and approaches.
E3. In general, what would you consider evidence of a "climate of mutual respect based on valuing each other's self-worth"?	This question asks about evaluation criteria for this principle generally. It inquires into evaluability of the principle based on being able to identify relevant evidence of effectiveness.

EXHIBIT 21.3. Illustrative Ratings Instrument for Adult Education Principles
Target Respondents: Adult Educators

Based on your experience, knowledge, and perspective as an adult educator, please rate each proposed adult education principle on the 5-point scales provided.

A. **Your ratings on clarity of guidance: How clear is the guidance offered to you as a teacher? To what extent is it clear to you what you should do to follow each principle? Please *check the box* in each row that best fits your opinion about the clarity of each principle.**

Principles	Very clear: I know what this means	Fairly clear	Partly clear, partly vague	Fairly vague	Very vague: I'm not sure what this means
1. *Create and maintain a climate of mutual respect based on valuing each other's self-worth.*					
2. *Make facilitation collaborative.*					
3. *Put praxis at the center of facilitation as part of an ongoing cycle of action and reflection.*					
4. *Foster critical reflection.*					
5. *Nurture and empower self-direction.*					

B. **Your ratings on utility of the principle: How useful is the principle to you as a teacher? To what extent can you use this principle in your teaching? (Check a box.)**

Principles	Very useful	Fairly useful	Somewhat useful	Not too useful	Not at all useful
1. *Create and maintain a climate of mutual respect based on valuing each other's self-worth.*					
2. *Make facilitation collaborative.*					
3. *Put praxis at the center of facilitation as part of an ongoing cycle of action and reflection.*					
4. *Foster critical reflection.*					
5. *Nurture and empower self-direction.*					

Principles were meant to change. Exhibit 21.4 presents the baseline in contrast with the reform principles.

The baseline consisted of behavioral and attitudinal norms rather than a manifestation of treaty agreements, as with the Paris Declaration Principles. Progress in reforming the development aid system involved judging the direction, distance, and pace of reform in 21 countries and 18 international agencies through in-depth case studies. The results of the evaluation showed country ownership had advanced farthest, meaning that adherence to the principle of country ownership was greatest compared with adherence to the other principles. Adherence to the principles of alignment and harmonization was progressing more unevenly, and managing for development results and mutual accountability advancing least (Wood et al., 2011, p. xv), that is, manifesting the lowest degree of adherence. How did the evaluation team arrive at these judgments?

Adherence to a Principles Evaluation Matrix

The evaluation began with core adherence questions: To what extent has the Paris Declaration been implemented in different countries and donor/agency systems? What are the important factors that have affected the relevance and implementation of the Paris Declaration and its potential effects on aid effectiveness and development results?

To answer this question at the country level, an operational matrix was developed as the main evaluation instrument. It provided a common data collection framework for national evaluation teams to assess implementation of the principles in each country and agency context. As a standardized framework, it facilitated comparative analysis at the synthesis level (cross-country and cross-agency). The overall implementation (adherence) question was then examined through a number of subquestions, with

EXHIBIT 21.4. International Development Aid Principles before and after 2005	
Baseline explicating how international development aid operated prior to 2005	**Paris Declaration reform principles adopted in 2005**
1. **Donor national interests:** Donor countries set priorities for aid based on their own national interests.	1. **Ownership:** *Developing countries set their own strategies for poverty reduction, improving their institutions, and tackling corruption.*
2. **Subservience:** In order to get aid, developing countries subsume and subordinate their priorities to those of donor countries.	2. **Alignment:** *Donor countries align behind these objectives and use local systems.*
3. **Bilateralism:** Donor countries each operate autonomously through bilateral agreements with recipient countries.	3. **Harmonization:** *Donor countries coordinate and simplify procedures and share information to avoid duplication.*
4. **Amount of aid:** Developing countries and donors focus on the amount of aid delivered.	4. **Results:** *Developing countries and donors shift focus to development results and results get measured.*
5. **No accountability to developing countries:** Donors are accountable only within their own countries and political systems.	5. **Mutual accountability:** *Donors and partners are accountable for development results.*

the operational matrix providing guidance on appropriate indicators and evidence to collect and analyze, as well as options for methods or forms of analysis that case study teams could employ. Country teams reviewed documents like government and donor strategic plans, memoranda of agreement on aid flows and priorities, and monitoring reports by governments and donor agencies to seek evidence of adherence to the principles. The evaluation teams interviewed key informants and experts as sources of data. They conducted surveys with people involved in all aspects of development aid. Country teams then wrote a summary of each country's development aid operational procedures and compared what they found with the Paris Declaration Principles. For example, using these multiple sources of evidence, the country evaluation teams could determine the extent to which aid priorities from donor countries were based on country priorities and the extent to which diverse donors were coordinating their aid packages. The country teams then converted this qualitative case data into a rating scale judgment on degree of progress since 2005. Exhibit 21.5 presents an overview of the rating matrix used for evaluating adherence to the Paris Declaration Principles. These ratings were applied to specific dimensions of reform for each country. The categorical ratings were backed up with and based on the diverse evidence gathered and the triangulated analysis conducted. Details of how this was done and the validity and reliability of the ratings are described extensively in the Operational Matrix for Country Evaluations (Paris Declaration Evaluation, 2011a) and the evaluation report Technical Annex (Paris Declaration Evaluation, 2011b).

Results of Adherence to the Principles

Having evaluated adherence to the principles, the evaluation of the Paris Declaration Principles turned to outcome questions:

▶ To what extent and how has the implementation of the Paris Declaration led to an improvement in the efficiency of aid delivery and the management and use of aid as well as better partnerships? (Process and intermediate outcomes)

▶ What contributions can aid effectiveness reforms plausibly be judged to have made to development results? (Specific impacts of the principles)

▶ Has the implementation of the Paris Declaration strengthened the contribution of aid to sustainable development results? If so, how? (Overall development outcomes)

As with evaluating adherence, multiple sources of data, both qualitative and quantitative, were used to support judgments about the degree and nature of development impacts. Exhibit 21.6 presents one example of the summary matrix used to rate degree of impact. These overall synthesis ratings were based on and backed up by detailed data and evidence from multiple sources (Paris Declaration Evaluation, 2011a).

This brief overview doesn't begin to do justice to the methodical, systematic, and rigorous data collection and analysis processes developed to evaluate adherence to and results of the Paris Declaration Principles. The point of the examples I've included here is to give a sense of what's possible, and, more specifically and importantly, to affirm that it is possible to evaluate principles meaningfully and credibly. All Paris Declaration evaluation methods, procedures, instruments, techniques, and reports are available online (Paris Declaration Evaluation, 2011c).

Meta-Evaluation of the Paris Declaration Evaluation

You may be wondering about the overall methodological quality of the evaluation of the implementation of the Paris Declaration Principles. *How trustworthy and credible*

EXHIBIT 21.5. Evaluation Ratings Matrix for Each Country's Adherence
to the Paris Declaration Development Aid Principles

Principles	Direction of implementation	Distance traveled in implementation	Pace of implementation
1. Recipient countries determine aid priorities	a. Substantial movement toward reform b. Some movement toward reform c. Little movement d. No movement toward reform e. Regression away from reform	a. Substantial b. Some c. Little d. None e. Regression	a. Fast b. Moderate c. Slow d. None e. Reverse
2. Alignment of donor countries with recipient country priorities	a. b. c. d. e. Same items as above	a. b. c. d. e. Same items as above	a. b. c. d. e. Same items as above
3. Donor agencies harmonize and coordinate development aid	a. b. c. d. e.	a. b. c. d. e.	a. b. c. d. e.
4. Both donors and recipients manage for results	a. b. c. d. e.	a. b. c. d. e.	a. b. c. d. e.
5. Mutual accountability	a. b. c. d. e.	a. b. c. d. e.	a. b. c. d. e.

Note. These ratings were completed by the country evaluation teams based on a synthesis of the multiple sources of data collected.

were the findings? I'm glad you asked. The national and global decision makers and policymakers who, it was hoped, would use the report's findings, could be expected to ask the same question. Thus, I was commissioned to conduct *an independent meta-evaluation:* an evaluation of the evaluation. Exhibit 21.7 presents the overall conclusions of the meta-evaluation, which took the form of an independent audit report. As noted earlier, more details about the organization, design, data collection, findings, and uses of the evaluation of the Paris Declaration Principles are presented in Chapter 25, where it is featured as a principles-focused evaluation exemplar.

Perhaps also worth noting: the evaluation received the 2012 Outstanding Evaluation of the Year Award by the American Evaluation Association.

Qualitative Coding of Principles

This chapter opened with an example of how to evaluate the meaningfulness and quality of principles using the GUIDE criteria. The illustrative example involved evaluating adult education principles for clarity of guidance, utility, inspirational value, developmental adaptability to diverse contexts, and evaluability. We then examined

---

EXHIBIT 21.6. Summary Matrix Used to Rate the Degree of Impact of Implementation of the Paris Declaration Principles

Conclusions on the effects of Paris Declaration implementation (judgments based on multiple sources of evidence)

Improvements in the efficiency of aid delivery to the sector	• Substantial impact • Some impact • Little impact • No impact • Regression
Improvements in the management and use of aid in the sector	• Substantial impact • Some impact • Little impact • No impact • Regression
Better (more inclusive and effective) partnerships in the sector	• Substantial impact • Some impact • Little impact • No impact • Regression
Contribution to sustainable development results	• Substantial impact • Some impact • Little impact • No impact • Regression
Have there been unintended consequences of the Paris Declaration for aid effectiveness in the sector (e.g., unintended impacts on particular groups including women and girls)?	

EXHIBIT 21.7. Independent Audit of the Evaluation of the Paris Declaration Principles

May 2011

An Independent Audit of the Evaluation

Readers and users of this Evaluation Report on the Paris Declaration and Aid Effectiveness may wonder, quite naturally, whether the findings can be trusted, whether the evaluation was conducted independently, and whether the evaluation process was rigorous. Just as an independent auditor's review is essential in establishing the credibility of corporate financial information to investors, stockholders and the general public, this audit of the Synthesis Evaluation speaks to the credibility of this report for intended users, policy makers, international aid stakeholders, and the global public. Given the importance of the Evaluation of the Implementation of the Paris Declaration, the Management Group commissioned this independent assessment of the evaluation. Indeed, it has become a standard in major high-stakes evaluations of this kind to commission an independent review to determine whether the evaluation meets generally accepted international standards of quality.

Prior to undertaking this review, I had no prior relationship with any members of the Management Group or the Core Evaluation Team. My associate and I had complete and unfettered access to any and all evaluation documents and data, and to all members of the International Reference Group, the Management Group, and the Core Evaluation Team. Our responsibility is to express an opinion on the quality of the Synthesis Evaluation.

Our audit included reviewing data collection instruments, templates, and processes; reviewing the partner country and donors evaluation reports on which the synthesis is based; directly observing two meetings of the International Reference Group where the evidence was examined and the conclusions revised accordingly; surveying participants in the evaluation process and interviewing key people involved in and knowledgeable about how the evaluation was conducted. The evaluation audit includes assessing both the report's findings and the technical appendix that details how findings were generated.

In our opinion, the findings and conclusions generated adhere closely and rigorously to the evaluation evidence collected. Obtaining high-quality evidence and thoughtfully analyzing that evidence was the constant theme of the evaluation. Both strengths and weaknesses in the evaluation are appropriately acknowledged. The comprehensive Technical Annex accurately describes data collection and analysis approaches. Partner country and donor evaluation reports, upon which the Synthesis Evaluation is based, were openly and transparently shared with the International Reference Group to allow peer review and make visible both strengths and limitations in those reports. Partner country reports were screened for adherence to quality standards with particular attention to the strength of evidence to support conclusions reached.

Those countries and donors that undertook this voluntary evaluation of the implementation of the Paris Declaration have engaged in systematic and in-depth reflection and evidence-based processes that make their conclusions and insights worthy of serious attention. The Final Report accurately captures those evidence-based conclusions and insights.

In our opinion, the Synthesis Report can be trusted as independent, evidence-based, and adhering to international standards for quality evaluation. Notwithstanding inevitable limitations inherent in such a complex and comprehensive evaluation initiative, the findings can be studied and used as trustworthy and credible.

[signature]

Michael Quinn Patton, Ph. D.
Independent Evaluator and Faculty,
The Evaluators' Institute

Sources: Patton and Gornick (2012, p. 65); Wood et al. (2011, p. vi).

---

how the evaluation of the Paris Declaration Principles assessed degree of recipient and donor countries' adherence to the principles and made judgments about the impacts of implementing the principles on sustainable development outcomes. This section examines how principles for helping youth overcome homelessness were evaluated for both adherence and outcomes.

Evidence of Adherence to Principles

Chapter 26 describes the development and evaluation of the program effectiveness principles for helping youth overcome homelessness. Chapter 3 concluded by listing the nine evidence-based principles that were the focus of evaluation. This section looks in greater depth at how the evidence on adherence to and effectiveness of principles was analyzed. First, a brief review of the principles that were being evaluated.

In 2012, six agencies serving homeless youth in Minneapolis and Saint Paul, Minnesota, began collaborating to evaluate the implementation and effectiveness of their shared principles. They first identified shared values and common principles and found that their work was undergirded and informed by eight principles. At the outset, these principles were just sensitizing concepts: labels and phrases without definition. Where there was a descriptive definition, it varied among the agencies.

1. Trauma-informed care
2. Nonjudgmental engagement
3. Harm reduction
4. Trusting youth–adult relationships
5. Strengths-based approach
6. Positive youth development
7. Holistic approach
8. Collaboration

(For definition of these principles, see Exhibit 3.1 in Chapter 3. A new, ninth principle, being *journey-oriented,* emerged from analysis of interviews with the youth.)

Working together, we designed a qualitative study to examine whether the principles actually guided the agency's work with youth and whether the outcomes the youth achieved could be linked to the principles. Nora Murphy, a graduate student at the University of Minnesota, was commissioned to conduct the study, which also served as her doctoral dissertation (Murphy, 2014). Selecting a diverse (maximum variation) sample of homeless youth who had been involved with several of the agencies, Murphy conducted 14 in-depth interviews with homeless youth and produced case studies based on the interviews with the youth and program staff, as well as a review of program case records. The results of the 14 case studies were then coded and

analyzed, and the findings synthesized to reveal overall patterns of principles' adherence and effectiveness.

The six agency executive directors participated in reviewing every case study to determine which principles were at work and their effectiveness in helping the youth meet their needs and achieve their goals. Key to evaluating the principles in practice was that *the youth interviewed were never asked directly about the principles.* This point deserves methodological emphasis. The youth were interviewed about their experiences and reflections on their experiences, but they were not asked about the principles. The analysis, then, involved coding the interviews to see if the experiences and reflections of the youth showed evidence of the principles being followed by program staff.

First, a word on qualitative coding. *Coding* means identifying quotations and data in the case studies that exemplify a pattern of interest. For example, the following three statements can all be quoted as *valuing evaluation.*

1. "Our program hasn't done evaluation in the past, but now that we've started, we're finding it's really valuable."
2. "We've learned that our staff values evaluation if it's designed to be useful. That's the key. Make it useful to staff."
3. "If a director values evaluation, the staff will value it. And vice versa."

Finding these three quotes in interviews with three different program staff and labeling them as passages related to "valuing evaluation" is an example of qualitative coding. Bringing the three quotes together for comparison and interpretation is an example of qualitative analysis. (For an in-depth discussion of qualitative coding, see Patton, 2015a, Ch. 8.)

The next section provides examples of quotations from one youth's interview, with case study excerpts, that were identified and coded as evidence of adherence to the principles.

Coding Principles:
Evidence of the Principles in Practice

Here's the format for what follows. A principle will be defined. Then an example of data supporting adherence to or the importance of that principle will be presented. All of the data examples are from one youth's interview and case study. The purpose is to illustrate one way in which qualitative data can be used to evaluate how, if at all, participants in a program experience the principles a program says guides its work with participants.

> **Principle 1:** *Trauma-informed care.* Recognize that most homeless youth have experienced trauma; build relationships, responses, and services on that knowledge.

Supporting Evidence of the Principle in Practice (From a Case Study Excerpt)

Throughout his time visiting drop-in centers, Thmaris (a homeless youth) has never stayed at a youth or adult shelter. He typically couch hops or stays with women he is dating. Some nights, he walks the skyway all night or sleeps in a stairwell. After staying in family shelters when he was younger, he has vowed to himself that he would never stay in another shelter again.

"When we first came to Minnesota that's all we did. We stayed in shelter[s] as a family. It was like traumatizing to me because [in shelters] you see like humans at their weakest point. You see them hungry, dirty. I didn't like that. I don't like being around a whole bunch of people that was . . . I'm not saying that I feel like I'm better than anybody because I definitely don't. But I just felt like it was too much to take in. It was too stressful, and it just made me want to cry. It was crazy. I don't want to go back to a shelter ever again."

Interpretation. The quote illustrates an example of the trauma a youth has experienced being homeless. The qualitative data validates, for this participant, the importance of offering trauma-informed care as a principle of effective practice. The full case study offers additional evidence of the participant's traumatic history and its effects on his homelessness and outlook about the future.

> **Principle 4:** *Trusting youth–adult relationships.* Build relationships by interacting with youth in an honest, dependable, authentic, caring, and supportive way.

Supporting Evidence of Principle 4 in Practice (From a Case Study Excerpt)

Thmaris had two caseworkers previous to Rahim but was transferred to Rahim when Rahim began working with youth under Healthy Transitions. This was a lucky move for Thmaris because this relationship developed into one that has been deeply meaningful to him.

"I just feel that ever since I turned 20 I realized that I'm an adult and that I have to make better choices, not just for me but the people around me. Didn't nobody help me with that but Rahim. . . . The things that he was able to do, he made sure that he did them. I remember days that I'd come down to Safe Zone, and I'd be like, Rahim, I haven't eaten in two days or, Rahim, I haven't changed my underwear in like a week or whatever. He would give me bus cards to get to and from interviews. He would give me Target cards to go take care of my personal hygiene. He would give me Cub cards to go eat. It was like every problem or every obstacle I threw in front of him, he made sure that I would overcome it with him. He was like the greatest mentor I ever had. I've never had nobody like that.

"Out of all the other caseworkers I had, nobody ever really sat me down and tried to work out a resolution for my problems. They always just gave me pamphlets like, 'Well, go call these people and see if they can do something for you.' Or, 'You should go to this building because this building has that, what you want.' It was like every time I come to him I don't have to worry about anything. He's not going to send me to the next man, put me on to the next person's caseload. He just always took care of me. If I would have never met Rahim, I would have been in a totally different situation, I would have went a totally different route."

Without the support of Rahim and the resources at the drop-in center, Thmaris is sure he would still be in a gang and dealing weed and would eventually end up in jail again. And it wasn't just that Rahim was there for him, it's also that Rahim has been with the drop-in center for more than 5 years. This consistency has meant a lot to Thmaris, who shared, "I just seen a lot of case managers come and go. Rahim is the only one that has never went anywhere. So many years have gone past, and Rahim is here."

"Everything I was doing [with Rahim] was productive. When you get that feeling like you're accomplishing something and you're doing good, it's like a feeling that you can't describe."

Interpretation. This case study excerpt illustrates one example of what a trusting relationship looks and feels like from one youth's perspective. The full case study portrays an ever-deepening relationship developing and the importance of that trusting relationship to this homeless young man.

Principle 5: *Strengths-based approach.* Start with and build on the skills, strengths, and positive characteristics of each youth.

Supporting Evidence of Principle 5 in Practice (from a Case Study Excerpt)

When Thmaris first thought about going back to school, he was planning to go just to get a student loan check like many of the homeless youth around him. But Rahim helped him see a different path. Knowing of Thmaris's past positive experiences with construction and building, Rahim urged him to consider careers that would allow him to work with his hands and to focus on the big picture. He also made sure that Thmaris had the support of a learning specialist from Saint Paul Public Schools, who helped Thmaris figure out what steps he would need to take to get from where he was then to his dream career of welding.

"The first time I ever talked to him about school. I was like, 'Yeah, man. I just feel like I should go to school and get a loan.' And he was like, 'Well, it's bigger than that. That loan money is going to be gone like that.' He didn't tell me, no, you shouldn't do that. He just said just think about the future. And I just thought about it. I was thinking and I was thinking. And then I was like, 'What if I went to school for something that I want to get a job in?' He was, 'Yeah, that's the best way to go.'

"I talked to him about construction, and he told me you already basically have experience in that because he knows all the jobs I had. So he was like you should go into something that's totally different but that pays a lot of money. Then I researched it and then just knew that I liked working with my hands. So I just put two and two together and was like, well, I want to go to school for welding. Ever since I learned how to weld it's like . . . I love it!"

Interpretation. These qualitative data illustrate how the program focused on supporting one participant's strengths, that is, working with his hands. The full case study provides a great deal of evidence about the importance of that support and encouragement to this youth.

> **Principle 9:** *Journey oriented.* **Interact with youth to help them understand the interconnectedness of past, present, and future as they decide where they want to go and how to get there.**

Supporting Evidence of the Principle in Practice (from a Case Study Excerpt)

He's proud that he's been able to overcome the challenges in his life in order to get a high school diploma and graduate from his welding program. Feeling successful has just fueled his ambition to experience more success.

"You don't know how it felt when I graduated high school. I was like, 'Wow, I did this on my own?' And it just felt so good. I'm thirsty again to get another certificate or diploma or whatever just because it's just the best feeling in the world. It's better than any drug. It's like, man, I don't even know how to explain it. It just felt like you just climbed up to the top of the mountain and just like you made it."

He feels that without the drop-in center and his case manager he might be in jail right now. He sees other young people "wasting their time" at the drop-in center and wishes he could tell them what he now knows.

"If you're still stuck in that stage where you don't know what you want to do with your life, then come here and sit down with a case manager. Try to talk to somebody, and they'll help you better your situation."

Interpretation. Many homeless youth live day to day, surviving almost moment to moment. The qualitative data from this case study showed the participant developing an understanding of his past, analysis of his present situation, and hope for the future. Developing a sense of future is an outcome of being journey-oriented.

Summary of Qualitative Coding of Principles

The preceding examples illustrate how qualitative data can be coded, analyzed, and interpreted to evaluate whether principles are evident in the experiences and reflections of program participants. Chapter 12 used the youth homelessness example as a way of examining how principles point to outcomes. Thus, more qualitative data and principles-focused coding examples are presented in Chapter 12. Chapter 26 provides still more qualitative data coding examples and explanations, for that chapter is where the youth homelessness evaluation is featured as a principles-focused evaluation exemplar. The final section in this chapter presents yet a different example of rigorous research on and evaluation of principles.

Rigorous Research on and Evaluation of Principles

Scaling Up Excellence tackles a challenge that confronts every leader and organization—spreading constructive beliefs and behavior from the few to the many. This book shows what it takes to build and uncover pockets of exemplary performance, spread those splendid deeds, and as an organization grows bigger and older—rather than slipping toward mediocrity or worse—recharge it with better ways of doing the work at hand.
—ROBERT I. SUTTON & HUGGY RAO (2014, p. 1)

This is how Sutton and Rao (2014) open their influential book *Scaling Up Excellence*. Scaling is an applied version of the challenge of generalization. Scholars worry about generalizing findings. Philanthropic foundations, policymakers, and social innovators worry about spreading effective programs. Sutton and Rao identified five principles to guide scaling.

1. Stoke the scaling engine.
2. Cut cognitive load.
3. Identify the right people to propel scaling.
4. Use social bonds to spread the right mind-set.
5. Clear the way for excellence.

The labels they gave to the principles do not make their meaning or guidance readily evident, but for my purpose in this chapter, I am focusing on their methods for evaluating principles, not, in this case, how clearly they are stated. They devote a chapter to each principle, explaining its implications, presenting the research evidence for its importance, and discussing how it can be implemented and evaluated. But how did they discover and validate the principles? They report that they began by gathering ideas and evidence, a process that took years.

We did case studies, reviewed theory and research, and huddled to develop insights about scaling challenges and how to overcome them. Little by little, this process changed from a private conversation between the two of us to ongoing conversations about scaling with an array of smart people. We were at the center of this process: making decisions about which leads, stories, and evidence to pursue; choosing which to keep, discard, or save for later; and weaving them together into (we hope) a coherent form. (p. 299)

They then analyzed the evidence to reach preliminary conclusions. As conclusions emerged, they presented what they had found to people who had read their prior publications and/or attended their classes and speeches. They recruited knowledgeable and thoughtful people to review, question, and enhance their work.

[The principles are] the product of years of give-and-take between us and many thoughtful people, not as an integrated perspective that we constructed in private and are now unveiling for the first time. Hundreds of people played direct roles in helping us, and thousands more played indirect roles—even if they didn't realize it. (p. 299)

To speak to issues of rigor and credibility, they have distilled their inquiry process into seven core methods, each of which they elaborate in the methodological appendix of the book.

1. Combing through research from the behavioral sciences and beyond
2. Conducting and gathering detailed case studies
3. Brief examples from diverse media sources
4. Targeted interviews and unplanned conversations
5. Presenting emerging scaling ideas to diverse audiences
6. Teaching a "*Scaling Up Excellence*" class to Stanford graduate students
7. Participation in and observation of scaling at the Stanford school (an executive professional development program)

What emerges from their description of their inquiry methods is portrayal of an ongoing, generative, and iterative process of integrating theory, research, and practice around gathering and making sense of the evidence and, ultimately, *distilling what they found into principles*. The principles constitute a form of generalized guidance derived from and based on lessons. The lessons led to principles.

Why Principles?

In explaining why they reported their findings in the form of principles, they emphasized that people engaged in a scaling
initiative cannot simply look up some right
answers and apply them. There is no recipe.

> In the case of scaling, there are so many dif-
> ferent aspects of the challenge, and the right
> answers vary so much across teams, organi-
> zations, and industries (and even across chal-
> lenges faced by a single team or organiza-
> tion), that it is impossible to develop a useful
> "paint by numbers" approach. Regardless of
> how many cases, studies, and books (includ-
> ing this one) you read, success at scaling will
> always depend on making constantly shifting,
> complex, and not easily codified judgments.
> (p. 298)

Summary and Conclusion

This chapter has presented data options
and analysis approaches for three types of
principles-focused evaluation: (1) evaluating the meaningfulness of principles, (2)
evaluating the degree of adherence to principles, and, if adhered to, (3) evaluating
the results and impacts of adherence. The
chapter opened with an example of how to
evaluate the meaningfulness and quality of
adult education principles using the GUIDE
criteria: clarity of guidance, utility, inspirational value, developmental adaptability to
diverse contexts, and evaluability. I then
examined how the evaluation of the Paris
Declaration Principles assessed degree of

recipient and donor country adherence to
the principles by measuring direction, distance, and pace of implementation, and
made judgments about the impacts of implementing the principles on sustainable
development outcomes. Next I discussed
how principles for helping youth overcome
homelessness were evaluated for both adherence and outcomes. The final example
was the rigorous research of Sutton and
Rao (2014) that generated five principles in
Scaling Up Excellence.

There are no routine or preferred methods for engaging in principles-focused
evaluation. This chapter has provided illustrations and options, not prescriptions for
favored methods. Qualitative, quantitative,
and mixed methods can be used. What is
critical is that the methods are appropriate to the context, credible to the intended
users of the evaluation, and useful to fulfill the intended purpose of the evaluation.
In essence, principles-focused evaluation is
utilization focused.

Practice Exercise

Identify a principle that informs practice
in an area of your interest and expertise.
How would you bring data to bear on the
effectiveness of that principle? Create a
principles-focused evaluation design and
data collection approach that is appropriate
for and well matched to the principle you've
identified. What do you have to do to ensure
that your principles-focused evaluation
design is also utilization focused?

CHAPTER 22

Principles-Focused Sampling

It is often easier to fight for a principle than to live up to it.
—ADLAI STEVENSON, American politician, diplomat,
and U.S. Ambassador to the United Nations

Principles-focused evaluation necessarily employs principles-focused sampling. This involves identifying and studying cases that illuminate the nature, implementation, outcomes, and implications of principles. Quantitatively, principles-focused probability sampling involves gathering data from a population or representative sample of people who can respond to questions about adherence to and experiences with the principles that are the focus of inquiry. Qualitatively, studying the implementation and outcomes of effectiveness principles is built on principles-focused purposeful sampling, a specific type of qualitative purposeful sampling. A mixed-methods design could include both a probability sample and a purposeful sample, each of which would be principles focused. This chapter will give examples to illustrate how the *E* for *evaluable* in the GUIDE framework includes identification of a sample that can be selected to study and evaluate adherence to and results of a principles-based program or initiative. I'll start with a concrete example.

Project SPIRIT: A Principles-Focused Sampling Example

Project SPIRIT is a program of Interfaith Action of Greater Saint Paul that provides after-school programming for African American and other youth in grades K–5 in four specific Saint Paul public schools. Participating students receive help with homework, exposure to the creative arts, and studies in African American history and culture, as well as social and emotional support. Parent involvement is a core element. With support from the Saint Paul Schools Foundation, Project SPIRIT has participated in a standardized quality assessment for after-school programs. That assessment showed that Project SPIRIT was meeting quality standards for after-school programs. Independent evaluations also showed that Project SPIRIT was meeting or exceeding outcome goals for student school attendance and growth in academic proficiency. What those evaluations did *not* do, however, was document and evaluate

Project SPIRIT's unique principles-driven cultural orientation and practice impacts.

Project SPIRIT focuses on the children developing several key traits—Strength, Perseverance, Imagination, Responsibility, Integrity, and Talent (SPIRIT)—to help cultivate student success. The program aims to provide experiences that facilitate the children becoming strong and learning to persevere, to use imagination, to be responsible, to live with integrity, and to develop their talent. The program is built on culturally specific, deeply rooted traditions that blend academic and cultural enrichment activities, drawing on African American traditions. Much of the curriculum is based on Kwanzaa principles: *Umoja* (Unity), *Kujichagulia* (Self-determination), *Ujima* (Collective Work and Responsibility), *Ujamaa* (Cooperative Economics), *Nia* (Purpose), *Kuumba* (Creativity), and *Imani* (Faith). Exhibit 22.1 presents the principles. Each month is devoted to a principle.

Evaluation Questions

1. To what extent are the principles clear, meaningful, and actionable? And, if so,

2. To what extent are they actually being followed? And, if so,

3. To what extent are they leading to specific desired results—that the children feel strong and are learning to persevere, to

use imagination, to be responsible, to live with integrity, and to develop their talent?

Evaluation Design

The evaluation began by developing criteria and methods for documenting and assessing the Kwanzaa principles in collaboration with Project SPIRIT staff. A pilot evaluation was undertaken to develop program observation protocols and interview instruments for students, parents, and staff. The evaluators examined with staff the curriculum, activities, and processes that were used each month in support of implementing the principle featured each month. The evaluation proposed that a portfolio be established for students to capture and document their work in relation to each principle. Students and parents would be interviewed about their knowledge of, experiences with, and perceived impacts of engaging the principles.

Principles-Focused Sampling Issues

1. What classroom activities should be sampled for observation to document principles-focused programming?

2. How should students, parents, and staff be sampled for in-depth interviews?

3. How should other key informants be

EXHIBIT 22.1. The Seven Kwanzaa Principles Adopted by Project SPIRIT

Umoja—*Unity* among African American people in mutual support

Kujichagulia—*Self-determination* as a people, individually and collectively

Ujima—*Collective work and shared responsibility* to help each other as needed to strengthen our community

Ujamaa—*Economic cooperation* to support community prosperity

Nia—Strong sense of *purpose* based on knowledge of African people's historical greatness

Kuumba—*Creativity* in contributing to our community

Imani—*Faith* in African American people and the rightness of our struggle

Source: Karenga (2008).

sampled for a survey about the program, including key informants' knowledge of and perspectives on the Kwanzaa principles?

Examples of the Principles-Focused Data from the Pilot Evaluation

The evaluation began with a small pilot study to learn how to ask students, parents, and staff about the principles. Seven students were interviewed from one of the four program sites in the pilot evaluation. Students' knowledge and understanding of the seven principles of Kwanzaa varied. All students interviewed could remember at least three of the seven principles, while one student remembered six and another remembered all seven. The two most remembered principles were *Kujichagulia* (self-determination) and *Nia* (purpose), but when asked which principle stood out most to them, students had varying answers. Most students had a hard time explaining why the principle they chose was important, and some seemed to have misconceptions about what the principle they chose really meant. For example, one student shared that *Umoja* carried the most meaning for him, but when asked why he actually described *Kuumba* (creativity).

Only one student named all seven principles. She was also able to clearly articulate why *Imani* (faith) was most important to her. She was not only the older of the only two students who had been in the program for 2 years, but she was also the only student who celebrates *Kwanzaa* at home. The combination of this longer dosage and reinforcement at home was interpreted as likely responsible for the fact that the principles seemed to have sunk in most deeply for her. Only a few of the other students indicated that they talked about the principles at home.

In pilot interviews with parents, several noted learning one or more of the Kwanzaa principles from their children, and noticing improvements in their children's self-esteem and confidence. Classroom observations included documenting teacher interactions with students and the recitations that students completed throughout 3-hour sessions. One of the recitations students memorized and recited, each in turn, in an Imani Circle affirmation group was:

"I Am Somebody": "I am capable and loveable. I am teachable, therefore I can learn. I can do anything I try. I will respect myself and others. I will do the best I can do each day. I will not waste time because time is too valuable and I am too precious and great. I am somebody."

High-Dosage Sampling

The pilot evaluation was just being completed as this was being written. Given the pilot results, the next phase of the evaluation will focus on a *high-dosage sample:* students and parents who have participated in the program multiple years to get a better sense of the cumulative impact of engaging with the principles over time. A survey will also be developed to measure knowledge of and get reactions to the principles from key informants who are in some way involved with the program.

The point here is not to report in detail on the Project SPIRIT program or evaluation, but to illustrate principles-focused sampling options and decision making. High-dosage sampling is an option for exploring how principles are manifested among those who have had the deepest engagement with them. Results from high-dosage sampling can then inform further design decisions about the value of documenting the effects of variability in dosage and engagement with the principles.

Purposeful Principles-Focused Evaluation Sampling

The logic and power of purposeful sampling lies in selecting information-rich cases for in-depth study. Information-rich cases are those from which one can learn a great deal about issues of central importance to the purpose of the inquiry, thus the term *purposeful sampling*. Studying information-rich cases yields insights and in-depth understanding rather than empirical generalizations. For example, if the purpose of an evaluation is to increase the effectiveness of a program in reaching lower socioeconomic groups, one may learn a great deal by studying in depth a small number of carefully selected poor families. Purposeful sampling focuses on selecting information-rich cases whose study will illuminate the questions under study (Patton, 2015a, Ch. 5).

Sampling and case selection are the foundation of any inquiry. What you find from your inquiry will be determined by the sample and cases you study. The type of sample you select should follow from and support inquiry into the questions you are asking. The purpose of a purposeful sample is to focus case selection strategically in alignment with the inquiry's purpose, primary questions, and data being collected.

For example, principles-focused sampling aims to elucidate the nature and implications of prescriptive admonitions like "Plan your work. Work your plan." What does this mean in practice for a specific group of practitioners? To what extent and in what ways, if at all, is this principle followed? And if followed, how does adhering to this principle affect behavior? The sample for inquiry would consist of people in organizations or professions that profess adherence to this principle. In my view, principles have become so widely touted as a basis for action and, as a result, such an important focus of inquiry that principles-focused sampling deserves its own category among purposeful sampling options (Patton, 2015a, p. 292).

Another example of principles-focused sampling is when diverse programs in a group are all adhering to the same principles but each adapting those principles to its own particular target population within its own context. An evidence-based effectiveness principles approach assumes that while the principles remain the same, there will necessarily and appropriately be adaptation within and across contexts in implementing them. Taken together, a set of principles provides a framework that guides cohesive approaches and solutions. Evidence for the effectiveness of principles can be derived from in-depth case studies of their implementation and implications. The results of the case studies are then synthesized across the diverse programs, all adhering to the same principles but each adapting those principles to its own particular target population within its own context. See Chapter 26 on effective principles for serving homeless youth for an example and discussion of principles-focused evaluation based on principles-focused sampling. The next chapter also discusses synthesizing findings about principles across diverse programs as a way of evaluating effectiveness to validate the extent to which a principles-based program is evidence-based.

Diverse Principles-Focused Sampling Examples

Part III presents exemplars of principles-focused initiatives and corresponding principles-focused evaluation approaches. As a cross-reference resource, Exhibit 22.2 summarizes the principles-focused sampling approach for each of the exemplars. Each principles-based program or initiative had to come up with a sampling strategy appropriate to the nature of the intervention and the purpose of the evaluation. Exhibit 22.2 provides a flavor of the variety of principles-focused sampling strategies that can be designed to match the nature and purpose of the evaluation.

Summary

The overall theme of this book is that evaluating principles is different from evaluating

Chapters	Focus	Number of principles	Purposeful sample
25	Paris Declaration on Aid Effectiveness, an international agreement	5	21 countries that volunteered to serve as case studies of the implementation and outcomes of the Paris Declaration Principles; 18 aid agencies that also volunteered to be case studies
26	Evidence-based effectiveness principles for working with homeless youth	9	Case studies of 14 homeless youth served over time by at least four different youth-serving agencies
27	Vibrant Communities Canada	5	Anti-poverty initiatives in 15 Canadian cities
28	Global Alliance for the Future of Food	6	All initiatives that the Global Alliance undertakes
29	Comprehensive Crop Research Program of the McKnight Foundation	8	Projects in four regions of the world: Eastern Africa, West Africa, Southern Africa, and the Andes
30	Agroecology principles	Varies by framework	Agroecological frameworks advocated by prominent agroecological researchers and research teams selected for their influence and diversity.

EXHIBIT 22.2. Principles-Focused Sampling Examples from Part III of This Book

projects. Principles-driven programs are different from goals-driven programs. Principles constitute *a different kind of evaluand* (focus for evaluation). As an evaluand, principles constitute a unit of analysis for sampling. In essence, principles-focused evaluation requires principles-focused sampling.

Practice Exercise

At the end of Chapter 1, I invited you to identify a principle that is important to you, one that informs and guides your life choices and decisions. Any kind of choice. Work. Family. Money. Relationships. Faith. I asked you to write it down, date it, and put it someplace where you could find it, refer to it, and use it in the practice exercises in this book. At the end of Chapter 6, I invited you to review and revise your principle based on the GUIDE criteria. Now it's time to pull out that principle again. What incidents, events, relationships, activities, achievements, or other things would you sample to examine what your principle means to you, the extent to which you are following it, and what outcomes flow from adherence to it? Create a principles-focused sample to generate data to evaluate the effectiveness of your principle in your work and/or life.

CHAPTER 23

Rendering Judgments
about the Effectiveness of Principles

> Evaluation is the act of judging the value, merit, worth, or significance of things. Those "things" can be performances, programs, processes, policies, or products, to name a few.
> —THOMAS A. SCHWANDT, *Evaluation Foundations Revisited* (2015, p. 1)

The "thing" evaluated can also be principles. The nature of the judgment rendered depends upon an evaluation's purpose. A formative evaluation renders judgment, typically in the form of feedback, about how something can be improved. A developmental evaluation renders judgment, in a timely manner, as real-time as possible, about what is emerging in complex dynamic systems and the implications of what is emerging. Accountability judgments concern whether resources and plans were followed as expected and specified contractually, and whether appropriate procedures and mandates were implemented. Knowledge-generating judgments concern contributions to what we know about how the world works. Exhibit 5.2 in Chapter 5 (page 28) presented a table showing how a principles-focused evaluation could serve these diverse purposes. The most challenging and highest-stakes purpose is rendering a summative judgment about overall merit, worth, and significance.

Part III of this book presents exemplars of principles-focused evaluations that rendered summative judgments.

▶ *Chapter 25.* The evaluation of the Paris Declaration on International Aid rendered overall judgment about the effectiveness of those principles for sustainable development results. The Paris Declaration Principles evaluation begins with development aid dominated by donor country agendas. Through case studies in 21 countries the evaluators identify both adherence and resistance to implementation of the principles. Where adherence is substantial, country priorities take center stage, and donors align their strategies with those priorities. The evidence is available in interviews with key informants, documents, survey responses, and tracking of money flows. The case studies also highlight those initiatives that flow from implementation of the principles and the results of those initiatives. The data from success cases show greater development impacts where resources are collaboratively channeled to priority issues. The evaluation reaches a summative judgment that implementation of the principles can enhance sustainable development results, but much greater and deeper adherence is needed. Essentially, the evaluation tells a story that has a beginning (the baseline), a middle (implementation activities), and a point-in-time ending (verifiable results to date).

▶ *Chapter 26.* The evaluation of shared principles among six agencies serving homeless youth rendered a judgment that those principles were effective and could be considered "evidence-based." The evaluation tells the story of implementation of the principles through case studies of 14 youth. Examples of the principles in practice as experienced by the youth show how the youth reacted to and were affected by the caseworkers who were adhering to the principles in their practice. Triangulation came from case documents and interviews with youth and staff.

▶ *Chapter 27.* The evaluation of community anti-poverty initiatives across Canada rendered judgment about the effectiveness of five core principles in guiding anti-poverty initiatives in diverse communities. The evaluation portrays a journey of ups and downs, and adaptation to the variations in communities, but with documentable and verifiable reductions in poverty that exceeded initial targets and can be linked, element by element, to the principles.

In each of these cases, the evaluation logic, as always, is connecting the dots, considering alternative explanations, and rendering judgment based upon the preponderance of evidence from multiple sources, both qualitative and quantitative. The nature of the evidence varied in each of these exemplary cases, but they shared a common evaluative reasoning process to reach the judgments rendered. In this chapter I'm going to focus on applying evaluation

reasoning to the evaluation of effectiveness principles to render overall judgments of merit, worth, and significance. The question I'll be addressing is: To what extent and in what ways is rendering judgments about the effectiveness of principles different from rendering such judgments about traditional evaluands, like projects and programs? My response is that the reasoning process is the same, but because principles constitute a different evaluand, the nature of the conclusions reached and judgments rendered needs to be adjusted and adapted to fit the nature of principles themselves.

The problem seems to be that we know what it means to say that a project, program, policy, or model "works," that it is effective, but what does it mean to say that a principle "works," or that a principle "is effective"? In a discussion with an experienced colleague on this point, he said that he found the problem "vexing." He couldn't quite grasp how one might render a summative judgment about the effectiveness of principles. To take on this challenge, I'll begin with what evaluative judgment processes have in common, regardless of evaluand, then turn to some of the nuances of rendering judgment about the effectiveness of principles.

Evaluative Reasoning

In his classic book *Evaluating with Validity,* House (1980) argued that designs or statistical analysis don't determine the validity of evaluation findings and judgments, but rather validity resides in the arguments that supported the use of these designs and analyses. He later reiterated this point: "All validity types necessarily rely on supporting arguments" (p. 31).

Davidson (2005, 2012, 2014) has elaborated what "sound evaluative reasoning" looks like:

> Reasoned answers that are clear, direct, and explicitly evaluative [are] . . . essentially the

methodological "core" of evaluation logic and methodology that defines our discipline. The absolutely fundamental difference between evaluation and other related activities, such as research, monitoring, performance measurement, and audit is that we ask and answer explicitly evaluative questions (i.e., questions about quality, value, and importance). (Davidson, 2014, p. 37)

Davidson has identified six steps to follow when reasoning evaluatively. Exhibit 23.1 summarizes her six steps and applies them to reaching evaluative judgments about principles.

EXHIBIT 23.1. Steps in Evaluative Reasoning Applied to Evaluating Effectiveness Principles

Generic steps in evaluative reasoning with validity*	Application to rendering judgments about the effectiveness of principles	Example from the evaluation of the Paris Declaration Principles for Development Aid
1. For each major evaluation question, list all relevant criteria of merit.	**GUIDE criteria** (Chapter 6) • Clarity of guidance • Usefulness • Inspiring • Developmental and adaptable • Evaluable **Criteria of merit** a. Meaningfulness of the principles to those using and affected by them b. Adherence to the principles c. Results of adherence	Criteria for judging adherence: • *Direction*—To what degree were the principles being implemented or resisted? • *Distance*—How extensively were the principles being implemented? • *Pace*—What was the speed of implementation?
2. Determine the relative importance of the criteria.	For formative evaluation: meaningfulness and adherence. For summative evaluation: results of adherence	Relative importance: 1. Direction 2. Distance 3. Pace
3. Define "how good is good," that is, what the "constellation of evidence" on each criterion would look like in order to say something was "good," "barely acceptable," "unacceptable," or "excellent."	A realistic, contextual in-depth description of what adherence to the principles and results looks like for the situation and context within which the evaluation is occurring. Create rating scales for degree of adherence and results.	Recipient countries determine aid priorities: a. Substantial movement toward reform b. Some movement toward reform c. Little movement d. No movement toward reform e. Regression away from reform

(continued)

Generic steps in evaluative reasoning with validity[*]	Application to rendering judgments about the effectiveness of principles	Example from the evaluation of the Paris Declaration Principles for Development Aid
4. Gather and analyze the right mix of evidence, being sure to triangulate using multiple sources.	Sample instances of the principles being implemented. Document variations in adherence. Get multiple and diverse perspectives on adherence and results.	21 country case studies; 18 international development agency case studies
5. Draw evaluative conclusions about performance on each of the criteria by interpreting the evidence (see #4 above) against the definitions of "how good is good."	Tell and document the story about how adherence to principles leads to results, or not.	Report rank-ordered direction and degree of adherence to the principles. Country ownership was greatest.
6. Synthesize these subevaluations (performances on several criteria) to draw overall evaluative conclusions about the program, policy, etc., as a whole.	Render judgment about the whole set of principles interacting together systemically, not just individual principles.	The evaluation synthesized the interrelationships among the five Paris Declaration Principles and rank-ordered degree of adherence and impacts.

[*]Davidson (2014, pp. 37–38).

Warranted Conclusions and Credible Judgments

Making judgments, especially high-stakes summative judgments, which involves determining the merit, worth, significance, and overall value of what is being evaluated, is fundamentally about reasoning and critical thinking. Warranted conclusions are those conclusions that are deemed credible because the story told by the preponderance of data is convincing within the context that the story is told. Evaluation as a field has become methodologically manic. Too many still think that rigor resides in particular methods. To the contrary, rigor is all about reasoning. That's why I repeat whenever I can the observation offered by Harvard physicist Percy W. Bridgman, Nobel Prize recipient in 1946 for discoveries in high-pressure physics: "The scientific method, so far as it is a method, is nothing more than doing one's damnedest with one's mind, no holds barred" (quoted in Waller, 2004, p. 106).

The larger problem, it seems to me, is the focus on methods and procedures as the basis for determining quality and rigor. The notion that methods are more or less rigorous decouples methods from context and the thinking process that determined what questions to ask, what methods to use, what analytical procedures to follow, and what inferences to draw from the findings.

Rigorous Thinking

No problem can withstand the assault of sustained thinking.

—VOLTAIRE, French philosopher

Rigorous thinking combines (1) critical thinking, (2) creative thinking, (3) evaluative thinking, (4) inferential thinking, and (5) practical thinking. *Critical thinking* involves questioning assumptions; acknowledging and dealing with preconceptions, predilections, and biases; diligently looking for negative and disconfirming cases that don't fit the dominant pattern; conscientiously examining rival explanations; relentlessly seeking diverse perspectives; and analyzing what and how you think, why you think that way, and the implications for your inquiry. (This section is drawn from Patton, 2015a, p. 702.)

Creative thinking means putting the data together in new ways to see the interactions among separate findings more holistically; synthesizing diverse themes in a search for coherence and essence while simultaneously developing comfort with ambiguity and uncertainty in the messy, complex, and dynamic real work; distinguishing signal from noise while also learning from the noise; asking wicked questions that enter into the intersections and tensions between the search for coherent meaning and persistent uncertainties and ambiguities; bringing artistic, evocative, and visualization techniques to data analysis and presentations; and inviting outside-the-box, off-the-wall, and beyond-the-ken perspectives and interpretations.

Evaluative thinking forces clarity about the inquiry purpose, who it is for, with what intended uses, to be judged by what quality criteria; it involves being explicit about what criteria are being applied in framing inquiry questions, making design decisions, determining what constitutes appropriate methods, and selecting and following analytical processes and being aware of and articulating values, ethical considerations, contextual implications, strengths and weaknesses of the inquiry, and potential (or actual) misinterpretations, misuses, and misapplications. In contrast with the perspective of rigor as strict adherence to a standardized process, evaluative thinking emphasizes the importance of understanding the sufficiency of rigor relative to context and situational factors.

Inferential thinking involves examining the extent to which the evidence supports the conclusions reached. Inferential thinking can be deductive, inductive, or abductive—and often draws on and creatively integrates all three analytical processes—but at its core, it is a fierce examination of and allegiance to where the evidence leads.

> A rigorously conducted evaluation will be convincing as a presentation of evidence in support of an evaluation's conclusions and will presumably be more successful in withstanding scrutiny from critics. Rigor is multifaceted and relates to multiple dimensions of the evaluation. . . . The concept of rigor is understood and interpreted within the larger context of validity, which concerns the "soundness or trustworthiness of the inferences that are made from the results of the information gathering process" (Joint Committee on Standards for Educational Evaluation, 1994, p. 145). . . . There is relatively broad consensus that validity is a property of an inference, knowledge claim, or intended use, rather than a property either of a research or evaluation study's findings. (Braverman, 2013, p. 101)

In reflecting on and writing about "what counts as credible evidence in applied research and evaluation practice," Sharon Rallis (2009), former president of the American Evaluation Association and an experienced researcher, emphasized rigorous reasoning: "I have come to see a *true scientist*, then, as one who puts forward her findings and the reasoning that led her to those findings for others to contest, modify, accept, or reject" (p. 171, emphasis added).

Practical thinking calls for assiduously integrating theory and practice; examining real-world implications of findings; inviting interpretations and applications from nonresearchers (e.g., community members, program staff, and participants), who can and will apply to the data what ordinary people refer to as "common sense"; and applying real-world criteria to interpreting the findings—criteria like understandability, meaningfulness, cost implications, and implications in addressing societal issues and problems.

Telling the Summative Story through Principles-Focused Contribution Analysis

The complex systems critique of traditional causal attribution approaches is that the language and concepts are overly deterministic. The word *cause* connotes singular, direct, and linear actions leading to clear, precise, and verifiable results: *X* caused *Y*. But such a direct, singular, linear causation is rare in the complex and dynamic interactions of human beings. More often, there are multiple causal influences and multiple outcomes. Contribution analysis reframes explanation of findings from cause-and-effect thinking to masking sense of influences and interactions. Contribution analysis (Mayne, 2008, 2011, 2012) was developed as an approach in program evaluation to examine a causal hypothesis (theory

of change) against logic and evidence to determine what factors could explain the findings. Attribution questions are different from contribution questions, as shown in Exhibit 23.2, which compares traditional evaluation causality questions (attribution), generic contribution analysis questions, and principles-focused contribution analysis questions.

Contribution Analysis Conclusions about Effectiveness Principles

The result of a principles contribution analysis is not definitive proof that the principles have made an important contribution but rather evidence and argumentation from which it is reasonable to draw conclusions about the degree and importance of the contribution, within some level of confidence. The aim is to get plausible association based on a preponderance of evidence, as in the judicial and forensic traditions. The question is whether a reasonable person would agree from the evidence and argument that the principles have made an important contribution to the observed result.

EXHIBIT 23.2. Comparing Attribution Questions, Generic Contribution Analysis Questions, and Principles-Focused Contribution Analysis Questions

Traditional causal attribution questions	Generic contribution analysis questions	Principles-focused contribution analysis questions
• Has the program caused the measured outcomes? • To what extent has the program caused the measured outcomes? • To what extent are the measured outcomes caused by the program?	• Has the program made a difference? That is, has the program made an important contribution to the observed results? • Has the program influenced the observed result? • How much of a difference has the program made? How much of a contribution?	• What logical and empirical connections can be made between degree of adherence with principles and the results of adherence? • How have principles interacted with other factors in a way that reasonably explains the results observed over time? • How substantively significant, interpretable, meaningful, and actionable are the pathway connections between adherence to principles and observed and documented changes?

A contribution analysis produces a contribution story that presents the evidence and other influences on observed and documented changes. A major part of that story may tell about behavioral changes that intended beneficiaries have made as a result of experiencing a program's principles, as in the case of the evaluation of principles for working with homeless youth.

Attributes of a Credible Principles Contribution Story

A credible principles-focused summative evaluation of contribution would entail the following:

▶ An in-depth description context for the evaluation that includes a baseline assessment of the forces affecting the situation at the beginning of the change process.

▶ A plausible theory of change about how and why the principles might be expected to contribute to desired changes.

▶ Description and documentation of the degree and nature of adherence to the principles, including variations in adherence and explanations for those variations insofar as they are known.

▶ Description and documentation of the observed changes and results.

▶ Analysis of the nature and strength of the connections and linkages between implementation of the principles and the observed changes ("connecting the dots" in the contribution story).

▶ Marshaling evidence in support of the assumptions behind the key linkages in the theory of change.

▶ Discussion of the roles of the other influencing factors and alternative explanations.

▶ Discussion of the strengths, weaknesses, and quality of the evidence provided.

Contribution analysis focuses on identifying likely influences. Such causes, which on their own are neither necessary nor sufficient, represent the kind of contribution role that many interventions play. Contribution analysis, like detective work, requires connecting the dots between what was done with the principles and what resulted, examining a multitude of interacting variables and factors, and considering alternative explanations and hypotheses, so that in the end we can reach an independent, reasonable, and evidence-based judgment based on the cumulative evidence. That is what was done in all three exemplary summative principles-focused evaluations in Part III, discussed at the beginning of this chapter. Outcome harvesting (Wilson-Grau, Chapter 32, in this volume) is a well-developed framework that uses contribution analysis for evaluating outcomes in complex dynamic systems characterized by multiple influences, multiple outcomes, and multiple interrelationships.

Presenting the Contribution Story and Supporting the Summative Judgment Made

Presentations depend on audience and purpose, and are therefore highly situational. In preparing a report or presentation, it is worth remembering (and here repeating) House's criteria of truth, beauty, and justice discussed in Chapter 15. Truth is a well-supported argument with relevant and credible data. Beauty is a coherent presentation in which the evidence inexorably leads to the conclusion and judgment. Justice is acknowledging and taking into account the political context and ramifications of whatever conclusions are reached and judgments made.

Truth is the *attainment* of arguments soundly made, beauty is the *attainment* of coherence well wrought, and justice is the *attainment* of politics fairly done. (House, 2014, p. 31)

Making Credible Summative Judgments about the Effectiveness of Principles

The suggestions in this chapter about how to make credible summative judgments about principles have adapted generic evaluation advice about validity and valuing to the particular challenges of focusing on principles as the evaluand. I'll conclude this chapter with six specific principles-focused bits of advice about rendering summative judgments.

1. *Make principles real to the readers and intended users of the evaluation.* People know what a program is and have a good idea what it means for it to be effective. But what does it mean for a principle to be effective? It helps to make the principle in question as concrete as possible. Describe the principle in action and practice. In the evaluation of principles for working with homeless youth, each of the nine principles is portrayed behaviorally. In presenting the principle of building trusting adult–youth relationships, the evaluation describes several such relationships. That makes it easier to understand how a trusting adult–youth relationship would contribute to a young person taking positive steps toward housing and a hopeful future. The details tell the story, making it understandable and credible. The mechanisms for change are embedded in but made explicit in the descriptive storytelling that portrays the principle in practice.

2. *Connect the dots between adherence to principles and results.* A summary judgment is a conclusion to a story, but is not the story. Imagine a romantic story that simply says the boy and girl got married, but tells nothing about how they met and what they did leading up to marriage. To conclude that a principle, or set of interacting principles, is effective requires a description of what effectiveness means as well as the detailed story line about how effectiveness unfolds as principles are followed.

3. *Support the summative judgment with multiple sources of evidence to increase credibility.* This means triangulation, which supports drawing warranted (convincing) conclusions generally but takes on added importance with principles because the evaluand is less well known, and therefore the evidence of effectiveness may have to be more convincing than traditional evaluation conclusions. Integrate and triangulate diverse sources of qualitative data: interviews, observations, document analysis. Any single source of data has strengths and weaknesses. Consistency of findings across types of data increases confidence in the confirmed patterns and themes of the principles' effectiveness. Integrating and triangulating quantitative and qualitative data in mixed-methods studies adds credibility to the conclusions reached and judgments made. Be creative with triangulation. Triangulate analysts by having more than one look at and think about the data, identifying patterns and themes of principles effectiveness (and ineffectiveness) and testing conclusions and explanations from different perspectives. This reduces concerns about the potential biases and selective perception of a single evaluation analyst.

4. *Argue with your arguments.* Acknowledge counterarguments, weak links in the story line, and omissions in the data. Don't oversell your conclusions and judgments. Modesty and humility are appropriate when trying to make sense of and explain complex dynamic phenomena.

   a. Generate and assess alternative conclusions and rival explanations. What are other ways of explaining what you've found? Guide the reader to the explanation that best fits the preponderance of evidence, but don't force the fit.

b. Consider an advocacy–adversary presentation using a debate format for examining the viability of conclusions. What are the evidence and arguments that support your conclusions? What are the contrary evidence and counterarguments? Devote a section to a "devil's advocate." The aim is to surface and address doubts and weaknesses that the reader or intended user may have as well as build on strengths and confirm solid conclusions.

c. Search for, analyze, and include negative or disconfirming evidence and cases. There are "exceptions that prove the rule" and exceptions that question the rule. In either case, look for and learn from exceptions to the patterns you've identified.

5. *Incorporate evidence and arguments from sources outside the evaluation.* In all three of the featured summative evaluations in Part III, evaluation data and conclusions were supported with relevant research findings, expert analysis, practitioner experiences, and relevant social science theory. For example, the format for reporting the evaluation findings and conclusions for each of the principles guiding work with homeless youth was:

a. Statement and definition of the principle

b. Why the principle is important

c. Outcomes from adhering to the principle

d. What the research says about the issue the principle addresses

e. Practice implications of the principle

f. Evaluation evidence

g. Bottom-line conclusion

6. *Context matters, so position findings, conclusions, and judgments as context sensitive, context dependent, and context specific.* The overall conclusion of the Paris Declaration

Principles evaluation was that *context matters*. In a volume of *New Directions for Evaluation* on valuing and rendering judgments, every contributor emphasized the importance of context (Julnes, 2012). Then there's a whole volume of *New Directions for Evaluation* devoted to illuminating how and why context matters (Rog, Fitzpatrick, & Conner, 2012). Summative judgments are no exception. Context is especially important for interpreting the effectiveness of principles because they have to be adapted to context, which is what the *D* for *developmental* addresses in the GUIDE framework.

Conclusion: What It Means for Principles to Work

In traditional project evaluation, a summative evaluation, if positive, validates a model for replication. When replicated, the model is subject to fidelity evaluation, which is aimed at ensuring that the model is implemented exactly as validated in the summative evaluation. As such, it may take on the moniker of being a "best practice." The next chapter will discuss the dangers and misrepresentations of that labeling. Regardless of how it is marketed, the point of a traditional summative evaluation is to judge the merit, worth, significance, *and replicability* of a standardized model.

A summative judgment that principles "work," that is, that they are effective, means something quite different. First, it means, or should mean, that the principles have been found to be meaningful to those following them, that they are being followed, and that in being followed they contribute to certain identifiable, desirable results. Moreover, a summative judgment based on the criteria in the GUIDE framework affirms that the principles provide meaningful guidance, are useful, inspire, support developmental and contextual adaptation, and are evaluable. Exhibit 23.3 summarizes these judgments about what it means for principles to be effective.

EXHIBIT 23.3. What It Means for Principles to Be Judged Effective

---

The GUIDE criteria specify what it means to render judgment that principles are effective, that that effectiveness is evidence based, and that the principles "work" in support of attaining desired results.

G The principles provide meaningful **guidance** about what to do and what not to do.

U The principles are **useful** in informing decision making about possible alternative actions, helping determine what path to take at metaphorical (or real) forks in the road.

I The principles inspire and motivate followers and adherents to walk the talk, stay the course, and otherwise be true to their principles.

D The principles have demonstrated **developmental** flexibility by being contextually adaptable, situationally relevant, and helpful in navigating complex dynamic systems.

> *Note:* This criterion alone is why a set of principles do not constitute a high-fidelity, standardized model; they are not rules; they are not formulaic; they have to be interpreted and adapted to context; meeting *the developmental criterion* means that the principles have shown meaningful, adaptable, and relevant guidance within diverse contexts, usually characterized as complex dynamic systems.

E The principles are evaluable, which has presumably been well demonstrated if a summative evaluation has been undertaken successfully.

Practice Exercise

In the practice exercise at the end of the last chapter (page 201), I asked you to generate a principles-focused sample to gather data for your personal effectiveness principle (first identified in the practice exercise at the end of Chapter 1 and revised in the practice exercise at the end of Chapter 6 based on the GUIDE framework.) So here's the question now: How would you render a summative judgment about the effectiveness of that principle in your work and life? Right at this point in time, what would be, *what is*, your judgment about (1) the meaningfulness of that principle to you, (2) your adherence to it, and (3) the results that emanate from whatever degree of adherence you manage? What evidence do you bring to bear on those judgments? What's the story line for your judgments? What's your contribution analysis? How does making a summative judgment about your principle's effectiveness position you for following that principle in the future? What's your recommendation to yourself? Go for it!

CHAPTER 24

Evaluating Principles for Evidence of Effectiveness

Three Kinds of Evidence-Based Judgments and Effective Principles in Contrast to Best Practices

The value of a principle is the number of things it will explain.
—RALPH WALDO EMERSON, American essayist and poet

It's an intriguing idea, that one should have evidence to support claims of effectiveness. Thus, the label "evidence-based" has become widely used to give credence to a variety of models, programs, treatments, and interventions—many of which lack any actual evidence of effectiveness other than the fervent beliefs of their advocates. The question is: "What counts as credible evidence in applied research and evaluation practice?" (Donaldson, Christie, & Mark, 2008). What kinds of evidence are appropriate for different purposes, programs, and situations? Evidence about program effectiveness involves systematically gathering and carefully analyzing data about the extent to which observed outcomes can be attributed to a program's interventions.

It is useful to distinguish three types of evidence-based conclusions:

1. *Single evidence-based program.* Rigorous and credible summative evaluation of a single program provides evidence for the effectiveness of that program and only that program. A "summative evaluation" is an overall judgment of merit, worth, and significance that sums up the evidence to make a determination of overall effectiveness for a particular, specific intervention.

2. *Evidence-based model.* Systematic meta-analysis (statistical aggregation) of the results of several programs all implementing the same model in a high-fidelity, standardized, and replicable manner, and (ideally) evaluated with randomized controlled trials, to determine overall effectiveness of the model. This is the basis for claims that a model is a "best practice."

3. *Evidence-based principles.* Synthesis of case studies, including both processes and outcomes, of a group of diverse programs all adhering to the same principles but each adapting those principles to its own particular target population within its own context. If the findings show that the principles have been implemented systematically, and

analysis connects implementation of the principles with desired outcomes through detailed and in-depth contribution analysis, the conclusion can be drawn that the practitioners are following effective evidence-based principles.

Exhibit 24.1 compares and contrasts the three types of evidence-based judgments of effectiveness.

Effective Principles in Contrast to Best Practices

A model is not something to be replicated but rather it is a demonstration of the feasibility of a principle.

—JOHN DEWEY, American philosopher and educational reformer

This chapter opened by delineating three kinds of evidence-based evaluation

EXHIBIT 24.1. Three Types of Evidence-Based Judgments of Effectiveness

	Effective program	Effective model	Effective principles
1. **Unit of analysis and comparison**	Single program	Multiple programs implementing the same model with high consistency and fidelity	Multiple programs serving different participants in diverse ways but all based on and following the same principles
2. **Example**	One program in one community for high school dropouts to get their general equivalency secondary school certificate.	25 separate programs in communities across the United States all follow *the same program model* to support high school dropouts to get their general equivalency secondary school certificate. They all gather the same outcome data in the same way.	10 different programs in communities across the United States implement different approaches to helping high school dropouts get their general equivalency secondary school certificate. Programs are adapted to different ethnic groups, poverty levels, jobs available for graduates, and other contextual factors, but all profess adherence to a common set of principles of adult education.
3. **Method**	*Program evaluation:* Document and measure program participants' outcomes (usually pre–post) and compare to desired outcomes; show that the outcomes can be attributed to the program.	*Meta-analysis:* Statistically aggregate and analyze common outcome data from multiple programs that all follow the same model and measure the same outcomes in the same way.	*Case studies synthesis:* Qualitative synthesis of patterns of principle implementation and effectiveness across a number of diverse programs based on case studies of a purposeful sample of participants.

(continued)

	Effective program	Effective model	Effective principles
4. **Methodological challenge**	Measuring outcomes; attributing outcomes to the program.	Measuring the fidelity of model implementation; getting high-quality data, consistent from multiple programs.	Identifying and coding principles in the case studies; determining the contribution of the principles to the observed and documented outcomes in the case studies.
5. **Conclusion and judgment**	The program is effective (or not).	The model is effective (or not).	The principles are effective (or not).
6. **Strength**	Solid evidence about the effectiveness of the program evaluated.	Credible, generalizable statistical evidence about the effectiveness of *the model.*	In-depth qualitative data about how principles are implemented under diverse conditions with diverse participants, what the principles mean to staff and participants in different contexts, and how they contribute to desired outcomes across contexts.

conclusions: summative evaluation of a single program, meta-evaluation of the same model implemented in different sites, and a synthesis of the effectiveness of principles-driven programs. To further understand the significance of evaluating effective principles, this section examines the limitations of the dominant "best-practices" approach to conceptualizing and judging effectiveness so as to better locate the niche and value of the principles-focused alternative.

Model Conceptualization and Adherence

Model adherence involves following precisely and systematically the steps and processes specified in a model in order to achieve the predetermined, standardized, and measurable results the model aims to achieve. The very nature and purpose of a model is to specify and predict what will result if the steps prescribed in the model are implemented systematically with high fidelity. For example, *Teaching Children to Read* by the National Reading Panel (2000) presents research-based best practices in reading instruction in five instructional areas: *phonemic awareness, phonics, vocabulary, fluency,* and *comprehension.*

In a similar vein, the U.S. Environmental Protection Agency (EPA; 2015) promotes *The Clean Energy-Environment Guide to Action: State Policies and Best Practices for Advancing Energy Efficiency, Renewable Energy, and Combined Heat and Power.* The guide includes 16 clean energy "best practices" that states can adopt to save energy, improve air quality, lower greenhouse gas emissions, and increase economic development. An example is building codes for energy efficiency. This illustrates the appropriate and useful contribution of best practices: research-based knowledge about specific actions that have been proven to produce predictable results across contexts.

The "Best-Practices" Mania

Designating a model a "best practice" has swept like wildfire through all sectors of society. Do an Internet search and prepare to be astounded by how much best-ness there is in the world. Governments and international agencies publish best practices for education, health, highways, and welfare reform, and on and on it goes. The "best practices"–disseminating business is thriving worldwide. Philanthropic foundations are anxious to discover, fund, and disseminate best practices. Corporations advertise that they follow best practices. Management consultants teach best practices. Identifying, following, and promoting "best practices" has led to the creation of best practices databases (e.g., Conference of Mayors, 2014). The trick is to determine if the proclaimed "best practices" actually constitute research-based knowledge about specific actions that have been proven to produce predictable results across contexts.

Why Real Best Practices Are Rare

"Best practices" are top of the mountain. They are not just effective practices, decent practices, better practices, promising practices, or smart practices—but *the best*. The connotation embedded in the phrase "best practice" is that there is a single best way to do something. Karl Popper, whose contributions to philosophy of science were monumental, argued that nothing could ultimately be proved, only disproved. Applied to best practices, this means we can never prove that a practice is the best, but we can distinguish practices that are poor and ineffective from those that are less poor and more effective, no small contribution. Popper identified a natural tendency for people to overgeneralize and speculate well beyond the data, thus the importance of carefully considering rival hypotheses

and falsification (claims that disprove the hypothesis). Science, he argued, was not so much a set of methods as a form of argumentation in which different interpretations are subjected to careful scrutiny and criticism.

Moreover, "best" is inevitably a matter of perspective and criteria. Like beauty, what is best will reside in the eye and mind of the beholder and the criteria, comparisons, and evidence that the beholder finds credible. In a world that manifests vast diversity, many paths exist for reaching a desired destination; some may be more difficult and some more costly, but such criteria reveal the importance of asking, "'Best' from whose perspective using what criteria?"

From a systems point of view, a major problem with many "best practices" is the way they are offered without attention to context. Suppose automobile engineers identified the best fuel injection system, the best transmission, the best engine cooling system, the best suspension system, and so forth. Let us further suppose, as is likely, that these best subsystems (fuel injection, etc.) come from different car models (Lexus, Infiniti, Audi, Mercedes, etc.). When one had assembled all the "best" systems from all the best cars, they would not constitute a working car. Each best part (subsystem) would have been designed to go together with other specifically designed parts for a specific model of car. They're not interchangeable. Yet a lot of best-practices rhetoric presumes context-free adoption.

Best-Practices Distortions in Practice

John Bare, vice president of the Arthur M. Blank Family Foundation in Atlanta, tells of teaching an evaluation class for nonprofit executives:

> I had one woman explain that her organization had a foundation grant to deliver health services to low income families. The funder required all grantees to adhere strictly to the preferred [best practice] implementation

model. To keep their funding, grantees had to deliver detailed reports to the funder describing how they were following the model. For this executive, however, her staff had discovered that they could get better results by varying the model based on the needs of client families. Varying the model was not permitted. To keep the funder happy while also pursuing authentic social change for client families, the organization decided to keep two sets of books. The group used one set of reports to satisfy the evaluation requirements of the funder. The second set of books accurately tracked the work and the outcomes. (2013, p. 86)

The assertion that a best practice has been discovered and must now be followed easily becomes a new orthodoxy, and then a mandate, when that alleged best practice aligns with the ideological preferences of the powerful. It is a dangerous, simpleminded, and authoritarian way to disguise preference as scientific knowledge.

Best Practices
and Evidence-Based Medicine

Gary Klein is a psychologist who has studied evidence-based medicine (EBM). Klein (2014) warns against the notion that "best practices" can become the foundation of EBM.

The concept behind EBM is certainly admirable: a set of best practices validated by rigorous experiments. EBM seeks to provide healthcare practitioners with treatments they can trust, treatments that have been evaluated by randomized controlled trials, preferably blinded. EBM seeks to transform medicine into a scientific discipline rather than an art form. What's not to like? We don't want to return to the days of quack fads and unverified anecdotes.

But we should only trust EBM if the science behind best practices is *infallible* and *comprehensive,* and that's certainly not the case. Medical science is not infallible. Practitioners shouldn't believe a published study just because it meets the criteria of randomized controlled trial design. Too many of these

studies cannot be replicated. Sometimes the researcher got lucky and the experiments that failed to replicate the finding never got published or even submitted to a journal (thus publication bias). In rare cases the researcher has faked the results. Even when the results can be replicated they shouldn't automatically be believed—conditions may have been set up in a way that misses the phenomenon of interest so a negative finding doesn't necessarily rule out an effect.

And medical science is not comprehensive. Best practices often take the form of simple rules to follow, but practitioners work in complex situations. EBM relies on controlled studies that vary one thing at a time, rarely more than two or three. Many patients suffer from multiple medical problems, such as Type 2 diabetes compounded with asthma. The protocol that works with one problem may be inappropriate for the others. EBM formulates best practices for general populations but practitioners treat individuals, and need to take individual differences into account. A treatment that is generally ineffective might still be useful for a sub-set of patients. Further, physicians aren't finished once they select a treatment; they often have to adapt it. They need expertise to judge whether a patient is recovering at an appropriate rate. Physicians have to monitor the effectiveness of a treatment plan and then modify or replace it if it isn't working well. A patient's condition may naturally fluctuate and physicians have to judge the treatment effects on top of this noisy baseline. . . .

Worse, reliance on EBM can impede scientific progress. If hospitals and insurance companies mandate EBM, backed up by the threat of lawsuits if adverse outcomes are accompanied by any departure from best practices, physicians will become reluctant to try alternative treatment strategies. (p. 1)

Embracing Humility
and Acknowledging Uncertainty

Commenting on the proliferation of supposed "best practices" in evaluation reports, Harvard-based evaluation research pioneer Carol Weiss (2002) advised wisely that evaluators should exercise restraint and demonstrate "a little more humility" about what we conclude and report to our sponsors and clients. Humility acknowledges, even embraces, uncertainty. An assertion of certainty about what is best fosters ideological orthodoxy, intolerance, self-righteousness, rigidity, and pride. In asserting the seven deadly sins—anger, covetousness, envy, gluttony, lust, sloth, and pride—Saint Thomas Aquinas considered pride to be chief among the deadly sins, not because of its inherent gravity but because of its potential for leading to still other sins. There's pridefulness in proclaiming that one is practicing what is "best." Humility, in contrast, acknowledges respectfully that others, looking at the same facts, may arrive at different interpretations and draw different conclusions and that in a different context others might effectively pursue different actions. Of course, exercising and rewarding humility is admittedly hard to do in a world that feeds on hype.

> What works in a poverty neighborhood in Chicago may not stand a ghost of a chance in Appalachia. We need to understand the conditions under which programs succeed and the interior components that actually constitute the program in operation, as well as the criteria of effectiveness applied. We need to look across . . . programs in different places under different conditions and with different features, in an attempt to tease out the factors that matter. . . . But even then, I have some skepticism about lessons learned, particularly in the presumptuous "best practices" mode. With the most elegant tools at our disposal, can we really confidently identify the elements that distinguished those program

realizations that had good results from those that did not? (Weiss, 2002, pp. 229–230)

Why This Matters

The allure and seduction of best-practice thinking poisons genuine dialogue about both what we know and the limitations of what we know. More specifically, it creates a mind-set that standardized, universal prescriptions are widely possible and the desired, most useful, and most prestigious form of knowledge. But *context matters,* greatly, consistently, and dramatically (Rog et al., 2012). In a highly diverse world of varying contexts and conditions, more generally applicable knowledge takes the form of principles that are formulated and implemented with attention to contextual adaptation. Principles can be evaluated for effectiveness and results, but the nature of the knowledge is different. Both have value, but they are built on different forms of knowledge and applied differently. Exhibit 24.2 contrasts principles with best practices.

Practice Exercise

Conduct an Internet search for "best practices" in your area of primary interest and expertise. What turns up? Assess what is presented as "best practices." How would you characterize those assertions? If what you find are not really "best practices," what would you call them? What's an appropriate designation? Why?

EXHIBIT 24.2. Best Practices Compared to Effectiveness Principles

	Best practices	Effective principles
1. **Definition and scope**	Research-based knowledge about specific actions that have been proven to produce predictable results across contexts.	Guidance for action derived from experience, expertise, values, research, and evaluation that must be interpreted and applied contextually.
2. **Example**	*Immunization for polio:* dosage, timing, mode of delivery, qualifications and training of immunizer, and precise procedures for storage, treatment, safety, and possible side effects.	*Immunization campaign:* voluntary participation; adapt the campaign to target population education levels, culture, societal norms, nature and quality of health system, religion, political environment, and history for polio and other immunization campaigns.
3. **Formulation and format**	Best practices are formulated as a model specifying the inputs, activities, and processes that will lead to desired and predictable outputs, outcomes, and impacts, which take the form of clear, specific, and measureable goals.	Principles are formulated as statements offering guidance, usually with a name for the principle (e.g., Occam's razor), followed by action-oriented wisdom: *In comparing explanations, choose the simplest that conforms with the preponderance of evidence.*
4. **Strengths**	• Applies across contexts • Standardized procedures • Standardized results	• Context sensitive • Situationally responsive • Adaptable
5. **Weaknesses**	• Becomes rigid and fixed • Resists change in the face of new knowledge and changed conditions • Inattentive to where it doesn't work (assumes universality)	• Can generate conflict over what the guidance means and how to apply it in context • Subject to various interpretations • May be too vague, general, and obtuse
6. **Evaluation criteria**	• High-fidelity implementation: following prescribed practices precisely • Standardized, replicable results regardless of context • Goal-oriented: specifies clear, specific, and measureable outcomes	• Leads to contextually sensitive action • Supports attaining contextually desired and appropriate results • Problem-focused: driven by addressing problems for which solutions are being created, but not enough may be known to set precise outcome targets

Summary of Parts I and II
Major Themes of Principles-Focused Evaluation

Part I introduced principles: What they are, why they matter, and their niche in program development and evaluation. Chapter 1 distinguished three kinds of principles: natural principles, moral principles, and effectiveness principles, and positioned this book as focusing on evaluating principles for effectiveness. Chapter 2 explained what principles-focused evaluation is and where it is most appropriate. Chapter 3 provided an overview of a number of diverse examples of principles-driven programs and change initiatives. Chapter 4 made the case that evaluating principles is new territory for evaluation, which has been and still is dominated by a project mind-set focused on measuring goal attainment. Principles as the *evaluand*, the thing evaluated, are different from projects and models as the unit of analysis for evaluation and must therefore be evaluated differently. Chapter 5 positioned principles-focused evaluation in relation to developmental evaluation and utilization-focused evaluation.

Part II has elaborated the nature and quality of principles. Chapter 6 presented the GUIDE framework for developing and evaluating principles, which identifies five characteristics of a high-quality

effectiveness principle: It provides guidance, is useful, inspires, supports ongoing development and adaptation, and is evaluable. Chapters 7–24 elaborated each of the GUIDE criteria. In so doing, I made conceptual distinctions (e.g., principles vs. rules), addressed issues (e.g., does the distinction between principles and rules matter?), suggested ways of helping groups identify and articulate their principles, and offered examples of principles-driven programs and principles-focused evaluation. By way of review and synthesis, this chapter, in transitioning to the case exemplars in Part III, concludes by reviewing 10 major themes presented in Parts I and II.

Synthesis of Themes for Principles-Focused Evaluation

1. Principles constitute a unique and important focus for evaluation. Evaluating principles is different from evaluating projects and programs and therefore requires particular approaches, skills, knowledge, and evaluation frameworks.

2. Principles are grounded in values about what matters to those who

develop, adopt, and attempt to follow them. The inspirational nature of values is grounded in those values, which express the things people care about.

3. Principles can and should be evaluated for effectiveness. This requires answering three questions at a minimum:

   a. Are the principles stated in a way that can be evaluated? Do they meet the GUIDE criteria for statements that are meaningful, actionable, and evaluable?

   b. To what extent are the principles being adhered to in practice?

   c. If they are adhered to, to what extent is following the principles leading to the desired results?

4. Principles are the rudder for navigating complex dynamic systems. Evaluating them confirms that the rudder can be used to steer and navigate *mare incognitum*.

5. Principles provide direction but not detailed prescription, so they offer opportunities to adapt to different contexts, changing understandings, and varied challenges. Thus, principles must be interpreted and applied contextually and situationally to ensure their relevance.

6. Principles require judgment in application, so their effectiveness is somewhat dependent on the quality of decision making and judgment rendering in applying and evaluating them.

7. Principles point to consequences, outcomes, and impacts.

8. Principles are distinct from rules, minimum specifications, and best-practice prescriptions.

9. Referring to something as a principle doesn't make it one. There's a lot of crap out there that poses as principles but fails to meet criteria for a meaningful and evaluable principle.

10. Principles-focused evaluation is most appropriate for principles-driven programs and people.

Principles Rule

Principles are distinct from rules, including but not limited to simple rules, rules of thumb, rules of engagement, the rule of law, procedural rules, operating rules, and rules about rules. I've devoted a whole chapter to distinguishing principles from rules. Still, in the parlance of the day, principles rule. By that I mean, principles are fundamental to making our way in the world. We can't have rules for everything. Principles are broader than rules and therefore have wider application. Where rules are needed and applicable, they provide clear, meaningful, and appropriate guidance. Stop at stop signs. Pay your taxes. Don't drink and drive. Principles, in contrast, provide more general guidance. Respect others if you want to be respected. Spend your time and energy on the things that are most important. Think evaluatively. And: PRINCIPLES RULE.

Principles-Focused Evaluability Assessment

I've devoted as much or more attention thus far to identifying and articulating principles as to evaluating them. This is because the work of principles-focused evaluation begins with evaluating the quality of the principles to be evaluated. In the early days of evaluation, evaluators were stymied by program goals that were vague, meaningless, vacuous, and immeasurable. The notion of evaluability assessment emerged as a way of determining if a program was ready for evaluation. This led to evaluators being involved in developing program goals that were clear, specific, and measurable and program logic models that specified how goals were to be achieved. In this way evaluation moved from being primarily a back-end activity (determining whether goals were achieved) to being a front-end activity (determining whether a program was ready for evaluation).

In similar fashion, principles-focused evaluation includes evaluability assessment:

Are principles stated in a way that can be evaluated? This means that the skills needed to do principles-focused evaluation include providing assistance in identifying and articulating principles that meet the GUIDE criteria.

Confusion about Principles

Part III moves from the general to the particular, providing specific examples and exemplars of principles-driven organizations, programs, and initiatives and corresponding principles-focused evaluations. In making this transition, I feel compelled to acknowledge that, as a homonym, principles can be confusing to discuss.

A freshman returned home from his first day in high school. His mother asked: "So, what did you learn on your first day?"

"I hate principals."

The mother gasped, "What in the world do you have against principles?"

"Principals make everything about rules, rules, rules. It's all about following the rules, or else."

"But principles are there to help us know what to do. They help us stop and think. Following principles makes us better people. You shouldn't hate principles. You should embrace them."

"Embrace?!" exclaimed the teenager. "No way. Our school has three principals and they are ugly, mean, nasty, and to be avoided at all costs. No one likes the principals except the principals. I want nothing to do with them."

"I don't know what to say," replied the mother, distraught. "Perhaps I should go meet with your teachers to find out about the principles for myself. I can't believe they're as bad as all that."

"Meet them? No way. You'll just get me in trouble."

"But we've tried to teach you to live by high standards and worthy principles."

"And I am. The first principle of success in high school is to stay away from principals. I intend to follow that principle fully, which means absolutely avoiding the principals. So what do we have for snacks? I'm starved."

Principles-Driven Initiatives with Principles-Focused Evaluations

Exemplars of Principles in Practice

Seek and you shall find.
—Biblical verse
(Matthew 7:7–8)

Principles abound. When you start paying attention, you'll find them everywhere. Like having an injured leg and suddenly noticing how many people limp, or being pregnant and noticing the number of expectant couples, or buying a new car and noticing how many like yours are on the road. Start watching for principles and you will be inundated. Principles for managing your money. Nutrition principles. Exercise principles. Relationship principles. Study principles. Physical health principles. Mental health principles. Marriage principles. Dating principles. You'll also notice lots of assertions claiming to be principles that aren't actually principles. The recurring message of this book is that all principles can be evaluated on whether they are clear and inspirational enough to follow (meaningfulness evaluation), whether those positing them are actually following them systematically (adherence evaluation), and, if they are followed, whether they yield the results hoped for (outcomes evaluation).

Part III of this book presents examples of principles-focused initiatives with principles-focused evaluations. Each chapter illustrates a different approach to and purpose for principles. Taken together, these examples take the somewhat abstract idea of principles and show what they

223

look like in practice for both change initiatives and evaluation of those initiatives.

> ▶ Part IIIA presents and discusses principles at three levels: global principles for development aid; program-level principles for working with homeless youth; and community-level principles for a community initiative (meso level). (See p. 225.) What these exemplars have in common is that they have all been completed. The case presentations are derived from their final reports.

> ▶ Part IIIB presents and discusses principles for three different agriculturally focused initiatives: a global alliance of philanthropic foundations; an international program working in Africa and South America; and the emergence of a new interdisciplinary field of scholarship and practice. (See p. 257 for an overview.) These examples are all still developing. The chapters are based on progress reports, interactions with key leaders, and developmental evaluation experiences with principles-focused evaluation.

Comparing and contrasting principles within these two groupings will illuminate different kinds of principles-focused initiatives and, correspondingly, appropriately matched kinds of principles-focused evaluation, each of which is unique.

Three Levels
of Principles-Based
Interventions
Macro (Global), Micro (Program),
and Meso (Community)

Chs.	Focus	No. of principles	Purpose	Scope	What is illustrated: Completed principles-focused evaluations
25	Paris Declaration on Aid Effectiveness, an international agreement	5	Drive reform	International negotiations among over 100 countries and international development agencies to change the relationships between donors of international aid and countries receiving aid	Macro level: Global principles and evaluation
26	Evidence-based effective principles for working with homeless youth	9	Document and increase effectiveness among collaborating agencies	Leaders of six diverse nonprofit youth-serving agencies in Minnesota	Micro level: Program principles
27	Vibrant Communities Canada	5	A principles-driven systems change initiative and emergent example of principles-focused evaluation potential	15 Canadian cities involved in poverty reduction; leaders in community anti-poverty programs across Canada meeting together to collaborate and learn	Meso level: Community initiative principles

CHAPTER 25

Principles Driving Reform
Evaluation of the Paris Declaration
on Aid Effectiveness

It is not the responsibility of knights errant to discover whether the afflicted, the enchained and the oppressed whom they encounter on the road are reduced to these circumstances and suffer this distress for their vices, or for their virtues: the knight's sole responsibility is to succour them as people in need, having eyes only for their sufferings, not for their misdeeds.
—MIGUEL DE CERVANTES SAAVEDRA, *Don Quixote*

The Paris Declaration on Aid Effectiveness

The Paris Declaration on Aid Effectiveness was endorsed in 2005 by over 100 countries and organizations, including the more developed aid donor countries like the United States, developing countries from around the world, and international development institutions like the World Bank, the United Nations Development Group, and the Organization for Economic Co-operation and Development (OECD). It was a landmark international agreement and the culmination of several decades of attempts to improve the quality of aid and its impact on development. The 2005 Paris Declaration on Aid Effectiveness remains the agreed-on international statement on the aid relationship. The Paris Declaration identified and endorsed five key principles of effective aid:

1. *Ownership:* Developing countries set their own strategies for poverty reduction, improve their institutions, and tackle corruption.

2. *Alignment:* Donor countries align behind these objectives and use local systems.

3. *Harmonization:* Donor countries coordinate, simplify procedures, and share information to avoid duplication.

4. *Results:* Developing countries and donors shift focus to development results and results get measured.

5. *Mutual accountability:* Donors and partners are accountable for development results.

In 2008, Accra, Ghana, was the site of the Third High Level Forum on Aid Effectiveness, an assembly that had been planned at the time of the original signing to review progress. The Accra forum reaffirmed the Paris Declaration Principles and added details in the form of an action agenda in support of the principles.

Evaluation Results

Evaluation of the Paris Declaration Principles illustrates how the evaluation process can drive implementation of reform. The independent evaluation found considerable variation among countries and agencies in implementing the principles and in the effects of implementation where it occurred. Context matters, and different country contexts led to different approaches to implementation of the principles. The Solomon Islands was different from Indonesia, Uganda different from Afghanistan, and Vietnam different from Bolivia. For each of the 21 countries for which case studies were done, the national evaluation team aggregated multiple sources of evidence to assess the extent, direction, and pace of implementation. The core evaluation team then synthesized the country and donor agency case studies and reached the following conclusion:

> Overall the Evaluation finds that of the five principles, country ownership has advanced farthest, with alignment and harmonisation progressing more unevenly, and managing for development results and mutual accountability advancing least. (Wood et al., 2011, p. xv)

Significance and Quality of the Paris Declaration Evaluation

The Paris Declaration included provisions for the regular monitoring and independent evaluation of how the principles and action agenda were implemented. That evaluation received the AEA's Outstanding Evaluation Award in 2012, recognition given for the successful completion of a single high-quality evaluation that "taken as a whole . . . should be considered exemplary of its kind and a potential model for other evaluators doing similar kinds of work." As near as I can tell, this evaluation is the most comprehensive principles-focused evaluation ever conducted. This chapter provides an overview of key aspects of the evaluation. The full evaluation and all supporting documents are available online.

The Paris Declaration Evaluation was organized and conducted as a joint international initiative. Joint evaluations involve multiple agencies and diverse international participants. Traditionally, international aid agencies like USAID commissioned and conducted their own individual agency evaluations, and that remains the dominant form of evaluation. But for major initiatives that involve multiple donors and recipients acting collaboratively, a joint evaluation was most appropriate.

The Evaluand: Evaluation of Adherence to Principles

As noted in Chapter 4, the profession of evaluation has been heavily oriented toward evaluation of projects and programs, but the Paris Declaration is neither. It is a set of principles and political commitments. As the evaluation's final report explained:

> The object of the Evaluation—an agreed set of principles and commitments to improve aid effectiveness—is not a project or programme, the more normal objects of development evaluation. In a broad sense it is more like a strategy, a domain where evaluation is beginning to be tested, but the Declaration campaign has less-clear boundaries than most strategies. Interesting common elements can also be found in the growing experience in evaluating policy influence. (Wood et al., 2011, p. 3)

Evaluation Focus, Design, and Methods

The overall purpose of the evaluation was to assess the relevance and effectiveness of the Paris Declaration and its contribution to aid effectiveness and ultimately to development effectiveness. It included 21 country-level evaluations that were designed within a common evaluation framework to ensure comparability of findings across countries while allowing flexibility for each country's specific interests. Each of these evaluations was conducted by independent evaluation teams managed by the respective partner country under the oversight of and with technical support from the core evaluation team and the Evaluation Secretariat.

The country-level evaluations were supplemented by 18 donor and multilateral development agency studies that assessed how the Paris Declaration was represented in the policies, strategies, and procedures of these donors and agencies. The studies mainly consisted of document reviews supplemented by interviews with key actors at headquarters level and in field offices. The studies were conducted by independent teams managed by the respective agencies' evaluation departments. See Exhibit 25.1 for a list of participating countries.

EXHIBIT 25.1. Countries Participating in the Paris Declaration Evaluation

Recipient	Population (thousand)	GNI per capita (USD)	Economy
Afghanistan	29,803	310	Low income
Bangladesh	162,221	580	Low income
Benin	8,935	750	Low income
Bolivia	9,863	1,630	Lower-middle income
Cambodia	14,805	650	Low income
Cameroon	19,522	1,190	Lower-middle income
Colombia	45,660	4,990	Upper-middle income
Cook Islands	22	5,000	Upper-middle income
Ghana	23,837	1,190	Lower-middle income
Indonesia	229,965	2,050	Lower-middle income
Malawi	15,263	290	Low income
Mali	13,010	680	Low income
Mozambique	22,894	440	Low income
Nepal	29,331	440	Low income
Philippines	91,983	1,790	Lower-middle income
Samoa	179	2,840	Lower-middle income
Senegal	12,534	1,040	Lower-middle income
South Africa	49,320	5,760	Upper-middle income
Uganda	32,710	460	Low income
Vietnam	87,280	1,000	Lower-middle income
Zambia	12,935	960	Low income

Note. Data are for 2009.

A literature review on aid effectiveness theory and practice, particularly at the country level, was conducted and used as a knowledge base to inform the evaluation questions, design, and data collection framework. In addition, several thematic studies were commissioned covering diverse subjects such as the applicability of the Paris Declaration in fragile situations, development sources beyond the current reach of the Paris Declaration, and the relationship between the Paris Declaration, aid effectiveness, and development effectiveness.

The final evaluation process and report provided a synthesis of all component evaluations and thematic studies, including the Phase 1 evaluation. It was prepared by a team of independent evaluators comprising Bernard Wood (Canada; team leader), Julia Betts (United Kingdom); Florence Etta (Nigeria); Julian Gayfer (United Kingdom); Dorte Kabell (Denmark); Naomi Ngwira (Malawi); Francisco Sagasti (Peru); and Mallika Samaranayake (Sri Lanka).

The evaluation addressed three main questions:

1. What are the factors that have shaped and limited the implementation of the Paris Declaration reforms and their effects? ("The Paris Declaration in Context")

2. What improvements have been made in aid effectiveness as targeted in the Paris Declaration? ("Contributions to Aid Effectiveness")

3. What contributions have improvements in aid effectiveness made to sustainable development results? ("Contributions to Development Results")

Following an introductory overview and context-setting chapter, evidence addressing each of the three evaluation questions was presented in three chapters. The report concluded with chapters on overall conclusions and recommendations. Part of what made this an outstanding evaluation is the exceptional clarity, coherence, and relevance of the final report in integrating and synthesizing mountains of evidence from diverse sources and methods in systematically addressing these complex evaluation questions. The evidence was artfully summarized, cross-referenced, and triangulated, and carefully linked to the resulting conclusions and recommendations. Exhibit 25.2 shows the integration of various components of the evaluation, including two phases of the evaluation conducted before and after the 2008 Accra High Level Forum.

The Evaluation Findings

The evaluation concluded that the five principles have proved relevant to improving the quality of aid and of the partnerships needed to make it work. However, "the ways in which the Declaration has been implemented have sometimes strained its relevance, but it remains unbroken, and has shown the resilience to withstand considerable change and turbulence" (Wood et al., 2011, p. xv).

The Declaration has raised expectations for rapid change, perhaps unrealistically, but also strengthened agreed norms and standards of better practice and partnership. There is ample evidence here that these standards [the principles] have been used to reinforce or legitimize demands—especially from partner countries—that good practice be observed.

There is no going back—expectations are more likely to keep rising than to diminish—so that the standard expected has permanently been raised for all engaged in development cooperation.

The Evaluation concludes that the changes made by the Declaration have not yet reduced the overall burdens of aid management as hoped. However, they have contributed to a better quality of aid, to more transparent and effective partnerships, and to supporting rising volumes of aid. Those cases identified

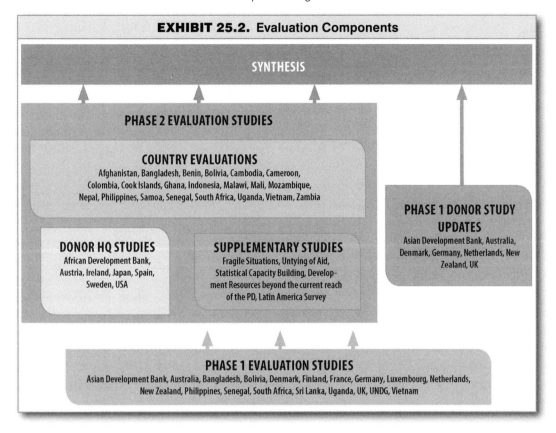

EXHIBIT 25.2. Evaluation Components

SYNTHESIS

PHASE 2 EVALUATION STUDIES

COUNTRY EVALUATIONS
Afghanistan, Bangladesh, Benin, Bolivia, Cambodia, Cameroon, Colombia, Cook Islands, Ghana, Indonesia, Malawi, Mali, Mozambique, Nepal, Philippines, Samoa, Senegal, South Africa, Uganda, Vietnam, Zambia

PHASE 1 DONOR STUDY UPDATES
Asian Development Bank, Australia, Denmark, Germany, Netherlands, New Zealand, UK

DONOR HQ STUDIES
African Development Bank, Austria, Ireland, Japan, Spain, Sweden, USA

SUPPLEMENTARY STUDIES
Fragile Situations, Untying of Aid, Statistical Capacity Building, Development Resources beyond the current reach of the PD, Latin America Survey

PHASE 1 EVALUATION STUDIES
Asian Development Bank, Australia, Bangladesh, Bolivia, Denmark, Finland, France, Germany, Luxembourg, Netherlands, New Zealand, Philippines, Senegal, South Africa, Sri Lanka, Uganda, UK, UNDG, Vietnam

where management burdens have been increased by introducing Declaration-style aid such as multi-donor funds do not outweigh these wider benefits.

In contrast with improvements in aid covered by the Declaration, the evaluation finds a critical lack of transparency and of reliable data on many of the other forms and flows of cooperation beyond the current scope of the Declaration. (Wood et al., 2011, p. xv)

Methodological Approach and Quality

Three Criteria for Assessing Implementation Progress: Direction, Distance, and Pace

The evaluation team created a clear and innovative framework for assessing implementation progress and rendering judgments about adherence to the principles by

countries and international aid agencies. Early on, at the first International Reference Group meeting of key stakeholders, the metaphor emerged of treating the implementation of Paris Declaration changes as a journey, which led to focusing the synthesis framework on three critical dimensions of that journey: *direction of travel on each principle, the pace of implementing the principles, and the distance traveled so far in implementation.*

As noted earlier, evidence was gathered from multiple sources to support the judgments rendered, mainly qualitative evidence but also sound quantitative data where available. Aggregating and synthesizing the massive amounts of data from case studies and secondary sources was greatly facilitated and given coherence by this simple but powerful template: *direction of travel* (toward implementing the principles or away from implementation), *distance of implementation* (degree of adherence to the principles), and *pace* (speed of implementation).

Exhibit 25.3 displays these three criteria for three dimensions of implementation: (1) stronger national strategies in compliance with the principles; (2) stronger detailed operational plans in support of implementing the principles; and (3) increased alignment of donor agency aid with the priorities, systems, and procedures of aid-recipient countries ("partner countries"). For more details about the methods and measures used in the evaluation, see Chapter 21, pp. 186–190.

Details about the evaluation's methods, analysis, findings, uses, governance, and funding have been fully documented in a special issue of the *Canadian Journal of Program Evaluation* (Patton, 2012b). What I shall highlight here are those elements of the evaluation that are especially relevant to principles-focused evaluation.

Adhering to the Paris Declaration Principles in Conducting the Evaluation

The evaluation was conducted according to and in compliance with the Paris Declaration Principles. This ensured that it was a genuinely and authentically *joint* endeavor that fully respected the interests and concerns of both aid-recipient countries and donor agencies, as well as the broader international community. Country ownership by aid-receiving countries was made a priority to ensure full participation and engagement. Country representatives participated in designing the synthesis matrix. Quality control was based on peer reviews and international participant feedback. Sufficient support was provided to make the evaluation a trilingual exercise (English, French, and Spanish) in order to ensure full participation in and access to all aspects of the evaluation. In-country evaluation team procurement was the

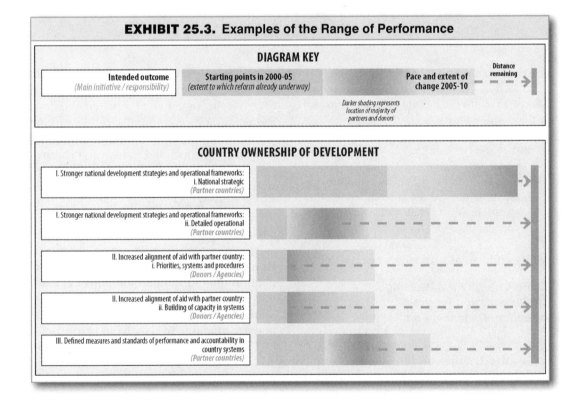

EXHIBIT 25.3. Examples of the Range of Performance

responsibility of partner countries and followed partner country processes. Indeed, from the beginning, the evaluation was conceptualized, designed, and implemented to adhere to—and support the implementation of—Paris Declaration Principles themselves. This was not always easy and resulted in administrative challenges and, in some cases, delays in implementation, but the evidence gathered in the meta-evaluation (evaluation of the evaluation, Patton & Gornick, 2012) supported the conclusion that the evaluation was a genuine and authentic joint endeavor.

Principles-Focused Evaluation and Adherence to Quality Evaluation Standards

The Development Assistance Committee (DAC) of the OECD established its own standards for evaluation in 2010, and the Network on Development Evaluation supports implementation of the standards. The DAC quality standards for evaluation provide relevant, appropriate, and useful guidance for conducting a complex, strategic, and principles-focused evaluation. The DAC standards proved highly appropriate and useful. The Evaluation Final Report Technical Annex includes a detailed analysis of how the DAC standards informed the evaluation (see pp. 218–221).

Context Matters

A constant refrain in the deliberations about and interpretation of evaluation findings was that *context matters*. The evaluation report comments: "the processes for improving aid effectiveness are political and not just technical, and . . . different contexts have a major impact on the possibilities for improving aid processes and strengthening aid's contributions to development results" (Wood et al., 2011, p. 3). This reinforces the case made throughout this book that principles are especially appropriate as a form of

guidance where change is occurring across highly diverse and complex contexts—and that principles-focused evaluation is necessary to evaluate principles-focused reform and change initiatives, like that represented by the Paris Declaration Principles for reforming international development aid.

Principles-Focused Evaluation Process Use

One of the major conceptual developments in scholarship on evaluation use of the past decade has been attention to process use. Process use concerns the impacts of an evaluation that go beyond the findings. It includes what is learned by those involved, the capacity for evaluation that is built through doing evaluation, and the variety of impacts that result from the fact that the inquiry is even being undertaken. The Paris Declaration Evaluation is an exemplar of the power and importance of process use. Two points deserve emphasis.

1. *The evaluation focused attention on the Paris Declaration, its principles, purposes, and effects.* For 5 years (Phases 1 and 2) the evaluation engaged a dedicated, knowledgeable, and diverse group of people in thinking about, gathering data on, and interpreting the effects of the Paris Declaration and Accra Action Agenda. A comprehensive and in-depth evaluation process involves defining terms, clarifying and focusing priority questions, operationalizing key concepts, formalizing the theory of change, establishing boundaries around the inquiry, building partnerships, constructing data collection protocols, building capacity to gather and analyze data, facilitating relations, and focusing attention on what is being evaluated: the implementation of the Paris Declaration and its effects on development aid. The final product, *The Evaluation of the Paris Declaration: Phase 2, Final Report,* was the culmination of all this effort. But

behind that report, both making it possible and extending its impact, is a large number of people around the world who have been deeply engaged in thinking about these issues and bringing evaluative thinking and methods to bear on critical questions of effectiveness, efficiency, and impact. It seems fair to suggest that the large and diverse group of people engaged in the many activities and distinct studies that, together, make up the whole of the evaluation, have thought as deeply about these issues as any group anywhere in the world. An evaluation process is not just talking about something. It means studying the thing being evaluated. At its best, as in this case, it involves deep intellectual and rigorous methodological inquiry. Thus, a major strength and accomplishment of the full 5-year inquiry was the very process of focusing in-depth attention on the Paris Declaration Principles. That focusing deepened the evaluation's impact significantly during Phase 2, the object of this nomination.

2. *Expanding knowledge of and engagement with the Paris Declaration Principles.* This second impact and example of process use follows directly from the first. The prior bullet point highlights the in-depth knowledge and understanding created among those engaged in the evaluation. This second point highlights the fact that the evaluation process increased awareness of and engagement with the Paris Declaration, as well as issues of aid effectiveness, well beyond what would have occurred without the evaluation. Policymakers, ministers, civil servants, agency directors and staff, NGOs, and others who were interviewed as part of country and donor studies became more aware of and thought more deeply about the Paris Declaration as a result of being interviewed. The evaluation, therefore, served a dissemination function even as the inquiry gathered data about the degree of knowledge about and engagement with the Paris Declaration. Members of national reference groups, country evaluation teams,

and donor study groups have all reported that the evaluation contributed to greater knowledge about and, in many cases, greater commitment to and implementation of the Paris Declaration. This exemplifies what has come to be known in the evaluation literature as "process use," which captures the fact that evaluation inquiries have an impact on the focus of inquiry quite apart from and well before the findings are reported.

Evaluation Financing and Resources

Evaluation reviews rarely report costs. I'm going to do so here to show how important this principles-focused evaluation was to those who commissioned and funded it, so the resources made available were sufficient to do a high-quality job. It was clear from the beginning that an international joint evaluation of this magnitude and scope would be costly. One of the elements that make this evaluation an exemplar is that the organizers used their great experience, credibility, and global contacts to raise sufficient funds to conduct a high-quality evaluation. An underresourced evaluation would be a poor evaluation in every respect, including poor quality and poor use. Moreover, it is yet another hallmark of this evaluation that the financing is also transparent.

The total cost of the two phases of the Paris Declaration Evaluation was €10.433.200 (US $13,121,317 as of June 6, 2012). The Phase 2 Evaluation cost €6.597.800 (US$8,295,782 in 2012).

The costs of country and donor/agency studies are based on a combination of reported actual costs and estimated costs for several countries and donors that did not report their costs. The cost must be weighed against the multibillion-dollar stakes in the aid reform effort and the uses of the evaluation as well as its scope covering 21 countries and 18 donors/agencies directly, and many more indirectly.

What Was at Stake?

In considering the costs of the evaluation, and the enormous resources expended, both financial and human, it is worth placing this evaluation in the context of what was at stake, as the evaluation report does in its opening preface:

> The Evaluation is important both for accountability and to point the way for future improvements. The underlying stakes are huge: better lives for billions of people (reflected in the approaching Millennium Development Goals for 2015); hundreds of billions of dollars expended; vital international relationships; and growing demands to see results from development aid. (Wood et al., 2011, p. xii)

Evaluation Leadership

The backstory of the evaluation of the Paris Declaration makes visible a critical evaluation role that is little understood and seldom visible: the leadership of those who commission evaluations and raise the funds to support their implementation. Niels Dabelstein, head of the Paris Declaration Evaluation Secretariat, and Ted Kliest, who provided leadership on the Management Committee, played key roles in ensuring that the evaluation was undertaken at all and, when undertaken, done with sufficient resources, integrity, methodological rigor, credibility, and evaluator independence to be useful in accordance with international evaluation standards. The evaluation would not have happened without their vision, principles, standards, experience, competence, and commitment.

People matter. A substantial body of research on evaluation credibility and use points to the importance of what has been called "the personal factor," which points to the interest, commitment, engagement, and leadership of key individuals as essential to conducting high-quality evaluations. Much of evaluation focuses on procedures, protocols, measures, methods, and analytical techniques. But none of that happens without people. The Paris Declaration Evaluation Secretariat brought vision and experienced leadership to this enterprise, without which it would not have happened. Assembling resources, garnering the support of key institutions, using networks to negotiate critical agreements, and finding competent people to manage and implement the evaluation are leadership functions. It was at this level of visionary leadership that key decisions were made and commitments engendered to base the evaluation of the Paris Declaration on the principles of the Declaration, to adhere throughout to the DAC standards for quality evaluations, and to take on such a complex, controversial, and challenging initiative in the face of many, many naysayers who loudly declared that this could not be done.

Having studied for years the factors that distinguish high-quality, useful evaluations from those that are neither, I would be remiss to not call attention to the great extent to which the Paris Declaration Evaluation is an exemplar of the critical role played by committed and effective leadership at all levels. Being privy to some of the background stories of things that had to be negotiated, problems that had to be solved, resources that had to be found, people who had to be engaged, crises that had to be handled, and challenges that had to be met, it is clear that a successful evaluation is about much, much more than systematic procedures, rigorous methods, careful analysis, and thoughtful, evidence-based judgments. The personal factor, exemplified in effective leadership, is at the core of evaluation success. That leadership included a vision of principles-focused evaluation as a pioneering approach to evaluation.

Lessons from the Paris Declaration Evaluation

I included six principles-focused evaluation exemplars in this book. At the conclusion of each example I extract some lessons about engaging in principles-focused evaluation.

1. *Principles constitute a distinct evaluand (focus of evaluation).* A set of political commitments expressed as principles is not a project, program, or policy, the usual objects of evaluation. Evaluating principles requires a customized framework that includes methods, measures, data collection, processes, procedures, analysis, and reporting appropriate to principles as a distinct kind of evaluand.

2. *Evaluators conducting principles-focused evaluation will need specialized capacity building.* They will also need support to understand and implement a principles-focused evaluation precisely because the nature of what is being evaluated (principles) is nontraditional and demands customization (the preceding lesson).

3. *A principles-focused evaluation will be expected to abide by the principles of the initiative being evaluated.* From the beginning, the Paris Declaration Evaluation was conceptualized, designed, and implemented to adhere to the Paris Declaration Principles themselves. For example, the principle of country ownership meant that country case studies were conducted by country evaluation teams. The principles of country–donor alignment and donor harmonization affected how the governance of the evaluation was structured and conducted. Conducting the evaluation in accordance with the principles was not always easy and resulted in administrative challenges and, in some cases, delays in implementation, but the credibility of the evaluation was ultimately dependent on adhering to the very principles being evaluated.

4. *A visible, high-stakes, principles-focused evaluation brings attention to the principles being evaluated.* The evaluation focused attention on the Paris Declaration, its principles, purposes, and effects. For 5 years the evaluation engaged a dedicated, knowledgeable, and diverse group of people in thinking about, gathering data on, and interpreting the implementation and effects of the Paris Declaration. The evaluation engaged a large number of people around the world in thinking about the meaning and implications of the Paris Declaration. By focusing in-depth attention on the Paris Declaration Principles, the evaluation expanded knowledge of and engagement with them. The evaluation process increased awareness of and engagement with the Paris Declaration, as well as issues of aid effectiveness, well beyond what would have occurred without it. Policymakers, ministers, civil servants, agency directors and staff, NGOs, and others who were interviewed as part of country and donor studies became more aware of and thought more deeply about the Paris Declaration as a result of being interviewed. The evaluation, therefore, served a dissemination function even as the inquiry gathered data about the degree of knowledge about and engagement with the Paris Declaration.

5. *Distance, direction, and pace offer a generic framework for evaluating implementation of principles.* Direction assesses whether implementation is moving forward or facing resistance and backsliding. Pace examines how fast implementation is occurring. Distance measures how far implementation has proceeded. These three dimensions provide a foundation for evaluating implementation of a wide variety of types of principles.

6. *Utilization-focused evaluation (focusing on intended use by intended users) provides a broad umbrella approach relevant to principles-focused evaluation.* The Paris Declaration principles-focused evaluation exemplified utilization-focused evaluation.

7. *Evaluating principles requires contextual sensitivity and adaptation.* The Paris Declaration Evaluation involved case studies of 21 countries and 18 international aid

agencies. Distance, direction, and pace of implementation varied by context. A major finding of the evaluation was that context matters. Principles-focused evaluation inherently involves examining contextual adaptations of the principles being evaluated.

8. *Synthesis as a form of analysis and reporting involves special conceptual and analytical skills.* The purpose of synthesis is to answer core evaluation questions by finding patterns and themes that elucidate the implementation and effects of principles across diverse context. Quantitative data can be aggregated. Qualitative data must be synthesized. Synthesizing findings about principles across contexts is a special and specialized form of sense making and evaluation (Patton, 2015a).

Concluding Reflections

The evaluation of the implementation of the Paris Declaration Principles is the largest, most comprehensive, and most complex principles-focused evaluation conducted to date. It wasn't called a "principles-focused evaluation" at the time because that designation as a type of evaluation did not yet exist. But looking back, we can identify it as a groundbreaking, leading-edge principles-focused evaluation. My involvement in the meta-evaluation of that evaluation planted the seed for this book.

CHAPTER 26

Discovering and Validating Effectiveness Principles to Help Youth Overcome Homelessness

Home is a notion that only nations of the homeless fully appreciate and only the uprooted comprehend.

—WALLACE STEGNER, *Angle of Repose*

It Begins with Committed and Principled People

When, in 1943, community banking pioneer and philanthropist Otto Bremer founded the Otto Bremer Foundation in Saint Paul, Minnesota, he included caring for orphaned children as part of the foundation's priorities. That concern turned into support for homeless youth in 2012. As part of grants to six agencies serving homeless youth, the foundation offered the agency leaders an opportunity for collaboration. Those agency directors came together to figure out how to address common and complex challenges. Among their concerns was frustration that traditional evaluation requirements, mainly reporting numbers served and placed in housing, did not tell the story of either the youth they served or how they worked with homeless youth. As they shared strategic plans, values statements, evaluation data, and stories about what they knew about young people's lives on the streets, they found that their

work was undergirded and informed by some common principles. Supported by the Otto Bremer Foundation, I helped them identify those principles. The six agencies were quite diverse, serving different parts of the metropolitan area and offering different services and programs, but the leaders shared a deep sense of commitment. Articulating shared principles let them state what they cared about and express what they had learned about working with troubled and homeless youth.

Exhibit 26.1 presents the integrating statement that interconnects the nine principles. This statement was the final product of the evaluation.

As the principles emerged and coalesced into a meaningful framework integrating values and knowledge about what works, I said: "You've drafted a powerful set of principles about how you believe homeless youth ought to be supported and engaged to overcome homelessness. You've found common ground. Your caring, commitments, and collective wisdom come through

---

EXHIBIT 26.1. Integration of the Nine Evidence-Based Guiding Principles to Help Youth Overcome Homelessness

The principles begin with the perspective that *youth are on a journey*; all of our interactions with youth are filtered through that journey perspective. This means we must be *trauma informed*, *nonjudgmental*, and work to *reduce harm*. By holding to these principles, we can build a *trusting relationship* that allows us to *focus on youths' strengths* and *opportunities for positive development*. Through all of this, we *approach youth as whole beings* through a *youth-focused collaborative system of support*.

Note: The full statement of each of the nine principles is presented in Exhibit 3.1 at the end of Chapter 3 (p. 18).

---

in the principles. The question is, are you walking the talk? Do your staff actually follow the principles? Would the experiences of the homeless youth you serve reflect the principles? Are you prepared to evaluate whether you are actually implementing the principles and, if so, how, if at all, the principles show up in the stories of the youth you've served?"

One highly experienced agency director immediately asked, "Can that be done? I've never heard of evaluating principles. How would we do it?"

An intense discussion about possibilities led quickly to an enthusiastic consensus. Not only were they interested in doing such an evaluation, they were enthusiastic about it and prepared to participate actively in any ways that would support the process. For the next 18 months, these busy agency directors and senior foundation staff, including the foundation executive director, devoted a half day a month to principles-focused evaluation, from question formulation, to design, to data interpretation, to reporting. Several said that those sessions together were one of the things they most looked forward to despite many competing demands on their time. Together, we designed a study to examine evidence for the implementation and effectiveness of these principles.

To actually conduct the evaluation, the foundation and the collaboration of agencies engaged an independent evaluator, Nora Murphy (then a PhD candidate). Nora brought her own deep social justice commitments and values to the work, which

immediately resonated with the agency leaders and foundation staff. She had excellent interviewing skills and proved to be a quick study of principles-focused developmental evaluation. She reflects on her principles-focused evaluation experiences in Chapter 34. She has described this evaluation in depth in a chapter in *Developmental Evaluation Exemplars: Principles in Practice* (Murphy, 2016).

Principles-Focused Evaluation Design and Results

Murphy conducted 14 in-depth case studies of homeless youth who had interacted with the agencies, including interviews with the youth and program staff, and reviews of case records. The results of the case studies were then synthesized through the nine-principle framework with active participation by the six agency leaders. The collaboration members reviewed every homeless youth case study to determine which principles were at work and the evidence for effectiveness of the principles in helping the youth meet their needs and achieve their goals. (See Chapter 21 on measuring principles for how the interview data were analyzed.)

The results showed that *all the participating organizations were adhering to the principles and that the principles were effective (even essential) in helping youth make progress out of homelessness.* While staff could not necessarily give a label to every principle at the time of the initial evaluation interviews, they clearly talked about and followed them in practice. In the interviews with the youth, their stories showed how the staffs' principles-based approaches made a critical difference in their journey through homelessness. In addition to the case studies, Murphy reviewed other available research to identify scholarly evidence and theory that elucidated the knowledge base supporting and explaining the effectiveness of each principle.

The principles-focused evaluation report is available online (Homeless Youth Collaborative, 2014). In that report, each principle is defined and discussed. For each principle, an opening summary statement explains why it matters, what key research shows, what the practice implications are, and concludes with illustrative quotes from the youth case studies. Excerpts from the case studies are presented that document the outcomes the youth experienced through engagement with the youth-serving agencies. (Chapter 13 presented an outcomes framework for the effectiveness principles supporting work with homeless youth.) Taken together, this set of principles has provided a cohesive framework that guides practice in working with homeless youth. The principles were evaluated and validated, informed by the voices of homeless youth. The next section gives one example of how the results for each principle were summarized for a general audience. This proved an effective format for reporting the results of the principles-focused evaluation. I include it here as much for the reporting format as for the substantive example of evaluating a principle in practice.

Excerpt from the Report

Principle 9: *Journey oriented:* Interact with youth to help them understand the interconnectedness of past, present, and future as they decide where they want to go and how to get there.

Why This Matters

▶ Young people are on a continuous life journey. We interact with them at a point in time and have the opportunity to help them sort through where they've been, understand what has influenced them, and think about where they want to go.

▶ Experiences (good and bad), achievements, failures, changing perspectives, maturing, external influences and resources, and self-awareness all impact the trajectory of a youth's journey.

▶ Intangible moments and influences can often have a greater impact on the lives of youth than external, tangible, and material gains (e.g., housing, employment, education).

▶ Youth need to learn how to work through their past and present as they move toward their future.

Outcomes for Youth

▶ Youth realize they have some control of and responsibility for their future.

▶ Youth understand and own their story in order to move forward.

▶ Youth are able to learn and grow from mistakes and achievements.

The Research Basis

▶ There is a clear distinction between changes and transitions. Change is largely external. Transition is our internal adjustment to that change. Becoming homeless might be a change that youth experience, but understanding themselves as "homeless youth" may result in a psychological transition.

▶ The "stages of change" theory is useful when understanding where a client is on his or her journey at a point in time. It helps youth and youth workers understand transition.

▶ Emerging adulthood is typically marked by uncertainty concerning future life choices and exploration of potential roles and paths. Homeless young adults experience this uncertainty without the parental and social supports that enable the general young adult population to access health care, education, employment, and stable housing.

▶ Research supports journey orientation as nonlinear. All people, regardless of age or status, experience their journey as sometimes forward, sometimes backward, and sometimes sideways.

▶ Youth are sometimes resistant to change that may appear positive due to:
  ▷ Fear of losing their current identity
  ▷ Disorientation and discomfort during the transition
  ▷ Risk of failing in a new beginning

▶ Research supports the important role that having a future orientation and hopefulness play in sustaining perseverance, increasing impulse control, and developing other positive attributes needed to move forward on one's journey. (See Murphy, 2014.)

Practice Implications

Being journey oriented requires providers to:

▶ Understand youth based on where they are in their journey and not judge them for what they currently believe (being nonjudgmental). Accept that a homeless young person probably cannot perceive a future beyond the current day or one that is safe and stable. Recognize that it will take healing and time to help a young person begin to have a positive future orientation.

▶ Create a platform with youth to understand the steps needed to make progress. Homeless youth do not instantly become non-homeless once they have secure housing.

▶ Help youth prepare for the future by understanding the skills they need to develop.

▶ Remember there will always be relapses along the way and that everyone's path is different. Plan to stick with the young person when they need support.

▶ Intentionally assess the shifts, changes, and/or adaptations needed in approach, strategy, and focus as youth move through transformational stages in their journey.

▶ Find a balance between managing current crises and navigating youth toward the future.

▶ Equip youth with the framework, language, and resources to support their personal journey of transformation.

▶ Understand that a youth's time with a youth-serving program is only a moment in the youth's journey. It is the staff's responsibility to support the youth's transition into and out of that moment.

▶ Acknowledge that staff are not responsible for designing the journey for youth. Staff needs to accept and honor that the youth have been and will be on their own journey.

Bottom Line

At its most basic level, being journey oriented is a commitment to help youth learn from each step forward, and steps backward, while understanding these steps as part of the journey. The following quotations from youth in interviews illustrate their experience of the journey-oriented principle.

  On self-awareness
  "I had to become strong. And I became strong at a young age. But then I reached my breaking point, and I fell. And I had to build myself back from the bottom to the top. . . . I am who I am because of my struggles and knowin' the people that I know, the community that I know, and the outreach that I have that has been

handed out to me . . . I found the real Pearl deep down in me inside. I had to reach down deep inside. It hurt—pain, suffered, tears, blood, sweat—to actually find the real me."

On being future focused

"Even though I had a lot a struggles—sometimes you have to struggle to get to a better place. It takes for you to be at your lowest place to get to your highest place. It takes time, patience. I want everybody to know there's hope. There's always hope. Don't ever give up. 'Cause life is what you make it."

Outcomes Snapshots

Fourteen in-depth case stories were written about youth who (1) were between the ages of 18 and 24 at the time of the interview, (2) were or had been homeless and unaccompanied by family, (3) utilized services provided by least two of the six organizations participating in the Homeless Youth Collaborative on Developmental Evaluation, (4) were identified by staff as being reasonably reflective and articulate, and (5) had made substantial progress toward their goals.

While the case stories relied heavily on the young people's accounts of their own journeys, data were also included from interviews with one staff person, nominated by each youth, who knew the youth well and who worked at one of the six organizations participating in the Homeless Youth Collaborative on Developmental Evaluation. Additional data were collected through a review of the young people's case files.

The primary text for writing the case story was the youth interview; priority was placed on using the participants' quotations when possible and, when paraphrasing, on keeping the intention of their words and story. Youth were provided the opportunity to review their story.

All fourteen complete cases are provided in Dr. Nora F. Murphy's dissertation (Murphy, 2014). What follows is one of the 14 snapshots of homeless youth. Snapshots are condensed versions of each case story and were created to address the question: When the principles are implemented, what are the results for youth? These snapshots present the status of each young person at the time of the interview, a bit about their journey with the agencies serving homeless youth, and concluding thoughts about what the engagement has meant to them and their outcomes.

Alexa

As you read the outcomes snapshot of Alexa, look for evidence of the journey-oriented principle discussed above.

Alexa is a resilient 22-year-old African American woman and committed mother of two: a daughter (age 2) and a son (age 4). She was born in Chicago and raised, along with her brother, by her single mother. Her father's presence was scarce; Alexa doesn't remember meeting him until she was 9 years old. She also has a sister by her father who grew up in a different home. Alexa and her family moved to Minnesota when she was 9, and she was raised with several cousins. She remembers this as a hard time. Her mother worked long hours, was in an abusive relationship, and did not pay much attention to the kids. Alexa felt her mom didn't love them because no matter what kind of violence the family experienced, her mother would always take her boyfriend back into their home. Alexa was angry, hurt, and "running the streets and getting in to some stuff." During this period, her uncle was killed less than a block from her home, and it nearly brought Alexa to her breaking point.

Looking back, Alexa observed that homelessness came on slowly over her lifetime, but accelerated when she entered into her own abusive relationship. Domestic abuse had been a fixture in her family history. She witnessed intimate partner violence against her mom, her aunties, and her cousin. As Alexa stated, "the cycle just kept goin' on and on." Sometimes she would try to leave her boyfriend, but wouldn't find what she was looking for in other relationships and would end up returning. She became pregnant at 17 with her first child while still in an abusive relationship and withdrew from her friends. She found it impossible to leave her boyfriend. "Every time somethin' happened to me—like he abused me—I'd try to find love somewhere else. And I end up gettin' pregnant twice with him. It made it no better—no better."

During those tumultuous years, Alexa visited a youth drop-in center regularly. She felt supported and accepted by the staff. As she described it, "whatever you want or need, the staff at the drop-in center can help you meet your needs and work towards your goals. . . . You just gotta know what you want to do and move forward with it." She noted that the staff at the drop-in center help young people regardless of choices they may have made in their lives: "If you have a past—like nobody judge you about it. So say, for instance, you used to do different drugs, other than smokin' weed, they don't judge you. They just help you—pretty much they help youth, period."

Alexa originally visited the drop-in center to meet her basic needs such as meals, showers, a place to sleep, and computer access. Since having children, she feels she's made even greater use of the resources at the drop-in center, working with a case manager toward the goals that she set for herself—going back to school, finding a job, and finding a place to live. She recalled how hard it was trying to find an apartment when she was pregnant and had no rental history. It was scary to think about living on her own. Her case manager helped her research housing options and helped Alexa get her name onto several waiting lists. Alexa was on several waiting lists, and when she was 3 months pregnant, her case

manager told her that she had moved to the top of one of the waiting lists and took her to sign the lease. Having her own apartment was important for many reasons, primarily because having a stable home contributed to Alexa's ability to keep her daughter when she was born.

Alexa couldn't always make enough money to meet her needs. The drop-in center helped her during those months when she couldn't afford her rent, and they helped her pay for school. When she dropped out mid-semester, she would incur fines that she couldn't pay that would have prevented her from reenrolling. The drop-in center was able to help cover the cost of the fines. This financial support helped her keep a stable home for herself and her children.

Alexa has been living in the same apartment for 3 years, and had a job for the last 2½ years. She has been going to school on and off, depending largely on whether her boyfriend was in jail. She recalls passing English and Reading while her boyfriend was in jail and then dropping out the following semester when he was released from jail. "I had to drop out. Couldn't go to school with two black eyes. So I just stopped going."

While Alexa was visiting the drop-in center, she was able to see a therapist there named Monica. "I see Monica a lot. So that helps me. She's a good support system to help me through a lot of things."

Alexa and Monica have been able to engage intellectually, as well as therapeutically, around understanding the domestic abuse cycle. This understanding has changed Alexa's narrative about her abuse by helping her see it in a systemic light rather than as a personal weakness. Alexa credits the work she has done with Monica with allowing her to see a different path for herself.

Her boyfriend was recently incarcerated, sentenced to several years for abusing Alexa. Alexa and Monica both shared that the strength and courage Alexa showed by pressing charges is one of her biggest accomplishments. Alexa feels that her ability to do this was, in part, a reflection of the progress she has made in therapy. With Alexa's ex-boyfriend in jail, she feels that she has been able to cultivate peace in her life. Since ending her abusive relationship and entering a healthier one, she has reduced her stress and symptoms of depression, and has had fewer migraine headaches. Again, she credits these changes largely to the work she has done with Monica. Talking to Monica helped her understand some of the choices she's made and believe that she deserves to be treated well by her intimate partner.

Alexa takes pride in the changes she's made and feels optimistic about her future. She is planning to reenroll in school for the fall and is looking for a townhome so that she and her children will have more space. Her son will be entering kindergarten in the fall, and she feels confident about the school she has chosen for him. She credits the support of staff at the drop-in center, particularly her case manager and therapist, as being critical in helping her stay in school, meet her needs, and furnish her new apartment.

"It was meant for them to be in my life. 'Cause if I didn't find Monica, I don't know what I'd do. Tamika also done came to my house and really helped me a lot. She knows I'll be strugglin' at some point in time. But she'll find a way to help me. Any person would be proud of the stuff that I've been through personally. I actually almost died from bein' abused. I'm proud of makin' it to 22. I'm proud that I'm a proud mother of two beautiful children. I'm proud that I have my own place. I'm proud that I don't have to depend on a person to take care of me and my kids, because that's my responsibility and nobody else's."

In order to get to where she is now, Alexa feels that she has had to address her relationships with abusive men and rebuild her relationships with the friends that she had shut out. The supportive, stable staff at the drop-in center helped her learn to open up and trust others. Alexa hopes other young people will take advantage of that resource.

"I'll tell them that this actually is a great place for you to get yourself together. And if you don't choose to do it right now, make sure you do it in the long run 'cause it takes time for a person to overcome all their obstacles. I'll explain to them it's a good support system. And if you're willin' to get that help and that support, then you can move forward."

Alexa is considering starting a nonprofit for abused women. She is proud of having the strength to get to where she is in her life today and wants to devote her hard-won knowledge and resilience to helping others.

Chapter Review

This chapter opened by describing the agency and foundation leaders who came together to collaborate around issues related to youth homelessness. They found that articulating and evaluating shared principles deepened their collaboration as well as their individual agencies' program effectiveness. The chapter then presented an example of how the evaluation of the principles was reported using the journey-oriented principle. An excerpt from one of the youth case studies (outcome snapshot) offered an opportunity to examine the kind of data collected to capture the experiences of homeless youth and analyze whether their experiences showed evidence of the principles at work. For more on how the case studies were analyzed and the qualitative data coded to evaluation adherence to and results of the principles, see Chapter 21, pp. 191–194. This chapter concludes with lessons about principles-focused evaluation from the youth homelessness collaborative.

Lessons from the Youth Homelessness Collaborative Experience

1. *Shared principles can provide a strong basis for meaningful collaboration.* The six agencies that participated in the principles-focused evaluation had not collaborated before. When the senior leadership of these agencies first came together under the auspices of the supporting foundation, it was not clear either whether there was a basis for collaboration or, if there was, what the focus would be. As they began sharing approaches, documents, commitments, visions, values, and concerns, they discovered that they shared principles. The process was emergent. They didn't come together or set out to identify principles. Rather, the principles emerged through the process of sharing. They didn't create the principles so much as they discovered them like a vein of gold running through the mountain of their collective experience and knowledge. They were already there, but they had to learn to see them, mine them, and recognize their value.

2. *Articulating and evaluating principles is a leadership function.* The senior leaders who participated in the developmental evaluation collaboration, both agency leadership and the chief executive officer of the supporting philanthropic foundation, devoted a half day a month to this effort over a period of 2 years. They did not delegate the work. They personally engaged in all aspects of the evaluation including formulating the core evaluation questions, designing the case study framework, identifying criteria for purposeful sampling selection, reviewing the interview instrument and questions, analyzing the case study data, and formulating the report format. The developmental evaluators facilitated this process, but the senior leadership made evaluation a priority and did the work, consistently and diligently.

3. *Principles-focused evaluators need astute and sensitive facilitation skills.* Helping program leaders articulate principles, engage in evaluation of those principles, and interpret evidence of effectiveness are critical facilitation skills that go well beyond standard methodological facilitation skills in participatory evaluations. Rapport and trust between program leaders and evaluators is essential because interacting around principles enters into potentially treacherous territory where leaders share their most fundamental values, concerns, fears, and hopes. Mutual respect and trust make it possible for the principles-focused evaluator to keep the focus on evidence and reality testing (what's really happening with the principles in the program) and to question assumptions without alienating or generating resistance from those who have articulated and care deeply about the principles.

4. *The implementation and effectiveness of principles can be evaluated through in-depth case studie*s. The interviews with homeless youth participants did not ask directly about the principles, but rather asked about the youths' experiences with the various youth-serving agencies. The interviews and case studies were then analyzed and coded to determine whether evidence of the implementation and impact of the principles were evident. (See Chapter 21 on measuring the effectiveness of principles.)

5. *Synthesizing the findings across multiple participants from diverse agencies constitutes a strong basis for evaluating the effectiveness of principles-driven services.* A qualitative synthesis across multiple and diverse agencies is different from a quantitative meta-analysis of multiple agencies all implementing the same model in the same way and generating standardized data. Qualitative synthesis cuts across diverse programs and participants to identify and validate cross-cutting patterns, themes, and, in this case, principles. (See Patton, 2015a.)

6. *Evidence-based, effective principles can be a basis for program development, staff*

development, participant engagement, strategic planning, staff hiring and orientation, and ongoing program evaluation. What began as a narrow and focused effort to identify common interests across the six agencies became a multifaceted organizational development process based on the findings and on the power of the principles to provide guidance across a range of organizational activities and responsibilities. The principles were formally adopted by the respective individual organizations. They were incorporated into strategic documents and organizational communications. They were used for staff training and development. In essence, they were incorporated into the respective organizational cultures as a foundation of effectiveness.

7. *Principles can be inspiring, and evaluation of principles can actually increase their meaningfulness and deepen commitment to the principles.* The principles-focused youth homelessness evaluation was the original basis and inspiration for the GUIDE framework for principles-driven initiatives (see Chapter 6 for the GUIDE framework). The agency and foundation leaders involved in the principles-focused evaluation have described significant impact on their leadership approach, deepening their capacity to provide principles-based leadership both within their agencies and in the larger communities they serve.

Concluding Reflections

This evaluation exemplifies a virtuous triangulation, which is like a virtuous cycle with reinforcing positive iterations that are increasingly positive as momentum accelerates. Principles-driven people (the six program directors) ran principles-based programs (the six programs serving homeless youth) and then collaborated in designing and implementing a principles-focused evaluation with a principles-driven evaluator. To understand the contribution made by and the importance of having a principles-driven evaluator at the center of this virtuous triangle, read Nora Murphy's reflections on being a principles-focused evaluator in Chapter 34.

My involvement as consultant to this evaluation provided the depth of direct experience with evaluating principles that formed the foundation of this book. My refrain throughout this book has been: *No principles, no principles-focused evaluation.* I would now add this acknowledgment: No youth homelessness principles-focused evaluation, no principles-focused evaluation book.

CHAPTER 27

Vibrant Communities Canada

A Principles-Driven Systems Change Initiative and Emergent Example of Principles-Focused Evaluation Potential

Chapter 25 discussed the evaluation of the Paris Declaration Principles, which reviewed the implementation and effectiveness of global principles aimed at reforming international development aid. Chapter 26 reported on effective principles for helping youth overcome homelessness. This chapter looks at community-level principles for fighting poverty. Taken together these chapters offer principles at a macro (global) level, micro (program) level, and now a meso (community and cross-community) level.

The Vibrant Communities (VC) collaboration began as an exemplar of a principles-driven systems change initiative. But its evaluation was not fully principles focused. Of course, principles-focused evaluation was not an explicit framework, approach, or option at the time. Nevertheless, the comprehensive evaluation conducted was partially principles focused. The evaluation demonstrates some of the confusion among innovators and the evaluation team about an evaluation focused on adherence to and implementation of the principles in practice versus also evaluating the effectiveness of the principles directly. Therein lies

a tale laden with important lessons, which this chapter will extract and highlight.

A Principles-Driven Community Change Initiative

In April 2002, representatives from 15 Canadian cities already involved in poverty reduction activities and the three national sponsors met for a 3-day forum in Guelph, Ontario, to create VC. They jointly developed an experiment designed to test a "new" way to tackle poverty, one that acknowledged the complex nature of poverty and the challenge of achieving scale in poverty-reduction efforts. The new way was not a model but a set of five core principles that local communities agreed to follow in mounting locally unique campaigns:

1. *Poverty reduction:* a focus on reducing poverty as opposed to alleviating the hardships of living in poverty

2. *Comprehensive thinking and action:* addressing the interrelated causes of poverty rather than its individual symptoms

3. *Multisectoral collaboration:* engaging individuals and organizations from at least four key sectors—business, government, the nonprofit sector, and persons who have experienced poverty—in a joint effort

4. *Community asset building:* building on a community's strengths rather than focusing on its deficits

5. *Learning and change:* embracing a long-term process of learning and change rather than simply undertaking a series of specific interventions

Chapter 7 discusses and praises the formulation of these principles because they make explicit the contrary principle that is not being followed (e.g., poverty reduction, not poverty alleviation; addressing causes, not symptoms).

VC was designed as a two-phase initiative. In the first phase, five communities—officially called Trail Builders—would receive a variety of supports from the three national sponsors to develop and implement poverty-reduction initiatives. This included a commitment to collectively assist 5,000 households in their journeys out of poverty and engage 450 leaders from the private, public, and nonprofit sectors and residents with lived experience to help lead local efforts. The remaining communities—unofficially called early adopters—would participate in the Pan-Canadian Learning Community (PCLC) and would follow the learnings of the Trail Builders (those communities that led the way).

VC became a 10-year initiative in which over a dozen urban collaborations across Canada worked together to reduce poverty. The results of the VC initiative are impressive and well documented (Cabaj, 2011a; Gamble, 2010, 2012; Leviten-Reid, 2007). The evaluative processes that produced the findings have also been detailed by Cabaj, Leviten-Reid, Vocisano, and Rawlins (2016). The overall evaluation synthesized results

and lessons from a plethora of different documents, data systems, and reports, including work by various evaluators working within and sometimes across different projects and communities. The evaluation used a range of tools, methods, processes, reporting approaches, and conceptual frameworks. Scores of diverse stakeholders were involved in a variety of capacities and relationships. Part of what is impressive about this case is the open and honest accounts of the evaluation's ups and downs, including times it stalled completely and had to be resurrected with new energy through a negotiated process and reworked design. The developmental evaluation mirrored the complexity, turbulence, uncertainty, nonlinearities, and adaptations of the initiative itself (Cabaj et al., 2016).

My focus here is on the lessons to be learned from the fact that the VC collaboration began as an exemplar of a principles-driven systems change initiative, but the initial evaluation did not make those principles the core of the evaluation approach and design. The evaluation eventually found its way back to the principles, but only as a secondary focus. My premise here, based on a retrospective interpretation of what occurred, is that the evaluation would have experienced fewer problems and been more useful all the way along had it been a principles-focused evaluation throughout. This is not a criticism of what was done. Principles-focused evaluation was not sufficiently conceptualized at that time to constitute an option. What might have happened had it been an option and used as the guiding evaluation framework is, admittedly, mere conjecture. But the VC evaluation offers a provocative case to speculate on what might have been had principles-focused evaluation been an explicit framework option at the time. It is also a cautionary tale about what can still happen when a principles-driven initiative is not matched with a principles-focused evaluation.

The Evaluation

The framework for evaluating the VC initiative was developed nationally. In early 2002, the national sponsors secured two evaluation firms experienced in community development and poverty-reduction efforts. A VC evaluation working group was established, composed of the national team leadership, contracted evaluators, and representatives from each community. The working group agreed that the core ingredients of the evaluation design would be:

▶ A common definition of poverty and indicators to measure progress in reducing poverty

▶ A shared methodology for gathering, analyzing, and reporting data on the effects of Trail Builder activities on local poverty using a national database

▶ The use of the logic model to describe and guide evaluation design and provide the basis for comparing how Trail Builders manifested the VC principles

So, the original evaluation framework included examining adherence to the principles but made logic model comparisons the basis for that judgment. This is where the evaluation became cumbersome.

After much wrangling about the complex and subjective nature of poverty, and a review of multiple definitions and measures commonly used in Canada, participants agreed that all Trail Builders would measure their progress in reducing poverty on the basis of five indicators: changes in household income of people affected by local activities, and changes in employment, financial assets, education and training, and housing. While communities would be free to employ additional indicators for their own use, these measures were considered "core" and "minimum" across all Trail Builder sites.

Committee members stumbled over the next part of the design. Try as they might, they could not settle on a shared approach to

track their shared core outcomes. While the group supported the principle of a shared methodology and national database, they struggled to develop a standard approach to gathering, analyzing, and reporting outcomes that could be usefully employed for a wide variety of interventions and settings. (Cabaj et al., 2016, p. 169)

The diversity of interventions across communities made standardized indicators intrusive and inappropriate, which led to resistance.

Although each group was able to confirm its poverty reduction targets, commit to their domains of action, and sketch out the broad strokes of how they would "add value" in making things happen in those areas, they generally felt ill prepared to elaborate more on this until they had an opportunity to test their ideas on the ground. "You can only do so much strategy work in a boardroom," remarked an experienced community leader from Saint John. VC evaluators would have to settle on a broad-strokes evaluation design until Trail Builders had a chance to develop their approaches further. (Cabaj et al., 2016, p. 170)

The use of the logic model as the primary tool to describe their strategy "amplified the difficulties" (Cabaj et al., 2016, p. 170). Logic models work well for projects and targeted programs but prove "too linear to be employed for a comprehensive, city-wide poverty reduction campaign (e.g., the establishment of a workforce development pipeline with scores of partners)" (p. 170). There were too many moving pieces for a logic model to handle. They took a pretty complex strategy and squeezed it into logic model boxes; the result did not resonate with the communities who couldn't see their complex and adaptive strategies in the simplistic standardization of the logic model.

Within 6 months of the Guelph meeting, the evaluation was stalled. While the expertise and professionalism of the evaluation team were valued, the tools and process were viewed as unproductive. "The air left the room during those evaluation discussions," recounted one person in Edmonton. "We had worked hard to get all these senior people in the room—including business leaders who don't usually get involved in these efforts because they don't like process—and the process was turning them off." In Victoria, the process was testing a carefully put together leadership group still trying to find its feet in the local effort. "We really had to hold back our leadership team [members], who felt that the process was narrow and confining. They were quite angry," observed one participant in the process. "We had even mused about backing out of the [VC] project at some point."

The evaluation was at a crossroads. While everyone in the partnership was committed to making evaluation a useful part of the initiative, cookie-cutter, linear evaluation designs were simply unable to deal with the cross-scale, highly emergent, and complex nature of Vibrant Communities. The group would have to go back to the drawing board and start all over. (Cabaj et al., 2016, pp. 170–171)

Evaluation Redesign

After several months of discussion and debate, the working group redesigned the evaluation based on complex dynamic systems thinking, theory of change formulation, and developmental evaluation for learning and adaptation.

The new evaluation design immediately proved its value. Trail Builders found it easier to craft, communicate, and operationalize their comprehensive approaches to reducing poverty. By early 2004, all six Trail Builder communities had developed a theory of change for their work that was approved by their local leadership teams and accepted by the national sponsors. Perhaps just as important, Trail Builders had embraced the "tight–loose" evaluation design that allowed them to adhere to a VC-wide methodology for

assessing their theory of change and develop their own customized strategy for assessing their diverse strategies and initiatives. All six Trail Builders were inventive in their evaluation efforts. . . .

Meanwhile, the national team elaborated and refined the Learning and Evaluation package. Their participation in each group's annual reflection session, in providing assistance to groups and filling out the statistical report, gave them insights into (and empathy for) how the methodology played out in each community. They regularly adjusted the criteria for reporting quantitative outcomes, adapted the process for facilitating annual reviews, and experimented with a "storytelling" format to describe each Trail Builder's theory of change. (Cabaj et al., 2016, p. 175)

Evaluating VC

In 2006, the national sponsors, local communities, and evaluators met to review their collective experiences, results, and learnings. "The first conclusion was that all VC participants had a much better handle on how differently VC principles played out on the ground in different settings" (Cabaj et al., 2016, p. 176). The national team identified nine points of variation in local efforts, including different definitions of poverty, geographic scales, time frames, and demographic focus. They also identified some common patterns across many communities, for example, the difference between delivering anti-poverty programming and engaging in systems change related to poverty. The evaluation synthesized results as well as lessons.

The results exceeded expectations. These initiatives had already affected 11,000 households and were projected to touch an additional 24,000 in the next several years. The participants of VC had dramatically exceeded their original targets of 5,000 households and were eager to set even higher targets for the next phase of their work. (Cabaj et al., 2016, p. 178)

The evaluation also synthesized cross-community learning.

> Perhaps the most significant learning across sites was an even deeper appreciation of the complex nature of poverty and poverty reduction. Whereas the entire initiative was based on the idea that successful poverty reduction required communities to attend to the multiple factors of poverty, participants tended to focus on the idea that there was a select number of "root causes" of poverty. Three years of trying to address these multiple factors revealed that they were in fact highly intertwined and that the lines of cause and effect connecting them ran in many different directions. . . .
>
> The tangled-up nature of poverty reaffirmed the case for comprehensive, cross-sectoral efforts to reduce poverty. The simple act of framing it as a complex challenge led sponsors and communities to conclude that their current poverty-reduction framework—which focused on five measures of poverty reduction—was inadequate for planning, communicating, and evaluating the work. They committed to creating a new, more holistic framework. (Cabaj et al., 2016, p. 278)

New evaluation questions were framed for the next phase of the initiative, but once again, evaluating the adherence to VC principles and the implications and results of being principles driven was not explicitly a priority. Yet, the importance of the principles does surface in the evaluation process and reporting.

> The first six Trail Builders had already demonstrated the necessity of customizing the VC principles to reflect their unique contexts. Moreover, each group continued to adapt its approaches—in ways ranging from modest to radical—over the 3 years. Getting the original cohort of communities to agree to a common set of fixed practices was impractical. Getting the new cohort of seven communities to adopt these practices—rather than develop their own community responsive version of VC practices—was downright wishful. (Cabaj et al., 2016, p. 179)

Interestingly, one reason the principles did not receive more direct evaluation attention as the evaluation was redesigned was the argument that "judging the merit or worth of the VC principles was misdirected because the case for the VC approach was already clear."

> If poverty was shaped by multiple root causes, then poverty-reduction strategies needed to tackle multiple causes concurrently and comprehensively. If strategies needed to be comprehensive, then communities had to work across artificial organizational and sectoral boundaries. If communities had to work across artificial boundaries, then they should focus on their assets (rather than their deficits). If the practice of comprehensive and multisectoral strategies was complex, then communities needed to work adaptively and focus on continual learning and change. Why should VC participants spend their time trying to prove these relatively self-evident principles?
>
> The central evaluative challenge, instead, was to assess the relative merit or worth of different ways to manifest VC principles. For example, what were the different multisectoral leadership models? What were the strengths and limitations of each model? What were the contexts and conditions under which each model thrived or withered? These were the questions that Trail Builders—and would-be replicators—wanted assessments to answer. . . .
>
> The task of reorganizing the outcome-tracking frameworks of Trail Builders to answer questions about the depth, durability, and complex nature of poverty reduction turned out to be somewhat easier. To do this, VC participants turned to the sustainable livelihood framework (SLF), formulated in international development circles (U.K. Department for International Development, 1999). Its major features included:
>
> ▶ An asset-based approach that framed and measured the progress of poverty reduction as a household's building of "resiliency assets" that could assist vulnerable households.
>
> ▶ A focus on building assets in a variety of

interrelated domains, including financial (e.g., income), physical (e.g., housing), social (e.g., supportive relationships), human (e.g., education), and personal (e.g., self-esteem, hope), reflecting the tangled-up nature of factors relating to poverty.

▶ A distinction between programmatic interventions, designed to directly help vulnerable households accumulate assets (e.g., a matched savings program for teen parents receiving social assistance), and strategic interventions that aimed to reshape the systems and contexts that make people vulnerable in the first place (e.g., welfare rules that prevent households from accumulating savings).

The framework so closely reflected the principles and new insights of VC that it seemed like a perfect match. Ironically, the members of the original evaluation team had proposed using the SLF approach in the early days of VC, only to be told it was too abstract and complex. "I think we had to experience poverty reduction work more deeply before we really understood how useful this approach was," remarked a Trail Builder from Edmonton. (Cabaj et al., 2016, pp. 179–180)

While the SL conceptual framework matched the VC principles well, the SL evaluation process did not. It was too standardized, cumbersome, and resource intensive to be practical and relevant. In the end, VC participants modified the SL approach, agreeing to track and report the number of people accumulating what kind of assets from each intervention. The primary focus became (1) assessing, not just describing, Trail Builder practices; (2) a more multidimensional framework for tracking reductions in poverty; and (3) the use of a modified version of contribution analysis.

Elaborating on VC Principles in Practice

Throughout the period of 2006 to 2011, the VC initiative produced over 200 papers, tools, and learning seminars that explored concepts and practices related to the major VC principles.

VC participants were largely satisfied with the progress in mapping out the emerging practice of VC: 13 communities had applied and tested the VC principles, and the general sentiment was that VC participants had done a thorough job of elaborating their experiences and practices and documenting their results. VC participants turned their attention to answering the last major evaluation question in the initiative: Was the VC approach sufficiently effective in reducing poverty that it was worth replicating? What capacities and enabling conditions were required for the approach to be effective? (Cabaj et al., 2016, p. 183)

An independent evaluation was subsequently commissioned that led to a 94-page end-of-campaign report titled *Evaluating Vibrant Communities: 2002–2010* (Gamble, 2010). The document described the intent, design, and activities of the overall initiative and reviewed the results to date. It presented nearly two dozen working conclusions about the VC approach, including an overarching principles-focused finding:

> ***There are a variety of "archetypes" for applying VC principles.*** There are at least four archetypes of comprehensive, multisectoral efforts to reduce poverty, organized around different drivers (i.e., programmatic push, policy change, transformational change, and bottom-up citizen engagement). (Cabaj et al., 2016, p. 184)

The external report also addressed limits and challenges of the approach:

> A good many Trail Builders struggled to make the VC approach work in their local context; the VC approach often caused tension and a perception of duplication with various other local initiatives; and the results of the effort were somewhat unpredictable. In fact, there was an informal bell curve of experiences; five groups that managed to create resilient and high-producing results; groups whose

efforts were fragile and whose results were inconsistent; and roughly one-third of the communities falling somewhere in between. (Cabaj et al., 2016, p. 185)

More data collection, more reflective practice, and more synthesis led to a widely read and justifiably acclaimed additional report titled *Inspired Learning: An Evaluation of Vibrant Communities National Supports: 2002–2012* (Gamble, 2012). This second report focused more on the national supports in VC.

In their chapter in the developmental evaluation exemplars book in which the VC initiative is featured, Cabaj and colleagues (2016) offer "seven major reflections on their experience that may contribute to the growing body of practice of developmental evaluation" (p. 189). They are insightful and significant lessons about the need for flexibility, adaptability, strong relationships, and the need to understand complexity and systems change. But none of their reflections focus on principles as the focus for evaluation. For this book, I asked Mark Cabaj and Jamie Gamble, the VC developmental evaluators with a deep understanding of principles-focused evaluation, to reflect on retrospective lessons. They kindly and thoughtfully agreed. Here are their insights, filtered through my interpretations of what is especially relevant for principles-focused evaluation.

Lessons from the VC Experience

1. *Evaluating adherence to principles is distinct from evaluating effectiveness of principles.* Neither those engaged in the anti-poverty initiative (as funders or doers) nor those evaluating it were sufficiently clear on the nuanced distinction between evaluating the manifestation of and fidelity to principles and also testing the effectiveness of the principles themselves. This distinction is critical.

2. *Evaluating the effectiveness of principles is not the same as evaluating the effectiveness of **practices** derived from principles.* The evaluation focused directly on documenting variations in anti-poverty practices, comparing practices across communities, identifying patterns and extrapolating themes and lessons from effective practices, and evaluating outcomes and impacts. These were important, indeed critical and useful, evaluation findings. The VC evaluations, both internal and external, remain exemplars in all of these respects. But the VC experience demonstrates that a principle can generate multiple and diverse practices in different contexts. Making the connection back to the generative principle that led to the practices to judge the effectiveness of the principle itself is a different empirical, conceptual, and inferential process.

3. *In a large-scale initiative, large in scope, vision, geography, and complexity, multiple and diverse stakeholders will have multiple and diverse views of principles, including their purpose, importance, uses, and evaluability.* Traditional planning and evaluation approaches with which people are most familiar will treat principles as a helpful framework to express shared values and commitments, but then turn quickly and decisively to creating logic models, identifying outcome indicators, and determining monitoring and reporting requirements. Treating principles as the evaluand, as the *focus* of evaluation, is not familiar territory and will not happen naturally without explicit attention. This means conceptualizing a set of principles as *an effectiveness framework* and evaluating principles for both adherence and effectiveness.

4. *Evaluating principles for effectiveness will require distinguishing principles from value statements, assumptions, shared beliefs, shared commitments, and/or other ways of expressing collaboration coherence.* The principles were viewed in many different ways at different times and places by various

stakeholders. Conceptualizing principles as an explicit effectiveness framework elevates their importance and raises the stakes for evaluation. That's a big step that would require facilitation, capacity building, and an appreciation of principles as more than a starting place, but as the foundation of ongoing collaborative engagement and effectiveness. The principles are easily neglected when moving on to practices, logic models, indicators, and reporting requirements. Principles-focused evaluation keeps the focus on principles.

5. *Principles support coherence in the face of great contextual variation and adaptation.* Chapter 2 emphasized that principles must be interpreted and applied contextually and situationally to ensure their relevance. VC manifested huge contextual variation and situational (community-specific) innovation and adaptability. The five VC principles provided an ongoing source of coherence and integration across that contextual variation.

6. *Principles are the rudder for navigating complex dynamic systems.* This point, also introduced in Chapter 2, is dramatically manifest in and validated by the VC experience. Systems thinking and complexity understandings were central to the VC initiative at every level and throughout all aspects of the initiative. The initiative ran into the most trouble when attempting to oversimplify through logical modelling and standardized indicators. When both the initiative and the evaluation stayed attuned to the principles framework, complexity could be embraced as the reality it is, not something to be fought or controlled, but to be engaged with as the way the world is and as a means for understanding and making sense of systems change and wicked problems. This includes "systems paradoxes," Jamie Gamble reflected, "in which principles are a response to things that we know to be important and relevant, but yet are not naturally prioritized within the existing system."

7. *Know when, and when not, to evaluate principles for effectiveness.* Mark Cabaj was especially reflective about the implications of raising the stakes for principles by evaluating their effectiveness and the challenges of doing so, which includes managing expectations among diverse stakeholders about what can be done given the complexities involved. A principle to guide determining when to evaluate principles is the following: *evaluate effectiveness when principles are conceptualized and hypothesized (even touted) as effective.* If they are window dressing, just a starting point to bring people together, or platitudes without action and outcome expectations, then evaluation is not called for. But where the principles are framed and positioned as guidance for bringing about meaningful change, that is, as *effective,* then those claims deserve, indeed demand, evaluation.

Finally, having studied the VC case and discussed it with Mark Cabaj and Jamie Gamble, the evaluators, I offer my own additional reflection and lesson based on the case:

8. *The evaluation of a principles-driven initiative should stay focused on evaluating the principles as a priority, both adherence to the principles, if adhered to, and the results (effectiveness) of that adherence.* Explicit and focused attention on the VC principles waxed and waned over the decade of the initiative, in part, I speculate, because an explicit principles-focused evaluation framework and approach did not exist at the time to match the principles-driven intervention. Developmental evaluation took them partway, as did complexity theory and systems thinking. But principles constitute a special—and specialized—approach to change and deserve a correspondingly special—and specialized—evaluation approach, to wit, *principles-focused evaluation.*

Concluding Reflections

This concludes the third of the three principles-focused evaluation exemplars based on completed evaluations. Both Mark Cabaj and Jamie Gamble, who played key roles in the VC evaluations, are long-time colleagues who contributed significantly to the development of developmental evaluation (Cabaj, 2011b; Cabaj et al., 2016; Gamble, 2008; Gamble, Van Sluys, & Watson, 2016). Now each has contributed to the development of principles-focused evaluation with feedback during the writing of and contributions to this book. In Chapter 20 Mark Cabaj has contributed the section "Weaving Together Principles and MIN SPEC Practices: The Case of Replicating Mentoring Models in Northern Alberta" (see pp. 175–176). In the Epilogue, Jamie Gamble has contributed reflections on the relationship between developmental evaluation and principles-focused evaluation (see pp. 395–396). They epitomize what it means to be reflective practitioners.

Three Different Agriculture-Focused Initiatives

Chs.	Focus	No. of principles	Purpose	Scope	What is illustrated: The evolution of principles in ongoing initiatives
28	Global Alliance for the Future of Food	6	Support and guide collaboration	A new coalition of some 30 philanthropic foundations committed to shifting food and agriculture systems toward greater sustainability, security, and equity	Using principles to support formation of a new collaboration
29	Comprehensive Crop Research Program of The McKnight Foundation	8	Provide coherence to a 20+-year-old, multifaceted agricultural development program	Senior leadership team members from three regions of Africa and the Andes working on agroecological intensification	Using principles to bring greater coherence to an ongoing collaboration
30	Agroecology principles	Varies by framework	Define an emerging field and paradigm of agricultural research and development	Targets agroecological researchers and practitioners worldwide	Using principles to define a new disciplinary field

CHAPTER 28

Collaborative Principles
Supporting Shared Commitment
The Global Alliance for the Future of Food

> I have always believed in the power of collaboration. Early on in my professional career, I realized that you can't develop all the competencies you need fast enough on your own. Furthermore, if you don't collaborate, your ideas will be limited to your own abilities. As a result, you will not be able to serve your clientele and thus can't achieve the anticipated impact.
>
> —VISHWAS CHAVAN, *Vishwasutras: Universal Principles for Living*

Collaborations are formed to support collective action. Leaders may collaborate. Diverse organizations and agencies may come together to learn from each other and increase their collective impact. Representatives from diverse communities may collaborate. Collaborations take many forms and involve varying degrees of commitment. But a central question for every collaboration is: *What brings people together and, once brought together, what holds them together?*

Some collaborations begin by articulating shared interests, for example, fighting poverty. Some identify and work toward common goals, like eradicating polio worldwide. Some come together for specific activities, like sponsoring a conference or community event. Some collaborations are formed as a community of practice for shared learning. What they all have in common is a belief that they can accomplish more together than separately. Many are inspired by this observation of renowned anthropologist Margaret Mead: "Never doubt that a small group of thoughtful, committed citizens can change the world; indeed, it's the only thing that ever has."

Evaluation frameworks have been developed to measure the cohesiveness and effectiveness of collaborations (Butterfoss, 2007; Mattessich, Murray-Close, & Monsey, 2001; Woodland, 2015). None of the existing evaluation frameworks are principles focused. However, one way people and organizations seeking to collaborate can find common ground is to identify and commit to shared principles. The Global Alliance for the Future of Food offers an exemplary case of principles-driven collaboration based on shared commitments. That led the Alliance to adopt principles-focused developmental evaluation as its evaluation framework.

The Global Alliance for the Future of Food

In June 2012, a group of more than 20 philanthropic organizations from around the world, driven by a sense of urgency, assembled in the United Kingdom for the first time to explore shared visions for advancing sustainable global agriculture and food systems in the face of climate change, resource destruction, and food insecurity. The meeting created a strong sense among the participating philanthropies that much could be achieved by combining energies behind practical strategies for shifting the planet to greater agriculture and food system sustainability, and helped identify potential synergies in vision that could catalyze the emergence of an international collaborative network.

Plurality is the strength of the Global Alliance bringing together foundations, despite differences, from countries across the globe with diverse interests and expertise, spanning health, agriculture, food, conservation, cultural diversity, and community well-being. At the core of the Global Alliance is a shared belief in the urgency of advancing sustainable global agriculture and food systems, and in the power of working together and with others to effect positive change.

The foundations came together in a facilitated session to determine how to work together. They began by agreeing on a definition of the problem:

They saw global food systems that increasingly:

▶ Are too dependent on fossil fuels and nonrenewable inputs that result in pollution and environmental damage and consume unsustainable quantities of scarce natural resources, leading to depletion of natural capital, especially water, soil, and biodiversity

▶ Erode human health, social cohesion, rural livelihoods, important social, cultural, and spiritual traditions; undermine the vital contributions of farming, fishing, and forest communities as innovators, producers, providers, and custodians; and are unresponsive to the

knowledge and priorities of citizens in determining food policies and practices from the local to global level

▶ Promote an economic system that privileges corporate culture; results in economic liabilities due to hidden costs, global trade vulnerabilities, and declining rural economies; threatens food security; and prevents the proliferation of sustainable food systems

They agreed that as an alliance of foundations, they would "provide a collective space to amplify the work of our individual organizations through a systemic approach to food system reform [and] . . . work collaboratively to bolster global efforts" (*https://futureoffood.org/about-us*). But how would they work together? What would guide their collaboration? What were they committing to?

They knew that they would need to articulate goals for the Alliance, identify strategies, establish priorities, and create working groups to carry out specific projects and activities. But all of this could not be done at once. They had come together around a common understanding of the problems to be addressed, but the question was how to go about addressing those problems. Where should they begin? The answer was to articulate shared principles. They weren't ready to agree on a common goal. They considered shared strategies but decided that identifying strategies would emerge from shared purpose. Principles were general enough to provide common ground while specific enough to provide shared direction, and collaboration principles did not conflict with any such statements by their individual foundations. Thus, over a period of 2 months in two face-to-face meetings with professional facilitation, they generated, reviewed, revised, and agreed on six overarching principles:

1. *Renewability.* Address the integrity of natural and social resources that are the

foundation of a healthy planet and future generations in the face of changing global and local demands.

2. *Resilience.* Support regenerative, durable, and economically adaptive systems in the face of a changing planet.

3. *Equity.* Promote sustainable livelihoods and access to nutritious and just food systems.

4. *Diversity.* Value our rich and diverse agricultural, ecological, and cultural heritage.

5. *Healthfulness.* Advance the health and well-being of people, animals, the environment, and the societies that depend on all three.

6. *Interconnectedness.* Understand the implications of the interdependence of food, people, and the planet in a transition to more sustainable food and agricultural systems.

Articulation of and agreement on the principles constituted a major breakthrough for the Alliance. They had come together with a sense that collective action was urgently needed, but they were struggling to get to action without some way of framing their shared commitments. The principles established what participating members were committing to and pointed the way to identifying goals, strategies, priorities, and specific activities. The system developed for working groups to use in reporting to the overall Alliance includes questions about how the principles are being addressed and followed in the activities and projects undertaken under the Alliance umbrella. The developmental evaluation approach adopted by the Alliance is principles focused. That is possible and appropriate because the Alliance is principles driven, and developmental evaluation is especially appropriate for supporting emergent and adaptive processes in complex, dynamic systems (Patton, 2011). The global food system is certainly a complex dynamic system. The

application of the principles would certainly be emergent and adaptive. Principles-focused developmental evaluation, which is also principles based (see Chapter 5), was thus a good fit. (For more on the Global Alliance for the Future of Food, go to their website at *www.futureoffood.org.*)

Application and Implication of the Principles

A major test of the utility of the principles occurred when the Global Alliance convened a group of important stakeholders to consider the role of animals in agriculture. Some advocated opposing animal agriculture as a major source of pollution (methane) and unsustainable production practices. Others were focused on the humane treatment of animals. Still others were focused on alternative and sustainable approaches to animal agriculture. After 2 days there was agreement that consensus might emerge around some shared principles for animal agriculture. But was a new set of principles needed specific to animal agriculture? Could the Global Alliance principles, already agreed to, be adapted to animal agriculture? It turned out they could, as shown in the draft document reproduced as Exhibit 28.1.

Lessons from the Global Alliance Experience

1. *Be clear about the purpose of identifying principles.* The Global Alliance principles were developed to identify how the diverse philanthropic members of the collaboration were going to work together. The collaboration began with a shared concern about the future of food and agriculture. But how would they work together for change? The principles answered that question.

2. *Developmental evaluation can provide a framework for development of principles.* As an

EXHIBIT 28.1. Global Alliance Principles Applied to Animal Agriculture

Principle title	Specific Global Alliance commitment expressed as a principle	Implications and application of the principle when applied to animal agriculture. We work to foster meat systems that . . .
1. **Renewability**	Address the integrity of natural and social resources that are the foundation of a healthy planet and future generations in the face of changing global and local demands.	support the renewability of natural and social resources and that contribute to increased integrity in the face of changing global dynamics.
2. **Resilience**	Support resilient, regenerative, durable, and economically adaptive systems that contribute to communities that foster the same characteristics.	are resilient, regenerative, durable, and economically adaptive, and that contribute to communities that foster the same characteristics.
3. **Equity**	Promote sustainable livelihoods and access to nutritious and just food systems.	address the inequitable access different people have to animal products and proteins, and seek ways to balance those inequities (so that communities that need more animal protein/nutrition can receive it, and those that are consuming animal products to the detriment of their own health are supported in their transition to more sustainable and healthful alternatives).
4. **Diversity**	Value our rich and diverse agricultural, ecological, and cultural heritage.	value the rich biological capital of animal diversity and understand, analyze, and support the varied role of animal agriculture in diverse cultures, diets, and agroecological systems.
5. **Healthfulness**	Advance the health and well-being of people, animals, the environment, and the societies that depend on all three.	contribute to the health of individuals, households, communities, regions, and nations and that attend to the health, humane treatment, and well-being of animals in animal agriculture.
6. **Interconnectedness**	Understand the implications of the interdependence of food, people, and the planet in a transition to more sustainable food and agricultural systems.	recognize the contribution of sustainable animal agriculture and meat consumption to culture, healthy ecosystems, local economies, and climate change mitigation.

innovative initiative addressing complex dynamic systems change globally, the Global Alliance adopted *developmental evaluation* to support development of the collaboration and its working group initiatives (see Chapter 5 on the principles of developmental evaluation). Serving as the developmental evaluator, I facilitated the development of the principles that helped ensure that they met the GUIDE criteria (Chapter 6). (Part IV of this book offers further guidance on developing principles.)

3. *Testing principles for strategic relevance, decision-making utility, and shared understanding can pave the way for final articulation and adoption.* In originally developing the first-draft statements of potential principles, participants came up with a test of strategic utility: did the principles constitute a diagnostic framework for analyzing the baseline conditions of several diverse agricultural systems? In small groups, knowledgeable participants used the principles to describe the current system of beef production in South America, shrimp production Southeast Asia, smallholder farms in the highlands of Tanzania, and an organic farm in California. The principles proved a powerful diagnostic framework that was a breakthrough in bringing along those who were uncertain about either the value of identifying principles or their utility. The diagnostic exercise also identified areas where wording changes were needed to clarify shared meaning and ensure applicability.

4. *Determine together whether the principles are a pick-and-choose list or an integrated whole.* The diagnostic exercise gave rise to the question of whether all the principles had to be applied to an initiative of the Global Alliance or whether they constituted a menu of options. This question generated intense discussion and a shared commitment to treat the six principles as a whole, integrated framework, not as a list of options. This also resolved a corresponding question of whether they were to be listed in some order of priority. All were determined to be equally important and essential to the work of the Global Alliance.

5. *Articulating shared principles can create a foundation for other shared commitments.* Once the Global Alliance principles were identified and adopted, the collaboration found it possible to move relatively quickly to articulate and adopt a shared vision, goal, and three-pronged strategy (see the website for details). There is no correct or even preferred order for developing such organizational commitments. Sometimes a shared goal is the starting point. Sometimes strategy leads the way. Or a statement of shared values or beliefs can come first. In this case, the members expressed a desire from the beginning to be principles driven as a way of answering the question: How will we address together the problem of the future of food? The issues that were clarified in that discussion paved the way for consensus on other shared commitments.

I think this was the case, in part, because these representatives of major philanthropic organizations came with different institutional perspectives on what constitutes a good goal statement, or strategy, or theory of change. These concepts can be divisive, not just because of substantive differences but because of strong institutionally different format preferences for what a goal statement should include and how it should be written. For example, do all goals have to be SMART goals (see Chapter 6)? Organizations differ widely in what constitutes a strategy. But principles come with less baggage, both substantively and format-wise, so there is more freedom to focus on finding common ground and meaning without the burden of choosing among competing formats. They could readily agree that they wanted to be a principles-driven alliance without knowing exactly what that might look like. Developmental evaluation supports that kind of openness, emergence, adaptability, and search for common ground as part of the developmental process.

6. *Becoming a principles-driven alliance led to ongoing principles-focused evaluation.* The Monitoring and Evaluation (M&E) Committee of the Global Alliance took on the task of creating a framework and template for distinct working groups to report on their activities, achievements, and impacts. Asking the working groups to report on how the principles informed their work became a centerpiece of the M&E reporting system. This ensures that the principles are not just boilerplate statements but are meaningfully embedded in and inform the ongoing work of the Global Alliance for the Future of Food.

7. *Applying the principles to new initiatives provided a way to test their continued meaningfulness and relevance.* A test of the applicability, relevance, adaptability, and utility of general principles was their relevance to specific new initiatives and areas on engagement like animal agriculture and seeds. As Exhibit 28.1 shows, the principles passed this test for animal agriculture. Instead of developing new principles specifically for animal agriculture, as initially proposed by some, the already-adopted principles proved adaptable and relevant to this new initiative arena.

Concluding Reflections

The Global Alliance for the Future of Food adopted developmental evaluation as the appropriate approach for helping them, as a new, evolving, and adapting collaboration, stay focused on their ambitious vision while navigating the turbulent realities of their complex, dynamic, global systems change initiatives. The Global Alliance principles emerged, then, from the developmental evaluation process. As that process unfolded, the monitoring and evaluation activities of the Global Alliance became increasingly principles focused. Being principles driven supports the Global Alliance in taking on large-scale, problem-solving initiatives that cross sector and geographic boundaries. Principles-focused evaluation, as a developmental evaluation approach, aims to ensure that rigorous and leading-edge conceptual and methodological approaches to evaluation are embedded in Global Alliance initiatives from the beginning and throughout all aspects of their work.

Thus, the foundation of the Global Alliance has been built on principles. Principles-focused evaluation, as the work of the Global Alliance unfolds, will examine the meaningfulness of the principles to members of the Alliance, adherence to the principles in the variety of initiatives sponsored by the Alliance, and the results of adhering to the principles. That is the ambitious evaluation agenda the Global Alliance has committed itself to and that the evaluation community will watch with great interest, for evaluating global systems change is a major challenge for the future (Patton, 2015c).

CHAPTER 29

Principles Enhancing Coherence

The McKnight Foundation
Collaborative Crop Research Program

> For apart from inquiry, apart from the praxis, individuals cannot be truly human. Knowledge emerges only through invention and re-invention, through the restless, impatient, continuing, hopeful inquiry human beings pursue in the world, with the world, and with each other.
>
> —PAULO FREIRE, *Pedagogy of the Oppressed* (1970, p. 72)

This chapter describes how a multifaceted, multilayered, and multidimensional international agriculture program developed principles to help bring coherence across a diverse and dynamic landscape of people, places, cultures, and activities.

Diversity, Complexity, and Contextual Variation

In 1993, the McKnight Foundation, based in Minneapolis, Minnesota, created a plant biology program that funded nine cross-cultural partnerships between U.S. scientists and scientists in Asia, South America, and Africa to stimulate research on neglected crops. In the ensuing decades, the program developed into the Collaborative Crop Research Program (CCRP) and expanded to 70 research projects addressing the food crisis in four of the most hunger-challenged regions in the world: West Africa, Southern Africa, Eastern Africa, and the Andes. The program evolved to focus on small-scale farmers and agricultural researchers in 12 countries working with 24 different crops addressing solutions across the agricultural spectrum, from breeding to agronomy to markets to food preparation to storage to postharvest value addition. The program's evolution flowed from accumulating experience and knowledge, engaging in systematic reflective practice about what was being learned, and strategic priority setting based on the program's deepened understanding of its niche and comparative advantage in supporting agricultural development among smallholder farmers.

McKnight's overarching crop research goal is to improve farm management by working with smallholder farmers to increase productivity, enhance livelihoods, and improve nutrition and food security. CCRP concentrates on improving locally important but underresearched crops such as tef, quinoa, fonio, amaranth, and others. Through research into the devastating bacterial crop disease banana wilt, for example,

CCRP helped farmers control the disease's spread by up to 95% in Kenya and over 80% in Uganda pilot sites. By supporting collaborative innovation processes in agriculture at the project level, important partnerships between community members, farmers, researchers, and other professionals develop, strengthening capacity in each region to nurture and sustain farmer-focused agricultural research.

Each of the four areas has a unique research focus. Projects in the Andes are designed to improve the livelihoods of people, households, and communities in Bolivia, Ecuador, and Peru by targeting crops and cropping systems important to Andean food security, such as quinoa and lupin. Research on millet- and sorghum-based systems in West Africa focuses on improving food security for small farmers in Burkina Faso, Mali, and Niger. Projects in Southern Africa focus on increasing the integration of edible legumes into the cropping systems of Malawi, Mozambique, and Tanzania. The work in Eastern Africa and the Horn of Africa aims to enhance crop productivity, marketing, and utilization to improve the livelihoods and nutrition of people in Uganda, Kenya, and Ethiopia, particularly those depending on underresearched crops of regional significance.

Each of the four areas has a regional team consisting of a regional representative, a liaison scientist, and a research methods specialist. The regional teams make grants that support research and provide grantees access to programwide practices and capacity-building resources and technical assistance. The overall global program is coordinated and supported by a cross-regional leadership team and two program codirectors.

Creating an Integrated Monitoring, Evaluation, and Planning Process

Prior to 2008, CCRP had no systematic evaluation requirements, frameworks, reflective practice process for programwide learning, or formal protocols for sharing project findings. Monitoring and evaluation consisted largely of projects documenting their research process and results. No systematic cross-project analysis was conducted. In 2008, in concert with an influx of funding from the Bill and Melinda Gates Foundation, the new McKnight Foundation international program director, also serving as the CCRP program director, initiated an evaluation process to enhance overall program coherence and deepen understanding of the interrelated systems that undergird all aspects of CCRP, as well as document results more rigorously. What emerged was the Integrated Monitoring, Evaluation, and Planning (IMEP) process based on developmental evaluation at a time when developmental evaluation was being created (Moore & Cady, 2016).

The evaluation team collaborated on the emergent developmental evaluation approach to support a number of conceptual developments in the program that have evolved since 2008 and continue to develop:

▶ Conceptualization of a programwide theory of change and capacity-building support for development of project-level theories of change;
▶ A complex adaptive systems approach to analyzing agricultural development needs and systems change intervention strategies;
▶ Work on integrating social and technical innovations;
▶ Incorporation of gender analysis into projects;
▶ Conceptualization and adoption of an agroecological intensification (AEI) approach as a basis for understanding and improving smallholder farmer production systems;
▶ Technical support at the project level to increase the quality of farmer–researcher collaborative and participatory research designs;
▶ Designs for research to generate options by context that would support contextualized scaling;

▶ A focus on farmer research networks for increasing impact; and

▶ Enhanced evaluation at the project level and cross-project synthesis studies.

These diverse program development initiatives involved people at the project, regional, and leadership team levels as well as consultants and resource personnel with specialized knowledge to help guide these developments.

While these multifaceted initiatives were aimed at bringing greater conceptual clarity and coherence to the program, so much change at so many levels and in so many ways had the opposite effect for many program participants and grantees. They struggled with all the conceptual developments as they tried to deal with each new element and figure out how the diverse elements interconnected, which was not at all obvious, either conceptually or operationally. I was playing an advisory role to the developmental evaluation specifically and

these program developments generally. In that capacity, being a part of discussions about how to bring greater coherence to the program while maintaining local autonomy and ownership, I suggested that articulation of core principles might provide coherence as a foundation to support the different levels of activity in the multiple conceptual frameworks that had emerged to support various aspects of the work. Over a period of 2 years, including two leadership team meetings that brought program leaders together from around the world, a multilayered and multidimensional framework of principles emerged (Miller, 2016). This chapter presents the principles framework as much for format (multidimensional) and organization (multilayered) as for content and substance. Some specific elements may not be clear to people not involved in the work. Don't let that distract you from taking in the overall framework, which begins with Exhibit 29.1 followed by presentation and elucidation of dimensions and layers.

EXHIBIT 29.1. CCRP Overarching Principles	
COLLABORATIVE	1. **Inclusion principle.** Convene multiple and diverse stakeholders to inform deliberations at all levels and locations of decision making.
	2. **Genuine collaboration principle.** Ensure *genuine* and *authentic* collaborative engagement.
CROP	*Throughout all aspects and stages of crop systems improvement work . . .*
	3. **Agroecology intensification (AEI) principle.** Apply agroecology concepts, knowledge, and principles.
	4. **Contextualization principle.** Conduct and use contextual analysis.
RESEARCH	*In all aspects and phases of cropping systems research, facilitate . . .*
	5. **Farmer–researcher co-creation principle.** Engage farmers as partners to ensure relevance and use of research processes and results.
	6. **Research for AEI impact principle.** Design and implement research to achieve impact (generating options by context for improving crop systems).
PROGRAM	7. **Values coherence principle.** Ensure that CCRP work is ethical and grounded in core values.
	8. **Systemic program coherence principle.** Ensure that the diverse levels, elements, dimensions, and locations of CCRP are interconnected.

Two Levels of Principles:
Both Substantive and Inclusive

Two levels of principles emerged as important to distinguish: overarching guiding principles and specific operating principles. Overarching principles provide *strategic* guidance. Operating principles can be thought of as providing *tactical* guidance. In the process of facilitating potential principles, some 30 members of the leadership team, working in small groups, generated possible principles. The evaluation team then organized those principles into overarching strategic principles and categorized the remaining principles as operating (tactical) principles. This increased ownership of the principles by including all principles identified in any of the small groups, making the list inclusive; but it also led to many principles. Distinguishing overarching strategic principles from tactical operating principles allowed us to generate a manageable number of overarching principles (eight), while including in the final framework any

principles viewed as important by any leadership team members. The principles were understood to be in draft form and subject to review and revision at future annual leadership team meetings. This flexibility allowed the program to take a principles-based approach that was both substantive and inclusive. This meant not creating an arbitrary ceiling on how many principles a program ought to have. In the end, eight overarching principles were identified for the overall program, two for each letter in the program name: CCRP (see Exhibit 29.1).

Each of the eight overarching principles was elaborated and specified through operating principles as shown in Exhibit 29.2.

Process for Developing the Principles

The multilayered structure of principles allowed the diverse perspectives of leadership team members to be captured and included without ending up with a long, unwieldy, and undifferentiated laundry list of

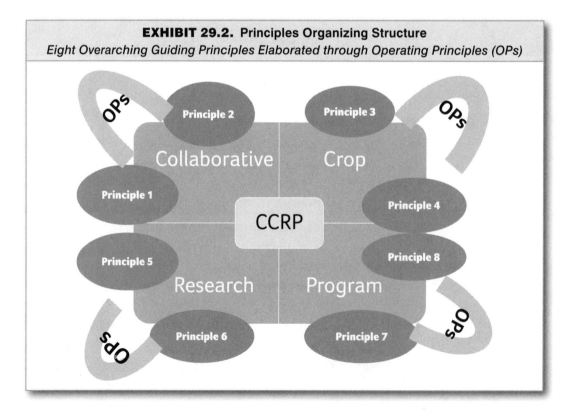

EXHIBIT 29.2. Principles Organizing Structure
Eight Overarching Guiding Principles Elaborated through Operating Principles (OPs)

OPs · OPs · OPs · OPs

Principle 2 · Principle 3 · Principle 1 · Principle 4 · Principle 5 · Principle 8 · Principle 6 · Principle 7

Collaborative · Crop · Research · Program

CCRP

principles. The leadership team consisted of some 40 people including senior program staff from the four regional communities of practice, technical and research liaisons and advisers, strategic advisers, evaluators, foundation leadership, and program partners. It's not important to get into specifics about these varied roles. What matters for our purpose here is that this was a large group of diverse people from around the world with different responsibilities in the program who came together annually for a week with a very full agenda to work through. Time for clarifying principles was no more than an hour or two in the whole agenda, though reference to specific principles or the principles in general was woven into discussion throughout the week.

The clarifying process involved my making a short presentation reviewing why the principles were being developed, their purpose, how they would be used to guide the work, and how their use would become part of the evaluation. The presentation included the GUIDE criteria for what constitutes a good principle though those criteria had not yet jelled into what is presented in this book as GUIDE. Indeed, it was in my work with the CCRP leadership team that the GUIDE criteria emerged and eventually cohered into the framework presented in Chapter 6.

The leadership team then divided into small groups of five to six people to articulate and clarify principles. They presented these to the whole group. I collected them and grouped similar principles together. As I participated in the leadership team meeting throughout the week, I listened for additional principles and interjected those already identified when discussion merited. For example, when discussion focused on how to strengthen the capacity of developing country researchers, I asked if the research principles might be incorporated in the capacity-building strategy and specific professional development work. The foundation international program director and developmental evaluator also helped monitor and bring attention to the principles. At the end of the leadership meeting week, I was given an opportunity to report back on how I had revised, synthesized, and organized the principles from the small groups. Following full-group feedback, I revised the principles again. Following the meeting, the draft principles were included in the proceedings with an invitation to send me further feedback. I then worked with the evaluation team and program leadership to refine and polish the principles. That's how the multilayered structure of principles emerged as a way to capture the diverse perspectives of leadership team members and include what they each felt was important without ending up with a long, unwieldy, and hard-to-use list of principles. For more details about the development of the principles as part of the program's developmental evaluation, see the "Journey of Discovery" by Marah Moore and Jane Maland Cady (2016).

In addition to differentiating overarching principles from operating principles, based on discussions and feedback, I identified potential dangers and traps that should be guarded against for each operating principles. Exhibit 29.3 presents the full CCRP principles framework, first presenting the two overarching principles for each letter in the CCRP name followed by a depiction of the interdependence and interaction between those two principles. That is followed by the operating principles and potential dangers and traps.

Caveats

What follows (the full principles framework) is a lot to absorb, but keep in mind that this is the fruit and culmination of 7 years of conceptual work aimed at bringing coherence to 65 research projects in four quite different regions in the world. These projects focused on smallholder farmers and agricultural researchers in 12 countries working with 24 different crops, addressing a wide variety of problems, and generating a diverse set of solutions appropriate to specific contexts.

EXHIBIT 29.3. CCRP Principles Framework

COLLABORATION PRINCIPLES

1. **Inclusion:** Convene multiple and diverse stakeholders to inform deliberations at all levels and locations of decision making.
2. **Genuine collaboration:** Ensure *genuine* and *authentic* collaborative engagement.

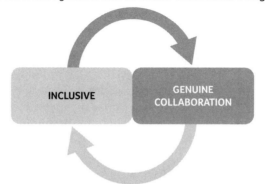

Operating principles	Desired outcomes	Dangers and traps
a. *Reciprocity:* Build trust based on shared interests and honest interactions.	a. Trust and mutual respect	a. Win–lose power plays: compliance mentality and behavior
b. *Mutuality:* Negotiate win–win agreements.	b. Shared ownership	b. Tokenism/one-sided control
c. *Realistic engagement:* Start where people are.	c. Sense of "we can do this"	c. Overwhelming
d. *Nudge:* Generate movement.	d. Movement, being engaged, process animated	d. Pushing too hard, too far, too fast

CROP SYSTEMS PRINCIPLES

Throughout all aspects and stages of crop systems improvement work . . .

3. **Agroecology intensification (AEI):** Apply agroecology concepts, knowledge, and principles.[*]
4. **Contextualization:** Conduct and use contextual analysis.

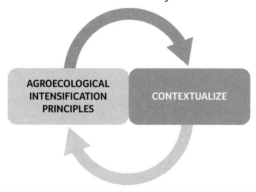

(continued)

Operating principles	Dangers, traps
a. Frame needs, diagnosis, the CCRP response, pathways of change, outcomes, and scaling potential through the lens of AEI and options by context analysis.	a. Unsystematic and idiosyncratic analysis, ad hoc interventions, non-contextualized findings, and simple, singular, linear recommendations
b. Value heterogeneity: Build on and enhance diversity.	b. Reduced diversity
c. Include multidimensional outcomes.	c. Single commodity outcomes (vs. *cropping systems* improvements)
d. Enhance resilience and sustainability.	d. Short-term, isolated, and immediate outcomes focus
e. Look for intersections and interactions among multiple, interrelated pathways of change (e.g., soil health and plant breeding).	e. Isolated, siloed interventions and outcomes
f. Take an integrated long-term perspective while producing short- and medium-term results (e.g., quinoa grants #1, #2, #3).	f. Short-term thinking

RESEARCH PRINCIPLES

In all aspects and phases of cropping systems research, facilitate . . .

5. **Farmer–researcher co-creation:** Engage farmers as partners to ensure relevance and use of research processes and results.
6. **Research for agroecological impact:** Design and implement research to achieve impact (generating options by context for improving crop systems).

Operating principles	Dangers, traps
a. Enhance quality through capacity building.	a. Expecting quality without support, guidance, and technical assistance
b. Integrate local and global research.	b. Isolated findings
c. Link social and technical inquiry.	c. Technically adequate research that is not relevant and useful

(continued)

Operating principles	Dangers, traps
d. Integrate farmer knowledge into the research.	d. Research isolated from existing contextual understandings and knowledge, and therefore less relevant and useful
e. Incentivize, support, and reinforce farmer participation to ensure responsiveness to farmers' needs, knowledge, problems, concerns, and constraints.	e. Weak farmer participation; researcher control (not genuine co-creation)
f. *Make the research process empowering:* Build social, technical, and methodological capital through the farmer–researcher co-creation process.	f. Narrow outcomes; little, if any, sustainable and resilient systems change
g. Implement phased and emergent design.	g. Project phases disconnected; lack of accumulation of capacity, findings, uses, and impacts
h. Be utilization focused: Don't collect data until and unless you know how it will be used.	h. Extraneous data, unused findings
i. Ensure two-way flow of communications between farmers and researchers throughout.	i. One-way, top-down, ineffective, alienating communications
j. Ensure secure data for access, aggregation, and future use locally and globally.	j. Lost data—inaccessible, unused, disaggregated

PROGRAM PRINCIPLES

7. **Values coherence:** Ensure that CCRP work is ethical and grounded in core values.
8. **Systemic program coherence:** Ensure that the diverse levels, elements, dimensions, and locations of CCRP are interconnected.

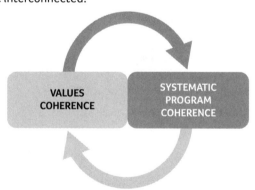

Values coherence operating principles	Dangers, traps
a. Clarify, reinforce, and incorporate core values: equity, gender, human rights, and ethical interactions.	a. Pretense of being value-free and neutral, purely technical orientation

(continued)

Values coherence operating principles	Dangers, traps
b. Keep the focus on smallholder, marginalized famers.	b. Slippery slope to supporting more advantaged farmers (often easier to work with)
c. Ensure respect for indigenous culture and knowledge.	c. Undermining indigenous culture with technical innovations and interventions
d. Empower.	d. Disempower
e. Avoid doing harm.	e. Inadvertently doing harm
f. Protect those at risk (be defensive when needed).	f. Being overwhelmed by powerful, well-resourced offensive initiatives
Systemic coherence operating principles	**Dangers, traps**
a. Integrate theory and practice.	a. Incoherence; isolated findings and outcomes
b. Reinforce systems and complexity thinking throughout.	b. Linear, simple thinking
c. Integrate monitoring and evaluation.	c. M&E done as compliance
d. Reflective practice, using the adaptive cycle.	d. Lack of shared learning
e. Connect levels, pathways, regions, outcomes.	e. Disconnected, incoherent, ineffective programming
f. Connect CCRP to other development institutions and initiatives.	f. Reduced impact
g. Ensure use of the theory of change.	g. Lack of program coherence across projects, regions, communities of practice, and pathways of change
h. Mutual accountability.	h. Accountability a burden, punitive, resisted
i. Administrative efficiency.	i-j-k. Poor resource use, not realizing potential
j. Effective stewardship and investment of scarce resources.	
k. Economies of scale in programming.	
l. Team leadership.	l. Individual agendas rule; lack of shared direction; conflict
m. Be a model of collaborative development.	m. No contribution to the field in its struggle for effective, values-based models

*For AEI principles, see Chapter 30 in this book.

Moreover, the framework (Exhivit 29.3) is a work in progress in accordance with the emergent and adaptive nature of developmental evaluation. The CCRP leadership team has adopted the principles as draft statements to be tried out, used, reviewed, and revised as the program gains experience with being explicitly principles driven. Being principles driven is not in question. The precise number and wording of principles is likely to change over time, especially the more detailed and longer list of operating principles.

Finally, I want to reiterate the caution that some elements, including potential pitfalls and dangers, may not be clear in the abbreviated form presented here. It's the overall nature, purpose, and structure of the principles framework that is focus here. So, review Exhibit 29.3 for the detailed CCRP principles framework.

The CCRP principles are intended to constitute an interrelated, mutually reinforcing, dynamically interconnected whole.

Lessons from the Collaborative Crop Research Program

1. *When coherence is the intended purpose of a set of principles, coherence constitutes a criterion for evaluating the set of principles.* As with any intent (goals, objectives, mission, strategy), the function of evaluation is to assess whether the intent is actually realized. The evaluation team participated in the principles development process by soliciting feedback about the perceived meaningfulness and relevance of individual principles, and the perceived coherence of the whole. That feedback supported revision of the principles, which remain a work in progress.

2. *Use of principles requires focused attention, facilitation, and evaluation.* At regional community of practice and global leadership meetings the principles are included in agenda materials and explicitly addressed as part of whatever business comes before the group. The scope of work of the evaluation team includes evaluation of the use of the principles in deliberations and decisions of the CCRP leadership and field participants. The fact that the evaluation is principles focused brings added attention to the principles, a manifestation of the classic evaluation principle that *what gets measured gets done.* The commitment to review and potentially revise the principles makes evaluation essential to provide information and feedback on which to base any revision process.

3. *Leadership support proved critical for persevering in development of the principles and using them to guide program deliberations and evaluate program developments.* The two co-directors kept attention focused on developing principles once the commitment to do so had been made. This included devoting time for principles development in the packed schedules of the overall, broadly based leadership team.

4. *Engaging people in the field in understanding and using the principles required a commitment to capacity building.* The notion of being principles driven was new to agricultural researchers, farmers, extension staff, and policymakers. Explaining the principles, both their purpose and their relevance, was essential to keep the statement of principles from just becoming window dressing.

5. *Distinguishing among levels and types of principles, overarching program principles versus specific operating principles, proved to be a breakthrough in focusing on core principles to support overall program coherence.* The inclusive participatory process for developing the principles generated a large number of candidates as potential core principles. The goals of getting to a manageable and meaningful number of principles while maintaining a sense of ownership of the principles among those who participated in developing and refining them were ultimately met by layering the principles. In

those layers were the voices and perspectives of diverse participants from the four regions of the world engaged in programming and research.

6. *Distinguishing overarching core program principles from specific subprogram-area principles proved an important and useful differentiation.* While the process began by generating the overarching core program principles, the need for an interest in specific subprogram-area principles emerged as an important way to enhance coherence between subprogram areas and the overall program. Thus subprogram principles were developed for agroecological research, farmer network engagement, and the integrated monitoring and evaluation initiative.

7. *The developmental evaluator played a crucial and ongoing role in clarifying principles and integrating them into program strategic work and evaluation.* In my role as evaluation consultant, in collaboration with the program's developmental evaluator, we advised and coached the development and adoption of principles. This is consistent with the more general role evaluators have come to play in clarifying conceptual elements of a program, like goals clarification or logic model development. In this case it was principles development.

8. *Going forward, serious and consistent evaluation of whether and how the principles are used will be important to integrating the principles into ongoing decision making and programming.* CCRP leadership has expressed this commitment, but evaluation has the responsibility of monitoring the extent to which that commitment is realized. Thus, principles-focused evaluation will be an important evaluation focus to realize the potential of principles-driven programming.

Concluding Reflections

What stands out to me about this principles-focused evaluation story is the transition from implicit principles to explicit articulation and focus on principles. The leaders of this program were principles driven from the beginning of their collaboration. They were strong conceptualizers, both thoughtful and action oriented, and committed to integrating theory and practice. They paid close attention to both processes and outcomes, to both achieving results and the importance of how those results were achieved. Undergirding and supporting this astute and committed leadership style were principles. Evidence of those principles regularly emerged in conversations, group deliberations, and decision making. I observed that evidence firsthand as a consultant to the program and the evaluation. The work on principles described in this chapter, then, did not create or generate principles, but rather brought them into the spotlight as an explicit framework for enhancing program coherence. The partnership between program leaders and the evaluation team was critical in this regard, as the observations made and questions asked by the evaluators propelled forward the process of articulating the principles and making them a core component of the evaluation framework and overall theory of change.

CHAPTER 30

Principles Defining
the Emergent Field of Agroecology

How Principles Inform and GUIDE Practices

Burning question: How can the entirety of a food system, including production, processing, transportation, financial intermediation, marketing, and consumption be ecologically sustainable, agriculturally productive, and economically efficient?

—Derived from V. ERNESTO MÉNDEZ, 2010, p. 1

Why agroecology? Perhaps a better title for this chapter would be "Principles Defining an Emergent Field That Aspires to Feed the Earth's Future Population of 10 Billion People with Healthy Food While Preserving the Environment and Saving the Planet for Future Generations." Why agroecology? The more than 20 philanthropic foundations that formed the Global Alliance for the Future of Food (Chapter 28) have adopted agroecology as the essential applied knowledge framework and best hope for realizing their sustainable food goals. The Collaborative Crop Research Program (CCRP) featured in the last chapter has also embraced agroecological intensification as its core science base and development strategy. *The bottom line:* You don't have to be an agricultural specialist for it to be worthwhile to know something about, appreciate, and learn from agroecology principles. You just have to be someone who likes food and cares about the future capacity of the Earth to feed people. So, in case you were thinking

about skipping this chapter, let me suggest that you give it a few more paragraphs. But feel free to get a snack for added sustenance before reading on.

The Emergence of Agroecology as an Applied Discipline Based on Principles

Disciplines given birth by the mother of all disciplines, philosophy, can be distinguished by their core burning questions. For sociology, the burning question is the Hobbesian question of order: What holds society or social groups together? What keeps societal groups from falling apart? Psychology asks why individuals think, feel, and act as they do. Political science asks, "What is the nature of power, how is it distributed, and with what consequences?" Economics studies how resources are produced and distributed. A foundational or burning question, like the mythic burning bush of Moses, blazes with heat (controversy) and light (wisdom) but is not consumed (is never fully answered).

Disciplines and subdisciplines reveal layers of questions. Biologists inquire into the nature and variety of life. Botanists ask how plants grow, while agriculturists investigate the production of food, and agronomists narrow their focus still further to field crops. To be sure, reducing any complex and multifaceted discipline to a single burning question oversimplifies the focus of that discipline. But what is gained is clarity about what distinguishes one lineage of inquiry from another. Moreover, and more important for my purpose here, the inquiry into any burning question follows scientific principles of investigation (what evidence is credible) and yields both natural principles (how the world works) and effectiveness principles (how to change the world). The combination of burning questions, natural principles, and effectiveness principles defines a field. The emergent field of agroecology illustrates this combination and the crucial role of principles in defining the field. The burning question of agroecology opened this chapter.

Discussion and debate about which principles are essential illustrates the critical role of principles in defining a field. Principles matter, thus the intensity of the engagement about which principles, worded in what ways, are essential. Evaluative thinking and judgment contribute to the principles clarification process. In particular, quite apart from the specifics of agroecology, this chapter, using agroecology as an example, will show how principles translate into and inform practices. I'll also demonstrate how to use the GUIDE principles evaluation framework (Chapter 6) to examine the quality of principles.

Tracing the History

Agroecologist Ernesto Méndez (2010) traces the emergence of agroecology to growing concerns about the negative environmental and social impacts of industrialized agriculture (or conventional agriculture) with its focus on maximizing yields and profits. Practices like mechanized soil tillage; excessive use of water, pesticides, and fertilizers; and extensive monocropping have degraded agricultural land. He notes that the term *agroecology* began appearing frequently in the sustainable agriculture literature in the 1970s, though the first textbook in the field (Gliessman, 2000) traces the roots of agroecology to writing on crop ecology in the late 1920s, and the first actual use of the term is credited to a Czechoslovakian agronomist, Basil Bensin, in 1930. In the past three decades agroecology has become "a vibrant field of research and practice, with increasing importance in policy, academic, and field applications" (Méndez, 2010, p. 1). Agroecology has been touted as "a global paradigm to challenge mainstream industrial agriculture" (Valenzuela, 2016).

Major agroecological initiatives are being funded by the philanthropic collaborations mentioned above as well as others like the AgroEcology Fund (*www.agroecologyfund. org*). Those initiatives, based on principles of agroecology, will need to be evaluated. We'll look at how principles-focused evaluation would approach that challenge.

Principles of Agroecology

Principles of agroecology apply to agroecosystems and aquacultures, though the inclusion of aquaculture is not always explicit.

Agroecosystems and aquacultures are communities of plants and animals interacting with their physical and chemical environments that have been modified by people to produce food, fiber, fuel and other products for human consumption and processing. Agroecology is the holistic study of agroecosystems, including all environmental and human elements. It focuses on the form, dynamics and functions of their interrelationships and the processes in which they are involved. An area used for agricultural production, e.g. a field or area of water devoted to aquaculture, is seen as a complex system in which ecological processes found under natural conditions also occur, e.g. nutrient cycling, predator/prey interactions, competition, symbiosis and successional changes. Implicit in agroecological research is the idea that, by understanding these ecological relationships and processes, agroecosystems can be manipulated to improve production and to produce more sustainably, with fewer negative environmental or social impacts and fewer external inputs. (Altieri, 1995)

The design of such systems is based on the application of the following kinds of ecological principles (Altieri & Toledo, 2005; Gliessman, 1992; Gliessman & Muramoto, 2010; Méndez, 2015; Méndez, Bacon, & Cohen, 2016):

1. Enhancing recycling of biomass, optimizing nutrient availability, and balancing nutrient flow.

2. Securing favorable soil conditions for plant growth, particularly by managing organic matter and enhancing soil biotic activity.

3. Minimizing losses due to flows of solar radiation, air, and water by way of microclimate management; water harvesting and soil management through increased soil cover.

4. Species and genetic diversification of the agroecosystem in time and space.

5. Enhance beneficial biological interactions and synergisms among agrobiodiversity components, resulting in the promotion of key ecological processes and services.

These principles can be applied by way of various techniques and strategies and would need to be expanded to include aquaculture. Each of these will have different effects on productivity, stability, and resiliency within the farm system, depending on the local opportunities, resource constraints and, in most cases, on the market. The ultimate goal of agroecological design is to integrate components so that overall biological efficiency is improved, biodiversity is preserved, and the agroecosystem productivity and its self-sustaining capacity is maintained. The goal is to design a quilt of agroecosystems within a landscape unit, each mimicking the structure and function of natural ecosystems (Altieri, 2016).

Comprehensive Approach to Agroecology

In his seminal textbook and influential website, Stephen Gliessman of the University of California, Santa Cruz, identified the comprehensive list of overarching agroecological principles presented in Exhibit 30.1. (*Note:* Specific and detailed operational principles identifying concrete practices within each category have been omitted here.)

Méndez adapted and used these principles to create a tool for analyzing the potential agroecological impact of agricultural interventions.

Analyzing the potential of agriculture interventions to do harm to food production systems and create opportunities to build resilience within them requires looking at the entire food system. This includes the agroecological, biological, farming and market, social and political systems, as well as the interactions between these components. A deep consideration of these sometimes complex interactions is necessary in order to ensure program interventions in one area of a food system do not have unintended negative effects in other dimensions of the food system and inadvertently increase vulnerability of households or the agroecosystem. The overall goal of this screening tool is to support productivity and income generation for smallholder farmers with a long term vision towards resilience. The tool utilizes a

EXHIBIT 30.1. Overarching Principles of Agroecology and Sustainability

1. Use renewable resources	10. Adjust to local environments
2. Minimize toxics	11. Diversify landscapes
3. Conserve resources	12. Diversify biota (e.g., intercrop; integrate animals in the system)
4. Conserve soil	
5. Conserve water	13. Diversify economics
6. Conserve energy	14. Empower people
7. Conserve genetic resources	15. Manage whole systems
8. Conserve capital	16. Maximize long-term benefits
9. Manage ecological relationships	17. Value health

Source: Gliessman (2014, 2015).

food system perspective and agroecological principles to guide those who design and implement agriculture and food security programs through a series of inquiries into how their interventions may affect the resilience of food systems and of those who depend on them. This application of agroecological principles to context analysis and program design is especially useful in minimizing the depletion of crucial natural capital of smallholder farmers. By identifying opportunities to leverage and maximize available resources in resource scarce environments, programs may enhance the resilience of productive, sustainable agroecosystems and the households, markets, and food systems which rely on them. (2010, p. 2)

These agroecological principles include:

1. Preservation and enhancement of agroecosystem diversity.
2. Conservation and enhancement of soil health and nutrient cycling.
3. Supporting ecological pest and disease regulating mechanisms.
4. Maximizing renewable energy potential.
5. Supporting and diversifying livelihoods to manage and mitigate risk exposure.
6. Prioritizing and enhancing local food production and food security.
7. Reducing dependence on external synthetic inputs.
8. Optimizing water use—preserving and regenerating water resources.
9. Integrating local and scientific knowledge.
10. Strengthening local organizations (Scarborough, Méndez, & Bisson, 2014).

Agroecological Principles in the CCRP

The preceding chapter presented the principles of The McKnight Foundation's CCRP. One of the eight core CCRP principles is agroecological intensification, which involves adhering to *agroecological principles*. As an adviser to CCRP, Ernesto Méndez adapted his work on agroecological principles to the CCRP framework and theory of change. This contributed to his development with colleagues of agroecological guiding principles for smallholder farmers in developing countries. Exhibit 30.2 presents some preliminary principles, subprinciples, and practices being used to guide agroecological research and practice. A key feature of Exhibit 30.2 is connecting principles to practices, that is, showing how principles lead to specific practices.

EXHIBIT 30.2. Preliminary List of Agroecological Principles to Use in Agroecological Research

Principles	Subprinciples	Practice examples
1. Conserve and enhance agroecosystem diversity at multiple levels.	• Preserve and enhance crop diversity • Preserve and enhance crop genetic diversity	• Intercropping • Agroforestry
2. Conserve and enhance soil health and nutrient cycling.	• Manage all soil properties: biological, physical, and chemical • Conserve and enhance soil organic matter	• Intercropping • Agroforestry • Green manuring
3. Conserve and enhance natural/ecological pest- and disease-regulating mechanisms.	• Minimize use of synthetic pesticides • Manage habitat to enhance natural enemies	• "Insectary" crops or hedgerows • Organic pest control
4. Minimize dependence on external synthetic inputs.	• Minimize use of synthetic pesticides • Minimize use of synthetic fertilizer	• Substitute with organic pesticides and fertilizers
5. Enhance agroecosystem performance without compromising the natural resource base.	• Improve ecological agroecosystem management efficiency • Improve economic agroecosystem management efficiency	• Farm planning • Cost–benefit analysis
6. Diversify livelihoods to manage and mitigate risk.	• Balance cash and subsistence production • Balance number of income sources	• Intercropping • Agroforestry • Cover cropping
7. Prioritize and enhance local food production for food security and food sovereignty.	• Link livelihood strategies for food security/food sovereignty	• Community food and seed centers • Agroecological food production
8. Strengthen local organizations.	• Support democratic farmer organizing • Strengthen farmer organization networks	• Organizational governance • Gender dynamics • Type and number of networks (density)
9. Integrate farmer/local and scientific knowledge.	• Create farmer scientist teams • Generate space for respectful dialogue	• Interest in research and in partnerships • Cultural competency
10. Maximize use of renewable resources and energy.	• Use on-farm or local resources • Minimize fossil fuel use	• Agroforestry • Composting
11. Conserve and optimize use of water.	• Reduce water waste/improve capture • Minimize water waste	• Rainwater capture • Contour ditches

Source: Agroecology Research Group, University of California, Santa Cruz.

Principles of Agroecology as an Organizing Heuristic for the Agroecology Knowledge Hub

Agroecology invites us to embrace the complexity of nature.
—OLIVIER DE SCHUTTER, Belgian legal scholar

This quote opens a proposal developed by Barbara Gemmill-Herren on using commonly accepted principles of agroecology as an organizing heuristic for the Agroecology Knowledge Hub of the UN's Food and Agriculture Organization (FAO). The proposal "recognizes and reflects salient features of the discipline, including its respect for principles, its inherent complexity, and the non-hierarchical form of knowledge creation." The proposal is framed around the following observation:

> There is a broad consensus that agroecology is built around a set of principles, derived both from ecological principles, and a strong ethic of valuing farmer and local knowledge. There is also the sense that these principles should provide—not prescriptive advice, but a "design framework" to be optimized and adapted to local contexts. (Gemmill-Herren, 2016, p. 5)

Origin of Agroecology Principles

The proposal traces the origins of agroecological principles to farmers. Reviewing the seminal literature on the origin of agroecology principles, the sense of "co-production" with farming communities is continuously reinforced. For example Gliessman (2015) notes that working alongside the campesino farmers in Mexico, the scientists studied their ecological foundations, and "in the process the principles of agroecology were born." This is very much the predominant view: that the basis of agroecological knowledge originates from the farmer. Farmers are viewed as discoverers as they proceed experimentally, by trial and error, observing what consequences follow from which combinations

and learning from what works. The science of agroecology builds on farmers' observations and experiences to document and explain the processes they have identified (Méndez et al., 2016).

Because agroecology adherents are committed to locally derived solutions and avoid any sense of being prescriptive, they are often described as being "more oriented toward offering a design framework for sustainable agroecosystems than they are prescriptions or blueprints for the construction or management of actual agroecosystems, and they do not dictate the specifics of an entire world food system. Nonetheless, agroecological principles do suggest the general elements of a sustainable food system" (Gliessman, 2014). Likewise, Méndez (2010) states that rather than a set of context-specific technologies, agroecology uses a set of principles that can be locally disseminated and adapted to multiple contexts. Of these elements, there is a general consensus on the following (Gliessman, 2014; Wezel et al., 2009):

1. Understanding of ecological relationships among the biota comprising a farming system and their interaction with natural systems. This aspect may be considered the *science* of agroecology, and draws heavily on modern ecological knowledge.

2. Effective and innovative agricultural *practices,* which value the knowledge of farmers and "undercut the distinction between the production of knowledge and its application" (Gliessman, 2014).

3. A social change or *social movement* aspect that advocates for fundamental changes in food systems.

Agroecology Knowledge Hub

The latest evidence of consensus about the principles-based nature of agroecology is establishment of an Agroecology Knowledge Hub by the FAO. It features 10 core elements of agroecology developed from principles:

> Agroecology has been defined as "the use of ecological principles for the design of agricultural systems." It is increasingly recognized that agroecology also addresses, in an indivisible way, economic and social dimensions in the food system. Agroecology offers more than a "design framework for sustainable agroecosystems." Agroecological principles should suggest the general elements of a sustainable food system. In alignment with this approach, FAO has identified 10 key elements, derived from the general principles articulated for agroecology. As projects, programmes and policies are developed to support agroecology, different elements may come to play in various configurations, with a strong blend between ecological and socio-economic elements. (FAO, 2017)

The Role of Evaluating Principles in Defining a Field

As the work of Steve Gliessman, Ernesto Méndez, Barbara Gemmill-Herren, and others illustrates, agroecology has developed as a field, and is still developing, through the identification, articulation, testing, refining, debating, and revising of principles. Undergirding and manifest throughout every aspect of principles development is principles-focused evaluation. I infer a set of evaluation criteria as the basis for the ongoing dialogue about what principles define the field of agroecology. Exhibit 30.3 presents these evaluation criteria as both a source of coherence and the basis for ongoing debate.

Lessons from Agroecology

1. *Generating alternative principles can facilitate dialogue and deliberation about the essential contributions of a new and emergent field of knowledge and practice.* In the case of agroecology, diverse sets of principles

provide evidence about areas of agreement as well as dimensions of difference and debate. Some sets of principles are quite comprehensive and multifaceted while others are short and focused. These differences help define the boundaries of this new field of inquiry and knowledge.

2. *Principles, by their very nature, emphasize the importance of context.* Agroecological principles encapsulate interdisciplinary knowledge and sustainable farming practices at a general level, but because agroecological systems vary significantly, the specific practices that follow from these principles within a given context will vary.

3. *Evaluating the principles on shared criteria is how the field advances.* Exhibit 30.3 shows how principles-focused evaluation supports evolution and further development of this emergent field of knowledge and practice. Evaluating the principles advances coherence of the field as a knowledge base emerges and coheres based on research and evaluation.

4. *Principles point to practices.* Exhibit 30.3 illustrates how principles can point to practices. Practices operationalize principles. The guidance in the GUIDE framework is guidance toward practices. This is a critical test for principles—that they can point to practices.

5. *Evaluating concrete practices is how the overarching principles are evaluated.* This is the critical role evaluation plays in linking principles and practices. The evaluation questions are: To what extent do principles point to specific practices? This is the guidance (G) criterion in the GUIDE framework. To what extent do the practices, if followed, demonstrate the effectiveness of the principles? This is the evaluable (E) criterion in the GUIDE framework.

6. *Defining a field of knowledge involves decisions about both what to include and what to exclude (boundary issues in systems approaches). Principles can inform that boundary-setting*

EXHIBIT 30.3. Six Evaluation Criteria for Judging Agroecological Principles Linked to GUIDE

Evaluation criteria	Definition and relevance	Source of debate	GUIDE framework corollary*
1. **Practical**	The principles must inform actual practices that farmers can use and that researchers can test.	Moving from concept to practice epitomizes the slip between cup and lip. Practicality varies by practice and context.	**G:** Guiding
2. **Relevant to small farmers**	The principles must be farmer based, farmer friendly, and farmer useful. Principles must be understandable by, meaningful to, and applicable by small farmers.	Small farmers are far from homogeneous in what they find relevant.	**U:** Useful
3. **Values consistent**	Principles are based on and consistent with values of ecosystem sustainability. Shared values provide the basis for a social movement that transforms the food system.	What to include in and how to articulate the values of sustainability is a matter of debate.	**I:** Inspiring
4. **Contextually adaptable**	The principles must be sufficiently general to be all-encompassing and field defining (consistent across contexts), while implementing the principles will necessarily and appropriately be adapted within and across contexts.	Adapting general principles to specific contexts involves knowledge, skill, farmer–researcher collaboration, and dealing with contextual complexities, all of which are matters of varied interpretation and implementation.	**D:** Developmental
5. **Scientifically credible**	Principles are based on and verifiable through empirical research.	Research findings are diverse, often conflicting, highly contextual, still emergent, and subject to varying interpretations.	**E:** Evaluable
6. **Effectively lead to desired outcomes and impacts**	The purpose of the principles is to increase the sustainability of agroecological systems while being agriculturally productive and efficient economically. Holistic systems thinking leads to holistic agroecological systems transformation.	The results of implementing agroecological principles are still emergent and a matter of debate as more evaluation findings accumulate globally across ecological and farming systems.	**E:** Evaluable

*See Chapter 6.

process. One critique of agroecology is that it ignores, or pays insufficient attention to, aquaculture. Exhibit 30.4 depicts an alternative framework for ecosystems that includes aquaculture. A relevant agroecological principle would be to include aquaculture explicitly and systematically in agroecological systems.

Concluding Reflections

This is the last of six principles-focused evaluation exemplars that make up Part III of this book. The first three exemplary cases focused on evaluations already completed: the evaluation of the implementation of the Paris Declaration principles for international development aid; the evaluation of six programs serving homeless youth; and the evaluation of the cross-Canada Vibrant Communities anti-poverty initiative. The second set of exemplars features initiatives and evaluations still unfolding, with stories that remain to be told: the Global Alliance for the Future of Food; the McKnight Foundation Collaborative Crop Research Program; and the development of the new interdisciplinary and applied field of agroecology.

At the end of each case I extrapolated lessons about principles-based initiatives and principles-focused evaluation. A major theme that cuts across those lessons and these six highly diverse initiatives is their use of principles as the rudder for navigating complex dynamic systems toward ambitious visions of a better world. These exemplars illustrate what it means for principles to manifest the GUIDE criteria. In each case the principles have provided guidance (G),

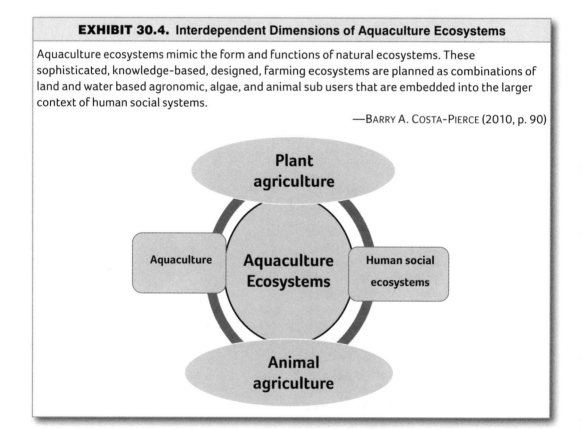

EXHIBIT 30.4. Interdependent Dimensions of Aquaculture Ecosystems

Aquaculture ecosystems mimic the form and functions of natural ecosystems. These sophisticated, knowledge-based, designed, farming ecosystems are planned as combinations of land and water based agronomic, algae, and animal sub users that are embedded into the larger context of human social systems.

—BARRY A. COSTA-PIERCE (2010, p. 90)

Plant agriculture

Aquaculture

Aquaculture Ecosystems

Human social ecosystems

Animal agriculture

proved useful (U), offered inspiration (I), supported developmental adaptation (D), and were evaluable (E). Since I began talking and writing about principles-focused evaluation 5 years ago, I've been asked what it looks like in practice. I've been asked for examples. These six exemplars are what principles-based initiatives and principles-focused evaluation look like in the trenches, where theory meets practice, and aspiration becomes action.

Parts I, II, and III of this book have focused on principles that guide projects, programs, initiatives, innovations, and change initiatives of all kinds. In the next part of the book, we leave the world of programming and turn to principles for evaluation. Evaluation models and approaches can be distinguished, and judged, by the principles that undergird them. Part IV, then, examines principles for evaluators and evaluations. As we move from program principles to evaluation principles, I offer you this meditation from Shakespeare's *The Comedy of Errors* by way of reflective preparation: "Every why hath a wherefore."

PART IV

Principles
for Evaluations
and Evaluators

Part I of this book introduced principles: What they are, why they matter, and their niche in program development and evaluation. Part II introduced the GUIDE framework for effectiveness principles and devoted several chapters to explaining, illustrating, and, hopefully, illuminating each letter in the GUIDE framework. Part III presented six case exemplars of principles-driven initiatives evaluated by principles-focused evaluations. Three of the exemplars are completed evaluations and three are still under way. Part IV now turns to principles for evaluations and evaluators.

Chapter 31 evaluates evaluation principles by examining principles that guide evaluations and evaluators, or at least purport to do so. Since the earlier parts of this book have examined program, project, organizational, and initiative principles, often critically, it seems only fair that we scrutinize published evaluation principles with the same fervor and intensity. Think of it as the proverbial admonition that *what's good for the goose is good for the gander*. Spoiler alert: It's not always a pretty picture.

Chapter 32 presents principles for *Outcome Harvesting*, an innovative approach that collects evidence of what has been achieved by an intervention and works backward to determine whether and how the efforts of social innovators and their interventions contributed to observed and documented changes. This chapter, by longtime colleague and friend Ricardo Wilson-Grau, shows how articulating principles can help define and illuminate an evaluation approach.

Chapters 33 and 34 offer reflections from two adept and experienced principles-focused evaluators about what it's like to do principles-focused evaluations and take on the identity of being a principles-focused evaluator. If you're considering journeying onto the principles pathway, you won't want to miss what Donna Podems and Nora Murphy have to say. In fact, even if you're not considering doing principles-focused evaluation, their experiences and insights are well worth reading.

What connects these chapters is *the personal factor,* the finding that caring and competent people make a difference, both in who conducts an evaluation and in distinguishing users of evaluations. Ricardo Wilson-Grau, Donna Podems, and Nora Murphy care about people in need, about evaluation use, and about conducting evaluations in ways that are true to their core values. I'll say more about each one in introducing their chapters. Here, in anticipation, is where these chapters will take you on *the principles pathway:*

▶ Chapter 31: where profession and principles become one

▶ Chapter 32: where theory and practice become one

▶ Chapter 33: where doing and naming become one

▶ Chapter 34: where personal and professional become one

Evaluating Evaluation Principles

Examining Principles That Guide Evaluations
and Evaluators

Evaluators spend other people's money doing evaluation, often huge amounts of money. They do so frequently, in every state and major city in the nation. They do so for nearly every major agency in the public sector and for an increasingly large number of private sector organizations, in academic and nonacademic settings. They are asked to address questions that often bear on the most controversial and persistent policy questions of our time. They do all this in competition with other groups who want to either do the evaluation or do something else with the evaluation money. With all this at stake, evaluators, their clients, and all the other stake-holders to evaluation realize that they stand to benefit from greater clarity about what to expect from evaluation. Codes of professional conduct are one way to begin to clarify these expectations.

—WILLIAM R. SHADISH, DIANNA NEWMAN, MARY ANN SCHEIRER,
and CHRISTOPHER WYE (1995, p. 3)

Codes of professional conduct take many forms, one of which is guiding principles. This chapter will review several sets of principles for evaluators. The thrust of this chapter is that principles-focused evaluation applies not just to program and organizational principles, but also to principles for evaluators, of which there turn out to be a great many displaying many-splendored variety. Principles for evaluators should be subject to principles-focused evaluation. The GUIDE framework can be applied to principles for evaluators. The evaluation questions for program principles are relevant to evaluation of principles for evaluations and evaluators:

1. To what extent are the evaluation principles meaningful?

2. To what extent are they adhered to?

3. If adhered to, to what extent do they lead to desired results?

Examples of Evaluation Principles

I've already presented some evaluation principles in this book. Exhibit 5.3 in Chapter 5 presented principles of utilization-focused evaluation (see p. 29). Exhibit 5.4 presented developmental evaluation principles (see p. 30). Exhibit 5.5 presented principles guiding principles-focused evaluation, to which we shall return in Chapter 35. Chapter 11 presented and discussed empowerment evaluation principles (see pp. 86–87).

In this chapter, we'll begin with the guiding principles of the AEA, then look at principles for data visualization, cultural competence, and collaborative approaches to evaluation. I'll close with several other sets of principles relevant to evaluation. My purpose is not to do a comprehensive, in-depth evaluation of these evaluation principles but to (1) show the diversity of evaluation principles available to guide practice, (2) emphasize that evaluation principles ought to be evaluated, and (3) illustrate how the GUIDE framework and criteria can be applied to sharpen evaluation principles.

AEA Guiding Principles

The AEA guiding principles for evaluators were published in 1995 (Shadish et al., 1995) and revised in 2004 (American Evaluation Association, 2004). The statements went through a number of public reviews at evaluation conferences and were assessed through invited critiques by evaluators. This led to several drafts and revisions over a couple of years before being approved and copyrighted by the AEA board of directors, and subsequently adopted by vote of the AEA membership. The principles were controversial from the outset. Some found the principles too vague, while others found them too specific to cover the full range of evaluation situations that occur. Some were concerned that they were too narrowly American (Western culture) to represent the evaluation profession globally (which they did not purport to do). Some thought they were unnecessary since disciplines (psychology, sociology, education) already had statements of principles that evaluators could draw on in particular subject areas. But, on the whole, the principles were welcomed as a significant, positive, and needed development signaling the growing maturity and stature of the profession (Chelimsky, 1995; Covert, 1995; Hendricks & Connor,

1995; House, 1995; Knott, 1995; Lovell, 1995; Newman, 1995; Rossi, 1995; Sanders, 1995). They have stood the test of time in that, more than two decades after adoption and minor revision, they remain the official principles of the AEA.

Several points about the principles deserve highlighting:

▶ The guiding principles were, and are, intended to apply to all kinds of evaluation.

▶ "The task to be done was to draft general guiding *principles* rather than highly specific *standards,* and the task force maintained that terminology throughout. Principles were understood to be conceptual rather than operational, giving guidance at the general level rather than at the level of how to make specific methodological or tactical decisions" (Shadish et al., 1995, p. 4). The Joint Committee Standards for Evaluation, supported by AEA, dealt with standards rather than principles, each of which was needed (Sanders, 1995).

▶ The five principles were not prioritized.

▶ The five principles were not viewed as independent from each other, "but overlap in many ways. Conversely, sometimes these principles will conflict, so that evaluators will have to choose among them. At such times evaluators must use their own values and knowledge of the setting to determine the appropriate response. Whenever a course of action is unclear, evaluators should solicit the advice of fellow evaluators about how to resolve the problem before deciding how to proceed" (Shadish et al., 1995, p. 21).

Restating the AEA Guiding Principles Using the GUIDE Criteria

The AEA guiding principles are stated as describing normative behaviors. They take the form of stating what evaluators do:

Evaluators conduct systematic, data-based inquiries.

I find this an awkward wording. The *G* (Guidance) criterion in the GUIDE framework stipulates that principles should be stated prescriptively, not descriptively:

> A principle is prescriptive. It provides advice and guidance on what to do, how to think, what to value, and how to act to be effective. It offers direction. The wording is imperative: *Do this.*

Restated in this format, the principle above becomes:

> Conduct systematic, data-based inquiries.

It's a small grammatical change that doesn't alter the substance of the principle but does, I think, alter the tone and feeling (inspirational nature) of the principle.

At any rate, for illustrative purposes, to let you decide whether such a change makes a difference, I have restated all five principles this way. Since I have the advantage of not needing to negotiate wording and format with a committee, or seek approval from the AEA board or membership, I am taking the liberty of offering this unofficial alternative. Have a look at Exhibit 31.1.

Principles for Evaluation Stakeholders and Primary Intended Users

Eleanor Chelimsky, one of our pioneers and thought leaders, had a particularly insightful concern and suggestion that, to my knowledge, has never been addressed, an omission I shall correct here. To appreciate her perspective and place her recommendation in context, let me tell you a bit about her. Between 1980 and 1994, Chelimsky, as

---

EXHIBIT 31.1. AEA Guiding Principles
Original and Restated

Original AEA Guiding Principles expressed as normative statements	AEA Guiding Principles as restated as prescriptive principles following the GUIDE format
What evaluators do . . .	**Guiding principles for evaluators**
A. Evaluators conduct systematic, data-based inquiries.	A. Conduct systematic, data-based inquiries.
B. Evaluators provide competent service to stakeholders.	B. Provide competent service to stakeholders.
C. Evaluators display honesty and integrity in their own behavior and attempt to ensure the honesty and integrity of the entire evaluation process.	C. Ensure the honesty and integrity of the entire evaluation process, including evaluators' behavior.
D. Evaluators respect the security, dignity, and self-worth of the respondents, program participants, clients, and other evaluation stakeholders with whom they interact.	D. Respect the security, dignity, and self-worth of respondents, program participants, clients, and other stakeholders.
E. Evaluators articulate and take into account the diversity of general and public interests and values that may be related to the evaluation.	E. Articulate and take into account the diversity of general and public interests and values that may be related to the evaluation.

*Source: American Evaluation Association (2004).

Assistant Comptroller General for Program Evaluation, established and directed the U.S. General Accounting Office's (GAO) Program Evaluation and Methodology Division (PEMD). The unit was charged with doing evaluations for Congress and improving GAO's methodological capabilities. With 80 to 100 people, PEMD had between 45 and 50 evaluations under way at any given time and produced 30 major products annually. When reviewing the AEA guiding principles, she was thinking about their relevance to her unit's diverse work as well as evaluations generally. But consider the diversity she dealt with: The PEMD unit did hugely influential evaluations on programs and policies as diverse as chemical weapons, drinking-age laws, Medicare, medical devices, AIDS education, highway safety, cancer research, taxation, welfare, immigration, and, indeed, the full range of federal initiatives of all kinds. PEMD used established methods rigorously, creatively employed old methods in new ways, and developed and demonstrated groundbreaking approaches to synthesis methods, prospective evaluation, mixed methods, and generation of rigorous and credible evaluation findings on hugely controversial, contested, and politicized issues. So given her context and depth of experience, what did Chelimsky propose?

She proposed that parallel principles were needed to guide stakeholders in their responsibilities in an evaluation. Such a statement of guiding principles for evaluation stakeholders, she hoped, would help create an "evaluation milieu" that would help evaluators "to be truthful about the program or policy that has been evaluated" (1995, p. 54). Inspired by Chelimsky's suggestion, Exhibit 31.2 provides parallel principles for evaluators and evaluation stakeholders.

EXHIBIT 31.2. AEA Guiding Principles with New Parallel Guiding Principles for Evaluation Stakeholders	
AEA Guiding Principles	Parallel guiding principles for evaluation stakeholders
Evaluators	*Evaluation stakeholders*, including those who commission, mandate, fund, use, and review evaluations
A. Conduct systematic, data-based inquiries.	A. Ensure adequate resources, access, and such other support as may be needed to ensure that evaluators can conduct systematic, data-based inquiries.
B. Provide competent service to stakeholders.	B. Be informed about the evaluator competences that will be needed to credibly provide needed information.
C. Ensure the honesty and integrity of the entire evaluation process.	C. Create an evaluation climate and conditions that support evaluator independence of judgment.
D. Respect the security, dignity, and self-worth of the respondents, program participants, clients, and other stakeholders.	D. Support an evaluation process that respects the security, dignity, and self-worth of the respondents, program participants, clients, and other stakeholders.
E. Articulate and take into account the diversity of general and public interests and values that may be related to the evaluation.	E. Support an evaluation process that articulates and takes into account the diversity of general and public interests and values that may be related to the evaluation.

An Inspiring Format

The brilliance of Chelimsky's suggestion lies in the message that evaluators and evaluation stakeholders are jointly responsible for how an evaluation is conducted, including its credibility, utility, and actual use. Parallel principles for evaluators and evaluation stakeholders drive that message home and give it substance.

Overarching and Operational Principles

Chapters 9, 17, and 27 presented examples of the value of distinguishing overarching and operational principles. Such a framework can be applied to the AEA guiding principles. "Each principle is illustrated by a number of statements to amplify the meaning of the overarching principle and to provide guidance for its application. These statements are illustrations" of how the principles might be applied in practice (Shadish et al., 1995, p. 21). The illustrative statements actually take the form of normative prescriptions and can be viewed as providing additional guidance to evaluators (Sanders, 1995, p. 48). Exhibit 31.3 adapts the illustrative normative prescriptions to statements of operating principles. See what you think of the relationship between the overarching principles and the more detailed operating principles.

EXHIBIT 31.3. AEA Guiding Principles Presented as Overarching and Operational Principles	
Reframed AEA guiding principles	**AEA illustrative statements adapted as operating principles for evaluators**
A. Conduct systematic, data-based inquiries.	1. Adhere to the highest appropriate technical standards, whether that work is quantitative or qualitative. 2. Explore with the client the shortcomings and strengths both of the various evaluation questions it might be productive to ask and the various approaches that might be used for answering those questions. 3. Communicate methods and approaches accurately and in sufficient detail to allow others to understand, interpret, and critique their work. 4. Discuss in a contextually appropriate way those values, assumptions, theories, methods, results, and analyses that *significantly* affect the interpretation of the evaluative findings.
B. Provide competent service to stakeholders.	1. Ensure that the evaluation team possesses the education, abilities, skills, and experience appropriate to undertake the tasks proposed in the evaluation. 2. Practice within the limits of your professional training and competence and decline to conduct evaluations that fall substantially outside those limits. 3. Continually seek to maintain and improve your competencies.
C. Ensure the honesty and integrity of the entire evaluation process.	1. Negotiate honestly with clients and relevant stakeholders the costs, tasks to be undertaken, limitations of methodology, scope of results likely to be obtained, and uses of data resulting from a specific evaluation. 2. Record and report all changes made in the originally negotiated project plans, and the reasons why the changes were made.

(continued)

Reframed AEA guiding principles	AEA illustrative statements adapted as operating principles for evaluators
	3. Be explicit about your own interests, and those of clients and other stakeholders, concerning the conduct and outcomes of an evaluation (including financial, political, and career interests). 4. Disclose any roles or relationships bearing on whatever is being evaluated that might pose a significant conflict of interest as an evaluator. 5. Do not misrepresent evaluation procedures, data, or findings and attempt to prevent or correct any substantial misuses of the evaluation by others. 6. Report any concerns that arise about procedures or activities that seem to produce misleading evaluative information or conclusions. 7. Disclose all sources of financial support for an evaluation, and the source of the request for the evaluation.
D. Respect the security, dignity, and self-worth of the respondents, program participants, clients, and other stakeholders.	1. Abide by current professional ethics and standards regarding risks, harms, and burdens that might be engendered to those participating in the evaluation. 2. Seek to maximize the benefits and reduce any unnecessary harms that might occur from the negative findings of an evaluation without compromising the integrity of the evaluation findings. 3. Conduct the evaluation and communicate results in a way that clearly respects the stakeholders' dignity and self-worth, especially when findings negatively affect the interests of some stakeholders. 4. Foster the social equity of the evaluation, so that those who give to the evaluation can receive some benefits in return. 5. Identify and respect differences among participants, such as differences in their culture, religion, gender, disability, age, sexual orientation, and ethnicity, and to be mindful of potential implications of these differences when planning, conducting, analyzing, and reporting their evaluations.
E. Articulate and take into account the diversity of general and public interests and values that may be related to the evaluation.	1. Include important perspectives and interests of the full range of relevant stakeholders, and justify any omissions. 2. Evaluate not only the immediate operations and outcomes of whatever is being evaluated, but also the broad assumptions, implications, and potential side effects of it. 3. Allow all relevant stakeholders to have access to evaluative information and actively disseminate that information to stakeholders as clearly and simply as accuracy allows so that clients and other stakeholders can easily understand the evaluation process and results. 4. Maintain a balance between client needs and other needs: explicitly identify and discuss any conflicts with the client and other relevant stakeholders, resolve them when possible, determine whether continued work on the evaluation is advisable if the conflicts cannot be resolved, and make clear any significant limitations on the evaluation that might result if the conflict is not resolved. 5. Do not ignore clear threats to the public good in any evaluation. 6. Go beyond an analysis of particular stakeholder interests when considering the welfare of society as a whole.

Truth-Speaking Principles

In reviewing the AEA guiding principles, Eleanor Chelimsky had another suggestion. She insisted that the principles for evaluators should explicitly include *speaking truth to power:* "Telling the truth to people who may not want to hear it is, after all, the chief purpose of evaluation" (1995, p. 54). But there are other evaluation perspectives on and approaches to power. For example: "Give voice to the voiceless" (Rodriguez-Bilella, 2016, p. 1).

Participatory, empowerment, culturally inclusive, and social justice approaches to evaluation seek to empower those whose voices are not typically heard (Fetterman, 2005; Hood, 2004; House, 2014; House & Howe, 2000; Kirkhart, 1995; Mertens, 1999). Plus, here's yet a third perspective. At the 2015 annual conference of the AEA in Chicago, a session on sharing evaluation failures was based on the principle of speaking truth to each other (Cooksy, Evergreen, Morris, & Patton, 2015). These three concerns suggest a trio of truth-speaking principles presented in Exhibit 31.4.

These principles meet the GUIDE criteria in my judgment. They provide guidance (G), are useful (U) if followed, are inspiring (I) as a vision of what evaluators are called on to do, can be adapted to a full of evaluation situations developmentally (D), and are evaluable (E).

Let's now move from the broad principles of overarching professional evaluation practice to a very focused set of principles for data visualization.

Design Principles for Data Visualization in Evaluation

Stephanie Evergreen (2017) has become the go-to person in evaluation for data visualization guidance. Her book *Effective Data Visualization: The Right Chart for the Right Data* (Evergreen, 2016) was an instant and well-deserved best-seller. Evergreen coauthored a chapter, "Design Principles for Data Visualization in Evaluation," that focuses on "two main concepts that work from models of cognition to support meaningful data visualizations—simplification and emphasis" (Evergreen & Metzner, 2013, p. 6). These concepts are subsequently used as main headings and referred to alternatively as guidelines, techniques, strategies, research findings, and best practices, but never actually delineated as principles or stated and presented in an explicit principles format. I infer, however, that the overarching principles are:

1. Simplify your presentations.
2. Emphasize your key points.

I further infer from the examples that one might distinguish overarching and operational principles, which, based on the guidance provided, I further infer might look something like Exhibit 31.5.

From Principles to Checklists

Since publication of the data visualization principles chapter, Evergreen has created two checklists, one for design of general evaluation and research reporting and another for design of data visualizations. The checklists are being widely disseminated, much lauded, and clearly proving useful to many evaluators, as they should. My own presentations could benefit from more

---

> **EXHIBIT 31.4.**
> **Truth-Speaking Principles**
>
> Evaluators . . .
>
> 1. Speak truth to power.
> 2. Give voice to the voiceless: Support and facilitate those whose truth is not typically heard by the powerful to speak their truths and have their truths heard.
> 3. Speak truth to each other.

EXHIBIT 31.5. Inferred Evergreen Design Principles for Effective Evaluation Presentations

Overarching principles	Operational principles
1. *Simplify your presentations.*	a. Keep the focus on the data. b. Avoid "visual noise." c. Segment complicated information in chunks. d. Avoid distracting detail.
2. *Emphasize your key points.*	a. Place graphics near their associated text. b. Use attention-guiding design elements. c. Avoid unnecessary decorative elements. d. Avoid clutter through overemphasis.

Source: Adapted from Evergreen and Metzner (2013).

adherence to them. That said, the items on the checklist are mostly rules. For example, here are five checklist items for "Type" from the Evaluation Report Layout Checklist (Evergreen, n.d.):

▶ Text fonts are used for narrative text.

▶ Long reading is in 9- to 11-point size.

▶ Body text has stylistic uniformity.

▶ Line spacing is 11–13 points.

▶ No more than three fonts are used.

The checklist also includes some operating principles, but no overarching principles. Here are examples of operating principles from the lists for alignment and graphics:

▶ Important elements are prominent.

▶ Grouped items logically belong together.

▶ Pictures/graphic elements are present.

▶ Visual theme is evident.

The checklist does not distinguish rules from principles, and doesn't need to, though they involve different kinds of advice. They are referred to as "elements of an evaluation report." My preference would be to distinguish rules from principles and group each together under the principle above that "grouped items logically belong together." I think such a regrouping would be more coherent and useful.

Principles for Culturally Competent Evaluation Practice

Cultural competence, by its very nature, calls for a flexible approach to evaluation. However, such an approach still has to be principled, and these principles must be articulated at the professional level.
— SAUMITRA SENGUPTA, RODNEY HOPSON, and MELVA THOMPSON-ROBINSON (2004, p. 15)

A special 2004 issue of *New Directions for Evaluation* was titled "In Search of Cultural Competence in Evaluation: Toward Principles and Practices." The volume did not promise actual principles (only the hope of moving toward them), has no entry for principles in the index, and does not explicitly offer any with the exception of the following:

We now believe that certain principles are given for culturally competent evaluation practice. Everyone should have a voice in an evaluation, but clearly not everyone can have his or her way. The evaluation should not unfairly punish individuals. The evaluation process should encourage and support people to use its findings to create meaningful change.

Other ideas are less clear, to our minds. (King, Nielsen, & Colby, 2004, p. 78)

However, one can infer cultural competence principles from other chapters[1]:

1. Include evaluators and observers who share a "lived experience" with the cultural groups being evaluated.

2. Ensure that the interests of the disadvantaged are represented and seriously considered.

3. Make multicultural validity a central concern in program evaluation.

4. Gather and report diverse cultural perspectives.

5. Include less powerful groups or individuals as stakeholders, such as racial, cultural, or language minority groups, in all aspects of the evaluation from design through interpreting results.

6. Speak the literal language of the participants.

7. Speak the figurative language of participants.

8. Share the benefits of inclusive and collaborative multicultural evaluation.

9. Develop flexible, responsive, and culturally appropriate assessment and evaluation approaches.

10. "Focus on the uniformity of purpose in program evaluation without unnecessary uniformity of procedure."

I draw these illustrative inferences to reemphasize the point, as I have throughout this book, that principles, or potential principles, don't often come ready-made. Principles-focused evaluators have to be able to recognize embedded and nascent principles, gently extract them, then mold and shape them, until they constitute principles. Then they

---

[1]Items 1–5 are derived from Hood (2004); items 6–8 are derived from Connor (2004); items 9 and 10 are derived from Symonette (2004).

are ready for the first evaluation test: finding out whether they are meaningful, useful, inspirational, and adaptable by those who would, in principle, adhere to them.

Fast-forward 7 years to adoption by AEA members of "a public statement on cultural competence in evaluation" (American Evaluation Association, 2011). That statement opens with the AEA guiding principle that states: "To ensure recognition, accurate interpretation, and respect for diversity, evaluators should ensure that the members of the evaluation team collectively demonstrate cultural competence" (p. 1). Beyond that overarching principle, the statement offers no other principles of culturally competent evaluation practice. What the statement does offer is several "core concepts [that] are foundational to the pursuit of cultural competence" (p. 1).

Exhibit 31.6 converts these core concepts into principles.

The practices identified and promoted in AEA's cultural competence statement could just as easily be treated as principles. Indeed, given the general nature of the guidance provided, I think they are better understood as principles than practices. The term *practices* suggests concrete behaviors. Principles provide more general guidance. At least that's how I think about the difference. But that distinction, principles versus practices, is a matter of personal preference and utility in this case, not a hard-and-fast categorical imperative. See what you think. Are the four statements below (American Evaluation Association, 2011, pp. 7–8) best thought of as practices or principles? Or does it matter?

1. Acknowledge the complexity of cultural identity.

2. Recognize the dynamics of power.

3. Recognize and eliminate bias in language.

4. Employ culturally appropriate methods.

EXHIBIT 31.6. AEA Culturally Competent Core Concepts Converted to Principles	
Culturally competent core concepts	**Conversion to principles for evaluators**
1. All evaluation reflects culturally influenced norms, values, and ways of knowing—making cultural competence integral to ethical, high-quality evaluation.	Make cultural competence integral to ethical, high-quality evaluation.
2. Given the diversity of cultures within the United States, cultural competence is fluid. An evaluator who is well prepared to work with a particular community is not necessarily competent in another.	Understand cultural competence as specific to each particular cultural community.
3. Cultural competence in evaluation requires that evaluators maintain a high degree of self-awareness and self-examination to better understand how their own backgrounds and other life experiences serve as assets or limitations in the conduct of an evaluation.	Examine and be aware of how your background and other life experiences serve as assets or limitations in the conduct of an evaluation.
4. Culture has implications for all phases of evaluation—including staffing, development, and implementation of evaluation efforts as well as communicating and using evaluation results.	Assess and apply cultural competence to all aspects of evaluation.
Source: American Evaluation Association (2011).	

Here's how I make the distinction between principles and practices. Treating the first statement as a principle, I'll offer an example of a corresponding practice.

Principle 1: Acknowledge the complexity of cultural identity.
   Practice implication: When facilitating introductions in a group invite people to describe the complexity of their identity *intersectionally* (expressing the interconnected nature of social categorizations such as race, class, and gender as they apply to a given individual or group, which creates overlapping and interdependent systems of disadvantage, for example, being a transgender, low-income African American).

Treating each of the four statements above as principles, see if you can identify specific practices that flow from each one.

Principles of Evaluative Thinking

The idea of fostering *evaluative thinking* is an increasingly important direction in the field of evaluation, particularly among people involved in evaluation capacity building (Buckley, Archibald, Hargraves, & Trochim, 2015, p. 375). Helping people learn to think and reason evaluatively has impacts beyond increasing the rigor, credibility, meaningfulness, and use of a particular evaluation. Start with the premise that a healthy and strong democracy depends on an informed citizenry. Evaluation's contribution, then, is to help ensure an informed electorate. Evaluation has a role to play in helping the citizenry weigh evidence and think evaluatively. This involves thinking processes that must be learned. It is not enough to have trustworthy and accurate information (the "informed" part of the "informed citizenry"). People must also know how to use information, that is, to weigh evidence, consider inevitable contradictions and inconsistencies, articulate values, interpret findings and examine assumptions, to note but a few of the things meant by "thinking evaluatively."

Philosopher Hannah Arendt was especially attuned to this foundation of democracy. Having experienced totalitarianism, then having fled it, she devoted much of her life to studying it and its opposite, democracy. She believed that thinking thoughtfully in public deliberations and acting democratically were intertwined. Totalitarianism is built on and sustained by deceit and thought control. In order to resist efforts by the powerful to deceive and control thinking, Arendt believed that people needed to practice thinking. Toward that end she developed "eight exercises in political thought" (Arendt, 1963). She wrote that "experience in thinking . . . can be won, like all experience in doing something, only through practice, through exercises" (p. 4). From this point of view, we might consider every evaluation an opportunity for those involved to practice thinking (Patton, 2002). In that spirit, Exhibit 31.7 offers some principles of evaluative thinking. These principles express both the logic and values of systematic evaluative inquiry, consistent with the AEA guiding principles presented earlier. However, these principles of evaluative thinking make explicit how reasoning and critical questioning undergird evaluation methods.

Principles for Guiding Collaborative Approaches to Evaluation

For excellence in the systematic and rigorous development of a set of principles, I know of no better example than the principles for use in guiding collaborative approaches to evaluation. The principles were developed to guide practice in situations "where evaluation knowledge is collaboratively produced by evaluators and stakeholders" (Shulha, Whitmore, Cousins, Gilbert, & al Hudib, 2016, p. 193). The principles were developed and tested in four phases over a 4-year multiple-method, multiphase study that involved

> two pilot phases exploring the desirability of developing a set of principles; an online questionnaire survey that drew on the expertise of 320 practicing evaluators to identify dimensions, factors or characteristics that enhance or impede success in collaborative approaches in evaluation (CAE); and finally a validation phase involving a subsample of 58 evaluators. (Shulha et al., 2016, p. 193)

Exhibit 31.8 presents the principles, which are viewed as "interconnected and loosely temporally ordered" (p. 193). The temporal order begins with the principle "Clarify motivation for collaboration." The ordering of principles then progresses clockwise, the second one being "Foster meaningful relationships." But these are not rigidly sequential steps. They are ordered and interconnected principles, each of which must be interpreted and adapted contextually.

The developers of the principles caution that they must be interpreted and applied contextually, and understood as an integrated set. Their warning in this regard constitutes generic wisdom that could be boilerplate for any set of principles:

> Two considerations are pivotal to the use of the principles. First, we contend that the set of principles is not a menu from which evaluators ought to choose in undertaking collaborative work. Adherence to individual principles is a matter of degree, as opposed to a "whether-or-not" proposition. In short, we see each principle as being essential to evaluation practice in a collaborative context; the extent

EXHIBIT 31.7. Illustrative Principles of Evaluative Thinking	
These are examples; they are not exhaustive of all possibilities.	
Principle	**Explanation**
1. Be clear.	Be clear about goals and purposes; be clear about what's being evaluated, what data will be collected, what judgments are to be made, and how results will be used—indeed, be as clear as possible about everything.
2. Be intentional.	Know what you want to do and why. Plan your work and work your plan. Think through what you're doing. Consider contingencies.
3. Be accountable.	Systematically examine the extent to which your intentions and hopes work out as planned and accomplish what you want to accomplish.
4. Be specific.	Specificity is related to clarity; specificity enhances mutual understanding and shared meanings.
5. Focus and prioritize.	Be purposeful in deciding what's worth doing and knowing; make decisions about priorities and own the consequences.
6. Be systematic.	Organize and document all that is done.
7. Make assumptions explicit.	Determine what can and cannot be subjected to empirical tests.
8. Draw conclusions.	Have data to support findings and logical explanations for conclusions.
9. Adapt to complexity.	Watch for and adapt to what emerges: nonlinear effects, dynamic interactions, and turbulence in complex dynamic systems.
10. Think systemically.	Examine interrelationships, perspectives, and boundaries, and their implications for evaluation.
11. Make criteria and standards for judgments explicit.	Judgments flow from criteria, values, and standards.
12. Limit generalizations and causal explanations to what data support.	Align conclusions about possible generalizations and attributions of causality with the nature of the data being interpreted.
13. Be culturally sensitive and competent.	Cultural variations and factors are critical to understanding.
14. Be contextually sensitive.	Context matters.
15. Be alert to unanticipated consequences.	Unintended consequences can be as important as those intended.

to which any given principle is important will depend entirely on contextual conditions, circumstances, and complexities. . . .

A second consideration is that the principles should not be prioritized a priori, we lay claim to only a loose temporal order. To reiterate, we reason that a decision about which principle to emphasize and when is likely to be contingent on the purpose of the evaluation, the stage of the evaluation, the context in which the [collaborative] application is being implemented, and the emergence of complexities as the evaluation unfolds. (Shulha et al., 2016, p. 198)

The article in the *American Journal of Evaluation* that presented the principles (Shulha et al., 2016) provides an explanation of each one, examples of how to apply each principle in practice, and evidence from the development process validating the importance of each principle based on feedback and analysis provided by practicing evaluators. This set of principles establishes a

high standard for how principles ought to be developed—and evaluated.

Methodological Principles

Science isn't about authority or white coats; it's about following a method. That method is built on core principles:

▶ precision and transparency
▶ being clear about your methods
▶ being honest about your results, and
▶ drawing a clear line between the results, on the one hand, and your judgment calls about how those results support a hypothesis.
　　　　　—BEN GOLDACRE, *Bad Science* (2009, p. 1)

Thus far this chapter has presented and discussed principles that provide guidance for how evaluations ought to be conducted. In this section I present examples of methodological principles. I do so without commentary. My purpose is to illustrate

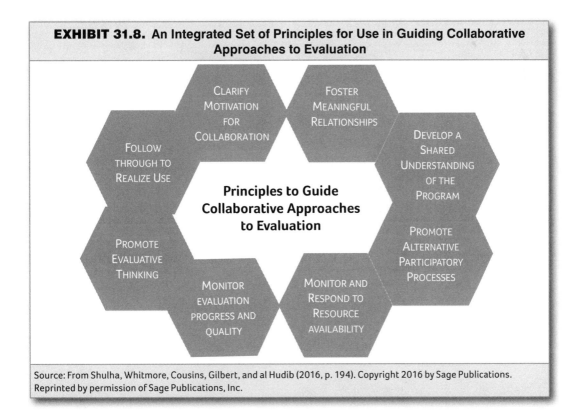

EXHIBIT 31.8. An Integrated Set of Principles for Use in Guiding Collaborative Approaches to Evaluation

CLARIFY MOTIVATION FOR COLLABORATION

FOSTER MEANINGFUL RELATIONSHIPS

FOLLOW THROUGH TO REALIZE USE

DEVELOP A SHARED UNDERSTANDING OF THE PROGRAM

Principles to Guide Collaborative Approaches to Evaluation

PROMOTE EVALUATIVE THINKING

PROMOTE ALTERNATIVE PARTICIPATORY PROCESSES

MONITOR EVALUATION PROGRESS AND QUALITY

MONITOR AND RESPOND TO RESOURCE AVAILABILITY

Source: From Shulha, Whitmore, Cousins, Gilbert, and al Hudib (2016, p. 194). Copyright 2016 by Sage Publications. Reprinted by permission of Sage Publications, Inc.

methodological principles as *a type of principle* to inform the data collection and analysis challenges of evaluation. More generally, the point of including these illustrations of methodological principles is to emphasize that empirical inquiry is not rigidly rules based but rather principles guided. An excellent example is an analysis of the logic of generalization through the lens of five principles common to experiments and ethnographies (Shadish, 1995). As Nobel Prize–winning physicist Percy Bridgman said, "There is no scientific method as such, but the vital feature of the scientist's procedures has been merely to do his utmost with his mind, no holds barred" (quoted in Waller, 2004, p. 106).

Exhibit 31.9 presents practical inquiry principles to get actionable answers. Exhibits 31.10 and 31.11 present principles specific to qualitative evaluation and principles for skilled in-depth interviewing. Taken together, these sets of principles illustrate and illuminate the nature and utility of methodological principles to guide evaluation. Adherence to these principles is evaluable as a form of principles-focused evaluation.

Evaluating Evaluation Principles

This chapter has presented and discussed several sets of principles for evaluators beginning with the AEA guiding principles, which I revised to better conform to the GUIDE criteria for high-quality effectiveness principles. I added three truth-speaking principles (Exhibit 31.4). Next came a review and critique of data visualization principles, followed by principles for culturally competent evaluation practice. That led to principles for evaluative thinking. We then examined the principles for use in guiding collaborative approaches to evaluation as an exemplar of how to develop empirically based and tested principles. The chapter closed with examples of methodological principles: practical inquiry principles to get actionable answers;

EXHIBIT 31.9. Practical Inquiry Principles to Get Actionable Answers

Evaluators, policy analysts, action and applied researchers, community change agents, and communications and organizational development specialists have studied extensively how to conduct inquiries that are useful and actually used. Here is a distillation of what has been learned expressed as principles.

Practical qualitative inquiry principles	Applying the principles in practice	Potential pitfalls
1. Frame the inquiry's purpose as practical and action oriented.	Be clear about the purpose of the study (e.g., to improve the program, practice, or policy based on feedback from knowledgeable interviewees).	Taking a purely academic approach that is interesting and may even yield an academic publication but is not action oriented.
2. Identify and work with people who can bring about change.	Actions and changes have to be done by people who can take action and make changes. Know who they are. Find out what they need to know to act.	Thinking in general audience terms without going through a process of identifying specific intended users and their intended uses (Patton, 2012a).

(continued)

Practical qualitative inquiry principles	Applying the principles in practice	Potential pitfalls
3. Ask action-oriented questions that will yield concrete answers.	Understand the problem at sufficient depth to generate solutions. Specific feedback from knowledgeable key informants may include: What doable improvements do well-informed people in the situation recommend? What practical solutions do they offer? What's the basis for their suggestions? What are the barriers to change? What are the factors supporting change?	Here are examples of interesting epistemological questions that are *not* directly actionable: How do people in a situation arrive at recommendations? How do recommendations emerge from lived experience? These questions make people's thinking process the focus rather than what to do to solve a problem.
4. Work with intended users to facilitate engagement with and interpretation of the findings.	Schedule data engagement sessions with key users as case studies are completed and qualitative analysis unfolds. Do so in a timely fashion that is meaningful and relevant to those who can take action.	Researchers often like to wait until their analysis is complete and ready for publication before sharing findings, attending only to their own timeline. This risks missing key decision points where findings could inform action and may miss opportunities to increase users' understanding and buy-in along the way.
5. Follow through and evaluate the extent to which recommended actions are implemented and if they are, whether they've solved the problem in whole or at least in part (or, alternatively, made the situation worse).	For those committed to having their findings used, the work is not done when the findings are reported. To optimize use, following up with intended users to support action is part of the full process of using findings to make a difference.	Failing to inquire into the unintended consequences and/or negative ripple effects of any findings acted on or recommended actions.

Sources: Patton (2008, 2011, 2012a, 2015a).

EXHIBIT 31.10. Twelve Principles for Qualitative Evaluation

1. Make real-world observations through *naturalistic inquiry*.

2. Stay open, responsive, and flexible through *emergent designs*.

3. Focus on information-rich cases through *purposeful sampling*.

4. Describe what you observe in detail and illuminate people's verbatim perspectives and meanings through rich, in-depth qualitative *data*.

5. Deepen your understanding through *direct personal experience* with and engagement in what you are studying.

6. Balance your critical and creative sides, your cognitive and affective processes, through a stance of *empathetic neutrality*.

7. Cultivate sensitivity to *dynamic processes and systems*.

8. Appreciate and do justice to each person, organization, community, or situation you study through attention to the particular: a *unique case orientation*.

9. Generate insight and understanding through bottom-up *inductive analysis*.

10. Broaden your analysis and interpretation through *contextual sensitivity*.

11. Integrate data through a *holistic perspective*.

12. Communicate authenticity and trustworthiness through *reflexivity:* Own your voice and perspective.

Source: Patton (2015a, p. 75).

EXHIBIT 31.11. Principles for In-Depth Interviewing

Interview principles	Illustrative examples
1. *Ask open-ended questions.* Ask relevant and meaningful open-ended questions that invite thoughtful, in-depth responses that elicit whatever is salient to the interviewee.	"What is a strong memory you have of your first year of high school?" *not* "Do you have any strong memories from high school?"
2. *Be clear.* Ask questions that are clear, focused, understandable, and answerable.	"What was most important to you about your experience?" *not* "What was important that you'll remember and can use and will tell people about and that made the program effective at least as you think about it now?"
3. *Listen.* Attend carefully to responses. Let the interviewees know that they've been heard. Respond appropriately to what you hear.	*Interviewer:* "That's very helpful. You've explained very well why that was important to you."

(continued)

Interview principles	Illustrative examples
4. *Probe as appropriate.* Follow up in complete responses with clarifying probes. Interviewees will only then learn what degree of depth and detail you seek through probes.	*Interviewer:* "It would be helpful to hear more about that. Tell me more about what happened and how you were involved."
5. *Observe.* Watch the interviewee to guide the interactive process. Acknowledge what is going on. Adapt the interview as appropriate to fit the reactions of the person interviewed. Every interview is also an observation.	*Interviewer:* "I can see that the question evoked strong emotions. Take your time, or if you'd like, we can change topics for the moment and come back to this later."
6. *Be both empathic and neutral.* Show interest and offer encouragement nonjudgmentally: empathic neutrality.	*Interviewer:* "I appreciate your willingness to share your story. Every story is unique, and we've heard all kinds of things. There's no right or wrong answer to any of these questions. What matters is that it's your story."
7. *Make transitions.* Help and guide the interviewee through the interview process.	*Interviewer:* "You've been describing how you got into the program. Now the next set of questions is about what you experienced in the program."
8. *Distinguish types of questions.* Separate purely descriptive questions from questions about interpretations and judgments. Distinguish behavior, attitude, knowledge, and feeling questions.	*Descriptive behavior question:* "What did you do in your art class?" *Interpretive opinion question:* "What were the strengths and weaknesses of the class in your opinion?"
9. *Be prepared for the unexpected.* The world can intrude during an interview. Be flexible and responsive.	Despite a commitment to a 2-hour interview, only a half hour may be available. Make the most of it. Interruptions occur. Things may emerge that need more time.
10. *Be present throughout.* Interviewees can tell when the interviewer is distracted, inattentive, or uninterested.	Checking the time regularly, glancing at your text messages, looking around instead of staying engaged with the person talking—these things are noticed.

principles for qualitative evaluation; and principles for skilled in-depth interviewing. Earlier in the book I presented and discussed empowerment evaluation principles, developmental evaluation principles, utilization-focused evaluation principles, and principles to guide principles-focused evaluation. That's a lot of principles! You may be forgiven if you're experiencing principles fatigue. But like the increased stamina that comes with regular exercise, your stamina, capacity, and expertise in being principles-focused will increase substantially with regular engagement, ongoing application, and dedicated reflective practice.

The thrust of this chapter has been to make the case that principles-focused evaluation applies not just to program and organizational principles, but also to principles for evaluators, of which there turn out to be a great many, displaying great variety. Principles for evaluators should be subject to principles-focused evaluation. The GUIDE framework can be applied to principles for evaluators. Evaluating adherence to evaluation principles is a source of our professional accountability and, indeed, stature as a principles-based profession. Being a principles-based profession improves and guides further development of our evaluation practices.

Practice Exercise

While this chapter has presented and discussed a number of evaluation principles, the inventory reviewed here is far from exhaustive. Search for other examples of evaluation, research, scientific inquiry, and/ or methodological principles. Select one example and review the principles put forth against the GUIDE criteria.

CHAPTER 32

Outcome Harvesting Evaluation
Practical Application of Essential Principles

RICARDO WILSON-GRAU

Based in Rio de Janeiro but working internationally, Ricardo Wilson-Grau has become deeply engaged with principles-focused developmental evaluation, contributing to both its theory and practice. He contributed substantively and substantially to conceptualization of the principles for developmental evaluation presented in Chapter 5. His contributions to my work on developmental evaluation and his reviews of early drafts of this book influenced his work on articulating principles for Outcome Harvesting—a principles-based evaluation approach that collects evidence of what has been achieved and works backward to determine whether and how the efforts of social innovators and their interventions contributed to observed and documented changes. Ricardo hosted me in Rio during the 2014 World Cup. During that time the idea for this book was taking shape, as was Ricardo's idea for this chapter. Ricardo epitomizes what it means to be a practical theoretician and a theory-based practitioner. He tests conceptual ideas and insights through his worldwide evaluation practice, and as he does so, *theory and practice become one.* That's what he has done in this chapter. I am grateful to Ricardo for honoring this book with his important and leading-edge work on the principles of Outcome Harvesting.

—M. Q. P.

Outcome Harvesting Evaluation

Outcome Harvesting is an evaluation approach for assessing and learning from social change. It is inspired and informed by Outcome Mapping and utilization-focused evaluation. Beginning in 2002, I developed the approach with colleagues to enable evaluators, grant makers, and managers to identify, formulate, verify, and make sense of changes that an intervention has influenced in a broad range of cutting-edge innovation and development projects and programs around the world. Over these years, I have led Outcome Harvesting evaluative exercises involving almost 500 nongovernmental organizations, networks, government agencies, funding agencies, community-based organizations, research institutes and university programs. Together with coevaluators, I have harvested outcomes in 143 countries on all seven continents through developmental, formative, and summative evaluations. Outcome Harvesting has been used in evaluations of a great diversity of initiatives including the following: human rights advocacy; political, economic, and environmental advocacy; arts and culture; health systems; information and communication technology; conflict and peace; water and sanitation; taxonomy for development; violence against women; rural development; organic agriculture; participatory democracy; waste management; public sector reform; good governance; eLearning; social accountability; and competition, among others.

The essence of Outcome Harvesting is achieving outcomes understood as (1) observable changes in the behavior of individuals, groups, communities, organizations, or institutions, plus (2) what the intervention did that plausibly contributed to them. Some examples of observable changes: a government minister publicly declares she will restrict untendered contracts to under 5% (an action); a civil society organization launches a campaign for governmental transparency (an activity); two political parties join forces to collaborate rather than compete in proposing transparency legislation (relationships); a legislature passes a new anticorruption law (policy); or a government implements norms and procedures for publishing all procurement records (practice). But these behavioral changes are only half an outcome. How the intervention's activities and outputs reasonably influenced each one of these changes is the other half.

The Niche for Outcome Harvesting

▶ *The purpose is social change.* Outcome Harvesting is well suited for situations in which an intervention aims to influence other societal actors to take the initiative to do something new and significantly different in any sphere of human endeavor—political, cultural, social, cultural, and environmental, among others.

▶ *The focus is primarily on outcomes rather than on the activities of an intervention.* Outcome Harvesting is designed for situations where decision makers (as "harvest users") are most interested in learning about what was achieved and how, and not about everything that a project, program, or organization did. In other words, there is an emphasis on effectiveness over efficiency or performance. The approach is also a good fit when the aim of the evaluation is to understand processes of change over time.

▶ *The programming context is complex.* Outcome Harvesting is suitable for programming contexts where relations of cause and effect are not fully understood. Conventional evaluation compares planned outcomes with what is actually achieved, and planned activities with what was actually done. In the complex environments that characterize most social change, however, objectives and the paths to achieving them are largely unpredictable and predefined objectives and theories of change must be modified over time to respond to changes in the context. Outcome Harvesting is particularly appropriate in these more dynamic and uncertain environments with many unintended outcomes, including negative ones.

▶ *The exercise is evaluative.* Outcome Harvesting can serve to track changes in the behavior of societal actors influenced by an intervention—that is, to monitor. It is designed, however, to go beyond this and support learning about those achievements.

(Monitoring combined with evaluation-based learning is commonly called M&E, or MEL.) It can be used for ongoing, mid-term, and end-of-term evaluations. It can be used by itself or in combination with other approaches.

Six Flexible Steps

An Outcome Harvest follows six interactive steps (see Exhibit 32.1):

1. Design the Outcome Harvest with evaluation questions based on the principal uses by the primary users of the process and findings.
2. Review documentary material to draft potential outcome descriptions of who changed their behavior, how the intervention contributed, and other relevant data such as the significance of the outcome.
3. Engage with human sources of information to complete outcome descriptions and formulate additional ones.
4. Substantiate the veracity of select outcome descriptions with independent third parties.
5. Analyze and interpret the outcome information to answer the evaluation questions.
6. Support the use of the Outcome Harvest findings.

Outcome Harvesting must be customized to the specific needs and context of each evaluation. In over 40 applications of the approach, I have never followed the six steps in the same way. Furthermore, the harvesting process itself is complex. The

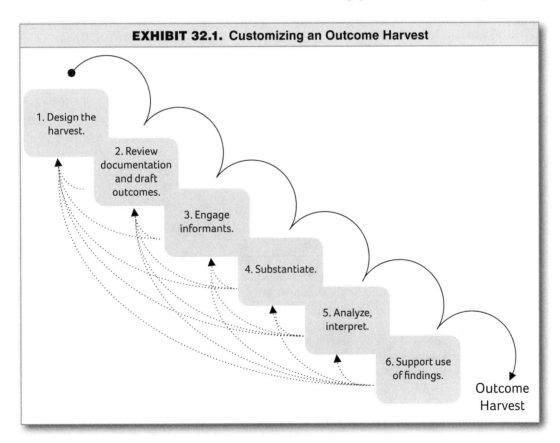

EXHIBIT 32.1. Customizing an Outcome Harvest

1. Design the harvest.
2. Review documentation and draft outcomes.
3. Engage informants.
4. Substantiate.
5. Analyze, interpret.
6. Support use of findings.

Outcome Harvest

evaluation plan evolves and adapts as the evaluation process unfolds.

My experience has shown that a successful Outcome Harvest must consider but not necessarily take each one of the six steps. For example, there may not be any written, audio, or visual documentation to review (step 2), or substantiation (step 4) may not be useful or feasible. More important, design decisions are made throughout the harvest and not just at the beginning. Users and uses may shift as outcomes are identified. New sources of outcomes may emerge. The people to be engaged as sources of information (step 3) will often depend on what is uncovered in the document review (step 2). What outcomes should be substantiated (step 4), by whom and how, is unknowable until you have the outcomes in hand. Similarly, how to analyze outcomes depends on what outcomes are harvested; how to interpret them may finally be clear only after you have seen them and the patterns they reveal (step 5). How to support use of the process and findings usually is not be evident right from the beginning. Consequently, Outcome Harvesting requires the application of principles in making decisions throughout the six steps of the harvest.

Outcome Harvesting as a Principles-Based Approach

I want to set the stage for introducing and explaining the principles of Outcome Harvesting by articulating why I resonate so strongly to a principles-based approach to evaluation. Over the decade that I developed Outcome Harvesting, there have been three constants that I believe explain the importance of the 10, for now, principles. The first constant was that all the 40+ projects, programs, and organizations I evaluated operated in substantially *complex* and *dynamic* situations. In the formative years, almost all the experiences were evaluating international social change networks or the

programs (vs. the grantees) of international development donors, ranging from private funders such as the Ford Foundation and the Open Society Institute to the multilateral UN and the World Bank. Their managers had found that conventional evaluation approaches were unworkable or at least not very useful because of the considerable uncertainty they had faced when planning their interventions and the dynamism they had encountered during implementation. Some had to cope with considerable disagreement about the nature of the challenge they were to confront and others on what they should do to address it. Some had to manage disagreement about both the challenge and what they could do about it. Thus, innovation and experimentation characterized their work. All of them had been unsure about the relations of cause and effect between what they planned to do and what they would achieve and, therefore, their results were substantially unknown until outcomes emerged.

As they implemented their interventions they had to cope with contextual turbulence and change. As the incidence of external actors and factors shifted constantly and often dramatically, so did their programming; unexpected needs and unforeseen results had become the norm. The complexity was so substantial that the managers agreed they had had to change their plans so much that it made no sense to assess if they had done and achieved what was in their original plans.

The second constant in the experience of developing Outcome Harvesting was the wide *diversity* represented by the projects, programs, and organizations who contracted me to evaluate their work. They ranged across the seven continents and a variety of social change and development topics.

The third constant was *participation* to meet a double-edged challenge: I had to develop a mode of evaluation that respond to very different content needs while ensuring evaluation rigor. The participatory evaluation solution I found was four dimensional.

Four Dimensions of Participatory Outcome Harvesting

First, the Outcome Mapping methodology created by the International Development Research Centre (IDRC) provided the brilliant concept of changes in societal actors as the bottom line for assessing social change and development. All of the stakeholders agreed that whatever the nature and context of their interventions, at the end of the day each one aimed to influence outcomes defined as individuals, groups, communities, or other organizations or institutions changing their actions, activities, relationships, policies, or practices. Thus, Outcome Harvesting offered a common conceptual denominator for social change and development results that resonated with all the stakeholders. It required, however, their participation in order to contextualize case by case the indicators of the specific outcomes they would consider important progress toward fulfilling their mission.

Second, Michael Quinn Patton's *Utilization-Focused Evaluation* (Patton, 2008, 2012a) provided an equally splendid approach to evaluation that focused on use from beginning to end. Everyone knew that the evaluation process would necessarily be a constant adaptation as data emerged. Involving the primary intended users in the decision making, including reconsideration of the principal intended uses, as the evaluation progressed made a lot of sense to everybody. In practice, the involvement of the primary users proved vitally important for the development of the Outcome Harvesting methodology, which would not have been possible without the contribution of the dozens of users who participated in the ongoing decision making during the evaluation process.

Third, every external evaluation I did was with one or two coevaluators who were content experts. I would take the methodological lead and they provided the subject-matter expertise. In the case of internal evaluations, someone from the project,

program, or organization being evaluated would fill the need for that expertise. As with the primary users, my coevaluators were essential to the development of the methodology. Of the many who have served as coevaluators with me, there are around a dozen who today make up the core of a vibrant community of practice. They include some former users who have become consultants and have Outcome Harvesting in their toolboxes.

Fourth, and closing a circle of usefulness, it quickly became clear that the most accurate identification and formulation of outcomes, in the first instance at least, is best made by the project or program staff who are closest to the action. They are the ones who know, and are motivated to share what they know, about whom they have influenced to change, in what ways, when, and where.

The Challenges of Customizing and Adapting Evaluations, While Maintaining Fidelity, Led to Identifying and Elaborating Outcome Harvesting Principles

Complexity, dynamism, and diversity plus a highly participatory process were the crucible in which the six steps of Outcome Harvesting were forged, along with the awareness that each of those steps had to be customized for each evaluation design and adapted in the course of the evaluation process. Over time, I found that the pressures created by complexity, constant change, diversity, and participation, coupled with the usual demands of my clients, tended to undermine fidelity to the concepts behind each Outcome Harvesting step. The methodology is counterintuitive in many ways. For example, in order to capture unintended outcomes, it is important to turn the normal evaluation process on its head and look first for what was achieved and only then determine how the intervention contributed. Similarly, the vibrant participation of those being evaluated runs against the ethos of the external, independent evaluation norm, even though in the substantiation step the evaluator verifies the accuracy and deepens the understanding of the information provided by the initial, internal sources. It was noteworthy that I also found that colleagues with less experience tended to have more difficulties maintaining these and many other characteristics of Outcome Harvesting as an alternative to—versus an improvement on—more conventional evaluation. In sum, I was concerned if not anguished to find as many misuses and abuses of Outcome Harvesting as creative advances in developing it further. Therefore, in the past year I have been promoting an understanding of what, based on my experience, are the principles underlying the six steps of Outcome Harvesting.

Because adapting Outcome Harvesting's six steps varies case by case, the guidance of the underlying principles is essential. In my experience, faulty application of Outcome Harvesting is due mainly to evaluators misunderstanding, misusing, or simply not taking into account all of the principles. All 10 principles, adapted of course to context, must be consciously considered to ensure an effective Outcome Harvest. Exhibit 32.2 presents an overview of the principles.

The 10 Principles of Outcome Harvesting

Principle 1: Ensure usefulness throughout the evaluation.

Since Outcome Harvesting is an evaluation approach that faces considerable uncertainty and dynamism at the moment of planning but also during implementation, its utilization focus must prevail from beginning to end. Thus, it is not only at the initial moment of design (step 1) that you focus on primary intended users and their principal uses, along with the consequences of establishing those boundaries. Why?

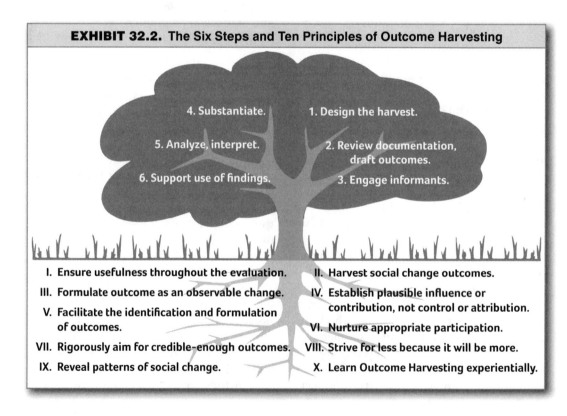

EXHIBIT 32.2. The Six Steps and Ten Principles of Outcome Harvesting

4. Substantiate.

5. Analyze, interpret.

6. Support use of findings.

1. Design the harvest.

2. Review documentation, draft outcomes.

3. Engage informants.

I. Ensure usefulness throughout the evaluation.

III. Formulate outcome as an observable change.

V. Facilitate the identification and formulation of outcomes.

VII. Rigorously aim for credible-enough outcomes.

IX. Reveal patterns of social change.

II. Harvest social change outcomes.

IV. Establish plausible influence or contribution, not control or attribution.

VI. Nurture appropriate participation.

VIII. Strive for less because it will be more.

X. Learn Outcome Harvesting experientially.

First, as the findings emerge, the users, as well as their uses, may change. For example, their staff begins to learn so much (in step 3) that sometimes the users will declare capacity building as a process use and even tap additional funds (step 1). Second, even if users and uses do not change, as the evaluation unfolds, decisions will be required to enhance the usefulness of the findings. For example, in the review of documentation (step 2) there may be so many potential outcomes that criteria have to be agreed on for how to prioritize the information to be collected. Or once the potential outcomes have been harvested, who should be engaged in order to complete them and identify additional outcomes (step 3) may turn out to be different than originally thought.

The danger of not keeping the focus of the harvest on its usefulness is demonstrated by a major evaluation for a leading Dutch funding agency. We whittled down the original 25 evaluation questions to five, all agreed on with the primary users when designing the evaluation. Over the months of implementing the evaluation, however, we never revisited those five questions in the light of the outcomes that were emerging, nor did we do so at the moment of using the outcome data to answer the evaluation questions. As a result, although we provided solid evidence-based answers and conclusions to the five questions, the answers to one question turned out to be useless and for another only partially useful. This was because the carefully crafted but negotiated questions did not express what the users really needed to know.

The lesson is that users and evaluators alike must accept a continuous responsibility to ensure the Outcome Harvesting process and findings correspond to original but also emergent uses, and to the evaluation questions derived from them. Only in this way can people "subjected" to an evaluation become the true subjects with agency and the corresponding empowerment that participation brings.

Principle 2: Harvest social change outcomes.

Like Outcome Mapping, Outcome Harvesting focuses on outcomes understood as societal actors changing the way they do things (or desisting from doing things). The criterion for a social change outcome is a modification in the character or nature of a behavior. The change may be comparatively small, but it must be a distinct change in an individual action or set of activities, a relationship, a policy, or a practice. Societal actors taking the initiative to do something new and significantly different generally means they alter or modify rather than improve what they had been doing. Therefore, a societal actor doing more of something or doing it better, while important, usually does not count as an outcome. For example, a government ministry reducing untendered contracts from 50% to 48% over those granted in the previous year would not count as an outcome whereas cutting in half the percentage of untendered contracts would be.

Furthermore, a societal actor not taking action or not changing course in a tumultuous situation can also be a social change outcome. For instance, stopping a torturer from torturing is an outcome, as is persuading an environmental minister to hold fast to regulations under the pressures engendered by an economic crisis.

I qualify with "generally" and "usually" because the context in the end determines if a change is an outcome. For example, the government of Denmark or Finland publishing its procurement records 3 years in a row would not be an outcome, whereas North Korea or Afghanistan doing so would probably be one. (The first two countries are at the top and the last two at the bottom of the Transparency International Corruption Perceptions Index 2015, at *www.transparency.org/cpi2015*.) So, an evaluator is well advised to define clearly with primary users what counts as an outcome and why, taking into account the context as well as the nature of the change.

Principle 3: Formulate an outcome as an observable change.

To qualify as having achieved an outcome, an individual, group, community, organization, or institution must demonstrate that it is doing something different. This often is not as straightforward as it appears. For example, many social change projects and programs carry out capacity-building work to strengthen the learning of knowledge (cognitive), attitudes (affective), and skills (psychomotor). They may be tempted to report as an outcome a societal actor's new understanding of an issue, or heightened awareness or sensitivity to the issue. As important as this learning may be, it does not count as outcomes until evidenced in changes in behavior. Thus, the outcome would be what the societal actor does differently as a result of that new knowledge, attitude, or skill.

For example, "civil society organizations are empowered" or "Members of Parliament have greater awareness of the need to legislate against corruption" are not outcomes. In contrast, "civil society organizations launch a social networking campaign against government corruption" and "a majority of parliamentarians vote to approve a new anti-corruption law" would be outcomes. There are, of course, exceptions, and they by and large depend on the context. For example, in a deeply patriarchal society, a man daring to attend a gender-awareness workshop for the first time is most likely an outcome, regardless of whether he subsequently takes action that demonstrates that his gender consciousness was raised during the workshop.

Equally important, through Outcome Harvesting you learn what the outcome was, and what the intervention did to contribute to it, but not necessarily the societal actor's motivation for the demonstrated novel behavior. New knowledge about the potential of social networking for advocacy work or greater understanding or awareness gained through the capacity development program may or may not be the reasons why the civil society organizations joined forces or why parliamentarians passed the law. The reasons why they took those actions could be any of a myriad of political, economic, social, cultural, or personal reasons that would have to be explored using other evaluative tools. Nonetheless, through Outcome Harvesting you can identify opinions about the actor's motivations or mix in a method to explain the new behavior, for example, engaging a trained psychologist to interview societal actors and render an expert opinion.

Principle 4: Establish plausible influence or contribution, not control or attribution.

An observable, demonstrated change in the behavior of another societal actor is necessary but not sufficient to consider it a result of the activities and outputs of an intervention and thus an outcome. There has to a reasonable relationship of cause–effect between what the intervention did and the outcome. To do this, Outcome Harvesting distinguishes between an intervention's outputs and its outcomes by the degree of control the intervention has over the result: outputs are controlled; outcomes are influenced. See Exhibit 32.3.

For example, in over two dozen evaluations of funding agency and donor programs that I have led, what the grantee did with the grant, as innovative as it often was, consistently was considered an output of the grant-making activity and not an outcome. The grantmaker's outcomes, albeit all indirect, were the changes in third parties influenced through the grantee's grant-funded activities. The Outcome Harvesting reasoning is that, on the one hand, the grantee was not influenced to change as a result of the grant but rather previously had decided to change and proposed how to do so in the funding proposal. On the other, through the funding agreement the grantmaker substantially controlled what

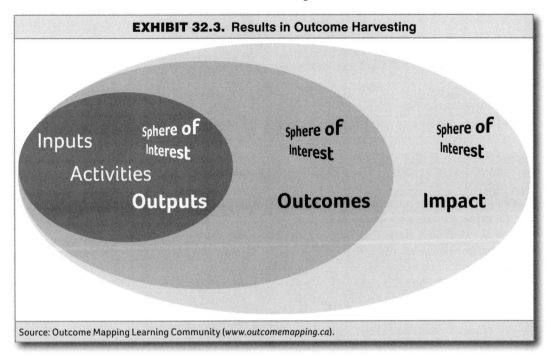

EXHIBIT 32.3. Results in Outcome Harvesting

Source: Outcome Mapping Learning Community (*www.outcomemapping.ca*).

was to be done with the funds. There are always exceptions, of course. For example, if a grantee unexpectedly changes strategy or direction as a result of a grantmaker's inspiration (but not of its funding), that may be a direct outcome. In the case of a conservative subsistence farmers' cooperative, a grant to convert to organic agriculture may sweeten the decision to take the enormous risks involved but not determine it. Thus, if the grantmaker facilitated the cooperative members' decision to take the great risk of investing their land and time to try out organic agriculture, then it could count as an outcome.

In addition to outcomes being directly or indirectly influenced and not controlled by an intervention's activities, they generally are only partially a result of the intervention. That is, an outcome can rarely be solely attributed to one intervention because in social change so many other actors and factors are present. In effect, an outcome is within an intervention's sphere of influence but not fully controlled; this contrasts with the intervention's inputs, activities, and outputs, which are basically controlled. There must be a reasonable cause–effect relationship of what the intervention did that in a small or large way, directly or indirectly, intentionally or not, contributed to, but did not control, the change. And, there will generally be other variables that contributed to the outcome.

Principle 5: Support the identification and formulation of outcomes.

Outcome Harvesting requires that evaluators serve as facilitators of a joint inquiry with the people who serve as sources of information. Evaluators are not experts wielding measuring sticks to assess what was done and what was achieved that can be attributed to the intervention. Instead, evaluators support the people who are providing information to craft concrete, verifiable descriptions of what has been achieved and how. This often requires overcoming the erroneous popular assumption that the Outcome Harvesting evaluator is testing informants and making judgments about what they know. The evaluator's role in harvesting data is to actively support their participation. For instance, one reason why evaluators review documentation (step 2) before engaging with sources of information (step 3) to review potential outcomes and identify additional ones is to demonstrate to program staff that the evaluators engage with them only after the evaluators have done everything they can to identify outcomes on their own. The evaluator is very hands on: "ping-ponging"—going back and forth two, three, or more times—to explain and exemplify what is required, raise questions, and suggest phrasing to arrive together at succinct, well-crafted, verifiable outcome descriptions.

For example, before engaging with the human sources of information, the evaluator attempts to find answers to questions about this incomplete but potential outcome (step 2) found in a report: "Members of Parliament vote to approve a new anti-corruption law." The evaluator looks in documentation or on the Internet for the date of the vote, the number of parliamentarians who voted in favor and against, and the name of the law. Only after exhausting the available documentary sources, the evaluator engages with live sources.

Furthermore, an outcome formulation must be intelligible to a reader without specialized knowledge about the topic or the context. The reader must be able to understand what changed solely from the outcome description. Thus, the evaluator does not simply passively raise questions or identify difficult-to-read phrases when engaging with the sources but suggests editing. For example, instead of declaring that the statement "two political parties joined forces to collaborate rather than compete in proposing transparency legislation" is unclear, the evaluator suggests alternative wording: "In May 2016, the Conservative and Socialist parties agreed to draft together a transparency law rather than individually propose two separate drafts." She or he

then asks the source if that rendering of the outcome is correct.

Evaluators also make sure the description provides sufficient concrete quantitative and qualitative information so that the formulation can be verified. This usually requires ping-ponging back and forth a couple of times. The evaluators do not, however, at this point make judgments about merit, value, or worth of the outcomes but support informants to do so, if that is part of the useful information being collected (steps 2 and 3). (The evaluators' interpretative role comes in step 5.) That is, the final formulation of the intervention's outcomes is determined by the sources of information and how the outcomes are formulated (see principle 9, on p. 318). Of course, the evaluators ensure the exercise is a professional, systematic, data-based inquiry that upholds the honesty and integrity of the entire evaluation process and generates credible data.

Principle 6: Nurture appropriate participation.

The participatory principle in Outcome Harvesting is a methodological imperative. Whether or not someone is a participant depends on his or her role in the evaluation. There are three categories. First, the focus on usefulness that undergirds the approach requires that primary intended users be periodically involved throughout the process and not just in the moment of design (step 1). As the evaluation unfolds, they revise and make new decisions about forthcoming steps, or even decide to return to an earlier step. For example, in the light of the potential outcomes extracted from documentation (step 2), users may modify an evaluation question. They may also decide different people should serve as sources of information to revise those draft outcomes and add others (step 3). Once the outcomes are in hand, they must make decisions about substantiation (step 4) and about the classification and interpretative lenses (step 5) as well. The appropriate support for their use of the process and findings (step 6) is often only possible to decide once the findings are reported.

Second, Outcome Harvesting engages with human sources of information (steps 3 and 4) based on their knowledge of what the intervention has achieved and how it was achieved, and on their availability. For example, generally the people to be consulted in the first instance are the intervention's staff in the field because they are closest to the action. They are the ones who know what changes in other societal actors their activities and outputs have influenced. They also are the people most motivated and willing to devote the time to sharing what they know—the outcomes will be their outcomes (not the evaluator's).

The third category of participants is the substantiators: individuals who are independent of the intervention but knowledgeable about one or more of the outcomes and give an authoritative opinion on the veracity of an outcome. They too require personalized attention. Again, evaluators are not assessing their knowledge but requesting that they share it. They should be approached individually, whether virtually or in person. Their responses should be reviewed for coherence. For example, if they say they only partially agree or disagree with an outcome formulation but do not explain why, evaluators should follow up with them. Often, disagreement is not with the accuracy of the written description of what was achieved or how, but with its completeness; the substantiator believes additional information should be included. The only way to be sure what substantiators mean is to engage with them so that their participation is effective.

Lastly, one of the principal obstacles to effective participation in Outcome Harvesting is misunderstanding the time required. First there is clock time. Primary users must understand that they will invest

hours (but probably not days) of time over the course of the Outcome Harvest. Even more crucially, people who serve as sources of information (step 3) must be prepared to also invest hours of time stretched over weeks; the first-time formulation of outcomes may take up to 1 hour each on average; getting it right may stretch those 60 minutes over days and perhaps weeks. On the other hand, substantiators only require a few minutes to respond by e-mail to give their opinion on an outcome. Of course, if they are interviewed it will take more of their time.

Regarding calendar time, since an Outcome Harvest usually requires that one step is completed before another can begin, meeting deadlines is vitally important. Nevertheless, a harvest will extend over a number of weeks and most probably 3, 4, or more months. Thus, the conventional 2–3 weeks of calendar (and clock) time of an evaluator or evaluation team going to the field to collect data and write up their report rarely will make sense for Outcome Harvesting.

Principle 7: Rigorously aim for credible-enough outcomes.

At the heart of all scientific debate throughout history has been the burning question: *What counts as credible evidence and by what criteria shall credibility be judged?*

—PATTON, 2015a, p. 695

Since Outcome Harvesting is a utilization-focused methodology, the criterion for quality and credibility of harvested data is deeply pragmatic: Thus, epistemologically, "what is useful, is true" (Patton, 2015a, p. 681). Nonetheless, one of the principal uses of evaluation findings is accountability to stakeholders other than the primary intended users. And because Outcome Harvesting is highly participatory, it must contend with scrutiny and questions about the trustworthiness of the process and the believability and accuracy of the findings. Since credibility depends in great measure on the trust and demonstrated competence of the evaluators, their application of rigorous evaluative thinking is a principal means to ensure that the quality of the data and the Outcome Harvesting exercise is credible, as well as useful.

Credibility is not only subjective but also relative. No findings have a 100% level of confidence and a 0% margin of error. Therefore, in Outcome Harvesting the goal is to generate data that are sufficiently credible—no more, no less—for the primary intended users' principal uses. For example, in the evaluation of 10 World Bank Institute projects, the 20% of outcomes whose accuracy was most questionable to me in my role of external evaluator were substantiated because this would make the whole set of outcomes credible enough for the audience of the evaluation. In the evaluation of a Ford Foundation global program, no substantiation at all was required because the purpose was limited to the program officer learning what her three dozen grantees considered were their outcomes—how they had contributed. In another instance, the three donors of a Latin American human rights network selected the outcomes that they wanted to be checked for accuracy with their own consultants in the region. Thus, the bottom line is that the Outcome Harvesting process and findings must be credible enough for the principal uses of the evaluation.

Principle 8: Strive for less because it will be more.

Through an evaluation using Outcome Harvesting there are crucial moments when evaluators must ensure that the information they are harvesting is both useful and plentiful enough to serve as evidence with which to answer the evaluation questions. Experience has shown that harvesting less will generally be more productive than scything for more, as counterintuitive

as it may appear. Formulating outcomes is time-consuming, regardless of whether the source of information provides the data in written or verbal form. For example, if you limit quantitatively the number of outcomes to 5–10, or to those of the top three priority projects, or to the most significant outcomes, your sources of information will be motivated to do everything they can to meet that goal, whereas asking for all the most significant outcomes motivates most people to do less.

Principle 9: Reveal patterns of social change.

The true value of an outcome harvest is not collecting individual outcomes demonstrating the way the change they represent happened over time. Exhibit 32.4 illustrates how a World Bank Institute project strengthening implementation of legislation on access to information across Latin America visualized the process of change represented by 22 outcomes it influenced over 24 months.

Principle 10: Learn Outcome Harvesting experientially.

Over the years, I have written extensively, given dozens of 1-, 2-, and 3-day workshops and answered hundreds of questions from people who learned about Outcome Harvesting and were trying to apply it. In addition, I myself have applied the methodology with over a dozen coevaluators who were new to Outcome Harvesting. It is clear to me that Outcome Harvesting is learned through experience. You understand the steps and principles by applying them. Equally important, with rare exceptions, the approach is learned best when that direct experience harvesting outcomes is supported through critical dialogue by one, two, or more colleagues—a coevaluator, a coach, a mentor, a methodologist—experienced in Outcome Harvesting. That is, the principle of learning Outcome Harvesting experientially can

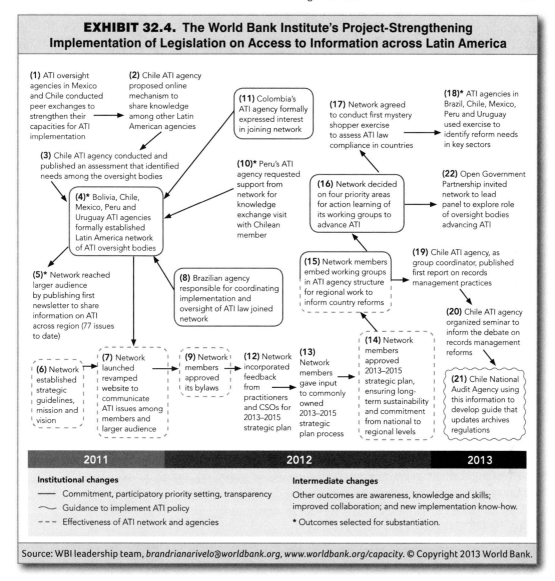

EXHIBIT 32.4. The World Bank Institute's Project-Strengthening Implementation of Legislation on Access to Information across Latin America

(1) ATI oversight agencies in Mexico and Chile conducted peer exchanges to strengthen their capacities for ATI implementation

(2) Chile ATI agency proposed online mechanism to share knowledge among other Latin American agencies

(11) Colombia's ATI agency formally expressed interest in joining network

(17) Network agreed to conduct first mystery shopper exercise to assess ATI law compliance in countries

(18)* ATI agencies in Brazil, Chile, Mexico, Peru and Uruguay used exercise to identify reform needs in key sectors

(3) Chile ATI agency conducted and published an assessment that identified needs among the oversight bodies

(10)* Peru's ATI agency requested support from network for knowledge exchange visit with Chilean member

(16) Network decided on four priority areas for action learning of its working groups to advance ATI

(22) Open Government Partnership invited network to lead panel to explore role of oversight bodies advancing ATI

(4)* Bolivia, Chile, Mexico, Peru and Uruguay ATI agencies formally established Latin America network of ATI oversight bodies

(8) Brazilian agency responsible for coordinating implementation and oversight of ATI law joined network

(15) Network members embed working groups in ATI agency structure for regional work to inform country reforms

(19) Chile ATI agency, as group coordinator, published first report on records management practices

(5)* Network reached larger audience by publishing first newsletter to share information on ATI across region (77 issues to date)

(20) Chile ATI agency organized seminar to inform the debate on records management reforms

(6) Network established strategic guidelines, mission and vision

(7) Network launched revamped website to communicate ATI issues among members and larger audience

(9) Network members approved its bylaws

(12) Network incorporated feedback from practitioners and CSOs for 2013–2015 strategic plan

(13) Network members gave input to commonly owned 2013–2015 strategic plan process

(14) Network members approved 2013–2015 strategic plan, ensuring long-term sustainability and commitment from national to regional levels

(21) Chile National Audit Agency using this information to develop guide that updates archives regulations

2011   **2012**   **2013**

Institutional changes
—— Commitment, participatory priority setting, transparency
〜 Guidance to implement ATI policy
- - - Effectiveness of ATI network and agencies

Intermediate changes
Other outcomes are awareness, knowledge and skills; improved collaboration; and new implementation know-how.
* Outcomes selected for substantiation.

Source: WBI leadership team, *brandrianarivelo@worldbank.org, www.worldbank.org/capacity.* © Copyright 2013 World Bank.

best be achieved by engaging in what Paulo Freire would have called social praxis (see Chapter 18).

In many professions, practical experience gained through being an apprentice, intern, trainee, mentee, or junior practitioner is widely considered to be an essential part of becoming competent. In my own professional life prior to becoming an evaluator, there are three examples that reinforce this principle that an innovation is best learned experientially and is often most effective when it is supported by someone more expert than the learner. The first example was in the 1970s when I directed the Latin American program of Friends World College. Through this university-level educational experiment students applied the principle: *define and pursue your own objectives through direct experience with what you want to learn about.* Thus, each student designed and carried out projects (internships, apprenticeships, volunteer work, travel, field study), complemented by reading and writing and supported by faculty and field advisers. This educational mode worked best for students who were open to the unconventional, self-directed, and self-critical. When successful—as measured by what students did with their lives afterward—it indeed enabled them "to become informed and responsible individuals who can approach their experience critically and creatively in order to transform themselves and contribute to the transformation of their world" (no less!). The two key ingredients were direct experience and the support of others.

The second experience was directing the Inforpress Centroamericana news agency from Guatemala in the 1980s. This agency became the source of choice worldwide for weekly bilingual economic and political analysis of events in this decade of revolution and counterinsurgency in Central America. The majority of the Spanish-language staff were university professors who fled the repression of academia. The English-language staff were bilingual, competent writers, but none were trained or experienced journalists. Thus, we had to train our own journalists in a highly politicized and violent context. All shared a belief in, as Quakers would say, speaking truth to power, or in the words of the 19th-century Swiss socialist Ferdinand Lassalle, "To tell the truth is revolutionary." They learned journalism on the job applying principles such as: *Every article must contain evidence-based analysis but not argue the position of any political faction.* Success resulted from the combination of doing economic and political analysis week in and week out, a trustworthy work environment, and mentoring by the two experienced journalists.

The third experience was in the early 1990s when I was a senior manager with Greenpeace International based in Amsterdam. One of the main principles of the most successful environmental campaigning organization at the time was: *In the face of environmental evil, take nonviolent, confrontational action.* This was a time when Greenpeace had been growing at 40% a year and expanding geographically. Multicultural Greenpeace campaigners learned the art and craft of applying principles such as this one by organizing and carrying out direct actions under the wing of more experienced Anglo-Saxon campaigners. There were some failures—including my own!—but learning experientially was the basis of successful campaigning.

In sum, the challenge of people making Outcome Harvesting their own, of developing the capacity to understand and apply the steps and principles, is, I believe, best achieved experientially—by harvesting outcomes . . . with the support of someone with more experience. Naturally, the need diminishes with . . . more experience.

Using Outcome Harvesting in a Principles-Focused Evaluation

By way of summary, Outcome Harvesting not only is underpinned by principles but can be used to evaluate program or intervention principles themselves. Say a useful evaluation question is "To what extent are we applying our principles to achieve outcomes?" Once you harvest the outcomes, you would assess how the intervention contributed evidence of the application of principles. Similarly, if you want to answer the question "How do our outcomes reflect our principles?" then you would examine the outcomes themselves for manifestations of the project's, the program's, or the organization's principles.

Furthermore, there is a third modality: you can harvest outcomes defined as the demonstration of principles in action: "To what extent are we contributing to the application of principles by other societal actors?" This could be done in a developmental, formative, or summative evaluation. In this way, Outcome Harvesting is a principles-based evaluation approach to use in doing principles-focused evaluations.

Finally, principles-focused evaluation can be used to evaluate the extent to which the principles of Outcome Harvesting are meaningful within a given context, the extent to which the Outcome Harvesting principles are adhered to in practice, and the extent to which the results of Outcome Harvesting are useful and actually used. Principles-focused evaluation is the appropriate framework for evaluation (and meta-evaluation) of principles-based evaluation approaches.

Acknowledgments

People who commented invaluably on a draft of this reflection on principles and Outcome Harvesting are: Emilia Bretan, Heather Britt, Mark Cabaj, Madeline Church, Barbara Klugman, Paul Kosterink, Jeph Mathias, John Mauremootoo, Kornelia Rassmann, Wolfgang Richert, Heidi Schaeffer, Goele Scheers, Richard Smith, Sara Vaca, and Bob Williams. I am most grateful for their innumerable contributions, but, of course, in the end the limitations of this reflection are mine alone since they are based on my experience with Outcome Harvesting.

CHAPTER 33

Reflections of a Principles-Focused Evaluator

What's in a Name?

DONNA PODEMS

Donna Podems is a principles-driven evalua-tor. She is first and foremost a principles-driven person, which makes it relatively natural for her to engage in principles-focused evaluation. I don't make these designations lightly and Donna wouldn't make them at all. Being prin-ciples driven isn't something she decided to be-come. It's who she is. It's who she's been since I first met her as an entering graduate student and became her PhD adviser in the customized program she created for her doctorate special-izing in evaluation.

Living and working in South Africa, Donna has become a global evaluator. As I was finish-ing this book she was completing a book on democratic evaluation using South Africa as a case study. She has written about feminist eval-uation (Bamberger & Podems, 2002; Podems, 2010, 2014b), utilization-focused evaluation (Podems, 2007), and evaluator competences (Podems, 2014a). These writings and her exten-sive evaluation practice have been anchored in principles. In this chapter she reflects on nam-ing principles-focused evaluation as a distinct approach in which *what she does and what she calls what she does become one*. My thanks to Donna for sharing her important and insightful reflections.

—M. Q. P.

Engaging with Principles

I was drawn to principles-focused evalua-tion before it had a designation, a title, or a label; drawn to it like a moth to a flame. En-gaging with principles, an often indiscern-ible yet very present determinant, tosses me smack into principles-focused evaluation. While I seem to consistently tangle with principles in nearly all my evaluation work, I am never explicitly asked to engage with them. Nor do I often start the evaluation process with a request to evaluate an orga-nization's principles. Rather, in evaluative processes I often stumble into confounding situations where principles-focused evaluation proves useful in a myriad of ways. This chapter looks at four evaluation processes that each bring a different lesson, and a different use, for principles-focused evaluation.

Grasping Principles-Focused Evaluation in a Grassroots Organization

What's in a name? Everything. Like the word *asshole*. Calling someone this word is not an endearment, a compliment, or meant to instill a sense of pride. A card game that encourages players to call each other this name is at the root of my first story, and takes place within an organization that purports to encourage and build the broken spirit and confidence of severely abused, neglected, and forgotten children.

The fieldwork for my doctoral dissertation took place in a small nonprofit organization (NPO) that worked with disadvantaged and abused children in Southern Africa. My research sought to understand how donors' M&E requirements influenced the nonprofit's culture and goals. This meant intensive observation and continued discussions with the NPO staff over a 2-year period. As a way to thank the NPO for allowing me to conduct my research, I volunteered to fill a role previously held by the very busy and overworked director: the M&E role.

The organization worked with boys between the ages of 12 and 15 who had committed a serious offense, such as rape or burglary, and rehabilitate them back into society. Their hope was to divert the boys from their path of crime, which was leading them straight into the formal penal system, a system that would likely have dire consequences on their young lives. Using my own research process and those required in my role as their M&E person, I was able to extract the organization's theory of use. The NPO believed that engaging the youth in various types of intensive outdoor therapy would instill a sense of self-pride, teach values, and enable these youth to reflect on their choices, understand right from wrong, and build their self-esteem. The staff played an integral role in every intervention and served as role models and mentors to the youth. With a feeling of self-worth and instilled values such as not harming others, the youth would reenter society on a path that led away from a life of crime.

The young boys came with assorted histories, though a common thread among most included being gang members, having been severely beaten or raped multiple times, not living with either parent, and no longer attending school. Anger and low self-esteem were common, and the boys often lashed out at others.

The NPO initiated the boys into their program through individual engagement, group discussion, and wilderness camps. The wilderness camps have tough days, including intense therapy, and long, hard hikes through the mountains, with the evenings more relaxed with organized leisure (e.g., movie night). It was during one of these evenings at the camp that I was invited to play a game of "Asshole" with the NPO staff and a few of the boys. Not being familiar with the card game, I sat down to play. And not being a great card player, I lost nearly every round. As the loser, I soon found out that the group had the enjoyment of calling me an "asshole" every . . . single . . . time. After the game thankfully finished, I crawled into my tent and cried.

Now, being a reflective researcher, I tried to reason through my response. Perhaps I had been overly sensitive. Maybe I only responded this way because I was tired. On the other hand, if I had this response, as a person with rather high (OK, maybe average) self-esteem, what effect does a game like this have on a young boy such as those in the program, a boy who likely comes from a place where he is beaten and called even worse names? Against my better judgment, though decidedly for research purposes, I decided to join the same card game the next night, with, as I soon found out, less experienced players.

I wasn't the "asshole" for the entire evening, and I was so happy, until I started watching the person who was consistently in that position, a young boy of perhaps 13. He became quieter as the game went on, with the group becoming louder and more demeaning in their obvious joy of calling him an asshole. He eventually shifted his response to loud, inappropriate laughter. No longer able to sit and watch, I ended the game proclaiming the group was too loud and we needed watch a movie. So I lied. However, at the time I just wanted to end the game—but we are not evaluating my principles here.

The next day, on the much-too-long hike, I created a situation where I had some time with this boy. I told him how I felt during this game when I had kept losing and being called an asshole, and eventually he opened up and talked about how horrible he felt and how much he hated the game. I asked him why he played, and he said that the counsellors played this game and he wanted to be accepted by them.

I would like to say that because of this finding, the game was never played again. While it was never played again with the participants when I was present, the staff continued to play it with each other. I found this consternating given that most staff members admitted in private to having the same reaction to losing ("I feel awful about myself") and to winning ("I am so glad you are the asshole"). How could staff, who were role models to these young boys, and who claim to have the principle of helping others believe in themselves, enjoy playing a game that made them feel good about themselves at the expense of others?

While this experience did not have a noteworthy ending for the NPO—they continued to play this game—my first foray into principles-focused evaluation had some key lessons. The interplay between an organization's principles and its actions illuminates key issues and opens a space for dialogue that can potentially inform change. Bumbling through this formidable dialogue showed that providing empirical data is not enough; effective facilitation skills, patience, and cultural competence are needed, as well as a client who is willing to engage in a facilitated discussion.

Using Principles-Focused Evaluation with an Explicitly Principled Organization

What's in a name? Everything. Like the word *evaluator*. I have never felt that the name *evaluator* encapsulates all that I do in my daily work life, and thus far it is not in "typical" evaluation processes (e.g., implementing a national learner education outcome evaluation) where I am most engaged with useful principles-focused evaluation. While principles are often one factor in most of my evaluations, it is habitually one that is easily pushed aside with the ever-popular "This doesn't answer the set evaluation questions" or the kindly "This is outside your scope, please remove it from the evaluation report." While I often find exploring principles to be useful, and therefore principles-focused evaluation to be illuminating, clients are not universally so enamored of it.

One organization that embraced (though they did not request) a principles-focused evaluation is the Canon Collins Educational and Legal Assistance Trust. Founded by an Anglican priest who was active in several radical political movements in the United Kingdom and who was later appalled by apartheid, the Trust supports several undertakings that aim to create and hold a space for activism and research to intermingle and bring about social change. Specifically, it works to build a community of change agents across Southern Africa who create and use research for social impact. Its approach is underpinned by a spirit of solidarity rooted in its history in the anti-apartheid struggle.

I was contacted by the Trust's South African manager 14 years after she first took part in one of my evaluation trainings, to conduct an evaluation process for one of its partner organizations. In writing this chapter, I asked the organization's Southern African manager a bit about its principles and how it chose evaluators.

"As an organization, we believe in the values of agency, learning, collaboration, solidarity, and fairness. With these values underlying our work, we strive to implement principles and practices that will enable these values to emerge and flourish. These values are actioned in our decision-making processes—the scholars we select for our scholarships, the partners we choose to work with, and even the funders we approach. They are also actioned in the way we engage collaboratively (in the spirit of solidarity) with our scholars and partners.

"Within the context of evaluation, we seek evaluators who share these values and who, in their own practice, can contribute to the strengthening and development of these values. We seek evaluators who will hold us to account on our values, and how we implement our programs, as well as the achievement of stipulated outcomes in our project and evaluation frameworks. Evaluation is a learning experience, rather than a grading experience. It is a process to promote learning and collaboration, and the overall result should be a more effective, robust, and wiser organization."

My earlier training had provided an insight into my evaluation approach and encouraged her to request that I lead an evaluative process with an NPO with whom they collaborated, a well-known yet cash-strapped community activist organization. The South African manager was under pressure to secure the NPO's second grant from a United Kingdom donor by demonstrating the NPO's achievement in its four donor-promised outcomes. Intimately involved with the NPO and its monitoring data, she realized that the outcomes and their related indicators did not adequately reflect the NPO's efforts and successes. Faced with the pressure to retain a grant that would sustain a small, yet vibrant and necessary NPO, she at the same time recognized that judging the NPO on its agreed-upon donor outcomes would not reflect the NPO's hard work. Furthermore, continuing to focus on achieving these outcomes would not significantly further the intended goal of activism and research leading to social change.

Given the NPO's focus on youth, I decided that I needed a youthful perspective and voice to inform the evaluation process. I brought on board a young, emerging South African evaluator who was familiar with the NPO, and the areas in which it worked. She recognized the NPO's importance in South Africa, and the conundrum we faced in evaluating it. Thus together we struggled with how to balance two very different intents.

Ultimately the South African manager guided the dual-purpose endeavor by tasking us to evaluate the program's fidelity, and to also explore what the NPO was doing that had useful and not-so-useful results. Therefore, she requested an evaluation that would meet the donor's needs for a review, and at the same time strengthen the NPO. As part of this process, we facilitated discussions that articulated the NPO's theory of change, and used this to suggest outcomes and indictors that better reflected and measured the NPO's intended results.

The Canon Collins Trust's principles, namely of helping and not harming, and of creating an enabling space for activism and research to bring about social change, informed the evaluation request and guided the evaluation design and implementation. This led to an evaluation that was truthful to the donor and candid with the NPO by recognizing its accomplishments and its challenges, and provided a pathway that supported the NPO in its quest to combine activism and research that would change the lives of disempowered people.

Using Principles-Focused Evaluation When Working with a University

What's in a name? Everything. Like "best practice." I am always a bit terrified when asked to identify an organization's best practice so that it can be applied elsewhere; I am expected to create a rule that if followed will bring about the same results. While I understand why this seems like a good idea to any organization (fidelity = results), life in the social world, in my experience anyway, just doesn't work that way.

When a local university approached me to identify their best practices that would then be used in "identical" health projects in two other countries, I was a bit wary. Yet the project intrigued me for two reasons. First, it was drawing on university professors (as opposed to NPOs) who mentored government health managers and clinic staff to address health issues that stemmed from poor management practices. Second? This intervention was taking place in the community in which I lived.

Early on in the project, I tentatively suggested that rather than identify best practices, I focus on identifying principles that guided the intervention. I explained that having a principle (or several principles) to guide a multicountry implementation would likely be more useful than a "best practice in this time and place and for these people as long as it's all the same and nothing else changes" concept. The program staff were wary, as they wanted something "concrete" to provide to their staff who would soon implement projects in other countries. Thus I moved forward with the intention of identifying best practices. I really did.

After countless hours of trying to understand an extremely complicated health system—including personal dynamics within that system; politics among national, local, and city authorities in providing health services; the cultural and infrastructural barriers that affected access to health delivery; and other dynamics—I was exhausted. I then weeded through project documents and held countless key informant interviews to understand how the project intended to bring about change. This was all before I began the "real" part of the evaluation.

The evaluation had some interesting findings, and as required by my contract, I provided a formal presentation to the university project staff with some suggested best practices. I then asked the project staff to stay a bit longer, and I provided a few principles that appeared to support their results and were likely applicable to their other sites. This led to good conversations, and the project staff agreed that using principles was likely a more helpful approach than best practices.

I then took a chance and pushed the envelope a bit further, identifying a few principles that would likely challenge other sites. One such principle was access to mentors. The data overwhelmingly showed that key advances in addressing the health system issues resulted from the university staff's availability to have impromptu discussions, mostly on weekends or after hours. Though this mentoring was one of the most lauded parts of the intervention, it was also university staff's uncompensated time. While in this case a best practice, it was also highly unlikely that NPO staff in the other countries could be available to this degree, for no pay. However, if I recommended the principle that underpinned this practice—"be available for, and responsible to, those you mentor"—it would likely be an approach that the other countries could appropriately apply to their context.

Having met the contractual agreement for best practices, we left them behind, and I facilitated further discussions to identify other useful key principles, which were then used to guide implementation in other countries.

Applying Principles-Focused Evaluation in Place of an Impact Evaluation

Collaboration. What's in this name? As my last example suggests, quite a bit. This short narrative describes how a principle of collaboration played out during a very frustrating evaluative process for all involved.

A well-known international foundation hired me to conduct an impact evaluation on its HIV and AIDS program in a Southern African country. For the past 4 years it had funded three HIV and AIDS organizations, each of which brought different knowledge, skill sets, and approaches to combatting HIV and AIDS. Specifically, the donor believed that in order to combat this issue among women and children, an intervention required the engagement of multiple partners, all bringing their area of expertise in health systems, human rights, or public awareness. Fundamental to the foundation's approach was its conviction that organizations that worked collectively would likely bring about change in the HIV and AIDS epidemic, and thus demonstrate the effectiveness of its principle of collaboration.

The foundation had budgeted an extremely limited amount of time for the evaluation and strongly suggested that I contact the lead NPO to organize program interviews and site visits. After contacting the NPO, I prepared my evaluation approach and arrived in the country, ready to implement my evaluation plan. Things did not go well for this plan.

The "lead" organization had set up several interviews that related to its work; however, the other foundation-funded NPOs had not been contacted. Assuming I had made an error, I apologized to the "lead" NPO and explained that since they managed the program, I had assumed that they would organize all the site visits.

A conversation ensued that clarified the situation. The NPO that I had contacted had thought I was referring to its program, which focused on one aspect of HIV and AIDS, and was completely unaware of any expected collaboration on a larger program. After several attempts, I made contact with the other two NPOs, and learned that these NPOs also had no idea that they were supposed to be collaborating with each other. Thus, while the foundation was supposedly advocating and supporting a principle of collaboration, this was a surprise to the NPOs that it funded. Because the bulk of the evaluation process was engaged with understanding these internal challenges, it did not meet the foundation's expectations of multiple external interviews and site visits and did not produce enough data for an impact evaluation, much to consternation of the foundation.

In retrospect, a formally named principles-focused evaluation framework would have been useful in several ways. The explicit structure would have provided a way in which to make sense of this exasperating situation and offered a legitimate evaluation approach with which to engage the foundation. For example, an evaluation report guided by a legitimate (e.g., named and published) approach may have provided an opportunity to use the findings to support a facilitated dialogue between the foundation and the NPOs. The potential result could have been the NPOs understanding and testing the collaboration principle, and the impact evaluation could then follow that explored how women and children infected and affected by HIV and AIDS benefited (or not) from a collaborative approach. However, that is what could have been. As it was, the report describing the evaluation process, its challenges, and the findings was rejected outright by the donor because it "didn't look like an impact evaluation."

Final Reflections

While we use values to make evaluative judgments, evaluations do not often explicitly identify, or judge, principles. Principles-focused evaluation does just that. This kind of evaluation is not for the shy, the faint-hearted, or the sensitive (though, ironically, I qualify for all three). After all, who wants to bring the news that organizations' actions do not reflect their principles?

The value and appropriateness of principles-focused evaluation need to be considered for each circumstance, as with any other type of evaluation, though in my experience, it fits many situations. As with my first example depicting a grassroots organization, it enables thoughtful engagement in situations where an evaluator struggles to understand and explain what is found in an evaluation process. In this case, its use is limited to the evaluator. However, even this is of critical importance for many of us working in the field, and often working alone. My second example, drawing on the experience of a trust, illustrates that when working with principles-based organizations, it can be a perfect fit. Here the organization recognized the utility in reflecting on its principles and drawing on them to guide and assess their practice. Using an organization's principles in this way likely supports a process and evaluative findings that are useful to the client. My third, university-based example suggests that even for organizations that are not as explicit in their principles, principles-focused evaluation provides a pathway to shift from antiquated thinking (best practices) to a new way that offers more useful application. The final example offers a few lessons. It shows how a donor's inflexibility over accepting findings that focused on misunderstanding in the application of its principles led to a waste of evaluation (and potentially program) resources. In fairness, it also demonstrates how it can be problematic for an evaluator to stumble into and use an as-yet-unidentified evaluation approach or a framework that is not yet explicit. The main lesson is that when the core of identified challenges stems from principles, such as an intervention's implementation differing from how and why it was funded, principle-focused evaluation provides a guiding light. Each example, in its unique way, illustrates how naming this approach and knowing its definitions and frameworks provides an evaluator with a potential transparent evaluation avenue for supporting conversations conducive to solving problems that result in effective change.

In my experience, the approach has proven to be at the same time exhausting and exhilarating. Naming this approach and providing concrete guidance in using it are critical to an emerging field that needs transparent, innovative approaches that aim to further a just society in a complex world. Naming and explaining this approach to students, potential clients, and fellow evaluators will encourage respect, understanding, recognition, and legitimacy, all of which will encourage utilization of findings. This in turn will move the now-named principles-focused evaluation toward being a part of mainstream evaluation.

CHAPTER 34

Waking Lumina

A Personal Principles-Based Evaluation Philosophy

NORA F. MURPHY

David Williams (2016) edited a volume of *New Directions for Evaluation* titled "Seven North American Evaluation Pioneers." Each chapter author, including the author of this book, described childhood and critical life events and experiences that contributed to becoming an evaluator and the approach to evaluation with which each author is associated. Robert Stake, Marvin Alkin, Michael Scriven, Daniel Stufflebeam, Eleanor Chelimsky, Ernie House, and I shared and interpreted stories from our personal as well as professional evaluation lives. In introducing the volume, Williams quoted Tom Schwandt (2002) to set the context for biographical inquiry into evaluation practice.

> When properly conceived as an activity of teaching and learning resulting in an action-oriented self-understanding, evaluation becomes more continuous with the ways we are as human beings in our everyday lives [p. xi] . . . , a way of understanding the self, a way we are as human beings in the world, or our ethical or moral orientation as human beings [p. 6], bring[ing] our notions of evaluating

and evaluation practice closer to the realities of thinking and doing in everyday life [p. 17].

That's what Nora Murphy has done in this chapter. Other important works that connect evaluators' personal lives with their professional practice include Marv Alkin's book *Evaluation Roots* (2013) and the AEA Oral History Project with life histories of and reflections from prominent evaluators, published in the *American Journal of Evaluation* (e.g., King, Shanker, Miller, & Mark, 2010). This chapter follows those exemplars.

I worked with Nora on the principles-focused evaluation of youth homelessness programs referred to often throughout this book and featured as an exemplar in Chapter 26. I came to know her story and her commitment to principles-focused evaluation during that work. I invited her to share her evaluation journey and am grateful for her courage and openness in doing so. She takes us to where the personal and professional not only intersect, but become one.

—M. Q. P.

A Personal Principles-Based Evaluation Philosophy

In 2008, my 2-year-old son, Ayrie, was diagnosed with recurrent respiratory papillomatosis. The disease causes benign cancer-like tumors to grow on the larynx, trachea, or lungs, causing noisy breathing, difficulty swallowing, and a quiet, raspy voice. There is no cure, but the tumors can be removed with repeated surgeries. (See International RRP ISA Center, 2016, for more information.)

Before the diagnosis, I believed following rules led to a life of success and happiness, where everything could be reduced to black or white, right or wrong, winners and losers. Doors seemed to open for me everywhere I went in the worlds of work and schooling. I accumulated awards, accolades, and promotions. From camp counselor, to high school teacher, to nonprofit manager, I finally found my way to evaluation. Playing and doing well at this game filled me with adrenaline, the buzz of competition, and the thrill of accomplishment—most of the time. But in my most private moments I admitted to myself that it also left me lonely, fearful that I was an imposter, and not feeling entirely proud of the way I performed my work. *Should we make major decisions about children's lives by sorted numbers*

Shiya (left) and Ayrie (right) Murphy.

on a spreadsheet? If we don't ask the most vulnerable people, the most impacted populations, how can we understand the consequences of our decisions? Does what's currently being mandated and counted deserve most of our attention, or do current mandates reflect easily collected data? These questions tugged at the corners of my mind, but I never articulated them. "Women," the world told me, "shouldn't be too loud, too opinionated, too aggressive, too boastful." Good rule follower that I was, I continually pushed these questions to the back of my mind and continued to follow the rules.

After Ayrie's diagnosis, my life careened out of control. I constantly fought our insurance company. Rules determined which doctors we could see, how many times we could see them, what diagnoses were acceptable, what procedures would be covered, and what medications could be prescribed. When I called insurance agents to advocate for my son, disembodied voices on the other end cared more about following rules than my son's life, valued compliance over humanity. The insurance company counted things (minutes, procedures, dollars), but not the things that mattered. They made decisions about my son's life based on spreadsheets and algorithms, distanced from what matters—a child. A life. At this same time I gave birth to my second son and I found myself parenting alone. Many times people's blind adherence to the rules made it impossible for me to care for my boys and threatened to push me beyond my breaking point.

Ayrie Mekai Jones Murphy died on September 29, 2010. He was 4½. My heart broke and the world grew heavy and dark. Nothing made sense. For a long time, I wished that I had died with Ayrie.

Through the brokenness and darkness I had to rebuild myself and our family. My younger son Shiya needed me, and he needed to grieve for his brother. And maybe, just maybe, the world needed me. (*This thought was so scary that it was only the echo of a whisper.*) I sensed that the only way I would be able to pull my way back to life was to live with purpose, passion, and a connection with something larger than myself—all things I had fought, diminished, or denied for my first 36 years. This process wasn't easy, especially because I didn't know who I was. In my personal spaces, I had often tried to become someone smaller—looked for ways to take up less space, to be less emotional. In my professional spaces, I tried to win the rationality game. I taught high school math and science, earned a master's degree in quantitative research methods, became a kick-ass Microsoft Excel wizard. I loved putting data and emotions in tiny bounded boxes. For most of my life I had been living by other people's rules, playing someone else's game.

I reflected on my parenting. I thought about the trauma my son endured, the trauma I and my family endured with him. I thought about all of the rules surrounding parenting—how much time kids should spend watching TV, how many vegetables they should eat, how long they should read each day, and on and on. When I sat at Ayrie's deathbed, none of this mattered. These rules, and the extent to which I followed them or didn't, were meaningless. I realized that I could drive myself crazy holding myself accountable for following ever-changing rules. *Did he have too much screen time when he was alive? Did he exercise enough? Was he reading enough words when he died?* Or, I could try to identify and focus on what mattered.

So what did matter? *Loved.* I loved him fiercely. I have no doubt he knew that. Not a day went by when I didn't hug him tightly and tell him I loved him over and over again. *Valued.* I valued his imagination, his laugh, his questions, his creativity, the spark in his eye. I valued what he taught me and the way he cared for his younger brother. I valued him and what he brought to our family and the world. *Walking with.* When I

could, I kept him safe. But I couldn't keep him safe from his own rapidly proliferating cells. In the end, the virus won. So I walked with him when he was scared. In the moments before he went under anesthesia, and in the moments when he came back, I know he felt safer because I was there and holding him, physically wrapping him with my fierce love. Ayrie knew he was loved, he was valued, and that I would walk with him when he was scared. That's all I did that truly mattered. I affectionately call this the "deathbed perspective"—the clarity that comes from sitting by a loved one's deathbed. What matters becomes clear, sometimes painfully so.

Five years later, these concepts have evolved to be principles that guide my personal relationships and life.

Love fiercely, freely, and fully and be open to receiving love.

Value myself and others, our unique qualities, gifts, and ways of being.

Walk with others through their journey, listening and bearing witness.

Every day I want Shiya (now 8) to know with certainty that he's loved and valued. I tell him that my heart is always connected to his through love. I value the silliness, empathy, and creativity he brings into our lives. I don't promise that I can keep him safe, but he knows I'll do my best and that I'll walk with him through life when he's scared. I'm dating someone I hope to be with for the rest of my life. Sometimes I worry that I drive him crazy with the number of times I tell him that I love him. But I don't want a day to pass where he wonders. He's brilliant and talented. I value what he brings to me, to my son, to our family, and to the world. And I want him to feel safe in our relationship. I want him to know that when we have the hard moments, days, and times, I will be gentle with him. I won't try to hurt him out of spite or whimsy.

Reimagining Myself as an Evaluator: My Guiding Principles for Professional Engagement

After my son's death, the only way I could find my way back to life was living with purpose and with passion, and connecting to something larger than myself. My guiding principles for personal relationships emerged as my North Star for my personal journey. But I wondered: *What is my purpose? Is it possible to find and fulfill my purpose through evaluation? If so, how? Can I reimagine myself as an evaluator that works in alignment with who I am becoming, not who I was?*

I kept asking myself these questions, noticing when evaluation made me feel heavy and drained or passionate and inspired. I started journaling about it, and one day, after several years of this self-study, an image popped into my head. I jotted it down on a coffee-stained napkin and sent the sketch to a graphic designer friend. I called the whole image "waking lumina" because I felt that the light inside me, which has been trying to wake me up for so long, was finally waking me. She produced the image in Exhibit 34.1.

I chose *light*. I've had moments when I've come into contact with my light and everything feels right. It's magical—a moment of divine connection with something greater than me. I can't always feel the light, but perhaps I can cultivate a way of being that increases how often I can sense my light.

I chose *connection*. We feel loved, valued, and safe in relationships when we connect to ourselves, to each other, to nature, to something larger than ourselves, to purpose.

I chose *social justice*. If the world isn't a more just and equitable place because I'm in it, then I haven't lived my life right. I don't say this from a place of hubris or ego, but from a belief that we can all make small contributions to increased justice and equity.

I chose *inspiration*. I want to be inspired. I want to inspire. Inspiration lets my light shine and helps the light in others shine. This world is so beautiful and amazing that if I'm not inspired, I'm not alive.

I engage my *heart, mind, and spirit* when I work toward light, connection, social justice, and inspiration. All create and contribute to different opportunities for

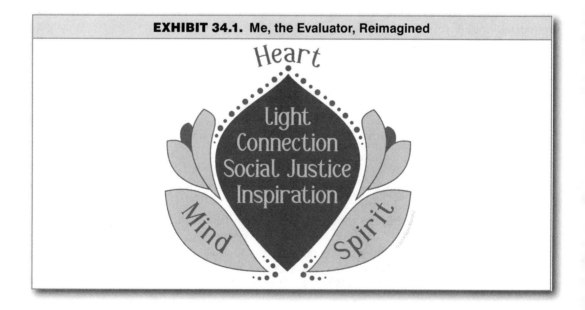

EXHIBIT 34.1. Me, the Evaluator, Reimagined

connection and different ways of knowing. If I only engage one or two of these, my work will be incomplete.

Exhibit 34.2 shows how I use these five principles in my work.

I didn't know how or if I would find a niche in evaluation that would let me work in this way. Something told me that I needed to try.

How I Came to Principles-Focused Evaluation

I met with Michael Quinn Patton in 2012 and spilled out my life story, not unlike the way I'm doing with you in this chapter. At the end of our second meeting, he asked if I'd be interested in working on a project with him—a developmental evaluation with six agencies that serve youth experiencing homelessness and a local family foundation. Um, yes?

This evaluation was conducted as part of the Otto Bremer Foundation's youth homelessness initiative, which included support for collaboration among six agencies serving homeless youth in the Twin Cities area. As part of this initiative, agencies identified nine shared principles and participated in a principles-based, utilization-focused developmental evaluation. Through the collaborative evaluation process, we hoped to (1) gain an understanding of the experiences of unaccompanied homeless youth, (2) understand how the shared principles of these organizations had been implemented in practice, and (3) explore the extent to which implementation of these principles helped lead to healthy youth development from the perspective of the youth.

I generated qualitative data through interviews with youth, street workers, agency staff, foundation staff, and case file reviews. From this data, I wrote 14 individual case studies, or stories as I preferred to call them. A cross-case analysis provided insight into how the principles were enacted, as well as how they supported a young person's healthy trajectory. The Reflective Practice Group (RPG), comprised of executive leadership from the six youth-serving organizations and the foundation, convened once per month for a period of nearly 2 years. The RPG made the principles come to life by engaging in the framing of the evaluation, engaging the shared meaning making of the data, and identifying implications for their individual organizations and for the system as a whole.

Analysis of the cases found that young people experiencing homelessness travel through unique journeys. Because they have experienced multiple traumas in their lives, their journeys may, at times, look nonlinear, scary, and confusing to people who care about them. Love is one of the

---

EXHIBIT 34.2. Guiding Principles for Professional Engagement

- Engage **heart, mind, and spirit** in all aspects of living my life: my relationship with myself, my relationship with others, my work, and the decisions I make.

- Make choices that let my **light** shine more brightly, and engage with others in a way that supports their ability to shine more brightly.

- Build and deepen **connections** between and among people, spirit, nature, passion, and purpose.

- Increase **social justice** and equity, recognizing my privilege and the opportunities it affords me to create change.

- **Inspire** and be inspired.

strongest motivating factors in their lives. The youth described going back to the people they love, and the behaviors that have helped them survive, even if these people and behaviors hurt them. Caring adults needed to support them without judgment, to help them take steps toward reducing harm in their lives, to help them develop in positive ways, and to create a path toward well-being. This requires caring adults to create and sustain one-on-one relationships with the young person, to work with adults in other sectors and systems who impact the young person's life, and to help the young person build community through lasting, healthy relationships with family, kin, and kith. Work with each young person must be highly individualized and contextualized, taking place over a long period of time (Murphy, 2014).

EXHIBIT 34.3. How My Guiding Principles for Professional Engagement Were Manifested in the Youth Homelessness Evaluation

Guiding principle	How it was manifested
Engage **heart, mind, and spirit** in all aspects of living my life: my relationship with myself, my relationship with others, my work, and the decisions I make.	Because I worked with the RPG as part of my dissertation research there was no question about whether I was engaging my mind. But the trust built among me and the group members was equally founded upon their ability to sense that I cared about the youth they served. They wanted to know that I wasn't someone driven only by the mind, by numbers, by a dissertation. They were fiercely protective of the young people they served and wanted to know that I had the same capacity to care.
Make choices that let my **light** shine more brightly, and engage with others in a way that supports their ability to shine more brightly.	I wrote the young people's stories based on interview transcripts and case files. I shared their stories with them before sharing them with anyone else, asking for feedback and permission. Every young person lit up, sharing sentiments such as "I can't wait to share this with my brother. I've never been able to explain myself so well before." Others wanted to turn their stories into music or use them as inipiration for poetry. I felt my light shine brighter when theirs did.
Build and deepen **connections** between and among people, spirit, nature, passion, and purpose.	The connection I made with youth engaged my heart and spirit as we shared tears of disappointments and hurts they chose to share with me. While I was interviewing them for the purposes of evaluation, I put them and their dignity at the center of our interactions. This built a bond of trust that helped create the space for them to share openly and honestly without feeling violated or used.
Increase **social justice** and equity, recognizing my privilege and the opportunities it affords me to create change.	Homeless youth are one of the most marginalized groups in our society. Privileging youth voice, as we did, is the only way to create change that will improve the system for youth according to what youth identify that they want and need.
Inspire and be inspired.	The young people's stories—their strength, their empathy, their dreams—inspired me. The commitment on behalf of the reflective group members to hear and uplift youth voice inspired me. I've heard from many that the case stories and principles we produced inspired them.

You can read more about this evaluation in Chapter 26. I introduce it here because this was the first project that allowed me to live my guiding principles for professional engagement (Exhibit 34.2). Exhibit 34.3 summarizes, in no particular order, how these principles showed up in the way I engaged with all aspects of the evaluation.

Journey-Oriented Developmental Evaluation for Social Justice and Equity

Realizing through the youth homelessness evaluation that I could evaluate in harmony with my guiding principles for professional engagement was a turning point for me. I wondered: *If I can conduct evaluations in harmony with my guiding principles for professional engagement, can I also conduct evaluations that reflect my beliefs regarding that about which I'm most passionate–increased social justice for the most vulnerable?* I had a professional life before evaluation that included working at a nursing home, teaching in an alternative high school, and working at a camp for children in foster care. Between these experiences and my journey through chronic illness and loss, I had developed some closely held beliefs about social justice, trauma, and healing.

Belief 1. All people share the same basic desires: to have their basic needs met; to love and be loved; to see and be seen; to have and realize their dreams; and to find belonging and purpose in communities.

Belief 2. The impact of trauma and systemic oppression prevents people from being able to meet their needs.

Belief 3. Healing occurs when we experience each other's humanity with love, acceptance, and open hearts and minds.

Belief 4. Working toward social justice (decreased oppression, increased equity) must happen simultaneously with healing.

I'm purposefully using the word *trauma* broadly to include multiple types of trauma such as psychological trauma, historical or intergenerational trauma, and race-based trauma. Psychological trauma is "a circumstance in which an event overwhelmed or exceeds a person's capacity to protect his or her psychic well-being and integrity" (Cloitre, Cohen, & Koenen, 2011, p. 3). Historical or intergenerational trauma is the devastating trauma of loss of culture and forcible removal from family and communities that remains unresolved and becomes a sort of "psychological baggage in a contemporary culture" (Evans-Campbell, 2008; Sotero, 2006). Race-based trauma occurs when someone experiences or witnesses specific events of danger related to race and/or lives in difficult social conditions because of the interrelationship between poverty and race (Dei, Karumanchery, & Karumanchery-Luik, 2004).

The drive to develop an evaluation practice guided by my principles for professional engagement (see Exhibit 34.3) and founded in my beliefs led me to my current niche as a developmental evaluator who supports systems change for increased social justice and equity. I actively choose evaluation projects related to innovative and collaborative approaches to systems change, with the goals of increasing social justice, opportunity, and equity, and decreasing oppression. My clients are typically foundations working to tackle a wicked problem in society. Wicked problems—like poverty, homelessness, police brutality, and racial disparities—do not have one source or one simple solution (Briggs, 2007). In fact, there are so many current and historical factors that created these problems, and such a wide array of things that must change before reaching a solution, that the task can seem daunting. To complicate matters further, once people start to make changes to the situation, other changes in the system occur as a result—anticipated or otherwise, visible or invisible—that make the path forward hard to see and constantly changing.

Through my work I have arrived at the hypothesis that (1) where there is a need for increased social justice and equity, people have experienced or are experiencing injustice and inequity, and (2) where there is injustice and inequity there is trauma. I realized that when designing an evaluation, I can choose to ignore trauma, or design an evaluation that creates the space to recognize trauma and promote healing. Years of questioning and reflecting, projects that went well and poorly, and half-written articles led me to my current approach, journey-oriented developmental evaluation for social justice and equity (JODE).

Why Journey Oriented? From a Forward-Thinking Orientation to a Journey Orientation

What does it mean to be *journey oriented*? Even in developmental evaluation, where we are attentive to complexity concepts, systems thinking, and co-creation, we can get trapped in a forward-thinking orientation, which I'll explain and contrast with journey orientation.

With a *forward-thinking orientation,* the first step is to identify the problem and describe the important context. Systems thinking requires that we try to understand the problem and important context from different perspectives, and complexity concepts require that we try to conceptualize the problem and surrounding context in a way that does not oversimplify and does not suggest that we could ever have a full understanding of the problem. Once the problem is identified and described, either a solution

is articulated and funding is sought to pay for implementation of the innovative solution *or* funding is sought to bring together people who will co-create an innovative solution. Together the co-creators are convened over time to implement the solution. Eventually the problem is solved or, more likely, the funding stream ends. Regardless of the reason, the initiative concludes. This typical chain of events is depicted in a simplified form in Exhibit 34.4.

Ideally, the developmental evaluator was engaged during step 1, but no later than step 3. During step 4, data are collected and timely feedback is provided, to support the development of the innovative solution. Eventually the project concludes, usually because the funding has ended. Attention is paid to the past during step 1 and if it surfaces during step 4, but the thrust of the work is forward oriented.

A journey orientation, by contrast, also looks backward, seeing the past, present, and future as intimately connected and ever changing. *A journey orientation in developmental evaluation is based on the belief that the past, present, and future are interconnected.* Our past and present are shaped by our experience, trauma, growth, and relationships. Our future is comprised of our hopes and dreams, for ourselves, our relationships, and the people we care about. Our past, present, and future intersect—physically, emotionally, mentally, and spiritually. Our understanding of the past, present, and future continually changes as the interrelated parts shape each other and new meanings emerge. This relationship is depicted in Exhibit 34.5.

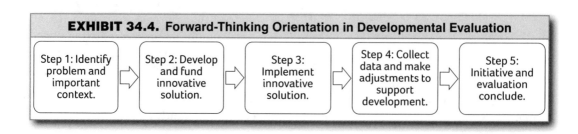

EXHIBIT 34.4. Forward-Thinking Orientation in Developmental Evaluation

Step 1: Identify problem and important context. ⇨ Step 2: Develop and fund innovative solution. ⇨ Step 3: Implement innovative solution. ⇨ Step 4: Collect data and make adjustments to support development. ⇨ Step 5: Initiative and evaluation conclude.

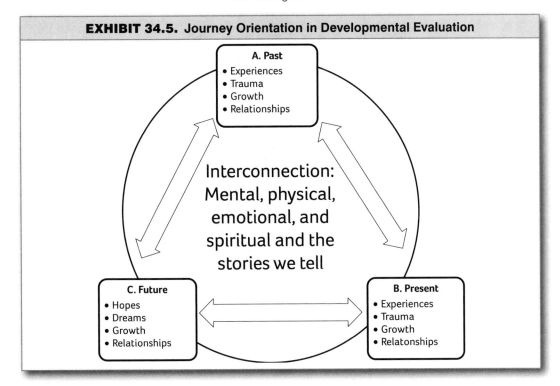

EXHIBIT 34.5. Journey Orientation in Developmental Evaluation

We make sense of ourselves and the world—in the past, present, and future—by the stories we tell ourselves and others. As our understanding of what happened in the past changes, so may our understanding and experience of the present and hopes for the future.

This thinking, while not commonly made explicit in the field of evaluation, has deep roots across cultures and times. Several ancient cultures believed in a sky goddess. The Egyptians believed in the goddess Nut, who symbolically swallowed the sun at night and gave birth to it each morning (see the depiction on page 338). For these cultures, humanity traveled on an endless journey of life, death, and rebirth, traveling through the underworld in dreams or visions and returning to the waking world with some small insight into the self or society. While I don't necessarily believe in Nut, I find her image—a woman stretched across the Earth to form the heavens—provocative. As I look at this picture, I see past, present, and future represented simultaneously.

The image encourages me to consider how someone travels through these interconnected concepts, as well as the continuing cycle of adaptation and learning between the individual and the surrounding culture.

Guiding Principles for JODE

So how do I make sense of everything I've shared so far in an evaluation context? Taken together, the set of guiding principles proposed in Exhibit 34.6 guides my decision making in a JODE context, incorporating my personal guiding principles—my beliefs about the relationship between social justice, trauma, and healing, grounded in what I've learned through my experience as a developmental evaluator.

Interestingly, in an *AEA365* blog post I wrote in 2015 (Murphy, 2015), I committed to asking myself a set of questions as I explore the intersection of evaluation, social justice, trauma, and healing. While writing this list of principles I looked back at the

The Egyptian goddess Nut.

blog post to see to what extent I was following the path I laid out for myself.

What gets placed at the center of the evaluation? Mertens (2015) suggests we place human rights and social justice at the center. I will be more intentional about doing so. This set of principles guides me to do so.

How do I attend to what's in the center? I consider methods that promote healing through deep listening, bearing witness, and creating opportunities for people to connect to their inner selves and to each other. This set of guiding principles asks me not only to promote healing, but to do

---

EXHIBIT 34.6. Guiding Principles for JODE for Social Justice

1. Focus on all aspects of the journey—past, present, or future—and their interrelationships.

2. Understand journeys as both individual and collective, shaped by our relationships with ourselves, with others, and society.

3. Recognize that the way we make sense of the journey—past, present, and future—is through stories we tell ourselves and others.

4. Identify and acknowledge trauma where it exists, respond with care, and create opportunities for healing.

5. Recognize the interconnection between and importance of people's physical, emotional, mental, and spiritual selves.

6. Identify and acknowledge growth, strengths, and assets, and create opportunities for empowerment and healing.

7. Relentlessly pursue well-being, social justice, and equity.

this with a journey orientation rather than a forward-thinking orientation.

For what purpose and to what ends do we evaluate? These guiding principles suggest that in addition to meeting the purposes of the developmental evaluation, I also work to promote healing, and increase well-being, social justice, and equity in a way that is true to the human experience.

Who is evaluating? I am guided by personal and professional principles and a foundational set of beliefs about the relationship between social justice, trauma, and healing. While these principles and beliefs may change over time, I suspect they won't change dramatically. I am transparent about the principles and beliefs with my clients and other stakeholders.

In Exhibit 34.7, I share some examples of how these principles are manifested in a JODE.

EXHIBIT 34.7. Journey-Orientation Guiding Principles and Developmental Evaluation

Guiding principle	JODE
1. Focus on all aspects of the journey—past, present, or future—and their interrelationships.	• Develop evaluation questions that address past, present, future, and the interrelationships between these elements. • As understandings of the past and present change, create space for people to understand, imagine, and reimagine hopes and dreams. Adjust the evaluation accordingly.
2. Understand journeys as both individual and collective, shaped by our relationships with ourselves, with others, and society.	• Apply systems thinking and seek to understand the problem and solutions through the lens of different boundaries, perspectives, and interrelationships. • Create opportunities for people in the system to see, understand, and learn from each other, reshaping boundaries and interrelationships.
3. Recognize that the way we make sense of the journey—past, present, and future—is through stories we tell ourselves and others.	• View stories as essential to making sense of the past, present, and future, and connections between them. • Allow space for the stories we tell ourselves and each other to change over time. • Identify new meanings as they emerge. Be curious about these changes.
4. Identify and acknowledge trauma where it exists, respond with care, and create opportunities for healing.	• Assume that where there is injustice and inequity, there is trauma. • Do not shy away from identifying and naming the injustice and inequity, and the systemic forces, structures, and beliefs that allow these to happen. • Select methods that provide appropriate opportunities for healing.
5. Recognize the interconnection between and importance of people's physical, emotional, mental, and spiritual selves.	• Rather than exploring physical, emotional, mental, and spiritual well-being as independent and siloed, support holistic thinking through the evaluation questions posed, methods selected, and interpretation of data collected.

(continued)

Guiding principle	JODE
6. Identify and acknowledge growth, strengths, and assets.	• In the situational analysis, seek to identify growth, strengths, and assets. • Reframe deficit thinking by focusing on possibilities, not problems. • Select methods that amplify growth, strengths, and assets.
7. Relentlessly pursue well-being, social justice, and equity.	• Follow the AEA's guiding principles for evaluators (2004) while fearlessly going beyond a focus on the welfare of society to a commitment to furthering social justice and equity for the most vulnerable. • Speak truth to power, even in extreme cases when the result might mean you do not get a contract in the initial phases or risk losing a contract in the implementation phase. • Include the voices and participation of the most vulnerable, marginalized, and silenced to the greatest extent possible while following the spirit of the program evaluation standards of the Joint Committee on Standards for Educational Evaluation (Yarbrough, Shulha, Hopson, & Caruthers, 2010).

How People Are Responding to a Principles-Focused Approach

Since the youth homelessness evaluation, I have conducted a number of principles-focused evaluations, all developmental evaluations in support of systems change. I've used them to support the shift to a youth-centered approach to adolescent sexual health in a metropolitan area, the shift toward a focus on well-being in the field of social change, and the shift to relationship-based education approaches in a large urban school district. The more I learn about how to do this work, the more questions I have: *What could I do better? What conditions set up this type of evaluation to be successful? Who decides what's increased social justice or equity? How do we better engage diverse thinking on our evaluation team? How do we better report in ways that engage the heart, mind, and spirit? Am I inspired? Are others inspired? Have I felt my light shine lately? Am I making a difference in the world? Do the people I love know that I love them?* Despite all of these questions I feel that I'm on the right

learning journey (albeit at the beginning), and so I continue down this path.

Not everyone I speak with loves the idea of principles. For some it feels too vague or squishy. But more often than not, people I'm working with around systems change for social justice are either ecstatic, relieved, curious, or all of the above when I describe a principles-focused approach. The positive feedback is largely focused around the idea that principles allow us to work together while we see the world as it actually is, see people as they are, bring people together around hard issues without asking for complete agreement or uniformity, and provide a framework for coherent systems change. Below I summarize some of the most frequent positive feedback I get.

▶ *Principles engage the world as it actually is.* By defining principles as the evaluand in a systems evaluation, evaluators can help organizations increase their capacity for trust and judgment and bring consistency to the work. The principles-driven work I've been engaged in seeks to look at the big picture from multiple perspectives and tries to honestly see and respond to the complexity of the situation and the diverse and dynamic needs of the people affected. And when things change (as we know they will), we don't have to start over or add new rules. We stop, take time to understand the changed context, and determine how the guiding principles help us respond thoughtfully to that change.

▶ *Principles see people as they are.* People are human. We are complex and messy. Each of us has a different path, different strengths, and different experiences. Successfully working with people means that you take the time to know all of this and respond accordingly. People want to be seen, want to be loved. We don't assume people equal numbers and widgets. We assume people don't move forward in straight lines or fit into neat data sets. We do this while allowing for variation and surprises.

▶ *Principles bring focus to collaborative and coherent systems change.* Principles-focused evaluation can be an effective way for people who work in different organizations and roles to communicate across boundaries, allowing them to agree on the concepts that guide their work but differ in how they operationalize those principles. The work might look different in different contexts, but the heart of the work is the same. A principles-based evaluation provides a promising way for organizations to collaborate in complex systems. Together, organizations can provide a cohesive response to a systems problem with contextual flexibility and adaptation.

▶ *Principles tackle hard issues.* Principles let people work in the same space without having to agree on everything, allowing them more space to work on hard issues. How, for example, should organizations who serve homeless youth interpret the principle of harm reduction? One organization follows this principle, in part, by giving out thousands of condoms each week.

A Catholic organization can't give out condoms at all. Both situations can coexist if they agree to approach youth with the intention of harm reduction rather than zero-tolerance. Both want to help youth self-identify risky behaviors, and work with them toward decreasing or stopping those behaviors. Adolescent health service providers who commit to providing culturally responsive services may do so through a lens of Afrocentric care, indigenous traditions and practices, a Christian background, or a focus on LGBTQ issues. All are OK, and all are necessary. The organizations allow the principles to guide their actions without agreeing on the "best" way to be culturally responsive.

What Does It Take to Work in a Principles-Driven Way with Clients?

All of my principles-focused work has been in the context of developmental evaluations in support of systems change for increased social justice and equity. This means people are collaborating from different organizations or vantage points in the systems and these individuals have decided that this is the time to work together for change. Other evaluators working with principles in a different way or different context may have very different feedback to share about what it takes to do this work with clients. Nonetheless, I offer you what I've learned.

▶ *Learning-oriented collaborations are based on trust and positive regard.* Working with principles is different in many ways than working with concrete goals and outcomes. Working with principles builds and strengthens trusting relationships. In my experience, principles-focused developmental evaluations require three essential ingredients: (1) trusting relationships, (2) positive regard, and (3) a commitment to learning. Things will fall apart when you take on big change, work toward social justice, and attempt to disrupt deeply entrenched and powered systems. These three essential ingredients bring things back together.

▶ *Principles-driven work takes time.* Engaging in principles-driven work at a systems level takes time because, depending on the group's process, the principles must be understood, operationalized, and implemented with consistency across the system. There needs to be a shared understanding of the language used, and how this translates to different contexts. This involves determining what the learning goals are related to the principles, collecting data, and bringing these data to the larger systems-level group. Ideally, the group working together for systems change collaboratively works together to look for patterns and reflect on implications, with each group member bringing his or her learning back to the organization. This requires a continuous cycle of learning and adaptation.

▶ *Principles-driven work is nonlinear and highly individualized.* A principles-based, big-picture-oriented approach often represents a culture shift for employees and managers. Principles require individuals to get comfortable with a certain level of ambiguity and messiness. Systems change, social justice work, and healing are all complex processes, not a linear progression toward an end. Sometimes things appear to be getting worse when, in fact, they are shifting in necessary ways before things can get better.

▶ *Principles-driven work requires high degrees of trust and judgment.* When systems are rule oriented, people know what to do in the event of conflict: they carry out the policies stated in manual and handbooks. People and organizations are judged on the degree to which they implement the rules listed in the rules manual or handbook. Professional judgment is less likely to be a factor in decision making. A principles-based approach, by contrast, requires a high degree of subjective judgment. Principles-driven work means saying to the staff, "Do what you think is right. I have confidence in your judgment." This raises the questions: *How does one make a judgment? How does one trust one's own judgment? How do people come to trust each other's judgment?* The two-part answer is: (1) building common understanding of the principles in theory and action, and (2) building trust: staff to staff, staff to management, and staff to youth. This leads to a larger question that will be critical for engaging in principles-driven systems change: *How do organizations and systems foster a culture of trust that empowers staff to exercise their professional judgment?*

▶ *Principles-driven work in a JODE context requires vulnerability.* I've learned that trust is often built during moments when people reveal their vulnerability—when sharing vulnerabilities is seen as a source of power rather than as something to fear, deny, or hide. A client I work with often shared this observation: "By being vulnerable you derive power. I trust that the mailman will come every day. What you do goes beyond building trust. Whatever it is about *you being you,* space is created for others to be vulnerable too. That's why this works, and why I was incredulous when you told me that you felt pressure to be something different. It's exactly those things that make you powerful." It's true that I sometimes feel led to share more of myself—my fears, my anxieties, my hopes—than I had anticipated, and this often leads to a place of deeper connection and better collaborative work.

▶ *Principles-driven work requires consistency.* Principles must be enacted throughout the entire system. For example, program leadership undergoing principles-based systems change reflected that both staff members and youth clients appreciated being treated as people on their own journey. Both groups appreciated opportunities to engage in their own positive development (Principle 1: Journey oriented, and Principle 3: Positive youth development). Trauma-informed care means being able to respond to staff trauma as well. One program administrator explained, "We're not only trying to know how to do trauma-informed care with young people, we're also trying to figure out how to do trauma-informed care with our staff to avoid further damage or burnout."

Conclusion

I'm a passionate person. I speak with force and conviction. I act with all of the energy that passion gives me. And I have to tell you, this has been uncomfortable for me. I interpreted signals I got from people and the social milieu that being a passionate person is a liability, a deficit, something to fix, something to overcome. Instead of interpreting myself as "a lot," I told myself I was "too much."

This path wasn't me. And, I now realize, it was unsustainable. Over time, my objective, logical, and rational identity drifted further and further from the core parts of my true self—my passion, emotions, sensitivities, and intuition. This split produced deep unhappiness in me, although I didn't understand it at the time. In this chapter, I shared how I came to discover principles in my personal life, and how I eventually found harmony between my true self and professional identity. I shared how I bring principles to bear on my professional decisions and how principles shape the way I currently work as an evaluator, and I reflected on what I've learned over the course of this 6-year journey. But I couldn't do this without telling you about me. I've told you who I am, what I believe, and how I came to believe this. It's not a traditional way to write a chapter in an evaluation book, but principles-based work isn't traditional. Neither am I.

Principles-Focused Evaluation in Practice

Tools and Checklist

An earthworm has five hearts.

Part I introduced principles: What they are, why they matter, and their niche in program development and evaluation. Part II presented the GUIDE framework and criteria for evaluating effectiveness principles. Part III provided exemplars of principles-based initiatives and principles-focused evaluations. Part IV reviewed principles for evaluators and offered reflections on principles-focused evaluations by principles-focused evaluators. Now we have arrived at the final section of the book, Part V.

The ancient Pythagoreans thought of five as *hieros gamos,* the marriage between heaven and earth. For Part V of this book, I reframe that as the marriage between theory and practice. These concluding chapters aim to be practical and practice oriented, suggesting how to apply the ideas, conceptual frameworks, and principles of previous chapters. Chapter 35 provides tools to use in conducting principles-focused evaluation. Chapter 36 provides a comprehensive checklist for the major elements of a principles-focused evaluation, identifying both tasks to be completed and facilitation challenges to address. Finally, the Epilogue offers responses to common questions I get asked about principles-focused evaluation.

These chapters, taken together, aim to both guide action and explain the basis for that guidance. Theories explain; they answer "why" questions; they posit hypotheticals; and they inform praxis. Practice involves acting; guidance on practice answers "how" questions; practice is enmeshed in reality; in-the-trenches practice brings praxis to life. Together,

345

in synthesis, the intersection of theory and practice provides the foundation for knowledge-based action, evoking the classic insight of Kurt Lewin, pioneer of applied social science: "There is nothing so practical as a good theory" (1951, p. 169). To which Gaffney and Anderson (1991) added this corollary proposition: "There is nothing so theoretically interesting as good practice."

But wait, there is a third leg to this stool: method. Methods are the bridge between theory and practice, which is what inspired psychologist Anthony G. Greenwald's (2012) riff on Lewin: "There is nothing so theoretical as a good method." Parts I and II of this book provided the conceptual framework for principles, essentially a theory positing a particular niche, purpose, and rationale for principles-focused evaluation matched to principles-based programs (a particular approach to theory of change). Part III provided practice-based exemplars, while Part IV provided insights from practitioners. Now, Part V adds further conceptual clarifications and new methods and tools. As you read, I invite you to keep in mind the theory–practice–method three-legged stool.

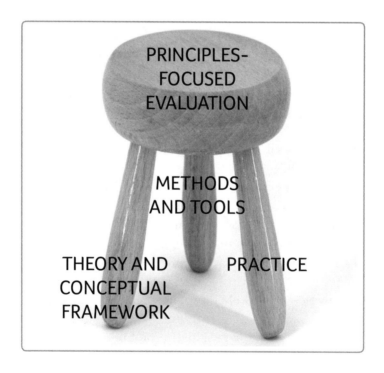

CHAPTER 35

Tools for Principles-Focused Evaluation

Technology is nothing. What's important is that you have a faith in people, that they're basically good and smart, and if you give them tools, they'll do wonderful things with them.
—STEVE JOBS, American entrepreneur, cofounder of Apple, Inc.

This chapter provides some tools for use in principles-focused evaluations. Because principles-focused evaluation often involves developing new principles or revising existing statements of principles, the first set of tools support assessing the quality of the principles to be evaluated. Principles are the evaluand, the focus of evaluation in principles-focused evaluation. This recalls the mantra that has run throughout this book: *No principles, no principles-focused evaluation.*

Here are the tools presented in this chapter.

▶ Exhibit 35.1 provides a checklist and guide for facilitating the development and review of principles.

▶ Exhibit 35.2 offers a tool for rating principles based on the GUIDE framework with a rubric for rating effectiveness principles.

▶ Exhibit 35.3 presents a rubric for assessing adherence to the principles of principles-focused evaluation.

▶ Appendix 35.1 lists exhibits presented

earlier in this book that can be used as tools.

A Word about Tools

These tools are not meant to be treated as fixed, standardized, validated, and rigid instruments. Both the format and the substance can be adapted to fit particular situations. Thus, the layout and design of the tools can be changed. The wording and sequencing of items in the checklists and rubrics can be changed and adapted. The size and categories of rating scales can be changed to fit your own preferences (even-numbered scales vs. odd-numbered scales). In essence, these are illustrative tools meant to suggest possibilities for principles-focused evaluation instrumentation in support of implementation and quality. They can be customized to fit specific contexts and situations.

Moreover, *you do not need permission to use these tools.* If you use them, you have the usual obligation to cite their source and reference their origin, but you do not need additional, explicit permission.

Checklist and Guide for Facilitating the Development and Review of Principles

Exhibit 35.1 provides guidance for facilitating the development and review of

principles. This general guidance, in the form of a checklist, identifies 10 key issues that typically need to be addressed when developing and reviewing principles. The checklist is presented as a series of steps, but the exact sequence and number of steps will vary. The left column identifies the issues that need to be addressed. The right column offers facilitation suggestions and options.

EXHIBIT 35.1. Checklist and Guide for Facilitating the Development and Review of Principles

Principles-focused evaluation often begins with development of new principles or review of existing principles, or both. Here are 10 things to consider when facilitating the development and review of principles.

Checklist items: Guide to and steps for developing and reviewing principles	Facilitation options, advice, and commentary
1. Determine who should be involved in generating or reviewing principles.	Those who are most involved will have the deepest knowledge about and feel the greatest ownership of the principles developed. Their capacity to participate in the principles-focused evaluation will also be significantly enhanced. These are likely to be the primary intended users for whom the principles-focused evaluation is designed.
2. Find out how the term *principles* is viewed among those with whom you will work.	Language matters. Connotations matter. Some terms carry baggage within a specific organizational or cultural context. Review documents and interview key informants to find out how the term *principles* has been used in the past and is currently perceived. Remember Thomas's theorem: *What is perceived as real is real in its consequences.* Find out the perceptions about principles and adapt your facilitation accordingly.
3. Examine existing documents within the setting where principles-focused evaluation will occur; look for patterns in the values expressed, the norms affirmed, and the issues raised that may affect the focus and content of principles.	Don't limit your review to documents that use the word *principles*. All kinds of documents can be relevant as background: strategic plans; staff guidelines; values statements; annual plan of work; mission, vision, and goal statements; public communications, including newsletters and website highlights. Use these documents to infer possible principles.

(continued)

Checklist items: Guide to and steps for developing and reviewing principles	Facilitation options, advice, and commentary
4. Set the organizational and situational context for developing and reviewing principles by explaining why principles are being developed and/or reviewed.	This context setting is usually done by someone in a leadership position, not the evaluator. A session to generate and review principles should be introduced by someone with credibility, authority, and prestige who can explain the rationale for and affirm the importance of engaging in principles-focused evaluation.
5. Provide a conceptual context for developing and reviewing principles by covering some basics that help get people ready to engage.	This is done by the evaluator. Some basics to consider in introducing principles-focused evaluation: • How treating principles as the evaluand (focus of evaluation) is different from goals and objectives, the traditional evaluands • How principles guide and how principles make a difference • The differences between principles and rules • Examples of principles and principles-focused evaluations These introductory issues are addressed in Chapters 1–5. Select relevant materials from those chapters for your introduction to the group you will be facilitating.
6. Introduce the GUIDE framework and criteria that will be used to develop high-quality effectiveness principles.	The timing of the introduction of the GUIDE framework can vary. Sometimes it is best to get the group quickly involved in the process by generating some draft principles and then reviewing what has been generated against the GUIDE criteria. For other groups, it is helpful to provide the GUIDE criteria before they begin generating statements of principles. When and how to introduce the GUIDE framework is a matter of facilitation strategy based on assessing what will work best for particular group.
7. Generate draft principles. Encourage creative thinking. Instruct group members not to worry about precise wording at this point. The initial task is to get an idea of what principles most resonate with those involved.	Some options for facilitating generation of draft principles: • Working on one principle at a time or drafting an initial list of several possibilities • Working in small groups or working together as a single group (which will depend on the size of the group involved and the amount of time available)

(continued)

Checklist items: Guide to and steps for developing and reviewing principles	Facilitation options, advice, and commentary
8. Facilitating identification of priority principles helps the group focus on a manageable number of the most relevant principles given its work. Some work on refining the wording of principles may occur at this point, but the process is still focused on identifying important principles that will guide the work and be meaningful to those involved, not finalizing wording.	Some options for facilitating focusing and priority setting: • Distinguish overarching principles from operational principles (see Chapters 17 and 29 for examples). • Aim for 5 to 10 principles, a number that is manageable. • Where there is disagreement about priorities, retain all principles that have support pending more systematic review in the next step.
9. Review the principles using the GUIDE criteria. Do this systematically.	Facilitation options: • Divide principles among individuals, pairs, or small groups so that each is working on only one principle using the GUIDE criteria. • Instead of using all five GUIDE criteria at once, review each principle against one criterion at a time; for example, rate all principles against the G (Guidance) criterion. • Make the review systematic and rigorous by using the principles rating rubric offered in Exhibit 35.2.
10. Together with the group, plan the next steps for principles development and review. Based on what the next steps are, establish a timeline for designing the principles-focused evaluation. Determine who should be involved in that design work.	Illustrative options for next steps: • A small group agrees to work with the evaluator on the wording and sequencing of principles, which will then be reviewed at a subsequent meeting. • Participants share the draft principles with others to get feedback. That feedback is brought back to a subsequent meeting for further revision of the principles. • Some pending decision, opportunity, or fork in the road is used as a test scenario of how principles provide guidance. The results of the simulation, or of a real test, can inform revision of the draft principles. • The group may decide to live with the draft principles for a while and get a feel for how to use them before finalizing the principles.

Tool for Rating Principles Based on the GUIDE Framework and Rubric for Rating Effectiveness Principles

Exhibit 35.2 provides a tool for rating principles based on the GUIDE framework. Each of the five GUIDE criteria has four dimensions for detailed rating. The rating scale varies for each GUIDE element. The column on the right is open to provide space for comments about how to improve each principle. The tool is designed to rate one principle at a time. The tool is complicated, presenting a number of dimensions for rating and changing rating scales. It is likely to require some careful study and practice using it to learn to use it effectively and efficiently.

Principles Guiding Principles-Focused Evaluation: Interconnectedness and Fidelity

Chapter 5 introduced the principles guiding principles-focused evaluation in relation to principles for utilization-focused evaluation and principles for developmental evaluation. For each of these sets of principles, the fidelity issue concerns determining what is essential to include in an approach to justify labeling that approach by its official designation. I have discussed the issue of fidelity with regard to utilization-focused evaluation and developmental evaluation (Patton, 2016b). I address the issue again here, drawing on my previous writing on this subject, followed by Exhibit 35.3, a fidelity checklist for engaging in principles-focused evaluation.

Just as fidelity is a central issue in efforts to replicate effective programs in new localities (Are the replications faithful to the original model on which they are based?),

evaluation fidelity concerns whether an evaluator following a particular model is faithful in implementing all the core steps, principles, and processes of that model. Here are examples of evaluation fidelity questions:

▶ What must be included in a "theory-driven evaluation" to justify its designation as *theory driven*? (Coryn, Noakes, Westine, & Schröter, 2011)

▶ What is the core of appreciative inquiry evaluation? (MacCoy, 2014; Preskill & Catsambas, 2006).

▶ What are the essential elements of Aboriginal program evaluations (Jacob & Desautels, 2014) or indigenous methods generally (Chilisa, 2012)?

▶ What must occur in a participatory evaluation to deem it *genuinely* participatory? (Cousins, Whitmore, & Shulha, 2014; Daigneault & Jacob, 2009). Cousins and Chouinard (2012) reviewed 121 pieces of empirical research on participatory evaluation published from 1997 through 2011 and also found great variation in approaches conducted under the "participatory" umbrella.

▶ What is essential to utilization-focused evaluation (Patton, 2012a)? I've seen a great many evaluations labeled *utilization-focused* that provided no evidence that primary intended users had been identified and engaged to focus the evaluation on those users' priorities.

▶ What are essential principles of developmental evaluation (Patton, 2016b)? An experienced developmental evaluation practitioner recently told me: "More often than not, I find, people say they are doing developmental evaluation, but they are not."

EXHIBIT 35.2. Tool for Rating Principles Based on the GUIDE Framework with a Rubric for Rating Effectiveness Principles

Principle to be evaluated:

GUIDE Rubric for Principles

G: GUIDING	Strongly agree	Agree	Neutral	Disagree	Strongly disagree	Comments: What needs to be improved?
G1. The principle is prescriptive; it provides advice and guidance on what to do, how to think, what to value, and how to act to be effective.						
G2. The principle provides clear direction.						
G3. The wording is imperative: *Do this . . . to be effective.*						
G4. The guidance is sufficiently distinct that it can be distinguished from contrary or alternative guidance.						
Overall guidance rating	Excellent	Good	Fair	Poor	Worthless	

U: USEFUL	Strongly agree	Agree	Neutral	Disagree	Strongly disagree	Comments: What needs to be improved?
U1. The principle is useful in making choices and decisions.						
U2. The principle's action implications are interpretable for use.						
U3. The principle's guidance is feasible.						
U4. The principle points the way toward desired results.						
Overall utility rating	Very useful	Fairly useful	Somewhat useful	Slightly useful	Useless	

(continued)

I: INSPIRING	Strongly agree	Agree	Neutral	Disagree	Strongly disagree	Comments: What needs to be improved?
I1. The values expressed by the principle are inspiring.						
I2. The principle incorporates and expresses ethical premises.						
I3. The principle is meaningful to what I do.						
I4. What the principle expresses matters to me.						
Overall inspiration rating	Very inspiring	Fairly inspiring	Somewhat inspiring	Slightly inspiring	Not at all inspiring	

D: DEVELOPMENTAL	Strongly agree	Agree	Neutral	Disagree	Strongly disagree	Comments: What needs to be improved?
D1. The principle is context sensitive—relevant to diverse contexts and situations.						
D2. The principle is *complexity relevant*: provides guidance for navigating complex dynamic systems.						
D3. The principle has an enduring quality: meaningful over time.						
D4. The principle is adaptable to emergent challenges in the face of change.						
Overall developmental rating	Highly applicable	Fairly applicable	Somewhat applicable	Slightly applicable	Not applicable	

(continued)

E: EVALUABLE	Strongly agree	Agree	Neutral	Disagree	Strongly disagree	Comments: What needs to be improved?
E1. The meaningfulness of the principle to those expected to follow it can be assessed.						
E2. It is possible to document and judge whether the principle is actually being followed (adhered to).						
E3. If adhered to, it is possible to document and judge what results from following the principle (to determine if following the principle takes you where you want to go).						
E4. It is possible to bring data to bear and render judgment about the overall effectiveness of the principle.						
Overall evaluability rating	Highly evaluable	Fairly evaluable	Somewhat evaluable	Slightly evaluable	Not at all evaluable	

Source: Created by Michael Quinn Patton and Charmagne Campbell-Patton.

354

Treating Essential Principles as Sensitizing Concepts

Before presenting Exhibit 35.3 listing the essential principles of principles-focused evaluation, let me describe how I think about them. As with developmental evaluation, I've wanted to avoid a recipe-like approach based on operationalizing key concepts and dimensions. Instead, again as with developmental evaluation, I view the essential principles for principles-focused evaluation as *sensitizing concepts*. That means that each of the principles must be explicitly addressed in a principles-focused evaluation, but how and the extent to which they are addressed depends on situation and context. This is a critical departure from the usual approach to *fidelity,* which has traditionally meant to implement an approach operationally in exactly the same way each time. Fidelity has meant adherence to a recipe or highly prescriptive set of steps and procedures. The essential principles of principles-focused evaluation, in contrast, provide guidance that must be interpreted and applied contextually—but *must* be applied in some way and to some extent if the evaluation is to be considered genuinely and fully principles focused.

In lieu of operationalizing fidelity criteria, I have designated this approach as *assessing the degree of manifest sensitivity.* In lieu of fidelity, I prefer to examine the *integrity* of an approach. For a principles-focused evaluation to have integrity, the essential principles-focused evaluation principles should be explicitly and contextually manifest in both processes and outcomes, in both design and use of findings. Thus, when I read a principles-focused evaluation report, or talk with those involved in a principles-focused evaluation, or listen to a principles-focused evaluation presentation at a conference, I should be able to see/detect/understand how these essential principles of principles-focused evaluation informed what was done and what resulted.

Let me elaborate just a bit, again drawing on my earlier writings. The notion of judging the integrity of an approach by assessing the degree of manifest sensitivity to essential principles flows from the notion of fieldwork guided by sensitizing concepts (Patton, 2007, 2015a). A sensitizing concept raises consciousness about something, alerts us to watch out for its relevance, and reminds us to engage with the concept throughout our fieldwork within a specific context. Essential principles of principles-focused evaluation sensitize us to what to include in principles-focused evaluation practice.

Consider the concept of the GUIDE framework. I have organized much of the book around the five GUIDE criteria. The *quality principle* in the list of principles for principles-focused evaluation presented in Exhibit 35.3 states: "Support development of effectiveness principles that meet the GUIDE criteria: They *Guide*; are *Useful*; *Inspire*; support *Developmental* adaptations; and are *Evaluable*." But I would not go so far as to say that if a principles-focused evaluation does not explicitly and formally use the GUIDE framework and criteria it is therefore not a principles-focused evaluation. There are other ways of addressing the quality criterion and quality principle. Thus, any principles-focused evaluation must address explicitly how the quality of principles is addressed and assessed, but that does not restrict the assessment to using the GUIDE criteria. I hope that's clear because I think it's important. Now, without further ado, Exhibit 35.3 presents the eight essential principles guiding principles-focused evaluation.

EXHIBIT 35.3. Essential Principles Guiding Principles-Focused Evaluation
A Tool for Assessing the Degree of Manifest Sensitivity (Fidelity) to Each Principle in a Principles-Focused Evaluation

Principles	Commentary on the importance of the principle	Rubric for assessing the degree of manifest sensitivity (fidelity)
1. *Matching principle*: Conduct principles-focused evaluations on principles-driven initiatives with principles-committed people. Principles are the evaluand (focus of evaluation).	*No principles, no principles-focused evaluation.* Matching is a general evaluation principle calling for the evaluation approach to match the evaluation situation and questions. This principle is a specific acknowledgment and application of that more general evaluation principle.	5. Excellent match between evaluation approach and the focus of the evaluation 4. Good match 3. Fair match 2. Poor match 1. Misalignment: the evaluation should not go forward
2. *Distinctions matter principle*: Distinguish types of principles: natural, moral, and effectiveness; distinguish principles from values, beliefs, lessons, rules, and proverbs.	I have documented throughout this book examples of statements labeled "principles" that don't come close to passing the GUIDE criteria. See Chapters 1–5 and 7–11 for examples of common confusions about what constitutes a principle and important distinctions to consider.	5. Very clear distinctions regarding what constitutes a principle 4. Fairly clear distinctions 3. Somewhat clear distinctions 2. Unclear distinctions 1. Confusion regarding what constitutes a principle
3. *Quality principle*: Support development of effectiveness principles that meet the GUIDE criteria: They *guide*; are *useful*; *inspire*; support *developmental* adaptations; and are *evaluable*.	I have organized much of the book around the five GUIDE criteria, but I would not go so far as to say that if a principles-focused evaluation does not explicitly and formally use the GUIDE framework and criteria that it is therefore not a principles-focused evaluation. There are other ways of addressing this quality principle. Thus, any principles-focused evaluation must address explicitly how the quality of principles is addressed and assessed, but that does not restrict the assessment to using the GUIDE criteria.	5. Very high-quality principles 4. Fairly high quality 3. Somewhat high quality 2. Poor quality 1. Principles need revision before the evaluation can be done

(continued)

Principles	Commentary on the importance of the principle	Rubric for assessing the degree of manifest sensitivity (fidelity)
4. **Evaluation rigor principle**: Systematically inquire into and evaluate effectiveness principles for both implementation (Are they followed?) and results (What difference do they make?).	This principle emphasizes that principles-focused evaluation should address both processes of implementation and results of adhering to principles. This is to counter the assertion and perception that principles-focused evaluation is entirely process oriented. The results of following principles are also a focus for evaluation.	5. Very rigorous 4. Fairly rigorous 3. Somewhat rigorous 2. Low rigor 1. Revise design to increase rigor
5. **Utilization focus principle**: Focus on intended use by intended users from beginning to end, facilitating the evaluation process to ensure utility and actual use.	The Joint Committee on Standards for Educational Evaluation (2012) makes utility the first standard of excellence for any evaluation. Principles-focused evaluation is conducted under the broad umbrella of utilization-focused evaluation (see Patton, 2008, 2012a).	5. Highly utilization focused 4. Fairly utilization focused 3. Somewhat utilization focused 2. Weak utilization focus 1. Revise the evaluation process and design to increase potential use.
6. **Beyond rhetoric principle**: Support using principles comprehensively; use them or lose them; don't let them become just a list; apply them across functions (staff development, working with clients, strategic planning, monitoring and evaluation).	This principle is included on this essential principles list because there is so much empty rhetoric about articulating principles, following principles, being principles driven, and "walking the talk" of principles. See Chapter 13 for an exemplar of using principles to guide all aspects of organizational and programmatic activity.	5. High degree of attention to and integration of principles throughout the work of the organization, program, or initiative 4. Fair degree of attention to and integration of principles 3. Some attention to and integration of principles 2. Little attention to and integration of principles 1. *Not* a principles-based organization, program, or initiative

(continued)

Principles	Commentary on the importance of the principle	Rubric for assessing the degree of manifest sensitivity (fidelity)
7. **Interconnections principle**: Interconnect principles. The eight principles of principles-focused evaluation are an interdependent, interconnected whole (not a pick-and-choose list). For any set of principles being evaluated, examine how individual principles are aligned (or not) and interconnect (or not).	Some lists of principles treat each principle as autonomous. That is not the case here. The eight principles guiding principles-focused evaluation reinforce each other and constitute a whole. Fidelity involves addressing all of the principles as essential.	5. Complete interconnections among principles 4. Considerable interconnections 3. Some interconnections 2. Little interconnection 1. No interconnections: a pick-and-choose list
8. **Learning principle**: Reflect on the strengths and weaknesses of the principles-focused evaluation process and results to learn and improve; engage in principles-focused reflective practice. Deepen learning about principles-driven programming and principles-focused evaluation; extract and apply lessons.	This principle acknowledges that principles-focused evaluation is relatively new, still developing, still adapting, still emerging, and much remains to be learned.	5. High-quality attention to learning 4. Some attention to learning, but not consistent 3. Little attention to learning 2. No systematic learning component in the evaluation 1. Pushback against learning as beyond the purpose of the evaluation

Exhibits as Tools

I have created exhibits throughout this book to summarize and illustrate critical lessons, key points, and core messages. Many of those exhibits can be used as tools or adapted for use in capacity building and design of principles-focused evaluations. The Appendix to this chapter identifies those exhibits that have high potential for use as tools. I have added commentary about how to use each exhibit. My comments are meant to be suggestive, not limiting. I mean simply to offer examples of how exhibits can be used as tools and facilitation guides.

Conclusion

This chapter has been about tools. The most important tool you possess is your mind. Rigor resides not in methods, but in rigorous reasoning. The GUIDE criteria provide guidance, but you have to figure out how to adapt them to whatever context and situation you encounter. GUIDE is a framework, not a formula. Principles provide direction, but are not rules. Principles have to be interpreted and their effectiveness evaluated. Tools may be useful, but you have to work with them and practice using them to realize their potential. Even then, with each new use you'll have to adjust them to fit your needs and disposition. This means there is much to do and much to learn, so go forth and engage in principles-focused evaluation as the occasion permits. And heed this advice from British poet George Herbert:

> Do not wait; the time will never be "just right." Start where you stand, and work with whatever tools you may have at your command, and better tools will be found as you go along.

Let's dub that the "Get on with it" principle. Get on with it.

APPENDIX 35.1. Exhibits as Tools

Exhibits for use as tools	Exhibit title	Page	Potential uses
Exhibit 1.1	Fourteen classic principles and corresponding evaluation questions	7–8	Illustrates the differences between moral principles, natural principles, and effectiveness principles.
Exhibit 3.1	Nine evidence-based guiding principles to help youth overcome homelessness	18	Presents an example of a set of guiding principles shared by multiple programs.
Exhibit 4.1	What evaluators do well and are still figuring out, and the emergent challenges for evaluation	22	Positions principles as an emergent evaluand (focus of evaluation) and new challenge for evaluation.
Exhibit 5.2	Principles-focused evaluation serving diverse purposes	28	Presents purpose distinctions for principles-focused evaluation: formative, summative, developmental, monitoring, accountability, and knowledge generation.
Exhibit 5.3	Principles of utilization-focused evaluation	29	Positions utilization-focused evaluation as the broad umbrella under which principles-focused evaluation takes place.
Exhibit 5.4	Developmental evaluation principles	30	When principles-focused evaluation serves a developmental evaluation purpose, the principles of developmental evaluation apply in conjunction with the principles of principles-focused evaluation.
Exhibit 5.5	Principles guiding principles-focused evaluation	31	Use in conjunction with Exhibit 35.3: "Essential principles guiding principles-focused evaluation: A tool for assessing the degree of manifest sensitivity (fidelity) to each principle in a principles-focused evaluation."
Exhibit 6.1	GUIDE for principles	38	Presents an overview of the GUIDE criteria for use in working with stakeholders, training, and teaching.
Exhibit 6.3	Example of a GUIDE framework application: Polio eradication principles	40	Provides a concrete illustration of the principle manifesting each GUIDE criterion.

(continued)

Exhibits for use as tools	Exhibit title	Page	Potential uses
Exhibit 6.4	GUIDE framework and rubric for effectiveness principles	43	Defines each GUIDE criterion and offers a sample quality-assessment rubric. This can be used in conjunction with Exhibit 35.2, "Tool for rating principles based on the GUIDE framework and rubric for rating effectiveness principles." Exhibit 6.4 is a simple introductory version of this more complicated and comprehensive tool.
Exhibit 7.2	Rules versus principles: Select examples	50	Gives examples of rules compared to principles in a number of areas like time management, investing, and exercise.
Exhibit 7.3	Principles versus rules	51	Six ways in which principles and rules vary.
Exhibit 7.4	Opposing principles for serving homeless youth	54	Demonstrates the value of articulating opposite or contrary principles as a way of clarifying and positioning a principle.
Exhibit 7.6	Contrasting a principle with a rule and an alternative principle	56	Uses evaluation as an example to highlight these distinctions.
Exhibit 8.1	Gottlieb's (2009) Six Pollyanna Principles converted to effectiveness principles and corresponding evaluation questions	63–64	Provides a concrete example of revising principles to meet the GUIDE criteria.
Exhibit 9.1	Skillful teaching: Assumptions versus principles	67	Illustrates how to reframe assumptions as principles using skillful teaching as the example.
Exhibit 9.2	Assumptions and personal truths reframed as overarching and operating principles for the skillful teacher	69	Demonstrates the difference between overarching and operating principles using the example of skillful teacher assumptions and truths.
Exhibit 9.3	Six principles of effective practice for adult educators, with commentary	71	Provides a review and critique of published adult education principles.
Exhibit 9.4	From lessons to principles and evaluation (reflective practice) questions	73	Illustrates how to generate evaluation questions from lessons and principles.
Exhibits 10.2 and 10.3	Parallel processes in extension and evaluation; Parallel extension and evaluation principles	79–81	Show how different fields of endeavor can have similar principles.

(continued)

Exhibits for use as tools	Exhibit title	Page	Potential uses
Exhibit 10.4	Common principles undergirding qualitative research inquiries and humanistic psychology therapies	82	Illustrates how separate arenas of action can be guided by the same principles.
Exhibit 11.1	Depiction of interrelated, mutually reinforcing, dynamic interconnections among CCRP principles	85	Graphically illustrates the interconnections and interdependence among a set of eight principles.
Exhibit 11.2	Autonomous principles in a framework compared to integrated and interdependent principles in a framework	87	Systematically compares two approaches to a set of principles, one in which each principle is autonomous and a contrasting one where the principles in the set are interrelated.
Exhibit 11.3	Generic evaluation questions for the sequence of truth and reconciliation principles	89	Illustrates the sequencing of principles in a holistic set.
Exhibit 12.1	Paris Declaration Principles of Aid Effectiveness: Baselines and outcomes	97	Depicts a framework for reporting changes in principles against a prior baseline at an earlier time.
Exhibit 12.2	Youth homelessness principles: examples of interim outcomes and corresponding evaluation questions	98	This exhibit could be used as a tool to organize and illustrate the relationship between principles, interim outcomes, evaluation questions, and overall program outcomes.
Exhibit 14.2	Criteria for evaluating research-derived principles applied to the TEC-VARIETY framework	114	Using principles for online teaching, this exhibit is a tool for identifying and articulating evaluation criteria and corresponding evaluation questions.
Exhibit 14.3	Examples of utilization-focused process and outcome evaluation questions for the TEC-VARIETY framework	115	Uses principles for online teaching to distinguish process evaluation and outcome evaluation questions.
Exhibit 15.1	Problem-focused versus principles-focused mission statements	123	Is useful in facilitating development of mission statements.
Exhibit 17.1	Working principles from the situation assessment	140	Shows how to differentiate overarching principles from more specific operational principles within overarching principles.

(continued)

Exhibits for use as tools	Exhibit title	Page	Potential uses
Exhibit 19.3	Example of adaptation and development of principles	159	This exhibit shows the transition from an original aspirational statement to a final convening question.
Exhibit 19.4	Evolving a civic communications ecosystem	165	Displays a visual graphic for depicting intersecting principles.
Exhibit 20.3	Translating change premises into effectiveness principles	171	Shows how to work with original action premises and revise them as effectiveness principles.
Exhibit 21.1	Applying the GUIDE criteria to the revised and focused principles for effective facilitation by adult educators	181	Demonstrates the use of the GUIDE framework to review and revise a specific set of draft principles.
Exhibit 21.2	Sample interview protocol: GUIDE-based evaluation questions for adult educators	182–184	Provides an example of a GUIDE-based set of questions for assessing the meaningfulness of a set of principles to those who are expected to adhere to them.
Exhibit 21.3	Illustrative ratings instrument for adult education principles	185	Shows how to create a ratings instrument for principles targeted to a specific group of people who are expected to adhere to a set of principles.
Exhibit 21.5	Evaluation ratings matrix for each country's adherence to the Paris Declaration development aid principles	188	Using the Paris Declaration development aid principles, a measurement matrix is presented.
Exhibit 21.6	Summary matrix used to rate degree of impact of implementation of the Paris Declaration Principles	189	Illustrates a principles-focused synthesis instrument for aggregating data across multiple sources.
Exhibit 22.2	Principles-focused sampling examples from Part III of this book	201	Reviews purposeful samples from exemplars in Part III of the book.
Exhibit 23.1	Steps in evaluative reasoning applied to evaluating effectiveness principles	204–205	Applies generic steps in evaluating reasoning to rendering judgments about the effectiveness of principles, with examples.

(continued)

Exhibits for use as tools	Exhibit title	Page	Potential uses
Exhibit 23.2	Comparing attribution questions, generic contribution analysis questions, and principles-focused contribution analysis questions	207	Distinguishing attribution from contribution evaluation questions can be useful in facilitating discussions of causality.
Exhibit 23.3	What it means for principles to be judged effective	211	Presents a succinct review of the GUIDE criteria.
Exhibit 24.1	Three types of evidence-based judgments of effectiveness	213–214	Distinguishes summative evaluation, meta-analysis, and qualitative synthesis.
Exhibit 24.2	Best practices compared to effectiveness principles	218	Compares best practices and effective principles on six criteria.
Exhibit 29.3	CCRP principles framework	270–273	Eight overarching guiding principles elaborated through operating principles. Shows the relationship between overarching and operating principles for a specific program.
Exhibit 30.2	Preliminary list of agroecological principles to use in agroecological research	280	Illustrates that social relationship between principles, subprinciples, and practices derived from principles.
Exhibit 31.1	AEA guiding principles: Original and restated	291	Illustrates conversion of a specific set of principles to the GUIDE format.
Exhibit 31.2	AEA guiding principles with new parallel guiding principles for evaluation stakeholders	292	Illustrates the adaptation of principles from one target audience to another.
Exhibit 31.3	AEA guiding principles presented as overarching and operational principles	293–294	Illustrates a differentiation between overarching and operational principles.
Exhibit 31.6	AEA culturally competent core concepts converted to principles	298	Illustrates the conversion of concepts to principles.
Exhibit 31.7	Illustrative principles of evaluative thinking	300	Illustrates principles for evaluators and evaluation stakeholders.
Exhibit 31.9	Practical inquiry principles to get actionable answers	302–303	Key learnings are expressed as principles.
Exhibit 31.10	Twelve principles for qualitative evaluation	304	Illustrates methodological principles.
Exhibit 31.11	Principles for in-depth interviewing	304–305	Illustrates methodological principles.

(continued)

Exhibits for use as tools	Exhibit title	Page	Potential uses
Exhibit 32.1	Customizing an outcome harvest	309	Depicts six steps
Exhibit 32.2	The six steps and ten principles of outcome harvesting	312	Ten principles related to the six steps
Exhibit 32.3	Results in outcome harvesting	315	Graphic display of levels of results
Exhibit 34.1	Me, the evaluator, reimagined	332	Graphically depicts the values of an evaluator.
Exhibit 34.2	Guiding principles for professional engagement	333	Illustrates professional principles adopted by one evaluator as an example of principles-focused evaluation practice.
Exhibit 34.3	How my guiding principles for professional engagement were manifested in the youth homelessness evaluation	334	Illustrates Nora Murphy's principles in practice.
Exhibit 34.4	Forward-thinking orientation in developmental evaluation	336	Steps in a developmental evaluation.
Exhibit 34.5	Journey orientation in developmental evaluation	337	Systems map of developmental evaluation. Use Exhibits 34.4 and 34.5 together as contrasting approaches.
Exhibit 35.1	Checklist and guide for facilitating the development and review of principles	348–350	Presents a tool to use in developing principles.
Exhibit 35.2	Tool for rating principles based on the GUIDE framework with a rubric for rating effectiveness principles	352–354	Presents a tool to use in applying the GUIDE framework in reviewing principles.
Exhibit 35.3	Essential principles guiding principles-focused evaluation: A tool for assessing the degree of manifest sensitivity (fidelity) to each principle in a principles-focused evaluation	356–358	The principles that are essential to principles-focused evaluation and therefore can be used to evaluate adherence and fidelity to principles-focused evaluation.
Exhibit 36.1	Principles-focused evaluation checklist: 10 steps to principles-focused evaluations that are useful—and actually used	367–377	Presents a comprehensive review of the major elements of a principles-focused evaluation identifying both tasks to be completed and facilitation challenges to address.

CHAPTER 36

Principles-Focused Evaluation Checklist

Here, then, is our situation at the start of the twenty-first century: We have accumulated stupendous know-how. We have put it in the hands of some of the most highly trained, highly skilled, and hard-working people in our society. And with that, they have indeed accomplished extraordinary things. Nonetheless, that know-how is often unmanageable. Avoidable failures are common and persistent, not to mention demoralizing and frustrating, across many fields—from medicine to finance, business to government. And the reason is increasingly evident: the volume and complexity of what we know has exceeded our individual ability to deliver its benefits correctly, safely, or reliably. Knowledge has both saved us and burdened us.

That means we need a different strategy for overcoming failure, one that builds on experience and takes advantage of the knowledge people have but somehow also makes up for our inevitable human inadequacies. And there is such a strategy— although it will seem almost ridiculous in its simplicity, maybe even crazy to those of us who spent years carefully developing ever more advanced skills and technologies.

It is a checklist.

—ATUL GAWANDE, *The Checklist Manifesto* (2010, p. 14)

This chapter presents a comprehensive, detailed 10-step principles-focused evaluation checklist that describes the primary tasks and major facilitation challenges of each step. The checklist both summarizes the major guidance provided throughout this book and serves as a review of that guidance. Basic premises are presented for each step to provide a context for the primary tasks and special facilitation challenges. Each step concludes with an overview of the *desired results* for that step.

The 10 steps in the checklist portray a simplified linear and sequential process. This can be helpful in proposing, planning, and managing a principles-focused evaluation and understanding the work involved in fulfilling each step. But in the real world the process is seldom neatly linear and sequential. Interdependencies and interactions among the steps make a principles-focused evaluation process complex, meaning it is typically emergent, nonlinear, dynamic, and adaptive. Use this checklist as you use principles, as big-picture guidance, providing direction, but be prepared to adapt that guidance to the real-world complexities of real-world evaluation and the people, situation, and context you're working with. Exhibit 36.1 presents the checklist.

EXHIBIT 36.1. Principles-Focused Evaluation Checklist
10 Steps to Principles-Focused Evaluations That Are Useful—and Actually Used

- Step 1. Assess and build program and organizational readiness for principles-focused evaluation.
- Step 2. Assess and enhance evaluator readiness and competence to undertake a principles-focused evaluation.
- Step 3. Identify, organize, and engage primary intended users for the principles-focused evaluation.
- Step 4. Using the GUIDE framework, conduct a principles-focused situation analysis jointly with primary intended users.
- Step 5. Identify primary intended uses by establishing the principles-focused evaluation's priority purposes.
- Step 6. Consider and build in process uses as appropriate.
- Step 7. Focus priority principles-focused evaluation questions relevant to evaluating principles.
- Step 8. Negotiate appropriate methods to generate credible findings and support intended use by intended users.
- Step 9. Review utilization-focused evaluation checklist for data collection, and analysis, reporting, and presentation strategies that enhance use.
- Step 10. Follow up with primary intended users to facilitate and enhance ongoing attention to the principles and ongoing principles-focused evaluation.

The checklist has two columns: primary *principles-focused evaluation (P-FE) premises for effectiveness* are in the left column. Because of the importance of capacity building and facilitation in P-FE, particular *capacity-building activities and facilitation challenges* are identified in the right column. Both kinds of premises are presented for each step. Each step concludes with an overview of the *desired results* for that step.

Step 1. Assess and build program and organizational readiness for principles-focused evaluation.

Effectiveness premises:	Facilitation premises: The P-FE evaluator must engage those involved in a P-FE in ways that will deepen their understanding of evaluation and commitment to use.
<ul><li>P-FE occupies a particular niche that is well matched to principles-based programs and principles-driven people.</li><li>Programs and organizations that are well matched to and ready to seriously engage in P-FE are more likely to participate in ways that are meaningful and result in use.</li><li>Use is more likely if key people who will be involved in and affected by the P-FE become interested and engaged.</li></ul>	<ul><li>Evaluability assessment includes examining if the program and organizational cultures are receptive to and ready for P-FE.</li><li>P-FE can include help in developing principles as well as evaluating them.</li></ul>
Primary tasks:	**Evaluation capacity-building work and facilitation challenges:**
1A. Assess the commitment of those commissioning and funding the evaluation to undertake a P-FE based on understanding *how principles guide.*	<ul><li>Explaining P-FE and assessing readiness for evaluation generally and P-FE specifically.</li></ul>

(continued)

Primary tasks:	Evaluation capacity-building work and facilitation challenges:
1B. Assess the context to illuminate *how principles make a difference.* • Review important documents, interview key stakeholders, and find out current perceptions about *both* principles and evaluation, and the connection between the two. • Conduct a baseline assessment of past approaches to principles and past evaluation uses. • To what extent does the context constitute a complex dynamic system that is especially appropriate for navigation through P-FE?	• Conducting individual and/or focus group interviews to get baseline information. • Building trust for honest discussions about how principles and evaluation are viewed. • Generating sufficient commitment of time and resources to do a high-quality P-FE, including developing principles that meet the GUIDE criteria.
1C. Introduce the GUIDE criteria as the framework within which the P-FE will be conducted (see Chapter 6). • When ready to engage, plan a launch workshop or event that will involve key stakeholders to both assess and build readiness for P-FE based on GUIDE.	• Explaining the GUIDE criteria and their relevance. • Engaging with the group to apply the GUIDE criteria. • Agreeing on what diverse stakeholders to involve in the launch workshop. • Generating commitment to engage in the full P-FE process.
1D. Based on the initial experience working with key stakeholders, assess what needs to be done next to further enhance readiness, build capacity, and move the evaluation forward.	• Planning, negotiating, and facilitating the commitment of key stakeholders to move forward with evaluation. • Generating commitment to strengthen evaluation capacity, as needed.

RESULTS of STEP 1: Primary intended users understand and are committed to P-FE

Primary intended users understand . . .

A. *How principles guide*
  1. Principles inform choices at forks in the road.
  2. Principles are grounded in values about what matters to those who develop, adopt, and attempt to follow them.
  3. Principles provide direction, but not detailed prescription, so they offer opportunities to adapt to different contexts, changing understandings, and varied challenges.
  4. Principles must be interpreted and applied contextually and situationally to ensure their relevance.
  5. Principles are the rudder for navigating complex dynamic systems.

B. *How principles make a difference*
  6. Principles, when based on experience, knowledge, and evidence about how to be effective, can enhance effectiveness.
  7. Principles require judgment in application so their effectiveness is somewhat dependent on the quality of decision making and judgment rendering in applying and evaluating them.

(continued)

8. Principles have opposites that point in contrary directions, so they force consideration of alternative courses of action based on comparing competing principles.
9. Principles point to consequences, outcomes, and impacts.
10. Principles can be evaluated for both process (implementation) and results so that their hypothetical effectiveness and relevance can be tested.

C. *The GUIDE criteria for effectiveness principles*
A high-quality effectiveness principle:

G—provides guidance
U— is useful
I—inspires
D—supports ongoing development and adaptation
E—is evaluable

D. *Primary intended users are committed and ready to . . .*
1. Undertake principles development work as needed so that the principles to be evaluated meet the GUIDE criteria.
2. Open their principles to evaluation.

Step 2. Assess and enhance evaluator readiness and competence to undertake a principles-focused evaluation.

Effectiveness premise: Facilitating and conducting a P-FE requires a particular philosophy and special skills.	**Facilitation premise:** P-FE facilitators need to know their strengths and limitations and develop the knowledge and skills needed to facilitate P-FEs.
Primary tasks:	**Evaluation capacity-building work and facilitation challenges:**
2A. Evaluator's self-assessment of *general competencies:* 1. Professional practice knowledge 2. Systematic inquiry skills 3. Situational analysis skills 4. Project management skills 5. Reflective practice competence 6. Interpersonal competence 7. Cultural competence	• As an evaluator, being rigorously reflective about your strengths and weaknesses. • In working with primary intended users, being forthright about those strengths and weaknesses. • Engaging in ongoing professional development to build on strengths and reduce weaknesses.
2B. Evaluator's self-assessment of specialized P-FE knowledge and skills. *The principles-focused evaluator knows:* 1. The principles of P-FE and how fidelity to those principles requires addressing them as an interconnected and interdependent whole (see Chapter 5). 2. The niche of P-FE within the larger landscape of evaluation options (see Chapter 4).	• Matching the evaluator's competencies with what is needed to work effectively with a particular group of primary intended users, evaluation situation, and the kinds of challenges posed by engaging in P-FE. • Learning by doing. Principles-focused evaluators will have to adapt to each P-FE situation and learn by engaging and adapting in that context.

(continued)

Primary tasks:	Evaluation capacity-building work and facilitation challenges:
3. The principles and practices of utilization-focused evaluation and developmental evaluation and how P-FE evaluation draws on those approaches (see Chapter 5). 4. Examples of principles-based programs and initiatives and how they were evaluated (see Part III of this book). 5. P-FE evaluation methods, measurement and data collection options, principles-focused sampling approaches, and how to render judgments about the effectiveness of principles (see Part IV of this book).	

2C. *Evaluator is principles driven.* Principles-driven social innovators and program staff will expect a principles-focused evaluator to be principles-driven.
  1. Know the Joint Committee's *Program Evaluation Standards* or OECD's evaluation standards for international development contexts.
  2. Know the AEA Guiding Principles for Evaluators (see Chapter 31).
	• Articulate your own guiding principles as an evaluator. (See Chapter 15, especially Bob Stake's six things evaluators care about [pp. 124–125] and Ernie House's articulation of truth, beauty, and justice criteria [p. 125].)
	• See examples of the principles of principles-focused evaluators in Chapters 16, 17, 18, 19, 33, 34, and 37.

2D. Assess the match between the *evaluator's substantive knowledge* and what will be needed in the evaluation, for example, education, international development, public health, early childhood, and so forth.	• Demonstrating sufficient substantive knowledge of the program being evaluated to have credibility with key stakeholders and be able to facilitate discussions on substantive issues. • Being able to connect to people with substantive knowledge to fill in any gaps in the evaluator's knowledge.
2E. Assess whether a single evaluator or a team is needed, and the combination of competencies that will be needed in a team approach.	• Working together as a team offers opportunity for mutual support and greater diversity of competencies brought to the evaluation but adds the complication of integrating team members into an effective working group.

RESULTS of STEP 2: The principles-focused evaluator is ready to undertake a P-FE.

The principles-focused evaluator has assessed, understands, and can articulate . . .

A. General competences needed and acquired to conduct the evaluation.
B. Specialized P-FE knowledge and skills for conducting the evaluation.

(continued)

C. Professional principles that will guide the P-FE and personal principles that make the evaluator principles-driven.

D. Appropriate substantive knowledge to do the job, either directly or indirectly (through networking).

Step 3. Identify, organize, and engage primary intended users for the P-FE.

Effectiveness premise: Identifying, organizing, and engaging primary intended users optimizes the *personal factor*, which emphasizes that an evaluation is more likely to be used if intended users are involved in ways they find meaningful, feel ownership of the evaluation, find the questions relevant, and care about the findings. Primary intended users are people who have a direct, identifiable stake in the evaluation.	**Facilitation premise:** The P-FE facilitator has a stake in evaluation use and therefore an interest in identifying and working with primary intended users to enhance use.
Primary tasks:	**Evaluation capacity-building work and facilitation challenges:**
3A. Be *utilization focused*. Identify and involve primary intended users who are: • Interested • Knowledgeable • Open • Connected to important stakeholder constituencies • Credible • Teachable • Committed and available for interaction throughout the evaluation process	• Determining real interest; building interest as needed; sustaining interest throughout the P-FE process. • Determining knowledge of users; increasing knowledge as needed. • Facilitating an evaluation climate of openness. • Working with primary intended users to examine stakeholder connections and their implications for use. • Building and sustaining credibility of the evaluation working group made up of primary intended users. • Outlining and facilitating a process that intended users want to be part of and will commit to.
3B. Involve intended users throughout all steps of the P-FE process.	• Building and enhancing the capacity of primary intended users to prioritize evaluation questions, make good design decisions, interpret data, and follow through to get findings used.
3C. Monitor ongoing availability, interest, and participation of primary intended users to keep the process energized and anticipate turnover of primary intended users.	• Getting feedback about how intended users are experiencing the P-FE process. • At the first indication of turnover, assessing the implications and planning to replace any primary intended users.

(continued)

RESULTS of STEP 3: The P-FE is utilization focused.

A. Primary intended users are identified, engaged, and committed to doing a P-FE that is utilization focused.
B. Primary intended users know and are committed engagement throughout the evaluation, not just at the beginning.
C. The evaluator and primary intended users have a process for building capacity as needed, for evaluating how the P-FE is unfolding throughout the process, and are prepared to use feedback and learning to make adjustments as needed.

Step 4. Using the GUIDE framework, conduct a principles-focused situation analysis jointly with primary intended users.

Effectiveness premise: Both principles use and evaluation use are dependent on people and context.	**Facilitation premise:** Situation analysis is ongoing.
Primary tasks:	**Evaluation capacity-building work and facilitation challenges:**
4A. Together the evaluator and primary intended users examine the principles of the program, organization, or initiative. To what extent do they meet the GUIDE criteria? Determine how much principles development work needs to be done for the principle to be evaluable. Generate or revise principles as needed to make them evaluable.	• Working with intended users to understand and apply the GUIDE criteria without their becoming overwhelmed.
4B. Identify contextual factors that will (or may) affect conduct of the evaluation; be prepared to monitor and deal with those contextual factors.	• Identifying and strategizing about critical factors that can affect the priority questions, evaluation design, and evaluation use. Distinguishing and strategizing about enabling factors that may enhance use.
4C. Attend to both • tasks that must be completed and • relationship dynamics that support getting tasks done	• Finding and facilitating an appropriate balance between tasks and relationships (outcomes and process).

RESULTS of STEP 4: The P-FE is centered on the GUIDE framework.

A. Principles that meet the GUIDE criteria have been identified or generated, or both.
B. Contextual and situational factors that may affect the evaluation have been identified.
C. The primary intended users and principles-focused evaluator have developed a working relationship that is moving the P-FE process forward.

(continued)

Step 5. Identify primary intended uses by establishing the principles-focused evaluation's priority purposes.

Effectiveness premises: Use flows from clarity about purpose. P-FE can serve a variety of evaluation purposes.	**Facilitation premise:** Evaluation options should be reviewed, screened, and prioritized by primary intended users to clarify the primary purposes and uses of the evaluation.

Primary tasks:	Evaluation capacity-building work and facilitation challenges:
5A. Review *alternative* purpose options with primary intended users to prioritize the evaluation's purpose. Options include: • *Improving* adherence to principles (formative evaluation) • Summative evaluation to render *overall judgments* about effectiveness of principles • Meeting *accountability* demands for compliance with principles • *Monitoring* adherence to principles • *Developmental* approach to P-FE to adapt principles to changing needs and complex contextual dynamics • Using P-FE to *generate knowledge* (lessons learned, synthesis of effective patterns across programs)	• Helping intended users distinguish evaluation purposes and the importance of differentiating intended uses. • Working with primary intended users to establish priorities and resolve conflicts over competing purposes, avoiding ambiguity or confusion about priorities. • Avoiding the temptation to dabble in a little bit of everything. • See Exhibit 5.5 in Chapter 5, pp. 30–31, on options for focusing a P-FE.

RESULTS of STEP 5: The priority purpose and primary intended use of the P-FE has been determined and agreed on.

A. Primary intended users understand the importance of having clarity of purpose.

Step 6. Consider and build in process uses as appropriate.

Effectiveness premises:	**Facilitation premises:**
• Process use can enhance findings use. • How an evaluation is facilitated and conducted can have impacts on those involved with the evaluation. • Process use is more effective if it is explicit, intentional, and purposeful.	• Evaluative thinking is learned and evaluation capacity is enhanced by involvement in a participatory, collaborative, and utilization-focused evaluation. • Process use for P-FE has the value of adding significant depth of engagement with principles among those involved in the evaluation.

(continued)

Primary tasks:	Evaluation capacity-building work and facilitation challenges:
6A. Review with primary intended users any alternative process use options that are especially relevant to P-FE. • Consider how **evaluative thinking might be infused into the organization culture** as part of doing the evaluation. • Consider how the way in which the evaluation is conducted and who is involved can **enhance shared evaluation understandings**. • Consider how the evaluation might be conducted in ways that **increase skills, knowledge, confidence, self-determination, and a sense of ownership** among those involved in the evaluation, included the program's staff and intended beneficiaries.	• Helping primary intended users understand process use options, and the potential importance of process uses as intentional, thereby adding value to the evaluation.
6B. Examine the relationship and interconnections between potential process uses and findings use.	Facilitating a complex systems understanding of how process uses and findings uses may be interconnected, interactive, and mutually interdependent.

RESULTS of STEP 6: The nature and extent of any process uses have been determined and incorporated into the evaluation process.

A. Primary intended users understand process use as distinct from but related to findings use.
B. Primary intended users understand the relationship and interconnections between potential process uses and findings use, especially how P-FE deepens engagement with principles.

Step 7. Focus on priority principles-focused evaluation questions relevant to evaluating principles.

Effectiveness premise: No evaluation can look at everything. Priorities have to be determined. Focusing is the process for establishing priorities.	Facilitation premise: P-FE asks questions specifically related to principles-based programming.

Primary tasks:	Evaluation capacity-building work and facilitation challenges:
7A. Review generic P-FE questions. 1. To what extent are the identified principles meaningful to those meant to follow the principles? 2. To what extent are the principles adhered to in practice? 3. If adhered to, to what extent do the principles guide followers to the results they hope to achieve?	• Helping primary intended users understand the implications of the questions asked. • Facilitating consideration of how answers to priority questions can be used. • Keeping the focus on evaluating the effectiveness of principles and not getting diverted into other evaluation possibilities, like participant satisfaction with the program (unless satisfaction is a principle).
7B. Develop additional evaluation questions specific to the evaluation context, primary intended users, and the intended uses of the evaluation.	

(continued)

RESULTS of STEP 7: Priority questions focused on the effectiveness of principles have been prioritized.

A. Generic P-FE questions have been reviewed and adapted to fit the context of the evaluation and priority information needs of primary intended users.
B. Evaluation questions specific to the context and program have been identified and prioritized.

Step 8. Negotiate appropriate methods to generate credible findings and support intended use by intended users.

Effectiveness premises:	**Facilitation premise:** Involving primary intended users in methods decisions increases their understanding of the strengths and weaknesses of the methods used and deepens their understanding of data collection decisions, which supports the commitment to use the resultant findings.
• Methods should be selected and the evaluation designed to support and achieve intended use by primary intended users. • P-FE involves some specific, customized methods choices, like principles-focused sampling.	

Primary tasks:	**Evaluation capacity-building and facilitation challenges:**
8A. Design the evaluation to answer questions about the meaningfulness of principles, adherence, and, if adhered to, the results of adherence. (See Chapter 21.)	• Making sure that primary intended users play an active role in reviewing methods to examine their appropriateness and credibility.
8B. Employ principles-focused purposeful sampling. (See Chapter 22.)	• Taking time to think through with intended users purposeful sampling choices and their implications.
8C. Ensure that the results obtained from the chosen methods will be able to be used as intended. (For utilization-focused methods and measurement decisions, see Patton, 2008, 2012a.)	• Finding the right level of engagement with intended users, the "sweet spot," neither overly technical, nor overly simplistic.
8D. Negotiate trade-offs between design and methods ideals and what can actually be implemented given inevitable constraints of resources and time.	• Negotiating criteria for methodological quality and what constitutes credible evidence among key stakeholders.
8E. Render judgments about the effectiveness of principles.	• Helping intended users understand contribution analysis. (See Chapter 23.)

RESULTS of STEP 8: An appropriate and credible principles-focused evaluation has been designed.

A. Methods and measures will answer priority questions.
B. Principles-focused sampling ensures a relevant sample for P-FE.
C. The P-FE design is utilization focused.
D. The design is realistic.
E. The design and data will lead to judgments about the effectiveness of the principles being evaluated.

(continued)

Step 9. Review utilization-focused evaluation checklist for data collection, and analysis, reporting, and presentation strategies that enhance use.

Effectiveness premise: P-FE is utilization focused, which is one of the principles of P-FE. *Note:* The utilization-focused checklist (Patton, 2012a) addresses additional issues that can affect the utility and actual use of an evaluation. This includes techniques for practicing and simulating evaluation use, organizing data to enhance use, and ethical considerations about working with primary intended users.	**Facilitation premises:** • Every evaluation is a utilization-focused capacity-building opportunity. • Primary intended users will judge the value of an evaluation by its credibility and use.

Primary tasks:	**Evaluation capacity-building work and facilitation challenges:**
9A. Know the research-derived factors that affect evaluation use and apply that knowledge throughout the evaluation.	• Helping primary intended users stay utilization focused. • Demonstrating the utility of P-FE as a specific type of evaluation and particular kind of use.

RESULTS of STEP 9: The P-FE is used by intended users in intended ways.

A. Research knowledge about ways of enhancing evaluation use is applied.
B. Capacity is built to undertake future P-FEs.

Step 10. Follow up with primary intended users to facilitate and enhance ongoing attention to the principles and ongoing principles-focused evaluation.

Effectiveness premise: Follow-up enhances use and increases the value of both principles and P-FE.	**Facilitation premises:** Adherence to principles is an ongoing commitment and challenge. Goals can be attained. Principles are not attained; they are adhered to beyond any one project, program, or initiative.

Primary tasks:	**Evaluation capacity-building work and facilitation challenges:**
10A. Plan and budget for follow-up.	• Encouraging primary intended users to find adequate time and resources to do a good job of following up findings to enhance use. This involves both user and evaluator time and resources.
10B. Make strategic choices about where to focus follow-up efforts.	• Keeping users engaged after the report has been disseminated. • Being a champion for use of the findings without becoming perceived as a champion for the program.

(continued)

Primary tasks:	Evaluation capacity-building work and facilitation challenges:
10C. Engage in systematic reflective practice about the P-FE and its processes and uses, with primary intended users.	• Involving the evaluation's primary intended users in reflective practice is a way to enhance their own capacities, provide feedback to the evaluator to deepen his or her own reflective practice, and bring closure to the evaluation process.

10D. Engage in personal reflective practice to support ongoing professional development.
  • Reflect on what went well, and not so well, throughout the evaluation.
  • Assess your essential competencies and skills as an evaluator.
  • Use what you learn to improve your practice and increase use.
	• Following up evaluations to learn what worked and didn't work, what was useful and not useful.
	• Committing time to serious reflective practice and learning for ongoing professional development.

RESULTS of STEP 10: The use of P-FE is enhanced, deepened, and reinforced.

A. Principles become more deeply embedded in and connected to practice.

B. Principles-focused evaluation is ongoing.

Conclusion and
Final Practice Exercise

Lately it occurs to me what a long, strange trip it's been.
—THE GRATEFUL DEAD, "Truckin'"

This quote opened the preface. It strikes me as a fitting final reflection. This book is now complete, but the journey is not. We are all, together, still on the early pathway of principles-focused evaluation. Where we go from here remains to be seen and experienced, and will be determined, in part, by your evaluation of principles-focused evaluation generally, and this book specifically.

Therefore, having arrived at this interim endpoint, I invite you to evaluate this book using the GUIDE criteria. A high-quality principle (1) provides guidance, (2) is useful, (3) inspires, (4) supports ongoing development and adaptation, and (5) is evaluable. A high-quality book does likewise.

G—From your perspective, what has been the quality, relevance, and meaningfulness of the guidance provided in this book?

U—How useful is the book likely to be to you? To what extent and in what ways has it already been useful, if any?

I—To what extent and in what ways, if at all, have you found the book inspirational?

D—To what extent can you adapt the book's guidance to your own developing context and needs?

E—What is your overall evaluation of the book?

Next Steps

What are your next steps based on your evaluation? Where do you go next on this journey?

Epilogue
Eleven Questions,
Eleven Principles-Focused Responses

Because answers exist only to *questions*.
—Mungara Tarou Krishnamurti,
contemporary Indian philosopher

All questions have responses, but not all responses are answers.
—Halcolm

When I do presentations on principles-focused evaluation and conduct workshops and webinars, some common questions get asked. This chapter offers my (MQP) responses. Why 11 questions? I'm glad you asked. These were the questions that surfaced most frequently in my presentations. It's that simple. Be relieved that I haven't responded to all 25 on my original list. As a preview of what's covered in this epilogue, here are the questions I'll address.

Questions

1. When you want to introduce people to principles and principles-focused evaluation, what example do you begin with?

2. You've said that as you got engaged in principles-focused evaluation, you started seeing principles everywhere. You've certainly collected lots of examples, both good and bad. Is there one particular instance where you came across principles in an unexpected place that really surprised you?

3. Was there someplace you were expecting to find principles and didn't? Or what you found was lousy?

4. You've made the case for principles-based initiatives to navigate complex dynamic systems and principles-focused evaluation data to support and inform that navigation. What can go wrong? What's the downside of being principles driven?

5. I think that I get the idea of principles-focused evaluation. I understand principles as an evaluand. But I'm not so clear about its niche. You talk about principles-focused evaluation having a particular niche, like a plant adapted to a particular ecosystem. What's the niche of principles-focused evaluation?

6. You make the case that principles provide guidance for change and point toward desired results. That's what a theory of change does. How is principles-based programming different from program theory, and how is principles-focused evaluation different from theory-driven evaluation? Or is it?

7. What's the relationship between logic models and principles?

8. What resistance do you encounter to the idea of principles-focused evaluation?

9. How are developmental evaluation and principles-focused evaluation connected?

10. What's next on the agenda for principles-focused evaluation?

11. What's the future research and evaluation agenda to deepen understanding and improve the practice of principles-focused evaluation?

Q&A

The greatest compliment that was ever paid me was when one asked me what I thought and attended to my answer.
—HENRY DAVID THOREAU, American writer

Question 1. When you want to introduce people to principles and principles-focused evaluation, what example do you begin with?

M. Q. P. Response

I have no standard example. I offer this principle: Find an example that is relevant to, understood by, and meaningful to the people you're addressing. In Minnesota, my home state, and the "Land of 10,000 Lakes," where more than a third of the population fish, I offer principles of fishing. In a conference in Orlando, Florida, I used Walt Disney's principles for Disney World. In Brazil, I worked with people on Paulo

Freire's pedagogical principles, which led to Chapter 18. In Denmark, I used design principles for Danish chairs as a contextually engaging way to start. Usually, people are expecting me to provide some example of program principles, but any given program will be of interest to only some people. Education programs. Human service interventions. International development aid projects. Anti-poverty initiatives. Exemplars exist of principles-based programs for all kinds of change efforts and I've presented a great many such exemplars throughout this book, including Chapter 3 and all six chapters in Part III. But no particular program example will interest everyone. However, we all sit in chairs. Product design is more commonly principles driven than most social innovations, so in Denmark I began with Danish chairs. Here's how that example emerged.

In 2016 the Trapholt Museum for Moderne Kunst in Kolding, Denmark, featured an exhibit called *Seven Danish Wonders,* featuring award-winning Danish chair designs by famous Danish designers (see Exhibit 35.1). I was in Kolding to keynote the Danish Evaluation Society conference, so I had a chance to visit the exhibit. Exemplars of Danish design include the People's Chair by Børge Mogensen; the Egg Chair by Arne Jacobsen; the Trinidad Chair by Nanna Detzel; the Chieftain Chair by Finn Juhl; the Hunting Chair by Børge Mogensen; the Wishbone Chair by Hans Wegner; the Rosewood Desk by Helge Vestergaard Jense; and the PK9 Chair by Poul Kjærholm. You can find them all online at *www.trapholt.dk*. The exhibit explained the design principles that the chairs had in common, despite each being quite unique. Here they are:

▶ Minimalism (i.e., minimal use of material)
▶ Organic functionality
▶ Pragmatic utility
▶ Affordability
▶ Aesthetic elegance

▶ Comfort

▶ Versatility

▶ Endurance

▶ Simplicity

▶ Inspiration

Practice Exercise

How would you rate the chair you are currently sitting as manifestation of those 10 principles? That's a principles-focused product evaluation. That's a good warm-up for doing principles-focused program evaluation, like stretching before jogging. It can get your head into and ready for thinking about principles the way stretching gets your muscles prepared for the road.

Question 2. You've said that as you got engaged in principles-focused evaluation, you started seeing principles everywhere. You've certainly collected lots of examples, both good and bad. Is there one particular instance where you came across principles in an unexpected place that really surprised you?

M. Q. P. Response

On August 4, 2016, the headline in the *Pine City Pioneer* was: Pine County, Mille Lacs Band Sign Joint Statement of Principles. Pine County, Minnesota, borders the state of Wisconsin, about an hour's drive north of Saint Paul, Minnesota, the state capital. The county population is about 30,000. It is one of the poorest counties in the state. The Mille Lacs Band of Ojibwe is a federally recognized American Indian tribe located in East Central Minnesota. The tribe has around 4,500 members, and the tribal homeland is the Mille Lacs Indian Reservation, parts of which are located in Pine County. Under treaty, the Ojibwe people have sovereign control of their land and govern their people. I have a cottage along the Snake River in Pine County where I go to enjoy the

woods and write. The *Pine City Pioneer* publishes weekly for about 3,000 subscribers. A headline about two local governments, one of which is American Indian, caught my eye.

The story was that leaders of Pine County and the Mille Lacs Band had negotiated and signed a joint statement of principles on government-to-government relations "that provides a foundation for working together in a way that is mutually beneficial."

While the Statement of Principles does not constitute a formal agreement, it does establish an umbrella framework whereby the County and the Band respect each other's authorities and seek to exercise their own authorities in a way that will protect the rights guaranteed by state, federal and tribal law. (Fischer, 2016, p. 2)

The agreement includes 18 fundamental principles. Here are some examples:

▶ Provide all people with equal access to justice and public safety.

▶ Ensure access to police and fire protection, emergency services, ambulance services.

▶ Work together for clean air and water.

▶ Help all people live in a clean, sanitary environment.

▶ Protect and respect natural resources and wildlife.

▶ Support access to safe, affordable housing, adequate health care, and hospital care.

▶ Ensure access to good roads, bridges, and transportation systems.

▶ Provide children with a good education and a safe home.

▶ Assist elderly persons to live in dignity with adequate nutrition, health care and housing.

▶ Ensure that all incarcerated persons have fair and equal treatment.

▶ Help all persons suffering from substance abuse to get adequate treatment.

The joint agreement states:

All persons deserve to live without fear or discrimination, to pursue employment, to pursue happiness, to exercise their religion, to have the protection of the law, to maintain their traditions and language to be healthy, to be safe, and to live from infancy to old age in peace and tranquility. (Fischer, 2016, p. 2)

Keep in mind that historically the relationship between whites and American Indians has been heavy on discrimination and conflict, and light on mutual understanding and respect. Pine County has not been an exception to that history. The content of this joint agreement, then, constitutes a historical breakthrough.

But why principles?

A formal legal agreement would require ratification by the Minnesota Legislature, the Band government, and the Pine County Board. It would take time, get caught up in state and tribal politics, and be subject to possible defeat by some opposition group objecting to particular language or clauses. Informal agreement on a commitment to shared principles requires no formal approval. Ironically, perhaps, the very informality of the agreement makes principles-focused monitoring and evaluation all the more important because that provides a mechanism and process to ensure adherence.

The agreement specifies how implementation will occur.

From a government-to-government communication perspective, the Chief Executive will designate personnel to conduct external relations with Pine County and set annual goals with Pine County. The Pine County Board likewise will designate county commissioners, the county administrator, or county department heads or their designees to conduct external relations with the Band, including setting annual goals. (Fischer, 2016, p. 2)

The emphasis in the statement of principles is on seeking better communication and understanding between the Mille Lacs Band and the county based on mutual respect, respect for the law, and a desire to provide better services to the people their governments serve. The desired results are to "improve relations and services, reduce tensions and conflicts, save both parties time and money, and improve the lives of Band members and all citizens of Pine County."

The Mille Lacs Band of Ojibwe and Pine County hereby state that it is in the best interests of the Band and the County to seek mutual agreements in the future on matters impacting Band members and citizens of the County. (Fischer, 2016, p. 2)

This story and agreement epitomize the need for and niche of principles-focused evaluation. It's a story that happens to be unfolding in the rural heartland of America, where I live. But it's a story that can emerge anywhere in the world. Be on the lookout. Principles-based collaborations may be emerging where you work and live. Indeed, they probably already have. Look around. See what you turn up.

Question 3. Was there someplace you were expecting to find principles and didn't? Or where what you found was lousy?

M. Q. P. Response

The *Where's Waldo?* books for children show crowds of people doing various things, and the reader is challenged to find a character named Waldo in the crowd wearing a red-and-white-striped shirt, distinctive hat, and glasses. Sometimes the illustrations include red-and-white striped objects as decoys to make it harder to spot Waldo. The *Where's Waldo?* books come to mind when I encounter books and articles that have principles in their titles but none of substance in the content. They are sometimes rich with axioms, concepts, definitions, postulates, fundamental assumptions, premises, operating prescriptions, models, common errors to be avoided, advice, exemplars, guidelines, standards, and tools—but *devoid of principles*. For example, the book *Principles of Evaluation and Research for Health Care Programs* (Perrin, 2014) is a fine methods text but fails to deliver on the promise of providing principles in the body of the book, table of contents, or index. I could offer many more examples. What's going on?

I offer two explanations, or perhaps, hypotheses. First, publishers, book editors, and marketing departments find that "principles" sell. (You may have astutely noted that I'm about to test that proposition anew.) Practitioners seek guidance, and a book title that promises principles in the title or subtitle is attractive. The fact that the book offers no principles is secondary to the marketing pizzazz.

Secondly, and related to the first point, we've come to accept sloppiness and overpromised hype in article and book titles. I sense that using the word *principles* as a generic title for an article or book means, "I'm going to talk about a lot of stuff and provide advice about that stuff so let me elevate my advice and opinions by calling them principles." The expectation is, I presume, that no one will notice the minor omission of actual principles in such publications since, it appears, the authors and editors have not noticed said omission. But henceforth, principles-focused evaluators do and will notice.

I close my critical response (one reviewer called it "snarky") to this question by offering a couple of principles to guide those who promise principles in the titles of their books, articles, and presentations. See Epilogue Exhibit 1.

Question 4. You've made the case for principles-based initiatives to navigate complex dynamic systems and principles-focused evaluation data to support and inform that navigation. What can go wrong? What's the downside of being principles driven?

M. Q. P. Response

Let me tell you a story, a cautionary tale, if you will.

The Union for Experimenting Colleges and Universities was founded in the innovative turbulence of the 1960s as an alternative doctoral program aiming to make PhDs more accessible to disadvantaged and underrepresented populations. It was conceived of as a principles-based rather than

EPILOGUE EXHIBIT 1. Principles to Guide Those Who Promise Principles in the Titles of Their Books, Articles, and Presentations

Overarching principles	Operational principles
1. *Deliver principles when you promise principles.*	a. Avoid simplifying your principles message to the point where you leave out the principles. b. Avoid emphasizing principles in a title unless you actually have principles to present.
2. *Distinguish principles from other forms of advice.*	a. Know the difference between principles and opinions, recommendations, beliefs, findings, strategies, guidelines, standards, goals, hypotheses, values, "best practices," hopes, dreams, and visions. b. State clearly what you are providing in your writings—and then provide what you have stated.

rules-based program. Its North Star principle was to *be learner centered.*

▶ Learners designed their own unique, customized doctoral programs based on their interests, experiences, and visions for their future.

▶ Learners selected their own doctoral committee members, including core faculty advisers, faculty with relevant subject matter expertise, and peer learners who completed the doctoral committee.

▶ Learners chaired their doctoral committees (as opposed to having faculty chairs).

▶ Learners had a number of options beyond doing a traditional dissertation including action projects, creative projects, and innovative forms of inquiry that constituted *projects demonstrating excellence.*

▶ Learners progressed at their own pace. There were no credit hours to fulfill or rigid deadlines to meet.

▶ The role of faculty was to support, empower, and serve as resources to learners, not tell them what to do or enforce rules and regulations.

In the early years I served as an adjunct faculty member, then became part-time, and eventually became full-time. For self-directed, highly motivated, and disciplined learners, the Union Institute was ideal. Several of the learners I worked with specialized in evaluation and have gone on to become distinguished and accomplished evaluators. Others I worked with have established themselves as recognized scholars and practitioners in interdisciplinary and applied fields like leadership development, community change, organizational transformation, global studies, and systems dynamics. Several went on to attain tenure in traditional universities, serve in senior government and philanthropic positions, or succeed in business.

But not everyone thrived. Some floundered trying to find a focus, changed their area of doctoral studies several times, had trouble conceptualizing a credible customized doctoral program of study and inquiry, and wrote poorly, which held them back. Most worked full time while trying to also do their doctoral program. Such learners could spend years working on their doctorate, going deeply into debt with student loans. After 10 years, learners no longer had to pay tuition, but by then they could be more than $100,000 in debt. Some never finished.

At faculty meetings we discussed this problem. We considered imposing deadlines and progress markers, but in the end, the principle of being learner centered prevailed. We would counsel learners that the program didn't seem like a good fit and advise them to cut their losses, but it was ultimately always their decision. The faculty was emphatically and determinedly committed to learner control, learner decision making, learner autonomy, and respect for learners as operating principles under the overarching principle of being learner centered.

The federal government student loan regulatory authorities and higher education accreditation agencies saw it differently. After external review, these oversight institutions required and imposed progress markers, standardized timelines, and procedures for dismissing learners who were not meeting requirements for quality and progress on time.

The Union Institute almost collapsed under the strain of new, externally imposed regulation. It has survived, but as a much different, and more traditional, institution of higher learning. Many of the pioneering faculty, including myself, left during or after the transition to a more rules-based program. With the advantage of hindsight, however, and upon deeper reflection, I think that the faculty became inflexibly and rigidly committed to a narrow and absolute articulation of what it meant to be learner centered. What should have been a guiding principle became an orthodoxy, indeed, a dogma, with no room for adaptation based on evidence of how some learners were suffering and the threats to the institution that came with failure to adapt. We became principles-driven purists, upholding an ideal of learner centeredness against what we saw as the increasingly rigid, procedurally dominated, and administration-centered cultures of most traditional universities.

This brief history does not begin to do justice to the complex dynamics, agonizing negotiations, contentious faculty meetings, and confrontational political mobilization among warring positions that escalated over several years until the Union Institute capitulated to overwhelming external regulatory forces. It was a difficult, tense, and ultimately sad time for those of us who had experienced Union's glory days and had the opportunity to work with learners who thrived under the learner-centered model. But in the context of this book, I look back and see a principle treated as if it was written on a stone tablet delivered from a higher education god that allowed for no flexibility and adaptation. *When a principle becomes a rule, it is no longer a principle.* Evaluatively, the learner-centered principle was certainly meaningful, and absolutely being adhered to, but we failed to deal with the evidence of devastating effects and consequences for some learners. *When adherence to a principle has undesirable, even unacceptable, consequences, adherence may need to be reinterpreted and adapted based on principles-focused evaluation evidence.*

Question 5. I think that I get the idea of principles-focused evaluation. I understand principles as an evaluand. But I'm not so clear about its niche. You talk about principles-focused evaluation having a particular niche, like a plant adapted to a particular ecosystem. What's the "niche" of principles-focused evaluation?

M. Q. P. Response

In 2012, the United States National Park Service Scientific Advisory Committee recommended that the parks' resources be managed "for continuous change that is not yet fully understood" (Kolbert, 2016, p. 26). That framing of the challenge calls out to me for principles-based management supported by principles-focused evaluation. More generally, principles-based management, programming, initiatives, collaborations, innovations, and reforms are the niche for principles-focused evaluation.

What is a niche? Consider the niches of warblers as described by ecologist Robert MacArthur (1958). A spruce tree in the northeastern coniferous forests of the United States can have several distinct niches for different types of warblers. This is a manifestation of Gause's principle of survival by differentiation. G. F. Gause, a biologist, was concerned with how natural selection occurs in evolution. He was testing Darwin's theory of survival of the fittest and finding that species could specialize and adapt to quite specific niches to survive as the fittest within that niche. Survival was key to evolutionary differentiation. But once specialized within a differentiated niche, a species could not only survive but thrive. Let's call this the *principle of thriving by differentiation*.

Under this conceptualization of a niche and its benefits, the niche of principles-focused evaluation can be considered wherever principles have emerged as the appropriate approach for guiding action, adhering to deeply held values, and navigating the uncertainties of complex dynamic systems. Principles-driven people create the niche for principles-focused evaluation.

The field of evaluation has given rise to a many-splendored cornucopia of alternative approaches geared to diverse challenges and specialized information and decision-making needs, for example, theory-driven evaluation, empowerment evaluation, performance indicators, impact evaluation, and collaborative evaluation. In my book *Utilization-Focused Evaluation,* I identify 90 alternative ways of focusing an evaluation (Patton, 2008, pp. 300–305). The challenge is matching the type of evaluation to the situation.

Alvin Roth and Lloyd Shapely won the 2012 Nobel Prize in Economic Sciences for their work in matching theory, which concerns how people and organizations find and select what they need and want, concerning everything from matching marriage partners, finding the right school, matching organ transplant donors with needy patients, and matching buyers with sellers. The challenge of matching an evaluation approach to the needs of a particular evaluation situation and specific primary intended users of evaluation revolves, in part, around the nature and characteristics of the evaluand (the focus of evaluation, the "thing" evaluated). Fundamentally, the niche of principles-focused evaluation is straightforward: It's where the evaluand is principles.

I would only add that the niche may not be readily recognized by those in it. For many principles-based programs, their principles remain implicit and their evaluability unrecognized because they don't know that principles-based programming is an explicit option. Evaluators, for their part, have not included principles-focused evaluation among the options they offer programs and stakeholders. Together, going forward, leaders of principles-based programs and principles-focused evaluators can make principles explicit and evaluable, using the GUIDE criteria. Once the niche is recognized and understood, principles-driven leaders and principles-focused evaluators can work together to support using effectiveness principles effectively.

Question 6. You make the case that principles provide guidance for change and point toward desired results. That's what a theory of change does. How is principles-based programming different from program theory, and how is principles-focused evaluation different from theory-driven evaluation? Or is it?

M. Q. P. Response

This question, or some version of it, has come up at virtually every presentation I've made, webinar I've offered, or workshop I've conducted on principles-focused evaluation. So it's an important question, suggesting how deeply embedded theory-of-change formulations have become as part of evaluation practice. (For explications of theory of change as an intervention and evaluation approach, see Pawson, Greenhalgh, Harvey, & Walshe, 2004; Pawson & Sridharan, 2009; Rogers & Funnell, 2011; Sridharan & Nakaima, 2012).

Here's how I think about the question.

There are both similarities and differences. Let's start with similarities, using parallel analogies. All governing structures (parliaments, nonprofit boards, neighborhood councils) and voting procedures (majority vote, consensus) are concerned with making decisions, but they do so in quite different ways. All telephones facilitate communications, but the features of phones vary tremendously. All religions are concerned with spirituality, but they offer quite different ways of experiencing the spiritual journey. All effectiveness evaluation frameworks are concerned with what works and why, but they provide different forms of engagement and inquiry. Theories of change and principles-based programs are both concerned with enhancing effectiveness but do so in different ways, in response to different conditions and different stakeholders. Epilogue Exhibit 2 highlights some of what I see as the similarities and differences. The differences strike me as substantial and important.

As the exhibit subtitle conveys, the distinctions in Epilogue Exhibit 2 are tendencies, predilections, and nuances, not absolute or categorical differences. Theories of

EPILOGUE EXHIBIT 2. Comparing Theory of Change as a Framework with Principles as a Framework		
Tendencies, Predilections, and Nuances, Not Absolute Differences		
Dimensions of comparison	**Theory of change**	**Principles**
1. Overall use and intention	*Same for both theories of change and principles:* Concerned with specifying an effective and evaluable pathway to desired results and change.	
2. Origin	Scholarly research and theory specifying causal mechanisms that lead to predictable outcomes.	Practitioners', change agents', and social innovators' values, experiences, commitments, and visions for a better world.
3. Formulation	Differentiating baseline conditions, intervention variables, change mechanisms, and hypothesized outcomes as a descriptive and predictive causal model.	Imperative statements that prescribe value-based actions that are believed (hypothesized) to be effective in moving toward desired results.
4. Theory orientation	A *theory of change* states how the desired results will be accomplished, for example, how the quality of life for immigrants will be improved; how poverty will be reduced; how educational attainment will be enhanced; or how youth will be developed. *The theory orientation is to predict and explain.*	A principles-driven initiative is undergirded by or provides the basis for a *theory of action* that articulates how the work will be done, for example, helping people help themselves. Such a theory of action can be applied to any problem—helping immigrants, poverty reduction, youth development, disease prevention—but the mission focus is on how the work will be done. *The theory orientation is to support action.*
5. Language	Scientific, research, and academic terminology. Scientists may find "principles" vague and overly value-laden.	Practitioner, policymaker, and ordinary people's terminology. Program staff and participants may find theory-of-change language off-putting, abstract, and too academic.
6. Focus	Focuses on predictive reliability, construct validity, explanatory power, and replicability.	Focuses on meaningfulness to adherents, interpretability, inspirational underpinnings, and adaptability to a great variety of conditions and situations.
7. Credibility	Highly credible among scholars and researchers.	Highly credible among people engaged in change efforts.
8. Approach to specification	Operationalizing variables; specificity and precision valued and expected.	Sensitizing concepts; comfortable with ambiguity, interpretative variability, and qualitative meaning making.

(continued)

Dimensions of comparison	Theory of change	Principles
9. Evaluability	Rigorous research designs under controlled conditions; meta-analysis.	Systematic inquiry across diverse situations; qualitative syntheses.
10. Approach to causality	Attribution analysis and predictive modeling.	Contribution analysis and nonlinear interactions in complex dynamic systems.
11. Peer review	Scholars, theorists, researchers.	Practitioners, activists, advocates, change agents

change and principles-based change initiatives draw on different traditions, appeal to different actors and audiences, employ different language, and constitute alternative ways of conceptualizing change. Each is useful. They are not so much in competition with each other as they are alternative ways of conceptualizing, making sense of, and evaluating change.

The process of engaging with either a theory of change or a set of principles takes time and involves multiple stakeholders over time. The way that realist theorists Pawson and colleagues (2004) have described the theory of change journey could be applied to the process of embedding a set of principles in a program and testing their effectiveness.

> Intervention theories have a long journey. They begin in the heads of policy architects, pass into the hands of practitioners and managers, and (sometimes) into the hearts and minds of clients and patients. Depending on the initiative, different groups will be crucial to implementation; sometimes the flow from management to staff (and through its different levels) will be the vital link; at other times the participation of the "general public" will be the key interchange. The critical upshot of this feature is that interventions carry not one, but several implicit mechanisms of action. The success of an intervention thus depends on the cumulative success of the entire sequence of these mechanisms as the programme unfolds. (p. 5)

So theories of change and sets of principles share a concern with articulating and testing the effectiveness of human efforts to bring about change. But I take exception to the assertion that sometimes prefaces the question: that principles are just a sloppy and vague formulation of an implicit theory of change. Nor do I accept the contrary position that theories of change are oversimplified, mechanistic, and reductionist models that dangerously mischaracterize a complex, turbulent, and uncertain world. Let's not turn this into dueling banjos, or a winner-take-all debate. Each has a niche, purpose, utility, and following. Understand and appreciate the similarities and differences, then choose your poison.

Question 7. What's the relationship between logic models and principles?

M. Q. P. Response

Sometimes in workshops the theory of change question arises first; sometimes this logic model question comes first; but they almost always come together. Here, I think, the differences are starker. Logic models specify quite specifically and mechanistically the inputs, activities, and processes that are to be followed to produce clear, specific, and measurable outcomes and impacts. Logic models work well in simple situations for simple problems with known parameters and known solutions. How to teach someone to drive a car or speak a foreign language lends itself to logic model specification. Principles, in contrast, provide direction in complex, dynamic situations where the relevant variables and processes are interconnected, interacting, and interdependent such that linear causal modeling is insufficient, probably oversimplified, quite possibly distorting, and problematic under conditions of complexity. Principles of parenting provide guidance and direction, but effective parenting cannot be reduced to a logic model.

Networks provide an illuminative example. The UNESCO Creative Cities Network is a forum where cities around the world that emphasize creativity as part of their identity and branding can share information and learn from each other. Some are quite large, some much smaller. At a conference held in Ostersund, Sweden, in connection with the network's 10th annual meeting in September 2016 ("Valuing and Evaluating Creativity for Sustainable Regional Development"), some called for applying traditional evaluation tools like logic models and SMART goals to evaluate the effectiveness of the network. My view was, and is, that a network is not a project or program. It's a dynamic, self-organizing organism. It doesn't need and shouldn't be burdened by a framework of results-based management, as advocated by some. It doesn't need targets and indicators of success. Such rigid, mechanistic fabrications hinder dynamism and adaptation. But the alternative is not anarchy and absence of accountability. Networks can be guided by principles, like transparent interactions, broad citizen participation, and letting a thousand flowers bloom. Principles-focused evaluation can assess the meaningfulness, adherence to, and results of following those and other principles. Frame programs and projects as logic models with SMART goals, if you will, but don't contaminate and restrain dynamic networks with them.

Africa-based community organizer John Wilson, whose reflections were featured in Chapter 16, commented (p. 135):

> Now, we live in the real world and won't change the demand for logic models and results-based approaches. They are here to stay, in the short and medium term at least. *But,* if we can give organizations the option *also* of articulating their principles, which they have anyway, we can then give them a tool to evaluate themselves against what really matters to them and a tool to help make strategic decisions with.
>
> This could mean that they still use the logic models without these taking them off course, because what will keep them effective is the principles-focused approach. I suspect it will also make them deal better with their logic models. They can approach these with more confidence rather than with trepidation, or loathing as is sometimes the case! It's a job to be done and managed, but not to be dominated by.

Thus, in that spirit, it is also quite possible to use a set of principles in parallel with a logic model. Each provides an approach to effectiveness, a framework for striving toward meaningful results through effective processes. My response to the second question in this chapter featured an agreement between Pine County commissioners and the Mille Lacs Band of American Indians. They agreed on principles and have designated representatives to set concrete goals on issues covered by the principles-based agreement. The goals they set will likely spawn joint programs that may have logic models. Perfectly reasonable and appropriate. The annual goals and supporting logic models may change as conditions change, challenges emerge, and learning together occurs, but the principles should endure. One likely evaluation focus in this example would be to examine the extent to which the goals and programs that develop out of this new collaboration are consistent with the joint principles.

The principles-based youth homelessness programs presented in Chapter 26 also have logic models, in part because they are required by funders. The principles provide an overarching direction and put their values into action while the logic models lay out the steps to be followed in helping youth get housing. They are complementary programming and evaluation approaches, each meeting different needs and funder requirements. Wise, sustainable, and enduring programs follow the principle of doing what has to be done as long as it can be done ethically and without violating fundamental principles. Logic models and principles can coexist and, when each serves its purpose well, generate synergies. Their separate as well as combined strengths and weaknesses offer great opportunities for *triple loop learning*—learning how to learn, instead of being locked into predetermined assumptions about each (G. Page, personal communication, 2016).

Question 8. What resistance do you encounter to the idea of principles-focused evaluation?

M. Q. P. Response

One form of resistance is cynicism, an attitude captured cryptically by American humorist Mark Twain's observation that "Principles have no real force except when one is well-fed." Let that sink in for a moment.

I encounter various kinds of resistance to principles-focused evaluation, each of which is quite appropriate, understandable, and sensible within the context that the resistance occurs. Epilogue Exhibit 3 presents some common pushbacks against principles-focused evaluation and potential ways of responding. *Trigger alert:* I'm told that some of my fabricated responses (items labeled "c") come across as "snarky." There's that word again. Do I detect a pattern? Naturally I was shocked to receive such feedback. But the responses aren't meant to be a script you'd follow. They are just ways of, hopefully, clarifying the nature of the resistance while having a little fun with the challenge of facing resistance. I confess that I sometimes think or imagine saying some version of the "c" responses in Epilogue Exhibit 3, but actually verbalizing those kinds of responses? Not likely.

EPILOGUE EXHIBIT 3. Points of Resistance to Principles-Based Programming and Principles-Focused Evaluation

Objection to principles as the focus of either programming and/or evaluation	Illustrative evaluator responses and possible reactions—*not all of which are recommended*—and, in any case, need to be adapted to the situation and people involved in the discussion.
1. "Principles are too mushy, vague, ambiguous, and unclear to be useful. I prefer clear, specific, and measurable goals."	a. "OK, SMART goals it is." b. "Before abandoning the principles approach, let's see if they can be made clearer, more specific, and more actionable while still being principles. Shall we give it a try?" c. "I understand. You're a narrow-minded, rigid, rules-based, best-practices addict with an obsessive–compulsive personality disorder scared to death of openness, flexibility, and situational adaption. No problem. I have just the evaluator for you!"

(continued)

Objection to principles as the focus of either programming and/or evaluation	Illustrative evaluator responses and possible reactions—*not all of which are recommended*—and, in any case, need to be adapted to the situation and people involved in the discussion.
2. "We'd love to do principles, but we're funded to do outcomes. Our funders are all about outcomes. I don't think they would resonate to principles as an approach."	a. "Perhaps it's not either/or. We can satisfy your funder's need for outcomes and a logic model, but since you seem to resonate to principles, suppose we dip a toe in the water a bit, so to speak, and add in a principles component. Once done, the funder might be intrigued as long as the outcomes evaluation takes priority. What do you think?" b. "It's good that you know your funder's preferences so well. We'll follow the Golden Rule: *Those who have the gold make the rules.*" c. "Let's be honest. You're blaming the funder. Just own your resistance. It's OK. Not everyone resonates to principles. It sounds like the dominant culture that drives the organization is more of a rigid, rules-based, best-practices culture with deep concerns about openness, flexibility, and situational adaption. No problem. I have just the evaluator for you—and your funder! Would you like their names?"
3. "Principles sounds soft. Our organization is all about being strategic. Strategy trumps principles. Or let me say it in a way that you'll understand: *Being strategic is our principle.*"	a. "*Be strategic* is an evaluable principle. Before abandoning the idea of principles, suppose we at least identify other principles that may guide your work and consider their implications." b. "I understand. Let's evaluate your strategy then. Strategy-focused evaluation is an alternative to principles-focused evaluation." c. "I understand your perspective. Strategy is, of course, a term taken from the military. Very macho. Very assertive. You don't want to be mistaken for some principles-driven, barefooted, half-naked, vegan agitator like Gandhi. If you'd like, we can feature those strong, big, strategic hands of yours on the cover of our evaluation report—but for now please take them off my knee."

(continued)

Objection to principles as the focus of either programming and/or evaluation	Illustrative evaluator responses and possible reactions—*not all of which are recommended*—and, in any case, need to be adapted to the situation and people involved in the discussion.
4. "Principles? Principles-focused evaluation? Is that the new flavor of the week? Seems like every month somebody's got a new change model or evaluation framework they're pitching. Give me a break! We picked up Stufflebeam's CIPP model in the 1970s, and we've had no reason to change since. Tried and true, road-tested and reliable. You want a principle, I'll give you a principle. *If it ain't broke, don't fix it.* That's our principle."	a. "CIPP is, indeed, classic. Have you seen the CIPP Evaluation Model Checklist (Context, Input, Process, and Product)? It's online. Stufflebeam put out a second edition in 2007. Vintage." b. "I don't think Dan Stufflebeam would feel like you were cheating on him, or being promiscuous, if you took a look at what's developed in evaluation since the 1970s." c. "I do have a tiny question: How would you even know if it's broke? I think your real principle may be *never change*! And it sure sounds like you're successfully adhering to that."
5. "Principles? Hmmm. . . . Well, we've already got a mission statement, goals and objectives, a needs assessment, a situation analysis, a strategic plan, a SWAT analysis, a values statement, a theory of change, a logic model, a systems map, a complexity graphic, a network analysis, a monitoring system, a formative evaluation task force, an external summative evaluation review team, a performance indicators system, an accountability framework, a cost–benefit analysis, a judgment rubric, a participatory and empowerment evaluation initiative—and some other stuff. Do any of those suffice for this principles-focused thing? But if not, and it's the new thing, we'd be happy to add it to our toolkit—as long as it doesn't take any major time or effort. As you can see, we're already kind of busy."	a. "Sorry I asked." b. "Have you ever heard of the principle *less is more*?" c. "Would you be willing to be featured on a panel at the American Evaluation Association annual conference about posttraumatic evaluation stress syndrome? Then we could get you some help. Or at least some meds."

Question 9. How are developmental evaluation and principles-focused evaluation connected?

M. Q. P. Response

This is another question that gets asked in virtually every workshop and webinar I do. I answered this question in Chapter 5 when I discussed the relationship between utilization-focused evaluation, developmental evaluation, and principles-focused evaluation. So I've had my shot at this question. Let me bring in another voice to offer another perspective.

Jamie Gamble is a longtime developmental evaluation practitioner and the principal of Imprint Consulting. He is a pioneer in conceptualizing developmental evaluation (Gamble, 2008) and a regular contributor to the field of developmental evaluation. He has supported innovation and development in a wide range of issues including poverty reduction, environmental sustainability, food security, public health and safety, citizen engagement, and the arts. I put this question to Jamie and invited him to add advice about how to use principles-focused evaluation to enhance the utility of developmental evaluation. My thanks to Jamie for sharing his wisdom. Pay close attention, folks. This is sound advice from a longtime developmental evaluation practitioner.

Jamie Gamble's Response

As Michael has posited throughout this book, principles help guide us through change. Developmental evaluators support social innovators in adaptation, and the concepts and approaches of principles-focused evaluation offer us a valuable resource for this role. Below are three ideas of how principles-focused evaluation can support developmental evaluations.

1. One of the niches of developmental evaluation is the preformative development of a potentially broad impact, scalable innovation (Patton, 2011, p. 311). In working with social innovators in the early stages of innovative initiatives, I often see their original ideas and aspirations for change articulated as vague principles. They are intuitively reacting to a pattern they see or shift in their environment that creates a novel

opportunity, and they formulate these observations into the essential elements for the action they want to take. These are implicit and tacit—yet untested—principles and form the basis for their design process. The developmental evaluator is well placed to help the social innovator articulate, refine, and validate these emerging principles. How you can help:

▶ Listen carefully to the way innovators describe their thinking and observe carefully the decisions they are making. How they express their intentions and their assessment of the key attributes of what they are working on tend to get clearer over time. Choices about strategy or resources tend to reveal implicit priorities. Social innovators are constantly responding to their observations and experiences, with deepened reflections about what they are trying to do.

▶ Feed back this evolving understanding about the emerging principles. This is useful to social innovators to further clarify their thinking, and even more useful to those working in close proximity to them to understand these underlying assumptions and how they are evolving.

▶ Help build in feedback loops, and design (and evaluate) quick experiments that can help social innovators explore their assumptions about effectiveness principles.

2. The process of innovation almost always involves some degree of collaboration. The developmental evaluator, working in close proximity to the innovators, will generally have a close view of the dynamics of the collaboration, and the inevitable conflict and stress that will surface from time to time. The developmental evaluator is well positioned to provide data and perspective that can help untangle the conflict and support things to productively move forward.

▶ One of the reasons that conflict emerges in a highly developmental situation is that there are key differences in assumptions about underlying effectiveness principles. In the early stages, collaborators agree in concept and begin to work together. As things unfold, people's assumptions about these principles become more focused, and resources get allocated accordingly. Developmental evaluators can help locate and name these different assumptions and support a process for testing assumptions. Sometimes the creation of a clear experimentation and learning plan allows contrasting assumptions about emerging principles to coexist so efforts can move forward.

▶ Another reason for conflict in these situations is the deviation from what are understood to be key moral principles that are guiding the initiative. Applying a principles-focused evaluation could help collaborators to examine the extent to which these values are followed in practice, and explore the implications of deviating from them.

▶ Collaborations that are highly productive get good at working through these conflicts. How can you, as the developmental evaluator, help them to develop the principles for working through these conflicts so they can do so more efficiently and effectively in the future?

3. Capacity for innovation and adaptation is an organizational skill that organizations can develop. There are principles in the field that can guide and inform how organizations go about systematic innovation. In my experience, each organization develops its own context-specific version of these field-level principles for intentional and ongoing innovation that is shaped by their culture, their preferences in a variety of areas, such as tolerance for risk, and the domain they operate in. In working with organizations over time, often in multiple initiatives, developmental evaluators are well placed to help organizations establish effectiveness principles for intentional and systematic innovation.

▶ Think about how you can build these principles for innovation into the evaluation design.

▶ What are opportunities for facilitating learning—and further development of field-level principles—across organizations that you are working with?

Question 10. What's next on the agenda for principles-focused evaluation?

M. Q. P. Response

In the opening of the book I distinguished effectiveness principles from moral principles. Moral principles tell us what is right. Effectiveness principles tell us what works. "Do unto others as you would have them do unto you" provides moral guidance. "Think globally, act locally" offers guidance about how to be effective. Both can be evaluated. Moral principles are evaluated on whether they are being followed, that is, whether you are behaving rightly. Effectiveness principles are evaluated on whether they are being followed *and* whether, in following them, you achieve what you want to achieve. This book has been concerned primarily with evaluating effectiveness principles, and I have offered the GUIDE criteria as a framework for doing so. I expect moral principles to garner more evaluation attention going forward, especially in the form of *rights-focused evaluation*.

Rights-Focused Evaluation

Traditional program evaluations have been concerned with whether project or program models were appropriately implemented and whether intended objectives were attained. While projects and programs remain a primary focus for evaluation, the new century has brought new challenges on the cutting edge of evaluation practice. As Chapter 4 documented and discussed, we are now engaged in evaluating strategies, systems change, community initiatives, ecosystem sustainability, social innovations, institutional transformations, collaborations, collective impact, complex dynamic systems changes, and effectiveness principles. These new evaluands, these different objects of evaluation, call for designs, methods, and approaches that go well beyond traditional project and program approaches. One emergent arena on the leading edge is rights-focused evaluation. Rights encompass and assert moral principles. How can rights be used as a framework for evaluation?

Former UN secretary-general Kofi A. Annan called on all agencies of the UN to mainstream human rights into their activities and programs. UN agencies developed the Statement of Common Understanding on Human Rights–Based Approaches to Development Cooperation and Programming. Central to the document are the following points:

1. All programmes of development cooperation, policies and technical assistance should further the realization of human rights as laid down in the Universal Declaration of Human Rights and other international human rights instruments.

2. Human rights standards contained in, and principles derived from, the Universal Declaration of Human Rights and other international human rights instruments guide all development cooperation and programming in all sectors and in all phases of the programming process. (UNICEF, 2004, Annex B, p. 91)

Human rights generate moral principles, which can be evaluated for meaningfulness and adherence.

Among these human rights principles are: universality and inalienability; indivisibility; interdependence and interrelatedness; non-discrimination and equality; participation and inclusion; accountability and the rule of law. (UNICEF, 2004, Annex B, p. 91)

Rights-focused evaluation appropriately matches rights-based programming. The evaluation implications were specified in the Common Understanding:

Human rights principles guide all programming in all phases of the programming process, including assessment and analysis, programme planning and design (including setting goals, objectives and strategies); implementation, monitoring and evaluation.

The following elements are necessary, specific, and unique to a human rights-based approach:

a) Assessment and analysis identify the human rights claims of rights-holders and the corresponding human rights obligations of duty-bearers, as well as the immediate, underlying, and structural causes when rights are not realized.

b) Programmes assess the capacity of rights-holders to claim their rights, and of duty-bearers to fulfill their obligations. They then develop strategies to build these capacities.

c) Programmes monitor and evaluate both outcomes and processes guided by human rights standards and principles. (UNICEF, 2004, Annex B, pp. 91–92)

Treaties and Rights-Focused Evaluation

Treaties and international agreements are a source of moral principles that can guide both programming and evaluation. The Canadian Charter of Rights and Freedoms and the aboriginal rights defined in the Constitution Act of 1982 and subsequent supreme court decisions, including the *Tsilhqot'in* decision, can be used as an evaluation framework (Canadian Evaluation Society, 2016; Marshall, 2016). In New Zealand, the Treaty of Waitangi provides a framework for evaluation (McKegg, 2016). In the United States, the Constitution's Bill of Rights and treaties with Native American groups have evaluation implications. At a global level, the United Nations Universal Declaration of Human Rights and the Convention on the Rights of the Child can be used to generate evaluation criteria (Campbell-Patton, 2016; Gready & Vandenhole, 2014).

Deborah Rugg, former director of the Inspection and Evaluation Division in the UN's Office of Inspection and Oversight Services, and former chair of the UN Evaluation Group (UNEG), has proposed a rights-based approach for engaging program participants.

> I believe that access to *evaluation itself is a right, like any other human right.* . . .
>
> I have concluded that we evaluators, *as good citizens,* need to start viewing our work and maturing profession, not only as a technical field with increasingly sound methodology, but more frequently and boldly as a tool for democracy and good governance. (Rugg, 2016, pp. 2–3)

Rugg (2016) has called for *an evaluation is your right campaign* for program participants. This would mean that the intended beneficiaries of a program have the right to know what the evidence is that a program in which they are participating has evidence of effectiveness (p. 7).

Principles to Guide Rights-Based Programming and Evaluation

Joachim Theis, on behalf of the NGO Save the Children, generated a comprehensive justification for rights-based evaluation based on moral principles.

> A rights-based approach promotes three main principles: the accountability of duty bearers, the participation of right holders, and equity/non-discrimination. It aims to increase impact and strengthen sustainability by addressing root causes, bringing about policy and practice changes, working together with others towards common goals and by changing power relations. The primary role of a rights-based development organisation is to contribute to the fulfilment of human rights by getting duty bearers to meet their obligations, and by empowering poor and exploited

people to claim their entitlements. Directly meeting needs and fulfilling rights helps people, but it does not necessarily strengthen the accountability of duty bearers. It also does not strengthen people's own ability to claim their rights. (2003, p. 1)

He articulated the importance of rights-based evaluation to support human rights initiatives.

> Monitoring the extent of the fulfilment and violation of human rights is a fundamental approach to promoting human rights. The collection and dissemination of data about unfulfilled rights and about rights violations puts pressure on duty bearers to meet their obligations to respect, protect and fulfil human rights. Human rights monitoring can help strengthen the compliance of duty bearers with human rights standards. (2003, p. 3)

I first encountered human rights as both a development framework and a corresponding human rights framework when Mahesh Patel, a thought leader with UNICEF, presented on this moral imperative for evaluation at the launching of the African Evaluation Society in Nairobi in 1999. He subsequently laid out this perspective in writing (Patel, 2001). Others have picked up the challenge (Berman, 2008; GIZ, 2011). But rights-focused evaluation remains an evaluation orphan, in my view. My hope is that principles-focused evaluation can provide some additional momentum to increase attention to evaluation of moral principles as well as effectiveness principles.

Evaluating Moral Principles

Psychologist Owen Flanagan has devoted his career to studying morality. His conclusions provide a window into the challenges of evaluating moral principles.

> There are multiple ways to live good human lives. Morality is fragile, subject to the vagaries of temperament, personality, gender,

class, culture, economics, and politics. Moral ideals are typically pictures of what kind of person from among the possibilities one ought to be, where "be" is intended in a deep, existentialist sense. Moral ideals call on one to be a person of a certain kind, not just to act in certain ways. (2017, p. 3)

Evaluating moral principles moves from individual morality to organizational, programmatic, and even societal morality. There is, it seems to me, a moral imperative to evaluate adherence to moral principles. Providing guidance for that imperative is a future challenge for principles-focused evaluation.

Question 11. What's the future research and evaluation agenda to deepen understanding and improve the practice of principles-focused evaluation?

M. Q. P. Response

This question comes most often from graduate students thinking about dissertations and theses.

The good news is that the research and evaluation agenda is wide open and needs attention. All three legs of the three-legged stool—the principles-focused evaluation conceptual framework/theory, principles-focused evaluation methods and tools, and principles-focused practice—need development, reflection, and evaluation. The GUIDE framework needs testing and validation. More exemplary cases are needed to deepen our learning, the six exemplars in Part III being merely a starting point. We need to document learnings and, certainly no less important, share failures in situations where principles-focused evaluation proved inappropriate, met resistance, or otherwise failed to be useful, meaningful, and/or credible. The tools, methods, and checklists I offer in Chapters 35 and 36, as well as elsewhere throughout this book, need to be tested, adapted, and revised to fit emergent challenges in real-world situations. An especially fruitful arena for inquiry will be how principles-focused evaluation intersects with and is used in combination with other evaluation approaches, as it inevitably will be. Then, of particular importance will be the reflective practice of principles-focused evaluators; Chapters 16, 17, 32, 33, and 34 exemplify open, insightful, probing, and deep reflective practice. *May these exemplars inspire your own reflective practice.* And, finally, as new cases are documented and presented, we will need new syntheses of the patterns and themes that cut across variations in principle-focused evaluation, and the implications of those variations for future applications and deepening practice. This form of synthesis evaluation is only possible with multiple case examples in different contexts (see Chapter 24 on synthesis evaluation and Exhibit 24.1, pp. 212–217).

The research and evaluation agenda is wide open. Research and evaluation are needed to further develop principles-focused evaluation. So, pick an inquiry issue that interests you. Find your niche. Follow your passion. Make your contribution. Leave your mark.

In so doing, you may help this new pathway among the many in the marvelous labyrinth that is evaluation become well trodden enough for others to follow and find value in the metaphorical inukshuk you create as guidance. In that spirit, we can each say with Sir Isaac Newton: "If I have seen further it is by standing on the shoulders of Giants." That's how you navigate a complex, dynamic labyrinth. That and, in this arena of action and through this particular labyrinth, being true to the principles of principles-focused evaluation.

References

Alkin, M. C. (2013). *Evaluation roots* (2nd ed.). Thousand Oaks, CA: SAGE.

Altieri, M. A. (1995). *Biodiversity and pest management in agroecosystems*. New York: Hayworth Press.

Altieri, M. A. (2016). Agroecology: Principles and strategies for designing sustainable farming systems. Retrieved from *www.agroeco.org/doc/news_docs/Agroeco_principles.pdf*.

Altieri, M. A., & Toledo, V. M. (2005). Natural resource managment among small scale farmers in semi-arid lands: Building on traditional knowledge and agroecology. *Annals of Arid Zone, 44*, 365–385.

American Evaluation Association. (2004). American Evaluation Association guiding principles for evaluators. Available at *www.eval.org/p/cm/ld/fid=51*.

American Evaluation Association. (2011). A public statement on cultural competence in evaluation. Retrieved from *www.eval.org/p/do/sd/topic=12&sid=61*.

Annette, K., Fauth, W., & Ahcan, A. (2015). The Blandin Foundation: The journey to a theory of philanthropy, *Foundation Review, 7*(4), 42–53.

Antunes, A. (2002). *Leitura do mundo no contexto da planetarização: Por uma pedagogia da sustentabilidade*. Unpublished doctoral dissertation, Faculdade de Educaçao da Universidade de São Paulo, São Paulo, Brazil.

Arendt, H. (1963). *Between past and future: Six exercises in political thought*. New Haven, CT: Meridian Books.

Bakiner, O. (2016). *Truth commissions: Memory, power, and legitimacy*. Philadelphia: University of Pennsylvania Press.

Bamberger, M., & Podems, D. R. (2002). Feminist evaluation in the international development context. In D. Seigart & S. Brisolara (Eds.), *New Directions for Evaluation, 96*, 83–96.

Bare, J. (2013). Evaluation, accountability, and social change. *Foundation Review, 1*(4), 84–104.

Bemelmans-Videc, M., Lonsdale, J., & Perrin, B. (2007). *Making accountability work*. London: Transaction.

Berman, G. (2008). *Undertaking a Human Rights-Based Approach: Lessons for Policy, Planning and Programming–Documenting Lessons Learned for the Human Rights-Based Approach to Programming: An Asia-Pacific Perspective–Implications for Policy, Planning and Programming*. Bangkok: UNESCO Bangkok.

Bonk, C. J., & Khoo, E. (2014). *Adding some TEC-VARIETY: 100+ activities for motivating and retaining learners online*. Bloomington, IN: Open Space Books.

Braverman, M. T. (2013). Negotiating measurement methodological and interpersonal considerations in the choice and interpretation of instruments. *American Journal of Evaluation, 34*(1), 99–114.

Briggs, L. (2007). *Tackling wicked problems: A public policy perspective.* Commonwealth of Australia, Australian Public Service Commission. Retrieved from *www.apsc.gov.au/__data/assets/pdf_file/0005/6386/wickedproblems.pdf.*

Brookfield, S. D. (1986). *Understanding and facilitating adult learning.* San Francisco: Jossey-Bass.

Brookfield, S. D. (2011). *Teaching for critical thinking: Tools and techniques to help students question their assumptions.* San Francisco: Jossey-Bass.

Brookfield, S. D. (2015). *The skillful teacher: On technique, trust, and responsiveness in the classroom* (3rd ed.). San Francisco: Jossey-Bass.

Buckley, J., Archibald, T., Hargraves, M., & Trochim, W. M. (2015). Defining and teaching evaluative thinking insights from research on critical thinking. *American Journal of Evaluation, 36*(3), 375–388.

Butterfoss, F. D. (2007). *Coalitions and partnerships in community health.* San Francisco: Jossey-Bass.

Cabaj, M. (Ed.). (2011a). *Cities reducing poverty: How vibrant communities are creating the comprehensive solutions to the most complex problem of our time.* Waterloo, ON, Canada: Tamarack Institute for Community Engagement.

Cabaj, M. (2011b). *Developmental evaluation: Experiences and reflections of 18 early adopters.* Master's thesis. University of Waterloo, ON, Canada.

Cabaj, M., & Leviten-Reid, E. (2006). *Understanding the potential and practice of comprehensive, multisectoral efforts to reduce poverty: The preliminary experiences of the vibrant communities trail builders.* Unpublished document. Waterloo, ON, Canada: Tamarack Institute for Community Engagement.

Cabaj, M., Leviten-Reid, E., Vocisano, D., & Rawlins, M. J. (2016). An example of patch evaluation: Vibrant Communities Canada. In M. Q. Patton, K. McKegg, & N. Wehipeihana (Eds.), *Developmental evaluation exemplars: Principles in practice* (pp. 163–191). New York: Guilford Press.

Cabaj, M., Makhoul, A., & Leviten-Reid, E.

(2006). *In from the field: Exploring the first poverty reduction strategies undertaken by Trail Builders in the Vibrant Communities initiative.* Waterloo, ON: Tamarack—An Institute for Community Engagement.

Campbell-Patton, C. (2015). Using reflective practice for developmental evaluation. AEA365 Blog, March 5, 2015. Retrieved from *http://aea365.org/blog/developmental-eval-week-charmagne-campbell-patton-on-using-reflective-practice-for-developmental-evaluation.*

Campbell-Patton, C. (2016, June). *Universal declaration of human rights and rights of the child as principles-focused evaluation frameworks.* Presentation, workshop on rights-based evaluation, annual conference of the Canadian Evaluation Society, St. John's, Newfoundland, Canada.

Campbell-Patton, C., & Patton, M. Q. (2010). Conceptualizing and evaluating the complexities of youth civic engagement. In L. R. Sherrod, J. Torney-Purta, & C. A. Flanagan (Eds.), *Handbook of research on youth civic engagement* (pp. 593–620). Hoboken, NJ: Wiley.

Canadian Evaluation Society. (2016). Response to the final report of the Truth and Reconciliation Commission of Canada. Available at *https://evaluationcanada.ca/news/6348.*

Canfield, J. (2015). *The success principles: How to get from where you are to where you want to be.* New York: William Morrow.

Carver, J., & Carver, M. (2001). *Carver's policy governance model in nonprofit organizations.* Retrieved from *www.carvergovernance.com/pg-np.htm.*

Chelimsky, E. (1995). Comments on the guiding principles. In W. R. Shadish, D. L. Newman, M. A. Scheirer, & C. Wye (Eds.), *New Directions for Evaluation, 66,* 53–54.

Chilisa, B. (2012). *Indigenous research methodologies.* Thousand Oaks, CA: SAGE.

Cloitre, M., Cohen, L. R., & Koenen, K. C. (2011). *Treating survivors of childhood abuse: Psychotherapy for the interrupted life.* New York: Guilford Press.

Commission to End Homelessness. (2006). Ten year plan to end homelessness in Minneapolis and Hennepin County. Available at *www.hennepin.us/-/media/hennepinus/your-government/projects-initiatives/documents/end-homelessness-10-year-plan.pdf.*

Conference of Mayors. (2014). Best practices.

Available at *www.nycom.org/resource-center/ success-stories/best-practices/10-meetings-and-training/607-2014-winter-legislative-expo.html.*

Connor, R. (2004). Developing and implementing culturally competent evaluation: A discussion of multicultural validity in two HIV prevention programs for Latinos. In M. Thompson-Robinson, R. Hopson, & S. Sen-Gupta (Eds.), *New Directions for Evaluation, 102,* 51–66.

Cooksy, L., Evergreen, S. D., Morris, M., & Patton, M. Q. (2015, November 13). *Exemplars of evaluation failure.* American Evaluation Association Annual Conference, Chicago, IL.

Cooperrider, D. (1990). Positive image, positive action: The affirmative basis of organizing. In S. Srivastva & D. Cooperrider (Eds.), *Appreciative management and leadership: The power of positive thought and action in organizations.* San Francisco: Jossey-Bass.

Coryn, C. L. S., Noakes, L. A., Westine, C. D., & Schröter, D. C. (2011). A systematic review of theory-driven evaluation practice from 1990 to 2009. *American Journal of Evaluation, 32*(2), 199–226.

Costa-Pierce, B. A. (2010). Sustainable ecological aquaculture systems: The need for a new social contract for aquaculture development. *Marine Technology Society Journal, 44*(3), 88–112.

Cousins, J. B. (2005). Will the real empowerment evaluation please stand up? In D. M. Fetterman & A. Wandersman (Eds.), *Empowerment evaluation principles in practice* (pp. 183–208). New York: Guilford Press.

Cousins, J. B., & Chouinard, J. A. (2012). *Participatory evaluation up close: An integration of research-based knowledge.* Charlotte, NC: Information Age.

Cousins, J. B., Whitmore, E., & Shulha, L. (2014). Arguments for a common set of principles for collaborative inquiry in evaluation. *American Journal of Evaluation, 34*(1), 7–22.

Covert, R. W. (1995). A twenty-year veteran's reflections on the guiding principles for evaluators. In W. R. Shadish, D. L. Newman, M. A. Scheirer, & C. Wye (Eds.), *New Directions for Evaluation, 66,* 35–46.

Daigneault, P. M., & Jacob, S. (2009). Toward accurate measurement of participation: Rethinking the conceptualization and operationalization of participatory evaluation.

American Journal of Evaluation, 30(3), 330–348.

Davidson, E. J. (2005). *Evaluation methodology basics: The nuts and bolts of sound evaluation.* Thousand Oaks, CA: SAGE.

Davidson, E. J. (2012). *Actionable evaluation: Getting succinct answers to the most important questions.* New Zealand: Real Evaluation.

Davidson, E. J. (2014). How "beauty" can bring truth and justice to life. In J. C. Griffith & B. Montrosse-Moorhead (Eds.), *New Directions for Evaluation, 142,* 31–43.

Dawes, M. (2013). Some general semantics principles. Available at *http://miltondawes. com/2013/04/21/some-general-semantics-principles.*

Dei, G., Karumanchery, L., & Karumanchery-Luik, N. (2004). The banality of racism: Living "within" the traumatic. *Counterpoints, 244,* 127–146. Available at *www.jstor.org/stable/42979562.*

Donaldson, S. I., Christie, C. A., & Mark, M. M. (Eds.). (2008). *What counts as credible evidence in applied research and evaluation practice?* Thousand Oaks, CA: SAGE.

Donaldson, S. I., Patton, M. Q., Fetterman, D., & Scriven, M. (2010). The 2009 Claremont debates: The promise and pitfalls of utilization-focused and empowerment evaluation. Available at *http://scholarship.claremont.edu/cgu_fac_pub/563.*

Eckberg, D. A. (2015). Vegetables, not dessert: Teaching sociological principles in an evaluation research course. *American Sociologist, 46*(4), 500–504.

Environmental Protection Agency. (2015). *The clean energy-environment guide to action: State policies and best practices for advancing energy efficiency, renewable energy, and combined heat and power.* Washington, DC: Author. Available at *www.epa.gov/sites/production/files/2015-08/documents/guide_action_full.pdf.*

Eoyang, G. (2009). Simple rules for complex times. *Attractors, 6*(8), 1. Available at *www. hsdinstitute.org/about-hsd-institute/simple-rules. html.*

Evans-Campbell, T. (2008). Historical trauma in American Indian/Native Alaska communities a multilevel framework for exploring impacts on individuals, families, and communities. *Journal of Interpersonal Violence, 23*(3), 316–338.

Evergreen, S. D. H. (2016). *Effective data visualization: The right chart for the right data.* Los Angeles: SAGE.

Evergreen, S. D. H. (2017). *Presenting data effectively: Communicating your findings for maximum impact* (2nd ed.). Los Angeles: SAGE.

Evergreen, S. D. H. (n.d.). Evaluation report layout checklist. Available at *https://dl.dropboxusercontent.com/u/22848961/EvalReportLayoutChecklist.pdf.*

Evergreen, S. D. H., & Metzner, C. (2013). Design principles for data visualization in evaluation. In T. Azzam & S. Evergreen (Eds.), *New Directions for Evaluation, 140,* 5–20.

Farber, N. (2013). 8 key principles to succeed: Action boarding made simple. *Psychology Today.* Retrieved from *www.psychologytoday.com/blog/the-blame-game/201309/8-key-principles-succeed.*

Fetterman, D. M. (2005). A window into the heart and soul of empowerment evaluation. In D. M. Fetterman & A. Wandersman (Eds.), *Empowerment evaluation principles in practice* (pp. 1–26). New York: Guilford Press.

Fetterman, D. M., Shakeh, J., Kaftarian, S. J., & Wandersman, A. H. (Eds.). (2014). *Empowerment evaluation: Knowledge and tools for self-assessment, evaluation capacity building, and accountability.* Thousand Oaks, CA: SAGE.

Fetterman, D. M., Wandersman, A., & Kaftarian, S. (2015). Empowerment evaluation is a systematic way of thinking: A response to Michael Patton. *Evaluation and Program Planning, 52,* 10–14.

Fischer, H. (2016). Pine County, Mille Lacs Band sign joint statement of principles. *Pine City Pioneer.* Retrieved from *www.pinecitymn.com/news/pine-county-mille-lacs-band-sign-joint-statement-of-principles/article_1c3e5e08–5b2e–11e6–8e7b-d7809a3aa1ed.html.*

Flanagan, O. (2017). *The geography of morals: Varieties of moral possibility.* New York: Oxford University Press.

Food and Agriculture Organization. (2017). *Agroecology knowledge hub.* Rome: Author. Available at *www.fao.org/agroecology/knowledge/10-elements/en/.*

Forss, K., Marra, M., & Schwartz, R. (Eds.). (2011). *Evaluating the complex: Attribution, contribution, and beyond.* New Brunswick, NJ: Transaction.

Freire, P. (1970). *Pedagogy of the oppressed.* New York: Herder & Herder.

Freire, P. (1997). *Pedagogia da autonomia: Saberes necessários à prática educativa.* São Paulo, Brazil: Paz e Terra.

Freire, P. (2000). *Pedagogia da indignação: Cartas pedagógicas e outros escritos.* São Paulo, Brazil: UNESP.

Freire, P. (2001). *Pedagogy of freedom: Ethics, democracy, and civic courage.* Lanham, MD: Rowman & Littlefield.

Freire, P., & Faundez, A. (1985). *Por uma pedagogia da pergunta.* São Paulo, Brazil: Paz e Terra.

Gadotti, M. (Ed.). (1996a). *Paulo Freire: Uma biobibliografia.* São Paulo, Brazil: Cortez/Instituto Paulo Freire.

Gadotti, M. (1996b). *Pedagogy of praxis: A dialectical philosophy of education.* Albany: State University of New York Press.

Gadotti, M. (2007). *Educar para um outro mundo possível.* São Paulo, Brazil: Publisher Brasil.

Gadotti, M. (2016). *The impact of Freire's pedagogy on contemporary education.* São Paulo, Brazil: Instituto Paulo Freire.

Gaffney, J. S., & Anderson, R. C. (1991). Two-tiered scaffolding: Congruent processes of teaching and learning. In E. H. Hiebert (Ed.), *Literacy for a diverse society: Perspectives, policies, and practices.* New York: Teachers College Press.

Gamble, J. (2008). *Developmental evaluation primer.* Montreal, Canada: J. W. McConnell Family Foundation. Available at *www.imprintinc.ca.*

Gamble, J. (2010). *Evaluating Vibrant Communities: 2002–2010.* Waterloo, ON, Canada: Tamarack Institute for Community Engagement.

Gamble, J. (2012). *Inspired learning: An evaluation of Vibrant Communities National Supports: 2002–2012.* Waterloo, ON, Canada: Tamarack Institute for Community Engagement.

Gamble, J., Van Sluys, S., & Watson, L. (2016). Fostering learning through developmental evaluation with a nontraditional arts organization and a traditional community funder. In M. Q. Patton, K. McKegg, & N. Wehipeihana (Eds.), *Developmental evaluation exemplars: Principles in practice* (pp. 83–102). New York: Guilford Press.

Gawande, A. (2010). *The checklist manifesto: How to get things right.* New York: Metropolitan Books.

Gemmill-Herren, B. (2016). *Agroecology Knowledge Hub Proposal.* Rome: United Nations, Food and Agriculture Organization.

GIZ. (2011). Selected resources on human rights-based monitoring and evaluation: Realizing human rights in development co-operation. Available at *www.giz.de/expertise/html/16809.html*.

Gliessman, S. R. (1992). Agroecology in the tropics: Achieving a balance between land use and preservation. *Environmental Management, 16*(6), 681–689.

Gliessman, S. R. (2000). *Agroecosystem sustainability: Developing practical strategies.* Boca Raton, FL: CRC Press.

Gliessman, S. R. (2014). *Agroecology: The ecology of sustainable food systems* (3rd ed.). Boca Raton, FL: CRC Press/Taylor & Francis.

Gliessman, S. R. (2015, September). *Agroecology: A global movement for food security and sovereignty.* Proceedings, International Symposium on Agroecology for Food Security and Nutrition, Food and Agriculture Organization, Rome, Italy.

Gliessman, S. R., & Muramoto, J. (2010). The conversion of strawberry production. In S. R. Gliessman & M. E. Rosemeyer (Eds.), *Converting to sustainable agroecosystems: Principles, processes, and practices* (pp. 117–131). Boca Raton, FL: CRC Press.

Goldacre, B. (2009). *Bad science.* London: 4th Estate.

Gottlieb, H. (2009). *The Pollyanna principles: Reinventing nonprofit organizations to create the future of our world.* Tucson, AZ: Renaissance Press.

Gready, P., & Vandenhole, W. (2014). *Human rights and development in the new millennium: Towards a theory of change.* New York: Routledge.

Greenwald, A. G. (2012). There is nothing so theoretical as a good method. *Perspectives on Psychological Science, 7,* 99–108.

Groover, J. (2012). Principles of success not taught in school. Available at *www.positivelypositive.com/2012/02/07/principles-of-success*.

Gutiérrez, F., & Prado, C. (1989). *Ecopedagogia e cidadania planetária.* São Paulo, Brazil: Instituto Paulo Freire/Cortez.

Guttentag, M., & Struening, E. L. (Eds.). (1975). *Handbook of evaluation research.* Beverly Hills, CA: SAGE.

Hayner, P. (2010). *Unspeakable truths: Transitional justice and the challenge of truth commissions.* New York: Routledge.

Heinlein, R. (1973). *The notebooks of Lazarus Long.* New York: G. P. Putnam's Sons.

Hendricks, M., & Connor, R. (1995). International perspectives on the guiding principles. In W. R. Shadish, D. L. Newman, M. A. Scheirer, & C. Wye (Eds.), *New Directions for Evaluation, 66,* 77–90.

Holladay, R. (2015). Four principles of change: Simple rules. Available at *www.adaptiveaction.org/blog/category/simple-rules*.

Holman, P. (2010). *Engaging emergence: Turning upheaval into opportunity.* San Francisco: Berrett-Koehler.

Holman, P. (2015). Complexity, self-organization, and emergence. In G. R. Bushe & R. J. Marshak (Eds.), *Dialogic organization development: The theory and practice of transformational change* (pp. 123–149). Oakland, CA: Berrett-Koehler.

Holman, P., Devane, T., & Cady, S. (2007). *The change handbook: The definitive resource on today's best methods for engaging whole systems* (2nd ed.). San Francisco: Berrett-Koehler.

Homeless Youth Collaborative on Developmental Evaluation. (2014). Nine evidence-based guiding principles to help youth overcome homelessness. Available at *www.terralunacollaborative.com/wp-content/uploads/2014/03/9-Evidence-Based-Principles-to-Help-Youth-Overcome-Homelessness-Webpublish.pdf*.

Hood, S. (2004). A journey to understand the role of culture in program evaluation: Snapshots and personal reflections of one African American evaluator. In M. Thompson-Robinson, R. Hopson, & S. SenGupta (Eds.), *New Directions for Evaluation, 102,* 21–38.

House, E. R. (1980). *Evaluating with validity.* Beverly Hills, CA: SAGE.

House, E. R. (1990). Methodology and justice. In K. A. Sirotnik (Ed.), *New Directions for Evaluation, 45,* 23–36.

House, E. R. (1995). Principled evaluation: A critique of the AEA guiding principles. In W. R. Shadish, D. L. Newman, M. A. Scheirer, & C. Wye (Eds.), *New Directions for Evaluation, 66,* 27–34.

House, E. R. (2014). Origins of the ideas in *Evaluating with Validity.* In J. C. Griffith & B. Montrosse-Moorhead (Eds.), *New Directions for Evaluation, 142,* 9–15.

House, E. R., & Howe, K. R. (2000). Deliberative democratic evaluation. In K. E. Ryan &

L. DeStefano (Eds.), *New Directions for Evaluation, 85*, 3–12.

Human Systems Dynamics. (2013). Adaptive action cycle. Available at *www.hsdinstitute.org/resources/adaptive-action.html*.

Huxley, A. (1949). Words and meaning: The functions of language. In S. I. Hayakawa, *Language in thought and action*. New York: Harcourt Brace Jovanovich.

International RRP ISA Center. (2016). What is RRP? Retrieved from *www.rrpwebsite.org*.

Jacob, S., & Desautels, G. (2014). Asessing the quality of Aboriginal program evaluations. *Canadian Journal of Program Evaluation, 29*(1), 62–86.

Joint Committee on Standards for Educational Evaluation. (1981). *Standards for Evaluations of Educational Programs, Projects, and Materials*. New York: McGraw-Hill.

Joint Committee on Standards for Educational Evaluation. (1994). *The program evaluation standards*. Thousand Oaks, CA: SAGE.

Journalism That Matters. (2016). Experience Engagement conference website. Available at *http://journalismthatmatters.org/experienceengagement*.

Julnes, G. (Ed.). (2012). Promoting valuation in the public interest: Informing policies for judging value in evaluation. *New Directions for Evaluation, 133*.

Kaner, S. (2014). *Facilitator's guide to participatory decision-making* (3rd ed.). San Francisco: Jossey-Bass.

Karenga, M. (2008). *Kwanzaa: A celebration of family, community and culture*. Los Angeles: University of Sankore Press.

King, J., Nielsen, J. E., & Colby, J. (2004). Lessons for culturally competent evaluation in the study of the multicultural initiative. In M. Thompson-Robinson, R. Hopson, & S. SenGupta (Eds.), *New Directions for Evaluation, 102*, 67–80.

King, J. A., Shanker, V., Miller, R. L., & Mark, M. M. (2010). The oral history of evaluation: The professional development of Marvin C. Alkin. *American Journal of Evaluation, 31*(2), 266–277.

King, M. L., Jr. (n.d.). Martin Luther King, Jr.'s principles of nonviolence. Available at *www.cpt.org/files/PW%20-%20Principles%20-%20King.pdf*.

Kinni, T. (2015). Conquering complexity with simple rules. *Insights by Stanford Business*. Available at *www.gsb.stanford.edu/insights/conquering-complexity-simple-rules*.

Kirkhart, K. E. (1995). Evaluation and social justice seeking multi-cultural validity. *American Journal of Evaluation, 16*(1), 1–12.

Klein, G. (2014). Evidence-based medicine. Retrieved from *www.edge.org/responses/what-scientific-idea-is-ready-for-retirement*.

Klein, J. (2016, May 30). Trump, the astute salesman, has seized America's prevailing mood: Nostalgia. *Time*, 29.

Kline, R. B. (2016). *Principles and practice of structural equation modeling*. New York: Guilford Press.

Knott, T. D. (1995). An independent consultant's perspective on the guiding principles. In W. R. Shadish, D. L. Newman, M. A. Scheirer, & C. Wye (Eds.), *New Directions for Evaluation, 66*, 69–76.

Kolbert, E. (2016, September 12). Into the wild. *New Yorker*, 5–26.

Ledger, B. (2014). *21 success principles: 21 powerful ways to help you immediately become more productive, happy and successful, for life!* Self-published.

Leviten-Reid, E. (2007). *Reflections on Vibrant Communities, 2002–2006*. Ottawa, ON, Canada: Caledon Institute.

Lewin, K. (1951). *Field theory in social science: Selected theoretical papers*. New York: Harper & Row.

Lidwell, W., Holden, K., & Butler, J. (2015). *Universal principles of design*. Beverly, MA: Rockport Publishers.

Lovell, R. G. (1995). Ethics and internal evaluators. In W. R. Shadish, D. L. Newman, M. A. Scheirer, & C. Wye (Eds.), *New Directions for Evaluation, 66*, 61–68.

MacArthur, R. (1958). Popular ecology of some warblers in the northeastern, coniferous forests. *Ecology, 39*, 599–619.

MacCoy, D. J. (2014). Appreciative inquiry and evaluation—getting to what works. *Canadian Journal of Program Evaluation, 29*(2), 104–127.

Marshall, A. (2016, June). *The Canadian Truth and Reconciliation Commission as a framework for rights-based evaluation*. Presentation at the annual conference of the Canadian Evaluation Society, St. John's, Newfoundland, Canada.

Martin, A. (2009). *La mémoire et le pardon: Les*

commissions de la vérité et de la réconciliation en Amérique latine. Paris: L'Harmattan.

Mattessich, P., Murray-Close, M., & Monsey, B. (2001). *Wilder collaboration factors inventory.* St. Paul, MN: Wilder Research. Available at *www.wilder.org/Wilder-Research/Research-Services/Pages/Wilder-Collaboration-Factors-Inventory.aspx.*

Mayne, J. (2008, May). Contribution analysis: An approach to exploring cause and effect. *ILAC Brief 16.* Available at *www.outcomemapping.ca/download.php?file=/resource/files/csette_en_ILAC_Brief16_Contribution_Analysis.pdf.*

Mayne, J. (2011). Exploring cause–effect questions using contribution analysis. In K. Forss, M. Mara, & R. Schwartz (Eds.), Evaluating the complex: Attribution, contribution and beyond. New Brunswick, NJ: Transaction.

Mayne, J. (2012). Contribution analysis: Coming of age? *Evaluation: The International Journal, 18*(3), 270–280.

McCambridge, R. (2016, June 13). New CEO stands on principle in midst of mental health system in chaos. *Nonprofit Quarterly* (NPQ) blog. *https://nonprofitquarterly.org/2016/06/13/new-ceo-stands-on-principle-in-midst-of-mental-health-system-in-chaos/*

McKegg, K. (2016, June). *New Zealand's Treaty of Waitangi as an evaluation framework.* Presentation at the annual conference of the Canadian Evaluation Society, St. John's, Newfoundland, Canada.

Mead, G. H. (1936). *Movements of thought in the nineteenth century* (C. W. Morris, Ed). Chicago: University of Chicago Press.

Méndez, V. E. (2010). Agroecology. In B. Warf (Ed.), *Encyclopedia of geography.* Thousand Oaks, CA: SAGE. Available at *www.uvm.edu/~agroecol/MendezVE_AgroecologyInEncyclopediaGeography__Electronic2010.pdf.*

Méndez, V. E. (2015). *A global performance assessment of agroecology for smallholder farmers.* Grant proposal developed by the Agroecology and Rural Livelihoods Group (ARLG), University of Vermont, Burlington, VT.

Méndez, V. E., Bacon, C. M., & Cohen, R. (2016) Agroecology as a transdisciplinary, participatory, and action-oriented approach. In V. E. Méndez, C. M. Bacon, R. Cohen, & S. Gliessman (Eds.), *Agroecology: A transdisciplinary, participatory, and action-oriented approach.* New York: CRC Press.

Méndez, V. E., Bacon, C. M., Cohen, R., & Gliessman, S. (Eds.). (2016). *Agroecology: A transdisciplinary, participatory and action-oriented approach.* New York: CRC Press.

Mertens, D. M. (1999). Inclusive evaluation: Implications of transformative theory for evaluation. *American Journal of Evaluation, 20*(1), 1–14.

Mertens, D. M. (2015, April 27). Donna M. Mertens on evaluation's contribution to solving wicked problems. *AEA365* blog post. Retrieved from *http://aea365.org/blog/mesi-week-donna-m-mertens-on-evaluations-contribution-to-solving-wicked-problems.*

Merton, R. K. (1976). Social knowledge and public policy. In *Sociological ambivalence* (pp. 156–179). New York: Free Press.

Miller, K. S. (2016). *Identifying the implicit guiding principles of the collaborative crop research program: Expanding principles-focused, developmental evaluation.* Unpublished doctoral dissertation, University of Minnesota, Minneapolis, Minnesota.

Miller, R. L., & Campbell, R. (2006). Taking stock of empowerment evaluation: An empirical review. *American Journal of Evaluation, 27*(3), 296–319.

Minnich, E. (2017). *The evil of banality: On the life and death importance of thinking.* New York: Rowman & Littlefield.

Moore, M., & Cady, J. M. (2016). Developmental evaluation in the McKnight Foundation's Collaborative Crop Research Program: A journey of discovery. In M. Patton, K. McKegg, & N. Wehipeihana (Eds.), *Developmental evaluation exemplars: Principles in practice* (pp. 143–162). New York: Guilford Press.

Murphy, N. F. (2014). *Developing evidence-based effective principles for working with homeless youth: A developmental evaluation of the Otto Bremer Foundation's support for collaboration among agencies serving homeless youth.* Minneapolis: University of Minnesota.

Murphy, N. F. (2015, May 25). Nora Murphy on the intersection of evaluation, social justice, trauma, and healing. *AEA365* blog post. Retrieved from *http://aea365.org/blog/nora-murphy-on-the-intersection-of-evaluation-social-justice-trauma-and-healing.*

Murphy, N. F. (2016). Nine guiding principles to help youth overcome homelessness: A principles-focused developmental evaluation.

In M. Patton, K. McKegg, & N. Wehipeihana (Eds.), *Developmental evaluation exemplars: Principles in practice* (pp. 63–82). New York: Guilford Press.

National Reading Panel. (2000). *Teaching children to read.* Washington, DC: Institute of Child Health and Human Development. Available at *www.nichd.nih.gov/publications/pubs/nrp/Documents/report.pdf.*

Newman, D. L. (1995). The future of ethics in evaluation: Dialoguing the dialogue. In W. R. Shadish, D. L. Newman, M. A. Scheirer, & C. Wye (Eds.), *New Directions for Evaluation, 66,* 99–110.

Owen, H. (2008). *Open Space Technology: A user's guide.* San Francisco: Berrett-Koehler.

Paris Declaration Evaluation. (2011a). Operational Matrix for Country Evaluations. Available at *www.oecd.org/dac/evaluation/dcdndep/referencedocumentsforphase2.htm.*

Paris Declaration Evaluation. (2011b). Technical annex 5: The evaluation of the Paris Declaration, Phase 2. Available at *http://pd-website.inforce.dk/content/pdf/PD-EN-annex5.pdf.*

Paris Declaration Evaluation. (2011c). Transparent and comprehensive documentation of the Paris Declaration Principles Phase 2 Evaluation. Available at *www.oecd.org/dac/evaluation/evaluationoftheimplementationoftheparisdeclaration.htm.*

Pascal, B. (1910). *Thoughts* (W. F. Trotter, Trans.). New York: Collier & Son.

Patel, M. (2001). *Human rights as an emerging development paradigm and some implications for programme planning, monitoring and evaluation.* Nairobi, Kenya: UNICEF.

Patton, M. Q. (1983). Similarities of extension and evaluation. *Journal of Extension, 21,* 14–21.

Patton, M. Q. (2002). A vision of evaluation that strengthens democracy. *Evaluation, 8*(1), 127–135.

Patton, M. Q. (2007). Process use as a usefulism. In J. B. Cousins (Ed.), *New Directions for Evaluation, 116,* 99–112.

Patton, M. Q. (2008). *Utilization-focused evaluation* (4th ed.). Thousand Oaks, CA: SAGE.

Patton, M. Q. (2011). *Developmental evaluation: Applying complexity concepts to enhance innovation and use.* New York: Guilford Press.

Patton, M. Q. (2012a). *Essentials of utilization-focused evaluation.* Thousand Oaks, CA: SAGE.

Patton, M. Q. (Ed.). (2012b). Special issue on evaluation of the Paris Declaration. *Canadian Journal of Program Evaluation, 27*(2).

Patton, M. Q. (2015a). *Qualitative research and evaluation methods* (4th ed.). Thousand Oaks, CA: SAGE.

Patton, M. Q. (2015b). Review of empowerment evaluation. *Evaluation and Program Planning, 52,* 15–18.

Patton, M. Q. (2015c). Transcultural global systems perspective: In search of Blue Marble evaluators. *Canadian Journal of Program Evaluation, 30*(3), 374–398.

Patton, M. Q. (2016a). The developmental evaluation mindset: Eight guiding principles. In M. Q. Patton, K. McKegg, & N. Wehipeihana (Eds.), *Developmental evaluation exemplars: Principles in practice* (pp. 289–312). New York: Guilford Press.

Patton, M. Q. (2016b). What is essential in developmental evaluation?: On integrity, fidelity, adultery, abstinence, impotence, long-term commitment, integrity, and sensitivity in implementing evaluation models. *American Journal of Evaluation, 37*(2), 250–265.

Patton, M. Q. (2017a). *Facilitating evaluation: principles in practice.* Los Angeles: SAGE.

Patton, M. Q. (2017b). Pedagogical principles of evaluation: Interpreting Freire. In M. Q. Patton (Ed.), *Pedagogy of evaluation: The contributions of Paulo Freire to global evaluation thinking and practice. New Directions for Evaluation, 155,* 39–55.

Patton, M. Q., Foote, N., & Radner, J. (2015). A foundation's theory of philanthropy: What it is, what it provides, how to do it. *Foundation Review, 7*(4), 7–20.

Patton, M. Q., & Gornick, J. (2012). Evaluation of the phase 2 evaluation of the implementation of the Paris Declaration: An independent review of strengths, weaknesses, and lessons. Available at *https://www.oecd.org/dac/evaluation/dcdndep/48620425.pdf.*

Pawson, R., Greenhalgh, T., Harvey, G., & Walshe, K. (2004). *Realist synthesis: An introduction.* Manchester, UK: ESRC Research Methods Programme.

Pawson, R., & Sridharan, S. (2009). Theory-driven evaluation of public health programmes. In A. Killoran & M. Kelly (Eds.), *Evidence-based public health: Effectiveness and efficiency* (pp. 43–61). Oxford, UK: Oxford University Press.

Perrin, K. M. (2014). *Principles of evaluation and*

research for health care programs. Burlington, MA: Jones & Bartlett Learning.

Podems, D. R. (2007). Process use: A case narrative from Southern Africa. In J. B. Cousins (Ed.), *New Directions for Evaluation, 116,* 87–97.

Podems, D. R. (2010). Feminist evaluation and gender approaches: There's a difference? *Journal of MultiDisciplinary Evaluation, 6*(14), 1–17.

Podems, D. R. (2014a). Evaluator competencies and professionalizing the field: Where are we now? *Canadian Journal of Program Evaluation, 28*(3), 127–136.

Podems, D. R. (2014b). Feminist evaluation for nonfeminists. In S. Brisolara, D. Seigart, & S. SenGupta (Eds.), *Feminist evaluation and research: Theory and practice* (pp. 113–141). New York: Guilford Press.

Preskill, H., & Catsambas, T. T. (2006). *Reframing evaluation through appreciative inquiry.* Thousand Oaks, CA: SAGE.

Preskill, S., & Brookfield, S. D. (2008). *Learning as a way of leading: Lessons from the struggle for social justice.* San Francisco: Jossey-Bass.

Rallis, S. F. (2009). Reasoning with rigor and probity: Ethical premises for credible evidence. In S. I. Donaldson, C. A. Christie, & M. Mark (Eds.), *What counts as credible evidence in applied research and evaluation practice* (pp. 168–180). Thousand Oaks, CA: SAGE.

Reynolds, C. (2001). Boids: Background and update. Available at *www.red3d.com/cwr/boids*.

Rodriguez-Bilella, P. (2016). Evaluations that make a difference: Evaluation stories around the world. Available at *https://evaluationstories.wordpress.com*.

Rog, D. J., Fitzpatrick, J. L., & Conner, R. F. (Eds.). (2012). Context: A framework for its influence on evaluation practice. *New Directions for Evaluation, 135.*

Rogers, E. (1962). *Diffusion of innovations.* New York: Free Press.

Rogers, E., & Shoemaker, F. (1971). *Communication of innovations.* New York: Free Press.

Rogers, P. J. (2011). Implications of complicated and complex characteristics for key tasks in evaluation. In K. Forss, M. Marra, & R. Schwartz (Eds.), *Evaluating the complex: Attribution, contribution, and beyond.* New Brunswick, NJ: Transaction.

Rogers, P. J. (2013, March 1). Addressing complexity. *Better Evaluation* (blog). Available at *http://betterevaluation.org/blog/addressing_complexity*.

Rogers, P. J., & Funnell, S. F. (2011). *Purposeful program theory: Effective use of theories of change and logic models.* San Francisco: Jossey-Bass.

Rogers, P. J., & Williams, B. (2006). Evaluation for practice improvement and organizational learning. In I. F. Shaw, J. C. Greene, & M. Mark (Eds.), *The SAGE handbook of evaluation* (pp. 76–97). Los Angeles: SAGE.

Romão, J. E. (2000). *Dialética da diferença: O projeto da Escola Cidadã frente ao projeto pedagógico neoliberal.* São Paulo, Brazil: Cortez.

Rosenstein, B., & Syna, H. D. (Eds.). (2015). Evaluation and social justice in complex sociopolitical contexts. *New Directions for Evaluation, 146.*

Rossi, P. (1995). Doing good and getting it right. In W. R. Shadish, D. L. Newman, M. A. Scheirer, & C. Wye (Eds.), *New Directions for Evaluation, 66,* 55–60.

Rotberg, R., & Thompson, D. (Eds.). (2000). *Truth versus justice: The morality of truth commissions.* Princeton, NJ: Princeton University Press.

Roth, K. (2016, June 9). A case against America. *New York Review of Books, 63,* 4–8.

Rothschild, S. (2012). *The non nonprofit: For-profit thinking and nonprofit success.* San Francisco: Jossey-Bass.

Rugg, D. (2016, June). *Social action and advocacy for evaluation: A citizen's right to know how effective programs really are.* Presentation and workshop at the annual conference of the Canadian Evaluation Society, St. John's, Newfoundland, Canada.

Samuelson, P. (2016). *It takes a community: Nine principles of highly effective youth service organizations.* Menlo Park, CA: Thrive Foundation for Youth.

Sanders, J. R. (1995). Standards and principles. In W. R. Shadish, D. L. Newman, M. A. Scheirer, & C. Wye (Eds.), *New Directions for Evaluation, 66,* 47–52.

Santhanam, K. (2015). Basic principles of Gandhism. In G. Ramachandran & T. K. Mahadevan (Eds.), *Gandhi: His relevance for our times.* Delhi, India: Gandhi Peace Foundation. Available at *www.mkgandhi.org/g_relevance/chap26.htm*.

Scarborough, G., Méndez, V. E., & Bisson, A. (2014). *Agroecological risk and resilience screening tool: Guidance for considering agroecological* impact of agriculture interventions and identifying opportunities to build resilience in food systems. Portland, OR: Mercy Corps. Available at *www.uvm.edu/~agroecol/ScarboroughEtAl_ARR_Screening%20Tool_V1.0_MC_14.pdf.*

Schoemaker, P. J. H., & Krupp, S. (2014, December 5). 6 principles that made Nelson Mandela a renowned leader. *Fortune.* Retrieved from *http://fortune.com/2014/12/05/6-principles-that-made-nelson-mandela-a-renowned-leader.*

Schwandt, T. A. (2002). *Evaluation practice reconsidered.* New York: Peter Lang.

Schwandt, T. A. (2015). *Evaluation foundations revisited: Cultivating a life of the mind for practice.* Stanford, CA: Stanford University Press.

Scriven, M. (1995). The logic of evaluation and evaluation practice. In D. M. Fournier (Ed.), *New Directions for Evaluation, 68,* 49–70.

Scriven, M. (2008). The concept of a transdiscipline: And of evaluation as a transdiscipline. *Journal of MultiDisciplinary Evaluation, 5*(10), 65–66.

Scriven, M. (2016). Roadblocks to recognition and revolution. *American Journal of Evaluation, 37*(1), 27–44.

SenGupta, S., Hopson, R., & Thompson-Robinson, M. (2004). Cultural competence in evaluation: An overview. In M. Thompson-Robinson, R. Hopson, & S. SenGupta (Eds.), *New Directions for Evaluation, 102,* 5–19.

Shadish, W. R. (1995). The logic of generalization: Five principles common to experiments and ethnographies. *American Journal of Community Psychology, 23,* 419–428.

Shadish, W. R., Newman, D. L., Scheirer, M. A., & Wye, C. (Eds.). (1995). Guiding principles for evaluators. *New Directions for Evaluation, 66.*

Shulha, L. M., Whitmore, E. J., Cousins, J. B., Gilbert, N., & al Hudib, H. (2016). Introducing evidence-based principles to guide collaborative approaches to evaluation: Results of an empirical process. *American Journal of Evaluation, 37*(2), 193–215.

Sirotnik, K. A. (Ed.). (1990). Evaluation and social justice: issues in public education. *New Directions for Evaluation, 45.*

Sotero, M. (2006). A conceptual model of historical trauma: Implications for public health practice and research. *Journal of Health Disparities Research and Practice, 1*(1), 93–108.

Sridharan, S., & Nakaima, A. (2012). Towards an evidence base of theory-driven evaluations:

Dome questions for proponents of theory-driven evaluation. *Evaluation, 18,* 378–395.

Stake, R. (2004). How far dare an evaluator go toward saving the world? *American Journal of Evaluation, 25*(1), 103–107.

Storkey, C. (2014). The Nelson Mandela way: 21 principles for passionate leaders. Retrieved from *http://calebstorkey.com/nelson-mandela.*

Sull, D., & Eisenhardt, K. M. (2012). Simple rules for a complex world. *Harvard Business Review.* Available at *https://hbr.org/2012/09/simple-rules-for-a-complex-world.*

Sunga, L. S. (2009). Ten principles for reconciling truth commissions and criminal prosecutions. In J. Doria, H.-P. Gasser, & M. C. Bassiouni (Eds.), *The legal regime of the International Criminal Court.* Leiden, The Netherlands: Martinus Nijhoff.

Sutton, R. I., & Rao, H. (2014). *Scaling up excellence: Getting to more without settling for less.* New York: Crown Business.

Symonette, H. (2004). Walking pathways toward becoming a culturally competent evaluator: boundaries, borderlands, and border crossings. In M. Thompson-Robinson, R. Hopson, & S. SenGupta (Eds.), *New Directions for Evaluation, 102,* 95–110.

Theis, J. (2003). *Rights-based monitoring and evaluation.* New York: Save the Children.

Tutu, D. (1997). *The essential Desmond Tutu.* Cape Town: David Philip.

UNICEF. (1959). Declaration of the Rights of the Child. Available at *www.unicef.org/malaysia/1959-Declaration-of-the-Rights-of-the-Child.pdf.*

UNICEF. (2004). The human rights-based approach: Statement of common understanding. Annex B, *The State of the World's Children.* Available at *www.unicef.org/sowc04/files/AnnexB.pdf.*

United Kingdom Department for International Development. (1999). Sustainable livelihoods guidance sheet: Introduction. Available at *www.livelihoodscentre.org/documents/20720/100145/Sustainable+livelihoods+guidance+sheets/8f35b59f-8207-43fc-8b99-df75d3000e86.*

Valenzuela, H. (2016). Agroecology: A global paradigm to challenge mainstream industrial agriculture. *Horticulture, 2*(2), 1–11.

Waller, J. (2004). *Fabulous science: Fact and fiction in the history of scientific discovery.* New York: Oxford University Press.

Weiss, C. H. (2002). "Lesson's learned": A comment. *American Journal of Evaluation, 23*(2), 229–230.

Westley, F., Zimmerman, B., & Patton, M. (2006). *Getting to maybe: How the world is changed.* Toronto: Vintage Canada.

Wezel, A., Bellon, S., Doré, T., Francis, C., Vallod, D., & David, C. (2009). Agroecology as a science, a movement and a practice: A review. *Agronomy for Sustainable Development, 29,* 503–515.

Whitman, C. (2016). The secret to abundance: Give what you want to receive. Retrieved from *http://christywhitman.com/the-secret-to-abundance-give-what-you-want-to-receive.*

Williams, B. (2014, November 16). A systems practitioner's journey. *AEA365* blog. *http://aea365.org/blog/?s=Bob+Williams&submit=Go*

Williams, B., & Hummelbrunner, R. (2011). *Systems concepts in action: A practitioner's toolkit.* Stanford, CA: Stanford University Press.

Williams, D. D. (Ed.). (2016). Seven North American evaluation pioneers. In D. Williams (Ed.), *New Directions for Evaluation, 150.*

Wood, B., Betts, J., Etta, F., Gayfer, J., Kabell, F. D., Ngwira, N., et al. (2011). *The evaluation of the Paris Declaration: Phase 2, final report.* Copenhagen, Denmark: Danish Institute for International Studies. Retrieved from *http://pd-website.inforce.dk/content/pdf/PD-EN-web.pdf.*

Woodland, R. (2015, August 15). Evaluating organizational collaboration. *AEA365* blog. Retrieved from *http://aea365.org/blog/pd-presenters-week-rebecca-woodland-on-evaluating-organizational-collaboration.*

Yarbrough, D. B., Shulha, L. M., Hopson, R. K., & Caruthers, F. A. (2010). *The program evaluation standards: A guide for evaluators and evaluation users* (3rd ed.). Thousand Oaks, CA: SAGE.

Zimmerman, B., Lindberg, C., & Plsek, P. (2001). *Edgeware: Insights from complexity science for healthcare leaders.* Irving, TX: VHA.

Author Index

Subject Index

About the Author

 **Michael Quinn Patton, PhD,** is an independent consultant who has been conducting program evaluations since the 1970s. Based in Minnesota, he was on the faculty of the University of Minnesota for 18 years and is a former president of the American Evaluation Association (AEA). His books include *Developmental Evaluation, Developmental Evaluation Exemplars, Qualitative Research and Evaluation Methods* (now in its fourth edition), and *Utilization-Focused Evaluation* (now in its fourth edition), among others. Dr. Patton is a recipient of the Alva and Gunnar Myrdal Evaluation Practice Award and the Paul F. Lazarsfeld Evaluation Theory Award, both from AEA, as well as the Lester F. Ward Distinguished Contribution to Applied and Clinical Sociology Award from the Association for Applied and Clinical Sociology. He is an active trainer and workshop presenter who has conducted applied research and evaluation on a broad range of issues and has worked with organizations and programs at the international, national, state, provincial, and local levels.